# Fractional Calculus and Hypergeometric Functions in Complex Analysis

# Fractional Calculus and Hypergeometric Functions in Complex Analysis

Editors

**Gheorghe Oros**
**Georgia Irina Oros**

Basel • Beijing • Wuhan • Barcelona • Belgrade • Novi Sad • Cluj • Manchester

*Editors*

Gheorghe Oros
Department of Mathematics
and Computer Science
University of Oradea
Oradea
Romania

Georgia Irina Oros
Department of Mathematics
and Computer Science
University of Oradea
Oradea
Romania

*Editorial Office*
MDPI
St. Alban-Anlage 66
4052 Basel, Switzerland

This is a reprint of articles from the Special Issue published online in the open access journal *Fractal and Fractional* (ISSN 2504-3110) (available at: www.mdpi.com/journal/fractalfract/special_issues/FCHF).

For citation purposes, cite each article independently as indicated on the article page online and as indicated below:

Lastname, A.A.; Lastname, B.B. Article Title. *Journal Name* **Year**, *Volume Number*, Page Range.

**ISBN 978-3-7258-1098-7 (Hbk)**
**ISBN 978-3-7258-1097-0 (PDF)**
doi.org/10.3390/books978-3-7258-1097-0

© 2024 by the authors. Articles in this book are Open Access and distributed under the Creative Commons Attribution (CC BY) license. The book as a whole is distributed by MDPI under the terms and conditions of the Creative Commons Attribution-NonCommercial-NoDerivs (CC BY-NC-ND) license.

# Contents

**About the Editors** . . . . . . . . . . . . . . . . . . . . . . . . . . . . . . . . . . . . . . . . . . . . . . vii

**Gheorghe Oros and Georgia Irina Oros**
Fractional Calculus and Hypergeometric Functions in Complex Analysis
Reprinted from: *Fractal Fract.* **2024**, *8*, 233, doi:10.3390/fractalfract8040233 . . . . . . . . . . . . . 1

**Najla M. Alarif and Rabha W. Ibrahim**
Specific Classes of Analytic Functions Communicated with a Q-Differential Operator Including a Generalized Hypergeometic Function
Reprinted from: *Fractal Fract.* **2022**, *6*, 545, doi:10.3390/fractalfract6100545 . . . . . . . . . . . . . 6

**Lei Shi, Muhammad Arif, Javed Iqbal, Khalil Ullah and Syed Muhammad Ghufran**
Sharp Bounds of Hankel Determinant on Logarithmic Coefficients for Functions Starlike with Exponential Function
Reprinted from: *Fractal Fract.* **2022**, *6*, 645, doi:10.3390/fractalfract6110645 . . . . . . . . . . . . . 24

**Georgia Irina Oros, Gheorghe Oros and Shigeyoshi Owa**
Subordination Properties of Certain Operators Concerning Fractional Integral and Libera Integral Operator
Reprinted from: *Fractal Fract.* **2023**, *7*, 42, doi:10.3390/fractalfract7010042 . . . . . . . . . . . . . 40

**Muhammad Bilal Khan, Adriana Cătaş, Najla Aloraini and Mohamed S. Soliman**
Some New Versions of Fractional Inequalities for Exponential Trigonometric Convex Mappings via Ordered Relation on Interval-Valued Settings
Reprinted from: *Fractal Fract.* **2023**, *7*, 223, doi:10.3390/fractalfract7030223 . . . . . . . . . . . . . 57

**Mohammad Faisal Khan amd Mohammed AbaOud**
Some New Applications of the Faber Polynomial Expansion Method for Generalized Bi-Subordinate Functions of Complex Order $\gamma$ Defined by $q$-Calculus
Reprinted from: *Fractal Fract.* **2023**, *7*, 270, doi:10.3390/fractalfract7030270 . . . . . . . . . . . . . 84

**Sadia Riaz, Timilehin Gideon Shaba, Qin Xin, Fairouz Tchier, Bilal Khan and Sarfraz Nawaz Malik**
Fekete–Szegö Problem and Second Hankel Determinant for a Class of Bi-Univalent Functions Involving Euler Polynomials
Reprinted from: *Fractal Fract.* **2023**, *7*, 295, doi:10.3390/fractalfract7040295 . . . . . . . . . . . . . 102

**Hari Mohan Srivastava, Waleed Adel, Mohammad Izadi and Adel A. El-Sayed**
Solving Some Physics Problems Involving Fractional-Order Differential Equations with the Morgan-Voyce Polynomials
Reprinted from: *Fractal Fract.* **2023**, *7*, 301, doi:10.3390/fractalfract7040301 . . . . . . . . . . . . . 119

**Mohammed Z. Alqarni, Ahmed Bakhet and Mohamed Abdalla**
Application of the Pathway-Type Transform to a New Form of a Fractional Kinetic Equation Involving the Generalized Incomplete Wright Hypergeometric Functions
Reprinted from: *Fractal Fract.* **2023**, *7*, 348, doi:10.3390/ fractalfract7050348 . . . . . . . . . . . . . 138

**Suha B. Al-Shaikh, Ahmad A. Abubaker, Khaled Matarneh, Mohammad Faisal Khan**
Some New Applications of the $q$-Analogous of Differential and Integral Operators for New Subclasses of $q$-Starlike and $q$-Convex Functions
Reprinted from: *Fractal Fract.* **2023**, *7*, 411, doi:10.3390/fractalfract7050411 . . . . . . . . . . . . . 150

**Isra Al-Shbeil, Jianhua Gong, Samrat Ray, Shahid Khan, Nazar Khan and Hala Alaqad**
The Properties of Meromorphic Multivalent $q$-Starlike Functions in the Janowski Domain
Reprinted from: *Fractal Fract.* **2023**, 7, 438, doi:10.3390/fractalfract7060438 . . . . . . . . . . . . . **173**

**Mohd Idris Qureshi, Tafaz Ul Rahman Shah, Junesang Choi and Aarif Hussain Bhat**
Three General Double-Series Identities and Associated Reduction Formulas and Fractional Calculus
Reprinted from: *Fractal Fract.* **2023**, 7, 700, doi:10.3390/fractalfract7100700 . . . . . . . . . . . . . **187**

**Adeel Ahmad, Jianhua Gong, Isra Al-Shbeil, Akhter Rasheed, Asad Ali1 and Saqib Hussain**
Analytic Functions Related to a Balloon-Shaped Domain
Reprinted from: *Fractal Fract.* **2023**, 7, 865, doi:10.3390/fractalfract7120865 . . . . . . . . . . . . . **213**

# About the Editors

**Gheorghe Oros**

Professor Gheorghe Oros was affiliated with the University of Oradea, Romania, now retired since 2015. After teaching mathematics in high school, he started as a lecturer at the University of Oradea in 1995. He obtained his Ph.D. at Babeș-Bolyai University, Cluj-Napoca in 1998 under the supervision of academician Petru T. Mocanu. He became a full Professor in 2001. His field of investigation is related to Complex Analysis and Geometric Function Theory. He has published over 100 research articles on this topic and continues to be an active researcher.

**Georgia Irina Oros**

Georgia Irina Oros has taught at the University of Oradea, Romania since 2004. She has been an associate professor at the Faculty of Informatics and Sciences, Department of Mathematics and Computer Science since 2013. She obtained her Ph.D. in 2006 in Geometric Function Theory at Babeș-Bolyai University, Cluj-Napoca, Romania under the supervision of Prof. Dr. Grigore Ștefan Sălăgean. She defended her habilitation thesis in 2018 at Babeș-Bolyai University, Cluj-Napoca, Romania. She has over 100 papers published in the field of Complex Analysis and Geometric Function Theory.

*Editorial*

# Fractional Calculus and Hypergeometric Functions in Complex Analysis

Gheorghe Oros and Georgia Irina Oros *

Department of Mathematics and Computer Science, University of Oradea, 410087 Oradea, Romania; gh_oros@yahoo.com
* Correspondence: georgia_oros_ro@yahoo.co.uk

## 1. Introduction

Fractional calculus has had a powerful impact on recent research, with many applications in different branches of science and engineering. Various branches of mathematics are also influenced by fractional calculus. Articles in the literature [1,2] discuss the history of fractional calculus and cite its many scientific and engineering applications, successfully highlighting the importance of this subject. Fractional operators are essential to the study of fractional calculus. For investigations utilizing fractional calculus, fractional operators are crucial resources. A brief history of fractional calculus operators is given in [3] and is further developed in [4]. Applications of fractional operators in complex analysis research are comprehensive, and interesting new results have been obtained in studies involving univalent functions theory, a topic which is also covered in [1].

This Special Issue aims to gather new research outcomes combining this prolific tool with another that generates exciting results when integrated into studies: hypergeometric functions.

The study of hypergeometric functions dates back 200 years. They appear in the works of Euler, Gauss, Riemann, and Kummer. Interest in hypergeometric functions has grown in the last few decades due to their applications in a large variety of scientific domains and many areas of mathematics. Hypergeometric functions are linked to the theory of univalent functions by L. de Branges' proof of Bieberbach's conjecture, published in 1985 [5], which uses the generalized hypergeometric function. After this connection was established, hypergeometric functions were studied intensely using geometric function theory.

Quantum calculus is also involved in studies alongside fractional calculus tools and different hypergeometric functions, as is nicely highlighted in [6].

This Special Issue compiles articles from researchers interested in any of these topics or a combination of them and their applications in different areas concerning complex analysis.

## 2. Overview of the Published Papers

After a thorough review procedure, 12 papers were selected for publishing in this Special Issue.

Najla M. Alarifi and Rabha W. Ibrahim (contribution 1) investigate the geometric properties of the generalized Prabhakar fractional differential operator in the open unit disk by using the concept of q–fractional calculus. The generalized operator is inserted in a special class of analytic functions. By using the methods of differential subordination and superordination theory, numerous fractional differential inequalities are proven. Additionally, this contribution investigates the potential application of these methods in the solution of special kinds of q–fractional differential equations.

The research presented by the authors Lei Shi, Muhammad Arif, Javed Iqbal, Khalil Ullah, and Syed Muhammad Ghufran (contribution 2) concerns the study of logarithmic-related problems of a certain subclass of univalent functions. A subclass of starlike functions connected with exponential mapping is introduced, and sharp estimates of the second Hankel determinant with the logarithmic coefficient as the entry are obtained for this class.

The well-known parametric formulas for initial coefficients in the Carathéodory class of functions serve as the methodological foundation for the proof. The authors discover that the bounds for the coefficients of a function and its inverse function can be obtained by transferring the logarithmic coefficients of functions. The results on Hankel determinants with logarithmic coefficients seem to be quite important, since bounds on coefficients of the inverse function are often a more challenging task to calculate. Since the exponential function belongs to a special class of hypergeometric functions, this work can serve as an inspiration for further research on univalent functions that are subordinated to a more general class.

The results presented by Georgia Irina Oros, Gheorghe Oros, and Shigeyoshi Owa (contribution 3) arise from a study regarding fractional calculus combined with the classical theory of differential subordination established for analytic complex valued functions. A new operator is introduced by applying the Libera integral operator and fractional integral of order $\lambda$ for analytic functions. Many subordination properties are obtained for this newly defined operator by using famous lemmas proved by important scientists concerned with geometric function theory, such as Eenigenburg, Hallenbeck, Miller, Mocanu, Nunokawa, Reade, Ruscheweyh, and Suffridge. Results regarding strong starlikeness and convexity of order $\lambda$ are also discussed, and an example shows how the outcome of this research can be applied. The operator defined in this work can be applied to the definition of new subclasses of analytic functions with certain geometric properties given by the characteristics of this operator that are already proven in this paper.

In the next paper (contribution 4), Muhammad Bilal Khan, Adriana Cătaş, Najla Aloraini, and Mohamed S. Soliman introduce left and right exponential trigonometric convex interval-valued mappings and review some of their important characteristics. The Hermite–Hadamard inequality for interval-valued functions is proven by utilizing fractional integrals with exponential kernels. Moreover, the idea of left and right exponential trigonometric convex interval-valued mappings is applied to show various findings for midpoint and Pachpatte-type inequalities. The authors also show that the results provided in this paper are expansions of several of the results that have already been demonstrated in prior publications. The suggested research following from this work generates variants that are applicable for conducting in-depth analyses of fractal theory, optimization, and research challenges in several practical domains, such as computer science, quantum mechanics, and quantum physics.

The investigation conducted by Mohammad Faisal Khan and Mohammed Abaoud (contribution 5) examines a new subclass of generalized bi-subordinate functions of complex order $\gamma$ connected to the $q$-difference operator. The upper bounds for generalized bi-subordinate functions of complex order $\gamma$ are obtained by using the Faber polynomial expansion technique. Coefficient bounds and the Fekete–Szegő problem are considered for functions in the newly defined class. The Ruscheweyh $q$-differential operator along with the Faber polynomial method are used to discuss the applications of the main results. The authors suggest that the method presented in this paper could be applied to define a number of new subclasses of meromorphic, multivalent, and harmonic functions and can be used to investigate a number of new properties of these classes.

The authors Sadia Riaz, Timilehin Gideon Shaba, Qin Xin, Fairouz Tchier, Bilal Khan, and Sarfraz Nawaz Malik investigate bi-univalent functions and Euler polynomials in their study (contribution 6). The Fekete–Szegő problem is solved by the authors, and bound estimates for the coefficients and an upper bound estimate for the second Hankel determinant are given for the new class of bi-univalent functions satisfying a certain subordination and involving Euler polynomials. The authors believe that their results could be extended for a class of certain $q$-starlike functions.

A new computational technique for solving some physics problems involving fractional-order differential equations, including the famous Bagley–Torvik method, is given by Hari Mohan Srivastava, Waleed Adel, Mohammad Izadi, and Adel A. El-Sayed (contribution 7). A collocation technique involving a new operational matrix that utilizes the Liouville–Caputo operator of differentiation and Morgan–Voyce polynomials is adapted in combination with the Tau spectral method. The differentiation matrix of fractional order that is used to convert the problem and its conditions into an algebraic system of equations with unknown coefficients is first presented. Then, the matrix is used to find the solutions to the proposed models. An error analysis for the method is proven to verify the convergence of the acquired solutions. To test the effectiveness of the proposed technique, several examples are simulated using the presented technique, and these results are compared with other techniques from the literature. In addition, the computational time is computed and tabulated to ensure the efficacy and robustness of the method. The outcomes of the numerical examples support the theoretical results and show the accuracy and applicability of the presented approach.

The authors Mohammed Z. Alqarni, Ahmed Bakhet, and Mohamed Abdalla (contribution 8) establish a generalization of the fractional kinetic equation using the generalized incomplete Wright hypergeometric function. This new generalization can be used to compute the change in chemical composition in stars such as the Sun. The pathway-type transform technique is then used to investigate the solutions to a fractional kinetic equation with specific fractional transforms. Furthermore, exceptional cases of the outcomes are discussed and graphically illustrated using MATLAB software. This work provides a thorough overview for further investigation into these topics in order to gain a better understanding of their implications and applications.

The next article (contribution 9) investigates the geometric properties of analytic functions using $q$-analogues of differential and integral operators. The authors Suha B. Al-Shaikh, Ahmad A. Abubaker, Khaled Matarneh, and Mohammad Faisal Khan define the $q$-analogues of a differential operator by using the basic idea of q-calculus and the definition of convolution. Using the newly constructed operator, the $q$-analogues of two new integral operators are established. Further, by employing these operators, new subclasses of the $q$-starlike and $q$-convex functions are defined. Sufficient conditions for the functions to belong to the newly defined classes are investigated, and certain subordination findings for the $q$-analogue differential operator are given. Certain novel geometric characteristics of the $q$-analogues of the integral operators in these classes are also obtained.

A comprehensive investigation to identify the uses of the Sălăgean $q$-differential operator for meromorphic multivalent functions is conducted by Isra Al-Shbeil, Jianhua Gong, Samrat Ray, Shahid Khan, Nazar Khan, and Hala Alaqad (contribution 10). In their paper, they extend the idea of the $q$-analogues of the Sălăgean differential operator for meromorphic multivalent functions using the fundamental ideas of $q$-calculus. With the help of this operator, the family of Janowski functions is extended by adding two new subclasses of meromorphic q-starlike and meromorphic multivalent q-starlike functions. The radii of starlikeness, partial sums, distortion theorems, and coefficient estimates are given for the new subclasses under investigation. The technique and ideas of this paper may stimulate further research in the theory of multivalent meromorphic functions, and additional generalized classes of meromorphic functions can be defined and investigated.

The next article (contribution 11) introduces three general double-series identities using Whipple transformations for terminating generalized hypergeometric $_4F_3$ and $_5F_4$ functions. By employing the left-sided Riemann–Liouville fractional integral on these identities, the authors Mohd Idris Qureshi, Tafaz Ul Rahman Shah, Junesang Choi, and Aarif Hussain Bhat show the ability to derive additional identities of the same nature successively. This research further presents various new transformation formulae, such as Bailey's quadratic transformation formula, the Clausen reduction formula, the Gauss quadratic transformation formula, the Karlsson reduction formula, the Orr reduction formula, and the Whipple quadratic transformation formula. The authors anticipate that these transformation and summation formulas, as well as those deducible from the same steps, will have applications in diverse fields, such as mathematical physics, statistics, and engineering sciences.

The authors Adeel Ahmad, Jianhua Gong, Isra Al-Shbeil, Akhter Rasheed, Asad Ali, and Saqib Hussain (contribution 12) define a new generalized domain obtained based on the quotient of two analytic functions. The sharp upper bounds of the modulus of the coefficients $a_2$, $a_3$, and $a_4$ are investigated, and the sharp upper bounds for the modulus of the second-order and third-order Hankel determinants are estimated for the normalized analytic functions belonging to the newly defined class in the generalized domain. This work provides a direction to define more interesting generalized domains and to extend to new subclasses of starlike and convex functions by using quantum calculus.

## 3. Conclusions

A printed book bearing the same title is available that contains the 12 papers published in this Special Issue on "Fractional Calculus and Hypergeometric Functions in Complex Analysis". This project has resulted in the publication of articles covering a wide range of topics. Because of this, scholars studying the applications of fractional calculus and hypergeometric functions in complex analysis and related fields should find this Special Issue to be interesting. This Special Issue's sequel is named "Fractional Calculus, Quantum Calculus, and Special Functions in Complex Analysis". In order to learn more about the suggested themes and perhaps contribute to the success of this new initiative by submitting research outputs, scholars interested in the field are welcome to visit the Special Issue homepage.

**Acknowledgments:** The Guest Editors of this Special Issue would like to thank all the authors who chose to submit their works and who helped make this Special Issue a success, as well as all the reviewers for their time, insightful feedback, and assistance in upholding high standards for the published materials. The Fractal and Fractional editors are also deserving of particular acknowledgment.

**Conflicts of Interest:** The authors declare no conflicts of interest.

**List of Contributions**

1. Alarifi, N.M.; Ibrahim, R.W. Specific Classes of Analytic Functions Communicated with a Q-Differential Operator Including a Generalized Hypergeometic Function. *Fractal Fract.* **2022**, *6*, 545. https://doi.org/10.3390/fractalfract6100545.
2. Shi, L.; Arif, M.; Iqbal, J.; Ullah, K.; Ghufran, S.M. Sharp Bounds of Hankel Determinant on Logarithmic Coefficients for Functions Starlike with Exponential Function. *Fractal Fract.* **2022**, *6*, 645. https://doi.org/10.3390/fractalfract6110645.
3. Oros, G.I.; Oros, G.; Owa, S. Subordination Properties of Certain Operators Concerning Fractional Integral and Libera Integral Operator. *Fractal Fract.* **2023**, *7*, 42. https://doi.org/10.3390/fractalfract7010042.
4. Khan, M.B.; Cătaş, A.; Aloraini, N.; Soliman, M.S. Some New Versions of Fractional Inequalities for Exponential Trigonometric Convex Mappings via Ordered Relation on Interval-Valued Settings. *Fractal Fract.* **2023**, *7*, 223. https://doi.org/10.3390/fractalfract7030223.
5. Khan, M.F.; AbaOud, M. Some New Applications of the Faber Polynomial Expansion Method for Generalized Bi-Subordinate Functions of Complex Order $\gamma$ Defined by $q$-Calculus. *Fractal Fract.* **2023**, *7*, 270. https://doi.org/10.3390/fractalfract7030270.
6. Riaz, S.; Shaba, T.G.; Xin, Q.; Tchier, F.; Khan, B.; Malik, S.N. Fekete–Szegö Problem and Second Hankel Determinant for a Class of Bi-Univalent Functions Involving Euler Polynomials. *Fractal Fract.* **2023**, *7*, 295. https://doi.org/10.3390/fractalfract7040295.
7. Srivastava, H.M.; Adel, W.; Izadi, M.; El-Sayed, A.A. Solving Some Physics Problems Involving Fractional-Order Differential Equations with the Morgan-Voyce Polynomials. *Fractal Fract.* **2023**, *7*, 301. https://doi.org/10.3390/fractalfract7040301.
8. Alqarni, M.Z.; Bakhet, A.; Abdalla, M. Application of the Pathway-Type Transform to a New Form of a Fractional Kinetic Equation Involving the Generalized Incomplete Wright Hypergeometric Functions. *Fractal Fract.* **2023**, *7*, 348. https://doi.org/10.3390/fractalfract7050348.
9. Al-Shaikh, S.B.; Abubaker, A.A.; Matarneh, K.; Khan, M.F. Some New Applications of the q-Analogous of Differential and Integral Operators for New Subclasses of q-Starlike and q-Convex Functions. *Fractal Fract.* **2023**, *7*, 411. https://doi.org/10.3390/fractalfract7050411.

10. Al-Shbeil, I.; Gong, J.; Ray, S.; Khan, S.; Khan, N.; Alaqad, H. The Properties of Meromorphic Multivalent q-Starlike Functions in the Janowski Domain. *Fractal Fract.* **2023**, *7*, 438. https://doi.org/10.3390/fractalfract7060438.
11. Qureshi, M.I.; Shah, T.U.R.; Choi, J.; Bhat, A.H. Three General Double-Series Identities and Associated Reduction Formulas and Fractional Calculus. *Fractal Fract.* **2023**, *7*, 700. https://doi.org/10.3390/fractalfract7100700.
12. Ahmad, A.; Gong, J.; Al-Shbeil, I.; Rasheed, A.; Ali, A.; Hussain, S. Analytic Functions Related to a Balloon-Shaped Domain. *Fractal Fract.* **2023**, *7*, 865. https://doi.org/10.3390/fractalfract7120865.

## References

1. Srivastava, H.M. An Introductory Overview of Fractional-Calculus Operators Based Upon the Fox-Wright and Related Higher Transcendental Functions. *J. Adv. Eng. Comput.* **2021**, *5*, 135–166. [CrossRef]
2. Baleanu, D.; Agarwal, R.P. Fractional calculus in the sky. *Adv. Differ. Equ.* **2021**, *2021*, 117. [CrossRef]
3. Kiryakova, V. A brief story about the operators of the generalized fractional calculus. *Fract. Calc. Appl. Anal.* **2008**, *11*, 203–220.
4. Baleanu, D.; Fernandez, A. On Fractional Operators and Their Classifications. *Mathematics* **2019**, *7*, 830. [CrossRef]
5. De Branges, L. A proof of the Bieberbach conjecture. *Acta Math.* **1985**, *154*, 137–152. [CrossRef]
6. Srivastava, H.M. Operators of basic (or q-) calculus and fractional q-calculus and their applications in geometric function theory of complex analysis. *Iran. J. Sci. Technol. Trans. A Sci.* **2020**, *44*, 327–344. [CrossRef]

**Disclaimer/Publisher's Note:** The statements, opinions and data contained in all publications are solely those of the individual author(s) and contributor(s) and not of MDPI and/or the editor(s). MDPI and/or the editor(s) disclaim responsibility for any injury to people or property resulting from any ideas, methods, instructions or products referred to in the content.

Article

# Specific Classes of Analytic Functions Communicated with a Q-Differential Operator Including a Generalized Hypergeometic Function

Najla M. Alarifi [1,*,†] and Rabha W. Ibrahim [2,†]

1 Department of Mathematics, Imam Abdulrahman Bin Faisal University, Dammam 31113, Saudi Arabia
2 Mathematics Research Center, Department of Mathematics, Near East University, Mersin 99138, Turkey
* Correspondence: nalareefi@iau.edu.sa
† These authors contributed equally to this work.

**Abstract:** A special function is a function that is typically entitled after an early scientist who studied its features and has a specific application in mathematical physics or another area of mathematics. There are a few significant examples, including the hypergeometric function and its unique species. These types of special functions are generalized by fractional calculus, fractal, $q$-calculus, $(q,p)$-calculus and $k$-calculus. By engaging the notion of $q$-fractional calculus (QFC), we investigate the geometric properties of the generalized Prabhakar fractional differential operator in the open unit disk $\nabla := \{\xi \in \mathbb{C} : |\xi| < 1\}$. Consequently, we insert the generalized operator in a special class of analytic functions. Our methodology is indicated by the usage of differential subordination and superordination theory. Accordingly, numerous fractional differential inequalities are organized. Additionally, as an application, we study the solution of special kinds of $q$–fractional differential equation.

**Keywords:** quantum calculus; fractional calculus; fractional differential equation; analytic function; subordination and superordination; univalent function; fractional differential operator

## 1. Introduction

The quantum fractional calculus (QFC, $q$-fractional calculus or Jackson calculus [1]) is an extension of the well-known fractional calculus. It has had applications in the investigation of the special functions, where it shows a central role to develop what is called the quantum groups [2]. As a result, it is established in the form of the Fock–Bargmann joining the theory of holomorphic functions [3]. Newly, the utilization of QFC covers the exacting solution for measurement systems and their presentation [4,5]. Moreover, QFC is operated in numerous complex physical systems, which can be selected in [6]. Temporarily special functions have good results in mathematical physics; therefore, it is a practical to imagine the ordinary special functions given by the new QFC. Likewise, the credit of the thermodynamics of QFC can be computed by the usage of QFC, where the structure of thermodynamics is conserved if one employed a suitable Jackson derivative instead of the normal thermodynamic derivative. Other applications can be located for the studies in optimization, control system, transform investigation, resolutions of the difference and fractional integral inequalities. In geometric function theory, researchers have formulated different classes of analytic functions using QFC. Recently, some fractional operators were generalized by assuming QFC. Recently, Hadid et al. [7] developed an expanded class of multivalent functions geometrically on the open unit disk using the QFC paradigm. In the framework of the quantum wavelet, Sabrine et al. [8] utilized the basis of quantum wavelets to present a novel uncertainty principle for the extended $q$-Bessel wavelet transform. Aldawish and Ibrahim [9] formulated a quantum symmetric differential operator and used it to investigate the geometric of some classes of analytic functions in a complex domain.

In this work, we carry on the investigation to explore some properties of the Prabhakar fractional differential operator [10,11] via the QFC.

We study the geometric characteristics of the generalized Prabhakar fractional differential operator in the open unit disk by using the concept of $q$–fractional calculus (QFC). In light of this, we introduce the generalized operator into a unique class of analytic functions. The use of differential subordination and superordination theories offers a clue to our approach. As a result, several fractional differential inequalities are categorized. In addition, as an application, we look at several types of solutions to $q$-fractional differential equations.

## 2. Fractional Operators

The Prabhakar integral operator acts on a normalized class of the analytic functions

$$h(\xi) \in \mathcal{H}[0,n] = \{h \in \nabla : h(\xi) = h_1 \xi^n + h_2 \xi^{n+1} + \ldots\},$$

as follows: [12–18]

$$\left(P_{\alpha,\beta}^{\gamma,\kappa} h\right)(\xi) = \int_0^\xi (\xi - \tau)^{\beta-1} \Xi_{\alpha,\beta}^{\gamma}[\kappa(\xi - \tau)^\alpha] h(\tau) d\tau \qquad (1)$$

$$= (h \cdot \varrho_{\alpha,\beta}^{\gamma,\kappa})(\xi),$$

$$\left(\alpha, \beta, \gamma, \kappa \in \mathbb{C}, \xi \in \nabla, \Re(\alpha), \Re(\beta) > 0\right)$$

such that [13]

$$\varrho_{\alpha,\beta}^{\gamma,\kappa}(\xi) := \xi^{\beta-1} \Xi_{\alpha,\beta}^{\gamma}(\kappa \xi^\alpha)$$

where

$$\Xi_{\alpha,\beta}^{\gamma}(\xi) = \sum_{n=0}^{\infty} \frac{\Gamma(\gamma+n)}{\Gamma(\gamma)\Gamma(\alpha n + \beta)} \frac{\xi^n}{n!}.$$

As a practicing, for $h(\xi) = \xi^{\varepsilon-1}$, we have [19]—Corollary 2.3

$$P_{\alpha,\beta}^{\gamma,\kappa} \xi^{\varepsilon-1} = \int_0^\xi (\xi - \tau)^{\beta-1} \Xi_{\alpha,\beta}^{\gamma}[\kappa(\xi - \tau)^\alpha] (\tau^{\varepsilon-1}) d\tau$$

$$= \Gamma(\varepsilon) \xi^{\beta+\varepsilon-1} \Xi_{\alpha,\beta+\varepsilon}^{\gamma}(\kappa \xi^\alpha).$$

Analogically, Prabhakar derivative is indicated by [11]

$$\left(\mathbb{D}_{\alpha,\beta}^{\gamma,\kappa} h\right)(\xi) = \frac{d^m}{d\xi^m}\left(P_{\alpha,m-\beta}^{-\gamma,\kappa} h(\xi)\right), \quad \xi \in \nabla. \qquad (2)$$

In view of the Caputo fractional operator, it is formulated as follows:

$$_m^C \mathbb{D}_{\alpha,\beta}^{\gamma,\kappa} h(\xi) = \int_0^\xi (\xi - \zeta)^{m-\beta-1} \Xi_{\alpha,m-\beta}^{-\gamma}[\kappa(\xi - \zeta)^\alpha]\left(\frac{d^m}{d\zeta^m} h(\xi)\right) d\zeta. \qquad (3)$$

$$= P_{\alpha,m-\beta}^{-\gamma,\kappa}\left(\frac{d^m}{d\xi^m} h(\xi)\right).$$

Note that

$$_m^C \mathbb{D}_{\alpha,\beta}^{\gamma,\kappa} h(\xi) = \mathbb{D}_{\alpha,\beta}^{\gamma,\kappa} h(\xi) - \sum_{k=0}^{m-1} \xi^{k-\beta} \Xi_{\alpha,k-\beta}^{-\gamma}[\kappa \xi^\alpha] h^{(k)}(0).$$

For instance, if we consider $h(\xi) = \xi^\lambda, \lambda \geq 1$, then by [19]—Corollary 2.3, we obtain

$$\begin{aligned}{}_1^C\mathbb{D}_{\alpha,\beta}^{\gamma,\kappa}(\xi^\lambda) &= \int_0^\xi (\xi-\zeta)^{1-\beta-1}\Xi_{\alpha,1-\beta}^{-\gamma}[\kappa(\xi-\zeta)^\alpha]\left(\frac{d}{d\zeta}h(\zeta)\right)d\zeta \\
&:= \int_0^\xi (\xi-\zeta)^{\mu-1}\Xi_{\alpha,\mu}^{-\gamma}[\kappa(\xi-\zeta)^\alpha]\left(\frac{d}{d\zeta}(\zeta^\lambda)\right)d\zeta \\
&= \lambda \int_0^\xi \zeta^{\lambda-1}(\xi-\zeta)^{\mu-1}\Xi_{\alpha,\mu}^{-\gamma}[\kappa(\xi-\zeta)^\alpha]d\zeta \\
&= \Gamma(\lambda+1)\xi^{\mu+\lambda-1}\Xi_{\alpha,\mu+\epsilon}^{-\gamma}[\kappa\xi^\alpha], \quad \mu := 1-\beta.\end{aligned}$$

Generally, we obtain

$$\begin{aligned}{}_m^C\mathbb{D}_{\alpha,\beta}^{\gamma,\kappa}(\xi^\lambda) &= \int_0^\xi (\xi-\zeta)^{m-\beta-1}\Xi_{\alpha,m-\beta}^{-\gamma}[\kappa(\xi-\zeta)^\alpha]\left(\frac{d^m}{d\zeta^m}(\zeta^\lambda)\right)d\zeta \\
&= \int_0^\xi (\xi-\zeta)^{k-\beta-1}\Xi_{\alpha,m-\beta}^{-\gamma}[\kappa(\xi-\zeta)^\alpha]\left(\frac{d}{d\zeta}(\zeta^\lambda)\right)d\zeta \\
&= (1-m+\lambda)_m \int_0^\xi \zeta^{\lambda-m}(\xi-\zeta)^{m-\beta-1}\Xi_{\alpha,m-\beta}^{-\gamma}[\kappa(\xi-\zeta)^\alpha]d\zeta \\
&= (1-m+\lambda)_m \int_0^\xi \zeta^{(\lambda-m+1)-1}(\xi-\zeta)^{m-\beta-1}\Xi_{\alpha,k-\beta}^{-\gamma}[\kappa(\xi-\zeta)^\alpha]d\zeta \\
&:= (\nu)_m \int_0^\xi \zeta^{\nu-1}(\xi-\zeta)^{\mu-1}\Xi_{\alpha,\mu}^{-\gamma}[\kappa(\xi-\zeta)^\alpha]d\zeta \\
&= (\nu)_m \Gamma(\nu)\,\xi^{\nu+\mu-1}\Xi_{\alpha,\mu+\nu}^{-\gamma}[\kappa\xi^\alpha],\end{aligned}$$

where $\mu := m-\beta$, $\nu := \lambda-m+1$ and $(\nu)_m = \dfrac{\Gamma(1+\lambda)}{\Gamma(1+\lambda-m)}$. Hence, we obtain

$$\begin{aligned}{}_m^C\mathbb{D}_{\alpha,\beta}^{\gamma,\kappa}(\xi^\lambda) &= \Gamma(1+\lambda)\xi^{\nu+\mu-1}\Xi_{\alpha,\mu+\nu}^{-\gamma}[\kappa\xi^\alpha] \\
&= \Gamma(m+\nu)\,\xi^{\nu+\mu-1}\Xi_{\alpha,\mu+\nu}^{-\gamma}[\kappa\xi^\alpha].\end{aligned}$$

*Modified Operators*

In this study, we deal with a special kind of analytic functions in $\nabla$ of the form (see [20])

$$h(\xi) = \xi + \sum_{n=\ell+1}^\infty h_n \xi^n, \quad \xi \in \nabla, \ell \in \mathbb{N} \qquad (4)$$

and denoted by $\Lambda_\ell$. The convolution product of two analytic functions $f$ and $g$ is given by

$$(f \times g)(\xi) = \left(\sum_{n=0}^\infty \phi_n \xi^n\right) \times \left(\sum_{n=0}^\infty \varphi_n \xi^n\right) = \sum_{n=0}^\infty \phi_n \varphi_n \xi^n.$$

**Proposition 1.** *For $h \in \Lambda_\ell$, consider the adjustment operator ${}^C\Delta_{\alpha,\beta,\ell}^{\gamma,\kappa,m} : \nabla \to \nabla$ by*

$${}^C\Delta_{\alpha,\beta,\ell}^{\gamma,\kappa,m} h(\xi) := \left(\frac{\xi^\beta}{\Xi_{\alpha,2-\beta}^{-\gamma}[\kappa\xi^\alpha]}\right)\left({}_m^C\mathbb{D}_{\alpha,\beta}^{\gamma,\kappa}\right)h(\xi).$$

*Then, ${}^C\Delta_{\alpha,\beta,\ell}^{\gamma,\kappa,m} h = {}^C\Delta_{\alpha,\beta,\ell}^{\gamma,\kappa,m} \times h \in \Lambda_\ell$.*

$$\left(\alpha, \beta, \gamma, \kappa \in \mathbb{C}, \xi \in \nabla\right).$$

**Proof.** Assume that $h \in \Lambda_\ell$. Then,

$$^{\mathcal{C}}\Delta_{\alpha,\beta,\ell}^{\gamma,\kappa,m} h(\xi) = \left(\frac{\xi^\beta}{\Xi_{\alpha,2-\beta}^{-\gamma}[\kappa\xi^\alpha]}\right)\left(^{\mathcal{C}}_m\mathbb{D}_{\alpha,\beta}^{\gamma,\kappa} h(\xi)\right)$$

$$= \left(\frac{\xi^\beta}{\Xi_{\alpha,2-\beta}^{-\gamma}[\kappa\xi^\alpha]}\right)\left(^{\mathcal{C}}_m\mathbb{D}_{\alpha,\beta}^{\gamma,\kappa}\left(\xi + \sum_{n=2}^{\infty} h_n \xi^n\right)\right)$$

$$= \left(\frac{\xi^\beta}{\Xi_{\alpha,2-\beta}^{-\gamma}[\kappa\xi^\alpha]}\right)\left(^{\mathcal{C}}_m\mathbb{D}_{\alpha,\beta}^{\gamma,\kappa}\xi + \sum_{n=\ell+1}^{\infty} h_n \,^{\mathcal{C}}_m\mathbb{D}_{\alpha,\beta}^{\gamma,\kappa}\xi^n\right)$$

$$= \left(\frac{\xi^\beta}{\Xi_{\alpha,2-\beta}^{-\gamma}[\kappa\xi^\alpha]}\right)\left(\Xi_{\alpha,2-\beta}^{-\gamma}[\kappa\xi^\alpha]\xi^{1-\beta} + \sum_{n=\ell+1}^{\infty} h_n \Gamma(n+1)\xi^{n-\beta}\Xi_{\alpha,n+1-\beta}^{-\gamma}[\kappa\xi^\alpha]\right)$$

$$= \xi + \sum_{n=\ell+1}^{\infty}\left(h_n \Gamma(n+1)\frac{\xi^{-\alpha}\Xi_{\alpha,n+1-\beta}^{-\gamma}[\kappa\xi^\alpha]}{\xi^{-\alpha}\Xi_{\alpha,2-\beta}^{-\gamma}[\kappa\xi^\alpha]}\right)\xi^n$$

$$= \xi + \sum_{n=\ell+1}^{\infty}\left(h_n \Gamma(n+1)\frac{\Xi_{\alpha,n+1-\beta}^{-\gamma}[\kappa]}{\Xi_{\alpha,2-\beta}^{-\gamma}[\kappa]}\right)\xi^n$$

$$:= \xi + \sum_{n=\ell+1}^{\infty} h_n \Sigma_n \xi^n$$

$$= \left(\xi + \sum_{n=\ell+1}^{\infty} \Sigma_n \xi^n\right) \times \left(\xi + \sum_{n=\ell+1}^{\infty} h_n \xi^n\right)$$

$$= \left(^{\mathcal{C}}\Delta_{\alpha,\beta,\ell}^{\gamma,\kappa,m} \times h\right)(\xi),$$

where

$$\Sigma_n := \Gamma(n+1)\frac{\Xi_{\alpha,n+1-\beta}^{-\gamma}[\kappa]}{\Xi_{\alpha,2-\beta}^{-\gamma}[\kappa]}.$$

This proves that $^{\mathcal{C}}\Delta_{\alpha,\beta,\ell}^{\gamma,\kappa,m} h \in \Lambda_\ell$. □

Note that the fractional integral corresponds to $[^{\mathcal{C}}\Delta_{\alpha,\beta,\ell}^{\gamma,\kappa,m} h](\xi)$ is given by the series

$$[^{\mathcal{C}}\mathbb{P}_{\alpha,\beta,\ell}^{\gamma,\kappa,m} h](\xi) = \xi + \sum_{n=\ell+1}^{\infty}\left(h_n \frac{\Xi_{\alpha,2-\beta}^{-\gamma}[\kappa]}{\Gamma(n+1)\Xi_{\alpha,n+1-\beta}^{-\gamma}[\kappa]}\right)\xi^n,$$

where

$$[^{\mathcal{C}}\Delta_{\alpha,\beta,\ell}^{\gamma,\kappa,m}](\xi) \times [^{\mathcal{C}}\mathbb{P}_{\alpha,\beta,\ell}^{\gamma,\kappa,m} h](\xi) = h(\xi)$$

and

$$[^{\mathcal{C}}\mathbb{P}_{\alpha,\beta,\ell}^{\gamma,\kappa,m}](\xi) \times [^{\mathcal{C}}\Delta_{\alpha,\beta,\ell}^{\gamma,\kappa,m} h](\xi) = h(\xi).$$

## 3. Quantum Formula

For a complex number $\omega \in \mathbb{C}$, the $\mathbb{Q}$-shifted factorials is given in the next structure [1]

$$(\omega; q)_\sigma = \prod_{\iota=0}^{\ell-1}(1 - q^\iota \omega), \quad \sigma \in \mathbb{N}, \; (\omega; q)_0 = 1. \tag{5}$$

Corresponding to (5) and in expressions of the well known gamma function, the Q-shifted formula is presented as follows:

$$(q^\omega; q)_\ell = \frac{\Gamma_q(\omega + \ell)(1-q)^\sigma}{\Gamma_q(\omega)}, \quad \Gamma_q(\omega) = \frac{(q;q)_\infty (1-q)^{1-\omega}}{(q^\omega;q)_\infty} \qquad (6)$$

where

$$\Gamma_q(\omega + 1) = \frac{\Gamma_q(\omega)(1-q^\omega)}{1-q}, \quad q \in (0,1).$$

and

$$(\omega; q)_\infty = \prod_{i=0}^{\infty}(1 - q^i \omega). \qquad (7)$$

Next is the difference operator for the formulation of the Jackson derivative

$$\Delta_q h(\xi) = \frac{h(\xi) - h(q\xi)}{\xi(1-q)}, \quad q \in (0,1) \qquad (8)$$

such that

$$\Delta_q(\xi^v) = \left(\frac{1-q^v}{1-q}\right)\xi^{v-1}.$$

Additionally, the idea of the $\mathfrak{Q}$–binomial formula satisfies the equality

$$(t - y)_\flat = \vartheta^\flat\left(\frac{-y}{t}; q\right)_\flat. \qquad (9)$$

The $q$-Mittag–Leffler function was described by the authors in [21] as follows:

$$\Xi_{v,\mu}^{\vartheta}[x]_q = \sum_{n=0}^{\infty} \frac{(q^\vartheta; q)_n}{(q;q)_n} \frac{\chi^n}{\Gamma_q(vn+\mu)}. \qquad (10)$$

In view of the above organization, we consider the $q$–Prabhakar differential operator as follows:

$$[^{\mathcal{C}}\Delta_{\alpha,\beta,\ell}^{\gamma,\kappa,m} h(\xi)]_q = \xi + \sum_{n=\ell+1}^{\infty} h_n [\Sigma_n]_q \xi^n, \qquad (11)$$

where

$$[\Sigma_n]_q := \Gamma_q(n+1)\frac{\Xi_{\alpha,n+1-\beta}^{-\gamma}[\kappa]_q}{\Xi_{\alpha,2-\beta}^{-\gamma}[\kappa]_q}.$$

Note that the quantum fractional integral corresponds to $[^{\mathcal{C}}\Delta_{\alpha,\beta,\ell}^{\gamma,\kappa,m} h]_q(\xi)$, which is given by the series

$$[^{\mathcal{C}}\mathbb{P}_{\alpha,\beta,\ell}^{\gamma,\kappa,m} h]_q(\xi) = \xi + \sum_{n=\ell+1}^{\infty} \frac{h_n}{[\Sigma_n]_q} \xi^n, \quad \xi \in \nabla.$$

Next, results show the sufficient conditions for the convexity and starlikeness of the $q$–operator for a special set of coefficients of $h(\xi)$.

**Proposition 2.** *Let $h$ be convex of order $\varrho, \varrho \in [0,1)$ with non–positive coefficients ($h_n \leq 0$). Moreover, let*

$$\sum_{n=\ell+1}^{\infty} \left(\frac{n(n-\varrho)}{1-\varrho}\right) h_n[\Sigma_n]_q \leq 1.$$

*Then,*

- $[^{\mathcal{C}}\Delta_{\alpha,\beta,\ell}^{\gamma,\kappa,m} h(\xi)]_q$ *is also convex of order $\varrho$.*

- It achieves the next upper and lower bounds

$$|\xi| - \frac{1-\varrho}{(\ell+1)(\ell+1-\varrho)}|\xi|^{\ell+1} \leq |[{}^C\Delta_{\alpha,\beta,\ell}^{\gamma,\kappa,m}h(\xi)]_q| \leq |\xi| + \frac{1-\varrho}{(\ell+1)(\ell+1-\varrho)}|\xi|^{\ell+1}$$

- and its derivative achieves the next upper and lower bounds

$$1 - \frac{1-\varrho}{(\ell+1-\varrho)}|\xi|^{\ell} \leq |[{}^C\Delta_{\alpha,\beta,\ell}^{\gamma,\kappa,m}h(\xi)]'_q| \leq 1 + \frac{1-\varrho}{(\ell+1-\varrho)}|\xi|^{\ell}.$$

- The above results are sharp such that the maximum function is given by the formula (see Figure 1)

$$[{}^C\Delta_{\alpha,\beta,\ell}^{\gamma,\kappa,m}h(\xi)]_q = \xi - \left(\frac{(1-\varrho)}{(\ell+1-\varrho)(\ell+1)}\right)\xi^{\ell+1}.$$

- Let

$${}^C\Delta_{\alpha,\beta,\ell}^{\gamma,\kappa,m}(\xi) := \xi + \sum_{n=\ell+1}^{\infty} [\Sigma_n]_q \xi^n, \quad \xi \in \nabla.$$

If ${}^C\Delta_{\alpha,\beta,\ell}^{\gamma,\kappa,m}(\xi)$ and $h(\xi)$ are a convex of order $\varrho$, then ${}^C\Delta_{\alpha,\beta,\ell}^{\gamma,\kappa,m}h(\xi)$ is convex of order $\rho$, where

$$\rho := \frac{\ell(\ell+1)(\ell+2-2\varrho)}{(\ell+1)^3 - 2\ell(\ell+2)\varrho + \ell\varrho^2 - 1}.$$

**Proof.** By the assumptions of the proposition, the convex function

$$h(\xi) = \xi - \sum_{n=\ell+1}^{\infty} h_n \xi^n, \quad \xi \in \nabla, \ell \in \mathbb{N}.$$

satisfies the inequality

$$\sum_{n=\ell+1}^{\infty} \left(\frac{n(n-\varrho)}{1-\varrho}\right) h_n [\Sigma_n]_q < 1.$$

In addition, in view of Lemma 2 [22], we have that $[{}^C\Delta_{\alpha,\beta,\ell}^{\gamma,\kappa,m}h(\xi)]_q$ is also convex of order $\varrho$. This completes the first part.

Now, the first part gives the following inequalities:

$$\left(\frac{(\ell+1)(\ell+1-\varrho)}{1-\varrho}\right) \sum_{n=\ell+1}^{\infty} h_n[\Sigma_n]_q \leq \sum_{n=\ell+1}^{\infty} n\left(\frac{n-\varrho}{1-\varrho}\right) h_n[\Sigma_n]_q \leq 1,$$

which yields

$$\sum_{n=\ell+1}^{\infty} h_n[\Sigma_n]_q \leq \frac{1-\varrho}{(\ell+1)(\ell+1-\varrho)}.$$

Moreover, we have

$$\sum_{n=\ell+1}^{\infty} nh_n[\Sigma_n]_q \leq \frac{1-\varrho}{(\ell+1-\varrho)}.$$

Consequently, we obtain the second part and third parts respectively. Clearly, the maximum sharp function is given by the formula

$$[{}^C\Delta_{\alpha,\beta,\ell}^{\gamma,\kappa,m}h(\xi)]_q = \xi - \left(\frac{(1-\varrho)}{(\ell+1-\varrho)(\ell+1)}\right)\xi^{\ell+1}.$$

A convolution property implies that

$$^C\Delta_{\alpha,\beta,\ell}^{\gamma,\kappa,m} h(\xi) = \left(^C\Delta_{\alpha,\beta,\ell}^{\gamma,\kappa,m} \times h\right)(\xi),$$

where $^C\Delta_{\alpha,\beta,\ell}^{\gamma,\kappa,m}$ and $h$ are convex of order $\varrho$. To show that $^C\Delta_{\alpha,\beta,\ell}^{\gamma,\kappa,m} h(\xi)$ is convex of order $\rho$, we have to show that

$$\sum_{n=\ell+1}^{\infty} n\left(\frac{n-\rho}{1-\rho}\right) h_n [\Sigma_n]_q \leq 1.$$

Since

$$\sum_{n=\ell+1}^{\infty} n\left(\frac{n-\varrho}{1-\varrho}\right) h_n \leq 1, \quad \sum_{n=\ell+1}^{\infty} n\left(\frac{n-\varrho}{1-\varrho}\right) [\Sigma_n]_q \leq 1,$$

then by the Cauchy–Schwarz inequality, we obtain

$$\sum_{n=\ell+1}^{\infty} n\left(\frac{n-\varrho}{1-\varrho}\right) \sqrt{h_n [\Sigma_n]_q} \leq 1, \quad \sqrt{h_n [\Sigma_n]_q} \leq \frac{1-\varrho}{n(n-\varrho)}.$$

However, $\frac{1-\varrho}{n(n-\varrho)} \leq \frac{(n-\varrho)(1-\rho)}{n(1-\varrho)(n-\rho)}$; thus, a computation yields

$$\rho := \frac{\ell(\ell+1)(\ell+2-2\varrho)}{(\ell+1)^3 - 2\ell(\ell+2)\varrho + \ell\varrho^2 - 1}.$$

Hence, in view of Lemma 2 [22], $^C\Delta_{\alpha,\beta,\ell}^{\gamma,\kappa,m} h(\xi)$ is convex of order $\rho$. This completes the last part of the result. □

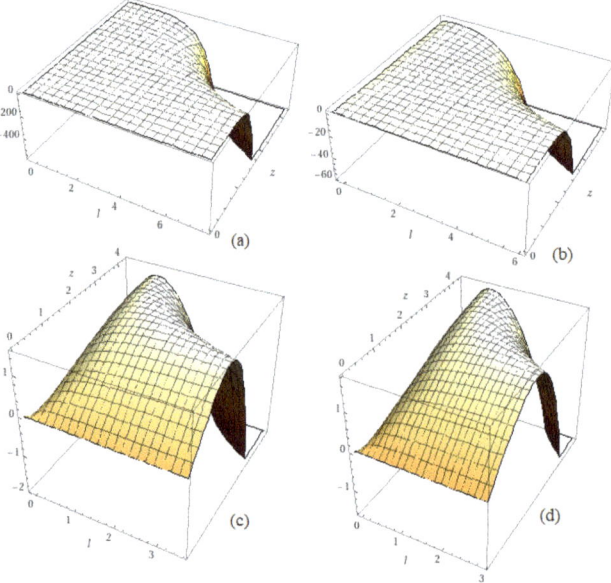

**Figure 1.** 3D–plot of the maximum function of convexity for $\varrho$, (**a**):0; (**b**):0.25; (**c**):0.5; (**d**): 0.6.

**Proposition 3.** Let $h$ be starlike of order $\varrho, \varrho \in [0,1)$ with non-positive coefficients ($h_n \leq 0$). Moreover, let
$$\sum_{n=\ell+1}^{\infty}\left(\frac{n-\varrho}{1-\varrho}\right)h_n[\Sigma_n]_q \leq 1.$$

Then,

- $[{}^C\Delta_{\alpha,\beta,\ell}^{\gamma,\kappa,m}h(\xi)]_q$ is also starlike of order $\varrho$.
- It achieves the next upper and lower bounds

$$|\xi| - \frac{1-\varrho}{\ell+1-\varrho}|\xi|^{\ell+1} \leq |[{}^C\Delta_{\alpha,\beta,\ell}^{\gamma,\kappa,m}h(\xi)]_q| \leq |\xi| + \frac{1-\varrho}{\ell+1-\varrho}|\xi|^{\ell+1}$$

- and its derivative achieves the next upper and lower bounds

$$1 - \frac{(1-\varrho)(\ell+1)}{(\ell+1-\varrho)}|\xi|^{\ell} \leq |[{}^C\Delta_{\alpha,\beta,\ell}^{\gamma,\kappa,m}h(\xi)]'_q| \leq 1 + \frac{(1-\varrho)(\ell+1)}{(\ell+1-\varrho)}|\xi|^{\ell}.$$

- The above results are sharp such that the maximum function is given by the formula (see Figure 2)

$$[{}^C\Delta_{\alpha,\beta,\ell}^{\gamma,\kappa,m}h(\xi)]_q = \xi - \left(\frac{1-\varrho}{\ell+1-\varrho}\right)\xi^{\ell+1}.$$

- If ${}^C\Delta_{\alpha,\beta,\ell}^{\gamma,\kappa,m}(\xi)$ and $h(\xi)$ are starlike of order $\varrho$ then ${}^C\Delta_{\alpha,\beta,\ell}^{\gamma,\kappa,m}h(\xi)$ is starlike of order $\rho$, where

$$\rho := \frac{\ell+1-\varrho^2}{\ell+2-2\varrho}.$$

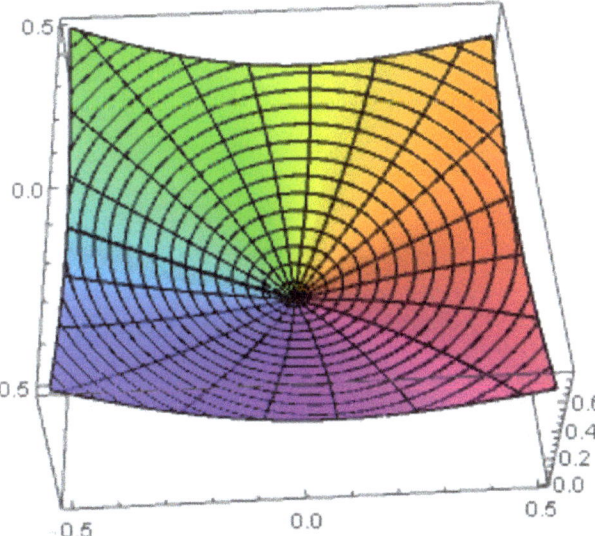

**Figure 2.** 3D–Plot of the maximum function of starlikeness for $\varrho = 0.5$.

**Proof.** Since $h$ has non-positive coefficients, then it can be written as follows:

$$h(\xi) = \xi - \sum_{n=\ell+1}^{\infty} h_n \xi^n, \quad \xi \in \nabla, \ell \in \mathbb{N}.$$

Moreover, since $h$ is starlike of order $\varrho$, where $\varrho \in [0,1)$, satisfies the inequality

$$\sum_{n=\ell+1}^{\infty} \left(\frac{n-\varrho}{1-\varrho}\right) h_n [\Sigma_n]_q \leq 1,$$

then in view of Lemma 1 [22], we have $[{}^C\Delta_{\alpha,\beta,\ell}^{\gamma,\kappa,m} h(\xi)]_q$ is also starlike of order $\varrho$. This completes the first part.

By the first part of this result, we obtain

$$\left(\frac{\ell+1-\varrho}{1-\varrho}\right) \sum_{n=\ell+1}^{\infty} h_n [\Sigma_n]_q \leq \sum_{n=\ell+1}^{\infty} \left(\frac{n-\varrho}{1-\varrho}\right) h_n [\Sigma_n]_q \leq 1,$$

which yields

$$\sum_{n=\ell+1}^{\infty} h_n [\Sigma_n]_q \leq \frac{1-\varrho}{\ell+1-\varrho}.$$

Consequently, we have

$$|[{}^C\Delta_{\alpha,\beta,\ell}^{\gamma,\kappa,m} h(\xi)]_q| \geq |\xi| - |\xi|^{\ell+1} \sum_{n=\ell+1}^{\infty} h_n [\Sigma_n]_q \geq |\xi| - |\xi|^{\ell+1} \left(\frac{1-\varrho}{\ell+1-\varrho}\right)$$

and

$$|[{}^C\Delta_{\alpha,\beta,\ell}^{\gamma,\kappa,m} h(\xi)]_q| \leq |\xi| + |\xi|^{\ell+1} \sum_{n=\ell+1}^{\infty} h_n [\Sigma_n]_q \leq |\xi| + |\xi|^{\ell+1} \left(\frac{1-\varrho}{\ell+1-\varrho}\right).$$

Combining the above two inequalities, we obtain the second part. By using the fact,

$$\sum_{n=\ell+1}^{\infty} n h_n [\Sigma_n]_q \leq 1 - \varrho + \frac{\varrho(1-\varrho)}{\ell+1-\varrho} = \frac{(\ell+1)(1-\varrho)}{\ell+1-\varrho}.$$

Therefore, a computation implies that

$$|[{}^C\Delta_{\alpha,\beta,\ell}^{\gamma,\kappa,m} h(\xi)]'_q| \geq 1 - |\xi|^{\ell} \sum_{n=\ell+1}^{\infty} n h_n [\Sigma_n]_q \geq 1 - \frac{(1-\varrho)(\ell+1)}{(\ell+1-\varrho)} |\xi|^{\ell}$$

and

$$|[{}^C\Delta_{\alpha,\beta,\ell}^{\gamma,\kappa,m} h(\xi)]'_q| \leq 1 + |\xi|^{\ell} \sum_{n=\ell+1}^{\infty} n h_n [\Sigma_n]_q \leq 1 + \frac{(1-\varrho)(\ell+1)}{(\ell+1-\varrho)} |\xi|^{\ell}.$$

Combining the above inequalities, we receive the third item. A direct calculation yields the maximum function placed as follows:

$$[{}^C\Delta_{\alpha,\beta,\ell}^{\gamma,\kappa,m} h(\xi)]_q = \xi - \left(\frac{1-\varrho}{\ell+1-\varrho}\right) \xi^{\ell+1},$$

which completes part four.

By the convolution definition, we have

$${}^C\Delta_{\alpha,\beta,\ell}^{\gamma,\kappa,m} h(\xi) = \left({}^C\Delta_{\alpha,\beta,\ell}^{\gamma,\kappa,m} \times h\right)(\xi),$$

where $^{C}\Delta_{\alpha,\beta,\ell}^{\gamma,\kappa,m}$ and $h$ are starlike of order $\varrho$. To show that $^{C}\Delta_{\alpha,\beta,\ell}^{\gamma,\kappa,m}h(\xi)$ is starlike of order $\rho$, we need to show that

$$\sum_{n=\ell+1}^{\infty}\left(\frac{n-\rho}{1-\rho}\right)h_n[\Sigma_n]_q \leq 1.$$

Since

$$\sum_{n=\ell+1}^{\infty}\left(\frac{n-\varrho}{1-\varrho}\right)h_n \leq 1$$

and

$$\sum_{n=\ell+1}^{\infty}\left(\frac{n-\varrho}{1-\varrho}\right)[\Sigma_n]_q \leq 1,$$

then in view of the Cauchy–Schwarz inequality, we obtain

$$\sum_{n=\ell+1}^{\infty}\left(\frac{n-\varrho}{1-\varrho}\right)\sqrt{h_n[\Sigma_n]_q} \leq 1,$$

where

$$\sqrt{h_n[\Sigma_n]_q} \leq \frac{1-\varrho}{n-\varrho}.$$

However,

$$\frac{1-\varrho}{n-\varrho} \leq \frac{(n-\varrho)(1-\rho)}{(1-\varrho)(n-\rho)};$$

thus, the equality of the above conclusion yields

$$\rho := \frac{\ell+1-\varrho^2}{\ell+2-2\varrho}.$$

Hence, in view of Lemma 1 [22], $^{C}\Delta_{\alpha,\beta,\ell}^{\gamma,\kappa,m}h(\xi)$ is starlike of order $\rho$. This completes the last part of the result. □

Note that the sufficient condition for convexity is

$$\Re\left(1+\frac{\xi h''(\xi)}{h'(\xi)}\right) > 0$$

and the class of all these functions is denoted by $C$. Moreover, the sufficient condition for the starlikeness is

$$\Re\left(\frac{\xi h'(\xi)}{h(\xi)}\right) > 0$$

and the class of all these functions is denoted by $S^*$.

Combining the two definitions to obtain the following functional using the $q$–operator:

**Definition 1.** *Let $h \in \Lambda_\ell$. Define a functional $[^{\epsilon}\mathbb{J}_{\alpha,\beta,\ell}^{\gamma,\kappa,m}h(\xi)]_q$ as follows:*

$$[^{\epsilon}\mathbb{J}_{\alpha,\beta,\ell}^{\gamma,\kappa,m}h(\xi)]_q = (1-\epsilon)\left(\frac{\xi[^{C}\Delta_{\alpha,\beta,\ell}^{\gamma,\kappa,m}h(\xi)]'_q}{[^{C}\Delta_{\alpha,\beta,\ell}^{\gamma,\kappa,m}h(\xi)]_q}\right) + \epsilon\left(1+\frac{\xi[^{C}\Delta_{\alpha,\beta,\ell}^{\gamma,\kappa,m}h(\xi)]''_q}{[^{C}\Delta_{\alpha,\beta,\ell}^{\gamma,\kappa,m}h(\xi)]'_q}\right). \quad (12)$$

The Formula (12) is a generalization of the functional appearing in [23]—P250 for a special type of convex integral operator. We advance to investigate extra properties utilizing the $[^{C}\Delta_{\alpha,\beta,\ell}^{\gamma,\kappa,m}]_q$.

## 4. Differential Inequalities

We consider the following results ([23]—P258–P266).

**Lemma 1.** *Define the following set for a positive integer $\ell$,*

$$\mathcal{H}[1,\ell] = \{\hbar : \hbar(\zeta) = 1 + h_\ell \zeta^\ell + h_{\ell+1}\zeta^{\ell+1} + \ldots\}.$$

*In addition, for $\wp > 0$, $\aleph \in (-1,1]$, the function $F \in \mathcal{H}[1,\ell]$ achieves*

$$G(\zeta) \prec \frac{1 + (\aleph + \wp\ell)\zeta}{1 - \zeta} + \frac{\ell\wp\aleph\zeta}{1 + \aleph\zeta} \equiv g(\zeta).$$

*If $g \in \mathcal{H}[1,\ell]$ is a solution of the differential equation*

$$\wp\zeta g'(\zeta) + G(\zeta).g(\zeta) = 1,$$

*then*

$$g(\zeta) \prec \frac{1-\zeta}{1+\aleph\zeta}, \quad \zeta \in \nabla,$$

*where $\prec$ indicates the subordination notion.*

**Lemma 2.** *Let $\phi \in \Lambda_\ell$. In addition, let $\lambda > 0$ and $\varsigma \in [0,1)$. If one of the following inequalities*

$$\frac{\zeta\phi'(\zeta)}{\phi(\zeta)} \prec \frac{1 + (1 - 2\varsigma + \ell\lambda)\zeta}{1 - \zeta} + \frac{\ell\lambda(1 - 2\varsigma)\zeta}{1 + (1 - 2\varsigma)\zeta} \equiv g(\zeta),$$

$$(1-\lambda)\left(\frac{\zeta\phi'(\zeta)}{\phi(\zeta)}\right) + \lambda\left(1 + \frac{\zeta\phi''(\zeta)}{\phi'(\zeta)}\right) \prec \frac{1 + (1 - 2\varsigma + \ell\lambda)\zeta}{1 - \zeta} + \frac{\ell\lambda(1 - 2\varsigma)\zeta}{1 + (1 - 2\varsigma)\zeta} \equiv g(\zeta),$$

*holds, then the $\lambda$-convex operator that acts on $\phi$*

$$\Phi_\lambda(\zeta) = \left(\frac{1}{\lambda}\int_0^\zeta \phi^{1/\lambda}(\tau)\tau^{-1}d\tau\right)^\lambda$$

*is starlike of order $\varsigma$.*

The main outcomes of this investigation are as follows:

**Theorem 1.** *Consider the functional in (12). If*

$$[^\epsilon \mathbb{J}_{\alpha,\beta,\ell}^{\gamma,\kappa,m} h(\zeta)]_q \prec \lambda(\zeta), \quad \zeta \in \nabla,$$

*where*

$$\lambda(\zeta) = \exp\left(\int_0^\zeta -\frac{[^\epsilon \mathbb{J}_{\alpha,\beta,\ell}^{\gamma,\kappa,m} h(\zeta)]_q}{\tau}d\tau\right)\left(\int_0^\zeta \frac{\exp\left(\int_0^z \frac{[^\epsilon \mathbb{J}_{\alpha,\beta,\ell}^{\gamma,\kappa,m} h(\zeta)]_q}{\tau}d\tau\right)}{\zeta}d\zeta + 1\right)$$

$$= 1 + \sum_{n=1+\ell}^{\infty} \lambda_n \zeta^n$$

*satisfies*

$$|\lambda_n| \leq 2 + \ell + (-1)^{n+1}\ell, \quad \ell \in \mathbb{N}, n \geq 1;$$

*then,*

$$[^\epsilon \mathbb{J}_{\alpha,\beta,\ell}^{\gamma,\kappa,m} h(\zeta)]_q \prec \frac{1-\zeta}{1+\zeta}, \quad \zeta \in \nabla.$$

**Proof.** Our aim is to apply Lemma 1. Clearly, $[{}^{\epsilon}\mathbb{J}_{\alpha,\beta,\ell}^{\gamma,\kappa,m}h(\xi)]_q \in \mathcal{H}[1,\ell]$, where $[{}^{\epsilon}\mathbb{J}_{\alpha,\beta,\ell}^{\gamma,\kappa,m}(0)]_q = 1$. Formulate a function as follows:

$$g(\xi) = \frac{1 + 2(\ell+1)\xi + \xi^2}{1 - \xi^2}$$
$$= 1 + 2(\ell+1)\xi + 2\xi^2 + 2(\ell+1)\xi^3 + 2\xi^4 + 2(\ell+1)\xi^5 + O(\xi^6)$$
$$= 1 + \sum_{n=\ell+1}^{\infty} \left(2 + \ell + (-1)^{n+1}\ell\right)\xi^n.$$

Obviously, $g(\xi)$ is convex univalent in $\nabla$ achieving (see Figure 3)

$$\Re\left(1 + \frac{\xi g''(\xi)}{g'(\xi)}\right) = \Re\left(1 + \frac{\frac{4\xi(\xi(\ell(\xi^2+3)+\xi(\xi+3)+3)+1))}{(1-\xi^2)^3}}{\frac{2(\ell(\xi^2+1)+(\xi+1)^2)}{(1-\xi^2)^2}}\right) > 0$$

for all $|\xi| < 1$ and $\ell > 0$. Obviously, $\lambda(\xi)$ is a solution of the differential equation

$$\xi \lambda'(\xi) + G(\xi) \cdot \lambda(\xi) = 1,$$

where $G(\xi) = [{}^{\epsilon}\mathbb{J}_{\alpha,\beta,\ell}^{\gamma,\kappa,m}h(\xi)]_q$. Since

$$\lambda(\xi) = 1 + \sum_{n=\ell+1}^{\infty} \lambda_n \xi^n$$

achieves

$$|\lambda_n| \leq 2 + \ell + (-1)^{n+1}\ell, \quad \ell \in \mathbb{N},$$

then we obtain the following inequality:

$$\lambda(\xi) \ll g(\xi), \quad \xi \subset \nabla,$$

where $\ll$ indicates the majority relation. Then, by [24]—Corollary 1 and for $|\xi| \in (0.28, \sqrt{2}-1)$, we have

$$\lambda(\xi) \prec g(\xi), \quad \xi \in \nabla.$$

By the concept of the subordination, there occurs a function $w(\xi), |w(\xi)| \leq |\xi| < 1$, $w(0) = 0$ then this implies that

$$\lambda(\xi) = g(w(\xi)), \quad \xi \in \nabla.$$

By letting $w(\xi) = \xi$, we obtain

$$[{}^{\epsilon}\mathbb{J}_{\alpha,\beta,\ell}^{\gamma,\kappa,m}h(\xi)]_q \prec g(\xi), \quad \xi \in \nabla,$$

where

$$g(\xi) = \frac{1 + 2(\ell+1)\xi + \xi^2}{1 - \xi^2}$$
$$= \frac{1 + (1+\ell)\xi}{1 - \xi} + \frac{\ell\xi}{1+\xi}.$$

Thus, by letting $\wp = \aleph = 1$ in Lemma 1, we confirm that

$$f(\xi) \prec \frac{1-\xi}{1+\xi},$$

which leads to the double inequality

$$[{}^{\epsilon}\mathbb{J}_{\alpha,\beta,\ell}^{\gamma,\kappa,m} h(\xi)]_q \prec g(\xi) \prec \frac{1-\xi}{1+\xi}.$$

Hence, we reach the fact

$$[{}^{\epsilon}\mathbb{J}_{\alpha,\beta,\ell}^{\gamma,\kappa,m} h(\xi)]_q \prec \frac{1-\xi}{1+\xi}, \quad \xi \in \nabla.$$

□

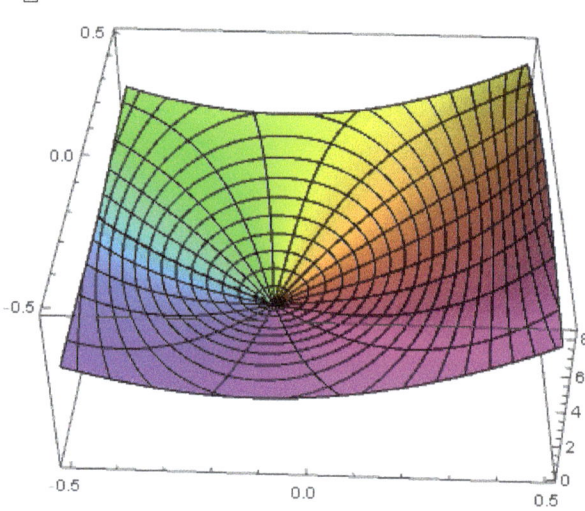

**Figure 3.** The plot of the convex function $g(\xi), \ell = 1, \lambda = 0.5$.

**Theorem 2.** *Consider the functional in (12). If*

$$[{}^{\lambda}\mathbb{J}_{\alpha,\beta,\ell}^{\gamma,\kappa,m} h(\xi)]_q \prec \lambda_\lambda(\xi), \quad \xi \in \nabla, \lambda > 0,$$

*where*

$$\lambda_\lambda(\xi) = \exp\left(\int_0^\xi -\frac{[{}^{\lambda}\mathbb{J}_{\alpha,\beta,\ell}^{\gamma,\kappa,m} h(\xi)]_q}{\lambda \tau} d\tau\right) \cdot \left(\int_0^\xi \frac{\exp\left(\int_0^\zeta \frac{[{}^{\lambda}\mathbb{J}_{\alpha,\beta,\ell}^{\gamma,\kappa,m} h(\xi)]_q}{\lambda \tau} d\tau\right)}{\lambda \zeta} d\zeta + 1\right)$$

$$= 1 + \sum_{n=1+\ell}^{\infty} \lambda_n(\lambda) \xi^n$$

*achieves*

$$|\lambda_n(\lambda)| \leq |2 - ((-1)^n - 1)\lambda \ell|, \quad \ell \in \mathbb{N}, n \geq 1,$$

then the $\lambda$-convex operator that acts on the q-operator $[{}^C\Delta_{\alpha,\beta,\ell}^{\gamma,\kappa,m}h(\xi)]_q$,

$$\Phi_\lambda(\xi) = \left(\frac{1}{\lambda}\int_0^\xi [{}^C\Delta_{\alpha,\beta,\ell}^{\gamma,\kappa,m}h(\xi)]_q^{1/\lambda}\tau^{-1}d\tau\right)^\lambda$$

is starlike in $\nabla$.

**Proof.** Our proof is based on Lemma 2. Eventually, $[{}^\lambda\mathbb{J}_{\alpha,\beta,\ell}^{\gamma,\kappa,m}h(\xi)]_q \in \mathcal{H}[1,\ell]$, where $[{}^\lambda\mathbb{J}_{\alpha,\beta,\ell}^{\gamma,\kappa,m}(0)]_q = 1$. Formulate a function as follows:

$$\begin{aligned}g(\xi) &= \frac{1+2(\ell\lambda+1)\xi+\xi^2}{1-\xi^2}\\ &= 1+2(\ell\lambda+1)\xi+2\xi^2+2(\ell\lambda+1)\xi^3+2\xi^4+2(\ell\lambda+1)\xi^5+O(\xi^6)\\ &= 1+\sum_{n=\ell+1}^\infty (2-((-1)^n-1)\ell\lambda)\,\xi^n.\end{aligned}$$

Obviously, $g(\xi)$ is convex univalent in $\nabla$ satisfying

$$\Re\left(1+\frac{\xi g''(\xi)}{g'(\xi)}\right) = \Re\left(1+\frac{\frac{4\xi(\xi(\ell\lambda(\xi^2+3)+\xi(\xi+3)+3)+1))}{(1-\xi^2)^3}}{\frac{2(\ell\lambda(\xi^2+1)+(\xi+1)^2)}{(1-\xi^2)^2}}\right) > 0$$

for all $|\xi|<1, \lambda>0$ and $\ell>0$. Clearly, $\lambda_\lambda(\xi)$ is a solution of the differential equation

$$\lambda\xi\,\lambda_\lambda'(\xi) + G(\xi).\lambda_\lambda(\xi) = 1,$$

where $G(\xi) = [{}^\lambda\mathbb{J}_{\alpha,\beta,\ell}^{\gamma,\kappa,m}h(\xi)]_q$. However,

$$\lambda_\lambda(\xi) = 1 + \sum_{n=\ell+1}^\infty \lambda_n(\lambda)\xi^n$$

satisfies

$$|\lambda_n(\lambda)| \leq |2-((-1)^n-1)\ell\lambda|, \quad \lambda>0, \ell\in\mathbb{N},$$

then we conclude that

$$\lambda_\lambda(\xi) \ll g(\xi), \quad \xi\in\nabla.$$

Then, by [24]—Corollary 1 and for $|\xi|\in(0.28,\sqrt{2}-1)$, we have

$$\lambda_\lambda(\xi) \prec g(\xi), \quad \xi\in\nabla.$$

Again the subordination definition implies that a function occurs with $u(\xi), |u(\xi)|\leq|\xi|<1, u(0)=0$ such that

$$\lambda_\lambda(\xi) = g(u(\xi)), \quad \xi\in\nabla.$$

By letting $u(\xi)=\xi$, we have

$$[{}^\lambda\mathbb{J}_{\alpha,\beta,\ell}^{\gamma,\kappa,m}h(\xi)]_q \prec g(\xi), \quad \xi\in\nabla,$$

where

$$[{}^\lambda\mathbb{J}_{\alpha,\beta,\ell}^{\gamma,\kappa,m}h(\xi)]_q = (1-\lambda)\left(\frac{\xi[{}^C\Delta_{\alpha,\beta,\ell}^{\gamma,\kappa,m}h(\xi)]_q'}{[{}^C\Delta_{\alpha,\beta,\ell}^{\gamma,\kappa,m}h(\xi)]_q}\right) + \lambda\left(1+\frac{\xi[{}^C\Delta_{\alpha,\beta,\ell}^{\gamma,\kappa,m}h(\xi)]_q''}{[{}^C\Delta_{\alpha,\beta,\ell}^{\gamma,\kappa,m}h(\xi)]_q'}\right)$$

and
$$g(\varsigma) = \frac{1 + 2(\ell\lambda + 1)\varsigma + \varsigma^2}{1 - \varsigma^2}$$
$$= \frac{1 + (1 + \ell\lambda)\varsigma}{1 - \varsigma} + \frac{\ell\lambda\varsigma}{1 + \varsigma}.$$

Thus, by considering $\varsigma = 0$ in Lemma 2, we attain that the $\lambda$-convex operator that acts on the $q$-operator $[^C\Delta_{\alpha,\beta,\ell}^{\gamma,\kappa,m} h(\xi)]_q$,

$$\Phi_\lambda(\xi) = \left(\frac{1}{\lambda} \int_0^\xi [^C\Delta_{\alpha,\beta,\ell}^{\gamma,\kappa,m} h(\xi)]_q^{1/\lambda} \tau^{-1} d\tau\right)^\lambda, \quad \lambda > 0,$$

is starlike in $\nabla$. □

**Theorem 3.** *Consider the operator $[^C\Delta_{\alpha,\beta,\ell}^{\gamma,\kappa,m} h(\xi)]_q$. Then,*

$$[^C\Delta_{\alpha,\beta,\ell}^{\gamma,\kappa,m} h(\xi)]_q \in \mathcal{S}^* \Rightarrow \left(\xi^{\nu-1} \int_0^\xi \left(\frac{[^C\Delta_{\alpha,\beta,\ell}^{\gamma,\kappa,m} h(\tau)]_q}{\tau}\right)^{\rho_1} \left(\frac{\mathbb{k}(\tau)}{\tau}\right)^{\rho_2} d\tau\right)^{1/\nu} \in \mathcal{S}^*\left(\frac{2\nu - 1}{2\nu}\right),$$

*where $\mathbb{k}$ is convex univalent function, $\nu > 1/2$ and $\rho_1 \geq 0, \rho_2 > 0$.*

*Moreover, if*
$$\mathbb{k}(\xi) = \frac{\xi}{1 - \xi}, \quad \rho_2 = 1,$$

*then*

$$[^C\Delta_{\alpha,\beta,\ell}^{\gamma,\kappa,m} h(\xi)]_q \in \mathcal{S}^* \Rightarrow \left(\xi^{\nu-1} \int_0^\xi \left(\frac{[^C\Delta_{\alpha,\beta,\ell}^{\gamma,\kappa,m} h(\tau)]_q}{\tau(1-\tau)^{1/\rho_1}}\right)^{\rho_1} d\tau\right)^{1/\nu} \in \mathcal{S}^*\left(\frac{2\nu - 1}{2\nu}\right),$$

*where $\mathbb{k}$ is convex univalent function and $\rho_1 \geq 0, \rho_2 > 0$.*

**Proof.** Let $\mathbb{k}(\xi) = \xi + \sum_{n=\ell+1}^\infty k_n \xi^n$. First, we must show that

$$\left(\xi^{\nu-1} \int_0^\xi \left(\frac{[^C\Delta_{\alpha,\beta,\ell}^{\gamma,\kappa,m} h(\tau)]_q}{\tau}\right)^{\rho_1} \left(\frac{\mathbb{k}(\tau)}{\tau}\right)^{\rho_2} d\tau\right)^{1/\nu} \in \Lambda_\ell. \tag{13}$$

By the definition of $[^C\Delta_{\alpha,\beta,\ell}^{\gamma,\kappa,m} h(\tau)]_q$, we have

$$I[F,G](\xi) := \left(\xi^{\nu-1} \int_0^\xi \left(\frac{[^C\Delta_{\alpha,\beta,\ell}^{\gamma,\kappa,m}h(\tau)]_q}{\tau}\right)^{\rho_1} \left(\frac{\Bbbk(\tau)}{\tau}\right)^{\rho_2} d\tau\right)^{1/\nu}$$

$$= \left(\xi^{\nu-1} \int_0^\xi \left(\frac{\tau + \sum_{n=\ell+1}^\infty h_n \Sigma_n \tau^n}{\tau}\right)^{\rho_1} \left(\frac{\tau + \sum_{n=\ell+1}^\infty k_n \tau^n}{\tau}\right)^{\rho_2} d\tau\right)^{1/\nu}$$

$$= \left(\xi^{\nu-1} \int_0^\xi \left(1 + \sum_{n=\ell+1}^\infty h_n \Sigma_n \tau^{n-1}\right)^{\rho_1} \left(1 + \sum_{n=\ell+1}^\infty k_n \tau^{n-1}\right)^{\rho_2} d\tau\right)^{1/\nu}$$

$$= \left(\xi^{\nu-1} \int_0^\xi \left(1 + \rho_1 \sum_{n=\ell+1}^\infty h_n \Sigma_n \tau^{n-1} + \ldots\right) \left(1 + \rho_2 \sum_{n=\ell+1}^\infty k_n \tau^{n-1} + \ldots\right) d\tau\right)^{1/\nu}$$

$$= \left(\xi^{\nu-1} \int_0^\xi \left(\left(1 + \rho_1 \sum_{n=\ell+1}^\infty h_n \Sigma_n \tau^{n-1}\right) + \ldots\right) d\tau\right)^{1/\nu}.$$

A direct integration yields the conclusion in (13). Since $\Bbbk(\xi)$ is convex in $\nabla$, then it belongs to $\mathcal{S}^*(1/2)$ (the class of starlike functions of order $1/2$). However, the multiplication of starlike functions is also starlike; then, the integral $I[F,G](\xi)$ is starlike of order $(2\nu-1)/2\nu$ (see [23]—P169). The second part comes from the first part, when $\Bbbk(\xi) = \xi/(1-\xi)$ and $\rho_2 = 1$. Hence, the proof. □

**Example 1.** *Consider the differential equation*

$$\left(\frac{\xi[^C\Delta_{\alpha,\beta,\ell}^{\gamma,\kappa,m}h(\xi)]_q'}{[^C\Delta_{\alpha,\beta,\ell}^{\gamma,\kappa,m}h(\xi)]_q}\right) = \left(\frac{1-\xi}{1+\xi}\right), \tag{14}$$

*and the solution is given by*

$$[^C\Delta_{\alpha,\beta,\ell}^{\gamma,\kappa,m}h(\xi)]_q = \frac{\xi}{(1-\xi)^2},$$

*which is starlike (see Figure 1), and hence, in view of Theorem 3, we have*

$$\left(\xi^{\nu-1} \int_0^\xi \left(\frac{[^C\Delta_{\alpha,\beta,\ell}^{\gamma,\kappa,m}h(\tau)]_q}{\tau(1-\tau)^{1/\rho_1}}\right)^{\rho_1} d\tau\right)^{1/\nu} \in \mathcal{S}^*\left(\frac{2\nu-1}{2\nu}\right),$$

*where $\rho_1 \geq 0$.*

**Example 2.** *Consider the differential equation*

$$\left(\frac{\xi[^C\Delta_{\alpha,\beta,\ell}^{\gamma,\kappa,m}h(\xi)]_q'}{[^C\Delta_{\alpha,\beta,\ell}^{\gamma,\kappa,m}h(\xi)]_q}\right) = 1, \tag{15}$$

*and the outcome of the above equation is formulated by*

$$[^C\Delta_{\alpha,\beta,\ell}^{\gamma,\kappa,m}h(\xi)]_q = \xi,$$

*which satisfies*

$$\Re\left(\frac{\xi[^C\Delta_{\alpha,\beta,\ell}^{\gamma,\kappa,m}h(\xi)]_q'}{[^C\Delta_{\alpha,\beta,\ell}^{\gamma,\kappa,m}h(\xi)]_q}\right) = 1 > 0;$$

thus, it is starlike. According to Theorem 3, we have

$$\left(\xi^{\nu-1}\int_0^\xi \left(\frac{1}{(1-\tau)^{1/\rho_1}}\right)^{\rho_1} d\tau\right)^{1/\nu} \in S^*\left(\frac{2\nu-1}{2\nu}\right),$$

where $\rho_1 \geq 0$.

## 5. Conclusions

From above, we conclude that the $q$–Prabhakar fractional differential operator of a complex variable can be studied in view of the geometric function theory by consuming a special class of analytic functions. Various differential inequalities are studied by the suggested operator and then its properties are investigated based on the concepts of subordination and superordination. A starlikeness of the operator implies a starlikeness of an integral formula, which indicates a solution of the well-known Briot–Bouquet differential equation (see Theorem 3). Finally, we presented the sharpness of convexity and starlikeness and estimate the corresponding extreme functions.

For future works, one can suggest the double QFC. Additionally, it is possible to extend the $q$–calculus to post quantum calculus, which is represented by the $(p,q)$-calculus. In reality, such a QFC extension cannot be achieved by simply replacing $q$ in the $q$-calculus with $q/p$. When $p = 1$ in the $(p,q)$–calculus, one can derive the $q$-calculus. The number of double QFC is determined by

$$[n]_{p,q} = \frac{p^n - q^n}{p - q}.$$

Moreover, the double QFC derivative is given by

$$\Delta_{p,q} h(\xi) = \frac{h(p\xi) - h(q\xi)}{\xi(p - q)}, \quad 0 < q < p \leq 1, \ \Delta_{p,q} h(0) = h'(0).$$

**Author Contributions:** Conceptualization, R.W.I. and N.M.A.; methodology, R.W.I. and N.M.A.; formal analysis, R.W.I.; inquiry, R.W.I. and N.M.A.; and financing acquisition, N.M.A. All authors have read and agreed to the published version of the manuscript.

**Funding:** This research received no external funding.

**Institutional Review Board Statement:** Not applicable.

**Informed Consent Statement:** Not applicable.

**Data Availability Statement:** In this investigation, no recorded data were collected or examined. This article does not allow for the exchange of data.

**Conflicts of Interest:** The authors declare no conflict of interest.

## References

1. Jackson, F.H. q-form of Taylor's theorem. *Messenger Math.* **1909**, *38*, 62–64.
2. Exton, H. *Q-Hypergeometric Functions and Applications*; John Wiley & Sons, Inc.: New York, NY, USA, 1983; Volume 355.
3. Celeghini, E.; Demartino, S.; Desiena, S.; Rasetti, M.; Vitiello, G. Quantum groups, coherent states, squeezing and lattice quantum mechanics. *Ann. Phys.* **1995**, *241*, 50–67. [CrossRef]
4. Biedenharn, L.C. The quantum group SUq (2) and a q-analogue of the boson operators. *J. Phys. A Math. Gen.* **1989**, *22*, L873. [CrossRef]
5. Ohnuki, Y.; Susumu, K. *Quantum Field Theory and Parastatistics*; University of Tokyo Press: Tokyo, Japan, 1982; pp. 100–110.
6. Zirar, H. Some applications of fractional calculus operators to a certain subclass of analytic functions defined by integral operator involving generalized Hypergeometric function. *Gen. Math. Notes* **2016**, *35*, 19–35.
7. Hadid, S.B.; Ibrahim, R.W.; Shaher, M. Multivalent functions and differential operator extended by the quantum calculus. *Fractal Fract.* **2022**, *6*, 354. [CrossRef]
8. Arfaoui, S.; Maryam, G.A.; Ben, M.A. Quantum wavelet uncertainty principle. *Fractal Fract.* **2021**, *6*, 8. [CrossRef]

9. Aldawish, I.; Ibrahim, R.W. Solvability of a new q-differential equation related to q-differential inequality of a special type of analytic functions. *Fractal Fract.* **2021**, *5*, 228. [CrossRef]
10. Pishkoo, A.; Darus, M. On Meijer's G-Functions (MGFs) and its applications. *Rev. Theor. Sci.* **2015**, *3*, 216–223. [CrossRef]
11. Prabhakar, T.R. A singular integral equation with a generalized Mittag-Leffler function in the kernel. *Yokohama Math. J.* **1971**, *19*, 7–15.
12. Garra, R.; Rudolf, G.; Federico, P.; Zivorad, T. Hilfer-Prabhakar derivatives and some applications. *App. Math. Comp.* **2014**, *242*, 576–589. [CrossRef]
13. Garra, R.; Roberto, G. The Prabhakar or three parameter Mittag-Leffler function: Theory and application. *Commun. Nonlinear Sci. Numer. Simul.* **2018**, *56*, 314–329. [CrossRef]
14. Giusti, A.; Ivano, C. Prabhakar-like fractional viscoelasticity. *Commun. Nonlinear Sci. Numer. Simul.* **2018**, *56*, 138–143. [CrossRef]
15. Derakhshan, M.H. New numerical algorithm to solve variable-order fractional integrodifferential equations in the sense of Hilfer-Prabhakar derivative. *Abstr. Appl. Anal.* **2021**, *2021*, 1–10. [CrossRef]
16. Eshaghi, S.; Alireza, A; Reza, K.G. Generalized Mittag-Leffler stability of nonlinear fractional regularized Prabhakar differential systems. *Int. J. Nonlinear Anal. Appl.* **2021**, *12*, 665–678.
17. Eghbali, N.; Aram, M.; Rassias, J. Mittag-Leffler-Hyers-Ulam stability of Prabhakar fractional integral equation. *Int. J. Nonlinear Anal. Appl.* **2021**, *12*, 25–33.
18. Michelitsch, T.M.; Federico, P.; Alejandro, P.R. On discrete time Prabhakar-generalized fractional Poisson processes and related stochastic dynamics. *Phys. A Stat. Mech. Appl.* **2021**, *565*, 125541. [CrossRef]
19. Kilbas, A.A.; Megumi, S.; Saxena, R.K. Saxena. Generalized Mittag-Leffler function and generalized fractional calculus operators. *Integral Transform. Spec. Funct.* **2004**, *15*, 31–49. [CrossRef]
20. Chen, M.P. On a class of starlike functions. *Nanta Math.* **1975**, *8*, 79–82.
21. Sharma, S.K.; Jain, R. On some properties of generalized q-Mittag Leffler function. *Math. Aeterna* **2014**, *4*, 613–619.
22. Srivastava, H.M.; Owa, S.; Chatterjea, S.K. A note on certain classes of starlike functions. *Rend. Semin. Mat. Univ. Padova* **1987**, *77*, 115–124.
23. Miller, S.S.; Mocanu, P.T. Differential Subordinations. In *Theory and Applications*; Marcel Dekker Inc.: New York, NY, USA; Basel, Switzerland, 2000.
24. Campbell, D.M. Majorization-subordination theorems for locally univalent functions, II. *Canad. J. Math.* **1973**, *25*, 420–425. [CrossRef]

Article

# Sharp Bounds of Hankel Determinant on Logarithmic Coefficients for Functions Starlike with Exponential Function

Lei Shi [1], Muhammad Arif [2,*], Javed Iqbal [2], Khalil Ullah [2] and Syed Muhammad Ghufran [2]

[1] School of Mathematics and Statistics, Anyang Normal University, Anyang 455002, China
[2] Department of Mathematics, Abdul Wali Khan University Mardan, Mardan 23200, Pakistan
* Correspondence: marifmaths@awkum.edu.pk

**Abstract:** Using the Lebedev–Milin inequalities, bounds on the logarithmic coefficients of an analytic function can be transferred to estimates on coefficients of the function itself and related functions. From this fact, the study of logarithmic-related problems of a certain subclass of univalent functions has attracted much attention in recent years. In our present investigation, a subclass of starlike functions $\mathcal{S}_e^*$ connected with the exponential mapping was considered. The main purpose of this article is to obtain the sharp estimates of the second Hankel determinant with the logarithmic coefficient as entry for this class.

**Keywords:** starlike function; exponential function; Hankel determinant; logarithmic coefficient

**MSC:** 30C45; 30C80

## 1. Introduction and Definitions

There is a long history of study on univalent functions in geometric function theory. Suppose that $\mathcal{A}$ is the family of analytic functions defined in the open unit disc $\mathbb{D} := \{z \in \mathbb{C} : |z| < 1\}$ normalized by

$$f(z) = z + \sum_{l=2}^{\infty} a_l z^l. \tag{1}$$

Let $\mathcal{S}$ indicate the family of normalized univalent functions. By the 1/4-theorem of Köebe, it is known that for each univalent function $f \in \mathcal{S}$, there exists an inverse function $f^{-1}$ defined at least on a disc of radius 1/4 with Taylor's series of the form

$$f^{-1}(w) := w + \sum_{n=2}^{\infty} B_n w^n, \quad (|w| < 1/4). \tag{2}$$

We say a function is bi-univalent in $\mathbb{D}$ if both $f$ and $f^{-1}$ are univalent in $\mathbb{D}$.

The coefficient conjecture that $|a_n| \leq n$ for $f \in \mathcal{S}$ proposed by Bieberbach [1] in 1916 has attracted many researchers to prove or disprove this result, until it was finally solved by De Branges [2] in 1985. During this period, some important subclasses of univalent functions were introduced and investigated. The most well-known subfamilies are convex functions $\mathcal{K}$ and starlike functions $\mathcal{S}^*$, defined, respectively, by

$$\mathcal{K} := \left\{ f \in \mathcal{A} : \Re\left(1 + \frac{zf''(z)}{f'(z)}\right) > 0, \quad z \in \mathbb{D} \right\} \tag{3}$$

and

$$\mathcal{S}^* := \left\{ f \in \mathcal{A} : \Re\frac{zf'(z)}{f(z)} > 0, \quad z \in \mathbb{D} \right\}. \tag{4}$$

Let $\alpha \in (0,1]$. If a function $f \in \mathcal{A}$ satisfies the condition

$$\left|\arg\frac{zf'(z)}{f(z)}\right| < \frac{\pi\alpha}{2}, \quad z \in \mathbb{D}, \tag{5}$$

it is called strongly starlike of order $\alpha$. Moreover, we say a function $f \in \mathcal{A}$ is strongly convex of order $\alpha$ if

$$\left|\arg\left(1+\frac{zf''(z)}{f'(z)}\right)\right| < \frac{\pi\alpha}{2}, \quad z \in \mathbb{D}. \tag{6}$$

For complex parameters $\alpha_1, \cdots, \alpha_l$ and $\beta_1, \cdots, \beta_m (\beta_j \neq 0, -1, -2, \cdots; j = 1, 2, \cdots, m)$, the generalized hypergeometric function $_lF_m(z)(\alpha_1, \cdots, \alpha_l; \beta_1, \cdots, \beta_m; z)$ is defined by

$$_lF_m(z)(\alpha_1,\cdots,\alpha_l;\beta_1,\cdots,\beta_m;z) := \sum_{n=0}^{\infty} \frac{(\alpha_1)_n \cdots (\alpha_l)_n}{(\beta_1)_n \cdots (\beta_m)_n} \frac{z^n}{n!} \quad (l \le m+1; l, m \in \mathbb{N}_0 := \mathbb{N} \cup \{0\}; z \in \mathbb{D}),$$

where $\mathbb{N}$ denotes the set of all positive integers, and $(\lambda)_k$ is the Pochhammer symbol defined by

$$(\lambda)_n = \begin{cases} 1, & n = 0, \\ \lambda(\lambda+1)(\lambda+2)\cdots(a+\lambda-1), & n \in \mathbb{N}; \lambda \in \mathbb{C}. \end{cases}$$

In recent years, many subclasses of analytic univalent functions or bi-univalent functions associated with the generalized hypergeometric function have been introduced and studied; see, for example, [3–8].

The logarithmic coefficients $\gamma_n$ of $f \in \mathcal{S}$ play an important role in estimation theory. They are given by the below formula:

$$\log\left(\frac{f(z)}{z}\right) = 2\sum_{n=1}^{\infty} \gamma_n z^n =: F_f(z), \quad z \in \mathbb{D}. \tag{7}$$

De Branges [2] obtained that for $n \ge 1$,

$$\sum_{l=1}^{n} l(n-l+1)|\gamma_n|^2 \le \sum_{l=1}^{n} \frac{n-l+1}{l}, \tag{8}$$

and the equality holds if and only if $f$ takes the form $\frac{z}{(1-e^{i\theta}z)^2}$ for some $\theta \in \mathbb{R}$. Clearly, this inequality gives the famous Bieberbach–Robertson–Milin conjectures about Taylor coefficients of $f$ belonging to $\mathcal{S}$ in its most general form. In 2005, Kayumov [9] solved Brennan's conjecture for conformal mappings by considering the logarithmic coefficients. For $n \ge 3$, it seems to be a more difficult work on the logarithmic coefficients problem. It is noted that the inequality $|\gamma_n| \le \frac{1}{n}$ holds for $f \in \mathcal{S}^*$, but it does not hold for the full class $\mathcal{S}$, even in an order of magnitude (see [3]). For some significant work on studying logarithmic coefficients, see [10–12].

For the given functions $g_1, g_2 \in \mathcal{A}$, the subordination between $g_1$ and $g_2$ (written as $g_1 \prec g_2$) if an analytic function $v$ appears in $\mathbb{D}$ comes with the restriction that $v(0) = 0$ and $|v(z)| < 1$ in such a manner that $f(z) = g(v(z))$ holds. $v$ is called a Schwarz function. Moreover, if $g_2$ in $\mathbb{D}$ is univalent, it is known that

$$g_1(z) \prec g_2(z), \quad (z \in \mathbb{D})$$

if and only if

$$g_1(0) = g_2(0) \quad \text{and} \quad g_1(\mathbb{D}) \subset g_2(\mathbb{D}).$$

By employing the principle of subordination, Ma and Minda [13] considered a unified version of the class $\mathcal{S}^*(\phi)$ in 1992 defined by

$$\mathcal{S}^*(\phi) := \left\{ f \in \mathcal{A} : \frac{zf'(z)}{f(z)} \prec \phi(z), \quad z \in \mathbb{D} \right\},$$

where $\phi$ is a univalent function with $\phi'(0) > 0$ and $\Re\phi > 0$. Additionally, the region $\phi(\mathbb{D})$ is star-shaped about the point $\phi(0) = 1$ and is symmetric along the real-line axis. In the past few years, numerous sub-families of the collection $\mathcal{S}$ have been examined as particular choices of the class $\mathcal{S}^*(\phi)$. For instance, if we choose $\phi(z) = \frac{1+(1-2\xi)z}{1-z}$ with $0 \leq \xi < 1$, then we achieve the class $\mathcal{S}^*(\xi) := \mathcal{S}^*\left(\frac{1+(1-2\xi)z}{1-z}\right)$ of the starlike function family of order $\xi$. It is noted that $\mathcal{S}^* := \mathcal{S}^*\left(\frac{1+z}{1-z}\right)$ is simply the familiar starlike function family. For more interesting related subclasses, see, for example, [14–16].

The Hankel determinant $\mathcal{H}_{q,n}(f)$ with $q, n \in \mathbb{N}$ for a function $f \in \mathcal{S}$ of the series form (1) was given by Pommerenke [17,18] as

$$\mathcal{H}_{q,n}(f) := \begin{vmatrix} a_n & a_{n+1} & \cdots & a_{n+q-1} \\ a_{n+1} & a_{n+2} & \cdots & a_{n+q} \\ \vdots & \vdots & \cdots & \vdots \\ a_{n+q-1} & a_{n+q} & \cdots & a_{n+2q-2} \end{vmatrix}.$$

In the literature, there are only a few references to the Hankel determinant for functions belonging to the general family of univalent functions. In [19], it was proved that $|\mathcal{H}_{2,n}(f)| \leq \lambda\sqrt{n}$, where $f \in \mathcal{S}$ and $\lambda$ is an absolute constant. The challenge of finding the sharp limits of Hankel determinants in a particular family of functions drew the attention of numerous mathematicians. For example, the sharp bound of $|\mathcal{H}_{2,2}(f)|$ for the sub-families $\mathcal{K}$ and $\mathcal{S}^*$ were calculated by Janteng et al. [20,21]. It is quite clear from the formulas given in (10) that the calculation of $|\mathcal{H}_{3,1}(f)|$ is far more challenging compared with finding the bound of $|\mathcal{H}_{2,2}(f)|$. In [22], Babalola investigated the bounds of the third-order Hankel determinant for the families of $\mathcal{K}$ and $\mathcal{S}^*$. Later, several authors [23–26] obtained some interesting results on $|\mathcal{H}_{3,1}(f)|$ for certain sub-families of analytic and univalent functions. In recent years, some sharp bounds of the third-order Hankel determinant were obtained for several subclass of univalent functions. Kowalczyk et al. [27] and Lecko et al. [28] proved that

$$|\mathcal{H}_{3,1}(f)| \leq \begin{cases} \frac{4}{135}, & \text{for } f \in \mathcal{K}, \\ \frac{1}{9}, & \text{for } f \in \mathcal{S}^*\left(\frac{1}{2}\right), \end{cases}$$

where $\mathcal{S}^*\left(\frac{1}{2}\right)$ indicate the starlike functions family of order $\frac{1}{2}$. For more contributions in this direction, see [29–38].

It seems a natural idea to generalize the Hankel determinant with logarithmic coefficients as entry. In [39,40], Kowalczyk et al. first introduced the Hankel determinant using logarithmic coefficients. Using the logarithmic coefficient as the element, we have

$$\mathcal{H}_{q,n}\left(F_f/2\right) = \begin{vmatrix} \gamma_n & \gamma_{n+1} & \cdots & \gamma_{n+q-1} \\ \gamma_{n+1} & \gamma_{n+2} & \cdots & \gamma_{n+q} \\ \vdots & \vdots & \cdots & \vdots \\ \gamma_{n+q-1} & \gamma_{n+q} & \cdots & \gamma_{n+2q-2} \end{vmatrix}. \quad (9)$$

In particular, it is noted that

$$\mathcal{H}_{2,1}(F_f/2) = \begin{vmatrix} \gamma_1 & \gamma_2 \\ \gamma_2 & \gamma_3 \end{vmatrix} = \gamma_1\gamma_3 - \gamma_2^2,$$

$$\mathcal{H}_{2,2}(F_f/2) = \begin{vmatrix} \gamma_2 & \gamma_3 \\ \gamma_3 & \gamma_4 \end{vmatrix} = \gamma_2\gamma_4 - \gamma_3^2,$$

If $f$ is given by (1), then its logarithmic coefficients are given by

$$\gamma_1 = \frac{1}{2}a_2 \tag{10}$$

$$\gamma_2 = \frac{1}{2}\left(a_3 - \frac{1}{2}a_2^2\right) \tag{11}$$

$$\gamma_3 = \frac{1}{2}\left(a_4 - a_2a_3 + \frac{1}{3}a_2^3\right) \tag{12}$$

$$\gamma_4 = \frac{1}{2}\left(a_5 - a_2a_4 + a_2^2a_3 - \frac{1}{2}a_3^2 - \frac{1}{4}a_2^4\right) \tag{13}$$

Let $f_\theta(z) := e^{-i\theta}f(e^{i\theta}z)$, $\theta \in \mathbb{R}$. It is observed that $\mathcal{H}_{2,1}(F_f/2)$ and $\mathcal{H}_{2,2}(F_f/2)$ are invariant under rotation since we have

$$\mathcal{H}_{2,1}(F_{f_\theta}/2) = \frac{e^{4i\theta}}{4}\left(a_2a_4 - a_3^2 + \frac{1}{12}a_2^4\right) = e^{4i\theta}\mathcal{H}_{2,1}(F_f/2)$$

and

$$\mathcal{H}_{2,2}(F_{f_\theta}/2) = e^{6i\theta}\left(\frac{1}{288}a_2^6 - \frac{1}{48}a_3a_2^4 - \frac{1}{24}a_2^3a_4 + \frac{1}{16}a_3^2a_2^2 - \frac{1}{8}a_5a_2^2 + \frac{1}{4}a_3a_2a_4 - \frac{1}{4}a_4^2 + \frac{1}{4}a_3a_5 - \frac{1}{8}a_3^3\right)$$
$$= e^{6i\theta}\mathcal{H}_{2,2}(F_f/2).$$

In 2014, Mendiratta R. et al. [41] introduced a subclass of starlike functions defined by

$$\mathcal{S}_e^* := \left\{f \in \mathcal{S} : \frac{zf'(z)}{f(z)} \prec e^z, \ z \in \mathbb{D}\right\}. \tag{14}$$

This class was later studied in [42] and generalized by Srivastava et al. [43], in which the authors determined the upper bound of the Hankel determinant. In 2019, Goel et al. [44] introduced a subclass of the starlike function $\mathcal{S}_{seg}^*$ defined by

$$\mathcal{S}_{seg}^* := \left\{f \in \mathcal{S} : \frac{zf'(z)}{f(z)} \prec \frac{2}{1+e^{-z}}, \ z \in \mathbb{D}\right\}.$$

The family $\mathcal{S}_{\sin}^*$ of starlike functions characterised by the condition

$$\mathcal{S}_{\sin}^* := \left\{f \in \mathcal{S} : \frac{zf'(z)}{f(z)} \prec 1 + \sin z, \ z \in \mathbb{D}\right\}$$

was first investigated by Cho et al. [45]. In virtue of $\sin z = \frac{e^{iz} - e^{-iz}}{2i}$, it is seen that the three function classes are associated with the exponential function. The exponential function $\varphi(z) = e^z$ has a positive real part in $\mathbb{D}$ and an image domain $\varphi(\mathbb{D}) = \{w \in \mathbb{C} : |\log w| < 1\}$ (see Figure 1). Let $\psi(z) = \frac{2}{1+e^{-z}}$. The function $\psi$ is called a modified sigmoid function. It maps $\mathbb{D}$ onto a domain $\Delta_{SG} := \{w \in \mathbb{C} : |\log(\frac{w}{2-w})| < 1\}$ (see Figure 2). Moreover, $\psi$ is convex and hence starlike with respect to $\psi(0) = 1$. For $f \in \mathcal{S}_{\sin}^*$, the quantity $\frac{zf'(z)}{f(z)}$ lies in an eight-shaped region in the right-half plane.

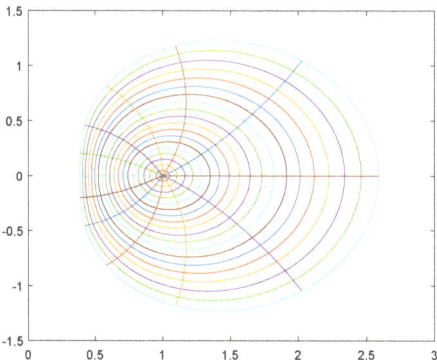

**Figure 1.** Image of $\mathbb{D}$ under $e^z$.

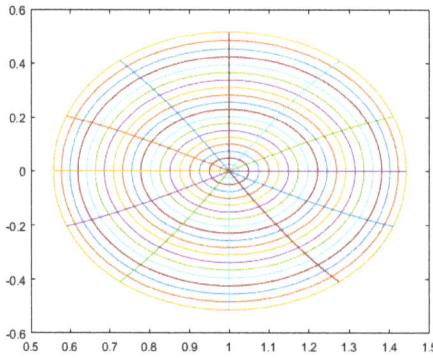

**Figure 2.** Image of $\mathbb{D}$ under $\frac{2}{1-e^{-z}}$.

Recently, Sevtap Sümer Eker et al. [46] obtained the sharp bounds for the second Hankel determinant of logarithmic coefficients for strongly starlike and strongly convex functions. In [47], the authors discussed the bounds of second Hankel determinants with logarithmic coefficients for the class $\mathcal{S}^*_{seg}$ and improved the estimation of the existing second Hankel determinant of logarithmic coefficients for the class $\mathcal{S}^*_{\sin}$.

In the present article, our aim is to calculate sharp bounds of the Hankel determinants with logarithmic coefficients as entry for the class $\mathcal{S}^*_e$.

## 2. Main Results

A function $p \in \mathcal{P}$ if and only if $\Re p(z) \geq 0$ for $z \in \mathbb{D}$ with the series expansion

$$p(z) = 1 + \sum_{n=1}^{\infty} c_n z^n, \quad z \in \mathbb{D}. \tag{15}$$

**Lemma 1** (see [48]). *Let $p \in \mathcal{P}$. Then, for some $x, \delta, \rho \in \overline{\mathbb{D}} := \{z \in \mathbb{C} : |z| \leq 1\}$, we have*

$$2c_2 = c_1^2 + \left(4 - c_1^2\right)x, \tag{16}$$

$$4c_3 = c_1^3 + 2c_1 x\left(4 - c_1^2\right) - x^2 c_1\left(4 - c_1^2\right) + 2\left(1 - |x|^2\right)\left(4 - c_1^2\right)\delta, \tag{17}$$

$$8c_4 = c_1^4 + x\left[c_1^2\left(x^2 - 3x + 3\right) + 4x\right]\left(4 - c_1^2\right) - 4(4 - c_1^2)(1 - |x|^2)$$
$$\left[c_1(x-1)\delta + \overline{x}\delta^2 - (1 - |\delta|^2)\rho\right]\left(4 - c_1^2\right). \tag{18}$$

Throughout this paper, in the following, we use $x$, $\delta$ and $\rho$ to denote some complex number satisfying $|x| \leq 1$, $|\delta| \leq 1$ and $|\rho| \leq 1$. Let $c_1 = c$, $|x| = t$ and $|\rho| = y$ be real numbers that lie in the intervals $[0, 2]$, $[0, 1]$ and $[0, 1]$, respectively.

**Theorem 1.** *Let $f \in \mathcal{S}_e^*$. Then,*

$$\left|\mathcal{H}_{2,1}(F_f/2)\right| = \left|\gamma_1 \gamma_3 - \gamma_2^2\right| \leq \frac{1}{16}. \tag{19}$$

*The inequality is sharp.*

**Proof.** Suppose that $f \in \mathcal{S}_e^*$. From the definition, we know it can be written in the form of a Schwarz function as

$$\frac{zf'(z)}{f(z)} = e^{w(z)}, \quad (z \in \mathbb{D}).$$

Define

$$p(z) := \frac{1 + w(z)}{1 - w(z)} = 1 + c_1 z + c_2 z^2 + c_3 z^3 + c_4 z^4 + \cdots, \quad (z \in \mathbb{D}). \tag{20}$$

It follows that

$$\begin{aligned}
w(z) &= \frac{1}{2}c_1 z + \left(\frac{1}{2}c_2 - \frac{1}{4}c_1^2\right)z^2 + \left(\frac{1}{8}c_1^3 - \frac{1}{2}c_1 c_2 + \frac{1}{2}c_3\right)z^3 \\
&\quad + \left(\frac{1}{2}c_4 - \frac{1}{2}c_1 c_3 - \frac{1}{4}c_2^2 - \frac{1}{16}c_1^4 + \frac{3}{8}c_1^2 c_2\right)z^4 + \cdots, \quad (z \in \mathbb{D}).
\end{aligned} \tag{21}$$

Using (1), we obtain

$$\begin{aligned}
\frac{zf'(z)}{f(z)} &= 1 + a_2 z + \left(2a_3 - a_2^2\right)z^2 + \left(a_2^3 - 3a_2 a_3 + 3a_4\right)z^3 \\
&\quad + \left(4a_5 - a_2^4 + 4a_2^2 a_3 - 4a_2 a_4 - 2a_3^2\right)z^4 + \cdots, \quad (z \in \mathbb{D}).
\end{aligned} \tag{22}$$

Using the series expansion of (21), we obtain

$$\begin{aligned}
e^{w(z)} &= 1 + \frac{1}{2}c_1 z + \left(\frac{1}{2}c_2 - \frac{1}{8}c_1^2\right)z^2 + \left(-\frac{1}{4}c_1 c_2 + \frac{1}{48}c_1^3 + \frac{1}{2}c_3\right)z^3 \\
&\quad + \left(\frac{1}{348}c_1^4 + \frac{1}{16}c_1^2 c_2 - \frac{1}{4}c_1 c_3 - \frac{1}{8}c_2^2 + \frac{1}{2}c_4\right)z^4 + \cdots, \quad (z \in \mathbb{D}).
\end{aligned} \tag{23}$$

Now, comparing (22) and (23) leads to

$$\begin{aligned}
a_2 &= \frac{1}{2}c_1, \\
a_3 &= \frac{1}{4}c_2 + \frac{1}{16}c_1^2, \\
a_4 &= \frac{1}{6}c_3 - \frac{1}{288}c_1^3 + \frac{1}{24}c_1 c_2, \\
a_5 &= \frac{1}{1152}c_1^4 - \frac{1}{96}c_1^2 c_2 + \frac{1}{48}c_1 c_3 + \frac{1}{8}c_4.
\end{aligned}$$

From (10)–(13), we have

$$\gamma_1 = \frac{1}{4}c_1, \qquad (24)$$

$$\gamma_2 = \frac{1}{8}c_2 - \frac{1}{32}c_1^2, \qquad (25)$$

$$\gamma_3 = \frac{1}{288}c_1^3 - \frac{1}{24}c_1c_2 + \frac{1}{12}c_3, \qquad (26)$$

$$\gamma_4 = \frac{1}{3072}c_1^4 + \frac{1}{128}c_1^2c_2 - \frac{1}{32}c_1c_3 - \frac{1}{64}c_2^2 + \frac{1}{16}c_4. \qquad (27)$$

From (24)–(26), we have

$$\left|\gamma_1\gamma_3 - \gamma_2^2\right| = \frac{1}{9216}\left|-c_1^4 - 24c_1^2c_2 + 192c_1c_3 - 144c_2^2\right|.$$

Since $\mathcal{H}_{2,1}(F_f/2)$ is rotationally invariant, we may assume that $c_1 = c \in [0, 2]$. Using (16) and (17) to express $c_2$ and $c_3$ in terms of $c_1 = c$, we obtain

$$\left|\gamma_1\gamma_3 - \gamma_2^2\right| = \frac{1}{9216}\left|-c^4 - 48c^2x^2\left(4-c^2\right) - 36x^2\left(4-c^2\right)^2 + 12xc^2\left(4-c^2\right) \right.$$
$$\left. + 96c\left(1 - |x|^2\right)\left(4-c^2\right)\delta\right|.$$

By replacing $|\delta| \leq 1$ and $|x| = t$, it follows that

$$\left|\gamma_1\gamma_3 - \gamma_2^2\right| \leq \frac{1}{9216}\left[c^4 + 48c^2t^2\left(4-c^2\right) + 96c\left(1-t^2\right)\left(4-c^2\right) \right.$$
$$\left. + 36t^2\left(4-c^2\right)^2 + 12c^2t\left(4-c^2\right)\right] =: \Omega(c,t).$$

Differentiating with respect to $t$, we have

$$\frac{\partial \Omega(c,t)}{\partial t} = \frac{1}{9216} \times 12\left(4-c^2\right)\left(2tc^2 - 16tc + c^2 + 24t\right).$$

As $c \in [0, 2]$, it is a simple exercise to show that $\frac{\partial \Omega(c,t)}{\partial t} \geq 0$ for $t \in [0, 1]$. Thus, we have $\Omega(c,t) \leq \Omega(c,1)$. Putting $t = 1$ gives

$$\left|\gamma_1\gamma_3 - \gamma_2^2\right| \leq \frac{1}{9216}\left[c^4 + 60c^2\left(4-c^2\right) + 36\left(4-c^2\right)^2\right] =: \omega(c).$$

Since $\omega'(c) \leq 0$ for $c \in [0, 2]$, we see that $\omega(c)$ is a decreasing function, and it gives its maximum value at $c = 0$. This yields

$$\left|\mathcal{H}_{2,2}(F_f/2)\right| \leq \frac{576}{9216} = \frac{1}{16}.$$

Equality is determined using (10)–(12) and

$$f_1(z) = z\exp\left(\int_0^z \frac{e^{t^2}-1}{t}dt\right) = z + \frac{1}{2}z^3 + \frac{1}{4}z^5 + \cdots. \qquad (28)$$

□

**Theorem 2.** *Let $f \in \mathcal{S}_e^*$. Then*

$$\left|\mathcal{H}_{2,2}(F_f/2)\right| = \left|\gamma_2\gamma_4 - \gamma_3^2\right| \leq \frac{1}{36}.$$

*This result is sharp.*

**Proof.** As $\mathcal{H}_{2,2}\left(F_f/2\right)$ is rotation-invariant, we assume that $c_1 = c \in [0,2]$. By using (24)–(27), we have

$$\left|\gamma_2\gamma_4 - \gamma_3^2\right| = \frac{1}{2654208}\Big(-59c^6 + 228c^4c_2 + 1056c^3c_3 - 720c^2c_2^2 - 5184c^2c_4$$
$$+ 8064cc_2c_3 - 5184c_2^3 + 20736c_2c_4 - 18432c_3^2\Big). \quad (29)$$

Suppose that $u = 4 - c^2$. An application of Lemma 1 leads to

$$\left|\gamma_2\gamma_4 - \gamma_3^2\right| = \frac{1}{2654208}\Big\{-5c^6 + 528c^3u\left(1 - |x|^2\right)\delta - 6c^4xu - 828c^2u^2x^2$$
$$- 912c^4x^2u - 288x^3u^2c^2 + 144x^4u^2c^2 - 4608u^2\left(1 - |x|^2\right)^2\delta^2$$
$$+ 2592ux^2c^2 + 648c^4ux^3 - 648x^3u^3 + 5184u^2x^3 - 2592c^3u\left(1 - |x|^2\right)x\delta$$
$$- 2592c^2u\bar{x}\left(1 - |x|^2\right)\delta^2 + 2592c^2u\left(1 - |x|^2\right)\left(1 - |\delta|^2\right)\rho$$
$$- 2016cxu^2\left(1 - |x|^2\right)\delta - 5184u^2|x|^2\left(1 - |x|^2\right)\delta^2$$
$$- 576cu^2x^2\left(1 - |x|^2\right)\delta + 5184u^2x\left(1 - |x|^2\right)\left(1 - |\delta|^2\right)\rho\Big\}.$$

Thus, we see that

$$\left|\gamma_2\gamma_4 - \gamma_3^2\right| = \frac{1}{2654208}\Big(v_1(c,x) + v_2(c,x)\delta + v_3(c,x)\delta^2 + \Phi(c,x,\delta)\rho\Big),$$

where

$$v_1(c,x) = -6\left(4 - c^2\right)x\Big[6\left(4 - c^2\right)x\left(-4x^2c^2 - 10xc^2 + 23c^2 - 72x\right) - 108c^4x^2$$
$$+ 152c^4x + c^4 - 432xc^2\Big] - 5c^6,$$
$$v_2(c,x) = -48\left(4 - c^2\right)\left(1 - |x|^2\right)c\Big[\left(12x^2 + 42x\right)\left(4 - c^2\right) + 54xc^2 - 11c^2\Big],$$
$$v_3(c,x) = -288\left(4 - c^2\right)\left(1 - |x|^2\right)\Big[\left(2|x|^2 + 16\right)\left(4 - c^2\right) + 9\bar{x}c^2\Big],$$
$$\Phi(c,x,\delta) = 2592\left(4 - c^2\right)\left(1 - |x|^2\right)\left(1 - |\delta|^2\right)\Big[2\left(4 - c^2\right)x + c^2\Big].$$

Now, by utilizing $|\delta| = y$, $|x| = t$ and taking $|\rho| \leq 1$, we achieve

$$\left|\gamma_2\gamma_4 - \gamma_3^2\right| \leq \frac{1}{2654208}\Big(|v_1(c,t)| + |v_2(c,t)|y + |v_3(c,t)|y^2 + |\Phi(c,t,\delta)|\Big),$$
$$\leq \frac{1}{2654208}[H(c,t,y)]. \quad (30)$$

where

$$H(c,t,y) = h_1(c,t) + h_2(c,t)y + h_3(c,t)y^2 + h_4(c,t)\left(1 - y^2\right). \quad (31)$$

with

$$\begin{aligned}
h_1(c,t) &= 6\left(4-c^2\right)t\left[6\left(4-c^2\right)t\left(4t^2c^2+10tc^2+23c^2+72t\right)+108c^4t^2\right.\\
&\quad \left.+152c^4t+c^4+432tc^2\right]+5c^6,\\
h_2(c,t) &= 48\left(4-c^2\right)\left(1-t^2\right)c\left[\left(12t^2+42t\right)\left(4-c^2\right)+54tc^2+11c^2\right],\\
h_3(c,t) &= 288\left(4-c^2\right)\left(1-t^2\right)\left[\left(2t^2+16\right)\left(4-c^2\right)+9tc^2\right],\\
h_4(c,t) &= 2592\left(4-c^2\right)\left(1-t^2\right)\left[2\left(4-c^2\right)t+c^2\right].
\end{aligned}$$

Let the closed cuboid be $\Delta := [0,2] \times [0,1] \times [0,1]$. We have to achieve the points of maxima of $H(c,t,y)$ in $\Delta$. By observing that $H(0,0,1) = 73728$, we know

$$\max H(c,t,y) \geq 73728, \quad (c,t,y) \in \Delta. \tag{32}$$

Denote $m_0 = 73728$. In the following, we aim to prove that $\max H(c,t,y) = m_0$ for all $(c,t,y) \in \Delta$. To show this, we first prove that the global maximum value of $H(c,t,y)$ can be obtained on the face of $y = 1$. On $t = 1$, $H(c,t,y)$ reduces to

$$q_1(c) := H(c,1,y) = -229c^6 - 4392c^4 + 10944c^2 + 41472, \quad c \in (0,2). \tag{33}$$

Solving $q_1'(c) = 0$, we obtain critical points $c = c_0 = 0$ and $c = c_1 \approx 1.0694$. Here, $c_0$ is the minimum points of $q_1$. Thus, $q_1$ attains its maximum $47901.1108$ at $c_1$. Clearly, it is impossible for $H(c,t,y)$ to obtain its global maximum on the face of $t = 1$. On $c = 2$, $H(c,t,y)$ reduces to

$$H(2,t,y) \equiv 320, \quad t, y \in [0,1]. \tag{34}$$

Obviously, the global maximal value of $H(c,t,y)$ also cannot be obtained on the face of $c = 2$. In the following, we assume that $c < 2$ and $t < 1$.

I. Let $(c,t,y) \in [0,2) \times [0,1) \times (0,1)$. Now, to find points of maxima in $\Delta$, we take partial derivative of (31) with respect to $y$. Since

$$h_3(c,t) - h_4(c,t) = 288\left(4-c^2\right)\left(1-t^2\right)(1-t)\left[\left(4-c^2\right)(16-2t)-9c^2\right], \tag{35}$$

it is easy to see that

$$\frac{\partial H}{\partial y} = h_2(c,t) + 2[h_3(c,t) - h_4(c,t)]y = 48\left(4-c^2\right)\left(1-t^2\right)M(c,t)y, \tag{36}$$

where

$$M(c,t) = 6ct(2t+7)\left(4-c^2\right) + (54t+11)c^3 + 12(1-t)\left[\left(4-c^2\right)(16-2t)-9c^2\right]. \tag{37}$$

Now, $\frac{\partial H}{\partial y} = 0$ yields

$$y = \frac{6ct\left(4-c^2\right)(2t+7) + c^3(54t+11)}{12(1-t)\left[\left(4-c^2\right)(2t-16) + 9c^2\right]}.$$

If $y_0$ is a critical point inside $\Delta$, then $y_0 \in (0,1)$, which is possible only if

$$6ct\left(4-c^2\right)(2t+7) + c^3(54t+11) + 12(1-t)\left(4-c^2\right)(16-2t) < 108(1-t)c^2, \tag{38}$$

and

$$c^2 > \frac{8(8-t)}{25-2t} =: h(t). \tag{39}$$

Then, we must obtain the solutions which satisfy both inequalities (38) and (39) for the existence of the critical points.

Since $h'(t) < 0$ for $(0,1)$, $h(t)$ is decreasing in $(0,1)$, hence, $c^2 > \frac{56}{23}$. A simple exercise shows that (38) does not hold in this case for all values of $t \in \left[\frac{1}{2}, 1\right)$, and there is no critical point of $H$ in $(0,2) \times (0,1) \times \left[\frac{1}{2}, 1\right)$. In fact, suppose that

$$Y(c,t) := \begin{aligned} & 6ct\left(4-c^2\right)(2t+7) + c^3(54t+11) + 12(1-t)\left(4-c^2\right)(16-2t) \\ & -108(1-t)c^2. \end{aligned}$$

It is easily obtained that

$$Y(c,t) \geq 672 - 276c^2 + 11c^3 + 6(-112 + 46c^2 + 9c^3)t =: L(c,t). \tag{40}$$

As it is observed that $L\left(c, \frac{1}{2}\right) \geq 0$ and $L(c,1) \geq 0$ for $c \in [0,2]$, we have

$$L(c,t) \geq \min\left\{L\left(c, \frac{1}{2}\right), L(c,1)\right\} \geq 0, \quad (c,t) \in [0,2] \times \left[\frac{1}{2}, 1\right). \tag{41}$$

Combining (40) and (41), we see (38) is impossible to hold for all $t \in \left[\frac{1}{2}, 1\right)$. This is to say that there are no critical points of $H(c,t,y)$ satisfying $y \in (0,1)$ with $t \in \left[0, \frac{1}{2}\right)$.

For $t < \frac{1}{2}$, we will prove that all the critical points of $H(c,t,y)$ with $y \in (0,1)$ have a maximum value no larger than $m_0$. Suppose that $(\hat{c}, \hat{t}, \hat{y})$ is a critical point of $H$ and $\hat{y} \in (0,1)$. To guarantee the inequalities (38) and (39) to be true simultaneously, we know that $\hat{t} < \frac{1}{2}$. Using (39), it follows that $\hat{c}^2 > h\left(\frac{1}{2}\right) = \frac{5}{2}$. By noting that $1 - t^2 \leq 1$ and $t < \frac{1}{2}$, it is not hard to observe that

$$h_1(c,t) \leq h_1\left(c, \frac{1}{2}\right) =: \kappa_1(c) \tag{42}$$

and

$$h_j(c,t) \leq \frac{4}{3} h_j\left(c, \frac{1}{2}\right) =: \kappa_j(c), \quad j = 2, 3, 4. \tag{43}$$

Hence, we obtain that

$$H(c,t,y) \leq \kappa_1(c) + \kappa_2(c)y + \kappa_3(c)y^2 + \kappa_4(c)\left(1 - y^2\right) =: \Theta(c,y). \tag{44}$$

A basic calculation shows that

$$\frac{\partial^2 \Theta(c,y)}{\partial y^2} = 2[\kappa_3(c) - \kappa_4(c)] = 3456\left(4 - c^2\right)\left(5 - 2c^2\right) \leq 0 \tag{45}$$

for $c^2 \in \left(\frac{5}{2}, 4\right]$. Thus, we know

$$\begin{aligned} \frac{\partial \Theta(c,y)}{\partial y} &\geq \frac{\partial \Theta(c,y)}{\partial y}\bigg|_{y=1} \\ &= \kappa_2(c) + 2[\kappa_3(c) - \kappa_4(c)] \\ &= 48\left(4 - c^2\right)\left(360 + 96c - 150c^2 + 14c^3\right) \geq 0 \end{aligned}$$

with $c \in \left(\sqrt{\frac{5}{2}}, 2\right]$. This leads to

$$\Theta(c, y) \leq \kappa_1(c) + \kappa_2(c) + \kappa_3(c) := \iota(c), \quad c \in \left(\sqrt{\frac{5}{2}}, 2\right]. \tag{46}$$

Now, a basic calculation shows that $\iota$ attains its maximum value 38095.55 at $c \approx 1.5811399$. Therefore, we conclude that

$$H(\hat{c}, \hat{t}, \hat{y}) \leq \Theta(\hat{c}, \hat{y}) \leq \iota(\hat{c}) < m_0. \tag{47}$$

This implies that the global maximum value of $H(c, t, y)$ in $\Delta$ cannot be obtained with $y \in (0, 1)$.

II. On the face of $y = 0$, we have

$$H(c, t, 0) = h_1(c, t) + h_4(c, t) =: R_1(c, t) \tag{48}$$

and

$$H(c, t, 1) = h_1(c, t) + h_2(c, t) + h_3(c, t) =: R_2(c, t). \tag{49}$$

It is noted that

$$R_2(c, t) - R_1(c, t) = h_2(c, t) + h_3(c, t) - h_4(c, t) = 48\left(4 - c^2\right)\left(1 - t^2\right)N(c, t), \tag{50}$$

where

$$N(c, t) = 12\left(4 - c^2\right)(1 + c)t^2 + \left(-432 + 168c + 162c^2 + 12c^3\right)t + 384 - 150c^2 + 11c^3. \tag{51}$$

For $t > \frac{7}{10}$ and $c \geq 1$, it is found that

$$\begin{aligned}
\frac{\partial N(c, t)}{\partial t} &= 24\left(4 - c^2\right)(1 + c)t - 432 + 168c + 162c^2 + 12c^3 \\
&\geq \frac{84}{5}\left(4 - c^2\right)(1 + c) - 432 + 168c + 162c^2 + 12c^3 \\
&= \frac{6}{5}\left(-304 + 196c + 121c^2 - 4c^3\right) =: \varrho(c).
\end{aligned}$$

As it is easy to see that $\varrho'(c) > 0$ for $c \in [1, 2)$, we know that $\varrho$ attains its minimum value at $c = 1$. Thus, we have

$$\varrho(c) \geq \varrho(1) = \frac{54}{5} > 0, \quad c \in [1, 2). \tag{52}$$

It follows that $\frac{\partial N(c,t)}{\partial t} \geq 0$ for all $c \in [1, 2)$. Therefore, we deduce that

$$N(c, t) \geq N\left(c, \frac{7}{10}\right) = \frac{1}{25}\left(2628 + 3528c - 1062c^2 + 338c^3\right) \geq 0. \tag{53}$$

On the other hand, if $c > \frac{7}{10}$ and $c < 1$, it is noted that $-432 + 168c + 162c^2 + 12c^3 \leq 0$ and

$$\begin{aligned}
N(c, t) &\geq 12\left(4 - c^2\right)(1 + c)t^2 + 384 - 150c^2 + 11c^3 \\
&\geq \frac{147}{25}\left(4 - c^2\right)(1 + c) + 384 - 150c^2 + 11c^3 \\
&= \frac{1}{25}\left(10188 + 588c - 3897c^2 + 128c^3\right) > 0.
\end{aligned}$$

Hence, we conclude that

$$N(c,t) \geq 0, \quad (c,t) \in [0,2) \times \left(\frac{7}{10}, 1\right). \tag{54}$$

This implies that $R_2(c,t) \geq R_1(c,t)$ and

$$H(c,t,0) \leq H(c,t,1), \quad (c,t) \in [0,2) \times \left(\frac{7}{10}, 1\right). \tag{55}$$

Thus, we have

$$\max H(c,t,0) \leq \max H(c,t,1), \quad (c,t) \in [0,2] \times \left[\frac{7}{10}, 1\right]. \tag{56}$$

For $t \leq \frac{7}{10}$, it is observed that

$$h_1(c,t) \leq h_1\left(c, \frac{7}{10}\right) =: \tau_1(c) \tag{57}$$

and

$$h_4(c,t) \leq \frac{100}{51} h_4\left(c, \frac{7}{10}\right) =: \tau_2(c). \tag{58}$$

Then, it follows that

$$H(c,t,0) = h_1(c,t) + h_4(c,t) \leq \tau_1(c) + \tau_2(c) =: \tau_3(c). \tag{59}$$

A basic calculation shows that $\tau_3$ attains its maximum value 72285.70 at $c = 0$. This means that

$$H(c,t,0) \leq m_0 \leq \max H(c,t,1), \quad (c,t) \in [0,2) \times \left[0, \frac{7}{10}\right]. \tag{60}$$

Combining (56) and (60), the global optimal value of $H$ is sure to be achieved on the face of $y = 1$. Now, we only need to find points of maxima on the faces $y = 1$ of $\Delta$. On $y = 1$, it is clear that

$$H(c,t,1) = h_1(c,t) + h_2(c,t) + h_3(c,t) =: U(c,t). \tag{61}$$

We note that

$$\begin{aligned}
U(c,t) &= 5c^6 + 6\left(4 - c^2\right)\left[88c^3 + \left(c^2 + 432c + 432\right)c^2 t\right. \\
&\quad + 8\left(19c^2 - 11c + 54\right)c^2 t^2 + 108\left(c^2 - 4c - 4\right)c^2 t^3\right] \\
&\quad + 36\left(4 - c^2\right)^2 \left[128 + 32ct + \left(23c^2 + 16c - 112\right)t^2\right. \\
&\quad \left. + 2\left(5c^2 - 16c + 36\right)t^3 + 4\left(c^2 - 4c - 4\right)t^4\right].
\end{aligned}$$

As we see that $c^2 - 4c - 4 \leq 0$, $5c^2 - 16c + 36 \geq 0$, $19c^2 - 11c + 54 \geq 0$ for $c \in [0,2]$ and $t^3 \leq t^2 \leq t$, it follows that

$$\begin{aligned}
U(c,t) &\leq 5c^6 + 6\left(4 - c^2\right)\left[88c^3 + \left(c^2 + 432c + 432\right)c^2 t + 8\left(19c^2 - 11c + 54\right)c^2 t\right] \\
&\quad + 36\left(4 - c^2\right)^2 \left[128 + 32ct + \left(23c^2 + 16c - 112\right)t^2 + 2\left(5c^2 - 16c + 36\right)t^2\right] \\
&= 5c^6 + 6\left(4 - c^2\right)\left[88c^3 + \left(153c^4 + 344c^3 + 864c^2\right)t\right] \\
&\quad + 36\left(4 - c^2\right)^2 \left[128 + 32ct + \left(33c^2 - 16c - 40\right)t^2\right] =: V(c,t).
\end{aligned}$$

In virtue of $t < 1$, we deduce that

$$V(c,t) \leq 5c^6 + 6\left(4-c^2\right)\left(153c^4 + 432c^3 + 864c^2\right)$$
$$+ 36\left(4-c^2\right)^2\left[128 + 32ct + \left(33c^2 - 16c - 40\right)t^2\right] =: W(c,t).$$

Define

$$S(c,t) := 128 + 32ct + \left(33c^2 - 16c - 40\right)t^2, \quad (c,t) \in [0,1) \times [0,1). \tag{62}$$

For $c < 1$, it is easily noted that $33c^2 - 16c - 40 \leq -23$ and

$$S(c,t) \leq 128 + 32ct - 23t^2 =: T(c,t), \quad (c,t) \in [0,1) \times [0,1). \tag{63}$$

It is seen that

$$t_0 = \frac{16}{23}c \in [0,1); \tag{64}$$

thus, we have

$$T(c,t) \leq \frac{4 \times (-23) \times 128 - 1024c^2}{4 \times (-23)} = 128 + \frac{256}{23}c^2 \leq 128 + 12c^2. \tag{65}$$

It follows that

$$W(c,t) \leq 5c^6 + 6\left(4-c^2\right)\left(153c^4 + 432c^3 + 864c^2\right) + 36\left(4-c^2\right)^2\left(128 + 12c^2\right)$$
$$= -481c^6 - 2592c^5 - 360c^4 + 10368c^3 - 9216c^2 + 73728 =: \chi(c).$$

To prove that $\chi(c) \leq 73728$ for $c \in [0,1)$, we need to show that

$$-481c^6 - 2592c^5 - 360c^4 + 10368c^3 - 9216c^2 \leq 0, \tag{66}$$

which is equivalent to

$$-481c^4 - 2592c^3 - 360c^2 + 10368c - 9216 \leq 0. \tag{67}$$

Let

$$\vartheta(c) := -481c^4 - 2592c^3 - 360c^2 + 10368c - 9216, \quad c \in [0,1). \tag{68}$$

It is clear that

$$\vartheta(c) \leq -481c^4 - 2592c^3 + 10368c - 9216 =: \hat{\vartheta}(c). \tag{69}$$

Since $\hat{\vartheta}'(c) \geq 0$ for $c \in [0,1)$, thus, we know that $\hat{\vartheta}(c) \leq \hat{\vartheta}(1) = -1921$. This implies that $\vartheta(c) \leq 0$. Then we obtain that $\chi(c) \leq 73728$ and thus $U(c,t) \leq 73728$ for all $(c,t) \in [0,1) \times [0,1)$.

For $c \in [1,2)$, it is found that

$$\frac{\partial V(c,t)}{\partial t} = 6(4-c^2)(153c^4 + 344c^3 + 864c^2) + 36(4-c^2)^2\left[32c + 2(33c^2 - 16c - 120)t\right]$$
$$\geq 6(4-c^2)(153c^4 + 344c^3 + 864c^2) + 36(4-c^2)^2(32c - 23t)$$
$$\geq 6(4-c^2)(153c^4 + 344c^3 + 864c^2) + 36(4-c^2)^2(32c - 23)$$
$$= 6(4-c^2)\left(153c^4 + 152c^3 + 1002c^2 + 768c - 552\right) \geq 0.$$

Thus, we have

$$\begin{aligned} V(c,t) &\leq V(c,1) \\ &= 5c^6 + 6\left(4-c^2\right)\left(153c^4 + 432c^3 + 864c^2\right) + 36\left(4-c^2\right)^2\left(33c^2 + 16c + 88\right) \\ &= 275c^6 - 2016c^5 - 7848c^4 + 5760c^3 + 14400c^2 + 9216c + 50688 =: \mu(c) \end{aligned}$$

In virtue of $\mu$ attaining its maximum 71992.07 at $c \approx 1.179235$, we know $U(c,t) \leq m_0$ for $(c,t) \in [1,2) \times [0,1)$. Thus, we claim that the maximum value of $U(c,t)$ is sure to exist in $(c,t) \in [0,1) \times [0,1)$ and hence has a maximum value no larger than $m_0$. Since $H(c,t,1) = U(c,t)$, and the global maximum value of $H$ is sure to exist on the face $y=1$ of $\Delta$, we obtain that $H(c,t,y) \leq m_0$ for $(c,x,y) \in \Delta$. From Equation (30), we can write

$$\left|\gamma_2\gamma_4 - \gamma_3^2\right| \leq \frac{m_0}{2654208} = \frac{73728}{2654208} = \frac{1}{36}.$$

If $f \in \mathcal{S}_e^*$, then the equality is determined by using (10)–(13) and

$$f_2(z) = z\exp\left(\int_0^z \frac{e^{(t^3)}-1}{t}dt\right) = z + \frac{1}{3}z^4 + \frac{5}{36}z^7 + \cdots. \tag{70}$$

This completes the proof. □

## 3. Conclusions

The Hankel determinants can be used in the study of singularities and power series with integral coefficients. Additionally, there are some of its applications in meromorphic functions in the literature. Therefore, to obtain the upper bounds of Hankel determinants for certain subclasses of univalent functions is an active topic in the field of geometric function theory. In the present work, we consider a family of starlike functions $\mathcal{S}_e^*$ connected with the exponential function. For functions in this class, we obtain some sharp results on the logarithmic coefficient-related problems. The method of proof is based on the well-known parametric formulas for initial coefficients in the Carathéodory class of functions. It was found that the logarithmic coefficients of functions can be transfered to obtain the bounds for the coefficients of a function and its inverse function. As the calculation of bounds on coefficients of the inverse function is often a more difficult task, our results on Hankel determinants with logarithmic coefficients seem to be of great significance. As the exponential function is a very special class of hypergeometric functions, this work may inspire some other investigations by considering univalent functions subordinated to a more general class. Additionally, it will be interesting if the sharp bounds of higher-order Hankel determinants can be obtained.

**Author Contributions:** The idea for the present paper come from M.A.; L.S., J.I. and K.U. completed the main calculations, and S.M.G. checked the results. All authors have read and agreed to the published version of the manuscript.

**Funding:** This work is supported by the Foundation for Excellent Youth Teachers of Colleges and Universities of Henan Province under Grant no. 2019GGJS195.

**Data Availability Statement:** Not applicable.

**Conflicts of Interest:** The authors declare that they have no conflict of interest.

## References

1. Bieberbach, L. Über dié koeffizienten derjenigen Potenzreihen, welche eine schlichte Abbildung des Einheitskreises vermitteln. Sitzungsberichte Preuss. *Akad. Wiss.* **1916**, *138*, 940–955.
2. De Branges, L. A proof of the Bieberbach conjecture. *Acta Math.* **1985**, *154*, 137–152. [CrossRef]
3. Duren, P. *Univalent Functions*; Grundlehren der mathematischen Wissenschaften; Springer: New York, NY, USA; Berlin/Heidelberg, Germany; Tokyo, Japan, 1983.

4. Goodman, A.W. *Univalent Functions*; Mariner: Tampa, FL, USA, 1983; Volumes 1–2.
5. Seaborn, J.B. *Hypergeometric Functions and Their Applications*; Springer Science & Business Media: New York, NY, USA, 2013.
6. Dziok, J.; Srivastava, H.M. Certain subclasses of analytic functions associated with the generalized hypergeometric function. *Integral Transform. Spec. Funct.* **2003**, *14*, 7–18. [CrossRef]
7. Hamzat, J.O.; Oluwayemi, M.O.; Alb Lupaş, A.; Wanas, A.K. Bi-Univalent Problems Involving Generalized Multiplier Transform with Respect to Symmetric and Conjugate Points. *Fractal Fract.* **2022**, *6*, 483. [CrossRef]
8. El-Deeb, S.M.; Alb Lupaş, A. Coefficient Estimates for the Functions with Respect to Symmetric Conjugate Points Connected with the Combination Binomial Series and Babalola Operator and Lucas Polynomials. *Fractal Fract.* **2022**, *6*, 360. [CrossRef]
9. Kayumov, I.P. On Brennan's conjecture for a special class of functions. *Math. Notes* **2005**, *78*, 498–502. [CrossRef]
10. Girela, D. Logarithmic coefficients of univalent functions. *Ann. Acad. Sci. Fenn. Math.* **2000**, *25*, 337–350.
11. Deng, Q. On the logarithmic coefficients of Bazilevič functions. *Appl. Math. Comput.* **2011**, *217*, 5889–5894. [CrossRef]
12. Roth, O. A sharp inequality for the logarithmic coefficients of univalent functions. *Proc. Am. Math. Soc.* **2007**, *135*, 2051–2054. [CrossRef]
13. Ma,W.C.; Minda, D. A unified treatment of some special classesof univalent functions. In *Conference Proceedings and Lecture Notes in Analysis, Proceedings of the Conference on Complex Analysis, Tianjin, China, 19–23 June 1992*; Li, Z., Ren, F., Yang, L., Zhang, S., Eds.; International Press: Cambridge, MA, USA, 1994; Volume I, pp. 157–169.
14. Sokół, J.; Stankiewicz, J. Radius of convexity of some subclasses of strongly starlike functions. *Zesz. Nauk. Politech. Rzesz. Mat.* **1996**, *19*, 101–105.
15. Alotaibi, A.; Arif, M.; Alghamdi, M.A.; Hussain, S. Starlikness associated with cosine hyperbolic function. *Mathematics* **2020**, *8*, 1118. [CrossRef]
16. Bano, K.; Raza, M. Starlike functions associated with cosine function. *Bull. Iran. Math. Soc.* **2020**, *47*, 1513–1532. [CrossRef]
17. Pommerenke, C. On the coefficients and Hankel determinants of univalent functions. *J. Lond. Math. Soc.* **1966**, *1*, 111–122. [CrossRef]
18. Pommerenke, C. On the Hankel determinants of univalent functions. *Mathematika* **1967**, *14*, 108–112. [CrossRef]
19. Hayman, W.K. On second Hankel determinant of mean univalent functions. *Proc. Lond. Math. Soc.* **1968**, *3*, 77–94. [CrossRef]
20. Janteng, A.; Halim, S.A.; Darus, M. Coefficient inequality for a function whose derivative has a positive real part. *J. Inequalities Pure Appl. Math.* **2006**, *7*, 1–5.
21. Janteng, A.; Halim, S.A.; Darus, M. Hankel determinant for starlike and convex functions. *Int. J. Math.* **2007**, *1*, 619–625.
22. Babalola, K.O. On $H_3(1)$ Hankel determinant for some classes of univalent functions. *Inequal. Theory Appl.* **2010**, *6*, 1–7.
23. Altınkaya, Ş.; Yalçın, S. Third Hankel determinant for Bazilevič functions. *Adv. Math.* **2016**, *5*, 91–96.
24. Bansal, D. Upper bound of second Hankel determinant for a new class of analytic functions. *Appl. Math. Lett.* **2013**, *26*, 103–107. [CrossRef]
25. Krishna, D.V.; Venkateswarlu, B.; RamReddy, T. Third Hankel determinant for bounded turning functions of order alpha. *J. Niger. Math. Soc.* **2015**, *34*, 121–127. [CrossRef]
26. Shanmugam, G.; Stephen, B.A.; Babalola, K.O. Third Hankel determinant for $\alpha$-starlike functions. *Gulf J. Math.* **2014**, *2*, 107–113. [CrossRef]
27. Kowalczyk, B.; Lecko, A.; Sim, Y.J. The sharp bound of the Hankel determinant of the third kind for convex functions. *Bull. Aust. Math. Soc.* **2018**, *97*, 435–445. [CrossRef]
28. Lecko, A.; Sim, Y.J.; Śmiarowska, B. The sharp bound of the Hankel determinant of the third kind for starlike functions of order 1/2. *Complex Anal. Oper. Theory* **2019**, *13*, 2231–2238. [CrossRef]
29. Khan, B.; Aldawish, I.; Araci, S.; Khan, M.G. Third Hankel Determinant for the Logarithmic Coefficients of Starlike Functions Associated with Sine Function. *Fractal Fract.* **2022**, *6*, 261. [CrossRef]
30. Raza, M.; Riaz, A.; Xin, Q.; Malik, S.N. Hankel Determinants and Coefficient Estimates for Starlike Functions Related to Symmetric Booth Lemniscate. *Symmetry* **2022**, *14*, 1366. [CrossRef]
31. Shi, L.; Shutaywi, M.; Alreshidi, N.; Arif, M.; Ghufran, M.S. The sharp bounds of the third-order Hankel determinant for certain analytic functions associated with an eight-shaped domain. *Fractal Fract.* **2022**, *6*, 223. [CrossRef]
32. Shi, L.; Arif, M.; Ullah, K.; Alreshidi, N.; Shutaywi, M. On Sharp Estimate of Third Hankel Determinant for a Subclass of Starlike Functions. *Fractal Fract.* **2022**, *6*, 437. [CrossRef]
33. Shi, L.; Arif, M.; Raza, M.; Abbas, M. Hankel Determinant Containing Logarithmic Coefficients for Bounded Turning Functions Connected to a Three-Leaf-Shaped Domain. *Mathematics* **2022**, *10*, 2924. [CrossRef]
34. Wang, Z.G.; Raza, M.; Arif, M.; Ahmad, K. On the third and fourth determinants for a subclass of analytic functions. *Bull. Malays. Math. Sci. Soc.* **2022**, *45*, 323–359. [CrossRef]
35. Zaprawa, P.; Obradović, M.; Tuneski, N. Third Hankel determinant for univalent starlike functions. *Rev. Real Acad. Cienc. Exactas Fís. Nat. Ser. A Mat.* **2021**, *115*, 1–6. [CrossRef]
36. Zaprawa, P. Third Hankel determinants for subclasses of univalent functions. *Mediterr. J. Math.* **2017**, *14*, 19. [CrossRef]
37. Shafiq, M.; Srivastava, H.M.; Khan, N.; Ahmad, Q.Z.; Darus, M.; Kiran, S. An upper bound of the third Hankel determinant for a subclass of $q$-starlike functions associated with $k$-Fibonacci numbers. *Symmetry* **2020**, *12*, 1043. [CrossRef]
38. Al-Shbeil, I.; Shaba, T.G.; Cătaş, A. Second Hankel Determinant for the Subclass of Bi-Univalent Functions Using q-Chebyshev Polynomial and Hohlov Operator. *Fractal Fract.* **2022**, *6*, 186. [CrossRef]

39. Kowalczyk, B.; Lecko, A. Second Hankel determinant of logarithmic coefficients of convex and starlike functions. *Bull. Aust. Math. Soc.* **2021**, *105*, 458–467. [CrossRef]
40. Kowalczyk, B.; Lecko, A. Second Hankel Determinant of logarithmic coefficients of convex and starlike functions of order alpha. *Bull. Malays. Math. Sci. Soc.* **2022**, *45*, 727–740. [CrossRef]
41. Mendiratta, R.; Nagpal, S.; Ravichandran, V. On a subclass of strongly starlike functions associated with exponential function. *Bull. Malays. Math. Sci. Soc.* **2015**, *38*, 365–386. [CrossRef]
42. Shi, L.; Srivastava, H.M.; Arif, M.; Hussain, S.; Khan, H. An investigation of the third Hankel determinant problem for certain subfamilies of univalent functions involving the exponential function. *Symmetry* **2019**, *11*, 598. [CrossRef]
43. Srivastava, H.M.; Khan, B.; Khan, N.; Tahir, M.; Ahmad, S.; Khan, N. Upper bound of the third Hankel determinant for a subclass of $q$-starlike functions associated with the $q$-exponential function. *Bull. Sci. Math.* **2021**, *167*, 102942. [CrossRef]
44. Goel, P.; Kumar, S. Certain class of starlike functions associated with Modified sigmoid function. *Bull. Malays. Math. Sci. Soc.* **2019**, *43*, 957–991. [CrossRef]
45. Cho, N.E.; Kumar, V.; Kumar, S.S.; Ravichandran, V. Radius problems for starlike functions associated with the sine function. *Bull. Iran. Math. Soc.* **2019**, *45*, 213–232. [CrossRef]
46. Sümer Eker, S.; Şeker, B.; Çekiç, B.; Acu, M. Sharp Bounds for the Second Hankel Determinant of Logarithmic Coefficients for Strongly Starlike and Strongly Convex Functions. *Axioms* **2022**, *11*, 369. [CrossRef]
47. Sunthrayuth, P.; Aldawish, I.; Arif, M.; Abbas, M.; El-Deeb, S. Estimation of the Second-Order Hankel Determinant of Logarithmic Coefficients for Two Subclasses of Starlike Functions. *Symmetry* **2022**, *14*, 2039. [CrossRef]
48. Kwon, O.S.; Lecko, A.; Sim, Y.J. On the fourth coefficient of functions in the Carathéodory class. *Comput. Methods Funct. Theory* **2018**, *18*, 307–314. [CrossRef]

*Article*

# Subordination Properties of Certain Operators Concerning Fractional Integral and Libera Integral Operator

**Georgia Irina Oros [1],\*, Gheorghe Oros [1] and Shigeyoshi Owa [2]**

[1] Department of Mathematics and Computer Science, Faculty of Informatics and Sciences, University of Oradea, 410087 Oradea, Romania
[2] 1 Decembrie 1918 University, 510009 Alba Iulia, Romania
\* Correspondence: georgia_oros_ro@yahoo.co.uk

**Abstract:** The results contained in this paper are the result of a study regarding fractional calculus combined with the classical theory of differential subordination established for analytic complex valued functions. A new operator is introduced by applying the Libera integral operator and fractional integral of order $\lambda$ for analytic functions. Many subordination properties are obtained for this newly defined operator by using famous lemmas proved by important scientists concerned with geometric function theory, such as Eenigenburg, Hallenbeck, Miller, Mocanu, Nunokawa, Reade, Ruscheweyh and Suffridge. Results regarding strong starlikeness and convexity of order $\alpha$ are also discussed, and an example shows how the outcome of the research can be applied.

**Keywords:** analytic function; libera integral operator; fractional integral of order $\lambda$; differential subordination; strongly of order $\alpha$

**MSC:** 30C45

---

**Citation:** Oros, G.I.; Oros, G.; Owa, S. Subordination Properties of Certain Operators Concerning Fractional Integral and Libera Integral Operator. *Fractal Fract.* **2023**, *7*, 42. https://doi.org/10.3390/fractalfract7010042

**Academic Editor:** Natália Martins

Received: 5 December 2022
Revised: 23 December 2022
Accepted: 27 December 2022
Published: 30 December 2022

**Copyright:** © 2022 by the authors. Licensee MDPI, Basel, Switzerland. This article is an open access article distributed under the terms and conditions of the Creative Commons Attribution (CC BY) license (https://creativecommons.org/licenses/by/4.0/).

## 1. Introduction

Ever since the theory of differential subordination was initiated by Miller and Mocanu in the work published in 1978 [1] and 1981 [2], it was intensely used since it proves useful at re-obtaining known results in easier manners and also for providing interesting results when associated to studies involving analytic functions. A line of research which developed nicely in the context of differential subordination theory resulted after incorporating different types of operators into the study. Integral operators are an important tool when such investigations are considered as a recent survey paper shows [3]. The research started with the integral operator introduced by Alexander in 1915 [4]. A widely investigated integral operator is the Libera integral operator, introduced in 1965 [5]. Due to its properties of preserving starlikeness and convexity, it has been associated with many studies (see for example, references [6–10]) and still provides important new outcomes if combined with differential operators, such as in [11], with a confluent hypergeometric function, such as in [12], or with a generalized distribution, such as in [13]. Generalizations of the Libera operator are also considered for recent studies in papers, such as in [14–17].

In the present investigation, the Libera integral operator is extended and combined with the fractional integral of order $\lambda$ for introducing a new fractional calculus operator. The idea was inspired by recent publications where the fractional integral is associated with the Mittag–Leffler confluent hypergeometric function [18–20], with the confluent hypergeometric function [21,22], with the Ruscheweyh and Sălăgean Operators [23], with the convolution product of the multiplier transformation and the Ruscheweyh derivative [24], with the convolution product of Sălăgean operator and Ruscheweyh derivative [25] or with other operators [26,27].

Consider the class of functions $f(z)$ of the form

$$f(z) = z + \sum_{k=2}^{\infty} a_k z^k$$

denoted by $A$ and called analytic functions in the open unit disk $U = \{z \in \mathbb{C} : |z| < 1\}$.

For $f(z) \in A$, Libera [5] introduced the integral operator $L_1(f(z))$ defined as

$$L_1(f(z)) = \frac{2}{z} \int_0^z f(t) dt$$

$$= z + \sum_{k=2}^{\infty} \left(\frac{2}{k+1}\right) a_k z^k.$$

Consider the following extension for the operator $L_1(f(z))$.

$$L_2(f(z)) = L_1(L_1(f(z)))$$

$$= z + \sum_{k=2}^{\infty} \left(\frac{2}{k+1}\right)^2 a_k z^k$$

and

$$L_n(f(z)) = L_1(L_{n-1}(f(z)))$$

$$= z + \sum_{k=2}^{\infty} \left(\frac{2}{k+1}\right)^n a_k z^k,$$

where $n \in \mathbb{N} = \{1, 2, 3, \ldots\}$, and $L_0(f(z)) = f(z)$.

For $f(z) \in A$, the extension called fractional integral of order $\lambda$ is used in [28,29] as:

$$I_z^\lambda(f(z)) = \frac{1}{\Gamma(\lambda)} \int_0^z \frac{f(t)}{(z-t)^{1-\lambda}} dt \quad (\lambda > 0),$$

where the multiplicity of $(z-t)^{\lambda-1}$ is removed by requiring $\log(z-t)$ to be real when $z - t > 0$, and $\Gamma(z)$ is the gamma function.

The following form in easily deduced:

$$I_z^\lambda(f(z)) = \frac{1}{\Gamma(2+\lambda)} z^{1+\lambda} + \sum_{k=2}^{\infty} \frac{k!}{\Gamma(k+1+\lambda)} a_k z^{k+\lambda}.$$

Using $I_z^\lambda(f(z))$, we consider

$$L_\lambda(f(z)) = \frac{\Gamma(2+\lambda)}{z^\lambda} I_z^\lambda(f(z))$$

$$= z + \sum_{k=2}^{\infty} \frac{k!\Gamma(2+\lambda)}{\Gamma(k+1+\lambda)} a_k z^k \quad (\lambda > 0). \tag{1}$$

It follows from the above that

$$L_0(f(z)) = \lim_{\lambda \to 0} L_\lambda(f(z)) = f(z)$$

and

$$L_1(f(z)) = z + \sum_{k=2}^{\infty} \left(\frac{2}{k+1}\right) a_k z^k.$$

**Definition 1.** Using the operator $L_\lambda(f(z))$ given by (1), we introduce

$$L_{n+\lambda}(f(z)) = L_n(L_\lambda(f(z)))$$
$$= z + \sum_{k=2}^{\infty} \left(\frac{2}{k+1}\right)^n \frac{k!\Gamma(2+\lambda)}{\Gamma(k+1+\lambda)} a_k z^k$$

and

$$L_{\lambda+n}(f(z)) = L_\lambda(L_n(f(z)))$$
$$= z + \sum_{k=2}^{\infty} \left(\frac{2}{k+1}\right)^n \frac{k!\Gamma(2+\lambda)}{\Gamma(k+1+\lambda)} a_k z^k$$

for $n = 0, 1, 2, \ldots$ and $0 < \lambda \leq 1$. Considering the expressions above, we have:

$$L_{n+\lambda}(f(z)) = L_{\lambda+n}(f(z)).$$

For $f(z) \in A$, $f(z)$ is said to be subordinate to $g(z)$, written $f(z) \prec g(z)$, if there exists a function $w(z)$ analytic in $U$ with $w(0) = 0$ and $|w(z)| < 1$ ($z \in U$), and such that $f(z) = g(w(z))$. If $g(z)$ is univalent in $U$, then $f(z) \prec g(z)$ if and only if $f(0) = g(0)$ and $f(U) \subset g(U)$ ([30,31]).

We note that $f(z) \in A$ belongs to the class of starlike functions of order $\alpha$ in $U$ if

$$\frac{zf'(z)}{f(z)} \prec \frac{1 + (1-2\alpha)z}{1-z} \quad (z \in U)$$

for $0 \leq \alpha < 1$ and that $f(z) \in A$ belongs to the class of convex functions of order $\alpha$ in $U$ if

$$1 + \frac{zf''(z)}{f'(z)} \prec \frac{1 + (1-2\alpha)z}{1-z} \quad (z \in U)$$

for $0 \leq \alpha < 1$.

In addition, the analytic function $p(z)$, $z \in U$, satisfies the condition

$$|\arg p(z)| < \frac{\pi}{2}\alpha \quad (z \in U)$$

for certain real values $\alpha > 0$ if

$$p(z) \prec \left(\frac{1+z}{1-z}\right)^\alpha \quad (z \in U).$$

In Section 2 of the paper, a series of properties are proved for the newly introduced operator $L_\lambda(f(z))$ given by (1) considering the theory of differential subordination and a well-known lemma from Miller and Mocanu [30,32]. The study on operator $L_\lambda(f(z))$ is continued in Section 3 with results obtained by using lemmas from Suffridge [33] and its improved form obtained by Hallenbeck and Ruscheweyh [34]. Results related to the Briot–Bouquet differential subordination involving the operator $L_\lambda(f(z))$ are also obtained in Section 3 by using a lemma from Eenigenburg, Miller, Mocanu and Reade [35]. The study considering the operator $L_\lambda(f(z))$ and known lemmas is concluded in Section 3 with two theorems that use a result proved by Nunokawa [36,37] for obtaining certain univalence conditions for the operator $L_\lambda(f(z))$. The necessary lemmas cited above are listed in every section before each new result that is obtained as application. In Section 4, strong starlikeness and convexity of order $\alpha$ are investigated regarding the operator $L_\lambda(f(z))$, and an example is also presented as an application for the new results.

## 2. Subordination Results Regarding $L_{n+\lambda}(F(Z))$

To consider some properties of $L_{n+\lambda}(f(z))$, the following result proved by Miller and Mocanu ([30,32]) (also from Jack [38]) will be considered in the study.

**Lemma 1** ([30,32,38]). *Let $w(z)$ be analytic in $U$ with $w(0) = 0$. Then, if $|w(z)|$ attains its maximum value on the circle $|z| = r < 1$ at a point $z_0 \in U$, then we have*

$$z_0 w'(z_0) = m w(z_0)$$

*and*

$$\operatorname{Re}\left(1 + \frac{z_0 w''(z_0)}{w'(z_0)}\right) \geq m,$$

*where $m \geq 1$.*

Using the lemma presented above, the following theorem can be stated and proved:

**Theorem 1.** *Consider the function $f(z) \in A$ satisfying the subordination*

$$\frac{L_{n+\lambda}(f(z))}{z} \prec \frac{\alpha(1+z)}{\alpha + (2-\alpha)z} \quad (z \in U) \tag{2}$$

*for certain real values $\alpha > 1$. The subordination (2) gives:*

$$\left|\frac{L_{n+\lambda}(f(z))}{z} - \frac{\alpha}{2}\right| < \frac{\alpha}{2} \quad (z \in U). \tag{3}$$

**Proof.** With condition (2), there exists an analytic function $w(z)$ satisfying the properties needed for the definition of subordination and

$$\frac{L_{n+\lambda}(f(z))}{z} = \frac{\alpha(1+w(z))}{\alpha + (2-\alpha)w(z)} \quad (z \in U). \tag{4}$$

Using relation (4) have that

$$|w(z)| = \left|\frac{\alpha\left(\frac{L_{n+\lambda}(f(z))}{z} - 1\right)}{\alpha - (2-\alpha)\frac{L_{n+\lambda}(f(z))}{z}}\right| < 1 \quad (z \in U),$$

and that

$$2\left|\frac{L_{n+\lambda}(f(z))}{z}\right|^2 - \alpha\left(\frac{L_{n+\lambda}(f(z))}{z} + \overline{\left(\frac{L_{n+\lambda}(f(z))}{z}\right)}\right) < 0 \tag{5}$$

for $z \in U$. Hence, inequality (3) holds. □

**Remark 1.** *The result (3) in Theorem 1 shows us that*

$$0 < \operatorname{Re}\left(\frac{L_{n+\lambda}(f(z))}{z}\right) < \alpha \quad (z \in U)$$

*for $\alpha > 1$.*

Let us consider the analytic function $f(z)$ such that

$$L_{n-1+\lambda}(f(z)) = \frac{z(4+5z-2z^2)}{(2-z)^2} \quad (z \in U).$$

Then, we see that

$$L_{n+\lambda}(f(z)) = \frac{2}{z}\int_0^z L_{n-1+\lambda}(f(t))dt$$
$$= \frac{2}{z}\int_0^z \frac{t(4+5t-2t^2)}{(2-t)^2}dt$$
$$= \frac{2z(1+z)}{2-z}. \quad (6)$$

The function obtained in (6) can be used in subordination (2) and satisfies the inequality (3) for $\alpha = 4$.

For an analytic function $f(z)$, the following result can be proved.

**Theorem 2.** *If $f(z) \in A$ satisfies*

$$\mathrm{Re}\left(\frac{L_{n-1+\lambda}(f(z))}{L_{n+\lambda}(f(z))} - 1\right) < \frac{1}{4(\alpha-1)} \quad (z \in U) \quad (7)$$

*for $1 < \alpha \leq 2$ or*

$$\mathrm{Re}\left(\frac{L_{n-1+\lambda}(f(z))}{L_{n+\lambda}(f(z))} - 1\right) < \frac{\alpha-1}{4} \quad (z \in U) \quad (8)$$

*for $\alpha > 2$, then*

$$\left|\frac{L_{n+\lambda}(f(z))}{z} - \frac{\alpha}{2}\right| < \frac{\alpha}{2} \quad (z \in U).$$

**Proof.** Consider an analytic function $w(z)$ that satisfies relation (4). We know that $w(0) = 0$, and we obtain from (4) that

$$\frac{z(L_{n+\lambda}(f(z)))'}{L_{n+\lambda}(f(z))} - 1 = \frac{zw'(z)}{w(z)}\left(\frac{w(z)}{1-w(z)} - \frac{(2-\alpha)w(z)}{\alpha+(2-\alpha)w(z)}\right). \quad (9)$$

Since

$$z(L_{n+\lambda}(f(z)))' = 2L_{n-1+\lambda}(f(z)) - L_{n+\lambda}(f(z)),$$

Equation (9) becomes

$$\frac{L_{n-1+\lambda}(f(z))}{L_{n+\lambda}(f(z))} - 1 = \frac{zw'(z)}{2w(z)}\left(\frac{w(z)}{1-w(z)} - \frac{(2-\alpha)w(z)}{\alpha+(2-\alpha)w(z)}\right).$$

For the considered function $w(z)$, assume that there exists a point $z_0 \in U$ such that

$$\max_{|z|\leq|z_0|}|w(z)| = |w(z_0)| = 1.$$

In this situation, we write $w(z_0) = e^{i\theta}$ $(0 \leq \theta < 2\pi)$ and

$$z_0 w'(z_0) = kw(z_0) \quad (k \geq 1).$$

Using the properties seen above, we have

$$\mathrm{Re}\left(\frac{L_{n-1+\lambda}(f(z_0))}{L_{n+\lambda}(f(z_0))} - 1\right) = \frac{k}{2}\mathrm{Re}\left(\frac{w(z_0)}{1-w(z_0)} - \frac{(2-\alpha)w(z_0)}{\alpha+(2-\alpha)w(z_0)}\right)$$
$$= \frac{k}{2}\left(\frac{1}{2} - \frac{(2-\alpha)(2-\alpha+\alpha\cos\theta)}{\alpha^2+(2-\alpha)^2+2\alpha(2-\alpha)\cos\theta}\right).$$

Considering a function $g(t)$ given by

we have
$$g(t) = \frac{2-\alpha+\alpha t}{\alpha^2+(2-\alpha)^2+2\alpha(2-\alpha)t} \quad (t=\cos\theta),$$

$$g'(t) = \frac{4\alpha(\alpha-1)}{(\alpha^2+(2-\alpha)^2+2\alpha(2-\alpha)t)^2} > 0.$$

Since $g(t)$ is increasing for $t = \cos\theta$, we obtain for $1 < \alpha \leq 2$ that

$$\mathrm{Re}\left(\frac{L_{n-1+\lambda}(f(z_0))}{L_{n+\lambda}(f(z_0))} - 1\right) \geq \frac{k}{4(\alpha-1)} \geq \frac{1}{4(\alpha-1)} \tag{10}$$

and

$$\mathrm{Re}\left(\frac{L_{n-1+\lambda}(f(z_0))}{L_{n+\lambda}(f(z_0))} - 1\right) \geq \frac{(\alpha-1)k}{4} \geq \frac{\alpha-1}{4} \quad (\alpha > 2). \tag{11}$$

Since (10) contradicts (7) and (11) contradicts (8), we say that there is no $w(z)$ such that $w(0) = 0$ and $|w(z_0)| = 1$ for $z_0 \in U$. This implies that

$$|w(z)| = \left|\frac{\alpha\left(\frac{L_{n+\lambda}(f(z))}{z} - 1\right)}{\alpha - (2-\alpha)\frac{L_{n+\lambda}(f(z))}{z}}\right| < 1 \quad (z \in U),$$

that is the inequality (5). □

Next, our result is

**Theorem 3.** *Consider the analytic function $f(z)$ satisfying the conditions*

$$\mathrm{Re}\left(\frac{L_{n+\lambda}(f(z))}{L_{n+1+\lambda}(f(z))} - \frac{L_{n-1+\lambda}(f(z))}{L_{n+\lambda}(f(z))} - 1\right) < \frac{1}{4(\alpha-1)} \quad (z \in U),$$

*for $1 < \alpha \leq 2$ or*

$$\mathrm{Re}\left(\frac{L_{n+\lambda}(f(z))}{L_{n+1+\lambda}(f(z))} - \frac{L_{n-1+\lambda}(f(z))}{L_{n+\lambda}(f(z))} - 1\right) < \frac{\alpha-1}{4} \quad (z \in U),$$

*for $\alpha > 2$. Then,*

$$\left|\frac{L_{n+1+\lambda}(f(z))}{L_{n+\lambda}(f(z))} - \frac{\alpha}{2}\right| < \frac{\alpha}{2} \quad (z \in U).$$

**Proof.** Consider a function $w(z)$ satisfying

$$\frac{L_{n+1+\lambda}(f(z))}{L_{n+\gamma}(f(z))} = \frac{\alpha(1+w(z))}{\alpha+(2-\alpha)w(z)} \quad (z \in U).$$

This shows that $w(0) = 0$.
Using

$$z(L_{n+1+\lambda}(f(z)))' = 2L_{n+\lambda}(f(z)) - L_{n+1+\lambda}(f(z))$$

and

$$z(L_{n+\lambda}(f(z)))' = 2L_{n-1+\lambda}(f(z)) - L_{n+\lambda}(f(z)),$$

we obtain that

$$\frac{L_{n+\lambda}(f(z))}{L_{n+1+\lambda}(f(z))} - \frac{L_{n-1+\lambda}(f(z))}{L_{n+\lambda}(f(z))} - 1 = \frac{zw'(z)}{2w(z)}\left(\frac{w(z)}{1-w(z)} - \frac{(2-\alpha)w(z)}{\alpha+(2-\alpha)w(z)}\right).$$

From this point on, the proof of this theorem is completed by following the same steps as for the proof of Theorem 2. □

**3. Applications of Subordinations by Suffridge**

We first introduce the following lemma proved by Suffridge [27].

**Lemma 2** ([27]). *If a function $p(z)$ is analytic in $U$ with $p(0) = 1$ and satisfies*
$$zp'(z) \prec h(z) \quad (z \in U)$$
*for some starlike function $h(z)$, then*
$$p(z) \prec \int_0^z \frac{h(t)}{t} \quad (z \in U).$$

Applying the above lemma, we have

**Theorem 4.** *Consider the analytic function $f(z)$ satisfying the following subordination*
$$\frac{L_{n-1+\lambda}(f(z)) - L_{n+\lambda}(f(z))}{z} \prec \frac{1 + (1-2\alpha)z}{2(1-z)} \quad (z \in U),$$
*for certain real values $\alpha$ ($0 \le \alpha < 1$).*
*Then*
$$\frac{L_{n+\lambda}(f(z))}{z} \prec \log\left(\frac{\sqrt{z}}{(1-z)^{1-\alpha}}\right) \quad (z \in U).$$

**Proof.** Consider the analytic function $p(z)$ with $p(0) = 1$ given by:
$$p(z) = \frac{L_{n+\lambda}(f(z))}{z}.$$

In addition, consider the starlike function of order $\alpha$ $h(z)$ given by
$$h(z) = \frac{1 + (1-2\alpha)z}{1-z} \quad (z \in U),$$
for $0 \le \alpha < 1$.
Since
$$zp'(z) = \frac{z(L_{n+\lambda}(f(z)))' - L_{n+\lambda}(f(z))}{z}$$
$$= \frac{2(L_{n-1+\lambda}(f(z)) - L_{n+\gamma}(f(z)))}{z}$$
and
$$\int_0^z \frac{h(t)}{t} dt = \int_0^z \left(\frac{1}{t} - \frac{2(1-\alpha)}{1-t}\right) dt$$
$$= \log\left(\frac{z}{(1-z)^{2(1-\alpha)}}\right),$$
by applying Lemma 2, we obtain that
$$\frac{L_{n-1+\lambda}(f(z)) - L_{n+\lambda}(f(z))}{z} \prec \frac{1}{2}\log\left(\frac{z}{(1-z)^{2(1-\alpha)}}\right) \quad (z \in U).$$

Hence, the proof is completed. □

Taking $\alpha = \frac{1}{2}$ in Theorem 4, the following corollary emerges:

**Corollary 1.** *If $f(z) \in A$ satisfies*

$$\frac{L_{n-1+\lambda}(f(z)) - L_{n+\lambda}(f(z))}{z} \prec \frac{1}{1-z} \quad (z \in U),$$

*then*

$$\frac{L_{n+\lambda}(f(z))}{z} \prec \frac{1}{2}\log\left(\frac{z}{1-z}\right) \quad (z \in U).$$

Hallenbeck and Ruscheweyh [28] obtained the following form for Lemma 2 given by Suffridge:

**Lemma 3** ([28]). *If a function $p(z)$ is analytic in $U$ with $p(0) = 1$ and satisfies*

$$p(z) + zp'(z) \prec h(z) \quad (z \in U)$$

*for some convex function $h(z)$, then*

$$p(z) \prec \frac{1}{z}\int_0^z h(t)dt \quad (z \in U).$$

Now, we prove the following result.

**Theorem 5.** *Consider the analytic function $f(z)$ satisfying the subordination*

$$2\frac{L_{n-1+\lambda}(f(z))}{z} - \frac{L_{n+\lambda}(f(z))}{z} \prec \log\left(\frac{z}{(1-z)^{2(1-\alpha)}}\right) \quad (z \in U),$$

*for certain real values of $\alpha$ ($0 \leq \alpha < 1$).*
*Then,*

$$\frac{L_{n+\lambda}(f(z))}{z} \prec \log\left(\frac{z}{(1-z)^{2(1-\alpha)}}\right) + \frac{2(1-\alpha)}{z}\log(1-z) + (1-2\alpha) \quad (z \in U).$$

**Proof.** Consider the analytic function $p(z)$, $z \in U$, with $p(0) = 1$, given by

$$p(z) = \frac{L_{n+\lambda}(f(z))}{z}.$$

Using it, we can write:

$$p(z) + zp'(z) = 2\frac{L_{n-1+\lambda}(f(z))}{z} - \frac{L_{n+\lambda}(f(z))}{z}.$$

Further, we know that a function $h(z)$ given by

$$h(z) = \log\left(\frac{z}{(1-z)^{2(1-\alpha)}}\right) \quad (z \in U)$$

satisfies

$$zh'(z) = \frac{1 + (1-2\alpha)z}{1-z}.$$

Thus, $h(z)$ is convex in $U$ because $zh'(z)$ is starlike of order $\alpha$ in $U$. Applying Lemma 3, we obtain

$$\frac{L_{n+\lambda}(f(z))}{z} \prec \frac{1}{z}\int_0^z \left(\log\left(\frac{t}{(1-t)^{2(1-\alpha)}}\right)\right)dt$$

$$= \frac{1}{z}\int_0^z (\log t - 2(1-\alpha)\log(1-t))dt$$

$$= \log\left(\frac{z}{(1-z)^{2(1-\alpha)}}\right) + \frac{2(1-\alpha)}{z}\log(1-z) + (1-2\alpha) \quad (z \in U).$$

□

Choosing $\alpha = \frac{1}{2}$ in Theorem 5, we obtain the following corollary.

**Corollary 2.** *Consider the analytic function $f(z)$ satisfying the following subordination:*

$$2\frac{L_{n-1+\lambda}(f(z))}{z} - \frac{L_{n+\lambda}(f(z))}{z} \prec \log\left(\frac{z}{1-z}\right) \quad (z \in U)$$

*Then,*

$$\frac{L_{n+\lambda}(f(z))}{z} \prec \log\left(\frac{z}{1-z}\right) + \frac{1}{z}\log(1-z) \quad (z \in U).$$

**Theorem 6.** *Consider the analytic function $f(z)$ satisfying the following subordination:*

$$2\frac{L_{n-1+\lambda}(f(z))}{z} - \frac{L_{n+\lambda}(f(z))}{z} \prec \frac{1+z}{1-z} \quad (z \in U).$$

*Then,*

$$\frac{L_{n+\lambda}(f(z))}{z} \prec \frac{2}{z}\log\left(\frac{1}{1-z}\right) - 1 \quad (z \in U). \tag{12}$$

**Proof.** Letting

$$p(z) = \frac{L_{n+\lambda}(f(z))}{z} \text{ and } h(z) = \frac{1+z}{1-z},$$

we have that $p(z)$ is analytic in $U$ with $p(0) = 1$, and $h(z)$ is convex in $U$. Since

$$\frac{1}{z}\int_0^z h(t)dt = \frac{1}{z}\int_0^z \left(\frac{1+t}{1-t}\right)dt$$

$$= \frac{2}{z}\log\left(\frac{1}{1-z}\right) - 1,$$

we have the subordination (12). □

Next, the lemma given below, proved by Eenigenburg, Miller, Mocanu and Reade [29], is used for obtaining a new result.

**Lemma 4** ([29]). *Let $h(z)$ be convex in $U$ with $\text{Re}(\beta h(z) + \gamma) > 0$ ($\beta \neq 0$). If $p(z)$ is analytic in $U$ with $p(0) = h(0)$, then the subordination*

$$p(z) + \frac{zp'(z)}{\beta p(z) + \gamma} \prec h(z) \quad (z \in U)$$

*satisfies*

$$p(z) \prec h(z) \quad (z \in U).$$

With this lemma, we have

**Theorem 7.** *Consider the analytic function $f(z)$ satisfying the following subordination:*

$$\frac{L_{n+1+\lambda}(f(z)) - 2L_{n-1+\lambda}(f(z))}{L_{n+\lambda}(f(z))} + \frac{2L_{n+\lambda}(f(z))}{L_{n+1+\lambda}(f(z))} \prec \frac{1+(1-2\alpha)z}{1-z} \quad (z \in U),$$

*for $0 \leq \alpha < 1$.*
*Then,*

$$\frac{L_{n+1+\lambda}(f(z))}{L_{n+\lambda}(f(z))} \prec \frac{1+(1-2\alpha)z}{1-z} \quad (z \in U).$$

**Proof.** Consider the analytic function $p(z)$, $z \in U$, with $p(0) = 1$, given by

$$p(z) = \frac{L_{n+1+\lambda}(f(z))}{L_{n+\lambda}(f(z))}.$$

In addition, consider the convex function of order $\alpha$ given by

$$h(z) = \frac{1+(1-2\alpha)z}{1-z}, \quad 0 \leq \alpha < 1,$$

$h(0) = 1$.
Taking $\beta = 1$ and $\gamma = 0$ in Lemma 4, we say that

$$p(z) + \frac{zp'(z)}{p(z)} \prec \frac{1+(1-2\alpha)z}{1-z} \quad (z \in U)$$

implies

$$p(z) \prec \frac{1+(1-2\alpha)z}{1-z} \quad (z \in U).$$

Since

$$\frac{zp'(z)}{p(z)} = 2\left(\frac{L_{n+\lambda}(f(z))}{L_{n+1+\lambda}(f(z))} - \frac{L_{n-1+\lambda}(f(z))}{L_{n+\lambda}(f(z))}\right),$$

we prove the theorem with Lemma 4. □

Next, we consider the following lemma proved by Nunokawa ([30,31]).

**Lemma 5** ([30,31])**.** *Let a function $p(z)$ be analytic in $U$ with $p(0) = 1$. If there exists a point $z_0$ ($|z_0| < 1$) such that*

$$|\arg(p(z))| < \frac{\pi}{2}\beta \quad (|z| < |z_0|)$$

*and*

$$|\arg(p(z_0))| = \frac{\pi}{2}\beta$$

*for some real $\beta > 0$, then*

$$\frac{z_0 p'(z_0)}{p(z_0)} = \frac{2ik\arg(p(z_0))}{\pi}$$

*for some real $k$ such that*

$$k \geq \frac{1}{2}\left(a + \frac{1}{a}\right) > 1,$$

*where*

$$(p(z_0))^{\frac{1}{\beta}} = \pm ia \quad (a > 0).$$

Now, we derive

**Theorem 8.** *Let $f(z) \in A$ and*

$$F(z) = \frac{L_{n+\lambda}(f(z)) - \alpha z}{(1-\alpha)z} + 2\frac{L_{n-1+\lambda}(f(z)) - \alpha z}{L_{n+\lambda}(f(z)) - \alpha z} - 2 \qquad (13)$$

*for $0 \leq \alpha < 1$. If $f(z)$ satisfies*

$$F(z)^2 - 1 \prec \frac{16z}{(1-z)^2} \quad (z \in U), \qquad (14)$$

*then,*

$$\text{Re}\left(\frac{L_{n+\lambda}(f(z))}{z}\right) > \alpha \quad (z \in U).$$

**Proof.** Consider the analytic function $p(z)$, $z \in U$, with $p(0) = 1$, given by:

$$p(z) = \frac{L_{n+\lambda}(f(z))}{z}.$$

For such $p(z)$, assume that there exists a point $z_0$ ($|z_0| < 1$) such that

$$\text{Re}\left(\frac{p(z) - \alpha}{1 - \alpha}\right) > 0 \quad (|z| < |z_0| < 1)$$

and

$$\text{Re}\left(\frac{p(z_0) - \alpha}{1 - \alpha}\right) = 0.$$

If

$$\frac{p(z_0) - \alpha}{1 - \alpha} \neq 0,$$

Lemma 5 gives us that

$$\frac{z_0 p'(z_0)}{p(z_0) - \alpha} = \frac{2ik}{\pi}\arg\left(\frac{p(z_0) - \alpha}{1 - \alpha}\right)$$

$$= \frac{2ik}{\pi}\arg(p(z_0) - \alpha)$$

for some real $k$ such that $k \geq \frac{1}{2}\left(a + \frac{1}{a}\right) > 1$ with

$$\left(\frac{p(z_0) - \alpha}{1 - \alpha}\right)^{\frac{1}{\beta}} = \pm ia \quad (a > 0).$$

It follows from the above that

$$\left\{\frac{p(z_0) - \alpha}{1 - \alpha} + \frac{z_0 p'(z_0)}{p(z_0) - \alpha}\right\} - 1 = F(z_0)^2 - 1$$

$$= (\pm ia \pm ik)^2 - 1$$

$$\leq -\left(a + \frac{a^2 + 1}{2a}\right)^2 - 1.$$

Let us consider a function $h(a)$ given by

$$h(a) = a + \frac{a^2 + 1}{2a} \quad (a > 0).$$

Then, $h(a)$ satisfies
$$h(a) \geq h\left(\sqrt{\frac{1}{3}}\right) = \sqrt{3}.$$

This gives us that
$$\left\{\frac{p(z_0) - \alpha}{1 - \alpha} + \frac{z_0 p'(z_0)}{p(z_0) - \alpha}\right\}^2 - 1 = F(z_0)^2 - 1 \leq -4.$$

Here, we define a function $g(z)$ by
$$g(z) = \frac{16z}{(1-z)^2} \quad (z \in U).$$

Then, $g(z)$ maps $U$ onto the domain with the slit $(-\infty, -4)$. This contradicts our condition (14).

Having the contradiction, we conclude that $p(z)$ satisfies the condition
$$\operatorname{Re}\left(\frac{p(z) - \alpha}{1 - \alpha}\right) = \operatorname{Re}\left(\frac{\frac{L_{n+\lambda}(f(z))}{z} - \alpha}{1 - \alpha}\right) > 0,$$

for all $z \in U$. Hence, the proof of the theorem is completed. □

Next, our theorem is

**Theorem 9.** *Consider a function $F(z)$ given by (13) where $f(z)$ is analytic in $U$ and $0 \leq \alpha < 1$. If $F(z)$ satisfies*
$$F(z) \prec \frac{1+z}{1-z} \quad (z \in U), \tag{15}$$

*then*
$$\operatorname{Re}\left(\frac{L_{n+\lambda}(f(z))}{z}\right) > \alpha \quad (z \in U).$$

**Proof.** Consider the analytic function $p(z)$ given by
$$p(z) = \frac{L_{n+\lambda}(f(z))}{z}.$$

Then, there exists a point $z_0$ ($|z_0| < 1$) such that
$$\operatorname{Re}\left(\frac{p(z) - \alpha}{1 - \alpha}\right) > 0 \quad (|z| < |z_0| < 1) \tag{16}$$

and
$$\operatorname{Re}\left(\frac{p(z_0) - \alpha}{1 - \alpha}\right) = 0. \tag{17}$$

If
$$\frac{p(z_0) - \alpha}{1 - \alpha} = 0,$$

by Lemma 5, we have
$$\frac{z_0 p'(z_0)}{p(z_0) - \alpha} = \frac{2ik}{\pi} \arg(p(z_0) - \alpha)$$

for some real $k \geq \frac{1}{2}\left(a + \frac{1}{a}\right) > 1$ with

$$\frac{p(z_0) - \alpha}{1 - \alpha} = \pm ia \quad (a > 0).$$

With the properties obtained so far, we can write

$$\frac{p(z_0) - \alpha}{1 - \alpha} + \frac{z_0 p'(z_0)}{p(z_0) - \alpha} = F(z_0) = \pm i(a + k).$$

Since

$$\operatorname{Re}\left(\frac{1+z}{1-z}\right) > 0 \quad (z \in U),$$

we say that

$$F(z) \not\prec \frac{1+z}{1-z} \quad (z \in U).$$

This means that there is no $z_0$ ($|z_0| < 1$) such that (16) and (17) are satisfied. Hence, we obtain the stated conclusion of the theorem.

$$\operatorname{Re}(p(z) - \alpha) = \operatorname{Re}\left(\frac{L_{n+\lambda}(f(z))}{z} - \alpha\right) > 0 \quad (z \in U).$$

□

**Remark 2.** *Considering $f(z)$ an analytic function in $U$ given by*

$$\frac{L_{n+\lambda}(f(z))}{z} = \frac{1}{1-z}$$

*and $\alpha = 0$ in Theorem 9, we have that*

$$F(z) = \frac{1+z}{1-z} \quad (z \in U).$$

*Therefore, $f(z)$ satisfies the subordination (15) for $\alpha = 0$. For such $f(z)$, we know that*

$$\operatorname{Re}\left(\frac{L_{n+\lambda}(f(z))}{z}\right) > \frac{1}{2} > 0 \quad (z \in U).$$

## 4. Results Regarding Strong Properties of Order $\alpha$

Let $f(z) \in A$ and $L_{n+\lambda}(f(z))$ be defined by (1) for $n = 0, 1, 2, \ldots$ and $0 \leq \lambda \leq 1$. For $f(z) \in A$ satisfying

$$\operatorname{Re}\left(\frac{L_{n+\lambda}(f(z))}{z}\right) > \alpha \quad (z \in U),$$

$f(z)$ is said to be strongly of order $\alpha$ in $U$ if $f(z)$ satisfies

$$\left|\arg\left(\frac{L_{n+\lambda}(f(z))}{z}\right)\right| < \frac{\pi}{2}\alpha \quad (z \in U),$$

where $0 \leq \alpha < 1$.

If $f(z) \in A$ satisfies

$$\left|\arg\left(\frac{zf'(z)}{f(z)}\right)\right| < \frac{\pi}{2}\alpha \quad (z \in U)$$

for $0 \leq \alpha < 1$, then $f(z)$ is said to be strongly starlike of order $\alpha$ in $U$. In addition, if $f(z) \in A$ satisfies
$$\left| \arg\left(1 + \frac{zf''(z)}{f'(z)}\right) \right| < \frac{\pi}{2}\alpha \quad (z \in U)$$
for $0 \leq \alpha < 1$, then we say that $f(z)$ is strongly convex of order $\alpha$ in $U$.

Let us consider a function $w(z)$ defined by
$$w(z) = \left(\frac{1+z}{1-z}\right)^{\alpha} \quad (z \in U)$$
for $0 \leq \alpha < 1$, then we see that
$$\arg w(z) = \alpha \arg\left(\frac{1+z}{1-z}\right) = \frac{\pi}{2}\alpha \quad (z \in U).$$

Thus, a function $f(z)$ given by
$$f(z) = \exp\left(\int_0^z \left(\frac{1+t}{1-t}\right)^{\alpha} dt\right)$$
is strongly starlike of order $\alpha$ in $U$ and a function $f(z) \in A$ given by
$$f'(z) = \frac{1}{z}\exp\left(\int_0^z \left(\frac{1+t}{1-t}\right)^{\alpha} dt\right)$$
is strongly convex of order $\alpha$ in $U$.

Now, we derive

**Theorem 10.** *If $f(z) \in A$ satisfies*
$$\left| \frac{L_{n-1+\lambda}(f(z))}{L_{n+\lambda}(f(z))} - 1 \right| < \frac{\alpha}{4}\mathrm{Re}\left(\frac{1+\beta z}{1-z}\right) \quad (z \in U)$$
*for some real $\alpha$ $(0 \leq \alpha < 1)$ and some real $\beta$ $(\beta \neq -1)$, then*
$$\left| \arg\left(\frac{L_{n+\lambda}(f(z))}{z}\right) \right| < \frac{\pi}{2}\alpha \quad (z \in U).$$

**Proof.** Define a function $p(z)$ by
$$p(z) = \frac{L_{n+\lambda}(f(z))}{z}.$$
Then, $p(z)$ is analytic in $U$, and $p(0) = 1$. This function $p(z)$ satisfies
$$\frac{zp'(z)}{p(z)} = 2\left(\frac{L_{n-1+\lambda}(f(z))}{L_{n+\lambda}(f(z))} - 1\right).$$

It follows from the above that

$$\left|\arg\left(\frac{L_{n+\lambda}(f(z))}{z}\right)\right| = |\arg(p(z))| = |\text{Im}(\log(p(z)))| = \left|\text{Im}\int_0^z (\log(p(t)))'dt\right|$$

$$= \left|\text{Im}\int_0^z \frac{p'(t)}{p(t)}dt\right| = \left|\text{Im}\int_0^z \frac{p'(\rho e^{i\theta})}{p(\rho e^{i\theta})}e^{i\theta}d\rho\right|$$

$$\leq \int_0^r \left|\text{Im}\left(\frac{p'(\rho e^{i\theta})}{p(\rho e^{i\theta})}e^{i\theta}\right)\right|d\rho \leq \int_{-r}^r \left|\frac{p'(\rho e^{i\theta})}{p(\rho e^{i\theta})}\right|d\rho$$

$$\leq \frac{r}{2}\int_0^{2\pi}\left|\frac{p'(re^{i\theta})}{p(re^{i\theta})}\right|d\theta = \frac{1}{2}\int_0^{2\pi}\left|\frac{re^{i\theta}p'(re^{i\theta})}{p(re^{i\theta})}\right|d\theta$$

$$= \int_0^{2\pi}\left|\frac{L_{n-1+\lambda}(f(re^{i\theta}))}{L_{n+\lambda}(f(re^{i\theta}))} - 1\right|dt < \frac{\alpha}{4}\int_0^{2\pi}\text{Re}\left(\frac{1+\beta re^{i\theta}}{1-re^{i\theta}}\right)d\theta$$

$$= \frac{\alpha}{4}\int_0^{2\pi}\left\{\frac{1-\beta}{2} + \left(\frac{1+\beta}{2}\right)\frac{1-r^2}{1+r^2-2r\cos\theta}\right\}d\theta = \frac{\pi}{2}\alpha,$$

because by Poisson integral

$$\frac{1}{2\pi}\int_0^{2\pi}\frac{1-r^2}{1+r^2-2r\cos\theta}d\theta = 1.$$

This completes the proof of the theorem. □

**Example 1.** *Consider a function $f(z) \in A$ given by*

$$L_{n+\lambda}(f(z)) = z\left(\frac{2}{2-z}\right)^{3\alpha} \quad (z \in U),$$

*with $0 \leq \alpha < 1$. Note that a function*

$$w(z) = \frac{2}{2-z}$$

*satisfies*

$$\left|w(z) - \frac{4}{3}\right| < \frac{2}{3} \quad (z \in U)$$

*and*

$$|\arg w(z)| < \frac{\pi}{6} \quad (z \in U).$$

*This gives us that*

$$\left|\arg\left(\frac{L_{n+\lambda}(f(z))}{z}\right)\right| < \frac{\pi}{2}\alpha \quad (z \in U).$$

*For such $f(z)$, we have*

$$\left|\frac{L_{n-1+\lambda}(f(z))}{L_{n+\lambda}(f(z))} - 1\right| = \frac{3}{2}\alpha\left|\frac{z}{2-z}\right| < \frac{3}{2}\alpha \quad (z \in U).$$

*Thus, if we consider a real $\beta$ such that $\beta \leq -11$, then $f(z)$ satisfies*

$$\left|\frac{L_{n-1+\lambda}(f(z))}{L_{n+\lambda}(f(z))} - 1\right| < \frac{3}{2}\alpha \leq \frac{\alpha(1-\beta)}{8} < \frac{\alpha}{4}\text{Re}\left(\frac{1+\beta z}{1-z}\right),$$

*for $z \in U$.*

## 5. Conclusions

The outcome of this paper falls within the research topic which concerns incorporating fractional calculus in geometric function theory by defining new fractional operators and conducting studies involving the theory of differential subordination. The operator used for the investigation denoted by $L_\lambda(f(z))$ is introduced in Definition 1 using fractional integral of order $\lambda$ defined in [28,29] and the Libera integral operator [5]. The necessary known definitions regarding the analytic functions are shown in the Introduction. Section 2 contains three theorems that show the results of the study conducted on the operator $L_\lambda(f(z))$ by applying a famous lemma from Miller and Mocanu [30,32] which is presented at the beginning of this section. Section 3 starts with recalling the lemma from Suffridge [33] which is used for obtaining the new results regarding the operator $L_\lambda(f(z))$ contained in Theorem 4 and Corollary 1. This lemma was modified by Hallenbeck and Ruscheweyh [34]. Their resulting lemma is first listed, and then Theorems 5 and 6 and Corollary 2 present the new results obtained by applying it to the operator $L_\lambda(f(z))$. A lemma from Eenigenburg, Miller, Mocanu and Reade [35] is next stated and used for obtaining the new result involving the operator $L_\lambda(f(z))$ presented in Theorem 7. A lemma proved by Nunokawa [36,37] is next listed and applied to the operator $L_\lambda(f(z))$ for the new outcome presented in Theorems 8 and 9. In Section 4, the basic definition regarding strong starlikeness and strong convexity of order $\alpha$ are recalled, and a new result concerning the strong starlikeness of order $\alpha$ of the operator $L_\lambda(f(z))$ is proved. An example is also provided in order to show a certain application of the theoretical result presented in Theorem 10.

As future uses of the results presented here, the operator $L_\lambda(f(z))$ given by (1) can be applied for defining new subclasses of analytic functions with certain geometric properties given by the characteristics of this operator already proven in this paper. The classes could be further investigated considering the strong starlikeness of order $\alpha$ of the operator $L_\lambda(f(z))$ having as inspiration recent studies such as [39].

**Author Contributions:** Conceptualisation, S.O.; methodology, G.I.O., G.O. and S.O.; software, G.I.O.; validation, G.I.O., G.O. and S.O.; formal analysis, G.I.O., G.O. and S.O.; investigation, G.I.O., G.O. and S.O.; resources, G.I.O. and S.O.; data curation, G.I.O. and S.O.; writing—original draft preparation, S.O.; writing—review and editing, G.I.O., G.O. and S.O.; visualisation, G.I.O.; supervision, S.O.; project administration, G.I.O.; funding acquisition, G.I.O. All authors have read and agreed to the published version of the manuscript.

**Funding:** This research received no external funding.

**Institutional Review Board Statement:** Not applicable

**Informed Consent Statement:** Not applicable

**Data Availability Statement:** Not applicable

**Conflicts of Interest:** The authors declare no conflict of interest.

## References

1. Miller, S.S.; Mocanu, P.T. Second order differential inequalities in the complex plane. *J. Math. Anal. Appl.* **1978**, *65*, 289–305. [CrossRef]
2. Miller, S.S.; Mocanu, P.T. Differential subordinations and univalent functions. *Mich. Math. J.* **1981**, *28*, 157–172. [CrossRef]
3. Ahuja, O.P.; Çetinkaya, A. A Survey on the theory of integral and related operators in Geometric Function Theory. In *Mathematical Analysis and Computing*; Mohapatra, R.N., Yugesh, S., Kalpana, G., Kalaivani, C., Eds.; ICMAC 2019. Springer Proceedings in Mathematics & Statistics; Springer: Singapore, 2021; Volume 344. [CrossRef]
4. Alexander, J.W. Functions which map the interior of the unit circle upon simple regions. *Ann. Math.* **1915**, *17*, 12–22. [CrossRef]
5. Libera, R.J. Some classes of regular univalent functions. *Proc. Am. Math. Soc.* **1965**, *16*, 755–758. [CrossRef]
6. Owa, S.; Srivastava, H.M. Some applications of the generalized Libera integral operator. *Proc. Jpn. Acad. Ser. A Math. Sci.* **1986**, *62*, 125–128. [CrossRef]
7. Nunokawa, M. On starlikeness of Libera transformation. *Complex Var. Elliptic Equ.* **1991**, *17*, 79–83. [CrossRef]
8. Acu, M. A preserving property of a generalized Libera integral operator. *Gen. Math.* **2004**, *12*, 41–45.
9. Oros, G.; Oros, G.I. Convexity condition for the Libera integral operator. *Complex Var. Elliptic Equ.* **2006**, *51*, 69–76. [CrossRef]
10. Szász, R. A sharp criterion for the univalence of Libera operator. *Creat. Math. Inf.* **2008**, *17*, 65–71.

11. Oros, G.I. New differential subordination obtained by using a differential-integral Ruscheweyh-Libera operator. *Miskolc Math. Notes* **2020**, *21*, 303–317. [CrossRef]
12. Oros, G.I. Study on new integral operators defined using confluent hypergeometric function. *Adv. Differ. Equ.* **2021**, *2021*, 342. [CrossRef]
13. Hamzat, J.O.; Oladipo, A.T.; Oros, G.I. Application of a Multiplier Transformation to Libera Integral Operator Associated with Generalized Distribution. *Symmetry* **2022**, *14*, 1934. [CrossRef]
14. Guney, H.O.; Owa, S. New extension of Alexander and Libera integral operators. *Turkish J. Math.* **2022**, *46*, 17. [CrossRef]
15. Chandralekha, S. Inclusion properties for subclasses of multivalent regular functions defined on the unit disk. *Malaya J. Mat.* **2021**, *9*, 684–689. [CrossRef]
16. Aouf, M.K.; Mostafa, A.O.; Bulboacă, T. Properties of a certain class of multivalent functions. *Bol. Soc. Parana Mat.* **2022**, *40*, 1–9. [CrossRef]
17. Kanwal, B.; Hussain, S.; Abdeljawad, T. On certain inclusion relations of functions with bounded rotations associated with Mittag-Leffler functions. *AIMS Math.* **2022**, *7*, 7866–7887. [CrossRef]
18. Ghanim, F.; Al-Janaby, H.F. An analytical study on Mittag-Leffler-confluent hypergeometric functions with fractional integral operator. *Math. Meth. Appl. Sci.* **2021**, *44*, 3605–3614. [CrossRef]
19. Ghanim, F.; Al-Janaby, H.F.; Bazighifan, O. Some New Extensions on Fractional Differential and Integral Properties for Mittag-Leffler Confluent Hypergeometric Function. *Fractal Fract.* **2021**, *5*, 143. [CrossRef]
20. Ghanim, F.; Bendak, S.; Al Hawarneh, A. Certain implementations in fractional calculus operators involving Mittag-Leffler-confluent hypergeometric functions. *Proc. R. Soc. A* **2022**, *478*, 20210839. [CrossRef]
21. Alb Lupaş, A. New Applications of the Fractional Integral on Analytic Functions. *Symmetry* **2021**, *13*, 423. [CrossRef]
22. Acu, M.; Oros, G.; Rus, A.M. Fractional Integral of the Confluent Hypergeometric Function Related to Fuzzy Differential Subordination Theory. *Fractal Fract.* **2022**, *6*, 413. [CrossRef]
23. Alb Lupaş, A. On Special Fuzzy Differential Subordinations Obtained for Riemann-Liouville Fractional Integral of Ruscheweyh and Sălăgean Operators. *Axioms* **2022**, *11*, 428. [CrossRef]
24. Alb Lupaş, A. New Applications of Fractional Integral for Introducing Subclasses of Analytic Functions. *Symmetry* **2022**, *14*, 419. [CrossRef]
25. Alb Lupaş, A. Subordination results for a fractional integral operator. *Probl. Anal. Issues Anal.* **2022**, *11*, 20–31. [CrossRef]
26. Wanas, A.K.; Hammadi, N.J. Applications of Fractional Calculus on a Certain Class of Univalent Functions Associated with Wanas Operator. *Earthline J. Math. Sci.* **2022**, *9*, 117–129. [CrossRef]
27. Srivastava, H.M.; Kashuri, A.; Mohammed, P.O.; Nonlaopon, K. Certain Inequalities Pertaining to Some New Generalized Fractional Integral Operators. *Fractal Fract.* **2021**, *5*, 160. [CrossRef]
28. Owa, S. On the distortion theorems I. *Kyungpook Math. J.* **1978**, *18*, 53–59.
29. Owa, S.; Srivastava, H.M. Univalent and starlike generalized hypergeometric functions. *Can. J. Math.* **1987**, *39*, 1057–1077. [CrossRef]
30. Miller, S.S.; Mocanu, P.T. *Differential Subordinations, Theory and Applications*; Marcel Dekker Inc.: New York, NY, USA, 2000.
31. Pommerenke, C. *Univalent Functions*; Vanderhoeck and Ruprecht: Göttingen, Germany, 1975.
32. Miller, S.S.; Mocanu, P.T. Briot-Bouquet differential equations and differential subordinations. *Complex Var.* **1997**, *33*, 217–237. [CrossRef]
33. Suffridge, T.J. Some remarks on convex maps on the unit disc. *Duke Math. J.* **1970**, *37*, 775–777. [CrossRef]
34. Hallenbeck, D.J.; Ruscheweyh, S. Subordination by convex functions. *Proc. Am. Math. Soc.* **1975**, *52*, 191–195. [CrossRef]
35. Eenigenburg, P.; Miller, S.S.; Mocanu, P.T.; Reade, M.O. On a Briot-Bouquet differential subordination. In *General Inequalities 3*; I.S.N.M. Birkhäuser Verlag: Basel, Switzerland, 1983; Volume 64, pp. 339–348.
36. Nunokawa, M. On properties of non-Carathéodory functions. *Proc. Jpn. Acad.* **1992**, *68*, 152–153. [CrossRef]
37. Nunokawa, M. On the order of strongly starlikeness of strongly convex functions. *Proc. Jpn. Acad.* **1993**, *69*, 234–237. [CrossRef]
38. Jack, I.S. Functions starlike and convex of order alpha. *J. Lond. Math. Soc.* **1971**, *3*, 469–471. [CrossRef]
39. Sümer Eker, S.; Şeker, B.; Çekiç, B.; Acu, M. Sharp Bounds for the Second Hankel Determinant of Logarithmic Coefficients for Strongly Starlike and Strongly Convex Functions. *Axioms* **2022**, *11*, 369. [CrossRef]

**Disclaimer/Publisher's Note:** The statements, opinions and data contained in all publications are solely those of the individual author(s) and contributor(s) and not of MDPI and/or the editor(s). MDPI and/or the editor(s) disclaim responsibility for any injury to people or property resulting from any ideas, methods, instructions or products referred to in the content.

Article

# Some New Versions of Fractional Inequalities for Exponential Trigonometric Convex Mappings via Ordered Relation on Interval-Valued Settings

Muhammad Bilal Khan [1,*], Adriana Căt̨aş [2,*], Najla Aloraini [3] and Mohamed S. Soliman [4]

[1] Department of Mathematics, COMSATS University Islamabad, Islamabad 44000, Pakistan
[2] Department of Mathematics and Computer Science, University of Oradea, 1 University Street, 410087 Oradea, Romania
[3] Department of Mathematics, College of Sciences and Arts Onaizah, Qassim University, P.O. Box 6640, Buraydah 51452, Saudi Arabia
[4] Department of Electrical Engineering, College of Engineering, Taif University, P.O. Box 11099, Taif 21944, Saudi Arabia
* Correspondence: bilal42742@gmail.com (M.B.K.); acatas@gmail.com (A.C.)

**Abstract:** This paper's main goal is to introduce left and right exponential trigonometric convex interval-valued mappings and to go over some of their important characteristics. Additionally, we demonstrate the Hermite–Hadamard inequality for interval-valued functions by utilizing fractional integrals with exponential kernels. Moreover, we use the idea of left and right exponential trigonometric convex interval-valued mappings to show various findings for midpoint- and Pachpatte-type inequalities. Additionally, we show that the results provided in this paper are expansions of several of the results already demonstrated in prior publications The suggested research generates variants that are applicable for conducting in-depth analyses of fractal theory, optimization, and research challenges in several practical domains, such as computer science, quantum mechanics, and quantum physics.

**Keywords:** left and right exponential trigonometric convex interval-valued mappings; Riemann–Liouville fractional integral operators having exponential kernels; Hermite–Hadamard inequalities

## 1. Introduction

It is common knowledge that mathematical subjects such as mathematical economy, probability theory, optimal control theory, and others depend heavily on convex function and convexity. Classical convexity has been expanded and generalized over time to include harmonic convexity, h-convexity, and p-convexity, among others. In reality, inequality is the basis for the ideas of convexity and convex function, and its significance cannot be overstated. One of the most significant classical inequalities, the Hermite–Hadamard (HH) inequality below, has recently received a lot of attention.

For a convex mapping $\omega : K \to \mathbb{R}$ on an interval $K = [z, v]$, the HH inequality is written as:

$$\omega\left(\frac{z+v}{2}\right) \leq \frac{1}{v-z}\int_{z}^{v}\omega(\varkappa)d\varkappa \leq \frac{\omega(z)+\omega(v)}{2}. \tag{1}$$

For all $z, v \in K$, with $K$ being a convex set. If $\omega$ is concave, then (1) is reversed.

The following inequality as the weighted generalization of (1) was established by Fejér in [1]. This important generalization of the HH inequality is known as the HH–Fejér inequality.

Let us consider $\omega : K = [z, v] \to \mathbb{R}$ a convex mapping on a convex set $K$, and $z, v \in K$. Then, we have

$$\omega\left(\frac{z+v}{2}\right) \leq \frac{1}{\int_z^v \mathcal{C}(\varkappa)d\varkappa} \int_z^v \omega(\varkappa)\mathcal{C}(\varkappa)d\varkappa \leq \frac{\omega(z)+\omega(v)}{2}. \qquad (2)$$

If $\mathcal{C}(\varkappa) = 1$, then we obtain (1) from (2). For a concave mapping, (2) is reversed. Different inequalities can be derived using distinct symmetric convex mappings, $\mathcal{C}(\varkappa)$.

Integral inequality (1) and (2) in various variants have also been extensively examined in [2–10] due to the differences between the ideas of convexity. In order to further their study and take advantage of the growing significance of fractional integrals, numerous writers have combined fractional integrals and Hermite–Hadamard-type inequalities. Recent advances in this field in different areas of mathematics can easily be seen and we refer readers to references [11–22].

Some fractional Hermite–Hadamard-type inequalities have been discovered in this way; for more information, see references [23–32]. This field of inequalities has many applications. Similarly, various other types of inequalities have found the bounds of mean inequalities. For more information, see also [33–43].

On the other hand, Moore initially presented interval analysis as a key method to manage interval uncertainty [44]. This has a wide range of applications [45–54]. Recently, Khan et al. also contributed to this field and defined different types of inequalities using crip theory and fuzzy theory, see [55–58].

In particular, researchers such as Chalco-Cano et al. [59,60], Costa and Román-Flores [61], Zhao et al. [62,63], An et al. [64], and others have studied a number of classical inequalities with interval-valued functions. Budak et al. [65] demonstrated the fractional Hermite–Hadamard inequality for the interval convex function as an additional extension. Since then, the authors of [66–76] have extensively investigated various additional improvements to and expansions of Hermite–Hadamard inequalities for different convex fuzzy-valued functions. Additionally, in [77], some Hermite–Hadamard- and Jensen-type inequalities for up and down convex fuzzy-number-valued functions were discovered. In this study, several Hermite–Hadamard-type inequalities for interval-valued left and right exponential trigonometric functions are established. The earlier inequalities described in [78–93] are generalized by our findings. For more information, see [94–99].

We establish some additional modifications for interval fractional Hermite–Hadamard-type inequalities as a result of [77,78,85,86]. Our findings clarify some previous questions. Furthermore, it is possible that the findings will be acknowledged as important approaches to investigating the study of interval-valued differential equations, interval optimization, and interval vector spaces, among other things. In Section 2, we provide an introduction. The idea of left and right exponential trigonometric $I$-$V$-$M$ is introduced in Section 3 along with several intervals fractional Hermite–Hadamard-type inequalities that are proven. Finally, several examples are provided in Section 4.

## 2. Preliminaries

Let $X_C$ be the space of all closed and bounded intervals of $\mathbb{R}$ and $\mathcal{I} \in X_C$ defined by

$$\mathcal{I} = [\mathcal{I}_*, \mathcal{I}^*] = \{\varkappa \in \mathbb{R} | \mathcal{I}_* \leq \varkappa \leq \mathcal{I}^*\}, (\mathcal{I}_*, \mathcal{I}^* \in \mathbb{R}). \qquad (3)$$

If $\mathcal{I}_* = \mathcal{I}^*$, then $\mathcal{I}$ is said to be degenerate. In this article, all intervals will be non-degenerate intervals. If $\mathcal{I}_* \geq 0$, then $[\mathcal{I}_*, \mathcal{I}^*]$ is called a positive interval. The set of all positive intervals is denoted by $X_C^+$ and defined as

$$X_C^+ = \{[\mathcal{I}_*, \mathcal{I}^*] : [\mathcal{I}_*, \mathcal{I}^*] \in X_C \text{ and } \mathcal{I}_* \geq 0\}.$$

Let $\lambda \in \mathbb{R}$ and $\lambda \cdot \Pi$ be defined by

$$\lambda \cdot \Pi = \begin{cases} [\lambda \Pi_*, \lambda \Pi^*] & \text{if } \lambda > 0, \\ \{0\} & \text{if } \lambda = 0, \\ [\lambda \Pi^*, \lambda \Pi_*] & \text{if } \lambda < 0. \end{cases} \qquad (4)$$

Then, the Minkowski difference $\mho - \Pi$, addition $\Pi + \mho$ and $\Pi \times \mho$ for $\Pi, \mho \in X_C$ are defined by

$$[\mho_*, \mho^*] + [\Pi_*, \Pi^*] = [\mho_* + \Pi_*, \mho^* + \Pi^*], \qquad (5)$$

$$[\mho_*, \mho^*] \times [\Pi_*, \Pi^*] = [\min\{\mho_* \Pi_*, \mho^* \Pi_*, \mho_* \Pi^*, \mho^* \Pi^*\}, \max\{\mho_* \Pi_*, \mho^* \Pi_*, \mho_* \Pi^*, \mho^* \Pi^*\}] \qquad (6)$$

$$[\mho_*, \mho^*] - [\Pi_*, \Pi^*] = [\mho_* - \Pi^*, \mho^* - \Pi_*]. \qquad (7)$$

**Remark 1.** *For given $[\mho_*, \mho^*]$, $[\Pi_*, \Pi^*] \in X_C$, we say that $[\mho_*, \mho^*] \leq_p [\Pi_*, \Pi^*]$ if and only if $\mho_* \leq \Pi_*$, $\mho^* \leq \Pi^*$ is a partial interval order relation [84].*

For $[\mho_*, \mho^*]$, $[\Pi_*, \Pi^*] \in X_C$, the Hausdorff–Pompeiu distance between intervals $[\mho_*, \mho^*]$ and $[\Pi_*, \Pi^*]$ is defined by

$$d_H([\mho_*, \mho^*], [\Pi_*, \Pi^*]) = \max\{|\mho_* - \Pi_*|, |\mho^* - \Pi^*|\}. \qquad (8)$$

It is a familiar fact that $(X_C, d_H)$ is a complete metric space, see [79,82,83].

## 3. Fractional Integral Operators of Real- and Interval-Valued Mappings

Now, we define and discuss some properties of fractional integral operators of real- and interval-valued mappings.

**Theorem 1.** *If $\omega : [z, v] \subset \mathbb{R} \to X_C$ is an interval-valued mapping (I·V·M) satisfying that $\omega(\varkappa) = [\omega_*(\varkappa), \omega^*(\varkappa)]$, then $\omega$ is Aumann integrable (IA-integrable) over $[z, v]$ when and only when $\omega_*(\varkappa)$ and $\omega^*(\varkappa)$ are both integrable over $[z, v]$ such that [79,81]*

$$(IA) \int_z^v \omega(\varkappa) d\varkappa = \left[ \int_z^v \omega_*(\varkappa) d\varkappa, \int_z^v \omega^*(\varkappa) d\varkappa \right]. \qquad (9)$$

**Definition 1.** *Let $\alpha > 0$ and $L([z, v], \mathbb{R})$ be the collection of all Lebesgue-measurable mapping on $[z, v]$. Then, the left and right Riemann–Liouville fractional integral with exponential kernels in connection of $\omega \in L([z, v], \mathbb{R})$ with order $\alpha > 0$ are, respectively, defined by [85]:*

$$\mathcal{I}_{z+}^{\alpha} \omega(\varkappa) = \frac{1}{\alpha} \int_z^{\varkappa} e^{\left(-\frac{1-\alpha}{\alpha}(\varkappa - v)\right)} \omega(v) dv, (\varkappa > z), \qquad (10)$$

and

$$\mathcal{I}_{v-}^{\alpha} \omega(\varkappa) = \frac{1}{\alpha} \int_{\varkappa}^v e^{\left(-\frac{1-\alpha}{\alpha}(v - \varkappa)\right)} \omega(v) dv, (\varkappa < v) \qquad (11)$$

**Definition 2.** *Let $\alpha > 0$ and $L([z, v], X_C)$ be the collection of all Lebesgue-measurable interval-valued mapping on $[z, v]$. Then, the left and right Riemann–Liouville fractional integral with exponential kernels in connection of $\omega \in L([z, v], X_C)$ with order $\alpha > 0$ are, respectively, defined by [86]*

$$\mathcal{I}_{z+}^{\alpha} \omega(\varkappa) = \left[ \mathcal{I}_{z+}^{\alpha} \omega_*(\varkappa), \mathcal{I}_{z+}^{\alpha} \omega^*(\varkappa) \right] = \frac{1}{\alpha} \int_z^{\varkappa} e^{\left(-\frac{1-\alpha}{\alpha}(\varkappa - v)\right)} [\omega_*(v), \omega^*(v)] dv, (\varkappa > z), \qquad (12)$$

and

$$\mathcal{I}_{v^-}^\alpha \omega(\varkappa) = [\mathcal{I}_{v^-}^\alpha \omega_*(\varkappa), \mathcal{I}_{v^-}^\alpha \omega^*(\varkappa)] = \frac{1}{\alpha} \int_\varkappa^v e^{(-\frac{1-\alpha}{\alpha}(v-\varkappa))} [\omega_*(v), \omega^*(v)] dv, (\varkappa < v), \tag{13}$$

**Definition 3.** *The mapping $\omega : [z, v] \to \mathbb{R}$ is called exponential trigonometric convex mapping on $[z, v]$ if [78]*

$$\omega(v\varkappa + (1-v)s) \leq \frac{\sin \frac{\pi v}{2}}{e^{1-v}} \omega(\varkappa) + \frac{\cos \frac{\pi v}{2}}{e^v} \omega(s). \tag{14}$$

*For all $\varkappa, s \in [z, v], v \in [0, 1]$, and $\varkappa \in [z, v]$. If (14) is reversed, then $\omega$ is called exponential trigonometric concave mapping on $[z, v]$.*

## 4. Left and Right Exponential Trigonometric Convex Interval-Valued Functions

In following results, we will use left and right Riemann–Liouville fractional integrals with left and right exponential kernels, and some nontrivial examples are also given to prove the validity of these integrals and results.

**Definition 4.** *The I-V·M $\omega : [z, v] \to X_C$ is called a left and right exponential trigonometric convex I-V·M on $[z, v]$ if*

$$\omega(v\varkappa + (1-v)s) \leq_p \frac{\sin \frac{\pi v}{2}}{e^{1-v}} \omega(\varkappa) + \frac{\cos \frac{\pi v}{2}}{e^v} \omega(s). \tag{15}$$

*For all $\varkappa, s \in [z, v], v \in [0, 1]$, where $\omega(\varkappa) \geq_p 0$ for all $\varkappa \in [z, v]$. If (15) is reversed, then $\omega$ is called a left and right exponential trigonometric concave I-V·M on $[z, v]$.*

**Theorem 2.** *Let $K$ be an invex set and $\omega : K \to X_C$ be a F-N-V·M given by*

$$\omega(\varkappa) = [\omega_*(\varkappa), \omega^*(\varkappa)], \forall \varkappa \in K. \tag{16}$$

*For all $\varkappa \in K$. Then $\omega$ is a left and right exponential trigonometric convex F-N-V·M on $K$ if and only if $\omega_*(\varkappa)$ and $\omega^*(\varkappa)$ are both exponential trigonometric convex mappings.*

**Proof.** Consider that $\omega_*(\varkappa)$ and $\omega^*(\varkappa)$ are both exponential trigonometric convex and concave mappings on $K$, respectively. Then, from (14), we have

$$\omega_*(v\varkappa + (1-v)s) \leq \frac{\sin \frac{\pi v}{2}}{e^{1-v}} \omega_*(\varkappa) + \frac{\cos \frac{\pi v}{2}}{e^v} \omega_*(s), \forall \varkappa, s \in K, v \in [0, 1],$$

and

$$\omega^*(v\varkappa + (1-v)s) \leq \frac{\sin \frac{\pi v}{2}}{e^{1-v}} \omega^*(\varkappa) + \frac{\cos \frac{\pi v}{2}}{e^v} \omega^*(s), \forall \varkappa, s \in K, v \in [0, 1].$$

Then, by (16), (8), and (10), we obtain

$$\omega(v\varkappa + (1-v)s)$$
$$= [\omega_*(v\varkappa + (1-v)s), \omega^*(v\varkappa + (1-v)s)],$$
$$\leq_p \frac{\sin \frac{\pi v}{2}}{e^{1-v}} [\omega_*(\varkappa), \omega^*(\varkappa)] + \frac{\cos \frac{\pi v}{2}}{e^v} [\omega_*(s), \omega^*(s)],$$

that is

$$\omega(v\varkappa + (1-v)s) \leq_p \frac{\sin \frac{\pi v}{2}}{e^{1-v}} \omega(\varkappa) + \frac{\cos \frac{\pi v}{2}}{e^v} \omega(s), \forall \varkappa, s \in K, v \in [0, 1].$$

Hence, $\omega$ is a left and right exponential trigonometric convex F-N-V·M on $K$.

Conversely, let $\omega$ be a left and right exponential trigonometric convex F-N-V·M on K. Then, for all $\varkappa, s \in K$ and $\mathfrak{v} \in [0,1]$, we have

$$\omega(\mathfrak{v}\varkappa + (1-\mathfrak{v})s) \leq_p \frac{\sin\frac{\pi\mathfrak{v}}{2}}{e^{1-\mathfrak{v}}}\omega(\varkappa) + \frac{\cos\frac{\pi\mathfrak{v}}{2}}{e^{\mathfrak{v}}}\omega(s).$$

Therefore, from (16), we have

$$\omega(\mathfrak{v}\varkappa + (1-\mathfrak{v})s) = [\omega_*(\mathfrak{v}\varkappa + (1-\mathfrak{v})s), \omega^*(\mathfrak{v}\varkappa + (1-\mathfrak{v})s)].$$

Again, from (16), (6), and (8), we obtain

$$\frac{\sin\frac{\pi\mathfrak{v}}{2}}{e^{1-\mathfrak{v}}}\omega(\varkappa) + \frac{\cos\frac{\pi\mathfrak{v}}{2}}{e^{\mathfrak{v}}}\omega(\varkappa) = \left[\frac{\sin\frac{\pi\mathfrak{v}}{2}}{e^{1-\mathfrak{v}}}\omega_*(\varkappa), \frac{\sin\frac{\pi\mathfrak{v}}{2}}{e^{1-\mathfrak{v}}}\omega^*(\varkappa)\right] + \left[\frac{\cos\frac{\pi\mathfrak{v}}{2}}{e^{\mathfrak{v}}}\omega_*(s), \frac{\cos\frac{\pi\mathfrak{v}}{2}}{e^{\mathfrak{v}}}\omega^*(s)\right].$$

For all $\varkappa, s \in K$ and $\mathfrak{v} \in [0,1]$. Then, by left and right exponential trigonometric convexity of $\omega$, we have for all $\varkappa, s \in K$ and $\mathfrak{v} \in [0,1]$ such that

$$\omega_*(\mathfrak{v}\varkappa + (1-\mathfrak{v})s) \leq \frac{\sin\frac{\pi\mathfrak{v}}{2}}{e^{1-\mathfrak{v}}}\omega_*(\varkappa) + \frac{\cos\frac{\pi\mathfrak{v}}{2}}{e^{\mathfrak{v}}}\omega_*(s),$$

and

$$\omega^*(\mathfrak{v}\varkappa + (1-\mathfrak{v})s) \leq \frac{\sin\frac{\pi\mathfrak{v}}{2}}{e^{1-\mathfrak{v}}}\omega^*(\varkappa) + \frac{\cos\frac{\pi\mathfrak{v}}{2}}{e^{\mathfrak{v}}}\omega^*(s).$$

Hence, the result follows. □

**Remark 2.** *If $\omega_*(\varkappa) = \omega^*(\varkappa)$, then we obtain the classical definition of exponential trigonometric convex mappings, see [78].*

We obtained some new definitions from the literature which will be helpful in investigating some classical and new results as special cases of the main results.

**Definition 5.** *Let $\omega : [z, v] \to X_C$ be an I-V·M. Then, $\omega(\varkappa)$ is given by*

$$\omega(\varkappa) = [\omega_*(\varkappa), \omega^*(\varkappa)].$$

*For all $\varkappa \in [z, v]$. Then, $\omega$ is a lower left and right exponential trigonometric convex (concave) I-V·M on $[z, v]$ if and only if*

$$\omega_*(\mathfrak{v}\varkappa + (1-\mathfrak{v})s) \leq (\geq) \frac{\sin\frac{\pi\mathfrak{v}}{2}}{e^{1-\mathfrak{v}}}\omega_*(\varkappa) + \frac{\cos\frac{\pi\mathfrak{v}}{2}}{e^{\mathfrak{v}}}\omega_*(s),$$

*and*

$$\omega^*(\mathfrak{v}\varkappa + (1-\mathfrak{v})s) = \frac{\sin\frac{\pi\mathfrak{v}}{2}}{e^{1-\mathfrak{v}}}\omega^*(\varkappa) + \frac{\cos\frac{\pi\mathfrak{v}}{2}}{e^{\mathfrak{v}}}\omega^*(s)$$

**Definition 6.** *Suppose that $\omega : [z, v] \to X_C$ is an I-V·M that is defined by*

$$\omega(\varkappa) = [\omega_*(\varkappa), \omega^*(\varkappa)]$$

*For all $\varkappa \in [z, v]$. Then, $\omega$ is an upper left and right exponential trigonometric convex (concave) I-V·M on $[z, v]$ if and only if*

$$\omega_*(\mathfrak{v}\varkappa + (1-\mathfrak{v})s) = \frac{\sin\frac{\pi\mathfrak{v}}{2}}{e^{1-\mathfrak{v}}}\omega_*(\varkappa) + \frac{\cos\frac{\pi\mathfrak{v}}{2}}{e^{\mathfrak{v}}}\omega_*(s),$$

*and*

$$\omega^*(\mathfrak{v}\varkappa + (1-\mathfrak{v})s) \leq (\geq) \frac{\sin\frac{\pi\mathfrak{v}}{2}}{e^{1-\mathfrak{v}}}\omega^*(\varkappa) + \frac{\cos\frac{\pi\mathfrak{v}}{2}}{e^{\mathfrak{v}}}\omega^*(s)$$

## 5. Riemann–Liouville Fractional Integrals Hermite–Hadamard-Type Inequalities

In the following section, we use the new concept of left and right exponential trigonometric convex interval-valued mapping to illustrate a few Riemann–Liouville fractional integrals Hermite–Hadamard-type inequalities having exponential kernels.

**Theorem 3.** *Let $\omega : [z, v] \to X_C^+$ be an I-V·M on $[z, v]$ given by $\omega(\varkappa) = [\omega_*(\varkappa), \omega^*(\varkappa)]$ for all $\varkappa \in [z, v]$. If $\omega$ is a left and right exponential trigonometric convex I-V·M on $[z, v]$ and $\omega \in L([z, v], X_C^+)$, then*

$$\sqrt{\frac{e}{2}}\omega\left(\frac{z+v}{2}\right) \leq_p \frac{1-\alpha}{2(1-e^{-\rho})}\left[\mathcal{I}_{z^+}^{\alpha}\omega(v) + \mathcal{I}_{v^-}^{\alpha}\omega(z)\right] \leq_p \frac{\rho}{1-e^{-\rho}}C(\rho)\frac{\omega(z)+\omega(v)}{2}. \quad (17)$$

*If $\omega(\varkappa)$ is a left and right exponential trigonometric concave I-V·M, then*

$$\sqrt{\frac{e}{2}}\omega\left(\frac{z+v}{2}\right) \geq_p \frac{1-\alpha}{2(1-e^{-\rho})}\left[\mathcal{I}_{z^+}^{\alpha}\omega(v) + \mathcal{I}_{v^-}^{\alpha}\omega(z)\right] \geq_p \frac{\rho}{1-e^{-\rho}}C(\rho)\frac{\omega(z)+\omega(v)}{2} \quad (18)$$

*where*

$$C(\rho) = \frac{4\rho + 2\pi e^{-\rho-1} + 4}{4\rho^2 + 8\rho + \pi^2 + 4} + \frac{2\pi e^{-1} + 4e^{-\rho-1}(e+\rho e)}{4\rho^2 - 8\rho + \pi^2 + 4}, \rho = \frac{1-\alpha}{\alpha}(v-z) \text{ and } 1 > \alpha > 0.$$

**Proof.** Let $\omega : [z, v] \to X_C^+$ be a left and right exponential trigonometric convex I-V·M. Then, by hypothesis, we have

$$\omega\left(\frac{z+v}{2}\right) \leq_p \frac{\sin\frac{\pi}{4}}{\sqrt{e}}\omega(\upsilon z + (1-\upsilon)v) + \frac{\cos\frac{\pi}{4}}{\sqrt{e}}\omega((1-\upsilon)z + \upsilon v).$$

After simplification, we find that

$$2\omega\left(\frac{z+v}{2}\right) \leq_p \sqrt{\frac{2}{e}}[\omega(\upsilon z + (1-\upsilon)v) + \omega((1-\upsilon)z + \upsilon v)].$$

Therefore, we have

$$2\omega_*\left(\frac{z+v}{2}\right) \leq \sqrt{\frac{2}{e}}[\omega_*(\upsilon z + (1-\upsilon)v) + \omega_*((1-\upsilon)z + \upsilon v)],$$

$$2\omega^*\left(\frac{z+v}{2}\right) \leq \sqrt{\frac{2}{e}}[\omega^*(\upsilon z + (1-\upsilon)v) + \omega^*((1-\upsilon)z + \upsilon v)].$$

Taking $\omega_*(.)$ and multiplying both sides by $e^{-\rho\upsilon}$ and integrating the obtained result with respect to $\upsilon$ from 0 to 1, we have

$$2\int_0^1 e^{-\rho\upsilon}\omega_*\left(\frac{z+v}{2}\right)d\upsilon \leq \sqrt{\frac{2}{e}}\left[\int_0^1 e^{-\rho\upsilon}\omega_*(\upsilon z + (1-\upsilon)v)d\upsilon + \int_0^1 e^{-\rho\upsilon}\omega_*((1-\upsilon)z + \upsilon v)d\upsilon\right].$$

Let $u = \upsilon z + (1-\upsilon)v$ and $\varkappa = (1-\upsilon)z + \upsilon v$. Then, we have

$$\begin{aligned}2\int_0^1 e^{-\rho\upsilon}\omega_*\left(\frac{z+v}{2}\right)d\upsilon &\leq \sqrt{\frac{2}{e}}\frac{1}{v-z}\int_z^v e^{(-\frac{1-\alpha}{\alpha}(v-u))}\omega_*(u)du + \frac{1}{v-z}\int_z^v e^{(-\frac{1-\alpha}{\alpha}(\varkappa-z))}\omega_*(\varkappa)d\varkappa \\ &= \sqrt{\frac{2}{e}}\frac{\alpha}{v-z}\left[\mathcal{I}_{z^+}^{\alpha}\omega_*(v) + \mathcal{I}_{v^-}^{\alpha}\omega_*(z)\right].\end{aligned} \quad (19)$$

Now, taking the right side of Equation (19), we have

$$\int_0^1 e^{-\rho\upsilon}\omega_*\left(\frac{z+v}{2}\right)d\upsilon = \frac{1-e^{-\rho}}{\rho}\omega_*\left(\frac{z+v}{2}\right). \quad (20)$$

From (19) and (20), we have

$$\frac{2}{\alpha} \cdot \frac{1-e^{-\rho}}{\rho} \omega_* \left(\frac{z+v}{2}\right) \leq \sqrt{\frac{2}{e}} \cdot \frac{1}{v-z} \left[\mathcal{I}^\alpha_{z^+} \omega_*(v) + \mathcal{I}^\alpha_{v^-} \omega_*(z)\right]. \tag{21}$$

Similarly, for $\omega^*(\varkappa)$, we have

$$\frac{2}{\alpha} \cdot \frac{1-e^{-\rho}}{\rho} \omega^* \left(\frac{z+v}{2}\right) \leq \sqrt{\frac{2}{e}} \cdot \frac{1}{v-z} \left[\mathcal{I}^\alpha_{z^+} \omega^*(v) + \mathcal{I}^\alpha_{v^-} \omega^*(z)\right]. \tag{22}$$

From (21) and (22), we have

$$\frac{2}{\alpha} \cdot \frac{1-e^{-\rho}}{\rho} \left[\omega_*\left(\frac{z+v}{2}\right), \omega^*\left(\frac{z+v}{2}\right)\right] \leq_p \sqrt{\frac{2}{e}} \cdot \frac{1}{v-z} \left[\left[\mathcal{I}^\alpha_{z^+} \omega_*(v) + \mathcal{I}^\alpha_{v^-} \omega_*(z)\right], \left[\mathcal{I}^\alpha_{z^+} \omega^*(v) + \mathcal{I}^\alpha_{v^-} \omega^*(z)\right]\right].$$

That is

$$\frac{2}{\alpha} \cdot \frac{1-e^{-\rho}}{\rho} \omega\left(\frac{z+v}{2}\right) \leq_p \sqrt{\frac{2}{e}} \cdot \frac{1}{v-z} \left[\mathcal{I}^\alpha_{z^+} \omega(v) + \mathcal{I}^\alpha_{v^-} \omega(z)\right]. \tag{23}$$

For the right side of Equation (17), since $\omega$ is a left and right exponential trigonometric convex $I$-$V$·$M$, we can deduce that

$$\omega(vz + (1-v)v) \leq_p \frac{\sin\frac{\pi v}{2}}{e^{1-v}} \omega(z) + \frac{\cos\frac{\pi v}{2}}{e^v} \omega(v), \tag{24}$$

and

$$\omega((1-v)z + vv) \leq_p \frac{\cos\frac{\pi v}{2}}{e^v} \omega(z) + \frac{\sin\frac{\pi v}{2}}{e^{1-v}} \omega(v). \tag{25}$$

Adding (24) and (25), we have

$$\omega(vz + (1-v)v) + \omega((1-v)z + vv) \leq_p [\omega(z) + \omega(v)] \left[\frac{\sin\frac{\pi v}{2}}{e^{1-v}} + \frac{\cos\frac{\pi v}{2}}{e^v}\right]. \tag{26}$$

Since $\omega$ is $I$-$V$·$M$, then we have

$$\begin{array}{l}\omega_*(vz + (1-v)v) + \omega_*((1-v)z + vv) \leq [\omega_*(z) + \omega_*(v)]\left[\frac{\sin\frac{\pi v}{2}}{e^{1-v}} + \frac{\cos\frac{\pi v}{2}}{e^v}\right],\\ \omega^*(vz + (1-v)v) + \omega^*((1-v)z + vv) \leq [\omega^*(z) + \omega^*(v)]\left[\frac{\sin\frac{\pi v}{2}}{e^{1-v}} + \frac{\cos\frac{\pi v}{2}}{e^v}\right].\end{array} \tag{27}$$

Taking $\omega_*(.)$ from (27) and multiplying the inequality with $e^{-\rho v}$, and integrating the resultant with $v$ from 0 to 1, we have

$$\begin{array}{l}\int_0^1 e^{-\rho v} \omega_*(vz+(1-v)v)dv \;+ \int_0^1 e^{-\rho v}\omega_*((1-v)z+vv)dv\\ \qquad \leq [\omega_*(z)+\omega_*(v)]\int_0^1 e^{-\rho v}\left[\frac{\sin\frac{\pi v}{2}}{e^{1-v}}+\frac{\cos\frac{\pi v}{2}}{e^v}\right]dv,\\ \qquad = \frac{4\rho+2\pi e^{-\rho-1}+4}{4\rho^2+8\rho+\pi^2+4} + \frac{2\pi e^{-1}+4e^{-\rho-1}(e+\rho e)}{4\rho^2-8\rho+\pi^2+4}[\omega_*(z)+\omega_*(v)].\end{array} \tag{28}$$

In a similar way to the above, for $\omega_*(.)$ we have

$$\begin{array}{l}\int_0^1 e^{-\rho v} \omega^*(vz+(1-v)v)dv \;+ \int_0^1 e^{-\rho v}\omega^*((1-v)z+vv)dv\\ \qquad \leq [\omega^*(z)+\omega^*(v)]\int_0^1 e^{-\rho v}\left[\frac{\sin\frac{\pi v}{2}}{e^{1-v}}+\frac{\cos\frac{\pi v}{2}}{e^v}\right]dv,\\ \qquad = \frac{4\rho+2\pi e^{-\rho-1}+4}{4\rho^2+8\rho+\pi^2+4} + \frac{2\pi e^{-1}+4e^{-\rho-1}(e+\rho e)}{4\rho^2-8\rho+\pi^2+4}[\omega^*(z)+\omega^*(v)].\end{array} \tag{29}$$

From (28) and (29), we have

$$\int_0^1 e^{-\rho v}\omega(vz+(1-v)v)dv + \int_0^1 e^{-\rho v}\omega((1-v)z+vv)dv$$
$$\leq_p \frac{4\rho+2\pi e^{-\rho-1}+4}{4\rho^2+8\rho+\pi^2+4} + \frac{2\pi e^{-1}+4e^{-\rho-1}(e+\rho e)}{4\rho^2-8\rho+\pi^2+4}[\omega(z)+\omega(v)]. \quad (30)$$

From (37) and (30), we have

$$\sqrt{\frac{e}{2}}\omega\left(\frac{z+v}{2}\right) \leq_p \frac{1-\alpha}{2(1-e^{-\rho})}\left[\mathcal{I}^\alpha_{z^+}\omega(v)+\mathcal{I}^\alpha_{v^-}\omega(z)\right] \leq_p \frac{\rho}{1-e^{-\rho}}C(\rho)\frac{\omega(z)+\omega(v)}{2}.$$

Hence, the required result. □

If we consider some mild restrictions on Theorem 3, then the following new and classical outcomes can be obtained.

**Remark 3.** *From Theorem 3, we can clearly see the following.*

*If one lays $\omega$ which is an upper left and right exponential trigonometric concave I-V·M on $[z,v]$, then one acquires the following inequality [98]:*

$$\sqrt{\frac{e}{2}}\omega\left(\frac{z+v}{2}\right) \supseteq_p \frac{1-\alpha}{2(1-e^{-\rho})}\left[\mathcal{I}^\alpha_{z^+}\omega(v)+\mathcal{I}^\alpha_{v^-}\omega(z)\right] \supseteq_p \frac{\rho}{1-e^{-\rho}}C(\rho)\frac{\omega(z)+\omega(v)}{2}. \quad (31)$$

*If $\alpha \to 1$, then*

$$\lim_{\alpha \to 1}\rho = \lim_{\alpha \to 1}\frac{1-\alpha}{\alpha}(v-z)=0, \text{ then}$$

$$\lim_{\alpha \to 1}\left(\frac{4\rho+2\pi e^{-\rho-1}+4}{4\rho^2+8\rho+\pi^2+4}+\frac{2\pi e^{-1}+4e^{-\rho-1}(e+\rho e)}{4\rho^2-8\rho+\pi^2+4}\right)=\frac{2\pi e^{-1}+4}{\pi^2+4}, \lim_{\alpha \to 1}\frac{1-\alpha}{2(1-e^{-\rho})}=\frac{1}{2(v-z)}.$$

Now from Theorem 3, we acquire the following result, which is also a new one:

$$\sqrt{\frac{e}{2}}\omega\left(\frac{z+v}{2}\right) \leq_p \frac{1}{v-z}\int_z^v \omega(\varkappa)d\varkappa \leq_p \frac{2\pi e^{-1}+4}{\pi^2+4}[\omega(z)+\omega(v)]. \quad (32)$$

If one lays $\alpha \to 1$ and $\omega$ which is an upper left and right exponential trigonometric concave I-V·M on $[z,v]$, then one can acquire the following inequality [98]:

$$\sqrt{\frac{e}{2}}\omega\left(\frac{z+v}{2}\right) \supseteq_p \frac{1}{v-z}\int_z^v \omega(\varkappa)d\varkappa \supseteq_p \frac{2\pi e^{-1}+4}{\pi^2+4}[\omega(z)+\omega(v)]. \quad (33)$$

Let $\alpha \to 1$ and $\omega_*(\varkappa) \neq \omega^*(\varkappa)$. Then, from Theorem 3, we achieve the Hermite–Hadamard inequality for the interval-valued left and right exponential trigonometric convex mapping, which is also a new one:

$$\sqrt{\frac{e}{2}}\omega\left(\frac{z+v}{2}\right) \leq_p \frac{1}{v-z}\int_z^v \omega(\varkappa)d\varkappa \leq_p \frac{2\pi e^{-1}+4}{\pi^2+4}[\omega(z)+\omega(v)]. \quad (34)$$

If $\omega_*(\varkappa) = \omega^*(\varkappa)$, then, from Theorem 3, we arrive at classical fractional Hermite–Hadamard inequality for the exponential trigonometric convex mapping.

$$\sqrt{\frac{e}{2}}\omega\left(\frac{z+v}{2}\right) \leq \frac{1-\alpha}{2(1-e^{-\rho})}\left[\mathcal{I}^\alpha_{z^+}\omega(v)+\mathcal{I}^\alpha_{v^-}\omega(z)\right] \leq \frac{\rho}{1-e^{-\rho}}C(\rho)\frac{\omega(z)+\omega(v)}{2}. \quad (35)$$

Let $\alpha \to 1$ and $\omega_*(\varkappa) = \omega^*(\varkappa)$. Then, from Theorem 3, we achieve the classical Hermite–Hadamard inequality for the exponential trigonometric convex mapping, see [78].

$$\sqrt{\frac{e}{2}}\omega\left(\frac{z+v}{2}\right) \leq \frac{1}{v-z}\int_z^v \omega(\varkappa)d\varkappa \leq \frac{2\pi e^{-1}+4}{\pi^2+4}[\omega(z)+\omega(v)]. \quad (36)$$

**Example 1.** Let $\alpha = \frac{1}{2}$, $\varkappa \in [0,1]$, and the I-V·M $\omega : [z, v] = [0, 1] \to X_C^+$, defined by $\omega(\varkappa) = [2\varkappa^2, 4\varkappa^2]$. Since left and right end point mappings $\omega_*(\varkappa) = 2\varkappa^2$, $\omega^*(\varkappa) = 4\varkappa^2$ are exponential trigonometric convex mappings, then $\omega(\varkappa)$ is a left and right exponential trigonometric convex I-V·M. We can clearly see that $\omega \in L([z, v], X_C^+)$ and

$$\sqrt{\frac{e}{2}}\omega_*\left(\frac{z+v}{2}\right) = \omega_*\left(\frac{5}{2}\right) = \frac{\sqrt{e}}{2\sqrt{2}}$$

$$\sqrt{\frac{e}{2}}\omega^*\left(\frac{z+v}{2}\right) = \omega^*\left(\frac{5}{2}\right) = \frac{\sqrt{e}}{\sqrt{2}}$$

$$\frac{\rho}{1-e^{-\rho}}C(\rho)\frac{\omega_*(z)+\omega_*(v)}{2} = \frac{8+2\pi e^{-2}}{2(16+\pi^2)(1-e^{-1})}$$

$$\frac{\rho}{1-e^{-\rho}}C(\rho)\frac{\omega^*(z)+\omega^*(v)}{2} = \frac{8+2\pi e^{-2}}{(16+\pi^2)(1-e^{-1})}.$$

Note that

$$\frac{1-\alpha}{2(1-e^{-\rho})}\left[\mathcal{I}_{z^+}^\alpha \omega_*(v) + \mathcal{I}_{v^-}^\alpha \omega_*(z)\right]$$
$$= \frac{1}{2(1-e^{-1})}\int_0^1 e^{-(1-\varkappa)} \cdot 2\varkappa^2 d\varkappa$$
$$+ \frac{1}{2(1-e^{-1})}\int_0^1 e^{-\varkappa} \cdot 2\varkappa^2 d\varkappa$$
$$= \frac{1}{1-e^{-1}}\left[1 - 2e^{-1} + 2 - 5e^{-1}\right]$$
$$= \frac{3-7e^{-1}}{1-e^{-1}}.$$

$$\frac{1-\alpha}{2(1-e^{-\rho})}\left[\mathcal{I}_{z^+}^\alpha \omega^*(v) + \mathcal{I}_{v^-}^\alpha \omega^*(z)\right]$$
$$= \frac{1}{2(1-e^{-1})}\int_0^1 e^{-(1-\varkappa)} \cdot 4\varkappa^2 d\varkappa$$
$$+ \frac{1}{2(1-e^{-1})}\int_0^1 e^{-\varkappa} \cdot 4\varkappa^2 d\varkappa$$
$$= \frac{2}{1-e^{-1}}\left[1 - 2e^{-1} + 2 - 5e^{-1}\right]$$
$$= \frac{2(3-7e^{-1})}{1-e^{-1}}.$$

Therefore,

$$\left[\frac{\sqrt{e}}{\sqrt{2}}, \frac{\sqrt{e}}{\sqrt{2}}\right] \leq_p \left[\frac{8+2\pi e^{-2}}{2(16+\pi^2)(1-e^{-1})}, \frac{8+2\pi e^{-2}}{(16+\pi^2)(1-e^{-1})}\right] \leq_p \left[\frac{3-7e^{-1}}{1-e^{-1}}, \frac{2(3-7e^{-1})}{1-e^{-1}}\right]$$

and Theorem 3 is verified.

The fractional integrals with exponential kernels can be used to describe Hermite–Hadamard-type inclusions involving midpoint as follows:

**Theorem 4.** Let $\omega : [z, v] \subset \mathbb{R} \to X_C^+$ be an I-V·M on $[z, v]$ given by $\omega(\varkappa) = [\omega_*(\varkappa), \omega^*(\varkappa)]$ for all $\varkappa \in [z, v]$. If $\omega$ is a left and right exponential trigonometric convex I-V·M on $[z, v]$ and $\omega \in L([z, v], X_C^+)$, then

$$\sqrt{\frac{e}{2}}\omega\left(\frac{z+v}{2}\right) \leq_p \frac{1-\alpha}{2\left(1-e^{-\frac{\rho}{2}}\right)}\left[\mathcal{I}_{\left(\frac{z+v}{2}\right)^+}^\alpha \omega(v) + \mathcal{I}_{\left(\frac{z+v}{2}\right)^-}^\alpha \omega(z)\right] \leq_p \frac{\rho}{2\left(1-e^{-\frac{\rho}{2}}\right)}B(\rho)\frac{\omega(z)+\omega(v)}{2}. \quad (37)$$

If $\omega(\varkappa)$ is a left and right exponential trigonometric concave I-V·M, then

$$\sqrt{\frac{e}{2}}\omega\left(\frac{z+v}{2}\right) \geq_p \frac{1-\alpha}{2\left(1-e^{-\frac{\rho}{2}}\right)}\left[\mathcal{I}_{\left(\frac{z+v}{2}\right)^+}^\alpha \omega(v) + \mathcal{I}_{\left(\frac{z+v}{2}\right)^-}^\alpha \omega(z)\right] \geq_p \frac{\rho}{1-e^{-\frac{\rho}{2}}}B(\rho)\frac{\omega(z)+\omega(v)}{2}, \quad (38)$$

where
$$B(\rho) = \frac{\pi\left(4e^{-1} - 2^{\frac{3}{2}}e^{-\frac{\rho+1}{2}}\right) - 2^{\frac{5}{2}}\rho e^{-\frac{\rho+1}{2}} + 2^{\frac{5}{2}}e^{-\frac{\rho+1}{2}}}{4\rho^2 - 8\rho + \pi^2 + 4} + \frac{8\rho + 2^{\frac{3}{2}}\pi e^{-\frac{\rho+1}{2}} - 2^{\frac{5}{2}}(\rho+1)e^{-\frac{\rho+1}{2}} + 8}{4\rho^2 + 8\rho + \pi^2 + 4}, \rho = \frac{1-\alpha}{\alpha}(v-z),$$
and $1 > \alpha > 0$.

**Proof.** Let $\omega : [z, v] \to X_C^+$ be a left and right exponential trigonometric convex I-V·M. Then, by hypothesis, we have

$$\omega\left(\frac{z+v}{2}\right) \leq_p \frac{\sin\frac{\pi}{4}}{\sqrt{e}}\omega\left(\frac{v}{2}z + \frac{2-v}{2}v\right) + \frac{\cos\frac{\pi}{4}}{\sqrt{e}}\omega\left(\frac{2-v}{2}z + \frac{v}{2}v\right).$$

After simplification, we find that

$$2\omega\left(\frac{z+v}{2}\right) \leq_p \sqrt{\frac{2}{e}}\left[\omega\left(\frac{v}{2}z + \frac{2-v}{2}v\right) + \omega\left(\frac{2-v}{2}z + \frac{v}{2}v\right)\right].$$

Therefore, we have

$$2\omega_*\left(\frac{z+v}{2}\right) \leq \sqrt{\frac{2}{e}}\left[\omega_*\left(\frac{v}{2}z + \frac{2-v}{2}v\right) + \omega_*\left(\frac{2-v}{2}z + \frac{v}{2}v\right)\right],$$

$$2\omega^*\left(\frac{z+v}{2}\right) \leq \sqrt{\frac{2}{e}}\left[\omega^*\left(\frac{v}{2}z + \frac{2-v}{2}v\right) + \omega^*\left(\frac{2-v}{2}z + \frac{v}{2}v\right)\right].$$

Taking $\omega_*(.)$ and multiplying both sides by $e^{-\frac{\rho v}{2}}$ and integrating the obtained result with respect to $v$ from 0 to 1, we have

$$2\int_0^1 e^{-\frac{\rho v}{2}}\omega_*\left(\frac{z+v}{2}\right)dv \leq \sqrt{\frac{2}{e}}\left[\int_0^1 e^{-\frac{\rho v}{2}}\omega_*\left(\frac{v}{2}z + \frac{2-v}{2}v\right)dv + \int_0^1 e^{-\frac{\rho v}{2}}\omega_*\left(\frac{2-v}{2}z + \frac{v}{2}v\right)dv\right].$$

Let $u = \frac{v}{2}z + \frac{2-v}{2}v$ and $\varkappa = \frac{2-v}{2}z + \frac{v}{2}v$. Then, we have

$$2\int_0^1 e^{-\frac{\rho v}{2}}\omega_*\left(\frac{z+v}{2}\right)dv \leq \sqrt{\frac{2}{e}}\frac{1}{v-z}\int_{\frac{z+v}{2}}^v e^{\left(-\frac{1-\alpha}{\alpha}(v-u)\right)}\omega_*(u)du + \frac{1}{v-z}\int_{\frac{z+v}{2}}^v e^{\left(-\frac{1-\alpha}{\alpha}(\varkappa-z)\right)}\omega_*(\varkappa)d\varkappa$$
$$= \sqrt{\frac{2}{e}}\frac{\alpha}{v-z}\left[\mathcal{I}^\alpha_{\left(\frac{z+v}{2}\right)^+}\omega_*(v) + \mathcal{I}^\alpha_{\left(\frac{z+v}{2}\right)^-}\omega_*(z)\right]. \tag{39}$$

Now, taking the right side of Equation (39), we have

$$\int_0^1 e^{-\frac{\rho v}{2}}\omega_*\left(\frac{z+v}{2}\right)dv = \frac{2(1-e^{-\rho})}{\rho}\omega_*\left(\frac{z+v}{2}\right). \tag{40}$$

From (39) and (40), we have

$$4 \cdot \frac{1-e^{-\rho}}{\rho}\omega_*\left(\frac{z+v}{2}\right) \leq \sqrt{\frac{2}{e}} \cdot \frac{2(1-z)}{v-z}\left[\mathcal{I}^\alpha_{\left(\frac{z+v}{2}\right)^+}\omega_*(v) + \mathcal{I}^\alpha_{\left(\frac{z+v}{2}\right)^-}\omega_*(z)\right]. \tag{41}$$

Similarly, for $\omega^*(\varkappa)$, we have

$$4 \cdot \frac{1-e^{-\rho}}{\rho}\omega^*\left(\frac{z+v}{2}\right) \leq \sqrt{\frac{2}{e}} \cdot \frac{2(1-z)}{v-z}\left[\mathcal{I}^\alpha_{\left(\frac{z+v}{2}\right)^+}\omega^*(v) + \mathcal{I}^\alpha_{\left(\frac{z+v}{2}\right)^-}\omega^*(z)\right]. \tag{42}$$

From (41) and (42), we have

$$2 \cdot \frac{1-e^{-\rho}}{\rho}\left[\omega_*\left(\frac{z+v}{2}\right), \omega^*\left(\frac{z+v}{2}\right)\right]$$
$$\leq_p \sqrt{\frac{2}{e}} \cdot \frac{1-z}{v-z}\left[\left[\mathcal{I}^\alpha_{\left(\frac{z+v}{2}\right)^+}\omega_*(v) + \mathcal{I}^\alpha_{v^-}\omega_*(z)\right], \left[\mathcal{I}^\alpha_{\left(\frac{z+v}{2}\right)^+}\omega^*(v) + \mathcal{I}^\alpha_{v^-}\omega^*(z)\right]\right].$$

That is

$$2 \cdot \frac{1-e^{-\rho}}{\rho} \omega\left(\frac{z+v}{2}\right) \leq_p \sqrt{\frac{2}{e}} \cdot \frac{1-z}{v-z}\left[\mathcal{I}^\alpha_{\left(\frac{z+v}{2}\right)^+}\omega(v) + \mathcal{I}^\alpha_{\left(\frac{z+v}{2}\right)^-}\omega(z)\right]. \tag{43}$$

For the right side of Equation (37), since $\omega$ is a left and right exponential trigonometric convex $I$-$V\cdot M$, we can deduce that

$$\omega\left(\frac{v}{2}z + \frac{2-v}{2}v\right) \leq_p \frac{\sin\frac{\pi v}{4}}{e^{\frac{2-v}{2}}}\omega(z) + \frac{\cos\frac{\pi v}{4}}{e^{\frac{v}{2}}}\omega(v), \tag{44}$$

and

$$\omega\left(\frac{2-v}{2}z + \frac{v}{2}v\right) \leq_p \frac{\cos\frac{\pi v}{4}}{e^{\frac{v}{2}}}\omega(z) + \frac{\sin\frac{\pi v}{4}}{e^{\frac{2-v}{2}}}\omega(v). \tag{45}$$

Adding (44) and (45), we have

$$\omega\left(\frac{v}{2}z + \frac{2-v}{2}v\right) + \omega\left(\frac{2-v}{2}z + \frac{v}{2}v\right) \leq_p [\omega(z) + \omega(v)]\left[\frac{\sin\frac{\pi v}{4}}{e^{\frac{2-v}{2}}} + \frac{\cos\frac{\pi v}{4}}{e^{\frac{v}{2}}}\right]. \tag{46}$$

Since $\omega$ is $I$-$V\cdot M$, then we have

$$\begin{aligned}\omega_*\left(\tfrac{v}{2}z+\tfrac{2-v}{2}v\right)+\omega_*\left(\tfrac{2-v}{2}z+\tfrac{v}{2}v\right) &\leq [\omega_*(z)+\omega_*(v)]\left[\tfrac{\sin\frac{\pi V}{4}}{e^{\frac{2-v}{2}}}+\tfrac{\cos\frac{\pi V}{4}}{e^{\frac{V}{2}}}\right],\\ \omega^*\left(\tfrac{v}{2}z+\tfrac{2-v}{2}v\right)+\omega^*\left(\tfrac{2-v}{2}z+\tfrac{v}{2}v\right) &\leq [\omega^*(z)+\omega^*(v)]\left[\tfrac{\sin\frac{\pi V}{4}}{e^{\frac{2-V}{2}}}+\tfrac{\cos\frac{\pi V}{4}}{e^{\frac{V}{2}}}\right].\end{aligned} \tag{47}$$

Taking $\omega_*(.)$ from (47) and multiplying the inequality by $e^{e^{-\frac{\rho v}{2}}}$, and integrating the resultant with $v$ from 0 to 1, we have

$$\begin{aligned}&\int_0^1 e^{e^{-\frac{\rho v}{2}}}\omega_*\left(\tfrac{v}{2}z+\tfrac{2-v}{2}v\right)dv + \int_0^1 e^{e^{-\frac{\rho v}{2}}}\omega_*\left(\tfrac{2-v}{2}z+\tfrac{v}{2}v\right)dv\\ &\leq [\omega_*(z)+\omega_*(v)]\int_0^1 e^{e^{-\frac{\rho v}{2}}}\left[\tfrac{\sin\frac{\pi v}{4}}{e^{\frac{2-v}{2}}}+\tfrac{\cos\frac{\pi v}{4}}{e^{\frac{v}{2}}}\right]dv,\\ &= \left(\frac{\pi\left(4e^{-1}-2^{\frac{3}{2}}e^{-\frac{\rho+1}{2}}\right)-2^{\frac{5}{2}}\rho e^{-\frac{\rho+1}{2}}+2^{\frac{5}{2}}e^{-\frac{\rho+1}{2}}}{4\rho^2-8\rho+\pi^2+4} + \frac{8\rho + 2^{\frac{3}{2}}\pi e^{-\frac{\rho+1}{2}} - 2^{\frac{5}{2}}(\rho+1)e^{-\frac{\rho+1}{2}}+8}{4\rho^2+8\rho+\pi^2+4}\right)[\omega_*(z)+\omega_*(v)].\end{aligned} \tag{48}$$

In a similar way as above, for $\omega^*(.)$ we have

$$\begin{aligned}&\int_0^1 e^{e^{-\frac{\rho v}{2}}}\omega^*\left(\tfrac{v}{2}z+\tfrac{2-v}{2}v\right)dv + \int_0^1 e^{e^{-\frac{\rho v}{2}}}\omega^*\left(\tfrac{2-v}{2}z+\tfrac{v}{2}v\right)dv\\ &\leq [\omega^*(z)+\omega^*(v)]\int_0^1 e^{-\rho v}\left[\tfrac{\sin\frac{\pi v}{4}}{e^{\frac{2-v}{2}}}+\tfrac{\cos\frac{\pi v}{4}}{e^{\frac{v}{2}}}\right]dv\\ &= \left(\frac{\pi\left(4e^{-1}-2^{\frac{3}{2}}e^{-\frac{\rho+1}{2}}\right)-2^{\frac{5}{2}}\rho e^{-\frac{\rho+1}{2}}+2^{\frac{5}{2}}e^{-\frac{\rho+1}{2}}}{4\rho^2-8\rho+\pi^2+4} + \frac{8\rho + 2^{\frac{3}{2}}\pi e^{-\frac{\rho+1}{2}} - 2^{\frac{5}{2}}(\rho+1)e^{-\frac{\rho+1}{2}}+8}{4\rho^2+8\rho+\pi^2+4}\right)[\omega^*(z)+\omega^*(v)].\end{aligned} \tag{49}$$

From (48) and (49), we have

$$\begin{aligned}&\int_0^1 e^{-\rho v}\omega\left(\tfrac{v}{2}z+\tfrac{2-v}{2}v\right)dv + \int_0^1 e^{-\rho v}\omega\left(\tfrac{2-v}{2}z+\tfrac{v}{2}v\right)dv\\ &\leq_p \left(\frac{\pi\left(4e^{-1}-2^{\frac{3}{2}}e^{-\frac{\rho+1}{2}}\right)-2^{\frac{5}{2}}\rho e^{-\frac{\rho+1}{2}}+2^{\frac{5}{2}}e^{-\frac{\rho+1}{2}}}{4\rho^2-8\rho+\pi^2+4} + \frac{8\rho + 2^{\frac{3}{2}}\pi e^{-\frac{\rho+1}{2}} - 2^{\frac{5}{2}}(\rho+1)e^{-\frac{\rho+1}{2}}+8}{4\rho^2+8\rho+\pi^2+4}\right)[\omega(z)+\omega(v)].\end{aligned} \tag{50}$$

From (43) and (50), we have

$$\sqrt{\frac{e}{2}}\omega\left(\frac{z+v}{2}\right) \leq_p \frac{1-\alpha}{2\left(1-e^{-\frac{\rho}{2}}\right)}\left[\mathcal{I}^\alpha_{\left(\frac{z+v}{2}\right)^+}\omega(v) + \mathcal{I}^\alpha_{\left(\frac{z+v}{2}\right)^-}\omega(z)\right] \leq_p \frac{\rho}{2\left(1-e^{-\frac{\rho}{2}}\right)}B(\rho)\frac{\omega(z)+\omega(v)}{2}.$$

Hence, the required result. □

**Remark 4.** *From Theorem 4, we can clearly see the following.*

*If one lays* $\omega$ *which is an upper left and right exponential trigonometric concave I-V·M on* $[z, v]$*, then one acquires the following inequality* [98]:

$$\sqrt{\frac{e}{2}}\omega\left(\frac{z+v}{2}\right) \supseteq_p \frac{1-\alpha}{2\left(1-e^{-\frac{\rho}{2}}\right)}\left[\mathcal{I}^{\alpha}_{\left(\frac{z+v}{2}\right)^+}\omega(v) + \mathcal{I}^{\alpha}_{\left(\frac{z+v}{2}\right)^-}\omega(z)\right] \supseteq_p \frac{\rho}{2\left(1-e^{-\frac{\rho}{2}}\right)}B(\rho)\frac{\omega(z)+\omega(v)}{2}. \quad (51)$$

*If* $\alpha \to 1$*, that is*

$$\lim_{\alpha \to 1}\rho = \lim_{\alpha \to 1}\frac{1-\alpha}{\alpha}(v-z) = 0, \text{then}$$

$$\lim_{\alpha \to 1}\frac{\rho}{1-e^{-\frac{\rho}{2}}} = \left(\frac{\pi\left(4e^{-1} - 2^{\frac{3}{2}}e^{-\frac{\rho+1}{2}}\right) - 2^{\frac{5}{2}}\rho e^{-\frac{\rho+1}{2}} + 2^{\frac{5}{2}}e^{-\frac{\rho+1}{2}}}{4\rho^2 - 8\rho + \pi^2 + 4} + \frac{8\rho + 2^{\frac{3}{2}}\pi e^{-\frac{\rho+1}{2}} - 2^{\frac{5}{2}}(\rho+1)e^{-\frac{\rho+1}{2}} + 8}{4\rho^2 + 8\rho + \pi^2 + 4}\right) = \frac{4(2\pi+4e)}{e(\pi^2+4)}, \lim_{\alpha \to 1}\frac{1-\alpha}{2\left(1-e^{-\frac{\rho}{2}}\right)} = \frac{1}{v-z}$$

*Then, we acquire the following result, which is also a new one:*

$$\sqrt{\frac{e}{2}}\omega\left(\frac{z+v}{2}\right) \leq_p \frac{1}{v-z}\int_z^v \omega(\varkappa)d\varkappa \leq_p \frac{2\pi+4e}{e(\pi^2+4)}[\omega(z)+\omega(v)] \quad (52)$$

*If one lays* $\alpha \to 1$ *and* $\omega$ *which is an upper left and right exponential trigonometric concave I-V·M on* $[z, v]$*, then one acquires the following inequality* [98]:

$$\sqrt{\frac{e}{2}}\omega\left(\frac{z+v}{2}\right) \supseteq_p \frac{1}{v-z}\int_z^v \omega(\varkappa)d\varkappa \supseteq_p \frac{2\pi+4e}{e(\pi^2+4)}[\omega(z)+\omega(v)] \quad (53)$$

*Let* $\alpha \to 1$ *and* $\omega_*(\varkappa) \neq \omega^*(\varkappa)$*. Then, from Theorem 4, we achieve the Hermite–Hadamard inequality for interval-valued left and right exponential trigonometric convex mapping, which is also a new one:*

$$\sqrt{\frac{e}{2}}\omega\left(\frac{z+v}{2}\right) \leq_p \frac{1}{v-z}\int_z^v \omega(\varkappa)d\varkappa \leq_p \frac{2\pi+4e}{e(\pi^2+4)}[\omega(z)+\omega(v)] \quad (54)$$

*If* $\omega_*(\varkappa) = \omega^*(\varkappa)$*, then, from Theorem 4, we arrive at classical fractional Hermite–Hadamard inequality for exponential trigonometric convex mapping.*

$$\sqrt{\frac{e}{2}}\omega\left(\frac{z+v}{2}\right) \leq \frac{1-\alpha}{2\left(1-e^{-\frac{\rho}{2}}\right)}\left[\mathcal{I}^{\alpha}_{\left(\frac{z+v}{2}\right)^+}\omega(v) + \mathcal{I}^{\alpha}_{\left(\frac{z+v}{2}\right)^-}\omega(z)\right] \leq \frac{\rho}{2\left(1-e^{-\frac{\rho}{2}}\right)}B(\rho)\frac{\omega(z)+\omega(v)}{2} \quad (55)$$

*Let* $\alpha \to 1$ *and* $\omega_*(\varkappa) = \omega^*(\varkappa)$*. Then, from Theorem 4, we achieve the classical Hermite–Hadamard inequality for exponential trigonometric convex mapping, see* [78].

$$\sqrt{\frac{e}{2}}\omega\left(\frac{z+v}{2}\right) \leq \frac{1}{v-z}\int_z^v \omega(\varkappa)d\varkappa \leq \frac{2\pi+4e}{e(\pi^2+4)}[\omega(z)+\omega(v)]. \quad (56)$$

Finally, we present the Pachpatte-type fractional integral inclusions. Moreover, in Theorem 5 we will establish a fractional integral inclusion, and discuss the several inclusions via a left and right exponential trigonometric convex I-V·M.

**Theorem 5.** *Let* $\omega, T : [z, v] \to X_C^+$ *be two I-V·Ms on* $[z, v]$ *defined by* $\omega(\varkappa) = [\omega_*(\varkappa), \omega^*(\varkappa)]$ *and* $T(\varkappa) = [T_*(\varkappa), T^*(\varkappa)]$ *for all* $\varkappa \in [z, v]$*. If* $\omega$ *and* $T$ *are two left and right exponential trigonometric convex I-V·Ms on* $[z, v]$ *and* $\omega \times T \in L([z, v], X_C^+)$*, then*

$$\frac{\alpha}{v-z}\left[\mathcal{I}^{\alpha}_{z^+}\omega(v) \times T(v) + \mathcal{I}^{\alpha}_{v^-}\omega(z) \times T(z)\right] \leq_p D(\rho)\Delta(z, v) + \frac{\pi e^{-\rho-1}(e^\rho+1)}{\rho^2+\pi^2}\nabla(z, v). \quad (57)$$

*If* $\omega(\varkappa)$ *and* $T(\varkappa)$ *are left and right exponential trigonometric concave I-V·Ms, then*

$$\frac{\alpha}{v-z}\left[\mathcal{I}^\alpha_{z^+}\omega(v)\times T(v)+\mathcal{I}^\alpha_{v^-}\omega(z)\times T(z)\right]\geq_p D(\rho)\Delta(z,v)+\frac{\pi e^{-\rho-1}(e^\rho+1)}{\rho^2+\pi^2}\nabla(z,v), \quad (58)$$

*where* $D(\rho) = -\frac{e^{-\rho-2}(8e^2-8\rho e^2+\pi^2 e^2+2\rho^2 e^2-\pi^2 e^\rho)}{2(\rho-2)(\rho^2-4\rho+\pi^2+4)} + \frac{8\rho-\pi^2 e^{-\rho-2}+\pi^2+2\rho^2+8}{2(\rho+2)(\rho^2+4\rho+\pi^2+4)}$, $\rho = \frac{1-\alpha}{\alpha}(v-z)$, $1 > \alpha > 0$, $\Delta(z,v) = [\Delta_*(z,v), \Delta^*(z,v)]$ *and* $\nabla(z,v) = [\nabla_*(z,v), \nabla^*(z,v)]$.

**Proof.** Since $\omega, T$ are both left and right exponential trigonometric convex I-V·Ms, taking left end points mappings, we have

$$\omega_*(\mathfrak{v}z+(1-\mathfrak{v})v) \leq \frac{\sin\frac{\pi\mathfrak{v}}{2}}{e^{1-\mathfrak{v}}}\omega_*(z)+\frac{\cos\frac{\pi\mathfrak{v}}{2}}{e^\mathfrak{v}}\omega_*(v),$$

and

$$T_*(\mathfrak{v}z+(1-\mathfrak{v})v) \leq \mathfrak{v}\frac{\sin\frac{\pi\mathfrak{v}}{2}}{e^{1-\mathfrak{v}}}T_*(z)+\frac{\cos\frac{\pi\mathfrak{v}}{2}}{e^\mathfrak{v}}T_*(v).$$

From the definition of left and right exponential trigonometric convex I-V·Ms, it follows that $0 \leq_p \omega(\varkappa)$ and $0 \leq_I T(\varkappa)$, so

$$\begin{aligned}&\omega_*(\mathfrak{v}z+(1-\mathfrak{v})v)\times T_*(\mathfrak{v}z+(1-\mathfrak{v})v)\\ &\leq \left(\frac{\sin\frac{\pi\mathfrak{v}}{2}}{e^{1-\mathfrak{v}}}\omega_*(z)+\frac{\cos\frac{\pi\mathfrak{v}}{2}}{e^\mathfrak{v}}\omega_*(v)\right)\left(\frac{\sin\frac{\pi\mathfrak{v}}{2}}{e^{1-\mathfrak{v}}}T_*(z)+\frac{\cos\frac{\pi\mathfrak{v}}{2}}{e^\mathfrak{v}}T_*(v)\right)\\ &= \left(\frac{\sin\frac{\pi\mathfrak{v}}{2}}{e^{1-\mathfrak{v}}}\right)^2\omega_*(z)\times T_*(z)+\left(\frac{\cos\frac{\pi\mathfrak{v}}{2}}{e^\mathfrak{v}}\right)^2\omega_*(v)\times T_*(v)\\ &+\left(\frac{\cos\frac{\pi\mathfrak{v}}{2}\sin\frac{\pi\mathfrak{v}}{2}}{e}\right)\omega_*(z)\times T_*(v)+\left(\frac{\cos\frac{\pi\mathfrak{v}}{2}\sin\frac{\pi\mathfrak{v}}{2}}{e}\right)\omega_*(v)\times T_*(z)\end{aligned} \quad (59)$$

Analogously, we have

$$\begin{aligned}&\omega_*((1-\mathfrak{v})z+\mathfrak{v}v)\times T_*((1-\mathfrak{v})z+\mathfrak{v}v)\\ &\leq \left(\frac{\cos\frac{\pi\mathfrak{v}}{2}}{e^\mathfrak{v}}\right)^2\omega_*(z)\times T_*(z)+\left(\frac{\sin\frac{\pi\mathfrak{v}}{2}}{e^{1-\mathfrak{v}}}\right)^2\omega_*(v)\times T_*(v)\\ &+\left(\frac{\cos\frac{\pi\mathfrak{v}}{2}\sin\frac{\pi\mathfrak{v}}{2}}{e}\right)\omega_*(z)\times T_*(v)+\left(\frac{\cos\frac{\pi\mathfrak{v}}{2}\sin\frac{\pi\mathfrak{v}}{2}}{e}\right)\omega_*(v)\times T_*(z)\end{aligned} \quad (60)$$

Adding (59) and (60), we have

$$\begin{aligned}&\omega_*(\mathfrak{v}z+(1-\mathfrak{v})v)\times T_*(\mathfrak{v}z+(1-\mathfrak{v})v)\\ &+\omega_*((1-\mathfrak{v})z+\mathfrak{v}v)\times T_*((1-\mathfrak{v})z+\mathfrak{v}v)\\ &\leq \left[\left(\frac{\sin\frac{\pi\mathfrak{v}}{2}}{e^{1-\mathfrak{v}}}\right)^2+\left(\frac{\sin\frac{\pi\mathfrak{v}}{2}}{e^{1-\mathfrak{v}}}\right)^2\right][\omega_*(z)\times T_*(z)+\omega_*(v)\times T_*(v)]\\ &+\frac{2\cos\frac{\pi\mathfrak{v}}{2}\sin\frac{\pi\mathfrak{v}}{2}}{e}[\omega_*(v)\times T_*(z)+\omega_*(z)\times T_*(v)]\end{aligned} \quad (61)$$

Multiplying (61) by $e^{-\rho\mathfrak{v}}$ and integrating the obtained result with respect to $\mathfrak{v}$ over $(0,1)$, we have

$$\begin{aligned}&\int_0^1 e^{-\rho\mathfrak{v}}\omega_*(\mathfrak{v}z+(1-\mathfrak{v})v)\times T_*(\mathfrak{v}z+(1-\mathfrak{v})v)\\ &+e^{-\rho\mathfrak{v}}\omega_*((1-\mathfrak{v})z+\mathfrak{v}v)\times T_*((1-\mathfrak{v})z+\mathfrak{v}v)d\mathfrak{v}\\ &\leq \Delta_*((z,v))\int_0^1 e^{-\rho\mathfrak{v}}\left[\left(\frac{\sin\frac{\pi\mathfrak{v}}{2}}{e^{1-\mathfrak{v}}}\right)^2+\left(\frac{\sin\frac{\pi\mathfrak{v}}{2}}{e^{1-\mathfrak{v}}}\right)^2\right]d\mathfrak{v}+2\nabla_*((z,v))\int_0^1 e^{-\rho\mathfrak{v}}\frac{\cos\frac{\pi\mathfrak{v}}{2}\sin\frac{\pi\mathfrak{v}}{2}}{e}d\mathfrak{v}\end{aligned}$$

It follows that

$$\begin{aligned}&\frac{\alpha}{v-z}\left[\mathcal{I}^\alpha_{z^+}\omega_*(v)\times T_*(v)+\mathcal{I}^\alpha_{v^-}\omega_*(z)\times T_*(z)\right]\\ &\leq D(\rho)\Delta_*((z,v))+\frac{\pi e^{-\rho-1}(e^\rho+1)}{\rho^2+\pi^2}\nabla_*((z,v))\end{aligned} \quad (62)$$

Similarly, for $\omega^*(\varkappa)$, we have

$$\frac{\alpha}{v-z}\left[\mathcal{I}_{z^+}^\alpha\,\omega^*(v)\times T^*(v)+\mathcal{I}_{v^-}^\alpha\,\omega^*(z)\times T^*(z)\right]$$
$$\leq D(\rho)\Delta^*((z,v))+\frac{\pi e^{-\rho-1}(e^\rho+1)}{\rho^2+\pi^2}\nabla^*((z,v)) \tag{63}$$

where

$$D(\rho) = \int_0^1 e^{-\rho v}\left[\left(\frac{\sin\frac{\pi v}{2}}{e^{1-v}}\right)^2+\left(\frac{\sin\frac{\pi v}{2}}{e^{1-v}}\right)^2\right]dv$$
$$= -\frac{e^{-\rho-2}(8e^2-8\rho e^2+\pi^2 e^2+2\rho^2 e^2-\pi^2 e^\rho)}{2(\rho-2)(\rho^2-4\rho+\pi^2+4)}+\frac{8\rho-\pi^2 e^{-\rho-2}+\pi^2+2\rho^2+8}{2(\rho+2)(\rho^2+4\rho+\pi^2+4)}$$

and

$$\int_0^1 e^{-\rho v}\frac{\cos\frac{\pi v}{2}\sin\frac{\pi v}{2}}{e}dv = \frac{\pi e^{-\rho-1}(e^\rho+1)}{\rho^2+\pi^2}$$

From (62) and (63), we have

$$\frac{\alpha}{v-z}\left[\mathcal{I}_{z^+}^\alpha\,\omega_*(v)\times T_*(v)\quad+\mathcal{I}_{v^-}^\alpha\,\omega_*(z)\times T_*(z),\ \mathcal{I}_{z^+}^\alpha\,\omega^*(v)\times T^*(v)+\mathcal{I}_{v^-}^\alpha\,\omega^*(z)\times T^*(z)\right]$$
$$\leq_p D(\rho)[\Delta_*((z,v)),\,\Delta^*((z,v))]+\frac{\pi e^{-\rho-1}(e^\rho+1)}{\rho^2+\pi^2}[\nabla_*((z,v)),\,\nabla^*((z,v))].$$

That is

$$\frac{\alpha}{v-z}\left[\mathcal{I}_{z^+}^\alpha\omega(v)\times T(v)+\mathcal{I}_{v^-}^\alpha\omega(z)\times T(z)\right]\leq_p D(\rho)\Delta(z,v)+\frac{\pi e^{-\rho-1}(e^\rho+1)}{\rho^2+\pi^2}\nabla(z,v).$$

and the theorem has been established. □

**Remark 5.** *From Theorem 5 we can clearly see the following.*

*If one lays $\omega$ which is an upper left and right exponential trigonometric concave I-V·M on $[z,v]$, then one acquires the following inequality* [98]:

$$\frac{\alpha}{v-z}\left[\mathcal{I}_{z^+}^\alpha\omega(v)\times T(v)+\mathcal{I}_{v^-}^\alpha\omega(z)\times T(z)\right]\supseteq_p D(\rho)\Delta(z,v)+\frac{\pi e^{-\rho-1}(e^\rho+1)}{\rho^2+\pi^2}\nabla(z,v). \tag{64}$$

*If $\alpha\to 1$, that is*

$$\lim_{\alpha\to 1}\rho = \lim_{\alpha\to 1}\frac{1-\alpha}{\alpha}(v-z) = 0,\text{ then}$$
$$\lim_{\alpha\to 1}\left(-\frac{e^{-\rho-2}(8e^2-8\rho e^2+\pi^2 e^2+2\rho^2 e^2-\pi^2 e^\rho)}{2(\rho-2)(\rho^2-4\rho+\pi^2+4)}+\frac{8\rho-\pi^2 e^{-\rho-2}+\pi^2+2\rho^2+8}{2(\rho+2)(\pi^2+4)}\right) = \frac{\pi^2-\pi^2 e^2+8}{2(\pi^2+4)},$$
$$\lim_{\alpha\to 1}\frac{\pi e^{-\rho-1}(e^\rho+1)}{\rho^2+\pi^2} = \frac{2}{\pi e}$$

*Then, we acquire the following result, which is also a new one:*

$$\frac{1}{v-z}\int_z^v \omega(\varkappa)\times T(\varkappa)d\varkappa\leq_p \frac{\pi^2-\pi^2 e^2+8}{4(\pi^2+4)}\Delta(z,v)+\frac{2}{\pi e}\nabla(z,v) \tag{65}$$

*If one lays $\alpha\to 1$ and $\omega$ which is an upper left and right exponential trigonometric concave I-V·M on $[z,v]$, then one acquires the following inequality* [98]:

$$\frac{1}{v-z}\int_z^v \omega(\varkappa)\times T(\varkappa)d\varkappa\supseteq_p \frac{\pi^2-\pi^2 e^2+8}{4(\pi^2+4)}\Delta(z,v)+\frac{2}{\pi e}\nabla(z,v) \tag{66}$$

Let $\alpha \to 1$ and $\omega_*(\varkappa) \neq \omega^*(\varkappa)$. Then, from Theorem 5, we achieve the Hermite–Hadamard inequality for interval-valued left and right exponential trigonometric convex mapping, which is also a new one:

$$\frac{1}{v-z}\int_z^v \omega(\varkappa) \times T(\varkappa)d\varkappa \leq_p \frac{\pi^2-\pi^2 e^2+8}{4(\pi^2+4)}\Delta(z,v) + \frac{2}{\pi e}\nabla(z,v). \qquad (67)$$

If $\omega_*(\varkappa) = \omega^*(\varkappa)$, then, from Theorem 5, we arrive at the classical fractional Hermite–Hadamard inequality for exponential trigonometric convex mapping:

$$\frac{\alpha}{v-z}\left[\mathcal{I}^\alpha_{z^+} \omega(v) \times T(v) + \mathcal{I}^\alpha_{v^-} \omega(z) \times T(z)\right] \leq D(\rho)\Delta(z,v) + \frac{\pi e^{-\rho-1}(e^\rho+1)}{\rho^2+\pi^2}\nabla(z,v). \qquad (68)$$

Let $\alpha \to 1$ and $\omega_*(\varkappa) = \omega^*(\varkappa)$. Then, from Theorem 5, we achieve the classical Hermite–Hadamard inequality for exponential trigonometric convex mapping, see [78].

$$\frac{1}{v-z}\int_z^v \omega(\varkappa) \times T(\varkappa)d\varkappa \leq \frac{\pi^2-\pi^2 e^2+8}{4(\pi^2+4)}\Delta(z,v) + \frac{2}{\pi e}\nabla(z,v). \qquad (69)$$

**Example 2.** Let $[z,v] = [0,1]$, $\alpha = \frac{1}{4}$, $\omega(\varkappa) = [\varkappa^2, 2\varkappa^2]$ and $T(\varkappa) = [2\varkappa^3, 4\varkappa^3]$. Since left and right end point mappings $\omega_*(\varkappa) = \varkappa^2$, $\omega^*(\varkappa) = 2\varkappa^2$, $T_*(\varkappa) = 2\varkappa^3$ and $T^*(\varkappa) = 4\varkappa^3$ are exponential trigonometric convex mappings, then $\omega(\varkappa)$ and $T(\varkappa)$ are both exponential trigonometric convex I-V·Ms. We can clearly see that $\omega(\varkappa) \times T(\varkappa) \in L([z,v], X_C^+)$ and

$$\frac{\alpha}{v-z}\left[\mathcal{I}^\alpha_{z^+} \omega_*(v) \times T_*(v) + \mathcal{I}^\alpha_{v^-} \omega_*(z) \times T_*(z)\right]$$
$$= \int_0^1 e^{-3(1-\varkappa)}(2\varkappa^5)d\varkappa + \int_0^1 e^{-3\varkappa}(2\varkappa^5)d\varkappa$$
$$= \left(\frac{80e^{-3}}{243} + \frac{52}{243}\right) + \left(\frac{80}{243} - \frac{1472e^{-3}}{243}\right)$$
$$= \left(\frac{44}{81} - \frac{464e^{-3}}{81}\right)$$

$$\frac{\alpha}{v-z}\left[\mathcal{I}^\alpha_{z^+} \omega^*(v) \times T^*(v) + \mathcal{I}^\alpha_{v^-} \omega^*(z) \times T^*(z)\right]$$
$$= \int_0^1 e^{-3(1-\varkappa)}(8\varkappa^5)d\varkappa + \int_0^1 e^{-3\varkappa}(8\varkappa^5)d\varkappa$$
$$= 4\left[\frac{44}{81} - \frac{464e^{-3}}{81}\right].$$

Note that

$$D(\rho)\Delta_*((z,v)) = \left(-\frac{e^{-5}(2e^2+\pi^2 e^2-\pi^2 e^3)}{2(1+\pi^2)} + \frac{50-\pi^2 e^{-5}+\pi^2}{10(25+\pi^2)}\right)[\omega_*(0) \times T_*(1) + \omega_*(1) \times T_*(1)]$$
$$= 2\left(\frac{50-\pi^2 e^{-5}+\pi^2}{10(25+\pi^2)} - \frac{e^{-5}(2e^2+\pi^2 e^2-\pi^2 e^3)}{2(1+\pi^2)}\right)$$

$$D(\rho)\Delta^*((z,v)) = \left(-\frac{e^{-5}(2e^2+\pi^2 e^2-\pi^2 e^3)}{2(1+\pi^2)} + \frac{50-\pi^2 e^{-5}+\pi^2}{10(25+\pi^2)}\right)[\omega^*(z) \times T^*(z) + \omega^*(v) \times T^*(v)]$$
$$= 8\left(\frac{50-\pi^2 e^{-5}+\pi^2}{10(25+\pi^2)} - \frac{e^{-5}(2e^2+\pi^2 e^2-\pi^2 e^3)}{2(1+\pi^2)}\right),$$

$$\frac{\pi e^{-\rho-1}(e^\rho+1)}{\rho^2+\pi^2}\nabla_*((z,v)) = \frac{\pi e^{-\rho-1}(e^\rho+1)}{\rho^2+\pi^2}[\omega_*(0) \times T_*(1) + \mho_*(1) \times T_*(0)] = 0,$$

$$\frac{\pi e^{-\rho-1}(e^\rho+1)}{\rho^2+\pi^2}\nabla_*((z,v)) = \frac{\pi e^{-\rho-1}(e^\rho+1)}{\rho^2+\pi^2}[\mho^*(1) \times T^*(1) + \mho^*(1) \times T^*(0)] = 0.$$

*Therefore, we have*

$$D(\rho)\Delta(z,v) + \frac{\pi e^{-\rho-1}(e^\rho+1)}{\rho^2+\pi^2}\nabla(z,v)$$
$$= \left(\frac{50-\pi^2 e^{-5}+\pi^2}{10(25+\pi^2)} - \frac{e^{-5}(2e^2+\pi^2 e^2-\pi^2 e^3)}{2(1+\pi^2)}\right)[2,8] + \frac{\pi e^{-\rho-1}(e^\rho+1)}{\rho^2+\pi^2}[0,0]$$
$$= \left(\frac{50-\pi^2 e^{-5}+\pi^2}{10(25+\pi^2)} - \frac{e^{-5}(2e^2+\pi^2 e^2-\pi^2 e^3)}{2(1+\pi^2)}\right)[2,8]$$

*It follows that*

$$\left(\frac{44}{81} - \frac{464e^{-3}}{81}\right)[2,4] \leq_p \left(\frac{50-\pi^2 e^{-5}+\pi^2}{10(25+\pi^2)} - \frac{e^{-5}(2e^2+\pi^2 e^2-\pi^2 e^3)}{2(1+\pi^2)}\right)[2,8].$$

*and Theorem 5 has been demonstrated.*

**Theorem 6.** *Let $\omega, T : [z,v] \to X_C^+$ be two I-V·Ms on $[z,v]$ defined by $\omega(\varkappa) = [\omega_*(\varkappa), \omega^*(\varkappa)]$ and $T(\varkappa) = [T_*(\varkappa), T^*(\varkappa)]$ for all $\varkappa \in [z,v]$. If $\omega$ and $T$ are two left and right exponential trigonometric convex I-V·Ms on $[z,v]$ and $\omega \times T \in L([z,v], X_C^+)$, then*

$$2\omega\left(\frac{z+v}{2}\right) \times T\left(\frac{z+v}{2}\right) \leq_p \frac{1-\alpha}{e(1-e^{-\rho})}\left[\mathcal{I}_{z^+}^\alpha \omega(v) \times T(v) + \mathcal{I}_{v^-}^\alpha \omega(z) \times T(z)\right] \tag{70}$$
$$+ \frac{\rho\pi e^{-\rho-1}(e^\rho+1)}{e(1-e^{-\rho})(\rho^2+\pi^2)}\nabla(z,v) + \frac{\rho}{e(1-e^{-\rho})}D(\rho)\Delta(z,v).$$

*If $\omega(\varkappa)$ and $T(\varkappa)$ are left and right exponential trigonometric concave I-V·Ms, then*

$$2\omega\left(\frac{z+v}{2}\right) \times T\left(\frac{z+v}{2}\right) \geq_p \frac{1-\alpha}{e(1-e^{-\rho})}\left[\mathcal{I}_{z^+}^\alpha \omega(v) \times T(v) + \mathcal{I}_{v^-}^\alpha \omega(z) \times T(z)\right] \tag{71}$$
$$+ \frac{\rho\pi e^{-\rho-1}(e^\rho+1)}{e(1-e^{-\rho})(\rho^2+\pi^2)}\nabla(z,v) + \frac{\rho}{e(1-e^{-\rho})}D(\rho)\Delta(z,v).$$

*where* $D(\rho) = -\frac{e^{-\rho-2}(8e^2-8\rho e^2+\pi^2 e^2+2\rho^2 e^2-\pi^2 e^\rho)}{2(\rho-2)(\rho^2-4\rho+\pi^2+4)} + \frac{8\rho-\pi^2 e^{-\rho-2}+\pi^2+2\rho^2+8}{2(\rho+2)(\rho^2+4\rho+\pi^2+4)}$, $\rho = \frac{1-\alpha}{\alpha}(v-z)$, $1 > \alpha > 0$, $\Delta(z,v) = [\Delta_*(z,v), \Delta^*(z,v)]$ *and* $\nabla(z,v) = [\nabla_*(z,v), \nabla^*(z,v)]$.

**Proof.** Consider $\omega, T : [z,v] \to X_C^+$ are left and right exponential trigonometric convex I-V·Ms. Then, by hypothesis, we have

$$\omega_*\left(\frac{z+v}{2}\right) \times T_*\left(\frac{z+v}{2}\right)$$
$$\leq \frac{1}{2e}\left[\begin{array}{l}\omega_*(vz+(1-v)v) \times T_*(vz+(1-v)v) \\ +\omega_*((1-v)z+(1-v)v) \times T_*((1-v)z+vv)\end{array}\right]$$
$$+ \frac{1}{2e}\left[\begin{array}{l}\omega_*((1-v)z+vv) \times T_*(vz+(1-v)v) \\ +\omega_*(vz+(1-v)v) \times T_*((1-v)z+vv)\end{array}\right]$$
$$\leq \frac{1}{2e}\left[\begin{array}{l}\omega_*(vz+(1-v)v) \times T_*(vz+(1-v)v) \\ +\omega_*((1-v)z+vv) \times T_*((1-v)z+vv)\end{array}\right]$$
$$+ \frac{1}{2e}\begin{array}{l}\left(\frac{\cos\frac{\pi v}{2}}{e^v}\omega_*(z) + \frac{\sin\frac{\pi v}{2}}{e^{1-v}}\omega_*(v)\right) \\ \times\left(\frac{\sin\frac{\pi v}{2}}{e^{1-v}}T_*(z) + \frac{\cos\frac{\pi v}{2}}{e^v}T_*(v)\right) \\ +\left(\frac{\sin\frac{\pi v}{2}}{e^{1-v}}\omega_*(z) + \frac{\cos\frac{\pi v}{2}}{e^v}\omega_*(v)\right) \\ \times\left(\frac{\cos\frac{\pi v}{2}}{e^v}T_*(z) + \frac{\sin\frac{\pi v}{2}}{e^{1-v}}T_*(v)\right)\end{array} \tag{72}$$
$$\leq \frac{1}{2e}\left[\begin{array}{l}\omega_*(vz+(1-v)v) \times T_*(vz+(1-v)v) \\ +\omega_*((1-v)z+vv) \times T_*((1-v)z+vv)\end{array}\right]$$
$$+ \frac{1}{2e}\left[\begin{array}{l}\frac{2\cos\frac{\pi v}{2}\sin\frac{\pi v}{2}}{e}\nabla_*((z,v)) \\ +\left[\left(\frac{\sin\frac{\pi v}{2}}{e^{1-v}}\right)^2+\left(\frac{\sin\frac{\pi v}{2}}{e^{1-v}}\right)^2\right]\Delta_*((z,v))\end{array}\right]$$

Multiplying (72) by $e^{-\rho v}$ and integrating over $(0,1)$, we find

72

$$\int_0^1 e^{-\rho v}\, \omega_*\left(\tfrac{z+v}{2}\right) \times T_*\left(\tfrac{z+v}{2}\right) dv$$
$$\leq \tfrac{1}{2e}\left[\int_z^v e^{-\rho v}\omega_*(\varkappa)\times T_*(\varkappa)dv + \int_z^v e^{-\rho v}\omega_*(s)\times T_*(s)\,dv\right]$$
$$+\tfrac{\nabla^*((z,v))}{2e}\int_0^1 e^{-\rho v}\tfrac{2\cos\tfrac{\pi v}{2}\sin\tfrac{\pi v}{2}}{e}dv + \tfrac{\Delta_*((z,v))}{2e}\int_0^1 e^{-\rho v}\left[\left(\tfrac{\sin\tfrac{\pi v}{2}}{e^{1-v}}\right)^2 + \left(\tfrac{\sin\tfrac{\pi v}{2}}{e^{1-v}}\right)^2\right]dv$$

$$\tfrac{1-e^{-\rho}}{\rho}\int_0^1 e^{-\rho v}\,\omega_*\left(\tfrac{z+v}{2}\right)\times T_*\left(\tfrac{z+v}{2}\right)$$
$$\leq \tfrac{\alpha}{2e(v-z)}\left[\mathcal{I}^\alpha_{z^+}\omega_*(v)\times T_*(v) + \mathcal{I}^\alpha_{v^-}\omega_*(z)\times T_*(z)\right] \qquad (73)$$
$$+\tfrac{\pi e^{-\rho-1}(e^\rho+1)}{2e(\rho^2+\pi^2)}\tfrac{\nabla_*((z,v))}{2e} + \tfrac{1}{2e}D(\rho)\tfrac{\Delta_*((z,v))}{2e}.$$

Similarly, for $\omega^*(\varkappa)$, we have

$$\tfrac{1-e^{-\rho}}{\rho}\omega^*\left(\tfrac{z+v}{2}\right)\times T^*\left(\tfrac{z+v}{2}\right)$$
$$\leq \tfrac{\alpha}{2e(v-z)}\left[\mathcal{I}^\alpha_{z^+}\omega^*(v)\times T^*(v) + \mathcal{I}^\alpha_{v^-}\omega^*(z)\times T^*(z)\right] \qquad (74)$$
$$+\tfrac{\pi e^{-\rho-1}(e^\rho+1)}{2e(\rho^2+\pi^2)}\tfrac{\nabla^*((z,v))}{2e} + \tfrac{1}{2e}D(\rho)\tfrac{\Delta^*((z,v))}{2e}.$$

From (73) and (74), we have

$$2\left[\omega_*\left(\tfrac{z+v}{2}\right)\times T_*\left(\tfrac{z+v}{2}\right), \omega^*\left(\tfrac{z+v}{2}\right)\times T^*\left(\tfrac{z+v}{2}\right)\right]$$
$$\leq_p \tfrac{1-\alpha}{e(v-z)}\left[\mathcal{I}^\alpha_{z^+}\omega_*(v)\times T_*(v) + \mathcal{I}^\alpha_{v^-}\omega_*(z)\times T_*(z), \mathcal{I}^\alpha_{z^+}\omega^*(v)\times T^*(v) + \mathcal{I}^\alpha_{v^-}\omega^*(z)\times T^*(z)\right]$$
$$+\tfrac{\rho\pi e^{-\rho-1}(e^\rho+1)}{e(1-e^{-\rho})(\rho^2+\pi^2)}[\nabla_*((z,v)), \nabla^*((z,v))] + \tfrac{\rho}{e(1-e^{-\rho})}D(\rho)[\nabla_*((z,v)), \nabla^*((z,v))],$$

where

$$D(\rho) = -\frac{e^{-\rho-2}(8e^2 - 8\rho e^2 + \pi^2 e^2 + 2\rho^2 e^2 - \pi^2 e^\rho)}{2(\rho-2)(\rho^2 - 4\rho + \pi^2 + 4)} + \frac{8\rho - \pi^2 e^{-\rho-2} + \pi^2 + 2\rho^2 + 8}{2(\rho+2)(\rho^2 + 4\rho + \pi^2 + 4)}.$$

Hence, the required result. □

**Remark 6.** *From Theorem 6 we can clearly see the following.*
*If one lays $\omega$ and $T$ which are upper left and right exponential trigonometric concave I-V·Ms on $[z,v]$, then one acquires the following inequality* [98]:

$$2\omega\left(\tfrac{z+v}{2}\right)\times T\left(\tfrac{z+v}{2}\right) \supseteq_p \tfrac{\alpha}{e(v-z)}\left[\mathcal{I}^\alpha_{z^+}\omega(v)\times T(v) + \mathcal{I}^\alpha_{v^-}\omega(z)\times T(z)\right]$$
$$+\tfrac{\rho\pi e^{-\rho-1}(e^\rho+1)}{e(1-e^{-\rho})(\rho^2+\pi^2)}\nabla(z,v) + \tfrac{\rho}{e(1-e^{-\rho})}D(\rho)\Delta(z,v). \qquad (75)$$

*If $\alpha \to 1$, that is*

$$\lim_{\alpha\to 1}\rho = \lim_{\alpha\to 1}\tfrac{1-\alpha}{\alpha}(v-z) = 0, \text{ then } \lim_{\alpha\to 1}\tfrac{1-\alpha}{e(1-e^{-\rho})} = \tfrac{1}{e(v-z)},$$

$$\lim_{\alpha\to 1}\tfrac{\rho}{e(1-e^{-\rho})}\left(-\tfrac{e^{-\rho-2}(8e^2 - 8\rho e^2 + \pi^2 e^2 + 2\rho^2 e^2 - \pi^2 e^\rho)}{2(\rho-2)(\rho^2 - 4\rho + \pi^2 + 4)} + \tfrac{8\rho - \pi^2 e^{-\rho-2} + \pi^2 + 2\rho^2 + 8}{2(\rho+2)(\pi^2+4)}\right) = \tfrac{\pi^2 - \pi^2 e^{-2} + 8}{2e(\pi^2+4)},$$

$$\lim_{\alpha\to 1}\tfrac{\rho\pi e^{-\rho-1}(e^\rho+1)}{e(1-e^{-\rho})(\rho^2+\pi^2)} = \tfrac{2}{\pi e^2}.$$

*Then, we acquire the following result, which is also a new one:*

$$2\omega\left(\tfrac{z+v}{2}\right)\times T\left(\tfrac{z+v}{2}\right) \leq_p \tfrac{2}{e(v-z)}\int_z^v \omega(\varkappa)\times T(\varkappa)d\varkappa + \tfrac{2}{\pi e^2}\Delta(z,v) + \tfrac{\pi^2 - \pi^2 e^2 + 8}{2e(\pi^2+4)}\nabla(z,v). \qquad (76)$$

*If one lays $\alpha \to 1$ and $\omega$ and $T$ which are upper left and right exponential trigonometric concave I-V·Ms on $[z,v]$, then one acquires the following inequality* [98]:

$$2\omega\left(\frac{z+v}{2}\right) \times T\left(\frac{z+v}{2}\right) \geq_p \frac{2}{e(v-z)} \int_z^v \omega(\varkappa) \times T(\varkappa)d\varkappa + \frac{2}{\pi e^2}\Delta(z,v) + \frac{\pi^2 - \pi^2 e^2 + 8}{2e(\pi^2+4)}\nabla(z,v). \tag{77}$$

Let $\alpha \to 1$, $\omega_*(\varkappa) \neq \omega^*(\varkappa)$ and $T_*(\varkappa) \neq T^*(\varkappa)$. Then, from Theorem 6 we achieve the Hermite–Hadamard inequality for interval-valued left and right exponential trigonometric convex mapping, which is also a new one:

$$2\omega\left(\frac{z+v}{2}\right) \times T\left(\frac{z+v}{2}\right) \leq_p \frac{2}{e(v-z)} \int_z^v \omega(\varkappa) \times T(\varkappa)d\varkappa + \frac{2}{\pi e^2}\Delta(z,v) + \frac{\pi^2 - \pi^2 e^2 + 8}{2e(\pi^2+4)}\nabla(z,v). \tag{78}$$

If $\omega_*(\varkappa) = \omega^*(\varkappa)$ and $T_*(\varkappa) \neq T^*(\varkappa)$, then, from Theorem 6, we achieve the classical fractional Hermite–Hadamard inequality for exponential trigonometric convex mapping

$$2\omega\left(\tfrac{z+v}{2}\right) \times T\left(\tfrac{z+v}{2}\right) \leq \frac{\alpha}{e(v-z)}\left[\mathcal{I}^\alpha_{z^+}\omega(v) \times T(v) + \mathcal{I}^\alpha_{v^-}\omega(z) \times T(z)\right] + \frac{\rho \pi e^{-\rho-1}(e^\rho+1)}{e(1-e^{-\rho})(\rho^2+\pi^2)}\nabla(z,v) + \frac{\rho}{e(1-e^{-\rho})}D(\rho)\Delta(z,v). \tag{79}$$

Let $\alpha \to 1$, $\omega_*(\varkappa) = \omega^*(\varkappa)$ and $T_*(\varkappa) \neq T^*(\varkappa)$. Then, from Theorem 6, we achieve the classical Hermite–Hadamard inequality for exponential trigonometric convex mapping, see [78]

$$2\omega\left(\frac{z+v}{2}\right) \times T\left(\frac{z+v}{2}\right) \leq \frac{2}{e(v-z)} \int_z^v \omega(\varkappa) \times T(\varkappa)d\varkappa + \frac{2}{\pi e^2}\Delta(z,v) + \frac{\pi^2 - \pi^2 e^2 + 8}{2e(\pi^2+4)}\nabla(z,v). \tag{80}$$

**Theorem 7.** *Let $\omega : [z,v] \subset \mathbb{R} \to X_C^+$ be an I-V·M on $[z,v]$ given by $\omega(\varkappa) = [\omega_*(\varkappa), \omega^*(\varkappa)]$ for all $\varkappa \in [z,v]$. If $\omega$ is a left and right exponential trigonometric convex I-V·M on $[z,v]$ and $\omega \in L([z,v], X_C^+)$, then*

$$\begin{aligned}
e\omega\left(\tfrac{z+v}{2}\right) &\leq_p \sqrt{\tfrac{e}{2}}\left[\omega\left(\tfrac{3z+v}{4}\right) + \omega\left(\tfrac{z+3v}{4}\right)\right] \\
&\leq_p \frac{1-\alpha}{2\left(1-e^{-\frac{\rho}{2}}\right)}\left[\mathcal{I}^\alpha_{z^+}\omega\left(\tfrac{z+v}{2}\right) + \mathcal{I}^\alpha_{\left(\frac{z+v}{2}\right)^+}\omega(v) + \mathcal{I}^\alpha_{\left(\frac{z+v}{2}\right)^-}\omega(z) + \mathcal{I}^\alpha_{v^-}\omega\left(\tfrac{z+v}{2}\right)\right] \\
&\leq_p \frac{\rho}{2\left(1-e^{-\frac{\rho}{2}}\right)}K(\rho)\left(\tfrac{\omega(z)+\omega(v)}{2} + \omega\left(\tfrac{z+v}{2}\right)\right) \\
&\leq_p \frac{\rho}{2\left(1-e^{-\frac{\rho}{2}}\right)}\left(1+\sqrt{\tfrac{e}{2}}\right)K(\rho)\tfrac{\omega(z)+\omega(v)}{2}.
\end{aligned} \tag{81}$$

*If $\omega(\varkappa)$ is a left and right exponential trigonometric concave I-V·M, then*

$$\begin{aligned}
e\omega\left(\tfrac{z+v}{2}\right) &\geq_p \sqrt{\tfrac{e}{2}}\left[\omega\left(\tfrac{3z+v}{4}\right) + \omega\left(\tfrac{z+3v}{4}\right)\right] \\
&\geq_p \frac{1-\alpha}{2\left(1-e^{-\frac{\rho}{2}}\right)}\left[\mathcal{I}^\alpha_{z^+}\omega\left(\tfrac{z+v}{2}\right) + \mathcal{I}^\alpha_{\left(\frac{z+v}{2}\right)^+}\omega(v) + \mathcal{I}^\alpha_{\left(\frac{z+v}{2}\right)^-}\omega(z) + \mathcal{I}^\alpha_{v^-}\omega\left(\tfrac{z+v}{2}\right)\right] \\
&\geq_p \frac{\rho}{2\left(1-e^{-\frac{\rho}{2}}\right)}K(\rho)\left(\tfrac{\omega(z)+\omega(v)}{2} + \omega\left(\tfrac{z+v}{2}\right)\right) \\
&\geq_p \frac{\rho}{2\left(1-e^{-\frac{\rho}{2}}\right)}\left(1+\sqrt{\tfrac{e}{2}}\right)K(\rho)\tfrac{\omega(z)+\omega(v)}{2},
\end{aligned} \tag{82}$$

*where*

$$K(\rho) = \frac{2\rho + 2\pi e^{-\frac{\rho+2}{2}} + 4}{\rho^2 + 4\rho + \pi^2 + 4} + \frac{2\pi e^{-1} + 2e^{-\frac{\rho}{2}}(2+\rho)}{\rho^2 - 4\rho + \pi^2 + 4}, \rho = \frac{1-\alpha}{\alpha}(v-z), \text{ and } 1 > \alpha > 0.$$

**Proof.** Taking $\left[z, \frac{z+v}{2}\right]$, we deduce that

$$\omega\left(\frac{3z+v}{4}\right) \leq_p \frac{\sin\frac{\pi}{4}}{\sqrt{e}}\omega\left(vz + (1-v)\frac{z+v}{2}\right) + \frac{\cos\frac{\pi}{4}}{\sqrt{e}}\omega\left((1-v)z + v\frac{z+v}{2}\right).$$

After simplification, we find that

$$2\omega\left(\frac{3z+v}{4}\right) \leq_p \sqrt{\frac{2}{e}}\left[\omega\left(vz + (1-v)\frac{z+v}{2}\right) + \omega\left((1-v)z + v\frac{z+v}{2}\right)\right].$$

Therefore, we have

$$2\omega_*\left(\frac{3z+v}{4}\right) \leq \sqrt{\frac{2}{e}}\left[\omega_*\left(vz + (1-v)\frac{z+v}{2}\right) + \omega_*\left((1-v)z + v\frac{z+v}{2}\right)\right],$$

$$2\omega^*\left(\frac{3z+v}{4}\right) \leq \sqrt{\frac{2}{e}}\left[\omega^*\left(vz + (1-v)\frac{z+v}{2}\right) + \omega^*\left((1-v)z + v\frac{z+v}{2}\right)\right].$$

Taking $\omega_*(.)$ and multiplying both sides by $e^{-\frac{\rho v}{2}}$ and integrating the obtained result with respect to $v$ from 0 to 1, we have

$$\int_0^1 e^{-\frac{\rho v}{2}}\omega_*\left(\frac{3z+v}{4}\right)dv \leq \sqrt{\frac{2}{e}}\left[\int_0^1 e^{-\rho v}\omega_*\left(vz + (1-v)\frac{z+v}{2}\right)dv + \int_0^1 e^{-\rho v}\omega_*\left((1-v)z + v\frac{z+v}{2}\right)dv\right].$$

Let $u = vz + (1-v)\frac{z+v}{2}$ and $\varkappa = (1-v)z + v\frac{z+v}{2}$. Then, we have

$$\int_0^1 e^{-\frac{\rho v}{2}}\omega_*\left(\frac{3z+v}{4}\right)dv \leq \sqrt{\frac{2}{e}}\frac{1}{v-z}\int_{\frac{z+v}{2}}^{v} e^{(-\frac{1-\alpha}{\alpha}(\frac{z+v}{2}-u))}\omega_*(u)du + \frac{1}{v-z}\int_{\frac{z+v}{2}}^{v} e^{(-\frac{1-\alpha}{\alpha}(\varkappa-z))}\omega_*(\varkappa)d\varkappa$$
$$= \sqrt{\frac{2}{e}}\frac{\alpha}{v-z}\left[\mathcal{I}^\alpha_{z^+}\omega_*\left(\frac{z+v}{2}\right) + \mathcal{I}^\alpha_{\left(\frac{z+v}{2}\right)^-}\omega_*(z)\right]. \tag{83}$$

Now, taking the right side of Equation (83), we have

$$\int_0^1 e^{-\frac{\rho v}{2}}\omega_*\left(\frac{3z+v}{2}\right)dv = \frac{2(1-e^{-\rho})}{\rho}\omega_*\left(\frac{3z+v}{4}\right). \tag{84}$$

From (83) and (84), we deduce that

$$\frac{2(1-e^{-\rho})}{\rho}\omega_*\left(\frac{3z+v}{4}\right) \leq \sqrt{\frac{2}{e}}\frac{1-\alpha}{v-z}\left[\mathcal{I}^\alpha_{z^+}\omega_*\left(\frac{z+v}{2}\right) + \mathcal{I}^\alpha_{\left(\frac{z+v}{2}\right)^-}\omega_*(z)\right]. \tag{85}$$

Similarly, for $\omega^*(.)$, from (85), we have

$$\frac{2(1-e^{-\rho})}{\rho}\omega^*\left(\frac{3z+v}{4}\right) \leq \sqrt{\frac{2}{e}}\frac{1-\alpha}{v-z}\left[\mathcal{I}^\alpha_{z^+}\omega^*\left(\frac{z+v}{2}\right) + \mathcal{I}^\alpha_{\left(\frac{z+v}{2}\right)^-}\omega^*(z)\right]. \tag{86}$$

From (85) and (86), we deduce that

$$\frac{2(1-e^{-\rho})}{\rho}\omega\left(\frac{3z+v}{4}\right) \leq_p \sqrt{\frac{2}{e}}\frac{1-\alpha}{v-z}\left[\mathcal{I}^\alpha_{z^+}\omega\left(\frac{z+v}{2}\right) + \mathcal{I}^\alpha_{\left(\frac{z+v}{2}\right)^-}\omega(z)\right]. \tag{87}$$

For the right side of Equation (81), since $\omega$ is a left and right exponential trigonometric convex $I$-$V$·$M$, then we can deduce that

$$\omega\left(vz + (1-v)\frac{z+v}{2}\right) \leq_p \frac{\sin\frac{\pi v}{4}}{e^{1-v}}\omega(z) + \frac{\cos\frac{\pi v}{4}}{e^v}\omega\left(\frac{z+v}{2}\right), \tag{88}$$

and

$$\omega\left((1-v)z + v\frac{z+v}{2}\right) \leq_p \frac{\cos\frac{\pi v}{4}}{e^v}\omega(z) + \frac{\sin\frac{\pi v}{4}}{e^{1-v}}\omega\left(\frac{z+v}{2}\right) \tag{89}$$

Adding (88) and (89), we have

$$\omega\left(\upsilon z + (1-\upsilon)\frac{z+v}{2}\right) + \omega\left((1-\upsilon)z + \upsilon\frac{z+v}{2}\right) \leq_p \left[\omega(z) + \omega\left(\frac{z+v}{2}\right)\right]\left[\frac{\sin\frac{\pi\upsilon}{4}}{e^{1-\upsilon}} + \frac{\cos\frac{\pi\upsilon}{4}}{e^\upsilon}\right]. \quad (90)$$

Since $\omega$ is I-V-M, then we have

$$\begin{aligned}\omega_*\left(\upsilon z + (1-\upsilon)\frac{z+v}{2}\right) + \omega_*\left((1-\upsilon)z + \upsilon\frac{z+v}{2}\right) &\leq \left[\omega_*(z) + \omega_*\left(\frac{z+v}{2}\right)\right]\left[\frac{\sin\frac{\pi\upsilon}{4}}{e^{1-\upsilon}} + \frac{\cos\frac{\pi\upsilon}{4}}{e^\upsilon}\right],\\ \omega^*\left(\upsilon z + (1-\upsilon)\frac{z+v}{2}\right) + \omega^*\left((1-\upsilon)z + \upsilon\frac{z+v}{2}\right) &\leq \left[\omega^*(z) + \omega^*\left(\frac{z+v}{2}\right)\right]\left[\frac{\sin\frac{\pi\upsilon}{4}}{e^{1-\upsilon}} + \frac{\cos\frac{\pi\upsilon}{4}}{e^\upsilon}\right].\end{aligned} \quad (91)$$

Taking $\omega_*(.)$ from (91) and multiplying the inequality by $e^{-\frac{\rho\upsilon}{2}}$, and integrating the resultant with $\upsilon$ from 0 to 1, we have

$$\begin{aligned}\int_0^1 e e^{-\frac{\rho\upsilon}{2}}\omega_*(\upsilon z &+ (1-\upsilon)\tfrac{z+v}{2})d\upsilon + \int_0^1 e e^{-\frac{\rho\upsilon}{2}}\omega_*((1-\upsilon)z + \upsilon\tfrac{z+v}{2})d\upsilon\\ &\leq [\omega_*(z) + \omega_*(\tfrac{z+v}{2})]\int_0^1 e e^{-\frac{\rho\upsilon}{2}}\left[\frac{\sin\frac{\pi\upsilon}{4}}{e^{1-\upsilon}} + \frac{\cos\frac{\pi\upsilon}{4}}{e^\upsilon}\right]d\upsilon,\\ &= \left(\frac{2\rho + 2\pi e^{-\frac{\rho+2}{2}} + 4}{\rho^2 + 4\rho + \pi^2 + 4} + \frac{2\pi e^{-1} + 2e^{-\frac{\rho}{2}}(2+\rho)}{\rho^2 - 4\rho + \pi^2 + 4}\right)[\omega_*(z) + \omega_*(\tfrac{z+v}{2})].\end{aligned} \quad (92)$$

In a similar way to the above, for $\omega_*(.)$ we have

$$\begin{aligned}\int_0^1 e e^{-\frac{\rho\upsilon}{2}}\omega^*(\upsilon z &+ (1-\upsilon)\tfrac{z+v}{2})d\upsilon + \int_0^1 e e^{-\frac{\rho\upsilon}{2}}\omega^*((1-\upsilon)z + \upsilon\tfrac{z+v}{2})d\upsilon\\ &\leq [\omega^*(z) + \omega^*(v)]\int_0^1 e^{-\rho\upsilon}\left[\frac{\sin\frac{\pi\upsilon}{4}}{e^{\frac{2-\upsilon}{2}}} + \frac{\cos\frac{\pi\upsilon}{4}}{e^{\frac{\rho}{2}}}\right]d\upsilon,\\ &= \left(\frac{2\rho + 2\pi e^{-\frac{\rho+2}{2}} + 4}{\rho^2 + 4\rho + \pi^2 + 4} + \frac{2\pi e^{-1} + 2e^{-\frac{\rho}{2}}(2+\rho)}{\rho^2 - 4\rho + \pi^2 + 4}\right)[\omega^*(z) + \omega^*(\tfrac{z+v}{2})].\end{aligned} \quad (93)$$

From (92) and (93), we have

$$\begin{aligned}\int_0^1 e^{-\rho\upsilon}\omega(\upsilon z &+ (1-\upsilon)\tfrac{z+v}{2})d\upsilon + \int_0^1 e^{-\rho\upsilon}\omega((1-\upsilon)z + \upsilon\tfrac{z+v}{2})d\upsilon\\ &\leq_p \left(\frac{2\rho + 2\pi e^{-\frac{\rho+2}{2}} + 4}{\rho^2 + 4\rho + \pi^2 + 4} + \frac{2\pi e^{-1} + 2e^{-\frac{\rho}{2}}(2+\rho)}{\rho^2 - 4\rho + \pi^2 + 4}\right)[\omega(z) + \omega(\tfrac{z+v}{2})].\end{aligned} \quad (94)$$

Combining (87) and (94), we have

$$\begin{aligned}\sqrt{\tfrac{\rho}{2}}\omega\left(\tfrac{3z+v}{2}\right) &\leq_p \frac{1-\alpha}{2\left(1-e^{-\frac{\rho}{2}}\right)}\left[\mathcal{I}_{z^+}^\alpha\omega\left(\tfrac{z+v}{2}\right) + \mathcal{I}_{\left(\frac{z+v}{2}\right)^-}^\alpha\omega(z)\right]\\ &\leq_p \frac{\rho}{2\left(1-e^{-\frac{\rho}{2}}\right)}K(\rho)\left(\frac{\omega(z)+\omega\left(\frac{z+v}{2}\right)}{2}\right),\end{aligned} \quad (95)$$

where

$$K(\rho) = \frac{2\rho + 2\pi e^{-\frac{\rho+2}{2}} + 4}{\rho^2 + 4\rho + \pi^2 + 4} + \frac{2\pi e^{-1} + 2e^{-\frac{\rho}{2}}(2+\rho)}{\rho^2 - 4\rho + \pi^2 + 4}.$$

Similarly, if we take the interval $\left[\frac{z+v}{2}, v\right]$, then, from (38), we find that

$$\begin{aligned}\sqrt{\tfrac{\rho}{2}}\left[\omega\left(\tfrac{z+3v}{2}\right)\right] &\leq_p \frac{1-\alpha}{2\left(1-e^{-\frac{\rho}{2}}\right)}\left[\mathcal{I}_{\left(\frac{z+v}{2}\right)^+}^\alpha\omega(v) + \mathcal{I}_{v^-}^\alpha\omega\left(\tfrac{z+v}{2}\right)\right]\\ &\leq_p \frac{\rho}{2\left(1-e^{-\frac{\rho}{2}}\right)}K(\rho)\left(\frac{\omega\left(\frac{z+v}{2}\right)+\omega(v)}{2}\right).\end{aligned} \quad (96)$$

Adding (95) and (96), we have

$$\sqrt{\tfrac{e}{2}}\left[\omega\left(\tfrac{3z+v}{2}\right)+\omega\left(\tfrac{z+3v}{2}\right)\right]$$
$$\leq_p \frac{1-\alpha}{2\left(1-e^{-\tfrac{\rho}{2}}\right)}\left[\mathcal{I}^\alpha_{z^+}\omega\left(\tfrac{z+v}{2}\right)+\mathcal{I}^\alpha_{\left(\tfrac{z+v}{2}\right)^+}\omega(v)+\mathcal{I}^\alpha_{\left(\tfrac{z+v}{2}\right)^-}\omega(z)+\mathcal{I}^\alpha_{v^-}\omega\left(\tfrac{z+v}{2}\right)\right] \quad (97)$$
$$\leq_p \frac{\rho}{2\left(1-e^{-\tfrac{\rho}{2}}\right)}K(\rho)\left(\tfrac{\omega(z)+\omega(v)}{2}+\omega\left(\tfrac{z+v}{2}\right)\right).$$

To achieve the first and fourth order relations in (81), again by taking

$$\begin{aligned}\omega\left(\tfrac{z+v}{2}\right) &= \omega\left(\tfrac{\tfrac{3z+v}{4}+\tfrac{z+3v}{4}}{2}\right)\\ &\leq_p \tfrac{\sin\tfrac{\pi}{4}}{\sqrt{e}}\omega(z)+\tfrac{\cos\tfrac{\pi}{4}}{\sqrt{e}}\omega(v)\\ &= \tfrac{1}{2}\sqrt{\tfrac{2}{e}}\omega(z)+\tfrac{1}{2}\sqrt{\tfrac{2}{e}}\omega(v)\end{aligned} \quad (98)$$

and

$$\begin{aligned}\omega\left(\tfrac{z+v}{2}\right) &= \omega\left(\tfrac{\tfrac{3z+v}{4}+\tfrac{z+3v}{4}}{2}\right)\\ &\leq_p \tfrac{\sin\tfrac{\pi}{4}}{\sqrt{e}}\omega\left(\tfrac{3z+v}{4}\right)+\tfrac{\cos\tfrac{\pi}{4}}{\sqrt{e}}\omega\left(\tfrac{z+3v}{4}\right)\\ &= \tfrac{1}{2}\sqrt{\tfrac{2}{e}}\omega\left(\tfrac{3z+v}{4}\right)+\tfrac{1}{2}\sqrt{\tfrac{2}{e}}\omega\left(\tfrac{z+3v}{4}\right).\end{aligned} \quad (99)$$

By using the inclusion relation (98) and (99), we obtain the first and fourth inclusions of (81). By combining the resultant inclusion and (97), we obtain the following relation:

$$\begin{aligned}e\omega\left(\tfrac{z+v}{2}\right) &\leq_p \sqrt{\tfrac{e}{2}}\left[\omega\left(\tfrac{3z+v}{2}\right)+\omega\left(\tfrac{z+3v}{2}\right)\right]\\ &\leq_p \tfrac{1-\alpha}{2\left(1-e^{-\tfrac{\rho}{2}}\right)}\left[\mathcal{I}^\alpha_{z^+}\omega\left(\tfrac{z+v}{2}\right)+\mathcal{I}^\alpha_{\left(\tfrac{z+v}{2}\right)^+}\omega(v)+\mathcal{I}^\alpha_{\left(\tfrac{z+v}{2}\right)^-}\omega(z)+\mathcal{I}^\alpha_{v^-}\omega\left(\tfrac{z+v}{2}\right)\right]\\ &\leq_p \tfrac{\rho}{2\left(1-e^{-\tfrac{\rho}{2}}\right)}K(\rho)\left(\tfrac{\omega(z)+\omega(v)}{2}+\omega\left(\tfrac{z+v}{2}\right)\right)\\ &\leq_p \tfrac{\rho}{2\left(1-e^{-\tfrac{\rho}{2}}\right)}\left(1+\sqrt{\tfrac{e}{2}}\right)K(\rho)\tfrac{\omega(z)+\omega(v)}{2}.\end{aligned}$$

Hence, the required result. □

**Remark 7.** *From Theorem 7 we can clearly see the following.*

*If one lays $\omega$ which is an upper left and right exponential trigonometric concave I-V·M on $[z,v]$, then one acquires the following inequality [98]:*

$$\begin{aligned}e\omega\left(\tfrac{z+v}{2}\right) &\supseteq_p \sqrt{\tfrac{e}{2}}\left[\omega\left(\tfrac{3z+v}{2}\right)\omega\left(\tfrac{z+3v}{2}\right)\right]\\ &\supseteq_p \tfrac{1-\alpha}{2\left(1-e^{-\tfrac{\rho}{2}}\right)}\left[\mathcal{I}^\alpha_{z^+}\omega\left(\tfrac{z+v}{2}\right)+\mathcal{I}^\alpha_{\left(\tfrac{z+v}{2}\right)^+}\omega(v)+\mathcal{I}^\alpha_{\left(\tfrac{z+v}{2}\right)^-}\omega(z)+\mathcal{I}^\alpha_{v^-}\omega\left(\tfrac{z+v}{2}\right)\right]\\ &\supseteq_p \tfrac{\rho}{2\left(1-e^{-\tfrac{\rho}{2}}\right)}K(\rho)\left(\tfrac{\omega(z)+\omega(v)}{2}+\omega\left(\tfrac{z+v}{2}\right)\right)\\ &\supseteq_p \tfrac{\rho}{2\left(1-e^{-\tfrac{\rho}{2}}\right)}\left(1+\sqrt{\tfrac{e}{2}}\right)K(\rho)\tfrac{\omega(z)+\omega(v)}{2}.\end{aligned} \quad (100)$$

*If $\alpha \to 1$, that is*

$$\lim_{\alpha\to 1}\rho = \lim_{\alpha\to 1}\tfrac{1-\alpha}{\alpha}(v-z) = 0, \text{ then}$$

$$\lim_{\alpha \to 1} \frac{\rho}{1-e^{-\frac{\rho}{2}}} \left( \frac{2\rho + 2\pi e^{-\frac{\rho+2}{2}} + 4}{\rho^2 + 4\rho + \pi^2 + 4} + \frac{2\pi e^{-1} + 2e^{-\frac{\rho}{2}}(2+\rho)}{\rho^2 - 4\rho + \pi^2 + 4} \right) = \frac{4(2\pi e^{-1} + 4)}{\pi^2 + 4}, \lim_{\alpha \to 1} \frac{1-\alpha}{2\left(1-e^{e^{-\frac{\rho}{2}}}\right)} = \frac{1}{v-z}$$

Then, we acquire the following result, which is also a new one:

$$\begin{aligned}
\frac{e}{2}\omega\left(\frac{z+v}{2}\right) &\leq_p \frac{1}{2}\sqrt{\frac{e}{2}}\left[\omega\left(\frac{3z+v}{2}\right) + \omega\left(\frac{z+3v}{2}\right)\right] \\
&\leq_p \frac{1}{v-z}\int_z^v \omega(\varkappa)d\varkappa \\
&\leq_p \frac{2\pi e^{-1}+4}{\pi^2+4}\left(\frac{\omega(z)+\omega(v)}{2} + \omega\left(\frac{z+v}{2}\right)\right) \\
&\leq_p \frac{2\pi e^{-1}+4}{\pi^2+4}\left(1+\sqrt{\frac{e}{2}}\right)\frac{\omega(z)+\omega(v)}{2}.
\end{aligned} \quad (101)$$

If one lays $\alpha \to 1$ and $\omega$ which is an upper left and right exponential trigonometric concave I-V·M on $[z, v]$, then one acquires the following inequality [98]:

$$\begin{aligned}
\frac{e}{2}\omega\left(\frac{z+v}{2}\right) &\geq_p \frac{1}{2}\sqrt{\frac{e}{2}}\left[\omega\left(\frac{3z+v}{2}\right) + \omega\left(\frac{z+3v}{2}\right)\right] \\
&\geq_p \frac{1}{v-z}\int_z^v \omega(\varkappa)d\varkappa \\
&\geq_p \frac{2\pi e^{-1}+4}{\pi^2+4}\left(\frac{\omega(z)+\omega(v)}{2} + \omega\left(\frac{z+v}{2}\right)\right) \\
&\geq_p \frac{2\pi e^{-1}+4}{\pi^2+4}\left(1+\sqrt{\frac{e}{2}}\right)\frac{\omega(z)+\omega(v)}{2}.
\end{aligned} \quad (102)$$

Let $\alpha \to 1$ and $\omega_*(\varkappa) \neq \omega^*(\varkappa)$. Then, from Theorem 7, we achieve the Hermite–Hadamard inequality for interval-valued left and right exponential trigonometric convex mapping, which is also a new one:

$$\begin{aligned}
\frac{e}{2}\omega\left(\frac{z+v}{2}\right) &\leq_p \frac{1}{2}\sqrt{\frac{e}{2}}\left[\omega\left(\frac{3z+v}{2}\right) + \omega\left(\frac{z+3v}{2}\right)\right] \\
&\leq_p \frac{1}{v-z}\int_z^v \omega(\varkappa)d\varkappa \\
&\leq_p \frac{2\pi e^{-1}+4}{\pi^2+4}\left(\frac{\omega(z)+\omega(v)}{2} + \omega\left(\frac{z+v}{2}\right)\right) \\
&\leq_p \frac{2\pi e^{-1}+4}{\pi^2+4}\left(1+\sqrt{\frac{e}{2}}\right)\frac{\omega(z)+\omega(v)}{2}.
\end{aligned} \quad (103)$$

If $\omega_*(\varkappa) = \omega^*(\varkappa)$, then, from Theorem 7, we arrive at the classical fractional Hermite–Hadamard inequality for exponential trigonometric convex mapping:

$$\begin{aligned}
e\omega\left(\frac{z+v}{2}\right) &\leq \sqrt{\frac{e}{2}}\left[\omega\left(\frac{3z+v}{2}\right) + \omega\left(\frac{z+3v}{2}\right)\right] \\
&\leq \frac{1-\alpha}{2\left(1-e^{-\frac{\rho}{2}}\right)}\left[\mathcal{I}^\alpha_{z^+}\omega\left(\frac{z+v}{2}\right) + \mathcal{I}^\alpha_{\left(\frac{z+v}{2}\right)^+}\omega(v) + \mathcal{I}^\alpha_{\left(\frac{z+v}{2}\right)^-}\omega(z) + \mathcal{I}^\alpha_{v^-}\omega\left(\frac{z+v}{2}\right)\right] \\
&\leq \frac{\rho}{2\left(1-e^{-\frac{\rho}{2}}\right)}K(\rho)\left(\frac{\omega(z)+\omega(v)}{2} + \omega\left(\frac{z+v}{2}\right)\right) \\
&\leq \frac{\rho}{2\left(1-e^{-\frac{\rho}{2}}\right)}\left(1+\sqrt{\frac{e}{2}}\right)K(\rho)\frac{\omega(z)+\omega(v)}{2}.
\end{aligned} \quad (104)$$

Let $\alpha \to 1$ and $\omega_*(\varkappa) = \omega^*(\varkappa)$. Then, from Theorem 7, we arrive at the classical Hermite–Hadamard inequality for exponential trigonometric convex mapping, see [78].

$$\begin{aligned}
\frac{e}{2}\omega\left(\frac{z+v}{2}\right) &\leq \frac{1}{2}\sqrt{\frac{e}{2}}\left[\omega\left(\frac{3z+v}{2}\right) + \omega\left(\frac{z+3v}{2}\right)\right] \\
&\leq \frac{1}{v-z}\int_z^v \omega(\varkappa)d\varkappa \\
&\leq \frac{2\pi e^{-1}+4}{\pi^2+4}\left(\frac{\omega(z)+\omega(v)}{2} + \omega\left(\frac{z+v}{2}\right)\right) \\
&\leq \frac{2\pi e^{-1}+4}{\pi^2+4}\left(1+\sqrt{\frac{e}{2}}\right)\frac{\omega(z)+\omega(v)}{2}.
\end{aligned} \quad (105)$$

To validate Theorem 7, we provide the following nontrivial example:

**Example 3.** Let $\alpha = \frac{1}{3}$, $\varkappa \in [0,1]$, and the I-V·M $\omega$ : $[z, v] = [0, 1] \to X_C^+$, defined by

$$\omega(\varkappa) = \left[2\varkappa^4, 4\varkappa^4\right].$$

Since left and right end point mappings $\omega_*(\varkappa) = 2\varkappa^4$, $\omega^*(\varkappa) = 4\varkappa^4$, are exponential trigonometric convex mappings then $\omega(\varkappa)$ is an exponential trigonometric convex I-V·M. We can clearly see that $\omega \in L([z, v], X_C^+)$ and

$$e\omega_*\left(\frac{z+v}{2}\right) = \frac{e}{8}$$

$$e\omega^*\left(\frac{z+v}{2}\right) = \frac{e}{4}$$

$$\sqrt{\frac{e}{2}}\left[\omega_*\left(\frac{3z+v}{2}\right) + \omega_*\left(\frac{z+3v}{2}\right)\right] = \sqrt{\frac{e}{2}}\frac{41}{64}$$

$$\sqrt{\frac{e}{2}}\left[\omega^*\left(\frac{3z+v}{2}\right) + \omega^*\left(\frac{z+3v}{2}\right)\right] = \sqrt{\frac{e}{2}}\frac{41}{32}$$

$$\frac{1-\alpha}{2\left(1-e^{-\frac{\rho}{2}}\right)}\left[\mathcal{I}_{z^+}^{\alpha}\omega_*\left(\frac{z+v}{2}\right) \quad +\mathcal{I}_{\left(\frac{z+v}{2}\right)^+}^{\alpha}\omega_*(v) + \mathcal{I}_{\left(\frac{z+v}{2}\right)^-}^{\alpha}\omega_*(z) + \mathcal{I}_{v^-}^{\alpha}\omega_*\left(\frac{z+v}{2}\right)\right]$$

$$= \frac{1}{1-e^{-1}}\left\{\int_0^{\frac{1}{2}} e^{-2\left(\frac{1}{2}-\varkappa\right)}\left(2\varkappa^4\right)d\varkappa + \int_0^{\frac{1}{2}} e^{-2\varkappa}(2\varkappa^4)d\varkappa\right\}$$

$$+ \frac{1}{1-e^{-1}}\left\{\int_{\frac{1}{2}}^{1} e^{-2(1-\varkappa)}\left(2\varkappa^4\right)d\varkappa + \int_{\frac{1}{2}}^{1} e^{-2\left(\varkappa-\frac{1}{2}\right)}(2\varkappa^4)d\varkappa\right\}$$

$$= \frac{1}{1-e^{-1}}\left\{\frac{3e}{2} - \frac{121e^{-1}}{8} + 2\right\}$$

$$\frac{1-\alpha}{2\left(1-e^{-\frac{\rho}{2}}\right)}\left[\mathcal{I}_{z^+}^{\alpha}\omega^*\left(\frac{z+v}{2}\right) \quad +\mathcal{I}_{\left(\frac{z+v}{2}\right)^+}^{\alpha}\omega^*(v) + \mathcal{I}_{\left(\frac{z+v}{2}\right)^-}^{\alpha}\omega^*(z) + \mathcal{I}_{v^-}^{\alpha}\omega^*\left(\frac{z+v}{2}\right)\right]$$

$$= \frac{1}{1-e^{-1}}\left\{\int_0^{\frac{1}{2}} e^{-2\left(\frac{1}{2}-\varkappa\right)}\left(4\varkappa^4\right)d\varkappa + \int_0^{\frac{1}{2}} e^{-2\varkappa}(4\varkappa^4)d\varkappa\right\}$$

$$+ \frac{1}{1-e^{-1}}\left\{\int_{\frac{1}{2}}^{1} e^{-2(1-\varkappa)}\left(4\varkappa^4\right)d\varkappa + \int_{\frac{1}{2}}^{1} e^{-2\left(\varkappa-\frac{1}{2}\right)}(4\varkappa^4)d\varkappa\right\}$$

$$= \frac{2}{1-e^{-1}}\left\{\frac{3e}{2} - \frac{121e^{-1}}{8} + 2\right\}.$$

$$\frac{\rho}{2\left(1-e^{-\frac{\rho}{2}}\right)}K(\rho)\left(\frac{\omega_*(z) + \omega_*(v)}{2} + \omega_*\left(\frac{z+v}{2}\right)\right) = \frac{9}{8(1-e^{-1})}\left(\frac{6+2\pi e^{-2}}{16+\pi^2} + \frac{2e^{-1}}{\pi}\right)$$

$$\frac{\rho}{2\left(1-e^{-\frac{\rho}{2}}\right)}K(\rho)\left(\frac{\omega^*(z) + \omega^*(v)}{2} + \omega^*\left(\frac{z+v}{2}\right)\right) = \frac{9}{4(1-e^{-1})}\left(\frac{6+2\pi e^{-2}}{16+\pi^2} + \frac{2e^{-1}}{\pi}\right)$$

$$\frac{\rho}{2\left(1-e^{-\frac{\rho}{2}}\right)}\left(1+\sqrt{\frac{e}{2}}\right)K(\rho)\frac{\omega_*(z) + \omega_*(v)}{2} = \frac{1}{1-e^{-1}}\left(1+\sqrt{\frac{e}{2}}\right)\left(\frac{6+2\pi e^{-2}}{16+\pi^2} + \frac{2e^{-1}}{\pi}\right)$$

$$\frac{\rho}{2\left(1-e^{-\frac{\rho}{2}}\right)}\left(1+\sqrt{\frac{e}{2}}\right)K(\rho)\frac{\omega^*(z) + \omega^*(v)}{2} = \frac{2}{1-e^{-1}}\left(1+\sqrt{\frac{e}{2}}\right)\left(\frac{6+2\pi e^{-2}}{16+\pi^2} + \frac{2e^{-1}}{\pi}\right).$$

That is

$$\left[\frac{e}{8}, \frac{e}{4}\right] \leq_p \left[\sqrt{\frac{e}{2}}\frac{41}{64}, \sqrt{\frac{e}{2}}\frac{41}{32}\right]$$
$$\leq_p \left[\frac{1}{1-e^{-1}}\left\{\frac{3e}{2} - \frac{121e^{-1}}{8} + 2\right\}, \frac{2}{1-e^{-1}}\left\{\frac{3e}{2} - \frac{121e^{-1}}{8} + 2\right\}\right]$$
$$\leq_p \left[\frac{9}{8(1-e^{-1})}\left(\frac{6+2\pi e^{-2}}{16+\pi^2} + \frac{2e^{-1}}{\pi}\right), \frac{9}{4(1-e^{-1})}\left(\frac{6+2\pi e^{-2}}{16+\pi^2} + \frac{2e^{-1}}{\pi}\right)\right]$$
$$\leq_p \left[\frac{1}{1-e^{-1}}\left(1+\sqrt{\frac{e}{2}}\right)\left(\frac{6+2\pi e^{-2}}{16+\pi^2} + \frac{2e^{-1}}{\pi}\right), \frac{2}{1-e^{-1}}\left(1+\sqrt{\frac{e}{2}}\right)\left(\frac{6+2\pi e^{-2}}{16+\pi^2} + \frac{2e^{-1}}{\pi}\right)\right].$$

Hence, Theorem 7 is verified.

## 6. Conclusions

This study discusses some fundamental properties and introduces the concepts of left and right exponential trigonometric interval-valued convex mappings. Furthermore, by utilizing the idea of fractional integrals having exponential kernels, we established some novel Hermite–Hadamard-type inequalities and proved certain conclusions for midpoint- and Pachpatte-type inequalities. Further research is necessary in this important area of interval-valued analysis that includes fractional integral operators. By utilizing the -integral, we plan to investigate the integral inequalities of fuzzy-interval-valued functions and some applications in interval optimizations.

**Author Contributions:** Conceptualization, M.B.K.; methodology, M.B.K.; validation, M.S.S. and A.C.; formal analysis, M.S.S.; investigation, M.B.K. and A.C.; resources, M.S.S. and A.C.; data curation, A.C.; writing—original draft preparation, M.B.K.; writing—review and editing, M.B.K., A.C. and M.S.S.; visualization, M.B.K.; supervision, M.B.K. and N.A.; project administration, M.B.K., A.C. and N.A. All authors have read and agreed to the published version of the manuscript.

**Funding:** The research was funded by the University of Oradea, Romania. The researchers also would like to acknowledge the Deanship of Scientific Research, Taif University, Saudi Arabia for funding this work.

**Data Availability Statement:** Not applicable.

**Acknowledgments:** The authors would like to thank the Rector, COMSATS University Islamabad, Islamabad 44000, Pakistan. The research was funded by the University of Oradea, Romania. The researchers also would like to acknowledge the Deanship of Scientific Research, Taif University, Saudi Arabia for funding this work.

**Conflicts of Interest:** The authors declare no conflict of interest.

## References

1. Fejér, L. Uberdie Fourierreihen, II. *Math. Naturwiss. Anz. Ungar Akad Wiss.* **1906**, *24*, 369–390.
2. Bombardelli, M.; Varošanec, S. Properties of h-convex functions related to the Hermite–Hadamard–Fejér inequalities. *Comput. Math. Appl.* **2009**, *58*, 1869–1877. [CrossRef]
3. Iscan, I. Some new Hermite–Hadamard type inequalities for s-geometrically convex functions and their applications. *arXiv* **2014**, arXiv:1305.6601.
4. Noor, M.A.; Noor, K.I.; Awan, M.U.; Li, J. On Hermite–Hadamard inequalities for h-preinvex functions. *Filomat* **2014**, *24*, 1463–1474. [CrossRef]
5. Latif, M.A.; Alomari, M. On Hadmard-type inequalities for h-convex functions on the co-ordinates. *Int. J. Math. Anal.* **2009**, *3*, 1645–1656.
6. Iscan, I. Hermite–Hadamard type inequalities for harmonically convex functions. *Hacet. J. Math. Stat.* **2014**, *43*, 935–942. [CrossRef]
7. Tseng, K.L.; Yang, G.S.; Hsu, K.C. Some inequalities for differentiable mappings and applications to Fejér inequality and weighted trapezoidal formula. *Taiwan J. Math.* **2011**, *15*, 1737–1747. [CrossRef]
8. Dragomir, S.S. Inequalities of Hermite–Hadamard type for h-convex functions on linear spaces. *Proyecciones* **2015**, *34*, 323–341. [CrossRef]
9. Zhao, T.H.; Castillo, O.; Jahanshahi, H.; Yusuf, A.; Alassafi, M.O.; Alsaadi, F.E.; Chu, Y.M. A fuzzy-based strategy to suppress the novel coronavirus (2019-NCOV) massive outbreak. *Appl. Comput. Math.* **2021**, *20*, 160–176.
10. Zhao, T.H.; Wang, M.K.; Chu, Y.M. On the bounds of the perimeter of an ellipse. *Acta Math. Sci.* **2022**, *42B*, 491–501. [CrossRef]
11. Zhao, T.H.; Wang, M.K.; Hai, G.J.; Chu, Y.M. Landen inequalities for Gaussian hypergeometric function. *RACSAM Rev. R Acad. A* **2022**, *116*, 53. [CrossRef]
12. Wang, M.K.; Hong, M.Y.; Xu, Y.F.; Shen, Z.H.; Chu, Y.M. Inequalities for generalized trigonometric and hyperbolic functions with one parameter. *J. Math. Inequal.* **2020**, *14*, 1–21. [CrossRef]
13. Zhao, T.H.; Qian, W.M.; Chu, Y.M. Sharp power mean bounds for the tangent and hyperbolic sine means. *J. Math. Inequal.* **2021**, *15*, 1459–1472. [CrossRef]
14. Chu, Y.M.; Wang, G.D.; Zhang, X.H. The Schur multiplicative and harmonic convexities of the complete symmetric function. *Math. Nachr.* **2011**, *284*, 53–663. [CrossRef]
15. Chu, Y.M.; Xia, W.F.; Zhang, X.H. The Schur concavity, Schur multiplicative and harmonic convexities of the second dual form of the Hamy symmetric function with applications. *J. Multivar. Anal.* **2012**, *105*, 412–442. [CrossRef]

16. Hajiseyedazizi, S.N.; Samei, M.E.; Alzabut, J.; Chu, Y.M. On multi-step methods for singular fractional q-integro-differential equations. *Open Math.* **2021**, *19*, 1378–1405. [CrossRef]
17. Jin, F.; Qian, Z.S.; Chu, Y.M.; Rahman, M. On nonlinear evolution model for drinking behavior under Caputo-Fabrizio derivative. *J. Appl. Anal. Comput.* **2022**, *12*, 790–806. [CrossRef]
18. Wang, F.Z.; Khan, M.N.; Ahmad, I.; Ahmad, H.; Abu-Zinadah, H.; Chu, Y.M. Numerical solution of traveling waves in chemical kinetics: Time-fractional fisher's equations. *Fractals* **2022**, *30*, 2240051. [CrossRef]
19. Chu, Y.M.; Siddiqui, M.K.; Nasir, M. On topological co-indices of polycyclic tetrathiafulvalene and polycyclic oragano silicon dendrimers. *Polycycl. Aromat. Compd.* **2022**, *42*, 2179–2197. [CrossRef]
20. Chu, Y.M.; Rauf, A.; Ishtiaq, M.; Siddiqui, M.K.; Muhammad, M.H. Topological properties of polycyclic aromatic nanostars dendrimers. *Polycycl. Aromat. Compd.* **2022**, *42*, 1891–1908. [CrossRef]
21. Chu, Y.M.; Numan, M.; Butt, S.I.; Siddiqui, M.K.; Ullah, R.; Cancan, M.; Ali, U. Degree-based topological aspects of polyphenylene nanostructures. *Polycycl. Aromat. Compd.* **2022**, *42*, 2591–2606. [CrossRef]
22. Chu, Y.M.; Muhammad, M.H.; Rauf, A.; Ishtiaq, M.; Siddiqui, M.K. Topological study of polycyclic graphite carbon nitride. *Polycycl. Aromat. Compd.* **2022**, *42*, 3203–3215. [CrossRef]
23. Iscan, I. Hermite–Hadamard–Fejér type inequalities for convex functions via fractional integrals. *arXiv* **2015**, arXiv:1404.7722.
24. Iscan, I.; Wu, S. Hermite–Hadamard type inequalities for harmonically convex functions via fractional integrals. *Appl. Math. Comput.* **2014**, *238*, 237–244.
25. Iscan, I.; Kunt, M.; Yazici, N. Hermite–Hadamard–Fejér type inequalities for harmonically convex functions via fractional integrals. *New Trends Math. Sci.* **2016**, *4*, 239–253. [CrossRef]
26. Sarikaya, M.Z.; Set, E.; Yaldiz, H.; Başak, N. Hermite–Hadamard's inequalities for fractional integrals and related fractional inequalities. *Math. Comput. Model.* **2013**, *57*, 2403–2407. [CrossRef]
27. Iscan, I. Generalization of different type integral inequalities for s-convex functions via fractional integrals. *Appl. Anal.* **2014**, *93*, 1846–1862. [CrossRef]
28. Noor, M.A.; Cristescu, G.; Awan, M.U. Generalized fractional Hermite–Hadamard inequalities for twice differentiable s-convex functions. *Filomat* **2015**, *29*, 807–815. [CrossRef]
29. Wang, J.R.; Li, X.Z.; Feckan, M.; Zhou, Y. Hermite–Hadamard-type inequalities for Riemann–Liouville fractional integrals via two kinds of convexity. *Appl. Anal.* **2013**, *92*, 2241–2253. [CrossRef]
30. Zhao, T.H.; Bhayo, B.A.; Chu, Y.M. Inequalities for generalized Grötzsch ring function. *Comput. Methods Funct. Theory* **2022**, *22*, 559–574. [CrossRef]
31. Zhao, T.H.; He, Z.Y.; Chu, Y.M. Sharp bounds for the weighted Hölder mean of the zero-balanced generalized complete elliptic integrals. *Comput. Methods Funct Theory* **2021**, *21*, 413–426. [CrossRef]
32. Zhao, T.H.; Wang, M.K.; Chu, Y.M. Concavity and bounds involving generalized elliptic integral of the first kind. *J. Math. Inequal.* **2021**, *15*, 701–724. [CrossRef]
33. Zhao, T.H.; Wang, M.K.; Chu, Y.M. Monotonicity and convexity involving generalized elliptic integral of the first kind. *RACSAM Rev. R Acad. A* **2021**, *115*, 46. [CrossRef]
34. Chu, H.H.; Zhao, T.H.; Chu, Y.M. Sharp bounds for the Toader mean of order 3 in terms of arithmetic, quadratic and contra harmonic means. *Math. Slovaca* **2020**, *70*, 1097–1112. [CrossRef]
35. Zhao, T.H.; He, Z.Y.; Chu, Y.M. On some refinements for inequalities involving zero-balanced hyper geometric function. *AIMS Math.* **2020**, *5*, 6479–6495. [CrossRef]
36. Zhao, T.H.; Wang, M.K.; Chu, Y.M. A sharp double inequality involving generalized complete elliptic integral of the first kind. *AIMS Math.* **2020**, *5*, 4512–4528. [CrossRef]
37. Khan, M.B.; Zaini, H.G.; Santos-García, G.; Noor, M.A.; Soliman, M.S. New Class Up and Down λ-Convex Fuzzy-Number Valued Mappings and Related Fuzzy Fractional Inequalities. *Fractal Fract.* **2022**, *6*, 679. [CrossRef]
38. Khan, M.B.; Santos-García, G.; Treanţă, S.; Noor, M.A.; Soliman, M.S. Perturbed Mixed Variational-Like Inequalities and Auxiliary Principle Pertaining to a Fuzzy Environment. *Symmetry* **2022**, *14*, 2503. [CrossRef]
39. Khan, M.B.; Zaini, H.G.; Macías-Díaz, J.E.; Soliman, M.S. Up and Down-Pre-Invex Fuzzy-Number Valued Mappings and Some Certain Fuzzy Integral Inequalities. *Axioms* **2023**, *12*, 1. [CrossRef]
40. Khan, M.B.; Othman, H.A.; Santos-García, G.; Noor, M.A.; Soliman, M.S. Some new concepts in fuzzy calculus for up and down λ-convex fuzzy-number valued mappings and related inequalities. *AIMS Math.* **2023**, *8*, 6777–6803. [CrossRef]
41. Zhao, D.; Chu, Y.M.; Siddiqui, M.K.; Ali, K.; Nasir, M.; Younas, M.T.; Cancan, M. On reverse degree based topological indices of polycyclic metal organic network. *Polycycl. Aromat. Compd.* **2022**, *42*, 4386–4403. [CrossRef]
42. Ibrahim, M.; Saeed, T.; Algehyne, E.A.; Alsulami, H.; Chu, Y.M. Optimization and effect of wall conduction on natural convection in a cavity with constant temperature heat source: Using lattice Boltzmann method and neural network algorithm. *J. Therm. Anal. Calorim.* **2021**, *144*, 2449–2463. [CrossRef]
43. Ibrahim, M.; Berrouk, A.S.; Algehyne, E.A.; Saeed, T.; Chu, Y.M. Numerical evaluation of exergy efficiency of innovative turbulators in solar collector filled with hybrid nanofluid. *J. Therm. Anal. Calorim.* **2021**, *145*, 1559–1574. [CrossRef]
44. Moore, R.E. *Interval Analysis*; Prentice-Hall: Englewood Cliffs, NJ, USA, 1966.
45. Chalco-Cano, Y.; Rufián-Lizana, A.; Román-Flores, H.; Jiménez-Gamero, M.D. Calculus for interval-valued functions using generalized Hukuhara derivative and applications. *Fuzzy Sets Syst.* **2013**, *219*, 49–67. [CrossRef]

46. Costa, T.M.; Chalco-Cano, Y.; Lodwick, W.A.; Silva, G.N. Generalized interval vector spaces and interval optimization. *Inf. Sci.* **2015**, *311*, 74–85. [CrossRef]
47. Osuna-Gómez, R.; Chalco-Cano, Y.; Hernández-Jiménez, B.; Ruiz-Garzón, G. Optimality conditions for generalized differentiable interval-valued functions. *Inf. Sci.* **2015**, *321*, 136–146. [CrossRef]
48. Lupulescu, V. Fractional calculus for interval-valued functions. *Fuzzy Sets Syst.* **2015**, *265*, 63–85. [CrossRef]
49. Zhao, T.H.; Shi, L.; Chu, Y.M. Convexity and concavity of the modified Bessel functions of the first kind with respect to Hölder means. *RACSAM Rev. R Acad. A.* **2020**, *114*, 96. [CrossRef]
50. Zhao, T.H.; Zhou, B.C.; Wang, M.K.; Chu, Y.M. On approximating the quasi-arithmetic mean. *J. Inequal. Appl.* **2019**, *2019*, 42. [CrossRef]
51. Zhao, T.H.; Wang, M.K.; Zhang, W.; Chu, Y.M. Quadratic transformation inequalities for Gaussian hyper geometric function. *J. Inequal. Appl.* **2018**, *2018*, 251. [CrossRef]
52. Chu, Y.M.; Zhao, T.H. Concavity of the error function with respect to Hölder means. *Math. Inequal. Appl.* **2016**, *19*, 589–595. [CrossRef]
53. Qian, W.M.; Chu, H.H.; Wang, M.K.; Chu, Y.M. Sharp inequalities for the Toader mean of order −1 in terms of other bivariate means. *J. Math. Inequal.* **2022**, *16*, 127–141. [CrossRef]
54. Zhao, T.H.; Chu, H.H.; Chu, Y.M. Optimal Lehmer mean bounds for the nth power-type Toader mean of n = −1, 1, 3. *J. Math. Inequal.* **2022**, *16*, 157–168. [CrossRef]
55. Khan, M.B.; Santos-García, G.; Budak, H.; Treanță, S.; Soliman, M.S. Some new versions of Jensen, Schur and Her-mite-Hadamard type inequalities for ($p$, $\mathfrak{J}$)-convex fuzzy-interval-valued functions. *AIMS Math.* **2023**, *8*, 7437–7470. [CrossRef]
56. Khan, M.B.; Othman, H.A.; Voskoglou, M.G.; Abdullah, L.; Alzubaidi, A.M. Some Certain Fuzzy Aumann Integral Inequalities for Generalized Convexity via Fuzzy Number Valued Mappings. *Mathematics* **2023**, *11*, 550. [CrossRef]
57. Khan, M.B.; Rakhmangulov, A.; Aloraini, N.; Noor, M.A.; Soliman, M.S. Generalized Harmonically Convex Fuzzy-Number-ValuedMappings and Fuzzy Riemann–Liouville Fractional Integral Inequalities. *Mathematics* **2023**, *11*, 656. [CrossRef]
58. Khan, M.B.; Catas, A.; Aloraini, N.; Soliman, M.S. Some Certain Fuzzy Fractional Inequalities for Up and Down $\hbar$-Pre-Invex via Fuzzy-Number Valued Mappings. *Fractal Fract.* **2023**, *7*, 171. [CrossRef]
59. Chalco-Cano, Y.; Flores-Franulic, A.; Román-Flores, H. Ostrowski type inequalities for interval-valued functions using generalized Hukuhara derivative. *Comput. Appl. Math.* **2012**, *31*, 457–472.
60. Chalco-Cano, Y.; Lodwick, W.A.; Condori-Equice, W. Ostrowski type inequalities and applications in numerical integration for interval-valued functions. *Soft Comput.* **2015**, *19*, 3293–3300. [CrossRef]
61. Costa, T.M.; Román-Flores, H. Some integral inequalities for fuzzy-interval-valued functions. *Inf. Sci.* **2017**, *420*, 110–125. [CrossRef]
62. Zhao, D.F.; An, T.Q.; Ye, G.J.; Liu, W. New Jensen and Hermite–Hadamard type inequalities for h-convex interval-valued functions. *J. Inequal. Appl.* **2018**, *2018*, 302. [CrossRef]
63. Zhao, D.F.; Ye, G.J.; Liu, W.; Torres, M. Some inequalities for interval-valued functions on time scales. *Soft Comput.* **2018**, *23*, 6005–6015. [CrossRef]
64. An, Y.R.; Ye, G.J.; Zhao, D.F.; Liu, W. Hermite–Hadamard type inequalities for interval (h1, h2)-convex functions. *Mathematics* **2019**, *7*, 436. [CrossRef]
65. Budak, H.; Tunç, T.; Sarikaya, M.Z. Fractional Hermite–Hadamard type inequalities for interval-valued functions. *Proc. Am. Math. Soc.* **2019**, *148*, 705–718. [CrossRef]
66. Costa, T.M. Jensen's inequality type integral for fuzzy-interval-valued functions. *Fuzzy Sets Syst.* **2017**, *327*, 31–47. [CrossRef]
67. Khan, M.B.; Noor, M.A.; Noor, K.I.; Chu, Y.M. New Hermite-Hadamard type inequalities for -convex fuzzy-interval-valued functions. *Adv. Differ. Equ.* **2021**, *2021*, 6–20. [CrossRef]
68. Khan, M.B.; Noor, M.A.; Abdeljawad, T.; Mousa, A.A.A.; Abdalla, B.; Alghamdi, S.M. LR-Preinvex Interval-Valued Functions and Riemann–Liouville Fractional Integral Inequalities. *Fractal Fract.* **2021**, *5*, 243. [CrossRef]
69. Ibrahim, M.; Berrouk, A.S.; Algehyne, E.A.; Saeed, T.; Chu, Y.M. Energetic and exergetic analysis of a new circular micro-heat sink containing nanofluid: Applicable for cooling electronic equipment. *J. Therm. Anal. Calorim.* **2021**, *145*, 1547–1557. [CrossRef]
70. Ibrahim, M.; Saeed, T.; Algehyne, E.A.; Khan, M.; Chu, Y.M. The effects of L-shaped heat source in a quarter-tube enclosure filled with MHD nanofluid on heat transfer and irreversibilities, using LBM: Numerical data, optimization using neural network algorithm (ANN). *J. Therm. Anal. Calorim.* **2021**, *144*, 2435–2448. [CrossRef]
71. Ibrahim, M.; Saleem, S.; Chu, Y.M.; Ullah, M.; Heidarshenas, B. An investigation of the exergy and first and second laws by two-phase numerical simulation of various nanopowders with different diameter on the performance of zigzag-wall micro-heat sink (ZZW-MHS). *J. Therm. Anal. Calorim.* **2021**, *144*, 1611–1621. [CrossRef]
72. Madhukesh, J.K.; Kumar, R.N.; Gowda, R.P.; Prasannakumara, B.C.; Ramesh, G.K.; Khan, M.I.; Khan, S.U.; Chu, Y.M. Numerical simulation of AA7072-AA7075/ water-based hybrid nanofluid flow over a curved stretching sheet with Newtonian heating: A non-Fourier heat flux model approach. *J. Mol. Liq.* **2021**, *335*, 116103. [CrossRef]
73. Li, J.; Alawee, W.H.; Rawa, M.J.; Dhahad, H.A.; Chu, Y.M.; Issakhov, A.; Abu-Hamdeh, N.H.; Hajizadeh, M.R. Heat recovery application of nanomaterial with existence of turbulator. *J. Mol. Liq.* **2021**, *326*, 115268. [CrossRef]
74. Chu, Y.M.; Hajizadeh, M.R.; Li, Z.; Bach, Q.V. Investigation of nano powders influence on melting process within a storage unit. *J. Mol. Liq.* **2020**, *318*, 114321. [CrossRef]
75. Chu, Y.M.; Yadav, D.; Shafee, A.; Li, Z.; Bach, Q.V. Influence of wavy enclosure and nanoparticles on heat release rate of PCM considering numerical study. *J. Mol. Liq.* **2020**, *319*, 114121. [CrossRef]

76. Chu, Y.M.; Ibrahim, M.; Saeed, T.; Berrouk, A.S.; Algehyne, E.A.; Kalbasi, R. Examining rheological behavior of MWCNT-TiO$_2$/5W40 hybrid nanofluid based on experiments and RSM/ANN modeling. *J. Mol. Liq.* **2021**, *333*, 115969. [CrossRef]
77. Khan, M.B.; Santos-García, G.; Noor, M.A.; Soliman, M.S. Some new concepts related to fuzzy fractional calculus for up and down convex fuzzy-number valued functions and inequalities. *Chaos Solitons Fractals* **2022**, *164*, 112692. [CrossRef]
78. Kadakal, M.; Iscan, I.; Agarwal, P. Exponential trigonometric convex function and Hermite-Hadamard type inequalities. *Math. Slovaca* **2021**, *71*, 43–56. [CrossRef]
79. Diamond, P.; Kloeden, P.E. Metric Spaces of Fuzzy Sets: Theory and Applications. *Fuzzy Sets Syst.* **1990**, *35*, 241–249. [CrossRef]
80. Bede, B. *Mathematics of fuzzy sets and fuzzy logic, volume 295 of Studies in Fuzziness and Soft Computing*; Springer: Berlin/Heidelberg, Germany, 2013.
81. Kaleva, O. Fuzzy differential equations. *Fuzzy Sets Syst.* **1987**, *24*, 301–317. [CrossRef]
82. Aubin, J.P.; Cellina, A. *Differential Inclusions: Set-Valued Maps and Viability Theory, Grundlehren der Mathematischen Wissenschaften*; Springer: Berlin/Heidelberg, Germany, 1984.
83. Aubin, J.P.; Frankowska, H. *Set-Valued Analysis*; Birkhäuser: Boston, MA, USA, 1990.
84. Zhang, D.; Guo, C.; Chen, D.; Wang, G. Jensen's inequalities for set-valued and fuzzy set-valued functions. *Fuzzy Sets Syst.* **2020**, *404*, 178–204. [CrossRef]
85. Ahmad, B.; Alsaedi, A.; Kirane, M.; Torebek, B.T. Hermite–Hadamard, Hermite–Hadamard–Fejér, Dragomir–Agarwal and Pachpatte type inequalities for convex functions via new fractional integrals. *J. Comput. Appl. Math.* **2019**, *353*, 120–129. [CrossRef]
86. Zhou, T.; Yuan, Z.; Du, T. On the fractional integral inclusions having exponential kernels for interval-valued convex functions. *Math. Sci.* **2021**, *2021*, 1–14. [CrossRef]
87. Ullah, N.; Khan, M.B.; Aloraini, N.; Treanţă, S. Some New Estimates of Fixed Point Results under Multi-Valued Mappings in G-Metric Spaces with Application. *Symmetry* **2023**, *15*, 517. [CrossRef]
88. Khan, M.B.; Santos-García, G.; Noor, M.A.; Soliman, M.S. New Hermite–Hadamard Inequalities for Convex Fuzzy-Number-Valued Mappings via Fuzzy Riemann Integrals. *Mathematics* **2022**, *10*, 3251. [CrossRef]
89. Khan, M.B.; Treanţă, S.; Soliman, M.S. Generalized Preinvex Interval-Valued Functions and Related Hermite–Hadamard Type Inequalities. *Symmetry* **2022**, *14*, 1901. [CrossRef]
90. Saeed, T.; Khan, M.B.; Treanţă, S.; Alsulami, H.H.; Alhodaly, M.S. Interval Fejér-Type Inequalities for Left and Right-λ-Preinvex Functions in Interval-Valued Settings. *Axioms* **2022**, *11*, 368. [CrossRef]
91. Khan, M.B.; Cătaş, A.; Alsalami, O.M. Some New Estimates on Coordinates of Generalized Convex Interval-Valued Functions. *Fractal Fract.* **2022**, *6*, 415. [CrossRef]
92. Ibrahim, M.; Saeed, T.; Hekmatifar, M.; Sabetvand, R.; Chu, Y.M.; Toghraie, D.; Iran, T.G. The atomic interactions between histone and 3LPT protein using an equilibrium molecular dynamics simulation. *J. Mol. Liq.* **2021**, *328*, 115397. [CrossRef]
93. Qureshi, M.Z.A.; Bilal, S.; Chu, Y.M.; Farooq, A.B. Physical impact of nano-layer on nano-fluid flow due to dispersion of magnetized carbon nano-materials through an absorbent channel with thermal analysis. *J. Mol. Liq.* **2021**, *325*, 115211. [CrossRef]
94. Ibrahim, M.; Saeed, T.; Hekmatifar, M.; Sabetvand, R.; Chu, Y.M.; Toghraie, D. Investigation of dynamical behavior of 3LPT protein-water molecules interactions in atomic structures using molecular dynamics simulation. *J. Mol. Liq.* **2021**, *329*, 115615. [CrossRef]
95. Xiong, P.Y.; Almarashi, A.; Dhadad, H.A.; Alawee, W.H.; Abusorrah, A.M.; Issakhov, A.; Abu-Hamhed, N.H.; Shafee, A.; Chu, Y.M. Nanomaterial transportation and exergy loss modeling incorporating CVFEM. *J. Mol. Liq.* **2021**, *330*, 115591. [CrossRef]
96. Wang, T.; Almarashi, A.; Al-Turki, Y.A.; Abu-Hamdeh, N.H.; Hajizadeh, M.R.; Chu, Y.M. Approaches for expedition of discharging of PCM involving nanoparticles and radial fins. *J. Mol. Liq.* **2021**, *329*, 115052. [CrossRef]
97. Xiong, P.Y.; Almarashi, A.; Dhadad, H.A.; Alawee, W.H.; Issakhov, A.; Chu, Y.M. Nanoparticles for phase change process of water utilizing FEM. *J. Mol. Liq.* **2021**, *334*, 116096. [CrossRef]
98. Zhou, T.C.; Du, T.S. Certain fractional integral inclusions pertaining to interval-valued exponential trigonometric convex functions. *J. Math. Inequal.* **2022**.
99. Qi, Y.; Wen, Q.; Li, G.; Xiao, K.; Wang, S. Discrete Hermite-Hadamard-type inequalities for (s, m)-convex function. *Fractals* **2022**, *30*, 2250160. [CrossRef]

**Disclaimer/Publisher's Note:** The statements, opinions and data contained in all publications are solely those of the individual author(s) and contributor(s) and not of MDPI and/or the editor(s). MDPI and/or the editor(s) disclaim responsibility for any injury to people or property resulting from any ideas, methods, instructions or products referred to in the content.

 *fractal and fractional*

Article

# Some New Applications of the Faber Polynomial Expansion Method for Generalized Bi-Subordinate Functions of Complex Order $\gamma$ Defined by $q$-Calculus

**Mohammad Faisal Khan [1,\*] and Mohammed AbaOud [2]**

[1] Department of Basic Sciences, College of Science and Theoretical Studies, Saudi Electronic University, Riyadh 11673, Saudi Arabia
[2] Department of Mathematics and Statistics, Imam Mohammad Ibn Saud Islamic University (IMSIU), Riyadh 11564, Saudi Arabia; maabaoud@imamu.edu.sa
\* Correspondence: f.khan@seu.edu.sa

**Abstract:** This work examines a new subclass of generalized bi-subordinate functions of complex order $\gamma$ connected to the $q$-difference operator. We obtain the upper bounds $\rho_m$ for generalized bi-subordinate functions of complex order $\gamma$ using the Faber polynomial expansion technique. Additionally, we find coefficient bounds $|\rho_2|$ and Feke–Sezgo problems $|\rho_3 - \rho_2^2|$ for the functions in the newly defined class, subject to gap series conditions. Using the Faber polynomial expansion method, we show some results that illustrate diverse uses of the Ruschewey $q$ differential operator. The findings in this paper generalize those from previous efforts by a number of prior researchers.

**Keywords:** quantum (or $q$-) calculus; analytic functions; univalent functions; $q$-derivative operator; convex functions; starlike functions; bi-univalent functions; Faber polynomial expansion

**MSC:** 05A30; 30C45; 11B65; 47B38

## 1. Introduction and Definitions

The set of all analytic functions $h(z)$ in the open unit disc $E = \{z : |z| < 1\}$ is denoted by the symbol $\mathfrak{A}$ and every $h \in \mathfrak{A}$ is normalized by

$$h(0) = 0 \text{ and } h'(0) = 1.$$

Thus, every function $h \in \mathfrak{A}$ can be expressed in the following form:

$$h(z) = z + \sum_{m=2}^{\infty} a_m z^m. \tag{1}$$

Furthermore, $\mathcal{S} \subset \mathfrak{A}$ and every $h \in \mathcal{S}$ is univalent in $E$. For $h_1, h_2 \in \mathfrak{A}$, and $h_1$ subordinate to $h_2$ in $E$, denoted by

$$h_1(z) \prec h_2(z), \; z \in E,$$

if there exists a function $w_0$, such that $w_0 \in \mathfrak{A}$, with $w_0(0) = 0$, and $|w_0(z)| < 1$, satisfying

$$h_1(z) = h_2(w_0(z)), \; z \in E.$$

Let $\mathcal{S}^*$ represent the class of starlike functions and every $h \in \mathcal{S}^*$, if

$$\operatorname{Re}\left(\frac{zh'(z)}{h(z)}\right) > 0, \; z \in E$$

and C represents the class of convex functions and every $h \in C$, if

$$1 + \operatorname{Re}\left(\frac{zh''(z)}{h'(z)}\right) > 0, \; z \in E.$$

In terms of subordination, these conditions are equivalent as follows:

$$\mathcal{S}^* = \left\{h \in \mathfrak{A} : \frac{zh'(z)}{h(z)} \prec \frac{1+z}{1-z}\right\}$$

and

$$\mathcal{C} = \left\{h \in \mathfrak{A} : 1 + \frac{zh''(z)}{h'(z)} \prec \frac{1+z}{1-z}\right\}.$$

Ma and Minda [1] stated that the aforementioned two classes can be generalized as follows:

$$\mathcal{S}^*(\varphi) = \left\{h \in \mathfrak{A} : \frac{zh'(z)}{h(z)} \prec \varphi(z)\right\}$$

and

$$\mathcal{C}(\varphi) = \left\{h \in \mathfrak{A} : 1 + \frac{zh''(z)}{h'(z)} \prec \varphi(z)\right\}.$$

where $\varphi(z)$ is a positive real part function and is normalized by the condition

$$\varphi(0) = 1, \; \varphi'(0) > 0$$

and $\varphi$ maps $E$ onto a region that is starlike with respect to 1 and symmetric with respect to the real axis. Ravichandran et al. [2] gave the extension of above two classes in the following way:

$$\mathcal{S}^*(\gamma, \varphi) = \left\{h \in \mathfrak{A} : 1 + \frac{1}{\gamma}\left(\frac{zh'(z)}{h(z)} - 1\right) \prec \varphi(z); \; \gamma \in \mathbb{C}\setminus\{0\}\right\}$$

and

$$\mathcal{C}(\gamma, \varphi) = \left\{h \in \mathfrak{A} : 1 + \frac{1}{\gamma}\left(\frac{zh''(z)}{h'(z)}\right) \prec \varphi(z); \; \gamma \in \mathbb{C}\setminus\{0\}\right\}.$$

These types of functions are referred to as Ma–Minda starlike and convex functions of $\gamma$, ($\gamma \in \mathbb{C}\setminus\{0\}$), respectively.

The Koebe one-quarter theorem (see [3]) states that the image of $E$ under every $h \in \mathcal{S}$ contains a disk of radius one-quarter centered at the origin. Thus, every function $h \in \mathcal{S}$ has an inverse $h^{-1} = g$,

$$g(h(z)) = z, \; z \in E$$

and

$$h(g(w)) = w, \; |w| < r_0(h), \; r_0(h) \geq \frac{1}{4}.$$

The series of the inverse function $g$ is given by

$$g(w) = w - a_2 w^2 + (2a_2^2 - a_3)w^3 - (5a_2^3 - 5a_2 a_3 + a_4)w^4 + \dots . \quad (2)$$

A function $h \in \mathfrak{A}$ is called bi-univalent in $E$ if both $h$ and $h^{-1}$ are univalent in $E$ and we denote the class of all bi-univalent functions by $\Sigma$.

Lewin [4] developed the idea of class $\Sigma$ and established that $|a_2| < 1.51$ for every $h \in \Sigma$. Styer and Wright [5] demonstrated the existence of $h \in \Sigma$ for which $|a_2| > \frac{4}{3}$. Since the creation of the class $\Sigma$, several researchers have been trying to determine how the geometric properties of the functions in the class and the coefficient bounds are related. Indeed, a strong foundation for the study of bi-univalent functions was laid by authors such as Lewin [4], Brannan and Taha [6], and Srivastava et al. [7]. Only non-sharp estimates of the initial coefficients were produced in these recent works. Coefficient estimates for general subclasses of analytic bi-univalent functions were also obtained in [8]. More recently, in [9], coefficient estimates for general subclasses of analytic bi-univalent functions were also obtained using the integral operator based upon Lucas polynomials, while Oros and Cotirla [10] defined a new subclass of $v$-fold bi-univalent functions and obtained coefficient estimates and the Fekete–Szego problem. However, the problem of a sharp coefficient bound for $|a_m|$, $(m = 3, 4, 5, \ldots)$ is still open.

Recently, Hamidi and Jahangiri [11,12] started to apply the Faber polynomial expansion method to find coefficient bounds $|a_m|$ for $m \geq 3$. The Faber polynomial method was introduced by Faber in [13] and its importance was discussed by Gong [14]. A number of new subclasses of bi-univalent functions have been introduced and studied by considering and involving the Faber polynomial expansion method. In the following article [15] Bult defined some new subclasses of bi-univalent functions and used the Faber polynomial technique to find general coefficient bounds $|a_m|$ for $m \geq 3$, and also discussed the unpredictable behavior of initial coefficient bounds. The general coefficient bounds $|a_m|$ $m \geq 3$ of analytic bi-univalent functions were also obtained recently, by using the subordination properties and Faber polynomial expansion method [16], and also using the same technique that Altinkaya and Yalcin [17] discussed concerning the interesting behavior of coefficient bounds for new subclasses of bi-univalent functions. Furthermore, many authors have applied the technique of Faber polynomials and determined some interesting results for bi-univalent functions.

Jackson [18] presented the idea of the $q$-calculus operator and defined $D_q$, while Ismail et al. [19] were the first to use the $q$-difference operator ($D_q$) to define a class of $q$-starlike functions. After that, many researchers introduced several subclasses of analytic functions related to $q$-calculus, (see, for details, [20–22]). The following articles on differential operators shall be used for the study of the applications of operators: [23–26].

In order to create some new subclasses of analytic and bi-univalent functions, the core definitions and ideas of $q$-calculus need to be discussed.

**Definition 1.** *For $\eta, q \in \mathbb{C}$, the $q$-shifted factorial $(\eta, q)_m$ is defined by*

$$(\eta, q)_m = \begin{cases} 1 & \text{if } m = 0, \\ (1 - \eta)(1 - \eta q) \ldots (1 - \eta q^{n-1}) & \text{if } (m \in \mathbb{N}). \end{cases} \tag{3}$$

*If $\eta \neq q^{-l}$, $(l \in \mathbb{N}_0)$, then it can be written as:*

$$(\eta, q)_\infty = \prod_{m=0}^{\infty} (1 - \eta q^m), \quad (\eta \in \mathbb{C} \text{ and } |q| < 1), \tag{4}$$

*when $\eta \neq 0$ and $q \geq 1$, $(\eta, q)_\infty$ diverges. Therefore, whenever we use $(\eta, q)_\infty$ then $|q| < 1$ will be assumed.*

**Remark 1.** *It is noted that when $q \to 1-$ in $(\eta, q)_m$, then (19) reduces to the Pochhammer symbol $(\eta)_m$ defined by*

$$(\eta)_m = \eta(\eta + 1) \ldots (\eta + m - 1) \quad \text{if } m \in \mathbb{N}.$$

*If $m = 0$, then $(\eta)_m = 1$.*

**Definition 2.** *The $(\eta, q)_m$ in (19) is precise with respect to the $q$-Gamma function, which is given below*

$$\Gamma_q(\eta) = \frac{(1-q)^{1-\eta}(q, q)_\infty}{(q^\eta, q)_\infty}, \quad (0 < q < 1),$$

or
$$(q^\eta, q)_m = \frac{(1-q)^m \Gamma_q(\eta+m)}{\Gamma_q(\eta)}, \quad (m \in \mathbb{N})$$

and q-factorial $[m]_q!$ is defined by:

$$[m]_q! = \prod_{k=1}^{m}[k]_q, \text{ if } (m \in \mathbb{N}) \tag{5}$$
$$= 1 \text{ if } m = 0.$$

It is important to note that ordinary calculus is a limiting case of quantum calculus. It is expected that a study of quantum difference operators will be crucial to the growth of q-function theory, which is essential for combinatory analysis. In addition, the differential and integral operators are widely used in geometric function theory. The most significant feature of our study is that we are investigating the properties of new class of analytic bi-univalent functions under a certain q-derivative operator. Geometric-function-theory-related research on this topic has still not been performed extensively.

In this paper, we first define the q-derivative (q-difference) operator and then consider this operator to define a new class of analytic bi-univalent functions of class $\Sigma$.

**Definition 3** ([18]). *For $h \in \mathfrak{A}$, the q-difference operator is defined as:*

$$D_q h(z) = \frac{h(qz) - h(z)}{z(q-1)}, \quad z \in E.$$

Note that, for $m \in \mathbb{N}$ and $z \in E$ and

$$D_q(z^m) = [m]_q z^{m-1}, \quad D_q\left(\sum_{m=1}^{\infty} a_m z^m\right) = \sum_{m=1}^{\infty} [m]_q a_m z^{m-1},$$

where $(0 < q < 1)$, is defined by

$$[m]_q = \frac{1-q^m}{1-q}, \text{ and } [0]_q = 0$$

and the q-number shift factorial is given by

$$[m]_q! = [1]_q[2]_q[3]_q \ldots [m]_q,$$
$$[0]_q! = 1.$$

The q-generalized Pochhammer symbol is defined by

$$[x]_{q,m} = \frac{\Gamma_q(x+m)}{\Gamma_q(x)}, \quad m \in \mathbb{N}, x \in \mathbb{C}. \tag{6}$$

**Remark 2.** *For $q \to 1-$, then $[x]_{q,m}$ reduces to $(x)_m = \frac{\Gamma(x+m)}{\Gamma(x)}$.*

Suppose that $\varphi$ is an analytic function with a positive real part in the unit disk $E$ satisfying
$$\varphi(0) = 1 \text{ and } \varphi'(0) > 0$$
and $\varphi(E)$ is symmetric with respect to the real axis and has the series

$$\varphi(z) = 1 + B_1 z + B_2 z^2 + B_3 z^3 + \ldots \text{ and } (B_1 > 0). \tag{7}$$

The $q$-calculus operator theory is used to solve a wide range of problems in heat transfer and other areas of mathematical physics and engineering that include cylindrical and spherical coordinates. Several remarkable characteristics of new subclasses of analytic functions have been found using $q$-differential operators, including new subclasses of convex and starlike functions. One of the classic areas of geometric function theory is the study of particular subclasses of starlike functions and its generalization. Therefore, by means of the $q$-difference operator $(D_q)$ defined in Definition 3 and inspired by the work introduced in [27], a new class of analytic bi-univalent functions of class $\Sigma$ is introduced. The original results will be proved in the following section using the Faber polynomial approach and two lemmas.

**Definition 4.** *Let $h$ be the form (1) and $h \in \mathfrak{J}(\lambda, \gamma, q; \varphi)$ if*

$$1 + \frac{1}{\gamma}\left(\frac{zD_q h(z) + \lambda z^2 D_q^2(h(z))}{(1-\lambda)h(z) + \lambda z D_q h(z)} - 1\right) \prec \varphi(z)$$

*and*

$$1 + \frac{1}{\gamma}\left(\frac{wD_q g(w) + \lambda w^2 D_q^2(g(w))}{(1-\lambda)g(w) + \lambda w D_q g(w)} - 1\right) \prec \varphi(w),$$

*where, $0 \leq \lambda \leq 1$, $\gamma \in \mathbb{C}\setminus\{0\}$, $z, w \in E$ and $g = h^{-1}$.*

**Note:** If both $h$ and its inverse map $g = h^{-1}$ are in $\mathfrak{J}(\lambda, \gamma, q; \varphi)$, then $h$ is called a generalized bi-subordinate function of complex order $\gamma$.

**Remark 3.** *For $\lambda = 0$, then we have $\mathfrak{J}(\lambda, \gamma, q; \varphi) = \mathfrak{J}(0, \gamma, q; \varphi)$ and for $\lambda = 1$, then we have $\mathfrak{J}(\lambda, \gamma, q; \varphi) = \mathfrak{J}(1, \gamma, q; \varphi)$.*

**Remark 4.** *For $q \to 1-$, then $\mathfrak{J}(\lambda, \gamma, q; \varphi) = \mathfrak{J}(\lambda, \gamma; \varphi)$, and introduced by Deniz in [28].*

## 2. The Faber Polynomial Expansion Method and Its Applications

For the function $h \in \mathfrak{A}$, Airault and Bouali ([29], page 184) used Faber polynomials to show that

$$\frac{zh'(z)}{h(z)} = 1 - \sum_{m=2}^{\infty}[R_{m-1}(a_2, a_3, \ldots a_m)]z^{m-1}, \qquad (8)$$

where

$$R_{m-1}(a_2, a_3, \ldots a_m) = \sum_{i_1 + 2i_2 + \ldots (m-1)i_{m-1} = m-1}^{\infty} A(i_1, i_2, i_3, \ldots, i_{m-1})\left(a_2^{i_1} a_3^{i_2} \ldots a_m^{i_{m-1}}\right)$$

and

$$A(i_1, i_2, i_3, \ldots, i_{m-1}) = (-1)^{(m-1)+2i_1+\cdots+mi_{m-1}}$$
$$\times \left(\frac{(i_1 + i_2 + i_3, \cdots + i_{m-1} - 1)!(m-1)}{(i_1!)(i_2!)(i_3!), \ldots (i_{m-1}!)}\right).$$

The first terms of the Faber polynomial $R_{m-1}$, $m \geq 2$, are given by (e.g., see ([30], page 52))

$$R_1 = -a_2, \quad R_2 = a_2^2 - 2a_3,$$
$$R_3 = -a_2^3 + 3a_2 a_3 - 3a_4),$$
$$R_3 = a_2^4 - 4a_2^2 a_3 + 4a_2 a_4 + 2a_3^2 - 4a_5).$$

Using the Faber polynomial technique for the analytic functions $h$, then the coefficients of its inverse map $g$ can be written as follows (see ([29], page 185)):

$$g(w) = h^{-1}(w) = w + \sum_{m=2}^{\infty} \frac{1}{m} R_{m-1}^m(a_2, a_3, \ldots, a_m) w^m,$$

where the coefficients of the $m$ parametric function are

$$R_1^p = pa_2,$$
$$R_2^p = \frac{p(p-1)}{2} a_2^2 + pa_3,$$
$$R_3^p = p(p-1)a_2 a_3 + pa_4 + \frac{p(p-1)(p-2)}{3!} a_2^3,$$
$$R_4^p = p(p-1)a_2 a_4 + pa_5 + \frac{p(p-1)}{2} a_3^2 + \frac{p(p-1)(p-2)}{2} a_2^2 a_3 + \frac{p!}{(p-4)!4!} a_2^4,$$

$$\vdots$$

$$R_{m-1}^p = \frac{p!}{(p-m)!m!} a_2^m + \frac{p!}{(p-m+1)!(m-2)!} a_2^{m-2} a_3 + \frac{p!}{(p-n+2)!(m-3)!} a_2^{m-3} a_4$$
$$+ \frac{p!}{(p-n+3)!(m-4)!} a_2^{m-4} \left( a_5 + \frac{p-n+3}{2} a_3^2 \right)$$
$$+ \frac{p!}{(p-n+4)!(m-5)!} a_2^{m-4} (a_6 + (p-m+3) a_3 a_4) + \sum_{i \geq 6} a_2^{m-i} Q_i,$$

and $Q_i$ is a homogeneous polynomial in the variables $a_2, a_3, \ldots, a_m$, for $6 \leq i \leq m$; see [31], page 349, and [29], pages 183 and 205. Particularly, the first three terms of $R_{m-1}^p$ are

$$\frac{1}{2} R_1^1 = -a_2, \quad \frac{1}{3} R_2^{-3} = 2a_2^2 - a_3,$$
$$\frac{1}{4} R_3^3 = -(5a_2^3 - 5a_2 a_3 + a_4).$$

In general, for $r \in \mathbb{Z}$ ($\mathbb{Z} := 0, \pm 1, \pm 2, \ldots$ and $m \geq 2$, there is an expansion of $R_m^r$ of the form:

$$R_m^r = r a_m + \frac{r(r-1)}{2} \mathcal{V}_m^2 + \frac{r!}{(r-3)!3!} \mathcal{V}_m^3 + \cdots + \frac{r!}{(r-m)!(m)!} \mathcal{V}_m^m,$$

where,

$$\mathcal{V}_m^r = \mathcal{V}_m^r(a_2, a_3 \ldots),$$

and by [32], we have

$$\mathcal{V}_m^v(a_2, \ldots, a_m) = \sum_{m=1}^{\infty} \frac{v!(a_2)^{\mu_1} \ldots (a_m)^{\mu_m}}{\mu_1!, \ldots, \mu_m!}, \text{ for } a_1 = 1 \text{ and } v \leq m.$$

The sum is taken over all nonnegative integers $\mu_1, \ldots, \mu_m$, which satisfy

$$\mu_1 + \mu_2 + \cdots + \mu_m = v,$$
$$\mu_1 + 2\mu_2 + \cdots + m\mu_m = m.$$

Clearly,

$$\mathcal{V}_m^m(a_1, \ldots, a_m) = \mathcal{V}_1^m,$$

and the first and last polynomials are

$$\mathcal{V}_m^m = a_1^m, \text{ and } \mathcal{V}_m^1 = a_m.$$

Geometric function theory has always placed a great deal of importance on establishing bounds for the coefficients. The size of the coefficients can determine a number of properties of analytic functions, including univalency, rate of growth, and distortion. Several scholars have employed a variety of techniques to resolve the aforementioned problems. Similar to univalent functions, the bounds of bi-univalent function coefficients have recently attracted a lot of attention. As a result of the significance of studying the coefficient problems described above, in this section, we consider the $q$-difference operator and Faber polynomial technique to obtain coefficient estimates $|\rho_m|$ of bi-univalent functions in the family $\mathfrak{J}(\lambda, \gamma, q; \varphi)$ and discuss the unpredictable behavior of initial coefficient bounds $|\rho_2|$ and Feke–Sezgo problems $|\rho_3 - \rho_2^2|$ in this family, subject to gap series conditions.

Using the Ruscheweyh differential operator, and Ruscheweyh $q$-differential operator, many scholars have defined new classes of convex and starlike functions. In this study, we also use the Ruscheweyh $q$-differential operator along with the Faber polynomial method and discuss the applications of our main results. We also investigate the Feketo–Sezego problem and some known consequences of our main results.

*Set of Lemmas*

The following well-known lemmas are required to prove our main theorems:

**Lemma 1** ([3]). *Let the function $p(z) = 1 + \sum_{m=1}^{\infty} p_m z^m$ and $\operatorname{Re}(p(z)) > 0$ for $z \in E$, then for $-\infty < \alpha < \infty$*

$$\left|p_2 - \alpha p_1^2\right| \leq \begin{cases} 2 - \alpha|p_1|^2 & \text{if } \alpha < \frac{1}{2} \\ 2 - (1-\alpha)|p_1|^2 & \text{if } \alpha \geq \frac{1}{2}. \end{cases}$$

**Lemma 2** ([28]). *Let the function $\phi(z) = \sum_{m=1}^{\infty} \phi_m z^m$ so that $|\phi(z)| < 1$ for $z \in E$, then*

$$\left|\phi_2 + \beta \phi_1^2\right| \leq \begin{cases} 1 - (1-\delta)|\beta|^2 & \text{if } \beta > 0 \\ 1 - (1+\delta)|\beta|^2 & \text{if } \beta \leq 0. \end{cases} \quad (9)$$

This paper uses the $q$-difference operator for $\xi \in \mathfrak{A}$, and the new class $\mathfrak{J}(\lambda, \gamma, q; \varphi)$ of generalized bi-subordinate functions of complex order $\gamma$ is defined. Next, in Theorem 1, upper bounds $\rho_m$ for generalized bi-subordinate functions of complex order $\gamma$ are proved and in Theorem 2 the initial coefficient bound $|\rho_2|$ and Feke–Sezgo problems $|\rho_3 - \rho_2^2|$ are investigated by putting the special value of parameters in the class $\mathfrak{J}(\lambda, \gamma, q; \varphi)$, and we obtain some new and known results. In Section 4, we use the Ruscheweyh $q$-differential operator and investigate some new characteristics of the class of generalized bi-subordinate functions of complex order $\gamma$ in the form of some new results. In Section 5, we give concluding remarks.

## 3. Main Results

**Theorem 1.** *Let $0 \leq \lambda \leq 1, \gamma \in \mathbb{C} \backslash \{0\}$. If both function $h(z) = z + \sum_{m=2}^{\infty} \rho_m z^m$ and its inverse map $g = h^{-1}$ are in $\mathfrak{J}(\lambda, \gamma, q; \varphi)$ and $\rho_k = 0, 2 \leq k \leq m-1$, then*

$$|\rho_m| \leq \frac{|\gamma| B_1}{([m]_q - 1)\left(1 + \lambda\left([m]_q - 1\right)\right)}, \quad (B_1 > 0).$$

**Proof.** If we write
$$\Lambda(h(z)) = (1-\lambda)h(z) + \lambda z D_q h(z),$$
then
$$h \in \mathfrak{J}(\lambda, \gamma, q; \varphi) \Leftrightarrow 1 + \frac{1}{\gamma}\left(\frac{zD_q(\Lambda(h(z)))}{\Lambda(h(z))} - 1\right) \prec \varphi(z)$$
and
$$g = h^{-1} \in \mathfrak{J}(\lambda, \gamma, q; \varphi) \Leftrightarrow 1 + \frac{1}{\gamma}\left(\frac{wD_q(\Lambda(g(w)))}{\Lambda(g(w))} - 1\right) \prec \varphi(w).$$

We notice that
$$a_m = 1 + \lambda\left([m]_q - 1\right)\rho_n$$
for
$$\Lambda(h(z)) = z + \sum_{m=2}^{\infty} a_m z^m.$$

Now, using the Faber polynomial expansion (8) for the power series $\mathfrak{J}(\lambda, \gamma, q; \varphi)$ yields:
$$1 + \frac{1}{\gamma}\left(\frac{zD_q(\Lambda(h(z)))}{\Lambda(h(z))} - 1\right) = 1 - \frac{1}{\gamma}\sum_{m=2}^{\infty}[R_{m-1}(a_2, a_3, \ldots a_m)]z^{m-1}, \qquad (10)$$

and for the inverse map $g = h^{-1}$, obviously, we have
$$1 + \frac{1}{\gamma}\left(\frac{wD_q(\Lambda(h(w)))}{\Lambda(h(w))} - 1\right) = 1 - \frac{1}{\gamma}\sum_{m=2}^{\infty} R_{m-1}(b_2, b_3, \ldots b_m)w^{m-1} \qquad (11)$$

where
$$b_m = 1 + \lambda\left([m]_q - 1\right)\tau_n = \frac{1}{m}R^m_{m-1}(a_2, a_3, \ldots, a_m).$$

By the definition of subordination, there exist two Schwarz functions
$$u(z) = \sum_{m=1}^{\infty} c_m z^m$$
and
$$v(w) = \sum_{m=1}^{\infty} d_m w^m,$$

Additionally, we have
$$\varphi(u(z)) = 1 - B_1 \sum_{m=1}^{\infty} R_m^{-1}(c_1, -c_2, \ldots (-1)^{m+1} c_m, B_1, B_2, \ldots B_m)z^m \qquad (12)$$
and
$$\varphi(v(w)) = 1 - B_1 \sum_{m=1}^{\infty} R_m^{-1}(d_1, -d_2, \ldots, (-1)^{m+1} d_m, B_1, B_2, \ldots B_m)w^m. \qquad (13)$$

In general (e.g., see [28]), the coefficients $R_m^p = R_m^p(k_1, k_2, \ldots, k_m, B_1, B_2, \ldots B_m)$ are given by

$$\begin{aligned}
R_m^p &= \frac{p!}{(p-m)!(m)!}k_1^m \frac{B_m}{B_1} + \frac{p!}{(p-m+1)!(m-2)!}k_1^{m-2}k_2 \frac{B_{m-1}}{B_1} \\
&+ \frac{p!}{(p-m+2)!(m-4)!}k_1^{m-3}k_3\left(\frac{B_{m-2}}{B_1}\right) \\
&+ \frac{p!}{(p-m+3)!(m-4)!}k_1^{m-4}\left[k_4\left(\frac{B_{m-3}}{B_1}\right) + \left(\frac{p-m+3}{2}\right)k_2^2\left(\frac{B_{m-2}}{B_1}\right)\right] \\
&+ \frac{p!}{(p-m+4)!(m-5)!}k_1^{m-5}\left[k_5\left(\frac{B_{m-4}}{B_1}\right) + (p-m+4)k_2k_3\left(\frac{B_{m-3}}{B_1}\right)\right] \\
&+ \sum_{j\geq 6} k_1^{m-j} Q_j,
\end{aligned}$$

where $Q_j$ in the variables $k_2, k_3, \ldots k_m$ is a homogeneous polynomial of degree $j$.

Evaluating the coefficients of Equations of (10) and (12) yields

$$\frac{1}{\gamma} R_{m-1}(a_2, a_3, \ldots a_m) = B_1 R_m^{-1}(c_1, -c_2, \ldots (-1)^m c_m, B_1, B_2, \ldots B_m). \tag{14}$$

However, using the facts $|c_m| \leq 1$ and $|d_m| \leq 1$ (e.g., see [3]), and under the assumption $2 \leq k \leq m-1$ and $a_k = 0$, respectively, we have

$$\frac{1}{\gamma}\left([m]_q - 1\right)a_m = \frac{1}{\gamma}\left([m]_q - 1\right)\left(1 + \lambda\left([m]_q - 1\right)\right)\rho_m = -B_1 c_{m-1}. \tag{15}$$

Evaluating the coefficients of Equations (11) and (13) yields

$$\frac{1}{\gamma} R_{m-1}(b_2, b_3, \ldots b_m) = B_1 R_m^{-1}(d_1, -d_2, \ldots (-1)^m d_m, B_1, B_2, \ldots B_m), \tag{16}$$

which by the hypothesis, we obtain

$$-\frac{1}{\gamma}\left([m]_q - 1\right)b_m = -B_1 d_{m-1}.$$

Note that, for, $2 \leq k \leq m-1$, $b_m = -a_m$ and $a_k = 0$; therefore

$$\frac{1}{\gamma}\left([m]_q - 1\right)a_m = \frac{1}{\gamma}\left([m]_q - 1\right)\left(1 + \lambda\left([m]_q - 1\right)\right)\rho_m = -B_1 d_{m-1}. \tag{17}$$

Taking the absolute values of either of Equations (15) or (17) we obtain the required bound.

This completes Theorem 1. □

For $\lambda = 0$, in Theorem 1, we obtain a new corollary, which is given below.

**Corollary 1.** *Let $\gamma \in \mathbb{C}\setminus\{0\}$. If both function $h(z)$ and its inverse map $g = h^{-1}$ are in $\mathfrak{J}(0, \gamma, q; \varphi)$ and $\rho_k = 0$, $2 \leq k \leq m-1$, then*

$$|\rho_m| \leq \frac{|\gamma| B_1}{[m]_q - 1}, \quad B_1 > 0.$$

For $\lambda = 1$, in Theorem 1, we obtain a new corollary, which is given below.

**Corollary 2.** Let $\gamma \in \mathbb{C}\setminus\{0\}$. If both function $h(z)$ and its inverse map $g = h^{-1}$ are in $\mathfrak{J}(1,\gamma,q;\varphi)$ and $\rho_k = 0, 2 \leq k \leq m-1$, then

$$|\rho_m| \leq \frac{|\gamma|B_1}{[m]_q\left([m]_q - 1\right)}, \quad B_1 > 0.$$

For $q \to 1-$ in Theorem 1, we obtain a known corollary that was proven in [28].

**Corollary 3** ([28]). Let $0 \leq \lambda \leq 1, \gamma \in \mathbb{C}\setminus\{0\}$. If both function $h(z)$ and its inverse map $g = h^{-1}$ are in $\mathfrak{J}(\lambda,\gamma;\varphi)$ and $\rho_k = 0, 2 \leq k \leq m-1$, then

$$|\rho_m| \leq \frac{|\gamma|B_1}{(m-1)(1+\lambda(m-1))}, \quad B_1 > 0.$$

For $\lambda = 0$, and $q \to 1-$ in Theorem 1, we obtain a known corollary that was proven in [28].

**Corollary 4** ([28]). Let $0 \leq \lambda \leq 1, \gamma \in \mathbb{C}\setminus\{0\}$. If both function $h(z)$ and its inverse map $g = h^{-1}$ are in $\mathfrak{J}(\gamma;\varphi)$ and $\rho_k = 0, 2 \leq k \leq m-1$, then

$$|\rho_m| \leq \frac{|\gamma|B_1}{m-1}, \quad B_1 > 0.$$

**Theorem 2.** Let $0 \leq \lambda \leq 1, \gamma \in \mathbb{C}\setminus\{0\}$. If both function $h(z) = z + \sum_{m=2}^{\infty} \rho_m z^m$ and its inverse map $g = h^{-1}$ are in $\mathfrak{J}(\lambda,\gamma,q;\varphi)$, then

$$|\rho_2| \leq \begin{cases} \sqrt{\dfrac{|\gamma|B_1}{\left\{\left([3]_q - 1\right)\left(1+\lambda\left([3]_q - 1\right)\right) - \left([2]_q - 1\right)\left(1+\lambda\left([2]_q - 1\right)\right)^2\right\}}} & \text{if } B_1 \geq |B_2| \\ \sqrt{\dfrac{|\gamma|B_2}{\left\{\left([3]_q - 1\right)\left(1+\lambda\left([3]_q - 1\right)\right) - \left([2]_q - 1\right)\left(1+\lambda\left([2]_q - 1\right)\right)^2\right\}}} & \text{if } B_1 < |B_2| \end{cases}$$

and

$$\left|\rho_3 - \rho_2^2\right| \leq \begin{cases} \dfrac{|\gamma||B_1|}{\left([3]_q - 1\right)\left(1+\lambda\left([3]_q - 1\right)\right)} & \text{if } B_1 \geq |B_2| \\ \dfrac{|\gamma||B_2|}{\left([3]_q - 1\right)\left(1+\lambda\left([3]_q - 1\right)\right)} & \text{if } B_1 < |B_2| \end{cases}$$

**Proof.** For $m = 2$, Equations (14) and (16), respectively, yield

$$\rho_2 = \frac{\gamma B_1 c_1}{\left([2]_q - 1\right)\left(1+\lambda\left([2]_q - 1\right)\right)} \quad \text{and} \quad \rho_2 = \frac{-\gamma B_1 d_1}{\left([2]_q - 1\right)\left(1+\lambda\left([2]_q - 1\right)\right)}. \quad (18)$$

If we take the absolute values of any of these two equations, and apply $|c_m| \leq 1$ and $|d_m| \leq 1$ (e.g., see Duren [3]), we obtain

$$|\rho_2| \leq \frac{|\gamma B_1|}{\left([2]_q - 1\right)\left(1+\lambda\left([2]_q - 1\right)\right)}.$$

For $m = 3$, Equations (14) and (16), respectively, yield

$$\frac{1}{\gamma}\left(\begin{array}{c} \left([3]_q - 1\right)\left(1+\lambda\left([3]_q - 1\right)\right)\rho_3 \\ -\left([2]_q - 1\right)\left(1+\lambda\left([2]_q - 1\right)\right)^2 \rho_2^2 \end{array}\right) = B_1 c_2 + B_2 c_1^2 \quad (19)$$

93

and

$$\frac{1}{\gamma}\left(\begin{array}{c}-\left([3]_q-1\right)\left(1+\lambda\left([3]_q-1\right)\right)\rho_3\\+\left\{\begin{array}{c}2\left([3]_q-1\right)\left(1+\lambda\left([3]_q-1\right)\right)\\-\left([2]_q-1\right)\left(1+\lambda\left([2]_q-1\right)\right)^2\end{array}\right\}\rho_2^2\end{array}\right)=B_1d_2+B_2d_1^2. \quad (20)$$

By combining the two equations mentioned above and finding $|\rho_2|$, we arrive at

$$\rho_2^2=\frac{\gamma(B_1c_2+B_2c_1^2+B_1d_2+B_2d_1^2)}{2\left\{\left([3]_q-1\right)\left(1+\lambda\left([3]_q-1\right)\right)-\left([2]_q-1\right)\left(1+\lambda\left([2]_q-1\right)\right)^2\right\}}.$$

Or

$$|\rho_2|^2\leq\frac{|\gamma|B_1\left(\left|c_2+\frac{B_2}{B_1}c_1^2\right|+\left|d_2+\frac{B_2}{B_1}d_1^2\right|\right)}{2\left\{\left([3]_q-1\right)\left(1+\lambda\left([3]_q-1\right)\right)-\left([2]_q-1\right)\left(1+\lambda\left([2]_q-1\right)\right)^2\right\}}. \quad (21)$$

If $B_2\leq 0$, and $\delta=\frac{B_2}{B_1}$, then by using Lemma 2 for (21), we obtain

$$|\rho_2|^2\leq\frac{|\gamma|B_1\left[1-\left(\frac{B_1+B_2}{B_1}\right)|c_1|^2\right]+\left[1-\left(\frac{B_1+B_2}{B_1}\right)|d_1|^2\right]}{2\left\{\left([3]_q-1\right)\left(1+\lambda\left([3]_q-1\right)\right)-\left([2]_q-1\right)\left(1+\lambda\left([2]_q-1\right)\right)^2\right\}}. \quad (22)$$

If $B_1+B_2>0$, then (22) yields

$$|\rho_2|\leq\sqrt{\frac{|\gamma|B_1}{\left\{\left([3]_q-1\right)\left(1+\lambda\left([3]_q-1\right)\right)-\left([2]_q-1\right)\left(1+\lambda\left([2]_q-1\right)\right)^2\right\}}}.$$

If $B_1+B_2<0$, then for the maximum values of $|c_1|=|d_1|$

$$|\rho_2|^2\leq\frac{2|\gamma|B_1\left[1-\left(\frac{B_1+B_2}{B_1}\right)\right]}{2\left\{\left([3]_q-1\right)\left(1+\lambda\left([3]_q-1\right)\right)-\left([2]_q-1\right)\left(1+\lambda\left([2]_q-1\right)\right)^2\right\}}$$

$$=\frac{-|\gamma||B_2|}{\left\{\left([3]_q-1\right)\left(1+\lambda\left([3]_q-1\right)\right)-\left([2]_q-1\right)\left(1+\lambda\left([2]_q-1\right)\right)^2\right\}}.$$

If $B_2>0$, and $\delta=\frac{B_2}{B_1}$, then by using Lemma 2 on (21), we obtain

$$|\rho_2|^2\leq\frac{|\gamma|B_1\left\{\left[1-\left(\frac{B_1-B_2}{B_1}\right)|c_1|^2\right]+\left[1-\left(\frac{B_1-B_2}{B_1}\right)|d_1|^2\right]\right\}}{2\left\{\left([3]_q-1\right)\left(1+\lambda\left([3]_q-1\right)\right)-\left([2]_q-1\right)\left(1+\lambda\left([2]_q-1\right)\right)^2\right\}}. \quad (23)$$

If $B_1-B_2>0$, then (23) yields

$$|\rho_2|\leq\sqrt{\frac{|\gamma|B_1}{\left\{\left([3]_q-1\right)\left(1+\lambda\left([3]_q-1\right)\right)-\left([2]_q-1\right)\left(1+\lambda\left([2]_q-1\right)\right)^2\right\}}}.$$

If $B_1 - B_2 < 0$, then for the maximum values of $|c_1| = |d_1|$, we have

$$|\rho_2|^2 \leq \frac{2|\gamma|B_1\left[1 - \left(\frac{B_1+B_2}{B_1}\right)\right]}{2\left\{\left([3]_q - 1\right)\left(1 + \lambda\left([3]_q - 1\right)\right) - \left([2]_q - 1\right)\left(1 + \lambda\left([2]_q - 1\right)\right)^2\right\}}$$

$$= \frac{|\gamma||B_2|}{\left\{\left([3]_q - 1\right)\left(1 + \lambda\left([3]_q - 1\right)\right) - \left([2]_q - 1\right)\left(1 + \lambda\left([2]_q - 1\right)\right)^2\right\}}.$$

Therefore

$$|\rho_2| \leq \sqrt{\frac{|\gamma||B_2|}{\left\{\left([3]_q - 1\right)\left(1 + \lambda\left([3]_q - 1\right)\right) - \left([2]_q - 1\right)\left(1 + \lambda\left([2]_q - 1\right)\right)^2\right\}}}.$$

Now we subtract (19) and (20), and $B_1 > 0$, we have

$$\rho_3 - \rho_2^2 = \frac{\gamma B_1}{2\left([3]_q - 1\right)\left(1 + \lambda\left([3]_q - 1\right)\right)}\left\{\left(c_2 + \frac{B_2}{B_1}c_1^2\right) - \left(d_2 + \frac{B_2}{B_1}d_1^2\right)\right\}. \quad (24)$$

If we take the absolute values of the two sides of (24), we obtain

$$\left|\rho_3 - \rho_2^2\right| \leq \frac{|\gamma|B_1\left\{\left|c_2 + \frac{B_2}{B_1}c_1^2\right| + \left|d_2 + \frac{B_2}{B_1}d_1^2\right|\right\}}{2\left([3]_q - 1\right)\left(1 + \lambda\left([3]_q - 1\right)\right)}.$$

(25)

If $B_2 \leq 0$, and $\delta = \frac{B_2}{B_1}$, then by using Lemma 2 on (25), we obtain

$$\left|\rho_3 - \rho_2^2\right| \leq \frac{|\gamma|B_1\left\{\left[1 - \left(\frac{B_1+B_2}{B_1}\right)\right]|c_1|^2 + \left[1 - \left(\frac{B_1+B_2}{B_1}\right)\right]|d_1|^2\right\}}{2\left([3]_q - 1\right)\left(1 + \lambda\left([3]_q - 1\right)\right)}. \quad (26)$$

If $B_1 + B_2 > 0$, then (26) yields

$$\left|\rho_3 - \rho_2^2\right| \leq \frac{|\gamma|B_1}{\left([3]_q - 1\right)\left(1 + \lambda\left([3]_q - 1\right)\right)}.$$

If $B_1 + B_2 < 0$, then for the maximum values of $|c_1| = |d_1|$, inequality (26) yields

$$\left|\rho_3 - \rho_2^2\right| \leq \frac{2|\gamma|B_1\left[1 - \left(\frac{B_1+B_2}{B_1}\right)\right]}{2\left([3]_q - 1\right)\left(1 + \lambda\left([3]_q - 1\right)\right)}$$

$$= \frac{-|\gamma||B_2|}{\left([3]_q - 1\right)\left(1 + \lambda\left([3]_q - 1\right)\right)}.$$

If $B_2 > 0$, and $\delta = \frac{B_2}{B_1}$, then by using Lemma 2 for (25) we obtain

$$\left|\rho_3 - \rho_2^2\right| \leq \frac{|\gamma|B_1\left\{\left[1 - \left(\frac{B_1-B_2}{B_1}\right)\right]|c_1|^2 + \left[1 - \left(\frac{B_1-B_2}{B_1}\right)\right]|d_1|^2\right\}}{2\left([3]_q - 1\right)\left(1 + \lambda\left([3]_q - 1\right)\right)}. \quad (27)$$

If $B_1 - B_2 > 0$, then (27) yields

$$\left|\rho_3 - \rho_2^2\right| \leq \frac{|\gamma|B_1}{\left([3]_q - 1\right)\left(1 + \lambda\left([3]_q - 1\right)\right)}.$$

If $B_1 - B_2 < 0$, then for the maximum values of $|c_1| = |d_1|$, the inequality (27) yields

$$\left|\rho_3 - \rho_2^2\right| \leq \frac{2|\gamma|B_1\left[1 - \left(\frac{B_1+B_2}{B_1}\right)\right]}{2\left([3]_q - 1\right)\left(1 + \lambda\left([3]_q - 1\right)\right)}$$

$$= \frac{|\gamma||B_2|}{\left([3]_q - 1\right)\left(1 + \lambda\left([3]_q - 1\right)\right)}.$$

This concludes the proof of Theorem 2. □

Taking $\lambda = 0$ in Theorem 2, we obtain a new corollary.

**Corollary 5.** *Let $0 \leq \lambda \leq 1, \gamma \in \mathbb{C}\setminus\{0\}$. If both function $h(z) = z + \sum\limits_{m=2}^{\infty} \rho_m z^m$ and its inverse map $g = h^{-1}$ are in $\mathfrak{J}(\gamma, q; \varphi)$, then*

$$|\rho_2| \leq \left\{ \begin{array}{ll} \sqrt{\frac{|\gamma||B_1|}{[3]_q - [2]_q}} & \text{if } B_1 \geq |B_2| \\ \sqrt{\frac{|\gamma||B_2|}{[3]_q - [2]_q}} & \text{if } B_1 < |B_2| \end{array} \right\}$$

and

$$\left|\rho_3 - \rho_2^2\right| \leq \left\{ \begin{array}{ll} \frac{|\gamma||B_1|}{[3]_q - 1} & \text{if } B_1 \geq |B_2| \\ \frac{|\gamma||B_2|}{[3]_q - 1} & \text{if } B_1 < |B_2| \end{array} \right\}.$$

Taking $\lambda = 1$ in Theorem 2, we obtain the following new corollary.

**Corollary 6.** *Let $0 \leq \lambda \leq 1, \gamma \in \mathbb{C}\setminus\{0\}$. If both function $h(z) = z + \sum\limits_{m=2}^{\infty} \rho_m z^m$ and its inverse map $g = h^{-1}$ are in $\mathfrak{J}(1, \gamma, q; \varphi)$, then*

$$|\rho_2| \leq \left\{ \begin{array}{ll} \sqrt{\frac{|\gamma|B_1}{\left\{\left([3]_q - 1\right)[3]_q - \left([2]_q - 1\right)[2]_q^2\right\}}} & \text{if } B_1 \geq |B_2| \\ \sqrt{\frac{|\gamma||B_2|}{\left\{[3]_q\left([3]_q - 1\right) - \left([2]_q - 1\right)[2]_q^2\right\}}} & \text{if } B_1 < |B_2| \end{array} \right\}$$

and

$$\left|\rho_3 - \rho_2^2\right| \leq \left\{ \begin{array}{ll} \frac{|\gamma|B_1}{[3]_q\left([3]_q - 1\right)} & \text{if } B_1 \geq |B_2| \\ \frac{|\gamma||B_2|}{[3]_q\left([3]_q - 1\right)} & \text{if } B_1 < |B_2| \end{array} \right\}.$$

Taking $q \to 1-$ in Theorem 2, we obtain the known corollary proved in [28].

**Corollary 7.** Let $0 \leq \lambda \leq 1, \gamma \in \mathbb{C}\setminus\{0\}$. If both function $h(z) = z + \sum_{m=2}^{\infty} \rho_m z^m$ and its inverse map $g = h^{-1}$ are in $\mathfrak{J}(\lambda, \gamma; \varphi)$, then

$$|\rho_3| \leq \left\{ \begin{array}{ll} \sqrt{\frac{|\gamma|B_1}{2(1+2\lambda)-(1+\lambda)^2}} & \text{if } B_1 \geq |B_2| \\ \sqrt{\frac{|\gamma||B_2|}{2(1+2\lambda)-(1+\lambda)^2}} & \text{if } B_1 < |B_2| \end{array} \right\}$$

and

$$\left|\rho_3 - \rho_2^2\right| \leq \left\{ \begin{array}{ll} \frac{|\gamma|B_1}{2(1+2\lambda)} & \text{if } B_1 \geq |B_2| \\ \frac{|\gamma||B_2|}{2(1+2\lambda)} & \text{if } B_1 < |B_2| \end{array} \right\}.$$

## 4. Applications

Kanas and Raducanu [21] defined the Ruscheweyh $q$-differential operator as follows: For $f \in \mathcal{A}$,

$$\mathcal{R}_q^\delta h(z) = h(z) * F_{q,\delta+1}(z) \qquad (\delta > -1, z \in E) \qquad (28)$$

where

$$F_{q,\delta+1}(z) = z + \sum_{m=2}^{\infty} \frac{F_q(m+\delta)}{[m-1]!\Gamma_q(1+\delta)} z^m = z + \sum_{m=2}^{\infty} \frac{[\delta+1]_{m-1}}{[m-1]!} z^m. \qquad (29)$$

We note that

$$\lim_{q \to 1^-} F_{q,\delta+1}(z) = \frac{z}{(1-z)^{\delta+1}}, \qquad \lim_{q \to 1^-} \mathcal{R}_q^\delta h(z) = h(z) * \frac{z}{(1-z)^{\delta+1}}.$$

Making use of (28) and (29), we have

$$\mathcal{R}_q^\delta h(z) = z + \sum_{m=2}^{\infty} \frac{F_q(m+\delta)}{[m-1]!\Gamma_q(1+\delta)} a_m z^m = z + \sum_{m=2}^{\infty} \psi_m a_m z^m \qquad (z \in E), \qquad (30)$$

where $F_q$ is the $q$-generalized Pochhammer symbol defined in (6) and

$$\psi_m = \frac{F_q(m+\delta)}{[m-1]_q!\Gamma_q(1+\delta)}. \qquad (31)$$

From (30), we note that

$$\begin{array}{rcl}
\mathcal{R}_q^0 h(z) & = & h(z), \\
\mathcal{R}_q^1 h(z) & = & zD_q h(z), \\
\mathcal{R}_q^\delta h(z) & = & \dfrac{zD_q^\delta(z^{\delta-1}h(z))}{[\delta]_q!} \quad (\delta \in \mathbb{N}).
\end{array}$$

We also have

$$D_q(\mathcal{R}_q^\delta h(z)) = 1 + \sum_{m=2}^{\infty} [m]_q \psi_m a_m z^{m-1}. \qquad (32)$$

**Remark 5.** When $q \to 1-$, then the Ruscheweyh $q$-differential operator reduces to the differential operator defined by Ruscheweyh [33].

**Definition 5.** Let $h$ be of the form (1) and $h \in \mathfrak{J}(\lambda, \gamma, \psi, q; \varphi)$ if

$$1 + \frac{1}{\gamma}\left(\frac{zD_q\left(\mathcal{R}_q^\delta h(z)\right) + \lambda z^2 D_q^2\left(\mathcal{R}_q^\delta h(z)\right)}{(1-\lambda)\mathcal{R}_q^\delta h(z) + \lambda z D_q\left(\mathcal{R}_q^\delta h(z)\right)} - 1\right) \prec \varphi(z)$$

and
$$1+\frac{1}{\gamma}\left(\frac{zD_q\left(\mathcal{R}_q^\delta g(z)\right)+\lambda w^2 D_q^2\left(\mathcal{R}_q^\delta g(w)\right)}{(1-\lambda)\left(\mathcal{R}_q^\delta g(w)\right)+\lambda w D_q\left(\mathcal{R}_q^\delta g(w)\right)}-1\right)\prec\varphi(w),$$

where $0\leq\lambda\leq 1, \gamma\in\mathbb{C}\setminus\{0\}, z,w\in E$ and $g=h^{-1}$.

**Theorem 3.** *Let $0\leq\lambda\leq 1, \gamma\in\mathbb{C}\setminus\{0\}$. If both function $h(z)=z+\sum\limits_{m=2}^{\infty}\rho_m z^m$ and its inverse map $g=h^{-1}$ are in $\mathfrak{J}(\lambda,\gamma,\psi,q;\varphi)$ and $\rho_k=0, 2\leq k\leq m-1$, then*

$$|\rho_m|\leq\frac{|\gamma|B_1}{\psi_m([m]_q-1)\left(1+\lambda\left([m]_q-1\right)\right)}.$$

**Proof.** If we write

$$\Lambda(h(z))=(1-\lambda)\mathcal{R}_q^\delta h(z)+\lambda z D_q\left(\mathcal{R}_q^\delta h(z)\right),$$

then

$$h\in\mathfrak{J}(\lambda,\gamma,\psi,q;\varphi)\Leftrightarrow 1+\frac{1}{\gamma}\left(\frac{zD_q\left(\Lambda\left(\mathcal{R}_q^\delta h(z)\right)\right)}{\Lambda\left(\mathcal{R}_q^\delta h(z)\right)}-1\right)\prec\varphi(z)$$

and

$$g=h^{-1}\in\mathfrak{J}(\lambda,\gamma,\psi,q;\varphi)\Leftrightarrow 1+\frac{1}{\gamma}\left(\frac{wD_q\left(\Lambda\mathcal{R}_q^\delta g(w)\right)}{\Lambda(g(w))}-1\right)\prec\varphi(w).$$

We see that
$$a_m=\psi_m\left(1+\lambda\left([m]_q-1\right)\right)$$

for
$$\Lambda(h(z))=z+\sum_{m=2}^{\infty}a_m z^m.$$

Now, an application of Faber polynomial expansion to the power series $\mathfrak{J}(\lambda,\gamma,\psi,q;\varphi)$ yields:

$$1+\frac{1}{\gamma}\left(\frac{zD_q(\Lambda(h(z)))}{\Lambda(h(z))}-1\right)=1-\frac{1}{\gamma}\sum_{m=2}^{\infty}[R_{m-1}(a_2,a_3,\ldots a_m)]z^{m-1},$$

After that, by using the similar method of Theorem 1, we can obtain Theorem 3. □

**Theorem 4.** *Let $0\leq\lambda\leq 1, \gamma\in\mathbb{C}\setminus\{0\}$. If both function $h(z)=z+\sum\limits_{m=2}^{\infty}\rho_m z^m$ and its inverse map $g=h^{-1}$ are in $\mathfrak{J}(\lambda,\gamma,\psi,q;\varphi)$, then*

$$|\rho_2|\leq\left\{\begin{array}{ll}\sqrt{\dfrac{|\gamma|B_1}{\left\{([3]_q-1)\left(1+\lambda([3]_q-1)\right)\psi_3-([2]_q-1)\left(1+\lambda([2]_q-1)\right)^2\psi_2^2\right\}}} & \text{if } B_1\geq|B_2|\\[2ex]\sqrt{\dfrac{|\gamma|B_2}{\left\{([3]_q-1)\left(1+\lambda([3]_q-1)\right)\psi_3-([2]_q-1)\left(1+\lambda([2]_q-1)\right)^2\psi_2^2\right\}}} & \text{if } B_1<|B_2|\end{array}\right\}$$

and

$$\left|\rho_3-\rho_2^2\right|\leq\left\{\begin{array}{ll}\dfrac{|\gamma|B_1}{([3]_q-1)\left(1+\lambda([3]_q-1)\right)\psi_3} & \text{if } B_1\geq|B_2|\\[2ex]\dfrac{|\gamma|B_2}{([3]_q-1)\left(1+\lambda([3]_q-1)\right)v} & \text{if } B_1<|B_2|\end{array}\right\}.$$

**Proof.** For $m = 2$, Equations (14) and (16), respectively, yield

$$\rho_2 = \frac{\gamma B_1 c_1}{\psi_2\left([2]_q - 1\right)\left(1 + \lambda\left([2]_q - 1\right)\right)} \text{ and } \rho_2 = \frac{-B_1 d_1}{\psi_2\left([2]_q - 1\right)\left(1 + \lambda\left([2]_q - 1\right)\right)}.$$

If we take the absolute values of any of these two equations, and apply $|c_m| \leq 1$ and $|d_m| \leq 1$ (e.g., see Duren [3]), we obtain

$$|\rho_2| \leq \frac{|\gamma B_1|}{\psi_2\left([2]_q - 1\right)\left(1 + \lambda\left([2]_q - 1\right)\right)}.$$

For $m = 3$, Equations (14) and (16), respectively, yield

$$\frac{1}{\gamma}\left(\begin{array}{l}\left([3]_q - 1\right)\left(1 + \lambda\left([3]_q - 1\right)\right)\psi_3 \rho_3 \\ -\left([2]_q - 1\right)\left(1 + \lambda\left([2]_q - 1\right)\right)^2 \psi_2^2 \rho_2^2\end{array}\right) = B_1 c_2 + B_2 c_1^2$$

and

$$\frac{1}{\gamma}\left(\begin{array}{l}-\left([3]_q - 1\right)\left(1 + \lambda\left([3]_q - 1\right)\right)\psi_3 \rho_3 \\ +\left\{\begin{array}{l}2\left([3]_q - 1\right)\left(1 + \lambda\left([3]_q - 1\right)\right)\psi_3 \\ -\left([2]_q - 1\right)\left(1 + \lambda\left([2]_q - 1\right)\right)^2 \psi_2^2\end{array}\right\}\rho_2^2\end{array}\right) = B_1 d_2 + B_2 d_1^2.$$

By using the similar method of Theorem 2, we can obtain the required result of Theorem 4. □

## 5. Conclusions

In order to introduce a new class of generalized bi-subordinate functions of complex order $\gamma$ in the open unit disk $E$, we used the idea of convolution and $q$-calculus in the current work. We produced estimates for the general coefficients in their Taylor–Maclaurin series expansions in the open unit disk $E$ for functions that belong to the class of analytic and bi-univalent functions. Our approach is mostly based on the Faber polynomial expansion technique. In addition, we listed some corollaries and applications of our primary findings.

The application of the idea of subordination and the Faber polynomial technique for producing findings involving the newly defined operators can be identified when additional research proposals are produced. Additionally, the method that has been presented in this paper might also apply to define a number of new subclasses of meromorphic, multivalent, and harmonic functions and can be investigated for a number of new properties of these classes. The only innovation in the types of studies that can be conducted in these classes will come from the researchers themselves and how the findings presented here motivate them.

**Author Contributions:** Both authors contributed equally to the writing of this paper. All authors have read and agreed to the published version of the manuscript.

**Funding:** The authors extend their appreciation to the Deanship of Scientific Research at Imam Mohammad Ibn Saud Islamic University for funding this work through Research Group no. RG-21-09-19.

**Data Availability Statement:** No data were used to support this study.

**Conflicts of Interest:** The authors declare no conflict of interest.

## References

1. Ma, W.C.; Minda, D. A unified treatment of some special classes of univalent functions. In *Proceedings of the Conference on Complex Analysis, Tianjin, China, 1 October 1992*; International Press: Tianjin, China, 1992; pp. 157–169.
2. Ravichandran, V.; Polatoglu, Y.; Bolcal, M.; En, A.S. Certain subclasses of starlike and convex functions of complex order. *Hacet. J. Math. Stat.* **2005**, *34*, 9–15.
3. Duren, P.L. Univalent functions. *Grundlehren der Mathematischen Wissenschaften*; Springer: New York, NY, USA, 1983; Volume 259.
4. Lewin, M. On a coefficient problem for bi-univalent functions. *Proc. Am. Math. Soc.* **1967**, *18*, 63–68. [CrossRef]
5. Styer, D.; Wright, D.J. Results on bi-univalent functions. *Proc. Am. Math. Soc.* **1981**, *82*, 243–248. [CrossRef]
6. Brannan, D.A.; Cluni, J. Aspects of contemporary complex analysis. In *Deterministic and Stochastic Scheduling: Proceedings of the NATO Advanced Study and Research Institute on Theoretical Approaches to Scheduling Problems, Durham, UK, 6–17 July 1981*; Academic Press: New York, NY, USA, 1981.
7. Srivastava, H.M.; Mishra, A.K.; Gochhayat, P. Certain subclasses of analytic and bi-univalent functions. *Appl. Math. Lett.* **2010**, *23*, 1188–1192. [CrossRef]
8. Srivastava, H.M.; Gaboury, S.; Ghanim, F. Coefficient estimates for some general subclasses of analytic and bi-univalent functions. *Afr. Mat.* **2017**, *28*, 693–706. [CrossRef]
9. Alb Lupas, A.; El-Deeb, S.M. Subclasses of bi-univalent functions connected with Integral operator based upon Lucas polynomial. *Symmetry* **2022**, *14*, 622. [CrossRef]
10. Oros, G.I.; Cotirla, L.I. Coefficient estimates and the Fekete-Szego problem for new classes of $m$-fold symmetric bi-univalentfunctions. *Mathematics* **2022**, *10*, 129. [CrossRef]
11. Hamidi, S.G.; Jahangiri, J.M. Faber polynomials coefficient estimates for analytic bi-close-to-convex functions. *C. R. Acad. Sci. Paris Ser. I* **2014**, *352*, 17–20. [CrossRef]
12. Hamidi, S.G.; Jahangiri, J.M. Faber polynomial coefficient estimates for bi-univalent functions defined by subordinations. *Bull. Iran. Math. Soc.* **2015**, *41*, 1103–1119.
13. Faber, G. Uber polynomische Entwickelungen. *Math. Ann.* **1903**, *57*, 1569–1573. [CrossRef]
14. Gong, S. *The Bieberbach Conjecture*; Translated from the 1989 Chinese Original and Revised by the Author, AMS/IP Studies in Advanced Mathematics, 12, MR1699322 (2000, 30029); American Mathematical Society: Providence, RI, USA, 1999.
15. Bulut, S. Faber polynomial coefficient estimates for certain subclasses of meromorphic bi-univalent functions. *C. R. Acad. Sci. Paris Ser. I* **2015**, *353*, 113–116. [CrossRef]
16. Hamidi, S.G.; Jahangiri, J.M. Faber polynomial coefficients of bi-subordinate functions. *C. R. Acad. Sci. Paris Ser. I* **2016**, *354*, 365–370. [CrossRef]
17. Altinkaya, S.; Yalcin, S. Faber polynomial coefficient bounds for a subclass of bi-univalent functions. *C. R. Acad. Sci. Paris Ser. I* **2015**, *353*, 1075–1080. [CrossRef]
18. Jackson, F.H. On $q$-functions and a certain difference operator. *Earth Environ. Sci. Tran. R. Soc. Edinb.* **1909**, *46*, 253–281. [CrossRef]
19. Ismail, M.E.H.; Merkes, E.; Styer, D. A generalization of starlike functions. *Complex Var. Theory Appl.* **1990**, *14*, 77–84. [CrossRef]
20. Aldweby, H.; Darus, M. Some subordination results on $q$-analogue of Ruscheweyh differential operator. *Abst. Appl. Anal.* **2014**, *2014*, 958563. [CrossRef]
21. Kanas, S.; Raducanu, D. Some class of analytic functions related to conic domains. *Math. Slovaca* **2014**, *64*, 1183–1196. [CrossRef]
22. Mahmood, S.; Sokol, J. New subclass of analytic functions in conical domain associated with rusacheweyh $q$-differential operator. *Results Math.* **2017**, *71*, 1–13. [CrossRef]
23. Huang, C.; Wang, J.; Chen, X.; Cao, J. Bifurcations in a fractional-order BAM neural network with four different delays. *Neural Netw.* **2021**, *141*, 344–354. [CrossRef]
24. Xu, C.; Mu, D.; Liu, Z.; Pang, Y.; Liao, M.; Aouiti, C. New insight into bifurcation of fractional-order 4D neural networks incorporating two different time delays. *Commun. Nonlinear Sci. Numer. Simul.* **2023**, *118*, 107043. [CrossRef]
25. Huang, C.; Liu, H.; Shi, X.; Chen, X.; Xiao, M.; Wang, Z.; Cao, J. Bifurcations in a fractional-order neural network with multiple leakage delays. *Neural Netw.* **2020**, *131*, 115–126. [CrossRef] [PubMed]
26. Xua, C.; Rahmanc, M.U.; Baleanu, D. On fractional-order symmetric oscillator with offset-boosting control. *Nonlinear Anal. Model Control* **2022**, *27*, 994–1008. [CrossRef]
27. Deniz, E. Certain subclasses of bi-univalent functions satisfying subordinate conditions. *J. Class. Anal.* **2013**, *2*, 49–60. [CrossRef]
28. Deniz, E.; Jahangiri, J.M.; Hamidi, S.G.; Kina, S.K. Faber polynomial coefficients for generalized bi-subordinate functions of complex order. *J. Math. Inequal.* **2018**, *12*, 645–653. [CrossRef]
29. Airault, H.; Bouali, H. Differential calculus on the Faber polynomials. *Bull. Sci. Math.* **2006**, *130*, 179–222. [CrossRef]
30. Bouali, A. Faber polynomials. Cayley-Hamilton equation and Newton symmetric functions. *Bull. Sci. Math.* **2006**, *130*, 49–70. [CrossRef]
31. Airault, H.; Ren, J. An algebra of differential operators and generating functions on the set of univalent functions. *Bull. Sci. Math.* **2002**, *126*, 343–367. [CrossRef]

32. Airault, H. Symmetric sums associated to the factorizations of Grunsky coefficients. In *Groups and Symmetries: From Neolithic Scots to John McKay*; CRM Proceedings and Lecture Notes; American Mathematical Society: Providence, RI, USA, 2009.
33. Ruscheweyh, S.T. New criteria for univalent functions. *Proc. Am. Math. Soc.* **1975**, *49*, 109–115. [CrossRef]

**Disclaimer/Publisher's Note:** The statements, opinions and data contained in all publications are solely those of the individual author(s) and contributor(s) and not of MDPI and/or the editor(s). MDPI and/or the editor(s) disclaim responsibility for any injury to people or property resulting from any ideas, methods, instructions or products referred to in the content.

Article

# Fekete–Szegö Problem and Second Hankel Determinant for a Class of Bi-Univalent Functions Involving Euler Polynomials

Sadia Riaz [1], Timilehin Gideon Shaba [2], Qin Xin [3], Fairouz Tchier [4], Bilal Khan [5,*] and Sarfraz Nawaz Malik [6,*]

[1] Department of Mathematics, National University of Modern Languages, Islamabad 44000, Pakistan; sadia.riaz@numl.edu.pk
[2] Department of Mathematics, Landmark University, Omu-Aran 251103, Nigeria; shabatimilehin@gmail.com or shaba.timilehin@lmu.edu.ng
[3] Faculty of Science and Technology, University of the Faroe Islands, Vestarabryggja 15, FO 100 Torshavn, Faroe Islands, Denmark; qinx@setur.fo
[4] Mathematics Department, College of Science, King Saud University, P.O. Box 22452, Riyadh 11495, Saudi Arabia; ftchier@ksu.edu.sa
[5] School of Mathematical Sciences and Shanghai Key Laboratory of PMMP, East China Normal University, 500 Dongchuan Road, Shanghai 200241, China
[6] Department of Mathematics, COMSATS University Islamabad, Wah Campus, Wah Cantt 47040, Pakistan
* Correspondence: bilalmaths789@gmail.com (B.K.); snmalik110@ciitwah.edu.pk or snmalik110@yahoo.com (S.N.M.)

**Abstract:** Some well-known authors have extensively used orthogonal polynomials in the framework of geometric function theory. We are motivated by the previous research that has been conducted and, in this study, we solve the Fekete–Szegö problem as well as give bound estimates for the coefficients and an upper bound estimate for the second Hankel determinant for functions in the class $\mathcal{G}_\Sigma(v,\sigma)$ of analytical and bi-univalent functions, implicating the Euler polynomials.

**Keywords:** analytic function; bi-univalent function; Fekete–Szegö problem; second Hankel determinant; Euler polynomials

## 1. Introduction

Let the collection of all functions $f$ be expressed by $\mathcal{A}$ and has the following form of series.

$$f(\xi) = \xi + \sum_{l=2}^{\infty} s_l \xi^l = \xi + s_2 \xi^2 + s_3 \xi^3 + \cdots + s_l \xi^l + \cdots, \quad s_l \in \mathbb{C}, \tag{1}$$

which are holomorphic in $\mathcal{U}$ where

$$\mathcal{U} = \{\xi \in \mathbb{C} : |\xi| < 1\}$$

in the complex plane. If a function never yields the same value twice, it is said to be univalent in $\mathcal{U}$. Mathematically

$$\xi_1 \neq \xi_2 \text{ for all points } \xi_1 \text{ and } \xi_2 \text{ in } \mathcal{U} \text{ implies } f(\xi_1) \neq f(\xi_2).$$

Let $\mathcal{S}$ represent the family of all univalent functions in $\mathcal{A}$ as well. As the families of starlike and convex functions of order $\phi$, respectively, the sets $\mathcal{S}^*(\phi)$ and $\mathcal{C}(\phi)$ are some of the significant and well-researched subclasses of $\mathcal{S}$, therefore, have been added here as follows (see [1,2]).

$$\mathcal{S}^*(\phi) = \left\{ f \in \mathcal{S} : \Re\left(\frac{\xi f'(\xi)}{f(\xi)}\right) > \phi, \ \phi \in [0,1), \ \xi \in \mathcal{U} \right\}$$

and
$$\mathcal{C}(\phi) = \left\{ f \in \mathcal{S} : \Re\left(1 + \frac{\xi f''(\xi)}{f'(\xi)}\right) > \phi, \ \phi \in [0,1), \ \xi \in \mathcal{U} \right\}.$$

**Remark 1.** *It is easy to seen that*
$$\mathcal{S}^*(0) = \mathcal{S}^* \quad \text{and} \quad \mathcal{C}(0) = \mathcal{C},$$
*where $\mathcal{S}^*$ and $\mathcal{C}$ are the well-known function classes of starlike and convex functions, respectively.*

Suppose $g$ and $f$ be analytical functions in $\mathcal{U}$. For an analytic function $w$ with
$$|\omega(\xi)| < 1 \text{ and } \omega(0) = 0 \ (\xi \in \mathcal{U}),$$
The function $f$ is considered to be subordinate to $g$ if the relation below holds, that is
$$g(\omega(\xi)) = f(\xi).$$
In addition to that, if the function $g \in \mathcal{S}$, then the following equivalency exists:
$$f(\xi) \prec g(\xi) \text{ if } g(0) = f(0)$$
and
$$f(\mathcal{U}) \subset g(\mathcal{U}).$$
For details, see [1]. The inverse function for every $f \in \mathcal{S}$, is defined by
$$\mathcal{F}(f(\xi)) = \xi, f(\mathcal{F}(w)) = w, \ \left(|w| < r_0(f), r_0(f) \geq \frac{1}{4}\right) \text{ and } (\xi, w \in \mathcal{U}),$$
where
$$\mathcal{F}(w) = w - s_2 w^2 + (2s_2^2 - s_3)w^3 + (-5s_2^3 + 5s_2 s_3 - s_4)w^4 + \cdots. \tag{2}$$

A function $f$ which is analytic is said to be bi univalent in $\mathcal{U}$ if both $f$ and $f^{-1}$ are univalent in $\mathcal{U}$. The classes of all such function is denoted by $\Sigma$.

The housebreaking research of Srivastava et al. [3] in fact, in the past decades, revitalized the examination of bi-univalent functions. Following the study of Srivastava et al. [3], numerous unique subclasses of the class $\Sigma$ were presented and similarly explored by numerous authors. The function classes $H_\Sigma(\gamma, \varepsilon, \mu.\varsigma; \alpha)$ and $H_\Sigma(\gamma, \varepsilon, \mu.\varsigma; \beta)$ as an illustration, were defined and Srivastava et al. [4] produced estimates for the Taylor–Maclaurin coefficients $|a_2|$ and $|a_3|$. Many authors were motivated by the work of Srivastava and have defined a number of other subclasses of analytic and bi-univalent functions, and for their defined functions classes different types of results were obtained. In this paper, motivated by the work of Srivastava, we define certain new classes of bi-univalent functions and obtain some remarkable results for our defined function's classes, including, for example, the initial bonds for the coefficients, the Fekete–Szegö problem and the second Hankel determinant.

The theory of special functions, originating from their numerous applications, is a very old branch of analysis. The long existing interest in them has recently grown due to their new applications and further generalizations. The contemporary intensive development of this theory touches various unexpected areas of applications and is based on the tools of numerical analysis and computer algebra system, used for analytical evolutions and graphical representations of special functions. Additionally, in Computer Science, special functions are used as activation functions, which play a significant role in this area. Particularly, orthogonal polynomials are an important and intriguing class of special functions. Many branches of the natural sciences contain them, including discrete mathematics, theta functions, continuous fractions, Eulerian series, elliptic functions, etc.; see [5,6], also [7–9].

In pure mathematics, the functions mentioned above have numerous uses. A lot of researchers have started working in a variety of fields as a result of the widespread use of these functionalities. Modern geometric function theory research focuses on the geometric features of special functions, including hypergeometric functions, Bessel functions, and certain other related functions. We refer to [10,11] and any relevant references in relation to some of the geometric characteristics of these functions. In this paper, we develop a new class of bi-univalent functions and use a particular special function, the Euler polynomial.

Using the generating function, the Eulers polynomials $\mathcal{E}_m(v)$ are frequently defined (see, e.g., [12,13]):

$$L(v,t) = \frac{2e^{tv}}{e^t + 1} = \sum_{m=0}^{\infty} \mathcal{E}_m(v) \frac{t^m}{m!}, \quad |t| < \pi \qquad (3)$$

An explicit formula for $\mathcal{E}_m(v)$ is given by

$$\mathcal{E}_n(v) = \sum_{m=0}^{n} \frac{1}{2^m} \sum_{k=0}^{m} (-1)^k \binom{m}{k} (v+k)^n$$

Now $\mathcal{E}_m(v)$ in terms of $\mathcal{E}_k$ can be obtained from the equation above as:

$$\mathcal{E}_m(v) = \sum_{k=0}^{m} \binom{m}{k} \frac{\mathcal{E}_k}{2^k} \left(v - \frac{1}{2}\right)^{m-k}. \qquad (4)$$

The initial Euler polynomials are:

$$\begin{aligned}
\mathcal{E}_0(v) &= 1 \\
\mathcal{E}_1(v) &= \frac{2v-1}{2} \\
\mathcal{E}_2(v) &= v^2 - v \\
\mathcal{E}_3(v) &= \frac{4v^3 - 6v^2 + 1}{4} \\
\mathcal{E}_4(v) &= v^4 - 2v^3 + v.
\end{aligned} \qquad (5)$$

Geometric function theory continues to struggle with the subject of determining bounds on the coefficients. The size of their coefficients can have an impact on a variety of aspects of analytic functions, including univalency, rate of growth, and distortion. The Fekete–Szegö problem, Hankel determinants, and many other formulations of efficient problems include an estimate of general or $l^{th}$ coefficient bounds. The coefficient concerns discussed above were addressed by several researchers using various approaches. Here, the functional of Fekete–Szegö for a function $f(\xi) \in \mathcal{S}$ is quite significant, and is denoted by $\mathcal{L}_\beta(f) = |s_3 - \beta s_2^2|$. By giving this functional, Fekete and Szegö [14] invalidated the Littlewood and Parley's claim that the modulus of coefficients of odd functions $f \in \mathcal{S}$ are less than or equal to 1. Much attention has been paid to the functional, especially in several subfamilies of univalent functions (see [15,16]).

Pommerenke [17] investigated and defined below the $l^{th}$-Hankel determinant, denoted by $H_s(l)(s, l \in \mathcal{N} = \{1, 2, 3, \cdots\})$, for any function $f \in \mathcal{S}$ in geometric function theory:

$$H_s(l) = \begin{vmatrix} j_l & j_{l+1} & \cdots & j_{l+s-1} \\ j_{l+1} & j_{l+2} & \cdots & j_{l+s} \\ j_{l+2} & j_{l+3} & \cdots & j_{l+s+1} \\ \vdots & \vdots & \cdots & \vdots \\ j_{l+s-1} & j_{l+s} & \cdots & j_{l+2(s-1)} \end{vmatrix}$$

For certain $s$ and $l$ values,

$$H_2(1) = \begin{vmatrix} j_1 & j_2 \\ j_2 & j_3 \end{vmatrix} = |j_3 - j_2^2| \text{ and } H_2(2) = \begin{vmatrix} j_2 & j_3 \\ j_3 & j_4 \end{vmatrix} = |j_2 j_4 - j_3^2|. \tag{6}$$

We see that the determinant $|H_2(1)|$ corresponds with the $\mathcal{L}_1(f)$, implying that $\mathcal{L}_\beta(f)$ is a generalization of $|H_2(1)|$. Following that, many additional subclasses of univalent functions paid close attention to the problem of determining bounds on coefficients. Recent research in this area includes the papers in [18,19].

In this study, we define the new subclass introduced and studied in the present paper, denoted by $\mathcal{G}_\Sigma(v,\sigma)$, consisting of bi-univalent functions satisfying a certain subordination involving Eulers polynomials. We solve the Fekete–Szegö problem for functions in the class $\mathcal{G}_\Sigma(v,\sigma)$ and in the special instances, as well as provide bound estimates for the coefficients.

**Definition 1.** *For $f \in \mathcal{G}_\Sigma(v,\sigma)$, suppose the following subordination is true:*

$$(1-\sigma)\frac{\xi f'(\xi)}{f(\xi)} + \sigma\left(\frac{f'(\xi) + \xi f''(\xi)}{f'(\xi)}\right) \prec L(v,\xi) = \sum_{m=0}^{\infty} \mathcal{E}_m(v)\frac{\xi^m}{m!} \tag{7}$$

*and*

$$(1-\sigma)\frac{w\mathcal{F}'(w)}{\mathcal{F}(w)} + \sigma\left(\frac{\mathcal{F}'(w) + w\mathcal{F}''(w)}{\mathcal{F}'(w)}\right) \prec L(v,w) = \sum_{m=0}^{\infty} \mathcal{E}_m(v)\frac{w^m}{m!}, \tag{8}$$

*where $\sigma \geq 0$, $v \in (\frac{1}{2}, 1]$, $\xi, w \in \mathcal{U}$, $L(v,w)$ is given by (3), and $\mathcal{F} = f^{-1}$ is given by (2). It could be seen that both the functions $f$ and and its inverse $\mathcal{F} = f^{-1}$ are univalent in $\mathcal{U}$, so we can conclude that the function $f$ is bi-univalent belonging to the function class $\mathcal{G}_\Sigma(v,\sigma)$.*

**Remark 2.** *Setting $\sigma = 0$ in Definition 1, we have bi-starlike function class $f \in \mathcal{S}_\Sigma^*(v)$, which fulfilled the following conditions:*

$$\frac{\xi f'(\xi)}{f(\xi)} \prec L(v,\xi) = \sum_{m=0}^{\infty} \mathcal{E}_m(v)\frac{\xi^m}{m!} \tag{9}$$

*and*

$$\frac{w\mathcal{F}'(w)}{\mathcal{F}(w)} \prec L(v,w) = \sum_{m=0}^{\infty} \mathcal{E}_m(v)\frac{w^m}{m!}, \tag{10}$$

*where $\xi, w \in \mathcal{U}$, $L(v,w)$ is given by (3), and $\mathcal{F} = f^{-1}$ is given by (2).*

**Remark 3.** *Setting $\sigma = 1$ in Definition 1, we have bi-convex function class $f \in \mathcal{C}_\Sigma(v)$, which fulfilled the following conditions:*

$$\frac{f'(\xi) + \xi f''(\xi)}{f'(\xi)} \prec L(v,\xi) = \sum_{m=0}^{\infty} \mathcal{E}_m(v)\frac{\xi^m}{m!} \tag{11}$$

*and*

$$\frac{\mathcal{F}'(w) + w\mathcal{F}''(w)}{\mathcal{F}'(w)} \prec L(v,w) = \sum_{m=0}^{\infty} \mathcal{E}_m(v)\frac{w^m}{m!}, \tag{12}$$

*where $L(v,w)$ is given by (3), and $\mathcal{F} = f^{-1}$ is given by (2).*

Next, let $\mathcal{P}$ represent the class including those functions, analytic in $\mathcal{U}$, and having series form given below as:

$$\alpha(\xi) = 1 + \sum_{l=1}^{\infty} \alpha_l \xi^l, \tag{13}$$

such that
$$\Re\{\alpha(\xi)\} > 0 \quad (\forall \xi \in \mathcal{U}).$$

**Lemma 1.** *[1] Let $\alpha \in \mathcal{P}$ be given by*

$$\alpha(\xi) = 1 + \alpha_1 \xi + \alpha_2 \xi^2 + \cdots \quad (\xi \in \mathcal{U}) \tag{14}$$

*then*

$$|\alpha_l| \leq 2 \quad (l \in \{1,2,3,\cdots\}). \tag{15}$$

**Lemma 2.** *[20] Let $\alpha \in \mathcal{P}$ be given by (14), then*

$$2\alpha_2 = \alpha_1^2 + x(4 - \alpha_1^2) \tag{16}$$

*and*

$$4\alpha_3 = \alpha_1^3 + 2\alpha_1(4 - \alpha_1^2)x - \alpha_1(4 - \alpha_1^2)x^2 + 2(4 - \alpha_1^2)(1 - |x|^2)\xi \tag{17}$$

*for some $x, \xi, |x| \leq 1$, and $|\xi| \leq 1$.*

## 2. Coefficients Bounds for the Functions of Class $\mathcal{G}_\Sigma(v, \sigma)$

**Theorem 1.** *Let $f \in \mathcal{G}_\Sigma(v, \sigma)$. Then:*

$$|s_2| \leq \sqrt{\Omega_1(\sigma, v)},$$

$$|s_3| \leq \frac{(2v-1)^2}{4(1+\sigma)^2} + \frac{2v-1}{4(1+2\sigma)}$$

*and*

$$|s_4| \leq \frac{(1+4\sigma)(2v-1)^3}{12(1+2\sigma)(1+\sigma)^3} + \frac{(15+45\sigma)(2v-1)^2}{48(1+\sigma)(1+2\sigma)^2} + \frac{4v^3 - 6v^2 + 1}{72(1+2\sigma)}$$

*where*

$$\Omega_1(\sigma, v) = \frac{(2v-1)^3}{|2(\sigma+1)(2\sigma + 2(\sigma-1)v^2 - 2(3\sigma+1)v+1)|}. \tag{18}$$

**Proof.** Let $f \in \Sigma$ given by (1) be in the class $\mathcal{G}_\Sigma(v, \sigma)$. Then

$$(1-\sigma)\frac{\xi f'(\xi)}{f(\xi)} + \sigma\left(\frac{f'(\xi) + \xi f''(\xi)}{f'(\xi)}\right) = L(v, a(\xi)) \tag{19}$$

and

$$(1-\sigma)\frac{w\mathcal{F}'(w)}{\mathcal{F}(w)} + \sigma\left(\frac{\mathcal{F}'(\xi) + w\mathcal{F}''(w)}{\mathcal{F}'(w)}\right) = L(v, b(w)) \tag{20}$$

We define $\alpha, \delta \in \mathcal{P}$ as follows:

$$\alpha(\xi) = \frac{1 + a(\xi)}{1 - a(\xi)} = 1 + \alpha_1 \xi + \alpha_2 \xi^2 + \alpha_3 \xi^3 + \cdots$$

$$\Rightarrow a(\xi) = \frac{\alpha(\xi) - 1}{\alpha(\xi) + 1} \quad (\xi \in \mathcal{U}) \tag{21}$$

and

$$\delta(w) = \frac{1 + b(w)}{1 - b(w)} = 1 + \delta_1 w + \delta_2 w^2 + \delta^3 w^3 + \cdots$$

$$\Rightarrow b(w) = \frac{\delta(w) - 1}{\delta(w) + 1} \quad (w \in \mathcal{U}). \tag{22}$$

From (21) and (22), we obtain

$$a(\zeta) = \frac{\alpha_1}{2}\zeta + \left(\frac{\alpha_2}{2} - \frac{\alpha_1^2}{4}\right)\zeta^2 + \left(\frac{\alpha_3}{2} - \frac{\alpha_1\alpha_2}{2} + \frac{\alpha_1^3}{8}\right)\zeta^3 + \cdots \quad (23)$$

and

$$b(w) = \frac{\delta_1}{2}w + \left(\frac{\delta_2}{2} - \frac{\delta_1^2}{4}\right)w^2 + \left(\frac{\delta_3}{2} - \frac{\delta_1\delta_2}{2} + \frac{\delta_1^3}{8}\right)w^3 + \cdots . \quad (24)$$

Taking it from (23) and (24), we have:

$$L(v, a(\zeta)) = \mathcal{E}_0(v) + \frac{\mathcal{E}_1(v)}{2}\alpha_1\zeta + \left[\frac{\mathcal{E}_1(v)}{2}\left(\alpha_2 - \frac{\alpha_1^2}{2}\right) + \frac{\mathcal{E}_2(v)}{8}\alpha_1^2\right]\zeta^2$$
$$+ \left[\frac{\mathcal{E}_1(v)}{2}\left(\alpha_3 - \alpha_1\alpha_2 + \frac{\alpha_1^3}{4}\right) + \frac{\mathcal{E}_2(v)}{4}\alpha_1\left(\alpha_2 - \frac{\alpha_1^2}{2}\right) + \frac{\mathcal{E}_3(v)}{48}\alpha_1^3\right]\zeta^3 + \cdots \quad (25)$$

and

$$L(v, b(w)) = \mathcal{E}_0(v) + \frac{\mathcal{E}_1(v)}{2}\delta_1 w + \left[\frac{\mathcal{E}_1(v)}{2}\left(\delta_2 - \frac{\delta_1^2}{2}\right) + \frac{\mathcal{E}_2(v)}{8}\delta_1^2\right]w^2$$
$$+ \left[\frac{\mathcal{E}_1(v)}{2}\left(\delta_3 - \delta_1\delta_2 + \frac{\delta_1^3}{4}\right) + \frac{\mathcal{E}_2(v)}{4}\delta_1\left(\delta_2 - \frac{\delta_1^2}{2}\right) + \frac{\mathcal{E}_3(v)}{48}\delta_1^3\right]w^3 + \cdots . \quad (26)$$

It follows from (19), (20), (25) and (26) that we have:

$$(1+\sigma)s_2 = \frac{\mathcal{E}_1(v)}{2}\alpha_1 \quad (27)$$

$$-(1+3\sigma)s_2^2 + 2(1+2\sigma)s_3 = \frac{\mathcal{E}_1(v)}{2}\left(\alpha_2 - \frac{\alpha_1^2}{2}\right) + \frac{\mathcal{E}_2(v)}{8}\alpha_1^2 \quad (28)$$

$$(1+7\sigma)s_2^3 - 3(1+5\sigma)s_2 s_3 + 3(1+3\sigma)s_4 = \frac{\mathcal{E}_1(v)}{2}\left(\alpha_3 - \alpha_1\alpha_2 + \frac{\alpha_1^3}{4}\right)$$
$$+ \frac{\mathcal{E}_2(v)}{4}\alpha_1\left(\alpha_2 - \frac{\alpha_1^2}{2}\right) + \frac{\mathcal{E}_3(v)}{48}\alpha_1^3 \quad (29)$$

$$-(1+\sigma)s_2 = \frac{\mathcal{E}_1(v)}{2}\delta_1 \quad (30)$$

$$(3+5\sigma)s_2^2 - 2(1+2\sigma)s_3 = \frac{\mathcal{E}_1(v)}{2}\left(\delta_2 - \frac{\delta_1^2}{2}\right) + \frac{\mathcal{E}_2(v)}{8}\delta_1^2 \quad (31)$$

$$-3(1+3\sigma)s_4 + (12+30\sigma)s_2 s_3 - (10+22\sigma)s_2^3 = \frac{\mathcal{E}_1(v)}{2}\left(\delta_3 - \delta_1\delta_2 + \frac{\delta_1^3}{4}\right)$$
$$+ \frac{\mathcal{E}_2(v)}{4}\delta_1\left(\delta_2 - \frac{\delta_1^2}{2}\right) + \frac{\mathcal{E}_3(v)}{48}\delta_1^3. \quad (32)$$

Adding (27) and (30) and further simplification, we have

$$\alpha_1 = -\delta_1, \ \alpha_1^2 = \delta_1^2 \ \text{and} \ \alpha_1^3 = -\delta_1^3. \quad (33)$$

When (27) and (30) are squared and added, the following result is obtained:

$$2(1+\sigma)^2 s_2^2 = \frac{\mathcal{E}_1^2(v)(\alpha_1^2 + \delta_1^2)}{4} \qquad (34)$$

$$\Rightarrow s_2^2 = \frac{\mathcal{E}_1^2(v)(\alpha_1^2 + \delta_1^2)}{8(1+\sigma)^2}. \qquad (35)$$

Additionally, adding (28) and (31) gives

$$2(1+\sigma)s_2^2 = \frac{2\mathcal{E}_1(v)(\alpha_2 + \delta_2) + \alpha_1^2(\mathcal{E}_2(v) - 2\mathcal{E}_1(v))}{4}$$

$$8(1+\sigma)s_2^2 = 2\mathcal{E}_1(v)(\alpha_2 + \delta_2) + \alpha_1^2(\mathcal{E}_2(v) - 2\mathcal{E}_1(v)). \qquad (36)$$

Applying (33) in (34)

$$\alpha_1^2 = \frac{4(1+\sigma)^2}{\mathcal{E}_1^2(v)} s_2^2. \qquad (37)$$

In (36), replacing $\alpha_1^2$ with the following results:

$$|s_2|^2 \leq \frac{2\mathcal{E}_1^3(v)(|\alpha_2| + |\delta_2|)}{2|2(1+\sigma)\mathcal{E}_1^2(v) - (1+\sigma)^2[\mathcal{E}_2(v) - 2\mathcal{E}_1(v)]|}. \qquad (38)$$

Applying Lemma 1 and (5), we obtain:

$$|s_2| \leq \sqrt{\Omega_1(\sigma, v)}$$

where $\Omega_1(\sigma, v)$ is given by (18).

Subtracting (31) and (28) and with some computation, we have

$$s_3 = s_2^2 + \frac{\mathcal{E}_1(v)(\alpha_2 - \delta_2)}{8(1+2\sigma)} \qquad (39)$$

$$s_3 = \frac{\mathcal{E}_1^2(v)\alpha_1^2}{4(1+\sigma)^2} + \frac{\mathcal{E}_1(v)(\alpha_2 - \delta_2)}{8(1+2\sigma)} \qquad (40)$$

Applying Lemma 1 and (5), we obtain:

$$|s_3| \leq \frac{(2v-1)^2}{4(1+\sigma)^2} + \frac{2v-1}{4(1+2\sigma)} \qquad (41)$$

By removing (32) from (29), we arrive at:

$$s_4 = \frac{(1+4\sigma)\mathcal{E}_1^3(v)}{12(1+3\sigma)(1+\sigma)^3}\alpha_1^3 + \frac{(15+45\sigma)\mathcal{E}_1^2(v)(\alpha_2 - \delta_2)}{96(1+\sigma)(1+2\sigma)(1+3\sigma)}\alpha_1 + \frac{\mathcal{E}_1(v)(\alpha_3 - \delta_3)}{12(1+3\sigma)}$$
$$+ \frac{[\mathcal{E}_2(v) - 2\mathcal{E}_1(v)](\alpha_2 + \delta_2)}{24(1+3\sigma)}\alpha_1 + \frac{[6\mathcal{E}_1(v) - 6\mathcal{E}_2(v) + \mathcal{E}_3(v)]}{144(1+3\sigma)}\alpha_1^3. \qquad (42)$$

Applying Lemma 1 and (5), we obtain:

$$|s_4| \leq \frac{(1+4\sigma)(2v-1)^3}{12(1+3\sigma)(1+\sigma)^3} + \frac{(15+45\sigma)(2v-1)^2}{48(1+\sigma)(1+2\sigma)(1+3\sigma)} + \frac{4v^3 - 6v^2 + 1}{72(1+3\sigma)}.$$

□

If we put $\sigma = 0$ in Theorem 1, then we have the next corollary.

**Corollary 1.** *Let* $f \in \mathcal{S}_{\Sigma}^{*}(v)$. *Then:*

$$|s_2| \leq \sqrt{\frac{(2v-1)^3}{|2(2v^2+2v-1)|}},$$

$$|s_3| \leq \frac{v(2v-1)}{2}$$

*and*

$$|s_4| \leq \frac{(2v-1)^3}{12} + \frac{15(2v-1)^2}{48} + \frac{4v^3 - 6v^2 + 1}{72}$$

For $\sigma = 1$, we arrive at the next corollary of Theorem 1.

**Corollary 2.** *Let* $f \in \mathcal{C}_{\Sigma}(v)$. *Then:*

$$|s_2| \leq \sqrt{\frac{(2v-1)^3}{|4(3-8v)|}},$$

$$|s_3| \leq \frac{(2v-1)(6v+13)}{192},$$

*and*

$$|s_4| \leq \frac{5(2v-1)^3}{384} + \frac{5(2v-1)^2}{96} + \frac{4v^3 - 6v^2 + 1}{288}.$$

## 3. Fekete–Szegö Inequalities for the Functions of Class $\mathcal{G}_{\Sigma}(v, \sigma)$

**Theorem 2.** *Let* $f \in \mathcal{G}_{\Sigma}(v, \sigma)$. *Then, for some* $\mu \in \mathbb{R}$,

$$\left|s_3 - \mu s_2^2\right| \leq \begin{cases} 2|1-\mu|\Omega_1(\sigma, v) & \left(|1-\mu|\Omega_1(\sigma, v) \geq \frac{2v-1}{4(1+2\sigma)}\right) \\ \frac{2v-1}{2(1+2\sigma)} & \left(|1-\mu|\Omega_1(\sigma, v) < \frac{2v-1}{4(1+2\sigma)}\right), \end{cases}$$

*where* $\Omega_1(\sigma, v)$ *is given by (18).*

**Proof.** From (39), we obtain:

$$s_3 - \mu s_2^2 = s_2^2 + \frac{\mathcal{E}_1(v)(\alpha_2 - \delta_2)}{8(1+2\sigma)} - \mu s_2^2$$

Applying the popular triangular inequality, we obtain:

$$|s_3 - \mu s_2^2| \leq \frac{2v-1}{4(1+2\sigma)} + |1-\mu|\Omega_1(\sigma, v)$$

If:

$$|1-\mu|\Omega_1(\sigma, v) \geq \frac{2v-1}{4(1+2\sigma)}$$

Furthermore, we obtain

$$|s_3 - \mu s_2^2| \leq 2|1-\mu|\Omega_1(\sigma, v)$$

where

$$|1-\mu| \geq \frac{2v-1}{4(1+2\sigma)\Omega_1(\sigma, v)}$$

and if:
$$|1-\mu|\Omega_1(\sigma,v) \leq \frac{2v-1}{4(1+2\sigma)}$$

then, we obtain:
$$|s_3 - \mu s_2^2| \leq \frac{2v-1}{2(1+2\sigma)}$$

where
$$|1-\mu| \leq \frac{2v-1}{4(1+2\sigma)\Omega_1(\sigma,v)}$$

and $\Omega_1(\sigma,v)$ is given in (18). □

By putting $\sigma = 0$ in the above Theorem 2, we obtain the following result.

**Corollary 3.** *Let $f \in \mathcal{S}_\Sigma^*(v)$. Then, for some $\mu \in \mathbb{R}$,*

$$\left|a_3 - \mu a_2^2\right| \leq \begin{cases} 2|1-\mu|\Omega_1(\sigma,v) & \left(|1-\mu|\Omega_1(\sigma,v) \geq \frac{2v-1}{4}\right) \\ \frac{2v-1}{2} & \left(|1-\mu|\Omega_1(\sigma,v) \leq \frac{2v-1}{4}\right), \end{cases}$$

*where*
$$\Omega_1(v) = \frac{(2v-1)^3}{|2(2v^2+2v-1)|}. \tag{43}$$

Letting $\sigma = 1$ in Theorem 2, we can obtain the next result.

**Corollary 4.** *Let $f \in \mathcal{C}_\Sigma(v)$. Then, for some $\mu \in \mathbb{R}$,*

$$\left|a_3 - \mu a_2^2\right| \leq \begin{cases} 2|1-\mu|\Omega_1(v) & \left(|1-\mu|\Omega_1(v) \geq \frac{2v-1}{12}\right) \\ \frac{2v-1}{6} & \left(|1-\mu|\Omega_1(v) \leq \frac{2v-1}{12}\right), \end{cases}$$

*where*
$$\Omega_1(v) = \frac{(2v-1)^3}{|4(3-8v)|}. \tag{44}$$

## 4. Second Hankel Determinant for the Class $\mathcal{G}_\Sigma(v,\sigma)$

**Theorem 3.** *Let the function $f(\xi)$ be in the class $\mathcal{G}_\Sigma(v,\sigma)$. Then:*

$$H_2(2) = \left|s_2 s_4 - s_3^2\right| \leq \begin{cases} T(2,v) & (B_1 \geq 0 \text{ and } B_2 \geq 0) \\ \max\left\{\left(\frac{2v-1}{4(1+2\sigma)}\right)^2, T(2,v)\right\} & (B_1 > 0 \text{ and } B_2 < 0) \\ \left(\frac{2v-1}{4(1+2\sigma)}\right)^2 & (B_1 \leq 0 \text{ and } B_2 \leq 0) \\ \max\{T(g_0,v), T(2,v)\} & (B_1 < 0 \text{ and } B_2 > 0). \end{cases}$$

*where*
$$T(2,v) = \frac{2(1+4\sigma)\mathcal{E}_1^4(v)}{3(1+3\sigma)(1+\sigma)^4} + \frac{\mathcal{E}_1(v)\mathcal{E}_3(v)}{18(1+\sigma)(1+3\sigma)} + \frac{\mathcal{E}_1^4(v)}{(1+\sigma)^4}$$

$$T(g_0,t) = \frac{\mathcal{E}_1^2(v)}{4(1+2\sigma)^2} + \frac{9B_2^4(1+\sigma)^4}{4(1+2\sigma)^2(1+3\sigma)B_1^3} + \frac{3B_2^3(1+\sigma)^2}{4(1+2\sigma)^2(1+3\sigma)B_1^2}.$$

$$B_1 = \mathcal{E}_1(v)\bigg[24\mathcal{E}_1^3(v)(1+4\sigma)(1+2\sigma)^2 + 2(6\mathcal{E}_1(v) - 6\mathcal{E}_2(v) + \mathcal{E}_3(v))(1+\sigma)^3(1+2\sigma)^2$$
$$+ 36\mathcal{E}_1^3(v)(1+3\sigma)(1+2\sigma)^2 - 24\mathcal{E}_1(v)(1+\sigma)^3(1+2\sigma)^2 + 9\mathcal{E}_1(v)(1+\sigma)^4(1+3\sigma) - 9\mathcal{E}_1^2(v)$$
$$(1+\sigma)^2(1+3\sigma)(1+2\sigma)\bigg]r^4$$

$$B_2 = \mathcal{E}_1(v)\bigg[3(1+2\sigma)(1+3\sigma)\mathcal{E}_1^2(v) + 4\mathcal{E}_1(v)(1+\sigma)(1+2\sigma)^2 + 4(\mathcal{E}_2(v) - 2\mathcal{E}_1(v))$$
$$(1+\sigma)(1+2\sigma)^2 + 8\mathcal{E}_1(v)(1+\sigma)(1+2\sigma)^2 - 6\mathcal{E}_1(v)(1+\sigma)^2(1+3\sigma)\bigg]r^2.$$

**Proof.** From (27) and (42), we have

$$s_2 s_4 = \frac{(1+4\sigma)\mathcal{E}_1^4(v)}{24(1+3\sigma)(1+\sigma)^4}\alpha_1^4 + \frac{(15+45\sigma)\mathcal{E}_1^3(v)(\alpha_2 - \delta_2)}{192(1+\sigma)^2(1+2\sigma)(1+3\sigma)}\alpha_1^2 + \frac{\mathcal{E}_1^2(v)(\alpha_3 - \delta_3)}{24(1+\sigma)(1+3\sigma)}\alpha_1$$
$$+ \frac{\mathcal{E}_1(v)[\mathcal{E}_2(v) - 2\mathcal{E}_1(v)](\alpha_2 + \delta_2)}{48(1+\sigma)(1+3\sigma)}\alpha_1^2 + \frac{\mathcal{E}_1(v)[6\mathcal{E}_1(v) - 6\mathcal{E}_2(v) + \mathcal{E}_3(v)]}{288(1+\sigma)(1+3\sigma)}\alpha_1^4$$

With some calculations, we have

$$s_2 s_4 - s_3^2 = \frac{(1+4\sigma)\mathcal{E}_1^4(v)}{24(1+3\sigma)(1+\sigma)^4}\alpha_1^4 + \frac{\mathcal{E}_1^3(v)(\alpha_2 - \delta_2)}{64(1+\sigma)^2(1+2\sigma)}\alpha_1^2 + \frac{\mathcal{E}_1^2(v)(\alpha_3 - \delta_3)}{24(1+\sigma)(1+3\sigma)}\alpha_1$$
$$+ \frac{\mathcal{E}_1(v)[\mathcal{E}_2(v) - 2\mathcal{E}_1(v)](\alpha_2 + \delta_2)}{48(1+\sigma)(1+3\sigma)}\alpha_1^2 + \frac{\mathcal{E}_1(v)[6\mathcal{E}_1(v) - 6\mathcal{E}_2(v) + \mathcal{E}_3(v)]}{288(1+\sigma)(1+3\sigma)}\alpha_1^4$$
$$- \frac{\mathcal{E}_1^4(v)}{16(1+\sigma)^4}\alpha_1^4 - \frac{\mathcal{E}_1^2(v)(\alpha_2 - \delta_2)^2}{64(1+2\sigma)^2}$$

By using Lemma 2,

$$\alpha_2 - \delta_2 = \frac{(4 - \alpha_1^2)(x - u)}{2} \tag{45}$$

$$\alpha_2 + \delta_2 = \alpha_1^2 + \frac{(4 - \alpha_1^2)(x + u)}{2} \tag{46}$$

and

$$\alpha_3 - \delta_3 = \frac{\alpha_1^3}{2} + \frac{4 - \alpha_1^2}{2}\alpha_1(x + u) - \frac{4 - \alpha_1^2}{4}\alpha_1(x^2 + u^2)$$
$$+ \frac{4 - \alpha_1^2}{2}\Big[(1 - |x|^2\xi) - (1 - |u|^2)w\Big] \tag{47}$$

for some $x, u, \xi, w$ with $|x| \leq 1$, $|u| \leq 1$, $|\xi| \leq 1$, $|w| \leq 1$, $|\alpha_1| \in [0, 2]$ and substituting $(\alpha_2 + \delta_2)$, $(\alpha_2 - \delta_2)$ and $(\alpha_3 - \delta_3)$, and after some straightforward simplifications, we have

$$s_2s_4 - s_3^2 = \frac{(1+4\sigma)\mathcal{E}_1^4(v)}{24(1+3\sigma)(1+\sigma)^4}\alpha_1^4 + \frac{\mathcal{E}_1^3(v)(4-\alpha_1^2)(x-u)}{128(1+\sigma)^2(1+2\sigma)}\alpha_1^2 + \frac{\mathcal{E}_1^2(v)}{48(1+\sigma)(1+3\sigma)}\alpha_1^4$$
$$+ \frac{\mathcal{E}_1^2(v)(4-\alpha_1^2)(x+u)}{48(1+\sigma)(1+3\sigma)}\alpha_1^2 - \frac{\mathcal{E}_1^2(v)(4-\alpha_1^2)(x^2+u^2)}{96(1+\sigma)(1+3\sigma)}\alpha_1^2$$
$$+ \frac{\mathcal{E}_1^2(v)(4-\alpha_1^2)[(1-|x|^2\zeta)-(1-|y|^2)w]}{48(1+\sigma)(1+3\sigma)} + \frac{\mathcal{E}_1(v)[\mathcal{E}_2(v)-2\mathcal{E}_1(v)]}{48(1+\sigma)(1+3\sigma)}\alpha_1^4$$
$$+ \frac{\mathcal{E}_1(v)[\mathcal{E}_2(v)-2\mathcal{E}_1(v)](4-\alpha_1^2)(x+u)}{96(1+\sigma)(1+3\sigma)}\alpha_1^2 + \frac{\mathcal{E}_1(v)[6\mathcal{E}_1(v)-6\mathcal{E}_2(v)+\mathcal{E}_3(v)]}{288(1+\sigma)(1+3\sigma)}\alpha_1^4$$
$$- \frac{\mathcal{E}_1^4(v)}{16(1+\sigma)^4}\alpha_1^4 - \frac{\mathcal{E}_1^2(v)(4-\alpha_1^2)^2(x-u)^2}{256(1+2\sigma)^2}$$

Let $r = \alpha_1$, assume without any restriction that $r \in [0,2]$, $\eta_1 = |x| \leq 1$, $\eta_2 = |u| \leq 1$ and applying triangular inequality, we have

$$|s_2s_4 - s_3^2| \leq \left\{ \frac{(1+4\sigma)\mathcal{E}_1^4(v)}{24(1+3\sigma)(1+\sigma)^4}r^4 + \frac{\mathcal{E}_1^2(v)}{48(1+\sigma)(1+3\sigma)}r^4 + \frac{\mathcal{E}_1^2(v)(4-r^2)}{24(1+\sigma)(1+3\sigma)}r \right.$$
$$+ \frac{\mathcal{E}_1(v)[\mathcal{E}_2(v)-2\mathcal{E}_1(v)]}{48(1+\sigma)(1+3\sigma)}r^4 + \frac{\mathcal{E}_1(v)[6\mathcal{E}_1(v)-6\mathcal{E}_2(v)+\mathcal{E}_3(v)]}{288(1+\sigma)(1+3\sigma)}r^4 + \left. \frac{\mathcal{E}_1^4(v)}{16(1+\sigma)^4}r^4 \right\}$$
$$+ \left\{ \frac{\mathcal{E}_1^3(v)(4-r^2)}{128(1+\sigma)^2(1+2\sigma)}r^2 + \frac{\mathcal{E}_1^2(v)(4-r^2)}{48(1+\sigma)(1+3\sigma)}r^2 \right.$$
$$+ \left. \frac{\mathcal{E}_1(v)[\mathcal{E}_2(v)-2\mathcal{E}_1(v)](4-r^2)}{96(1+\sigma)(1+3\sigma)}r^2 \right\}(\eta_1 + \eta_2) + \left\{ \frac{\mathcal{E}_1^2(v)(4-r^2)}{96(1+\sigma)(1+3\sigma)}r^2 \right.$$
$$- \left. \frac{\mathcal{E}_1^2(v)(4-r^2)}{48(1+\sigma)(1+3\sigma)}r \right\}(\eta_1^2 + \eta_2^2) + \frac{\mathcal{E}_1^2(v)(4-\alpha_1^2)^2}{256(1+2\sigma)^2}(\eta_1 + \eta_2)^2$$

and equivalently, we have

$$|s_2s_4 - s_3^2| \leq Y_1(v,r) + Y_2(v,r)(\eta_1 + \eta_2) + Y_3(v,r)(\eta_1^2 + \eta_2^2) + Y_4(v,r)(\eta_1 + \eta_2)^2 \quad (48)$$
$$= J(\eta_1, \eta_2)$$

where

$$Y_1(v,r) = \left\{ \frac{(1+4\sigma)\mathcal{E}_1^4(v)}{24(1+3\sigma)(1+\sigma)^4}r^4 + \frac{\mathcal{E}_1^2(v)}{48(1+\sigma)(1+3\sigma)}r^4 + \frac{\mathcal{E}_1^2(v)(4-r^2)}{24(1+\sigma)(1+3\sigma)}r \right.$$
$$+ \frac{\mathcal{E}_1(v)[\mathcal{E}_2(v)-2\mathcal{E}_1(v)]}{48(1+\sigma)(1+3\sigma)}r^4 + \frac{\mathcal{E}_1(v)[6\mathcal{E}_1(v)-6\mathcal{E}_2(v)+\mathcal{E}_3(v)]}{288(1+\sigma)(1+3\sigma)}r^4$$
$$+ \left. \frac{\mathcal{E}_1^4(v)}{16(1+\sigma)^4}r^4 \right\} \geq 0$$

$$Y_2(v,r) = \left\{ \frac{\mathcal{E}_1^3(v)(4-r^2)}{128(1+\sigma)^2(1+2\sigma)}r^2 + \frac{\mathcal{E}_1^2(v)(4-r^2)}{48(1+\sigma)(1+3\sigma)}r^2 \right.$$
$$+ \left. \frac{\mathcal{E}_1(v)[\mathcal{E}_2(v)-2\mathcal{E}_1(v)](4-r^2)}{96(1+\sigma)(1+3\sigma)}r^2 \right\} \geq 0$$

$$Y_3(v,r) = \left\{ \frac{\mathcal{E}_1^2(v)(4-r^2)}{96(1+\sigma)(1+3\sigma)}r^2 - \frac{\mathcal{E}_1^2(v)(4-r^2)}{48(1+\sigma)(1+3\sigma)}r \right\} \leq 0$$

$$Y_4(v,r) = \frac{\mathcal{E}_1^2(v)(4-\alpha_1^2)^2}{256(1+2\sigma)^2} \geq 0$$

where $0 \leq r \leq 2$. We now maximize the function $J(\eta_1, \eta_2)$ in the closed square

$$\Psi = \{(\eta_1, \eta_2) : \eta_1 \in [0,1], \eta_2 \in [0,1]\} \quad for \quad r \in [0,2].$$

The maximum of $J(\eta_1, \eta_2)$ with reference to $r$ must be explored, taking into consideration the cases where $r=0, r=2$, and $r \in (0,2)$. Given a fixed value of $r$, the coefficients of the function $J(\eta_1, \eta_2)$ in (48) are dependent on $m$.

**The First Case**
When $r = 0$,

$$J(\eta_1, \eta_2) = Y_4(v,0) = \frac{\mathcal{E}_1^2(v)}{16(1+2\sigma)^2}(\eta_1 + \eta_2)^2.$$

Clearly the function $J(\eta_1, \eta_2)$ attains its maximum at $(\eta_1, \eta_2)$ and

$$max\{J(\eta_1, \eta_2) : \eta_1, \eta_2 \in [0,1]\} = J(1,1) = \frac{\mathcal{E}_1^2(v)}{4(1+2\sigma)^2}. \tag{49}$$

**The Second Case**
In the case of $r = 2$, $J(\eta_1, \eta_2)$ is represented as a constant function with regard to $m$, giving us

$$J(\eta_1, \eta_2) = Y_1(v,2) = \left\{ \frac{2(1+4\sigma)\mathcal{E}_1^4(v)}{3(1+2\sigma)(1+\sigma)^4} + \frac{\mathcal{E}_1(v)\mathcal{E}_3(v)}{18(1+\sigma)(1+2\sigma)} + \frac{\mathcal{E}_1^4(v)}{(1+\sigma)^4} \right\}.$$

**The Third Case**
When $r \in (0,2)$, let $\eta_1 + \eta_2 = d$ and $\eta_1 \cdot \eta_2 = Y$ in this case, then (48) can be of the form

$$J(\eta_1, \eta_2) = Y_1(v,r) + Y_2(v,r)d + (Y_3(v,r) + Y_4(v,r))d^2 - 2Y_3(v,r)l = Y(d,q) \tag{50}$$

where, $d \in [0,2]$ ald $q \in [0,1]$. Now, we need to investigate the maximum of

$$Y(d,q) \in \Theta = \{(d,q) : d \in [0,2], q \in [0,1]\}. \tag{51}$$

By differentiating $Y(d,q)$ partially, we have

$$\frac{\partial Y}{\partial c} = Y_2(v,r) + 2(Y_3(v,r) + Y_4(v,r))d = 0$$

$$\frac{\partial Y}{\partial l} = -2Y_3(v,r) = 0.$$

These findings demonstrate that $Y(d,r)$ has no critical point in the square $\Psi$, and, consequently, $J(\eta_1, \eta_2)$ has no critical point in the same region.
Because of this, the function $J(\eta_1, \eta_2)$ is unable to reach its maximum value inside of $\Psi$. The maximum of $J(\eta_1, \eta_2)$ on the square's $\Psi$ boundary will then be examined.
For $\eta_1 = 0$, $\eta_2 \in [0,1]$ (also, for $\eta_2 = 0, \eta_1 \in [0,1]$) and

$$J(0, \eta_2) = Y_1(v,r) + Y_2\eta_2 + (Y_3(v,r) + Y_4(v,r))\eta_2^2 = D(\eta_2). \tag{52}$$

Now, since $Y_3(v,r) + Y_4(v,r) \geq 0$, then we have

$$D'(\eta_2) = Y_2(v,r) + 2[Y_3(v,r) + Y_4(v,r)]\eta_2 > 0$$

which implies that $D(\eta_2)$ is an increasing function. Therefore, for a fixed $r \in [0,2)$ and $v \in (1/2, 1]$, the maximum occurs at $\eta_2 = 1$. Thus, from (52),

$$\max\{r(0,\eta_2) : \eta_2 \in [0,1]\} = J(0,1)$$
$$= Y_1(v,r) + Y_2(v,r) + Y_3(v,r) + Y_4(v,r). \quad (53)$$

For $\eta_1 = 1, \eta_2 \in [0,1]$ (also, for $\eta_2 = 1$, $\eta_1 \in [0,1]$) and

$$J(1,\eta_2) = Y_1(v,r) + Y_2(v,r) + Y_3(v,r) + Y_4(v,r) + [Y_2(v,r)$$
$$+2Y_4(v,r)]\eta_2 + [Y_3(v,r) + Y_4(v,r)]\eta_2^2 = N(\eta_2) \quad (54)$$

$$N'(\eta_2) = [Y_2(v) + 2Y_4(v)] + 2[Y_3(v) + Y_4(v)]\eta_2. \quad (55)$$

We know that $Y_3(v) + Y_4(v) \geq 0$, then

$$N'(\eta_2) = [Y_2(v) + 2Y_4(v)] + 2[Y_3(v) + Y_4(v)]\eta_2 > 0.$$

Therefore, the function $N(\eta_2)$ is an increasing function and the maximum occurs at $\eta_2 = 1$. From (54), we have

$$\max\{J(1,\eta_2) : \eta_2 \in [0,1]\} = J(1,1)$$
$$= Y_1(v,r) + 2[Y_2(v,r) + Y_3(v,r)] + 4Y_4(v,r). \quad (56)$$

Hence, for every $r \in (0,2)$, taking it from (53) and (56), we have

$$Y_1(v,r) + 2[Y_2(v,r) + Y_3(v,r)] + 4Y_4(v,r)$$
$$> Y_1(v,r) + Y_2(v,r) + Y_3(v,r) + Y_4(v,r).$$

Therefore,

$$\max\{J(\eta_1,\eta_2) : \eta_1 \in [0,1], \eta_2 \in [0,1]\}$$
$$= Y_1(v,r) + 2[Y_2(v,r) + Y_3(v,r)] + 4Y_4(v,r).$$

Since,
$$D(1) \leq N(1) \quad for \quad r \in [0,2] \quad and \quad v \in [1,1],$$

then
$$\max\{J(\eta_1,\eta_2)\} = J(1,1)$$

occurs on the boundary of square $\Psi$.

Let $T : (0,2) \to \mathbb{R}$ defined by

$$T(v,r) = \max\{J(\eta_1,\eta_2)\} = J(1,1) = Y_1(v,r) + 2Y_2(v,r) + 2Y_3(v,r) + 4Y_4(v,r). \quad (57)$$

Now, inserting the values of $Y_1(v,r), Y_2(v,r), Y_3(v,r)$ and $Y_4(v,r)$ into (57) and with some calculations, we have

$$T(v,r) = \frac{\mathcal{E}_1^2(v)}{4(1+2\sigma)^2} + \frac{B_1}{576(1+\sigma)^4(1+2\sigma)^2(1+3\sigma)}r^4 + \frac{B_2}{48(1+\sigma)^2(1+2\sigma)^2(1+3\sigma)}r^2,$$

where

$$B_1 = \mathcal{E}_1(v)\left[24\mathcal{E}_1^3(v)(1+4\sigma)(1+2\sigma)^2 + 2(6\mathcal{E}_1(v) - 6\mathcal{E}_2(v) + \mathcal{E}_3(v))(1+\sigma)^3(1+2\sigma)^2\right.$$
$$+ 36\mathcal{E}_1^3(v)(1+3\sigma)(1+2\sigma)^2 - 24\mathcal{E}_1(v)(1+\sigma)^3(1+2\sigma)^2 + 9\mathcal{E}_1(v)(1+\sigma)^4(1+3\sigma) - 9\mathcal{E}_1^2(v)$$
$$\left.(1+\sigma)^2(1+3\sigma)(1+2\sigma)\right]r^4$$

$$B_2 = \mathcal{E}_1(v)\left[3(1+2\sigma)(1+3\sigma)\mathcal{E}_1^2(v) + 4\mathcal{E}_1(v)(1+\sigma)(1+2\sigma)^2 + 4(\mathcal{E}_2(v) - 2\mathcal{E}_1(v))\right.$$
$$\left.(1+\sigma)(1+2\sigma)^2 + 8\mathcal{E}_1(v)(1+\sigma)(1+2\sigma)^2 - 6\mathcal{E}_1(v)(1+\sigma)^2(1+3\sigma)\right]r^2.$$

If $T(v,r)$ achieves a maximum value inside of $r \in [0,2]$ and by using some basic mathematics, we have

$$T'(v,r) = \frac{B_1}{144(1+\sigma)^4(1+2\sigma)^2(1+3\sigma)}r^3 + \frac{B_2}{24(1+\sigma)^2(1+2\sigma)^2(1+3\sigma)}r.$$

In virtue of the signs of $B_1$ and $B_2$, we must now investigate the sign of the function $T'(v,r)$.
**1st result:**
Suppose $B_1 \geq 0$ and $B_2 \geq 0$ then,
$T'(v,r) \geq 0$. This shows that $T(v,r)$ is an increasing function on the boundary of $r \in [0,2]$ that is $r = 2$. Therefore,

$$\max\{T(v,r) : r \in (0,2)\} = \frac{2(1+4\sigma)\mathcal{E}_1^4(v)}{3(1+3\sigma)(1+\sigma)^4} + \frac{\mathcal{E}_1(v)\mathcal{E}_3(v)}{18(1+\sigma)(1+3\sigma)} + \frac{\mathcal{E}_1^4(v)}{(1+\sigma)^4}$$

**2nd result:**
If $B_1 > 0$ and $B_2 < 0$ then,

$$T'(v,r) = \frac{B_1 r^3 + 6B_2 r(1+\sigma)^2}{144(1+\sigma)^4(1+2\sigma)^2(1+3\sigma)} = 0 \tag{58}$$

at critical point

$$r_0 = \sqrt{\frac{-6B_2(1+\sigma)^2}{B_1}} \tag{59}$$

is a critical point of the function $T(v,r)$. Now,

$$T''(r_0) = \frac{-B_2}{8(1+\sigma)^2(1+2\sigma)^2(1+3\sigma)} + \frac{B_2}{24(1+\sigma)^2(1+2\sigma)^2(1+3\sigma)} > 0.$$

Therefore, $r_0$ is the minimum point of the function $T(v,r)$. Hence, $T(v,r)$ can not have a maximum.
**3rd result:**
If $B_1 \leq 0$ and $B_2 \leq 0$ then,
$$T'(v,r) \leq 0.$$
Therefore, $T(v,r)$ is a decreasing function on the interval $(0,2)$. Consequently,

$$\max\{T(v,r) : r \in (0,2)\} = T(0) = \frac{\mathcal{E}_1^2(v)}{4(1+2\sigma)^2}. \tag{60}$$

**4th result:**
If $B_1 < 0$ and $B_2 > 0$

$$T''(v_0, r) = \frac{-B_2}{12(1+\sigma)^2(1+2\sigma)^2(1+3\sigma)} < 0.$$

Therefore, $T''(v,r) < 0$. Hence, $g_0$ is the maximum point of the function $T(v,r)$ and $r = g_0$ is the maximum value. Likewise

$$\max\{T(v,r) : r \in (0,2)\} = T(g_0, s)$$

$$T(g_0, t) = \frac{\mathcal{E}_1^2(v)}{4(1+2\sigma)^2} + \frac{9B_2^4(1+\sigma)^4}{4(1+2\sigma)^2(1+3\sigma)B_1^3} + \frac{3B_2^3(1+\sigma)^2}{4(1+2\sigma)^2(1+3\sigma)B_1^2}.$$

□

Taking $\sigma = 0$ in Theorem 3, we have the next corollary.

**Corollary 5.** *Let the function $f(\xi)$ given by (1) be in the class $\mathcal{S}_\Sigma^*(v)$. Then:*

$$H_2(2) = \left|a_2 a_4 - a_3^2\right| \leq \begin{cases} T(2,v) & (B_1 \geq 0 \text{ and } B_2 \geq 0) \\ \max\left\{\frac{(2v-1)^2}{16}, T(2,v)\right\} & (B_1 > 0 \text{ and } B_2 < 0) \\ \frac{(2v-1)^2}{16} & (B_1 \leq 0 \text{ and } B_2 \leq 0) \\ \max\{T(g_0, v), T(2,v)\} & (B_1 < 0 \text{ and } B_2 > 0). \end{cases}$$

where

$$T(2,v) = \frac{5\mathcal{E}_1^4(v)}{3} + \frac{\mathcal{E}_1(v)\mathcal{E}_3(v)}{18}$$

$$T(g_0, v) = \frac{\mathcal{E}_1^2(v)}{4} + \frac{3B_2^4(3B_2 + B_1)}{4B_1^3}.$$

$$B_1 = \mathcal{E}_1(v)[60\mathcal{E}_1^3(v) + 2(\mathcal{E}_3(v) - 6\mathcal{E}_2(v)) - 3\mathcal{E}_1(v) - 9\mathcal{E}_1^2(v)]r^4$$
$$B_2 = \mathcal{E}_1(v)[3\mathcal{E}_1^2(v) - 2(2\mathcal{E}_2(v) - \mathcal{E}_1(v))]r^2.$$

Taking $\sigma = 1$ in Theorem 3, we have the next corollary.

**Corollary 6.** *Let the function $f(\xi)$ given by (1) be in the class $\mathcal{C}_\Sigma(v)$. Then:*

$$H_2(2) = \left|a_2 a_4 - a_3^2\right| \leq \begin{cases} T(2,v) & (B_1 \geq 0 \text{ and } B_2 \geq 0) \\ \max\left\{\frac{(2v-1)^2}{144}, T(2,v)\right\} & (B_1 > 0 \text{ and } B_2 < 0) \\ \frac{(2v-1)^2}{144} & (B_1 \leq 0 \text{ and } B_2 \leq 0) \\ \max\{T(g_0, v), T(2,v)\} & (B_1 < 0 \text{ and } B_2 > 0). \end{cases}$$

where

$$T(2,v) = \frac{11\mathcal{E}_1^4(v)}{96} + \frac{\mathcal{E}_1(v)\mathcal{E}_3(v)}{144}$$

$$T(g_0, v) = \frac{\mathcal{E}_1^2(v)}{36} + \frac{B_2^4}{B_1^3} + \frac{B_2^2}{12B_1^2}.$$

$$B_1 = \mathcal{E}_1(v)[2376\mathcal{E}_1^3(v) + 144(\mathcal{E}_3(v) - 6\mathcal{E}_2(v)) - 288\mathcal{E}_1(v) - 432\mathcal{E}_1^2(v)]r^4$$
$$B_2 = \mathcal{E}_1(v)[36\mathcal{E}_1^2(v) - 24(\mathcal{E}_1(v) - 3\mathcal{E}_2(v))]r^2.$$

## 5. Conclusions

The many well-known mathematicians have been studied the special functions, as well as polynomials in the recent years, due to the fact that they are used in a wide variety of mathematical and other scientific fields as indicated in the introduction section. The subject of this paper is a novel subclass of analytical and univalent functions which have been defined by using Euler polynomial. We solved the Fekete–Szegö problem, as well as provided bound estimates for the coefficients and an upper bound estimate for the second Hankel determinant for functions in the class $\mathcal{G}_\Sigma(v,\sigma)$. One can extend the above results for a class of certain $q$-Starlike functions, as mentioned in [21–27].

**Author Contributions:** Conceptualization, Q.X. and B.K.; Methodology, Q.X. and B.K.; Software, T.G.S. and F.T.; Validation, S.R. and S.N.M.; Formal analysis, S.R. and S.N.M.; Investigation, Q.X. and B.K.; Resources, T.G.S. and F.T.; Writing—original draft, B.K.; Writing—review & editing, S.N.M.; Visualization, T.G.S.; Supervision, S.R. and B.K.; Project administration, F.T.; Funding acquisition, F.T. All authors have read and agreed to the published version of the manuscript.

**Funding:** This research received no external funding.

**Acknowledgments:** This research was supported by the researchers Supporting Project Number (RSP2023R401), King Saud University, Riyadh, Saudi Arabia.

**Data Availability Statement:** No data is used in this work.

**Conflicts of Interest:** The authors declare no conflict of interest.

## References

1. Duren, P.L. Univalent Functions. In *Grundlehren der Mathematischen Wissenschaften. Band 259*; Springer: New York, NY, USA; Berlin/Heidelberg, Germany; Tokyo, Japan, 1983.
2. Srivastava, H.M.; Owa, S. *Current Topics in Analytic Function Theory*; World Scientific: Singapore, 1992.
3. Srivastava, H.M.; Mishra, A.K.; Gochhayat, P. Certain subclasses of analytic and bi-univalent functions. *Appl. Math. Lett.* **2010**, *23*, 1188–1192. [CrossRef]
4. Srivastava, H.M.; Gaboury, S.; Ghanim, F. Coefficient estimates for some general subclasses of analytic and bi-univalent functions. *Afr. Mat.* **2017**, *28*, 693–706. [CrossRef]
5. Fine, N.J. *Basic Hypergeometric Series and Applications, Mathematical Surveys and Monographs*; American Mathematical Society: Providence, RI, USA, 1988; Volume 27.
6. Andrews, G.E. *q*-Series: Their Development and Application in Analysis, Number Theory, Combinatorics, Physics, and Computer Algebra. In *Conference Series in Mathematics*; American Mathematical Society: Providence, RI, USA, 1986; Volume 66.
7. Koornwinder, T.H. Orthogonal polynomials in connection with quantum groups. In *Orthogonal Polynomials, Theory and Practice*; Nevai, P., Ed.; Kluwer Academic Publishers: Dordrecht, The Netherlands, 1990; Volume 294, pp. 257–292.
8. Koornwinder, T.H. Compact quantum groups and q-special functions. In *Representations of Lie Groups and Quantum Groups, Pitman Research Notes in Mathematics Series*; Baldoni, V., Picardello, M.A., Eds.; Longman Scienti1c & Technical: NewYork, NY, USA, 1994; Volume 311, pp. 46–128.
9. Vilenkin, N.J.; Klimyk, A.U. *Representations of Lie Groups and Special Functions*; Kluwer Academic Publishers: Dordrecht, The Netherlands, 1992; Volume I–III.
10. Dziok, J.; Srivastava, H.M. Certain subclasses of analytic functions associated with the generalized hypergeometric function. *Integral Transform. Spec. Funct.* **2003**, *14*, 7–18. [CrossRef]
11. Srivastava, H.M. Some families of Mittag-Leffler type functions and associated operators of fractional calculus. *TWMS J. Pure Appl. Math.* **2016**, *7*, 123–145.
12. Srivastava, H.M. Some formulas for the Bernoulli and Euler polynomials at rational arguments. *Math. Proc. Camb. Philos. Soc.* **2000**, *129*, 77–84. [CrossRef]
13. Kac, V.; Cheung, P. Quantum Calculus. In *Universitext*; Springer: New York, NY, USA, 2002.
14. Fekete, M.; Szego, G. Eine bemerkung uber ungerade schlichte funktionen. *J. Lond. Math. Soc.* **1993**, *8*, 85–89. [CrossRef]
15. Srivastava, H.M.; Shaba, T.G.; Murugusundaramoorthy, G.; Wanas, A.K.; Oros, G.I. The fekete-Szego functional and the Hankel determinant for a certain class of analytic functions involving the Hohlov operator. *AIMS Math.* **2022**, *8*, 340–360. [CrossRef]
16. Saliu, A.; Al-Shbeil, I.; Gong, J.; Malik, S.N.; Aloraini, N. Properties of *q*-Symmetric Starlike Functions of Janowski Type. *Symmetry* **2022**, *14*, 1907. [CrossRef]

17. Pommerenke, C. On the coefficients and Hankel determinants of univalent functions. *Pro-Ceedings Lond. Math. Soc.* **1966**, *41*, 111–122. [CrossRef]
18. Zhang, H.-Y.; Srivastava, R.; Tang, H. Third-Order Hankel and Toeplitz Determinants for Starlike Functions Connected with the Sine Function. *Mathematics* **2019**, *7*, 404. [CrossRef]
19. Khan, B.; Aldawish, I.; Araci, S.; Khan, M.G. Third Hankel Determinant for the Logarithmic Coefficients of Starlike Functions Associated with Sine Function. *Fractal Fract.* **2022**, *6*, 261. [CrossRef]
20. Libera, R.J.; Zlotkiewicz, E.J. Coefficient Bounds for the Inverse of a Function with Derivative. *Proc. Am. Math. Soc.* **1983**, *87*, 251–257. [CrossRef]
21. Hu, Q.; Shaba, T.G.; Younis, J.; Khan, B.; Mashwani, W.K.; Caglar M. Applications of $q$-derivative operator to Subclasses of bi-Univalent Functions involving Gegenbauer polynomial. *Appl. Math. Sci. Eng.* **2022**, *30*, 501–520. [CrossRef]
22. Khan, B.; Liu, Z.G.; Srivastava, H.M.; Khan, N.; Darus, M.; Tahir, M. A study of some families of multlivalent $q$-starlike functions involving higher-order q-derivatives. *Mathematics* **2020**, *8*, 1490 [CrossRef]
23. Khan, B.; Liu, Z.-G.; Srivastava, H.M.; Araci, S.; Khan, N.; Ahmad, Z. Higher-order $q$-derivatives and their applications to subclasses of multivalent Janowski type $q$-starlike functions. *Adv. Differ. Equ.* **2021**, 440. [CrossRef]
24. Taj, Y.; Zainab, S.; Xin, Q.; Tawfiq, F.M.O.; Raza, M.; Malik, S.N. Certain Coefficient Problems for $q$-Starlike Functions Associated with $q$-Analogue of Sine Function. *Symmetry* **2022**, *14*, 2200. [CrossRef]
25. Shi, L.; Arif, M.; Iqbal, J.; Ullah, K.; Ghufran, S.M. Sharp Bounds of Hankel Determinant on Logarithmic Coefficients for Functions Starlike with Exponential Function. *Fractal Fract.* **2022**, *6*, 645. [CrossRef]
26. Riaz, S.; Nisar, U.A.; Xin, Q.; Malik, S.N.; Raheem, A. On Starlike Functions of Negative Order Defined by q-Fractional Derivative. *Fractal Fract.* **2022**, *6*, 30. [CrossRef]
27. Al-shbeil, I.; Gong, J.; Khan, S.; Khan, N.; Khan, A.; Khan, M.F.; Goswami, A. Hankel and Symmetric Toeplitz Determinants for a New Subclass of q-Starlike Functions. *Fractal Fract.* **2022**, *6*, 658. [CrossRef]

**Disclaimer/Publisher's Note:** The statements, opinions and data contained in all publications are solely those of the individual author(s) and contributor(s) and not of MDPI and/or the editor(s). MDPI and/or the editor(s) disclaim responsibility for any injury to people or property resulting from any ideas, methods, instructions or products referred to in the content.

Article

# Solving Some Physics Problems Involving Fractional-Order Differential Equations with the Morgan-Voyce Polynomials

Hari Mohan Srivastava [1,2,3,4,*], Waleed Adel [5,6], Mohammad Izadi [7] and Adel A. El-Sayed [8,9]

[1] Department of Mathematics and Statistics, University of Victoria, Victoria, BC V8W 3R4, Canada
[2] Department of Medical Research, China Medical University Hospital, China Medical University, Taichung 40402, Taiwan
[3] Department of Mathematics and Informatics, Azerbaijan University, 71 Jeyhun Hajibeyli Street, AZ1007 Baku, Azerbaijan
[4] Center for Converging Humanities, Kyung Hee University, 26 Kyungheedae-ro, Dongdaemun-gu, Seoul 02447, Republic of Korea
[5] Department of Technology of Informatics and Communications, Université Française D'Egypte, Ismailia Desert Road, Cairo 11837, Egypt
[6] Department of Mathematics and Engineering Physics, Faculty of Engineering, Mansoura University, Mansoura 35516, Egypt
[7] Department of Applied Mathematics, Faculty of Mathematics and Computer, Shahid Bahonar University of Kerman, Kerman 76169-14111, Iran
[8] Department of Mathematics, Faculty of Science, Fayoum University, Fayoum 63514, Egypt
[9] Department of Mathematics, College of Education, University of Technology and Applied Sciences, Al-Rustaq 329, Oman
* Correspondence: harimsri@math.uvic.ca

**Abstract:** In this research, we present a new computational technique for solving some physics problems involving fractional-order differential equations including the famous Bagley–Torvik method. The model is considered one of the important models to simulate the coupled oscillator and various other applications in science and engineering. We adapt a collocation technique involving a new operational matrix that utilizes the Liouville–Caputo operator of differentiation and Morgan–Voyce polynomials, in combination with the Tau spectral method. We first present the differentiation matrix of fractional order that is used to convert the problem and its conditions into an algebraic system of equations with unknown coefficients, which are then used to find the solutions to the proposed models. An error analysis for the method is proved to verify the convergence of the acquired solutions. To test the effectiveness of the proposed technique, several examples are simulated using the presented technique and these results are compared with other techniques from the literature. In addition, the computational time is computed and tabulated to ensure the efficacy and robustness of the method. The outcomes of the numerical examples support the theoretical results and show the accuracy and applicability of the presented approach. The method is shown to give better results than the other methods using a lower number of bases and with less spent time, and helped in highlighting some of the important features of the model. The technique proves to be a valuable approach that can be extended in the future for other fractional models having real applications such as the fractional partial differential equations and fractional integro-differential equations.

**Keywords:** fractional-order equations; collocation method; Liouville–Caputo's fractional derivative operator; error analysis; Tau method

## 1. Introduction

Fractional calculus is a branch of mathematics that deals with the study of derivatives and integrals of non-integer order. It has been around since the late 17th century when Gottfried Leibniz first proposed the concept of fractional derivatives, which has developed into a powerful tool for simulating different physical problems in many areas such as physics, chemistry, engineering, economics, and biology. The concept of fractional calculus was initially met with skepticism due to its unfamiliarity and lack of intuitive understanding. However, over time, its usefulness has been recognized and there have been various definitions and properties. These definitions vary depending on the context in which it is used, which in general have a common definition as the study of derivatives and integrals with non-integer orders. This means that instead of taking derivatives or integrals concerning a single variable (as in traditional calculus), fractional calculus allows for derivatives or integrals to be taken concerning multiple variables simultaneously. This allows for more complex phenomena such as memory effects, diffusion processes, and chaotic systems that might be difficult to solve using traditional definitions. In addition, fractional derivatives are useful in many fields such as physics, engineering, economics, and finance. For example, Zhao et al. [1] investigated the possible application of fractional definitions to simulate a class of nonlinear fractional Langevin equations with important application in fluid dynamics. In addition, Zhang et al. [2] employed an exponential Euler scheme for simulating the multi-delay Caputo–Fabrizio fractional-order differential equations with application in control theory. Additionally, other applications of fractional calculus in several branches of science and engineering include the simulation of the model of viscoelastic materials in engineering applications and financial markets in economics. They can also be used to describe chaotic systems in physics and other fields. There are various definitions of the fractional order including the Riemann–Liouville operator [3], Grünwald–Letnikov operator [4], Liouville–Caputo operator [5] and Weyl–Riesz operator [6]. Each of these definitions adheres to some advantages and disadvantageous over the other and the most widely used of these applications is the Liouville–Caputo and Riemann–Liouville operators. There is a close relationship between these two definitions since they can be converted through some regularity assumption [7]. The Liouville–Caputo fractional operator is considered a powerful tool for solving fractional differential equations (FDEs) that have been used widely for simulating different complex problems. The Liouville–Caputo fractional operator is a generalization of the classical derivative operator and can be used to solve FDEs with non-integer order derivatives. It has the advantage of simulating physical phenomena that involve memory effects or non-local interactions. In addition, it allows for more accurate solutions since it takes into account memory effects and it provides more flexibility when solving FDEs; because it can be applied to any function that can be expressed as a power expansion series. This was one of the reasons to be used for the simulation of non-integer models. For example, the definition of the Liouville–Caputo operator has been used in simulating disease models. Bonyah et al. [8] simulated the definition of the Liouville–Caputo for investigating the dynamics of the COVID-19 infection. In addition, the time-dependent influenza model has been studied in [9] to provide insight into the dynamics of such a model and to provide measure precautions to stop its spread. Additionally, Gao et al. [10] proposed a new fractional numerical differentiation formula for the Liouville–Caputo fractional derivative and tested the new formulae for multiple applications. Additionally, the constant proportional Liouville–Caputo operators were employed in [11] for simulating the dynamics of the HIV disease model to understand its dynamics and ways of spread. Han et al. identified some solutions for the variable-coefficient fractional-in-space KdV equation in [12]. Some basic therapies and applications of the fractional differential equations have been illustrated in [13] while [14,15] provided some parametric and argument variations of the operators related to fractional calculus. With the importance of such definitions, the Liouville–Caputo operator is of importance in helping to understand such behavior of complex models.

Numerical simulation using collocation and spectral methods is a powerful tool for solving complex problems in engineering and science. It is a method of approximating solutions to differential equations by utilizing computational techniques such as collocation and spectral methods. Collocation methods are used to approximate solutions to various differential equations by representing them as a linear combination of basis functions. Spectral methods are used to approximate solutions to differential equations by representing them as an infinite series of (orthogonal) polynomials. Both of these techniques have been widely used in the field of computational science, with applications ranging from fluid dynamics to quantum mechanics. Collocation techniques have been widely used for acquiring accurate results for these models using different types of bases. The main idea of this technique is that the solution to a differential equation can be represented as a linear combination of basis functions. These basis functions can be chosen from a variety of sources including polynomials or other types. For example, Izadi et al. [16] investigated the solution of the waste plastic management model in the ocean system using the Morgan–Voyce polynomials. In addition, Adel et al. [17] employed a collocation method of Genocchi polynomials for simulating the solution to the fourth-order singular singularly perturbed and Emden–Fowler problems, which have significant importance in physics. Izadi et al. [18] developed a collocation approach with a new definition of the Chelyshkov polynomials to solve the fractional delay differential equations. Additionally, El-Gamel et al. [19] adapted the Genocchi collocation method for solving a class of high-order boundary value problems. The B-spline bases have been used to simulate physical models as well as other basis functions. For example, De Boor [20] was the first to introduce the basic definitions of the B-spline basis, and then researchers have been using it to simulate real-life models. Kaur et al. [21] employed the adaptive wavelet optimized finite difference technique combined with the B-spline polynomial for the solution of random partial differential equations. Zahra et al. [22] developed a robust uniform B-spline collocation method for solving the generalized PHI-four equation. In addition, a cubic B-spline collocation algorithm has been used to solve the Newell–Whitehead–Segel type equations in [23]. Additionally, the combination of the wavelet along with other polynomials has been used in the simulation of different models [24] and Alqhtani et al. [25] simulated a high-dimensional chaotic Lorenz system using the Gegenbauer wavelet polynomials. The coefficients in the linear combination are determined by solving an optimization problem that minimizes the error between the approximate solution and the exact solution. This approach is particularly useful when dealing with boundary value problems since it allows for accurate approximations near the boundaries without having to solve for all points in between. Spectral methods on the other hand are based on the idea that solutions to differential equations can be represented as an infinite series of orthogonal polynomials. These polynomials can be chosen from a variety of sources including the Chebyshev polynomials [26] which have been used in the simulation of the fractional diffusion-wave equation by Atta et al. [27]. Another type of polynomials is the Legendre polynomials [28], which is also used for solving the linear Fredholm integro-differential equations accompanied by the Galerkin method by Fathy et al. [29]. In addition, Abdelhakem et al. [30] employed the pseudo-spectral matrices method for treating some models using the Legendre polynomials. More general orthogonal polynomials such as Hermite [31] or Laguerre polynomials [32] have also been used in practical simulations. This approach is particularly useful when dealing with initial value problems since it allows for accurate approximations at all points in time without having to solve for all points in between. Both of these techniques have been extensively studied over the past few decades, leading to significant advances in their accuracy and efficiency. They have become essential tools for solving complex problems in engineering and science, allowing researchers to accurately simulate physical phenomena with unprecedented accuracy and speed.

One of these polynomials that prove to have an effective role in simulating and acquiring efficient results is the Morgan–Voyce polynomials (MVP). This type of polynomial is a family of polynomials that was developed in the early 20th century by the American mathematician and physicist, Edward L. Morgan, see [33]. Polynomials were initially developed as a tool to study the behavior of certain physical systems, such as electrical circuits and mechanical systems. These polynomials have since become an important tool in many areas of mathematics; for example, in algebraic geometry to study curves and surfaces defined by polynomial equations and in number theory to study Diophantine equations and prime numbers. Many researchers have recently been using the MVP accompanied by the collocation technique to solve engineering problems. For example, the MVP has been used to simulate a class of high-order differential equations by Türkyilmaz et al. in [34]. Additionally, Tarakci et al. [35] adapted a combination of the MVP with cubic and quadratic terms with the collocation strategy to simulate the nonlinear ordinary differential equations. Functional integro-differential equations of Volterra-type have been solved using the MVP collocation approach by Özel et al. [36]. In addition, Izadi et al. [37] employed the MVP to simulate the fractional Lotka–Volterra population model. Furthermore, Izadi et al. [38] employed the shifted MVP for solving a class of nonlinear diffusion equations. Additionally, Bushra et al. [39] proposed a collocation scheme for solving the Bratu problem with the aid of the MVP. With the little work on the application of the MVP, we are interested in expanding the application of such polynomials to fractional models.

In this research study, we are mainly interested in finding an accurate solution to a class of fractional order boundary value problems in the form

$$\omega_1 \mathbb{D}^2 g(t) + \omega_2 \mathbb{D}^\zeta g(t) + \omega_3 g(t) = \vartheta(t), \tag{1}$$

with the initial conditions

$$g(0) = g_0, \quad g'(0) = g_1. \tag{2}$$

Here, $\omega_1, \omega_2, \omega_3$, and $\vartheta(t)$ in Equation (1) are constant coefficients depending on the application type and the source term, respectively. In addition, $g_0$ and $g_1$ are the starting values for the problem's solution and $\mathbb{D}^\zeta$ is the fractional-order operator defined in Liouville–Caputo sense with the fractal value $1 < \zeta < 2$. To the best of our knowledge, this is the first time that the MVP is utilized for solving the model (1). This model incorporates a different form of fractional differential equations. One of the main models represented by the model (1) is the Bagley–Torvik model. This model has been used to simulate the motion of a rigid plate immersed in a Newtonian fluid and also describes the behavior of a system of coupled oscillators and was first discovered by Torvik and Begly [40]. Since then, it has been widely studied and applied to various fields such as nonlinear optics, fluid mechanics, and plasma physics. With the importance of this type of model, numerous analytical and numerical techniques have been employed to find accurate solutions to these problems. For examples, we mention neuro-swarming computational solver [41], cubic B-spline method [42], Haar wavelet [43], fractional Meyer neural network [44] and other related techniques. For more details and information, the reader may refer to the works [45–47] and references therein.

In this paper, we interfered in simulating this model using the MVP with the definition of the fractional order in terms of the Liouville–Caputo fractional derivative. We adapt the proposed collocation method accompanied by the Tau method for simulating a different model of fractional order having real-life applications. We use MVP as the basis function in the collocation method because it has multiple advantages. Some of the advantages of the proposed technique using the MVP are the ability to accurately approximate functions with fewer terms than other methods, their ability to represent complex functions with a single equation, and their ability to be used in a wide variety of applications. Additionally, they can be used to solve equations that would otherwise be difficult or impossible to solve using traditional methods. On the other hand, there are some drawbacks to the complexity of the equations involved and they may not always provide an optimal solution for certain types of problems. The novelty of the paper lies within the following few points:

- A novel operational matrix of fractional order is derived in the sense of the Liouville–Caputo fractional derivative for the MVP.
- The technique is a combination of the collocation technique with the Tau method.
- The method converts the nonlinear fractional differential equation into a system of algebraic equations that are solved easily.
- The convergence analysis is performed to prove the error bound for the technique.
- The proposed technique is adapted for solving various examples with the application including the Bagley–Torvik and Bratu models.

- The acquired results prove that the technique is better than the other methods in terms of error and computational cost.
- The proposed algorithm can be extended to more complex problems having real-life applications.

The organization of the rest of this paper can be summarized as the following. Section 2 provides the basic definitions and preliminaries related to the fractional calculus that will be used later in the subsequent sections. The main relations and definitions of the MVP are introduced in Section 3 with a derivation of the new fractional order matrix of differentiation. In Section 4, the derivation of the integer and fractional operational matrix of derivatives is illustrated in detail and the Tau-collocation technique is demonstrated for solving the general model. In addition, the convergence analysis for the proposed technique is provided in detail in the same section to prove the convergence of the developed method. Several examples are introduced in Section 5 to validate the theistical results in light of the absolute error and computational time. Finally, Section 6 presents the conclusion of the study and some possible future work for the study.

## 2. Preliminaries and Notations

In this part, we will provide some of the fundamentals that will be needed in later sections. We begin with the following definitions.

**Definition 1** ([48]). *Assume that $g(t)$ is continuously differentiable $k-$times. The operator of fractional-order derivative in the Liouville–Caputo sense is defined by:*

$$\mathbb{D}^\zeta g(t) = \begin{cases} Y^{k-\zeta} g^{(k)}(t), & k-1 < \zeta < k, \\ g^{(k)}(t), & \zeta = k, \quad k \in \mathbb{N}, \end{cases} \tag{3}$$

*where*

$$Y^\zeta g(t) = \frac{1}{\Gamma(\zeta)} \int_0^t \frac{g(t)}{(t-\tau)^{1-\zeta}} d\tau, \quad \zeta > 0, \quad t > 0. \tag{4}$$

The linearity properties for Liouville–Caputo's operator hold as

$$\mathbb{D}^\zeta (a_1 \, g_1(t) + a_2 \, g_2(t)) = a_1 \, \mathbb{D}^\zeta g_1(t) + a_2 \, \mathbb{D}^\zeta g_2(t), \tag{5}$$

where $a_1, a_2$ are constants.

The above principle Definition 1 of the Liouville–Caputo fractional-order operator is utilized to obtain the following results for polynomials. Below, we use these facts,

$$\mathbb{D}^\zeta a_1 = 0, \quad a_1 \text{ is a constant}, \tag{6}$$

$$\mathbb{D}^\zeta t^m = \begin{cases} \frac{\Gamma(1+m)}{\Gamma(1+m-\zeta)} t^{m-\zeta}, & m \in \mathbb{N}_0 \land m \geq \lceil \zeta \rceil \text{ or } m \notin \mathbb{N}_0 \land m > \lfloor \zeta \rfloor, \\ 0, & m \in \mathbb{N}_0 \land m < \lceil \zeta \rceil, \end{cases} \tag{7}$$

where the ceiling and floor functions are $\lceil \zeta \rceil, \lfloor \zeta \rfloor$, respectively. Additionally, if $\zeta \in \mathbb{N}$, then the classical differential operator of integer-order is obtained, see [48].

In what follows, we use the following theorem, a proof of which can be found in [49]. Before we proceed, let us mention that by $\mathbb{D}^{n\zeta}$ we denote $\mathbb{D}^{n\zeta} := \mathbb{D}^\zeta \cdot \mathbb{D}^\zeta \cdots \mathbb{D}^\zeta$, $n$ times.

**Theorem 1** (Generalized Taylor's formula). *Let assume that $0 < \zeta \leq 1$ and for $n = 0, 1, \ldots, m$ we have $\mathbb{D}^{n\zeta}(g(t)) \in C(0, \mathcal{T}]$, where $\mathcal{T} > 0$. Then, the function $g(t)$ can be stated in the power series form given by*

$$g(t) = \sum_{n=0}^{m} \frac{t^{n\zeta}}{\Gamma(1+n\zeta)} \mathbb{D}^{n\zeta} g(0^+) + \frac{t^{(m+1)\zeta}}{\Gamma(1+(m+1)\zeta)} \mathbb{D}^{(m+1)\zeta} g(\kappa), \quad \forall t \in [0, \mathcal{T}],$$

for some $\kappa \in (0, \mathcal{T})$.

**Corollary 1.** *Under the assumptions of Theorem 1 if we have $|\mathbb{D}^{(m+1)\zeta}(g(t))| \leq M_{\max}$, then the following upper bound holds*

$$\left| g(t) - \sum_{n=0}^{m} \frac{t^{n\zeta}}{\Gamma(1+n\zeta)} \mathbb{D}^{n\zeta} g(0^+) \right| \leq \frac{t^{(m+1)\zeta}}{\Gamma(1+(m+1)\zeta)} M_{\max}, \quad \forall t \in [0, \mathcal{T}].$$

Next, we will provide the details of the Morgan–Voyce polynomials.

## 3. Morgan–Voyce Polynomials

Let us provide the details and properties of the MVP [34,36,39] that will be needed to treat model (1).

**Definition 2.** *The Morgan–Voyce polynomials of the degree $m \geq 1$ in the variable t is explicitly expressed in the power formula*

$$MV_m(t) = \sum_{i=0}^{m} \binom{m+i+1}{m-i} t^i, \quad m \in \mathbb{N}. \tag{8}$$

Additionally, the Morgan–Voyce polynomials, $MV_m(t)$, can be constructed by taking the next recurrence relation

$$MV_{m+2}(t) = (t+2) MV_{m+1}(t) - MV_m(t), \quad m \geq 0, \tag{9}$$

where $MV_0(t) = 1$, $MV_1(t) = t + 2$. A few examples of these Morgan–Voyce polynomials are

$$MV_2(t) = t^2 + 4t + 3,$$
$$MV_3(t) = t^3 + 6t^2 + 10t + 4,$$
$$MV_4(t) = t^4 + 8t^3 + 21t^2 + 20t + 5,$$
$$MV_5(t) = t^5 + 10t^4 + 36t^3 + 56t^2 + 35t + 6.$$

Moreover, $MV_m(t)$ are the solution of the following second kind ordinary differential equation

$$(t^2 + 4t)u_m''(t) + (3t+6)u_m'(t) - m(m+2)u_m(t) = 0, \tag{10}$$

where $u_m(t) = MV_m(t)$, $m = 0, 1, \ldots$ values. These polynomials $MV_m(t)$ over the interval $(-4, 0)$ are orthogonal with regard to the weight function $\sqrt{4-(t+2)^2}$.

### 3.1. Morgan–Voyce Polynomials Operational Matrices of Derivatives

In this subsection, the operational matrices of Morgan–Voyce polynomials in the integer and fractional-orders of derivatives will be proposed. On the $[0, \mathcal{T}]$ Lebesgue integrable space, consider $g(t)$ to be a square integrable function defined on it. Assume $g(t)$ can be expressed as an infinite series linear independent combination of the terms of MVP as the following formula:

$$g(t) = \sum_{i=0}^{\infty} d_i MV_i(t). \tag{11}$$

Using truncation for the infinite series terms to have only $(m+1)$–terms, then Equation (11) becomes as

$$g(t) \approx g_m(t) = \sum_{i=0}^{m} d_i MV_i(t) = D_m^T \Psi_m(t), \tag{12}$$

where
$$D_m^T = [d_0, d_1, \ldots, d_m], \quad (13)$$
and
$$\Psi_m(t) = [MV_0(t), MV_1(t), \ldots, MV_m(t)]^T. \quad (14)$$

Consider now the following vector form:
$$\mathfrak{P}_m(t) = [1, t, t^2, \ldots, t^m]^T, \quad (15)$$

then, we can use Equation (15) to write the $\Psi_m(t)$ of Equation (14) as follows:
$$\Psi_m(t) = W \mathfrak{P}_m(t), \quad (16)$$

where $W$ is $(m+1) \times (m+1)$ non-singular square matrix

$$W = \begin{pmatrix} w_{0,0} & 0 & 0 & 0 & \cdots & 0 \\ w_{1,0} & w_{1,1} & 0 & 0 & \cdots & 0 \\ w_{2,0} & w_{2,1} & w_{2,2} & 0 & \cdots & 0 \\ \vdots & \vdots & \vdots & \vdots & \vdots & \vdots \\ w_{m,0} & w_{m,1} & w_{m,2} & \cdots & w_{m,m-1} & w_{m,m} \end{pmatrix}.$$

The components of the matrix $W$ are given by

$$(w_{r,s})_{0 \leq r,s \leq m} = \begin{cases} 1, & r = s, \\ \dfrac{\Gamma(r+s+2)}{\Gamma(r-s+1)\Gamma(2s+2)}, & r > s, \\ 0, & \text{otherwise.} \end{cases} \quad (17)$$

Clearly, $\det(W) = 1$, which indicates that $W$ is non-singular. The matrix $W$ of dimension $5 \times 5$ is given as an example as follows:

$$W = \begin{pmatrix} 1 & 0 & 0 & 0 & 0 \\ 2 & 1 & 0 & 0 & 0 \\ 3 & 4 & 1 & 0 & 0 \\ 4 & 10 & 6 & 1 & 0 \\ 5 & 20 & 21 & 8 & 1 \end{pmatrix}.$$

Therefore, through Equation (16), we gain
$$\mathfrak{P}_m(t) = W^{-1} \Psi_m(t). \quad (18)$$

### 3.2. $MV(t)$ Polynomials Integer-Order Operational Matrix of Derivatives

In this subsection, we deduce the integer-order derivative of the vector $\Psi(t)$ as follows:
$$\frac{d}{dt} \Psi_m(t) = Q^{(1)} \mathfrak{P}_m(t), \quad (19)$$

where $Q^{(1)} = \left(q_{lj}^{(1)}\right)$ is $(m+1) \times (m+1)$ operational matrix of derivatives of integer-order contains the derivatives coefficients for $MV(t)$. Here, $Q^{(1)}$ is $(m+1) \times (m+1)$ singular square matrix

$$Q^{(1)} = \begin{pmatrix} 0 & 0 & 0 & 0 & \cdots & 0 \\ q_{1,1} & 0 & 0 & 0 & \cdots & 0 \\ q_{2,1} & q_{2,2} & 0 & 0 & \cdots & 0 \\ \vdots & \vdots & \vdots & \vdots & \vdots & \vdots \\ q_{m,1} & q_{m,2} & q_{m,3} & \cdots & q_{m,m} & 0 \end{pmatrix},$$

where the components of $Q^{(1)}$ can be determined directly by using

$$q^{(1)}_{1\leq l,j\leq m} = \begin{cases} 0, & l < j, \\ \dfrac{j\,\Gamma(l+j+2)}{\Gamma(l-j+1)\,\Gamma(2j+2)}, & l \geq j. \end{cases} \tag{20}$$

Consider the case $m = 5$ as an example for the first-order derivative operational matrix, $Q^{(1)}$, as follows

$$Q^{(1)} = \begin{pmatrix} 0 & 0 & 0 & 0 & 0 & 0 \\ 1 & 0 & 0 & 0 & 0 & 0 \\ 4 & 2 & 0 & 0 & 0 & 0 \\ 10 & 12 & 3 & 0 & 0 & 0 \\ 20 & 42 & 24 & 4 & 0 & 0 \\ 35 & 112 & 108 & 40 & 5 & 0 \end{pmatrix}_{6\times 6}.$$

Hence, via the two Equations (19) and (20), we can obtain the classical derivatives integer-order operational matrix of order more than the first order as the following:

$$\frac{d^k}{dt^k}\Psi_m(t) = Q^{(k)}\,\mathfrak{P}_m(t) = \left(Q^{(1)}\right)^k \mathfrak{P}_m(t), \quad k = 1, 2, \ldots. \tag{21}$$

*3.3. $MV(t)$ Polynomials Fractional-Order Operational Matrix of Derivatives*

Below, we will investigate the processes that enable us to obtain the fractional-order operational matrix of Morgan–Voyce polynomials. According to (16) we have $\Psi_m(t) = W\,\mathfrak{P}_m(t)$. Then, we get

$$\mathbb{D}^\zeta \Psi_m(t) = \mathbb{D}^\zeta(W\,\mathfrak{P}_m(t)) = W\,\mathbb{D}^\zeta[1, t, t^2, \ldots, t^m]^T.$$

Using Equation (7) to obtain

$$\mathbb{D}^\zeta \Psi_m(t) = W\left[0, \frac{2}{\Gamma(2-\zeta)}t^{(1-\zeta)}, \frac{3}{\Gamma(3-\zeta)}t^{(2-\zeta)}, \ldots, \frac{\Gamma(m+1)}{\Gamma(m+1-\zeta)}t^{(m-\zeta)}\right]^T$$

$$= W \begin{bmatrix} 0 & 0 & 0 & \cdots & 0 \\ 0 & \frac{2}{\Gamma(2-\zeta)}t^{-\zeta} & 0 & \cdots & 0 \\ 0 & 0 & \frac{3}{\Gamma(3-\zeta)}t^{-\zeta} & \cdots & 0 \\ \vdots & \vdots & \vdots & \ddots & \vdots \\ 0 & 0 & 0 & \cdots & \frac{\Gamma(m+1)}{\Gamma(m+1-\zeta)}t^{-\zeta} \end{bmatrix} \begin{bmatrix} 1 \\ t \\ t^2 \\ \vdots \\ t^m \end{bmatrix} \tag{22}$$

$$= t^{-\zeta}\,W\,Y\,\mathfrak{P}_m(t),$$

where

$$Y = \begin{bmatrix} 0 & 0 & 0 & \cdots & 0 \\ 0 & \frac{2}{\Gamma(2-\zeta)} & 0 & \cdots & 0 \\ 0 & 0 & \frac{3}{\Gamma(3-\zeta)} & \cdots & 0 \\ \vdots & \vdots & \vdots & \ddots & \vdots \\ 0 & 0 & 0 & \cdots & \frac{\Gamma(m+1)}{\Gamma(m+1-\zeta)} \end{bmatrix}. \tag{23}$$

Using Equation (18), we have

$$\mathbb{D}^\zeta \Psi_m(t) = t^{-\zeta}\,W\,Y\,W^{-1}\,\Psi_m(t). \tag{24}$$

Hence, $(t^{-\zeta}\,W\,Y\,W^{-1})$ is called the fractional-order operational matrix for $\mathbb{D}^\zeta \Psi_m(t)$.

## 4. Proposed Methodology and Convergence Analysis

In this section, we will provide details on the main steps for finding the solution of model Equation (1) using the proposed Tau-collocation method. In addition, we will prove the convergence of the suggested method to ensure that the method convergence to the required solution.

### 4.1. Proposed Methodology

We will now illustrate the main steps for finding the solution of model Equation (1) using the proposed Tau-collocation method. Consider Equation (1), firstly. Then, by using the content of Section 3 especially Equations (12) and (16), in addition to Equations (21) and (24) to obtain the following matrix form:

$$\omega_1 D_m^T Q^{(2)} W^{-1} \Psi_m(t) + \omega_2 D_m^T t^{-\zeta} W Y W^{-1} \Psi_m(t) + \omega_3 D_m^T \Psi_m(t) = \vartheta(t), \quad t \in (0, \mathcal{T}]. \tag{25}$$

The residual related to Equation (25) can be computed through

$$t^\zeta R(t) = t^\zeta \omega_1 D_m^T Q^{(2)} W^{-1} \Psi_m(t) + \omega_2 D_m^T W Y W^{-1} \Psi_m(t) + t^\zeta \omega_3 D_m^T \Psi_m(t) - t^\zeta \vartheta(t). \tag{26}$$

Through application of the Tau method (see for example [50]) to have

$$\int_0^{\mathcal{T}} t^\zeta R(t) \Psi_m^j(t)\, dt = 0, \quad 0 \leq j \leq m. \tag{27}$$

Additionally, the initial conditions that given in Equation (2) can be re-expressed in the matrix form as follows:

$$D_m^T \Psi_m(0) = g_0, \quad D_m^T Q^{(1)} \Psi_m(0) = g_1. \tag{28}$$

Using Equations (25) and (28) a system of algebraic equations is created to represent the unknown expansion coefficients $d_i$ of dimension $(m+1)$. The resultant algebraic system will be solved using the Gaussian elimination method. As a result, it is possible to compute the appropriate numerical solution in Equation (12) for the model (1). In the next subsection, we will prove the convergence of the method.

### 4.2. Convergence of Morgan–Voyce Bases

In the final stage, we pay attention to the convergence of Morgan–Voyce polynomial functions in the space of $L^2[0, \mathcal{T}]$, where $\mathcal{T} > 0$. As mentioned in (11), every square-integrable function $g(t) \in L^2[0, \mathcal{T}]$ can be represented in terms of Morgan–Voyce polynomials in an infinite series form. However, we practically consider only $(m+1)$ terms series expansion as given in (12). It follows that we restrict ourselves to the finite-dimensional subspace $S_m$ defined by

$$S_m = \text{Span}\langle MV_0(t), MV_1(\tau), \ldots, MV_m(\tau)\rangle.$$

Additionally, let us define the error between $g(t)$ and its approximation $g_m(t)$ by $E_m(t) = g(t) - g_m(t)$. Next, we assert that by increasing $m$, the error converges to zero in the $L^2$ norm. Also, by $\|\cdot\|_2$ we denote the $L^2$ norm of a function over $[0, \mathcal{T}]$.

**Theorem 2.** *Assume that* $0 < \delta := \zeta/2 \leq 1$ *and for* $n = 0, 1, \ldots, m+1$ *we have* $\mathbb{D}^{n\delta} g(t) \in C(0, \mathcal{T}]$. *Suppose further that* $g_m(t) = D_m^T \Psi_m(t)$ *in (12) represents the best possible approximation for* $g(t)$ *out of* $S_m$. *Then, the following estimate for the error* $E_m(t)$ *is valid:*

$$\|E_m(t)\|_2 \leq \frac{M_{\max}}{\left(\Gamma(1+2(m+1)\delta)\right)^{\frac{1}{2}}} \frac{\mathcal{T}^{\frac{1}{2}+(m+1)\delta}}{\Gamma(1+(m+1)\delta)},$$

*where* $\left|\mathbb{D}^{(m+1)\delta} g(t)\right| \leq M_{\max}$, *for* $t \in [0, \mathcal{T}]$.

**Proof.** Owing to the fact that $0 < \delta \leq 1$ and in accordance to Theorem 1, the generalized Taylor form of $g(t)$ is represented as follows:

$$G_m(t) = g(0^+) + \frac{t^\delta}{\Gamma(1+\delta)}\mathbb{D}^\delta g(0^+) + \ldots + \frac{t^{m\delta}}{\Gamma(1+m\delta)}\mathbb{D}^{m\delta}g(0^+).$$

By applying Corollary 1, the associated upper bound is given by

$$|G_m(t) - g(t)| \leq \frac{t^{(m+1)\delta}}{\Gamma(1+(m+1)\delta)}M_{\max}, \quad 0 < t < \mathcal{T}. \tag{29}$$

By virtue of the fact that the approximate solution $g_m(t) \in S_m$ represents the finest approximation to $g(t)$, we have, consequently,

$$\|g(t) - g_m(t)\|_2 \leq \|g(t) - f(t)\|_2, \quad \forall f \in S_m.$$

Employing in particular $f(t) = G_m(t)$ in the forgoing inequality reveals that

$$\|g(t) - g_m(t)\|_2^2 \leq \|g(t) - G_m(t)\|_2^2 = \int_0^{\mathcal{T}} |g(t) - G_m(t)|^2 \, dt.$$

By (29) and the definition of the error term, we immediately find that

$$\|E_m(t)\|_2^2 \leq \left[\frac{M_{\max}}{\Gamma(1+(m+1)\delta)}\right]^2 \int_0^{\mathcal{T}} t^{2(m+1)\delta} dt.$$

By computing the integral, we obtain

$$\|E_m(t)\|_2^2 \leq \left[\frac{M_{\max}}{\Gamma(1+(m+1)\delta)}\right]^2 \frac{\mathcal{T}^{1+2(m+1)\delta}}{\Gamma(1+2(m+1)\delta)}.$$

The proof in finished by performing the square roots on the last expression. □

## 5. Numerical Simulations

This section presents several examples that are solved numerically using our proposed method, i.e., the Morgan–Voyce operational matrix method (MVOMM). The numerical results of these examples support the analytical investigation and demonstrate the feasibility of the introduced technique. In the paper, two types of errors are used to evaluate the performance of the model: the $L^2$ error and the $L_\infty$ error. The $L^2$ error measures the average squared difference between the true values and the predicted values, while the $L_\infty$ error measures the maximum absolute difference between the true values and the predicted values. Additionally, the simulations were run using a Core-i7 laptop with 16 GB RAM and the used software is Mathematica 11.0.

**Example 1** ([51–53]). *Consider the following inhomogeneous Bagley–Torvik initial value problem:*

$$\mathbb{D}^2 g(t) + \mathbb{D}^\zeta g(t) + g(t) = \vartheta(t), \quad \zeta \in (1,2),\ t \in (0,1),\ g(0) = 1,\ g(1) = 3, \tag{30}$$

*where*

$$\vartheta(t) = t^3 + \frac{6}{\Gamma(4-\zeta)}t^{3-\zeta} + 7t + 1.$$

*The exact solution of Equation (30) is given by* $g(t) = t(t^2 + 1) + 1$.

We apply the investigated method to have the following result as described. In Table 1, we present numerical results for $g(t)$ and its approximation $g_m(t)$ at various points in the interval $[0,1]$, obtained using the MVOMM with $m = 3$. The results in this table demonstrate the high accuracy of the MVOM method. The CPU time that takes through obtaining these results at $m = 3$ is 3.766 s. For comparison, we also include results obtained using the VIM and FIM methods from Mekkaouii and Hammouch [52]. The last column in the table shows the exact values problem. As can be seen from the table, the MVOM technique with $m = 3$ yields more accurate results than the VIM, FIM, and LDG approaches. Table 2 presents $L^2$-error and $L_\infty$-error results using our suggested method MVOMM in addition to the comparison with these results obtained via Lucas wavelet scheme (LWS) [53]. From these results, we obtain the accuracy of the proposed method. For further illustration, we introduce Figure 1, which shows the absolute error (left), and (right) the approximate solutions $\tilde{\zeta} = 1.9, 1.8, 1.7, 1.5, 1.3$ for Example 1 with $m = 3$. Clearly, from Figure 1, the accuracy and efficiency of the MVOMM is useful for obtaining the numerical solutions in several cases. In addition, it can be noticed from the figure that while changing the value of the fractional order $\tilde{\zeta}$, the value of the solution is increasing. This proves that the change in the fractional order has an impact on the simulation of the results.

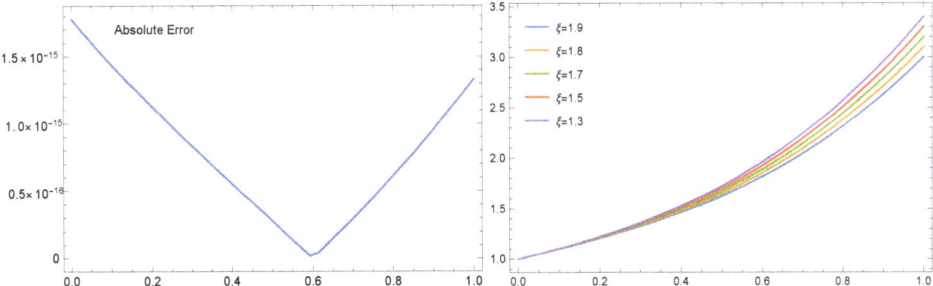

**Figure 1.** The absolute error (**left**), while (**right**) the numerical solution for different fractional-order cases of $\tilde{\zeta}$ for Example 1 with $m = 3$.

**Table 1.** Approximate solution result comparisons for the methods in [51,52], and the proposed method for Example 1, $\zeta = 1.5$, and $m = 3$.

| $t$ | LDG [51] | VIM [52] | FIM [52] | MVOMM | Exact |
|---|---|---|---|---|---|
| 0.10 | 1.101000000 | 1.183140356 | 1.103763584 | 1.100999999 | 1.101000 |
| 0.25 | 1.265624999 | 1.438783940 | 1.269040456 | 1.265624999 | 1.265625 |
| 0.30 | 1.326999999 | – | – | 1.326999999 | 1.327000 |
| 0.40 | 1.463999999 | – | – | 1.463999999 | 1.464000 |
| 0.50 | 1.625000000 | 1.519844510 | 1.623997167 | 1.624999999 | 1.625000 |
| 0.60 | 1.816000000 | – | – | 1.815999999 | 1.816000 |
| 0.75 | 2.171875000 | 0.830835570 | 2.166900262 | 2.171875000 | 2.171875 |
| 0.80 | 2.312000000 | – | – | 2.312000000 | 2.312000 |
| 0.90 | 2.629000000 | – | – | 2.629000000 | 2.629000 |

**Table 2.** Comparison of the strategy used in the present study for Example 1 with distinct errors and the LWS introduced in [53].

| Error Type | LWS [53] ($k = 0$, $H = 4$) | LWS [53] ($k = 1$, $H = 4$) | MVOMM ($m = 3$) |
|---|---|---|---|
| $L^2$-error | $5.9 \times 10^{-15}$ | $4.9 \times 10^{-15}$ | $1.78 \times 10^{-15}$ |
| $L_\infty$-error | $9.3 \times 10^{-15}$ | $7.8 \times 10^{-15}$ | $8.98 \times 10^{-16}$ |

**Example 2** ([51]). *In our next experiment, we will show that MVOM method can handle problems with discontinuities. To keep things simple, we will consider a model problem that only has one discontinuous point, but it is possible to extend the method to handle a larger number of discontinuities. We will consider a fractional-order Bagley–Torvik equation with an initial value and a discontinuous right-hand side.*

$$\mathbb{D}^2 g(t) + \mathbb{D}^{1.5} g(t) + g(t) = \vartheta(t), \quad t \in (0, 2), \quad g(0) = g'(0) = 0, \tag{31}$$

where

$$\vartheta(t) = \begin{cases} 2 + t^2 + \frac{4t^{0.5}}{\sqrt{\pi}}, & 0 \leq t < t_1, \\ 1 + 7t + t^3 + \frac{8t^{1.5}}{\sqrt{\pi}}, & t_1 \leq t \leq t_2. \end{cases}$$

In this case, $t_1$ is a point where the discontinuity occurs. The exact solutions to the problem are $g(t) = t^2$ for the variable t in the interval $I_1 = [0, t_1)$ and $g(t) = t(t^2 + 1) + 1$ for t in the interval $I_2 = [t_1, t_2]$. We will assume that the discontinuous point $t_1$ coincides with a mesh node.

For the purposes of this example, we will set $I_1 = [0, 1)$ and $I_2 = [1, 2]$. Using $m = 3$, we obtain the following approximations:

$$\begin{aligned} g_3(t) &= -4.44089 \times 10^{-16} + t^2 - 3.45025\, 10^{-16} t^3, \quad t \in I_1, \\ g_3(t) &= 1 + t - 1.77636 \times 10^{-15} t^2 + t^3, \quad t \in I_2. \end{aligned} \quad (32)$$

For Example 2, through both intervals $I_1$, $I_2$ and with $m = 3$, we obtain all the results via our suggested technique (MVOMM), reported in Equation (32), Table 3, Figures 2 and 3. The results that were obtained by Equation (32) indicate the approximate solutions were approximately consistent with the analytical solutions. Table 3 represented the absolute error, which is very tiny. Figure 2 shows the exact and approximate solutions (right), and the absolute error (left) at $t \in I_1$. Figure 3 presents the exact and approximate solutions (right), and the absolute error (left) where $t \in I_2$. Moreover, when $m = 3$, the CPU time required to produce these results at $t \in I_1$, $t \in I_2$ are 0.720 s, 0.858 s, respectively. Based on the presented results, we can say that our proposed algorithm gives high accuracy and efficiency.

**Table 3.** Absolute error comparisons for the presented method for Example 2, $\zeta = 1.5$, $m = 3$.

| $t \in I_1$ | Absolute Errors | $t \in I_2$ | Absolute Errors |
|---|---|---|---|
| 0.0 | $4.44089 \times 10^{-16}$ | 1.0 | $8.88178 \times 10^{-15}$ |
| 0.1 | $4.37773 \times 10^{-16}$ | 1.1 | $8.70304 \times 10^{-15}$ |
| 0.2 | $4.20204 \times 10^{-16}$ | 1.2 | $8.51763 \times 10^{-15}$ |
| 0.3 | $3.93453 \times 10^{-16}$ | 1.3 | $8.31890 \times 10^{-15}$ |
| 0.4 | $3.59589 \times 10^{-16}$ | 1.4 | $8.10019 \times 10^{-15}$ |
| 0.5 | $3.20684 \times 10^{-16}$ | 1.5 | $7.85483 \times 10^{-15}$ |
| 0.6 | $2.78806 \times 10^{-16}$ | 1.6 | $7.57616 \times 10^{-15}$ |
| 0.7 | $2.36027 \times 10^{-16}$ | 1.7 | $7.25753 \times 10^{-15}$ |
| 0.8 | $1.94416 \times 10^{-16}$ | 1.8 | $6.89226 \times 10^{-15}$ |
| 0.9 | $1.56044 \times 10^{-16}$ | 1.9 | $6.47371 \times 10^{-15}$ |
| 1.0 | – | 2.0 | $5.99520 \times 10^{-15}$ |

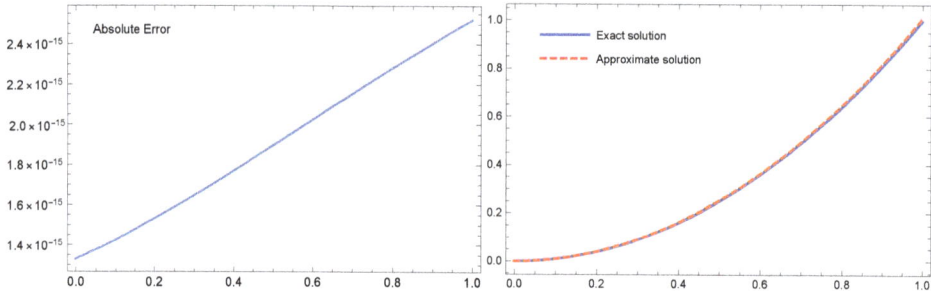

**Figure 2.** The exact and an approximate are shown on the right, while the absolute error is shown on the left for Example 2 where $t \in I_1$ and $m = 3$.

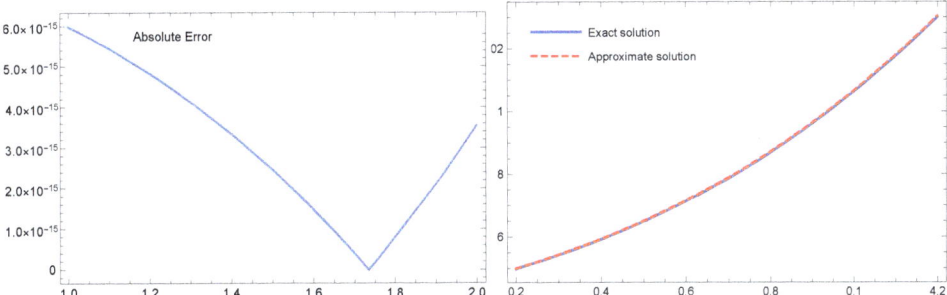

**Figure 3.** The exact and an approximate are shown on the right, while the absolute error is shown on the left for Example 2 where $t \in I_2$ and $m = 3$.

**Example 3** ([51]). *For the last examination, we choose a case study that is representative of the types of issues encountered in the modeling of electrical and mechanical oscillations, in order to make the example more applicable and realistic to real-world situations:*

$$a_1 \mathbb{D}^2 g(t) + a_2 g(t) = f_0 \cos(\varrho t), \quad f_0, \varrho > 0, \tag{33}$$

with the original state

$$g(0) = g_0, \quad g'(0) = 0, \quad 0 < t \leq \tau.$$

In our analysis of Equation (33), we only considered the cases where the forcing function is a sinusoidal wave with an amplitude of $f_0$ and a frequency of $\varrho$. Using the MVOM scheme, we examined three different vibration problems for $a_1$ and $a_2$ values of 1. We obtain the numerical solution for these cases as the following:

Case I: $f_0 = 0$, $g_0 = 1$, and $\tau = 1$. The analytical solution is $g(t) = \cos(t)$.
Case II: $f_0 = 0.01$, $g_0 = 0$, $\varrho = 1$, and $\tau = 1$. The precise solution $g(t) = 0.005\, t \sin(t)$.
Case III: $f_0 = 1$, $g_0 = 0$, and $\tau = 1$. The true solution is $g(t) = \frac{1}{1-\varrho^2}(\cos(\varrho t) - \cos(t))$, where $\varrho^2 \neq 1$. Here, we have $\varrho = 6$.

The proposed approach that was explained in the preceding Section is used to compute the absolute error for the three cases of Example 3. It is visible from analyzing the outcomes of Table 4 that were generated by the proposed methodology and the results produced by the method provided in [51] that the results provided by the proposed scheme are more accurate than those published in [51]. Additionally, the CPU time of our method is better than of [51] because we have few terms of the expansion series $m = 4, 6$ only. We obtain the CPU time in these different cases (Case I, Case II, and Case III), which are 0.093, 0.110, and 0.125 s, respectively. A great degree of precision is also provided by the proposed method for solving oscillation problems.

Figures 4–6 are reported at $m = 6$ for Example 3 through three different cases of oscillations. Figure 4 gives the absolute error on left, the analytic and an approximation solutions on right for Case I. Figure 5 presents the absolute error on left, the exact and numerical solutions on right for Case II. Figure 6 indicates the absolute error on left, the exact and an approximation solutions on right for Case III. At first glance of these three figures, we notice a great degree of agreement between the exact and the numerical solution.

**Table 4.** Absolute error comparisons for the presented method for Example 3.

| | Case I | | Case II | | Case III | |
|---|---|---|---|---|---|---|
| $t$ | LDG [51] | MVOMM ($m=4$) | LDG [51] | MVOMM ($m=4$) | LDG [51] | MVOMM ($m=6$) |
| 0.0 | – | $2.22 \times 10^{-16}$ | – | $2.42 \times 10^{-20}$ | – | $3.95 \times 10^{-20}$ |
| 0.1 | $1.95 \times 10^{-8}$ | $4.44 \times 10^{-16}$ | $7.76 \times 10^{-10}$ | $1.14 \times 10^{-15}$ | $1.12 \times 10^{-9}$ | $7.12 \times 10^{-17}$ |
| 0.2 | $1.36 \times 10^{-8}$ | $1.89 \times 10^{-15}$ | $5.38 \times 10^{-10}$ | $3.58 \times 10^{-15}$ | $5.91 \times 10^{-10}$ | $1.92 \times 10^{-16}$ |
| 0.3 | $9.66 \times 10^{-9}$ | $3.33 \times 10^{-15}$ | $3.79 \times 10^{-10}$ | $6.32 \times 10^{-15}$ | $1.92 \times 10^{-8}$ | $3.07 \times 10^{-16}$ |
| 0.4 | $9.96 \times 10^{-9}$ | $4.89 \times 10^{-15}$ | $3.94 \times 10^{-10}$ | $8.86 \times 10^{-15}$ | $3.11 \times 10^{-8}$ | $4.18 \times 10^{-16}$ |
| 0.5 | $1.02 \times 10^{-8}$ | $6.22 \times 10^{-15}$ | $4.01 \times 10^{-10}$ | $1.11 \times 10^{-14}$ | $1.92 \times 10^{-8}$ | $5.31 \times 10^{-16}$ |
| 0.6 | $5.06 \times 10^{-9}$ | $7.44 \times 10^{-15}$ | $2.01 \times 10^{-10}$ | $1.33 \times 10^{-14}$ | $5.55 \times 10^{-9}$ | $6.33 \times 10^{-16}$ |
| 0.7 | $9.44 \times 10^{-9}$ | $8.77 \times 10^{-15}$ | $3.72 \times 10^{-10}$ | $1.55 \times 10^{-14}$ | $1.88 \times 10^{-8}$ | $7.27 \times 10^{-16}$ |
| 0.8 | $3.58 \times 10^{-9}$ | $1.01 \times 10^{-14}$ | $1.42 \times 10^{-10}$ | $1.78 \times 10^{-14}$ | $1.62 \times 10^{-8}$ | $8.18 \times 10^{-16}$ |
| 0.9 | $4.79 \times 10^{-9}$ | $1.10 \times 10^{-14}$ | $1.89 \times 10^{-10}$ | $1.94 \times 10^{-14}$ | $9.71 \times 10^{-9}$ | $9.03 \times 10^{-16}$ |
| 1.0 | $3.18 \times 10^{-15}$ | $1.08 \times 10^{-14}$ | $1.19 \times 10^{-16}$ | $1.87 \times 10^{-14}$ | $1.12 \times 10^{-19}$ | $9.15 \times 10^{-16}$ |

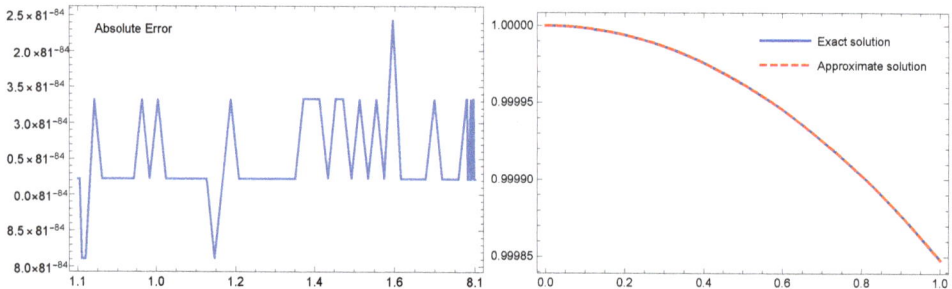

**Figure 4.** For Example 3, Case I with $m=6$: the absolute error is shown on (**left**), the analytic and the approximation solutions are presented on (**right**).

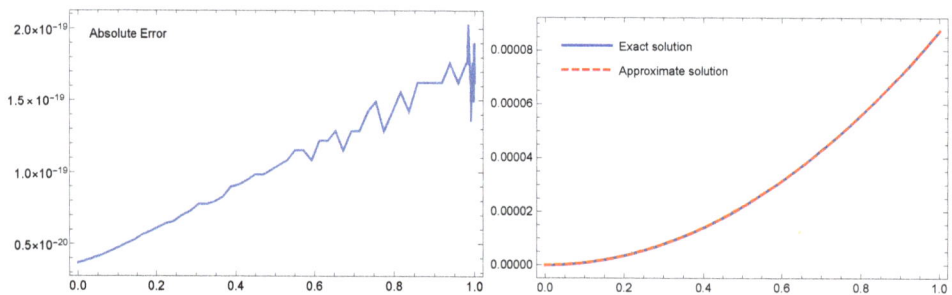

**Figure 5.** For Example 3, Case II with $m=6$: the absolute error is shown on (**left**), and the analytic and an approximation solutions are presented on (**right**).

**Example 4** ([53,54]). *Let us select the initial-value Bagley–Torvik equation of the fractional order*

$$\mathbb{D}^2 g(t) + \mathbb{D}^{1.5} g(t) + g(t) = \vartheta(t), \quad t \in [0,1],$$
$$\vartheta(t) = t^3 + \frac{8}{\sqrt{\pi}} t^{\frac{3}{2}} + 5t, \qquad (34)$$

*with the boundary conditions*

$$g(0) = g(1) = 0.$$

*The corresponding exact solution for Example 4 takes the form* $g(t) = t^3 - t$.

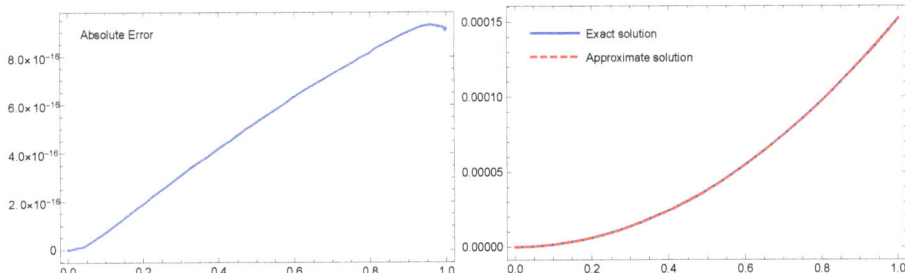

**Figure 6.** For Example 3, Case III with $m = 6$: the absolute error is shown on the (**left**), and the analytic and an approximation solutions are presented on the (**right**).

We use the suggested method for solving this problem numerically. Additionally, some comparisons are made between the obtained results of MVOMM and the LWS and the reproducing kernel Hilbert space (RKHS) reported in [53,54]. By using the LWS, the obtained solution is [53]

$$\bar{g}_3(t) = t^3 - 2.33591 \times 10^{-13} t^2 - t + 2.22045 \times 10^{-16}.$$

While the results with $m = 3$ using our method are as follows:

$$g_3(t) = t^3 - 2.66454 \times 10^{-15} t^2 - t. \tag{35}$$

For Example 4 at $m = 3$, we acquire all findings using our recommended technique (MVOMM), which is provided in Equation (35), Table 5, Table 6 and Figure 7. Equation (35) shows that the approximations were roughly congruent with the analytical solutions. Table 5, represented a comparison of the present study's exact solution with the absolute inaccuracy of the techniques developed in [53,54]. Table 6, displays findings for $L^2$-error and $L^\infty$-error utilizing our recommended approach MVOMM as well as a comparison to results obtained via [53]. Figure 7 presents the absolute error (left) and the numerical and true solutions (right). All results are obtained with CPU time 0.813 s (including all numerical results and plotting the figures). The results derived from these Tables and Figures for Example 4 provide a strong indication of the superiority of the presented Tau-collocation algorithm. In terms of accuracy and efficiency, the proposed method was found to outperform the other methods considered.

**Table 5.** Comparison of the present study's exact solution with the absolute inaccuracy of the RKHS [54] and LWS [53], relative to Example 4.

| $t$ | Exact | RKHS [54] ($n = 20$) | RKHS [54] ($n = 40$) | LWS [53] ($H = 4$) | MVOMM ($m = 3$) |
|---|---|---|---|---|---|
| 0.2 | −0.192000 | $1.890 \times 10^{-4}$ | $5.700 \times 10^{-5}$ | $9.575 \times 10^{-15}$ | $4.547 \times 10^{-16}$ |
| 0.4 | −0.336000 | $2.537 \times 10^{-4}$ | $7.131 \times 10^{-5}$ | $3.758 \times 10^{-14}$ | $1.080 \times 10^{-15}$ |
| 0.6 | −0.384000 | $2.168 \times 10^{-4}$ | $5.992 \times 10^{-5}$ | $8.426 \times 10^{-14}$ | $1.833 \times 10^{-15}$ |
| 0.8 | −0.288000 | $1.198 \times 10^{-4}$ | $3.312 \times 10^{-5}$ | $1.497 \times 10^{-13}$ | $2.672 \times 10^{-15}$ |
| 1.0 | 0 | 0 | 0 | 0 | 0 |

**Table 6.** Comparison between the LWS introduced in [53] and the current study for Example 4 with various errors.

| Error Type | LWS [53] ($k = 0$, $H = 4$) | LWS [53] ($k = 1$, $H = 4$) | MVOMM ($m = 3$) |
|---|---|---|---|
| $L^2$-error | $8.5 \times 10^{-14}$ | $2.2 \times 10^{-13}$ | $3.55 \times 10^{-15}$ |
| $L^\infty$-error | $1.6 \times 10^{-13}$ | $5.0 \times 10^{-13}$ | $1.88 \times 10^{-15}$ |

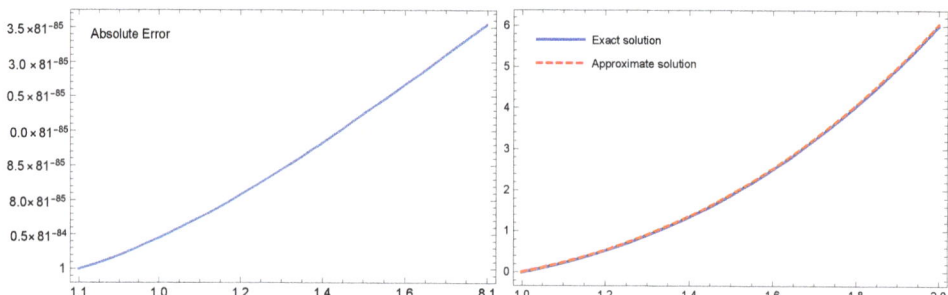

**Figure 7.** The absolute error (**left**), while the numerical and approximate solutions (**right**) for Example 4 with $m = 3$.

**Example 5** ([55–57]). *Finally, we turn our attention to another form of equation, which is know as the fractional-order Bratu differential equation type:*

$$\mathbb{D}^\zeta g(t) - 2e^{g(t)} = 0, \quad t \in [0,1], \; \zeta \in (1,2], \tag{36}$$

*with the initial conditions*

$$g(0) = g'(0) = 0.$$

*The exact solution that corresponds to Example 5 at $\zeta = 2$ is $g(t) = -2\ln(\cos(t))$.*

The following results are obtained by applying our recommended approach for solving this problem numerically and comparing the outcomes with those reported in [55–57]. The developed methods are the compact finite difference method (CFDM), the reproducing kernel Hilbert space method (RKM), and the combined spectral Bessel quasilinearization method (Bessel-QLM), respectively. For Example 5, we obtain all the results utilizing our advised method (MVOMM), and these are presented in Tables 7 and 8 and Figure 8. Table 7, introducing comparisons of the absolute error between the current methodology and the other research approaches, CFDM and RKM published in [55,56] with $m = 6$. The computational time (CPU time) in the case of $m = 6$ is 0.282 s using our suggested method. Table 8 reported a comparison between the recommended approach MVOMM and this given in [55] with $L^2$-error and $L^\infty$-error at $\zeta = 2$ and diverse values of $m$. Additionally, the CPU time in different values of $m$ is reported in the last column of Table 8. Figure 8, listed the achieved absolute error for $\zeta = 2$ (left) and the numerical values at several values of the fractional-order term $\zeta = 2, 1.9, 1.8, 1.7, 1.5, 1.3$ (right) with $m = 6$. These Tables and Figures for numerical results of Example 5 give clear evidence of the proposed method's superiority. The proposed method was found to perform better than the other existing numerical procedures taken into consideration in terms of efficiency and accuracy.

**Table 7.** Comparison of the absolute inaccuracy between the MVOMM and the CFDM and RKM used in the previous studies [55–57] using $\zeta = 2$ for Example 5.

| $t$ | CFDM [55] | RKM [56] | Bessel-QLM ($M = 7$) [57] | MVOMM ($m = 6$) |
|---|---|---|---|---|
| 0.1 | $7.1 \times 10^{-6}$ | $1.67 \times 10^{-5}$ | $4.20 \times 10^{-8}$ | $2.75 \times 10^{-17}$ |
| 0.2 | $1.23 \times 10^{-5}$ | $3.10 \times 10^{-7}$ | $1.22 \times 10^{-7}$ | $3.016 \times 10^{-17}$ |
| 0.3 | $1.71 \times 10^{-5}$ | $1.13 \times 10^{-6}$ | $1.86 \times 10^{-7}$ | $1.65 \times 10^{-16}$ |
| 0.4 | $2.26 \times 10^{-5}$ | $2.12 \times 10^{-4}$ | $2.61 \times 10^{-7}$ | $1.87 \times 10^{-16}$ |
| 0.5 | $2.90 \times 10^{-5}$ | $2.90 \times 10^{-6}$ | $3.55 \times 10^{-7}$ | $8.05 \times 10^{-17}$ |
| 0.6 | $3.69 \times 10^{-5}$ | $4.10 \times 10^{-6}$ | $4.10 \times 10^{-7}$ | $1.32 \times 10^{-16}$ |
| 0.7 | $4.72 \times 10^{-5}$ | $6.50 \times 10^{-6}$ | $5.79 \times 10^{-7}$ | $2.19 \times 10^{-16}$ |
| 0.8 | $6.14 \times 10^{-5}$ | $7.50 \times 10^{-6}$ | $6.83 \times 10^{-7}$ | $1.67 \times 10^{-16}$ |
| 0.9 | $8.32 \times 10^{-5}$ | $3.35 \times 10^{-6}$ | $3.04 \times 10^{-7}$ | $2.79 \times 10^{-16}$ |
| 1.0 | $1.29 \times 10^{-5}$ | $4.37 \times 10^{-8}$ | $3.23 \times 10^{-5}$ | $2.52 \times 10^{-16}$ |

**Table 8.** Comparison of the highest absolute errors for Example 5 using $\xi = 2$ and various values of $m$ from [55] and our proposed approach.

| CFDM [55] | | MVOMM | | |
|---|---|---|---|---|
| $N = m$ | $L_\infty$-Error | $m$ | $L_\infty$-Error | CPU Time (s) |
| 5 | $1.67 \times 10^{-3}$ | 2 | $1.42 \times 10^{-8}$ | 0.185 |
| 10 | $8.32 \times 10^{-5}$ | 4 | $5.61 \times 10^{-13}$ | 0.225 |
| 20 | $4.43 \times 10^{-6}$ | 6 | $4.11 \times 10^{-16}$ | 0.282 |
| 40 | $2.38 \times 10^{-7}$ | 8 | $8.34 \times 10^{-16}$ | 0.586 |
| 80 | $1.36 \times 10^{-8}$ | 10 | $1.47 \times 10^{-16}$ | 1.592 |

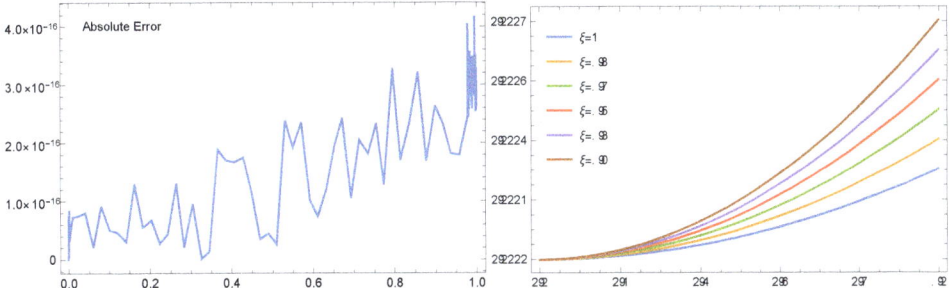

**Figure 8.** The absolute error (**left**) and the numerical solution (**right**) for various fractional-order cases of $\xi$ for Example 5 with $m = 6$.

## 6. Conclusions

In this research manuscript, we propose a novel technique based on the collocation strategy to acquire the approximate and numerical solutions for a class of fractional-order differential equations with various applications in science. To achieve this purpose, we utilize a novel operational matrix of fractional order for the Morgan–Voyce polynomials defined in the Liouville–Caputo sense combined with the collocation and Tau method. This approach involves converting the fractional order model into an algebraic system of equations with unknown coefficients, which are then solved to find these coefficients efficiently. A rigorous error analysis for the presented Tau-collocation technique shows that the proposed technique converges to the required solution. Several examples are illustrated to highlight the efficiency of the technique including the well-known Bagley–Torvik and Bratu equations and other models with different fractional orders. The results are compared with other relevant available techniques from the literature which support the proposition of a more accurate solution with fewer bases. These results provide insight into the behavior of the solution of the investigated models. In addition, the robustness of the proposed algorithm is verified by providing computational time which supports the claim. The method successfully provides accurate results highlighting the importance of the solved model, especially of the Bagley–Torvik model which have applications in simulating coupled oscillator. Thus, the provided methods are considered promising techniques for simulating similar models and can be extended to some more complex problems in the future including fractional partial differential equations with real-life applications.

**Author Contributions:** Conceptualization, W.A., A.A.E.-S. and M.I.; methodology W.A., M.I. and A.A.E.-S.; software, A.A.E.-S. and W.A.; validation, A.A.E.-S., W.A. and M.I.; formal analysis, H.M.S., M.I., W.A. and A.A.E.-S.; funding acquisition, H.M.S.; investigation, W.A., A.A.E.-S. and M.I.; writing—original draft preparation, A.A.E.-S., W.A. and M.I.; writing—review and editing, H.M.S., M.I., W.A. and A.A.E.-S. All authors have read and agreed to the published version of the manuscript.

**Funding:** This research received no external funding.

**Data Availability Statement:** Not Applicable.

**Acknowledgments:** The authors would like to thank the anonymous reviewers and editor for providing helpful comments and suggestions which further improved the quality of this work.

**Conflicts of Interest:** The authors declare no conflict of interest.

## References

1. Zhao, K. Existence, stability and simulation of a class of nonlinear fractional Langevin equations involving nonsingular Mittag-Leffler kernel. *Fractal Fract.* **2022**, *6*, 469. [CrossRef]
2. Zhang, T.; Li, Y. Exponential Euler scheme of multi–delay Caputo–Fabrizio fractional–order differential equations. *Appl. Math. Lett.* **2022**, *124*, 107709. [CrossRef]
3. Yu, F. Integrable coupling system of fractional soliton equation hierarchy. *Phys. Lett. A* **2009**, *373*, 3730–3733. [CrossRef]
4. Bonilla, B.; Rivero, M.; Trujillo, J.J. On systems of linear fractional differential equations with constant coefficients. *Appl. Math. Comput.* **2007**, *187*, 68–78. [CrossRef]
5. Diethelm, K.; Ford N.J. Analysis of fractional differential equations. *J. Math. Anal. Appl.* **2002**, *265*, 229–248. [CrossRef]
6. Momani, S.; Ibrahim, R.W. On a fractional integral equation of periodic functions involving Weyl-Riesz operator in Banach algebras. *J. Math. Anal. Appl.* **2008**, *339*, 1210–1219. [CrossRef]
7. Podlubny, I.; Chechkin, A.; Skovranek, T.; Chen, Y.; Jara, B.M.V. Matrix approach to discrete fractional calculus II: Partial fractional differential equations. *J. Comput. Phys.* **2009**, *228*, 3137–3153. [CrossRef]
8. Bonyah, E.; Hammouch, Z.; Koksal, M.E. Mathematical modeling of coronavirus dynamics with conformable derivative in Liouville-Caputo sense. *J. Math.* **2022**, *2022*, 353343. [CrossRef]
9. Saraswat, A.K.; Goyal, M. Numerical simulation of time–dependent influenza model with Atangana–Baleanu non–integer order derivative in Liouville–Caputo sense. *Pramana* **2022**, *96*, 104. [CrossRef]
10. Gao, G.H.; Sun, Z.Z.; Zhang, H.W. A new fractional numerical differentiation formula to approximate the Caputo fractional derivative and its applications. *J. Comput. Phys.* **2014**, *259*, 33–50. [CrossRef]
11. Günerhan, H.; Dutta, H.; Dokuyucu, M.A.; Adel, W. Analysis of a fractional HIV model with Caputo and constant proportional Caputo operators. *Chaos Solit. Fract* **2020**, *139*, 110053. [CrossRef]
12. Han, C.; Wang, Y.L. Numerical solutions of variable-coefficient fractional-in-space KdV equation with the Caputo fractional derivative. *Fractal Fract.* **2022**, *6*, 207. [CrossRef]
13. Kilbas, A.A.; Srivastava, H.M.; Trujillo, J.J. Theory and Application of Fractional Differential Equations. In *North-Holland Mathematics Studies*; Elsevier: Amsterdam, The Netherlands, 2006; Volume 204. [CrossRef]
14. Srivastava, H.M. Some parametric and argument variations of the operators of fractional calculus and related special functions and integral transformations. *J. Nonlinear Convex Anal.* **2021**, *22*, 1501–1520. [CrossRef]
15. Srivastava, H.M. An introductory overview of fractional-calculus operators based upon the Fox-Wright and related higher transcendental functions. *J. Adv. Engrg. Comput.* **2021**, *5*, 135–166.
16. Izadi, M.; Parsamanesh, M.; Adel, W. Numerical and stability investigations of the waste plastic management model in the ocean system. *Mathematics* **2022**, *10*, 4601.
17. Adel, W. A numerical technique for solving a class of fourth-order singular singularly perturbed and Emden-Fowler problems arising in astrophysics. *Int. J. Appl. Comput. Math.* **2022**, *8*, 220. [CrossRef]
18. Izadi, M.; Yüzbaşı, Ş.; Adel, W. A new Chelyshkov matrix method to solve linear and nonlinear fractional delay differential equations with error analysis. *Math. Sci.* **2022**. [CrossRef]
19. El-Gamel, M.; Mohamed, N.; Adel, W. Numerical study of a nonlinear high order boundary value problems using Genocchi collocation technique. *Int. J. Appl. Comput. Math.* **2022**, *8*, 143. [CrossRef]
20. De Boor, C. On calculating with B-splines. *J. Approx. Theory* **1972**, *6*, 50–62. [CrossRef]
21. Kaur, N.; Goyal, K. An adaptive wavelet optimized finite difference B-spline polynomial chaos method for random partial differential equations. *Appl. Math. Comput.* **2022**, *415*, 126738. [CrossRef]
22. Zahra, W.K.; Ouf, W.A.; El-Azab, M.S. A robust uniform B-spline collocation method for solving the generalized PHI-four equation. *Appl. Appl. Math.* **2016**, *11*, 24. [CrossRef]
23. Zahra, W.K.; Ouf, W.A.; El-Azab, M.S. Cubic B-spline collocation algorithm for the numerical solution of Newell Whitehead Segel type equations. *Electron. J. Math. Anal. Appl.* **2014**, *2*, 81–100. [CrossRef]
24. Ricker, N. Wavelet functions and their polynomials. *Geophysics* **1944**, *9*, 314–323.
25. Alqhtani, M.; Khader, M.M.; Saad, K.M. Numerical simulation for a high-dimensional chaotic Lorenz system based on Gegenbauer wavelet polynomials. *Mathematics* **2023**, *11*, 472.
26. Mason, J.; Handscomb, D. *Chebyshev Polynomials*; Chapman and Hall: New York, NY, USA; CRC: Boca Raton, FL, USA, 2003. [CrossRef]
27. Atta, A.G.; Abd-Elhameed, W.M.; Youssri, Y.H. Shifted fifth-kind Chebyshev polynomials Galerkin-based procedure for treating fractional diffusion-wave equation. *Int. J. Mod. Phys. C* **2022**, *33*, 2250102. [CrossRef]
28. Szeg, G. *Orthogonal Polynomials*; American Mathematical Soc.: Providence, RI, USA, 1939; Volume 23.
29. Fathy, M.; El-Gamel, M.; El-Azab, M.S. Legendre-Galerkin method for the linear Fredholm integro-differential equations. *Appl. Math. Comput.* **2014**, *243*, 789–800. [CrossRef]

30. Abdelhakem, M.; Moussa, H. Pseudo-spectral matrices as a numerical tool for dealing BVPs, based on Legendre polynomials' derivatives. *Alex. Eng. J.* **2023**, *66*, 301–313.
31. Zhang, C.; Khan, B.; Shaba, T.G.; Ro, J.S.; Araci, S.; Khan, M.G. Applications of q-Hermite polynomials to subclasses of analytic and bi-univalent functions. *Fractal Fract.* **2022**, *6*, 420. [CrossRef]
32. Wanas, A.K.; Lupaş, A.A. Applications of Laguerre polynomials on a new family of bi-prestarlike functions. *Symmetry* **2022**, *14*, 645. [CrossRef]
33. Swamy, M.N.S. Further properties of Morgan-Voyce polynomials. *Fibonacci Quart.* **1968**, *6*, 167–175. [CrossRef]
34. Türkyilmaz, B.; Gürbüz, B.; Sezer, M. Morgan-Voyce polynomial approach for solution of high-order linear differential-difference equations with residual error estimation. *Düzce Üniv. J. Sci. Tech.* **2016**, *4*, 252–263. [CrossRef]
35. Tarakci, M.; Özel, M.; Sezer, M. Solution of nonlinear ordinary differential equations with quadratic and cubic terms by Morgan–Voyce matrix-collocation method. *Turk. J. Math.* **2020**, *44*, 906–918.
36. Özel, M.; Kurkcu, O.K.; Sezer, M. Morgan-Voyce matrix method for generalized functional integro-differential equations of Volterra-type. *J. Sci. Arts* **2019**, *19*, 295–310
37. Izadi, M.; Yüzbaşı, Ş.; Adel, W. Accurate and efficient matrix techniques for solving the fractional Lotka–Volterra population model. *Physica A* **2022**, *600*, 127558. [CrossRef]
38. Izadi, M.; Zeidan, D. A convergent hybrid numerical scheme for a class of nonlinear diffusion equations. *Comp. Appl. Math.* **2022**, *41*, 318.
39. Kashiem, B.E. Morgan-Voyce Approach for Solution Bratu Problems. *Emir. J. Eng. Res.* **2021**, *26*, 3. [CrossRef]
40. Torvik, P.J.; Bagley, R.L. On the appearance of the fractional derivative in the behavior of real materials. *J. Appl. Mech.* **1984**, *51*, 294–298. [CrossRef]
41. Guirao, J.L.; Sabir, Z.; Raja, M.A.Z.; Baleanu, D. Design of neuro-swarming computational solver for the fractional Bagley–Torvik mathematical model. *Eur. Phys. J. Plus* **2022**, *137*, 245.
42. Shi, L.; Tayebi, S.; Arqub, O.A.; Osman, M.S.; Agarwal, P.; Mahamoud, W.; Abdel-Aty, M.; Alhodaly, M. The novel cubic B-spline method for fractional Painlevé and Bagley–Trovik equations in the Caputo, Caputo–Fabrizio, and conformable fractional sense. *Alex. Eng. J.* **2023**, *65*, 413–426. [CrossRef]
43. Deshi, A.B.; Gudodagi, G.A. Numerical solution of Bagley–Torvik, nonlinear and higher order fractional differential equations using Haar wavelet. *SeMA J.* **2022**, *79*, 663–675. [CrossRef]
44. Sabir, Z.; Raja, M.A.Z.; Sadat, R.; Ahmed, K.S.; Ali, M.R.; Al-Kouz, W. Fractional Meyer neural network procedures optimized by the genetic algorithm to solve the Bagley–Torvik model. *J. Appl. Anal. Comput.* **2022**, *12*, 2458–2474. [CrossRef]
45. Yüzbaşı, Ş.; Yıldırım, G. Numerical solutions of the Bagley–Torvik equation by using generalized functions with fractional powers of Laguerre polynomials. *Int. J. Nonlinear Sci. Numer. Simul.* **2022**. [CrossRef]
46. Ding, Q.; Wong, P.J. A higher order numerical scheme for solving fractional Bagley–Torvik equation. *Math. Methods Appl. Sci.* **2022**, *45*, 1241–1258. [CrossRef]
47. Izadi, M.; Yüzbaşı, Ş.; Cattani, C. Approximating solutions to fractional-order Bagley–Torvik equation via generalized Bessel polynomial on large domains. *Ric. Mat.* **2021**, 1–27. [CrossRef]
48. Podlubny, I. *Fractional Differential Equations, Mathematics in Science and Engineering*; Academic Press: New York, NY, USA, 1999. [CrossRef]
49. Odibat, Z.M.; Shawagfeh, N.T. Generalized Taylor's formula. *Appl. Math. Comput.* **2007**, *186*, 286–293. [CrossRef]
50. Abd Elaziz El-Sayed, A.; Boulaaras, S.; Sweilam, N.H. Numerical solution of the fractional-order logistic equation via the first-kind Dickson polynomials and spectral tau method. *Math. Methods Appl. Sci.* **2021**, Early View. https://doi.org/10.1002/mma.7345.
51. Izadi, M.; Negar, M.R. Local discontinuous Galerkin approximations to fractional Bagley–Torvik equation. *Math. Methods Appl. Sci.* **2020**, *43*, 4798–4813. [CrossRef]
52. Mekkaoui, T.; Hammouch, Z. Approximate analytical solutions to the Bagley–Torvik equation by the fractional iteration method. *Ann. Univ. Craiova Math. Comput.* **2012**, *39*, 251–256. [CrossRef]
53. Koundal, R.; Kumar, R.; Srivastava, K.; Baleanu, D. Lucas wavelet scheme for fractional Bagley–Torvik equations: Gauss–Jacobi approach. *Int. J. Appl. Comput. Math.* **2022**, *8*, 3. [CrossRef]
54. Sakar, M.G.; Saldır, O.; Akgül, A. A novel technique for fractional Bagley–Torvik equation. *Proc. Natl. Acad. Sci. USA* **2019**, *89*, 539–545.
55. Gharechahi, R.; Arabameri, M.; Bisheh-Niasar, M. Numerical solution of fractional Bratu's initial value problem using compact finite difference scheme. *Progr. Fract. Differ. Appl.* **2021**, *7*, 103–115. [CrossRef]
56. Babolian, E.; Javadi, S.; Moradi, E. RKM for solving Bratu-type differential equations of fractional order. *Math. Methods Appl. Sci.* **2016**, *39*, 1548–1557. [CrossRef]
57. Izadi, M.; Srivastava, H.M. Generalized Bessel quasilinearization technique applied to Bratu and Lane–Emden type equations of arbitrary order. *Fractal Fract.* **2021**, *5*, 179.

**Disclaimer/Publisher's Note:** The statements, opinions and data contained in all publications are solely those of the individual author(s) and contributor(s) and not of MDPI and/or the editor(s). MDPI and/or the editor(s) disclaim responsibility for any injury to people or property resulting from any ideas, methods, instructions or products referred to in the content.

*fractal and fractional*

Article

# Application of the Pathway-Type Transform to a New Form of a Fractional Kinetic Equation Involving the Generalized Incomplete Wright Hypergeometric Functions

Mohammed Z. Alqarni [1,†], Ahmed Bakhet [2,†] and Mohamed Abdalla [1,*]

1. Department of Mathematics, Faculty of Science, King Khalid University, Abha 61471, Saudi Arabia
2. Department of Mathematics, Faculty of Science, Al-Azhar University, Assiut 71524, Egypt
* Correspondence: moabdalla@kku.edu.sa
† These authors contributed equally to this work.

**Abstract:** We present in this paper a generalization of the fractional kinetic equation using the generalized incomplete Wright hypergeometric function. The pathway-type transform technique is then used to investigate the solutions to a fractional kinetic equation with specific fractional transforms. Furthermore, exceptional cases of our outcomes are discussed and graphically illustrated using MATLAB software. This work provides a thorough overview for further investigation into these topics in order to gain a better understanding of their implications and applications.

**Keywords:** incomplete Wright hypergeometric functions; pathway-type transform; fractional kinetic equations

Citation: Alqarni, M.Z.; Bakhet, A.; Abdalla, M. Application of the Pathway-Type Transform to a New Form of a Fractional Kinetic Equation Involving the Generalized Incomplete Wright Hypergeometric Functions. *Fractal Fract.* 2023, 7, 348. https://doi.org/10.3390/fractalfract7050348

Academic Editors: Gheorghe Oros and Georgia Irina Oros

Received: 14 February 2023
Revised: 16 April 2023
Accepted: 21 April 2023
Published: 23 April 2023

**Copyright:** © 2023 by the authors. Licensee MDPI, Basel, Switzerland. This article is an open access article distributed under the terms and conditions of the Creative Commons Attribution (CC BY) license (https://creativecommons.org/licenses/by/4.0/).

## 1. Introduction

Fractional-order differential equations have fractional derivatives instead of integer derivatives [1–5]. A kinetic equation is one of the essential kinds of fractional-order differential equations. Its importance is reflected in the fact that it has received increased attention in electrodynamics, control systems, economics, hydrodynamics, physics, geophysics, and mathematics. Furthermore, fractional-order kinetic (reaction-type) equations play a significant role as tools of mathematics that are frequently employed to describe a variety of physical and astrophysical phenomena (see [6–10]). For example, reaction-type (kinetic) equations can explain how nuclei are created and destroyed during chemical (thermonuclear) processes. A formal representation of reactions characterized by a time-dependent quantity $\mathbf{E} = \mathbf{E}(\xi)$ is given by the following Cauchy problem (see, for example, [11]):

$$\frac{d\mathbf{E}}{d\xi} = -\delta(\mathbf{E}) + p(\mathbf{E}), \quad \mathbf{E}(0) = \mathbf{E}_0, \tag{1}$$

where $\mathbf{E}_0$ is the initial data and $\delta$ and $p$ are the destruction and production rate of $\mathbf{E}$, respectively. Furthermore, Haubold and Mathai studied a special case of this Cauchy problem [11] given by

$$\frac{d\mathbf{E}}{d\xi} = -\vartheta \mathbf{E}, \quad \vartheta \in \mathbb{R}^+, \quad \mathbf{E}(0) = \mathbf{E}_0. \tag{2}$$

Equation (2) is known as the standard kinetic equation. They also gave a representation in the form of a fractional equation as follows:

$$\mathbf{E}(\xi) - \mathbf{E}_0 = -\vartheta \, {}_0\mathbb{D}_\xi^{-1} \mathbf{E}(\xi), \quad \vartheta, \xi \in \mathbb{R}^+, \tag{3}$$

where $_0\mathbb{D}_\xi^{-\nu}$ is the fractional integral operator [1] given by

$$_0\mathbb{D}_\xi^{-\nu} f(\xi) = \frac{1}{\Gamma(\nu)} \int_0^\xi (\xi - s)^{\nu-1} f(s) ds, \ \nu \in \mathbb{R}^+. \tag{4}$$

Many generalizations and solutions of the fractional-order kinetic equation have recently been developed, utilizing a variety of fractional integral transforms including the fractional Laplace transform [12–16], fractional Sumudu transform [17–19], Hadamard fractional integrals [20–22], fractional pathway transform [23,24] and Prabhakar-type operators [25], which have been extensively studied. In particular, Khan et al. [14] presented solutions for fractional kinetic equations associated with the $(p,q)$-extended $\tau$-hypergeometric and confluent hypergeometric functions using the Laplace transform, while Hidan et al. [15] discussed a technique for the Laplace transformation of solutions of fractional kinetic equations involving extended $(k,t)$-Gauss hypergeometric matrix functions. In addition, Abubakar [16] derived solutions for fractional kinetic equations using the $(p,q;l)$-extended $\tau$-Gauss hypergeometric function. Gaining insight from the last recently mentioned manuscripts, this paper provides an in-depth exploration of fractional kinetic equations and their solutions by using the generalized incomplete Wright hypergeometric function and pathway-type transform technique. We provide a comprehensive overview that is sure to give researchers plenty to think about when it comes to implications and applications. Overall, this work should be regarded as required reading for anyone interested in learning more about these themes.

## 2. Preliminaries

Here, we highlight a few concepts that would be helpful for future discussion.

The Gauss hypergeometric function given by

$$\mathbf{F}(\theta_1, \theta_2, \theta_3; z) = \sum_{j=0}^\infty \frac{(\theta_1)_j (\theta_2)_j}{(\theta_3)_j} \frac{z^j}{j!}, \quad z \in \mathbb{C}, \tag{5}$$

will be convergent absolutely and uniformly under the condition $|z| < 1$. Here, $\theta_1, \theta_2$, and $\theta_3$ are complex parameters with $\theta_3 \in \mathbb{C} \setminus \mathbb{Z}_0^-$, and

$$(\theta_1)_j = \frac{\Gamma(\theta_1 + j)}{\Gamma(\theta_1)} = \begin{cases} \theta_1(\theta_1+1)\cdots(\theta_1+j-1), & j \in \mathbb{N}, \ \theta_1 \in \mathbb{C} \\ 1, & j = 0; \ \theta_1 \in \mathbb{C} \setminus \{0\}, \end{cases} \tag{6}$$

is known to be the Pochhammer symbol of $\theta_1$, whereas $\Gamma(v)$ is the standard gamma function, defined as

$$\Gamma(\theta) = \int_0^\infty v^{\theta-1} e^{-v} dv, \quad \theta \in \mathbb{C} \setminus \mathbb{Z}_0^-. \tag{7}$$

Moreover, we define the lower and upper incomplete gamma functions, as shown in [26], as

$$\gamma(\theta; x) = \int_0^x v^{\theta-1} e^{-v} dv, \quad \theta \in \mathbb{C} \setminus \mathbb{Z}_0^-, \tag{8}$$

and

$$\Gamma(\theta; x) = \int_x^\infty v^{\theta-1} e^{-v} dv, \quad \theta \in \mathbb{C} \setminus \mathbb{Z}_0^-, \tag{9}$$

respectively. The decomposition formula of $\Gamma(\theta)$ can be preformed using Equations (8) and (9) as follows:

$$\gamma(\theta; x) + \Gamma(\theta; x) = \Gamma(\theta). \tag{10}$$

The incomplete Pochhammer symbols $(\theta; x)_n$ and $[\theta; x]_n$ are defined by

$$(\theta; x)_n = \frac{\gamma(\theta + n; x)}{\Gamma(\theta)} \tag{11}$$

and

$$[\theta; x]_n = \frac{\Gamma(\theta + n; x)}{\Gamma(\theta)}. \tag{12}$$

Similar to Equation (10), a decomposition of $(\theta)_n$ can be given by the functions in Equations (11) and (12) as follows:

$$(\theta; x)_n + [\theta; x]_n = (\theta)_n, \tag{13}$$

Wright's $(\tau - Gauss)$ hypergeometric function was first studied in [27] as follows:

$$_2\mathbf{R}_1(\vartheta_1, \vartheta_2; \vartheta_3; \tau; \eta) = \frac{\Gamma(\vartheta_3)}{\Gamma(\vartheta_2)} \sum_{j=0}^{\infty} \frac{(\vartheta_1)_j \Gamma(\vartheta_2 + \tau j)}{\Gamma(\vartheta_3 + \tau j)} \frac{\eta^j}{j!} \quad (\tau \in \mathbb{R}^+, \ |\eta| < 1), \tag{14}$$

where $\vartheta_1, \vartheta_2$, and $\vartheta_3$ are complex parameters such that $\Re(\vartheta_1) > 0, \Re(\vartheta_2) > 0$, and $\Re(\vartheta_3) > 0$.

In addition, the incomplete Wright's hypergeometric function was studied in [28] as follows:

$$_2\Gamma_1(\vartheta_1, \vartheta_2; \vartheta_3; \tau; \eta) = \frac{\Gamma(\vartheta_3)}{\Gamma(\vartheta_2)} \sum_{j=0}^{\infty} \frac{[\vartheta_1; x]_j \Gamma(\vartheta_2 + \tau j)}{\Gamma(\vartheta_3 + \tau j)} \frac{\eta^j}{j!} \quad (\tau \in \mathbb{R}^+, \ |\eta| < 1) \tag{15}$$

and

$$_2\gamma_1(\vartheta_1, \vartheta_2; \vartheta_3; \tau; \eta) = \frac{\Gamma(\vartheta_3)}{\Gamma(\vartheta_2)} \sum_{j=0}^{\infty} \frac{(\vartheta_1; x)_j \Gamma(\vartheta_2 + \tau j)}{\Gamma(\vartheta_3 + \tau j)} \frac{\eta^j}{j!} \quad (\tau \in \mathbb{R}^+, \ |\eta| < 1), \tag{16}$$

where $\vartheta_1, \vartheta_2$, and $\vartheta_3$ are complex parameters such that $\Re(\vartheta_1) > 0, \Re(\vartheta_2) > 0$, and $\Re(\vartheta_3) > 0$. Recent developments and expansions of Wright's hypergeometric function can be found, for example, in [29,30].

The family of the generalized incomplete Wright's hypergeometric functions of the $p$ numerator and $q$ denominator is given by [28]

$$_p\Gamma_q^{(\tau)} \left[ \begin{array}{c} (\theta_p, x); \\ \eta_q; \end{array} z \right] = {_p\Gamma_q^{(\tau)}} \left[ \begin{array}{c} (\theta_1, x), \theta_2, \ldots, \theta_p; \\ \eta_1, \eta_2, \ldots, \eta_q; \end{array} z \right]$$
$$= \frac{\Gamma(\eta_1), \ldots, \Gamma(\eta_q)}{\Gamma(\theta_2), \ldots, \Gamma(\theta_p)} \sum_{n=0}^{\infty} \frac{[\theta_1, x]_n \Gamma(\theta_2 + n\tau) \ldots \Gamma(\theta_p + n\tau)}{\Gamma(\eta_1 + n\tau) \Gamma(\eta_2 + n\tau) \ldots \Gamma(\eta_q + n\tau)} \frac{z^n}{n!}, \tag{17}$$

where $\vartheta_p, \eta_q \in \mathbb{C}, \tau > 0, p = q + 1, p, q \in \mathbb{N}_0, |z| < 1$, and

$$_p\gamma_q^{(\tau)} \left[ \begin{array}{c} (\theta_p, x); \\ \eta_q; \end{array} z \right] = {_p\gamma_q^{(\tau)}} \left[ \begin{array}{c} (\theta_1, x), \theta_2, \ldots, \theta_p; \\ \eta_1, \eta_2, \ldots, \eta_q; \end{array} z \right]$$
$$= \frac{\Gamma(\eta_1), \ldots, \Gamma(\eta_q)}{\Gamma(\theta_2), \ldots, \Gamma(\theta_p)} \sum_{n=0}^{\infty} \frac{(\theta_1, x)_n \Gamma(\theta_2 + n\tau) \ldots \Gamma(\theta_p + n\tau)}{\Gamma(\eta_1 + n\tau) \Gamma(\eta_2 + n\tau) \ldots \Gamma(\eta_q + n\tau)} \frac{z^n}{n!}, \tag{18}$$

where $\vartheta_p, \eta_q \in \mathbb{C}, \tau > 0, p = q + 1$, and $p, q \in \mathbb{N}_0, |z| < 1$.

The generalized incomplete hypergeometric functions ${}_p\Gamma_q^{(\tau)}$ and ${}_p\gamma_q^{(\tau)}$ satisfy the following decomposition formula:

$${}_p\Gamma_q^{(\tau)}\left[\begin{array}{c}(\theta_p,x);\\ \eta_q;\end{array} z\right] + {}_p\gamma_q^{(\tau)}\left[\begin{array}{c}(\theta_p,x);\\ \eta_q;\end{array} z\right] = {}_p\mathbf{R}_q^{(\tau)}\left[\begin{array}{c}\theta_p;\\ \eta_q;\end{array} z\right] \quad (19)$$

**Remark 1.** *Some special cases of the generalized incomplete Wright's hypergeometric functions are as follows:*

(i) By setting $\tau = 1$ in Equations (17) and (18) and employing the relation in Equation (6), we have the extended incomplete Gauss hypergeometric function (see [31]):

$$\begin{aligned}{}_p\Gamma_q\left[\begin{array}{c}(\theta_p,x);\\ \eta_q;\end{array} z\right] &= {}_p\Gamma_q\left[\begin{array}{c}(\theta_1,x),\theta_2,\ldots,\theta_p;\\ \eta_1,\eta_2,\ldots,\eta_q;\end{array} z\right]\\ &= \sum_{n=0}^{\infty}\frac{[\theta_1,x]_n\,(\theta_2)_n+\ldots(\theta_p)_n}{(\eta_1)_n\ldots(\eta_q)_n}\frac{z^n}{n!},\end{aligned} \quad (20)$$

where $\vartheta_p, \eta_q \in \mathbb{C}, \tau > 0, p = q+1, p, q \in \mathbb{N}_0, |z| < 1$, and

$$\begin{aligned}{}_p\gamma_q\left[\begin{array}{c}(\theta_p,x);\\ \eta_q;\end{array} z\right] &= {}_p\gamma_q\left[\begin{array}{c}(\theta_1,x),\theta_2,\ldots,\theta_p;\\ \eta_1,\eta_2,\ldots,\eta_q;\end{array} z\right]\\ &= \sum_{n=0}^{\infty}\frac{(\theta_1,x)_n\,(\theta_2)_n+\ldots(\theta_p)_n}{(\eta_1)_n\ldots(\eta_q)_n}\frac{z^n}{n!},\end{aligned} \quad (21)$$

where $\vartheta_p, \eta_q \in \mathbb{C}, \tau > 0, p = q+1$, and $p, q \in \mathbb{N}_0, |z| < 1$.

As an immediate consequence of Equations (20) and (21), we have the following decomposition formula:

$${}_p\Gamma_q\left[\begin{array}{c}(\theta_p,x);\\ \eta_q;\end{array} z\right] + {}_p\gamma_q\left[\begin{array}{c}(\theta_p,x);\\ \eta_q;\end{array} z\right] = {}_p\mathbf{F}_q\left[\begin{array}{c}\theta_p;\\ \eta_q;\end{array} z\right], \quad (22)$$

in terms of the generalized hypergeometric function.

(ii) If we put $p = 2$ and $q = 1$ into Equations (17) and (18), we obtain

$$\begin{aligned}{}_2\Gamma_1^{(\tau)}\left[\begin{array}{c}(\theta_2,x);\\ \eta_1;\end{array} z\right] &= {}_p\Gamma_q^{(\tau)}\left[\begin{array}{c}(\theta_1,x),\theta_2;\\ \eta_1;\end{array} z\right]\\ &= \frac{\Gamma(\eta_1)}{\Gamma(\theta_2)}\sum_{n=0}^{\infty}\frac{[\theta_1,x]_n\,\Gamma(\theta_2+n\tau)}{\Gamma(\eta_1+n\tau)\Gamma(\eta_2+n\tau)}\frac{z^n}{n!},\end{aligned} \quad (23)$$

$(\tau > 0, |z| < 1)$,

and

$$\begin{aligned}{}_2\gamma_1^{(\tau)}\left[\begin{array}{c}(\theta_2,x);\\ \eta_1;\end{array} z\right] &= {}_2\gamma_1^{(\tau)}\left[\begin{array}{c}(\theta_1,x),\theta_2;\\ \eta_1;\end{array} z\right]\\ &= \frac{\Gamma(\eta_1))}{\Gamma(\theta_2)}\sum_{n=0}^{\infty}\frac{(\theta_1,x)_n\,\Gamma(\theta_2+n\tau)}{\Gamma(\eta_1+n\tau)}\frac{z^n}{n!},\end{aligned} \quad (24)$$

$(\tau > 0, |z| < 1)$.

Equations (23) and (24) contain the following decomposition formula as a direct result:

$${}_2\Gamma_1^{(\tau)}\left[\begin{array}{c}(\theta_1,x),\theta_2;\\ \eta_1;\end{array} z\right] + {}_2\gamma_1^{(\tau)}\left[\begin{array}{c}(\theta_1,x),\theta_2;\\ \eta_1;\end{array} z\right] = {}_2\mathbf{R}_1^{(\tau)}\left[\begin{array}{c}\theta_1,\theta_2;\\ \eta_1;\end{array} z\right] \quad (25)$$

for the Wright hypergeometric function in (14).

The derivative formulas for generalized incomplete Wright's hypergeometric functions are as follows (see [28]):

$$\frac{d^n}{dz^n}\left\{ {}_p\Gamma_q^{(\tau)}\left[\begin{matrix}(\theta_1,x),\theta_2,\ldots,\theta_p;\\ \eta_1,\eta_2,\ldots,\eta_q;\end{matrix}z\right]\right\}$$
$$=\frac{(\theta_1)_n\,\Gamma(\theta_2+n\tau)\ldots\Gamma(\theta_p+n\tau)}{\Gamma(\eta_1+n\tau)\Gamma(\eta_2+n\tau)\ldots\Gamma(\eta_q+n\tau)}$$
$$\times {}_p\Gamma_q^{(\tau)}\left[\begin{matrix}(\theta_1+n,x),\theta_2+n\tau,\ldots,\theta_p+n\tau;\\ \eta_1+n\tau,\eta_2+n\tau,\ldots,\eta_q+n\tau;\end{matrix}z\right] \quad (26)$$

and

$$\frac{d^n}{dz^n}\left\{ {}_p\gamma_q^{(\tau)}\left[\begin{matrix}(\theta_1,x),\theta_2,\ldots,\theta_p;\\ \eta_1,\eta_2,\ldots,\eta_q;\end{matrix}z\right]\right\}$$
$$=\frac{(\theta_1)_n\,\Gamma(\theta_2+n\tau)\ldots\Gamma(\theta_p+n\tau)}{\Gamma(\eta_1+n\tau)\Gamma(\eta_2+n\tau)\ldots\Gamma(\eta_q+n\tau)}$$
$$\times {}_p\gamma_q^{(\tau)}\left[\begin{matrix}(\theta_1+n,x),\theta_2+n\tau,\ldots,\theta_p+n\tau;\\ \eta_1+n\tau,\eta_2+n\tau,\ldots,\eta_q+n\tau;\end{matrix}z\right]. \quad (27)$$

The pathway-type transform ($\mathbf{K}_\omega$ transform) is defined in [23,24] as

$$\mathbf{K}_\omega[f(t),s] = F(s) = \int_0^\infty [1+(\omega-1)s]^{\frac{-t}{\omega-1}} f(t)dt \quad \omega > 1, \quad (28)$$

with

$$\lim_{\omega\to 1^+}[1+(\omega-1)s]^{\frac{-t}{\omega-1}} = e^{-st}. \quad (29)$$

The Laplace transform ($L[.,.]$) is generalized by this transformation; which can be seen from

$$\lim_{\omega\to 1}\mathbf{K}_\omega[f(t),s] = L[f(t),s]. \quad (30)$$

The two useful properties of the $\mathbf{K}_\omega$ transform are as follows:

$$\mathbf{K}_\omega[1,s] = \frac{\omega-1}{\ln[1+(\omega-1)s]} \quad (31)$$

and

$$\mathbf{K}_\omega\left[\frac{t^n}{n!},s\right] = \left\{\frac{\omega}{\ln[1+(\omega-1)s]}\right\}^{n+1}. \quad (32)$$

Furthermore, using the convolution theorem of the $\mathbf{K}_\omega$ transform [23], we see that Equation (4) may be represented by

$$\mathbf{K}_\omega[{}_0\mathbb{D}_t^{-\lambda}f(t),s] = \left[\frac{\omega-1}{\ln[1+(\omega-1)s]}\right]^\lambda \mathbf{K}_\omega[f(t),s] \quad \lambda\in\mathbb{C}. \quad (33)$$

## 3. Statement of Results

In this section, we solve the fractional kinetic equation associated with the $\tau$-generalized incomplete hypergeometric functions using the method of the $\mathbf{K}_\omega$ transform.

**Theorem 1.** Let $\lambda > 0, d > 0, z \in \mathbb{C}$, and $\tau > 0$. Then, we conclude that the solution of the $\tau$-generalized incomplete hypergeometric function's fractional kinetic equation

$$\mathbf{E}(z) - \mathbf{E}_0 \, {}_p\Gamma_q^{(\tau)}(z) = -d^\lambda \, {}_0\mathbb{D}_z^{-\lambda}\mathbf{E}(z), \tag{34}$$

is given by

$$\begin{aligned}\mathbf{E}(z) =& \mathbf{E}_0 \frac{\Gamma(\eta_1),\ldots,\Gamma(\eta_q)}{\Gamma(\theta_2),\ldots,\Gamma(\theta_p)} \sum_{n=0}^{\infty} \frac{[\theta_1, x]_n \, \Gamma(\theta_2 + n\tau)\ldots\Gamma(\theta_p + n\tau)}{\Gamma(\eta_1 + n\tau)\Gamma(\eta_2 + n\tau)\ldots\Gamma(\eta_q + n\tau)} \\ &\times \sum_{m=0}^{\infty} (-1)^m (d)^{m\lambda} \frac{z^{m\lambda + n}}{(m\lambda + n)!}.\end{aligned} \tag{35}$$

**Proof.** By using the $\mathbf{K}_\omega$ transform of both sides of Equation (34) and using Equations (32) and (33), we have

$$\begin{aligned}&\mathbf{K}_\omega\big[\mathbf{E}(z)\big]\Big[1 + d^\lambda \Big\{\frac{\omega - 1}{\ln\{1 + (\omega - 1)r\}}\Big\}^\lambda\Big] \\ &= \mathbf{E}_0 \frac{\Gamma(\eta_1),\ldots,\Gamma(\eta_q)}{\Gamma(\theta_2),\ldots,\Gamma(\theta_p)} \sum_{n=0}^{\infty} \frac{[\theta_1, x]_n \, \Gamma(\theta_2 + n\tau)\ldots\Gamma(\theta_p + n\tau)}{\Gamma(\eta_1 + n\tau)\Gamma(\eta_2 + n\tau)\ldots\Gamma(\eta_q + n\tau)} \\ &\times \Big[\frac{\ln\{1 + (\omega - 1)\}}{\omega - 1}\Big]^{-n-1}\end{aligned} \tag{36}$$

and

$$\begin{aligned}\mathbf{K}_\omega\big[\mathbf{E}(z)\big] =& \mathbf{E}_0 \frac{\Gamma(\eta_1),\ldots,\Gamma(\eta_q)}{\Gamma(\theta_2),\ldots,\Gamma(\theta_p)} \sum_{n=0}^{\infty} \frac{[\theta_1, x]_n \, \Gamma(\theta_2 + n\tau)\ldots\Gamma(\theta_p + n\tau)}{\Gamma(\eta_1 + n\tau)\Gamma(\eta_2 + n\tau)\ldots\Gamma(\eta_q + n\tau)} \\ &\Big[\frac{\ln\{1 + (\omega - 1)r\}}{\omega - 1}\Big]^{-n-1} \sum_{m=0}^{\infty} \frac{(-1)^m}{m!}\Big[\frac{d(\omega - 1)}{\ln\{1 + (\omega - 1)r\}}\Big]^{m\lambda} \\ =& \mathbf{E}_0 \frac{\Gamma(\eta_1),\ldots,\Gamma(\eta_q)}{\Gamma(\theta_2),\ldots,\Gamma(\theta_p)} \sum_{n=0}^{\infty} \frac{[\theta_1, x]_n \, \Gamma(\theta_2 + n\tau)\ldots\Gamma(\theta_p + n\tau)}{\Gamma(\eta_1 + n\tau)\Gamma(\eta_2 + n\tau)\ldots\Gamma(\eta_q + n\tau)} \\ &\times \sum_{m=0}^{\infty} (-1)^m \, d^{m\lambda}(\omega - 1)^{n+m\lambda+1}\Big[\ln\{1 + (\omega - 1)r\}\Big]^{-(n+m\lambda+1)}.\end{aligned} \tag{37}$$

Now, when we take the inverse of the $\mathbf{K}_\omega$ transform and apply Equation (32), we have the desired result. □

**Theorem 2.** Let $\lambda > 0, d > 0, z \in \mathbb{C}$, and $\tau > 0$. Then, we conclude that the solution of the $\tau$-generalized incomplete hypergeometric function's fractional kinetic equation

$$\mathbf{E}(z) - \mathbf{E}_0 \Big\{\frac{d}{dz} \, {}_p\Gamma_q^{(\tau)}(z)\Big\} = -d^\lambda \, {}_0\mathbb{D}_t^{-\lambda}\mathbf{E}(z), \tag{38}$$

is given by

$$\begin{aligned}\mathbf{E}(z) =& \mathbf{E}_0 \Big[\frac{\theta_1(\theta_2 + \tau)\ldots(\theta_p + \tau)}{(\eta_1 + \tau)\ldots(\eta_q + \tau)}\Big] \sum_{n=0}^{\infty} \frac{[\theta_1 + 1, x]_n \, (\theta_2 + \tau)_n \ldots (\theta_p + \tau)_n}{(\eta_1 + \tau)_n(\eta_2 + \tau)_n \ldots (\eta_q + \tau)_n} z^n \\ &\times \sum_{m=0}^{\infty} \frac{(-1)^m (dz)^{m\lambda}}{(m\lambda + n)!}.\end{aligned} \tag{39}$$

**Proof.** By taking the $\mathbf{K}_\omega$ transform of both sides of Equation (38) and using Equations (26), (32), and (33), we find

$$\mathbf{K}_\omega\left[\mathbf{E}(z)\right]\left[1+d^\lambda\left\{\frac{\omega-1}{\ln\{1+(\omega-1)r\}}\right\}^\lambda\right]$$

$$=\mathbf{E}_0\left[\frac{\theta_1(\theta_2+\tau)\ldots(\theta_p+\tau)}{(\eta_1+\tau)\ldots(\eta_q+\tau)}\right]\sum_{n=0}^\infty\frac{[\theta_1+1,x]_n\,(\theta_2+\tau)_n\ldots(\theta_p+\tau)_n}{(\eta_1+\tau)_n(\eta_2+\tau)_n\ldots(\eta_q+\tau)_n} \quad (40)$$

$$\times\left[\frac{\ln\{1+(\omega-1)r\}}{\omega-1}\right]^{-n-1}$$

and

$$\mathbf{K}_\omega\left[\mathbf{E}(z)\right]=\mathbf{E}_0\left[\frac{\theta_1(\theta_2+\tau)\ldots(\theta_p+\tau)}{(\eta_1+\tau)\ldots(\eta_q+\tau)}\right]\sum_{n=0}^\infty\frac{[\theta_1+1,x]_n\,(\theta_2+\tau)_n\ldots(\theta_p+\tau)_n}{(\eta_1+\tau)_n(\eta_2+\tau)_n\ldots(\eta_q+\tau)_n}$$

$$\left[\frac{\ln\{1+(\omega-1)r\}}{\omega-1}\right]^{-n-1}\sum_{m=0}^\infty\frac{(-1)^m}{m!}\left[\frac{d(\omega-1)}{\ln\{1+(\omega-1)r\}}\right]^{m\lambda} \quad (41)$$

$$=\mathbf{E}_0\left[\frac{\theta_1(\theta_2+\tau)\ldots(\theta_p+\tau)}{(\eta_1+\tau)\ldots(\eta_q+\tau)}\right]\sum_{n=0}^\infty\frac{[\theta_1+1,x]_n\,(\theta_2+\tau)_n\ldots(\theta_p+\tau)_n}{(\eta_1+\tau)_n(\eta_2+\tau)_n\ldots(\eta_q+\tau)_n}$$

$$\times\sum_{m=0}^\infty(-1)^m\,d^{m\lambda}(\omega-1)^{n+m\lambda+1}\left[\ln\{1+(\omega-1)r\}\right]^{-(n+m\lambda+1)}.$$

By taking the inverse of the $\mathbf{K}_\omega$ transform of both sides of Equation (41) and applying Equation (32), we readily obtain the desired result. □

Now, we give the results for the solution of the fractional kinetic equation of the ${}_p\gamma_q^{(\tau)}$-generalized incomplete hypergeometric function in Equation (27), which are given in the following two theorems:

**Theorem 3.** *Let $\lambda>0, d>0, z\in\mathbb{C}$, and $\tau>0$. Then, the solution of the fractional kinetic equation of the $\tau$-generalized incomplete hypergeometric functions*

$$\mathbf{E}(z)-\mathbf{E}_0\,{}_p\gamma_q^{(\tau)}(z)=-d^\lambda\,{}_0\mathbb{D}_z^{-\lambda}\mathbf{E}(z), \quad (42)$$

*is given by*

$$\mathbf{E}(z)=\mathbf{E}_0\frac{\Gamma(\eta_1),\ldots,\Gamma(\eta_q)}{\Gamma(\theta_2),\ldots,\Gamma(\theta_p)}\sum_{n=0}^\infty\frac{(\theta_1,x)_n\,\Gamma(\theta_2+n\tau)\ldots\Gamma(\theta_p+n\tau)}{\Gamma(\eta_1+n\tau)\Gamma(\eta_2+n\tau)\ldots\Gamma(\eta_q+n\tau)}$$

$$\times\sum_{m=0}^\infty(-1)^m(d)^{m\lambda}\frac{z^{m\lambda+n}}{(m\lambda+n)!}. \quad (43)$$

**Proof.** The proof here runs in parallel with that for Theorem 1. The details have been omitted. □

**Theorem 4.** *Let $\lambda>0, d>0, z\in\mathbb{C}$, and $\tau>0$. Then, the solution of the fractional kinetic equation of the $\tau$-generalized incomplete hypergeometric functions*

$$\mathbf{E}(z)-\mathbf{E}_0\left\{\frac{d}{dz}\,{}_p\gamma_q^{(\tau)}(z)\right\}=-d^\lambda\,{}_0\mathbb{D}_t^{-\lambda}\mathbf{E}(z), \quad (44)$$

is given by

$$\begin{aligned} \mathbf{E}(z) = &\mathbf{E}_0 \left[ \frac{\theta_1(\theta_2+\tau)\dots(\theta_p+\tau)}{(\eta_1+\tau)\dots(\eta_q+\tau)} \right] \sum_{n=0}^{\infty} \frac{(\theta_1+1,x)_n \, (\theta_2+\tau)_n \dots (\theta_p+\tau)_n}{(\eta_1+\tau)_n (\eta_2+\tau)_n \dots (\eta_q+\tau)_n} z^n \\ &\times \sum_{m=0}^{\infty} \frac{(-1)^m (dz)^{m\lambda}}{(m\lambda+n)!}. \end{aligned} \quad (45)$$

**Proof.** This proof follows a similar pattern to that of Theorem 2. The specifics have been left out. □

### 4. Illustrative Examples

The following are some examples of the special cases of the solution to fractional kinetic equations, including the $\tau$-generalized incomplete hypergeometric functions,

(i) If we have $p = 2$ and $q = 1$, then Equation (34) reduces to

$$\mathbf{E}(z) - \mathbf{E}_0 \, {}_2\Gamma_1^{(\tau)}(z) = -d^\lambda \, {}_0\mathbb{D}_z^{-\lambda} \mathbf{E}(z), \quad (46)$$

whose solution is

$$\mathbf{E}(z) = \mathbf{E}_0 \frac{\Gamma(\eta_1)}{\Gamma(\theta_2)} \sum_{n=0}^{\infty} \frac{[\theta_1,x]_n \, \Gamma(\theta_2+n\tau)}{\Gamma(\eta_1+n\tau)} \sum_{m=0}^{\infty} (-1)^m (d)^{m\lambda} \frac{z^{m\lambda+n}}{(m\lambda+n)!}. \quad (47)$$

(ii) When we have $p = 2$ and $q = 1$, then Equation (42) reduces to

$$\mathbf{E}(z) - \mathbf{E}_0 \, {}_2\gamma_1^{(\tau)}(z) = -d^\lambda \, {}_0\mathbb{D}_z^{-\lambda} \mathbf{E}(z), \quad (48)$$

whose solution is

$$\mathbf{E}(z) = \mathbf{E}_0 \frac{\Gamma(\eta_1)}{\Gamma(\theta_2)} \sum_{n=0}^{\infty} \frac{(\theta_1,x)_n \, \Gamma(\theta_2+n\tau)}{\Gamma(\eta_1+n\tau)} \sum_{m=0}^{\infty} (-1)^m (d)^{m\lambda} \frac{z^{m\lambda+n}}{(m\lambda+n)!}. \quad (49)$$

(iii) When we have $p = 2, q = 1$ and $\tau = 1$, then Equation (34) reduces to

$$\mathbf{E}(z) - \mathbf{E}_0 \, {}_2\Gamma_1(z) = -d^\lambda \, {}_0\mathbb{D}_z^{-\lambda} \mathbf{E}(z) \quad (50)$$

and its solution is

$$\mathbf{E}(z) = \mathbf{E}_0 \sum_{n=0}^{\infty} \frac{[\theta_1,x]_n \, (\theta_2)_n}{(\eta_1)_n} \sum_{m=0}^{\infty} (-1)^m (d)^{m\lambda} \frac{z^{m\lambda+n}}{(m\lambda+n)!}. \quad (51)$$

(iv) When we have $p = 2$ and $q = 1$, then Equation (38) reduces to a hypergeometric function

$$\mathbf{E}(z) - \mathbf{E}_0 \left\{ \frac{d}{dz} \, {}_2\Gamma_1^{(\tau)}(z) \right\} = -d^\lambda \, {}_0\mathbb{D}_t^{-\lambda} \mathbf{E}(z), \quad (52)$$

given by

$$\begin{aligned} \mathbf{E}(z) = &\mathbf{E}_0 \left[ \frac{\theta_1(\theta_2+\tau)}{(\eta_1+\tau)} \right] \sum_{n=0}^{\infty} \frac{[\theta_1+1,x]_n \, (\theta_2+\tau)_n}{(\eta_1+\tau)_n} z^n \\ &\times \sum_{m=0}^{\infty} \frac{(-1)^m (dz)^{m\lambda}}{(m\lambda+n)!}. \end{aligned} \quad (53)$$

(v) When we substitute $p = 2$ and $q = 1$, then Equation (44) reduces to

$$\mathbf{E}(z) - \mathbf{E}_0 \left\{ \frac{d}{dz} \, {}_2\gamma_1^{(\tau)}(z) \right\} = -d^\lambda \, {}_0\mathbb{D}_t^{-\lambda} \mathbf{E}(z) \quad (54)$$

and its solution is

$$\mathbf{E}(z) = \mathbf{E}_0 \left[ \frac{\theta_1(\theta_2 + \tau)}{(\eta_1 + \tau)} \right] \sum_{n=0}^{\infty} \frac{(\theta_1 + 1, x)_n \, (\theta_2 + \tau)_n}{(\eta_1 + \tau)_n} z^n \\ \times \sum_{m=0}^{\infty} \frac{(-1)^m (dz)^{m\lambda}}{(m\lambda + n)!}. \tag{55}$$

## 5. Comments on the Graphical Interpretations

Figure 1 depicts the plots of solutions to Equation (35) with parametric values $\mathbf{E}_0 = 1, q = 20, p = 21$, and $z = 0.5, \cdots, 5$ for various values of $\lambda = 0.1, 0.2, \cdots, 0.9$ in Figure 1a and with fixed values of $x = 2$, $d = 0.2$, and $\tau = 1$. In Figure 1b, we fix the values to $\tau = 1$, $d = 1$ and $\lambda = 0.5$ and generate graphs for various values of $x = 0.1, \cdots, 2$. The valid region of convergence of the solutions is given by the time interval $z = 0.5, \cdots, 5$. Figure 2 exhibits 2D plots of the solutions to Equation (43) for various values of $\lambda$ and $x$ in Figure 2a and Figure 2b, respectively, with fixed values of $\tau = 1, d = 1$, and $\mathbf{E}_0 = 1$. The graphical findings show that the region of convergence of the solutions was continually dependent on the parameters $\lambda$ and $x$. As a result, evaluating the behavior of the solutions for various parameters and time periods revealed that $\mathbf{E}(z)$ was always positive. Furthermore, we could change the values of $\lambda, x, \tau$, and $d$ to obtain more accurate results.

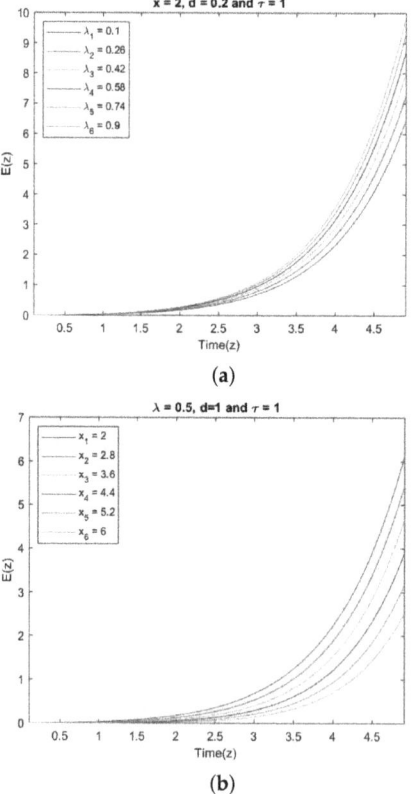

**Figure 1.** Graphs of the solution to Equation (35) with various values of $\lambda$ in (**a**) and various values of $x$ in (**b**).

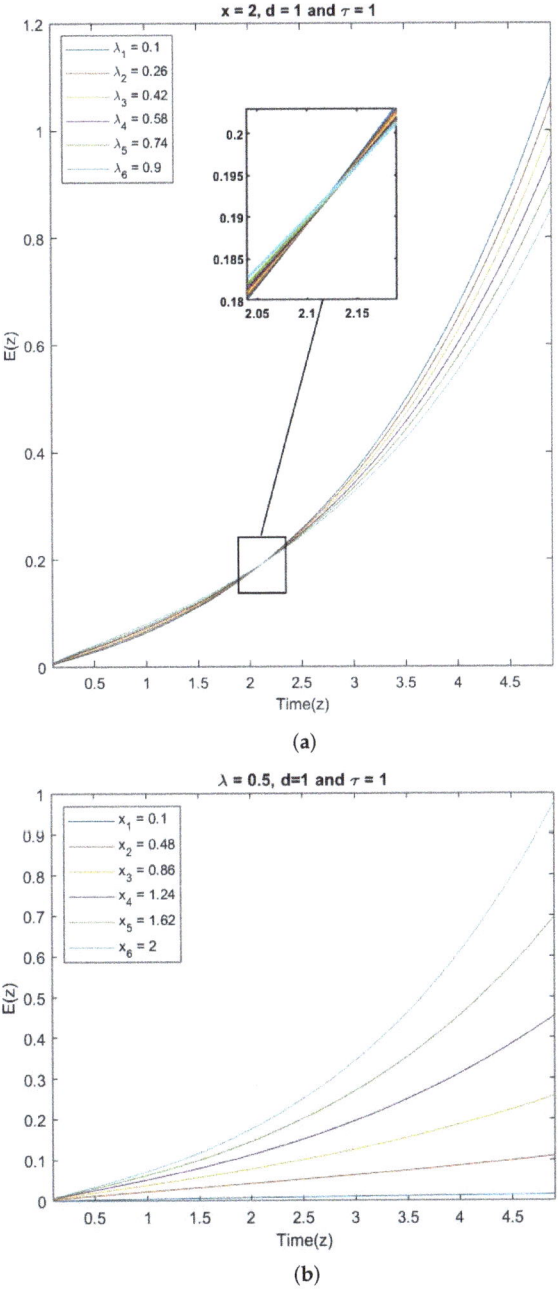

**Figure 2.** Graphs of the solution to Equation (43) with various values of $\lambda$ in (**a**) and various values of $x$ in (**b**).

## 6. Conclusions

Because of the usefulness and great importance of the kinetic equation in some astrophysical issues, fractional kinetic equations have been investigated to describe the various phenomena governed by anomalous reactions in dynamical systems [6–9]. Several authors have recently presented solutions to various families of fractional kinetic equations involving special functions using the Laplace transform, Sumudu transform, Prabhakar-type operators, Hadamard fractional integrals, and pathway-type transform based on these principles (see, for example, [10–25]).

Motivated by the above works, the authors developed a new and generalized form of the fractional kinetic equation involving the generalized incomplete Wright hypergeometric function. This new generalization can be used to compute the change in chemical composition in stars such as the Sun. The manifold generality of the Mittag-Leffler function was discussed in terms of the solution to the above fractional kinetic equation by applying a pathway-type transform. Furthermore, a graphical representation of the solutions was provided to demonstrate the behavior of these solutions and to analyze special situations for fractional kinetic equations.

**Author Contributions:** Methodology, M.A.; Software, M.Z.A.; Formal analysis, A.B.; Investigation, A.B. and M.A.; Data curation, M.Z.A.; Writing—original draft, M.Z.A.; Writing—review & editing, A.B. and M.A.; Supervision, M.A. All authors have read and agreed to the published version of the manuscript.

**Funding:** This work was funded by the Deanship of Scientific Research at King Khalid University through a large group research project under grant number RGP2/25/44.

**Data Availability Statement:** No data were used to support this study.

**Conflicts of Interest:** This work does not have any conflict of interest.

## References

1. Abbas, S.; Benchohra, M.; Guerekata, G.M.N. *Topics in Fractional Differential Equations*; Springer: New York, NY, USA, 2012.
2. Zhou, Y. *Basic Theory of Fractional Differential Equations*; World Scientific: Singapore, 2014.
3. Abbas, M.I.; Ragusa, M.A. Solvability of Langevin equations with two Hadamard fractional derivatives via Mittag-Leffler functions. *Appl. Anal.* **2020**, *101*, 3231–3245.
4. Bakhet, A.; He, F. On the matrix version of extended Struve function and its application on fractional calculus. *Filomat* **2022**, *36*, 3381–3392. [CrossRef]
5. Youssri, Y.H.; Abd-Elhameed, W.M.; Ahmed, H.M. New fractional derivative ex-pression of the shifted third-kind Chebyshev polynomials: Application to a type of non-linear fractional pantograph differential equations. *J. Funct. Spaces* **2022**, 3966135.
6. Saxena, R.K.; Mathai, A.M.; Haubold, H.J. On fractional kinetic equations. *Astrophys. Space Sci.* **2002**, *282*, 281–287. [CrossRef]
7. Saxena, R.K.; Mathai, A.M.; Haubold, H.J. On generalized fractional kinetic equations. *Phys. A* **2004**, *344*, 657–664.
8. Saxena, R.K.; Kalla, S.L. On the solutions of certain fractional kinetic equations. *Appl. Math. Comput.* **2008**, *199*, 504–511. [CrossRef]
9. Chaurasia, V.B.L.; Pandey, S.C. On the new computable solution of the generalized fractional kinetic equations involving the generalized function for the fractional calculus and related functions. *Astrophys. Space Sci.* **2008**, *317*, 213–219. [CrossRef]
10. Kolokoltsov, V.N.; Troeva, M. A new approach to fractional kinetic evolutions. *Fractal Fract.* **2022**, *6*, 49. [CrossRef]
11. Haubold, H.J.; Mathai, A.H. The fractional kinetic equation and thermonuclear functions. *Astrophys. Space Sci.* **2000**, *327*, 53–63. [CrossRef]
12. Habenom, H.; Oli, A.; Suthar, D.L. $(p,q)$-Extended Struve function: Fractional integrations and application to fractional kinetic equations. *J. Math.* **2021**, *2021*, 5536817.
13. Sharma, K.P.; Bhargava, A.; Suthar, D.L. Application of the Laplace transform to a new form of fractional kinetic equation involving the composition of the Galue Struve function and the Mittageffler function. *Math. Probl. Eng.* **2022**, *2022*, 5668579. [CrossRef]
14. Khan, O.; Khan, N.; Choi, J.; Nisar, K.S. A type of fractional Kinetic equations associated with the $(p,q)$-extented $\tau$-hypergeomtric and confluent hypergeomtric functions. *Nonlinear Funct. Anal. Appl.* **2021**, *26*, 381–392.
15. Hidan, M.; Akel, M.; Abd-Elmageed, H.; Abdalla, M. Solution of fractional kinetic equations involving extended $(k,t)$-Gauss hypergeometric matrix functions. *AIMS Math.* **2022**, *7*, 14474–14491. [CrossRef]
16. Abubakar, U.M. Solutions of fractional kinetic equations using the $(p,q;l)$-extended $\tau$-Gauss hypergeometric function. *J. New Theory* **2022**, *38*, 25–33. [CrossRef]
17. Purohit, S.D.; Ucar, F. An application of $q$-Sumudu transform for fractional $q$-kinetic equation. *Turk. J. Math.* **2018**, *42*, 726–734. [CrossRef]
18. Agarwal, P.; Ntouyas, S.K.; Jain, S.; Chand, M.; Singh, G. Fractional kinetic equations involving generalized $k$-Bessel function via Sumudu transform. *Alex. Eng. J.* **2018**, *57*, 1937–1942. [CrossRef]

19. Yagci, O.; Sahin, R. Solutions of fractional kinetic equations involving generalized Hurwitz-Lerch Zeta functions using Sumudu transform. *Commun. Fac. Sci. Univ. Ank. Ser. A1 Math. Stat.* **2021**, *70*, 678–689. [CrossRef]
20. Akel, M.; Hidan, M.; Boulaaras, S.; Abdalla, M. On the solutions of certain fractional kinetic matrix equations involving Hadamard fractional integrals. *AIMS Math.* **2022**, *7*, 15520–15531. [CrossRef]
21. Ahmed, W.; Salamoon, A.; Pawar, D. Solution of fractional kinetic equation for Hadamard type fractional integral via Mellin transform. *Gulf. J. Math.* **2022**, *12*, 15–27. [CrossRef]
22. Abdalla, M.; Akel, M. Contribution of using Hadamard fractional integral operator via Mellin integral transform for solving certain fractional kinetic matrix equations. *Fractal Fract.* **2022**, *6*, 305. [CrossRef]
23. Kumar, D. Solution of fractional kinetic equation by a class of integral transform of pathway type. *J. Math. Phys.* **2013**, *54*, 043509. [CrossRef]
24. Mathur, G.A.R. Solution of fractional kinetic equations by using integral transform. *AIP Conf. Proc.* **2020**, *2253*, 020004.
25. Dorrego, G.A.; Kumar, D. A generalization of the kinetic equation using the Prabhakar-type operators. *Honam Math. J.* **2017**, *39*, 401–416.
26. Chaudhry, M.A.; Zubair, S.M. *On a Class of Incomplete Gamma Functions with Applications*; Chapman and Hall/CRC: Boca Raton, FL, USA, 2002.
27. Virchenko, N.; Kalla, S.L.; Al-Zamel, A. Some results on a generalized hypergeometric function. *Integral Transforms Spec. Funct.* **2001**, *12*, 89–100. [CrossRef]
28. Nisar, K.S.; Rahman, G.; Mubeen, S.; Arshad, M. The incomplete Pochhammer symbols and their application to generalized hypergeometric functions. *Int. Bull. Math. Res.* **2017**, *4*, 1–13.
29. Khan, N.; Usman, T.; Aman, M.; Al-Omari, S.; Araci, S. Computation of certain integral formulas involving generalized Wright function. *Adv. Differ. Equ.* **2020**, 1–10. [CrossRef]
30. Ghaffar, A.; Saif, A.; Iqbal, M.; Rizwan, M. Two classes of integrals involving extended Wright type generalized hypergeometric function. *Commun. Math. Appl.* **2019**, *10*, 599–606. [CrossRef]
31. Srivastava, H.M.; Chaudhry, M.A.; Agarwal, R.P. The incomplete Pochhammer symbols and their applications to hypergeometric and related functions. *Integral Transform. Spec. Funct.* **2012**, *23*, 659–683. [CrossRef]

**Disclaimer/Publisher's Note:** The statements, opinions and data contained in all publications are solely those of the individual author(s) and contributor(s) and not of MDPI and/or the editor(s). MDPI and/or the editor(s) disclaim responsibility for any injury to people or property resulting from any ideas, methods, instructions or products referred to in the content.

*Article*

# Some New Applications of the $q$-Analogous of Differential and Integral Operators for New Subclasses of $q$-Starlike and $q$-Convex Functions

Suha B. Al-Shaikh [1,*], Ahmad A. Abubaker [1], Khaled Matarneh [1] and Mohammad Faisal Khan [2]

[1] Faculty of Computer Studies, Arab Open University, Riyadh 11681, Saudi Arabia; a.abubaker@arabou.edu.sa (A.A.A.); k.matarneh@arabou.edu.sa (K.M.)
[2] Department of Basic Sciences, College of Science and Theoretical Studies, Saudi Electronic University, Riyadh 11673, Saudi Arabia; f.khan@seu.edu.sa
* Correspondence: s.alshaikh@arabou.edu.sa

**Citation:** Al-Shaikh, S.B.; Abubaker, A.A.; Matarneh, K.; Khan, M.F. Some New Applications of the $q$-Analogous of Differential and Integral Operators for New Subclasses of $q$-Starlike and $q$-Convex Functions. *Fractal Fract.* **2023**, *7*, 411. https://doi.org/10.3390/fractalfract7050411

Academic Editors: Hari Mohan Srivastava, Gheorghe Oros and Georgia Irina Oros

Received: 7 March 2023
Revised: 5 May 2023
Accepted: 17 May 2023
Published: 19 May 2023

**Copyright:** © 2023 by the authors. Licensee MDPI, Basel, Switzerland. This article is an open access article distributed under the terms and conditions of the Creative Commons Attribution (CC BY) license (https://creativecommons.org/licenses/by/4.0/).

**Abstract:** In the geometric function theory of complex analysis, the investigation of the geometric properties of analytic functions using $q$-analogues of differential and integral operators is an important area of study, offering powerful tools for applications in numerical analysis and the solution of differential equations. Many topics, including complex analysis, hypergeometric series, and particle physics, have been generalized in $q$-calculus. In this study, first of all, we define the $q$-analogues of a differential operator ($DR_{\lambda,q}^{m,n}$) by using the basic idea of $q$-calculus and the definition of convolution. Additionally, using the newly constructed operator ($DR_{\lambda,q}^{m,n}$), we establish the $q$-analogues of two new integral operators ($F_{\lambda,\gamma_1,\gamma_2,\ldots\gamma_l}^{m,n,q}$ and $G_{\lambda,\gamma_1,\gamma_2,\ldots\gamma_l}^{m,n,q}$), and by employing these operators, new subclasses of the $q$-starlike and $q$-convex functions are defined. Sufficient conditions for the functions ($f$) that belong to the newly defined classes are investigated. Additionally, certain subordination findings for the differential operator ($DR_{\lambda,q}^{m,n}$) and novel geometric characteristics of the $q$-analogues of the integral operators in these classes are also obtained. Our results are generalizations of results that were previously proven in the literature.

**Keywords:** analytic functions; convolution; quantum (or $q$-) calculus; $q$-difference operator; $q$-integral operator; $q$-starlike and $q$-convex functions; differential subordination

**MSC:** 05A30; 30C45; 11B65; 47B38

## 1. Introduction and Definitions

Since the dawn of analytic function theory, when Alexander [1] introduced the first integral operator in 1915, differential and integral operators have been the subject of scholarly research. Novel combinations of differential and integral operators are constantly being invented (see [2,3]). Sălăgean and Ruscheweyh operators have great importance in research [4–7]. Recent research on differential and integral operators from several perspectives, including quantum calculus, has produced remarkable findings that have applications in other branches of physics and mathematics. Some fascinating uses of differential and integral operators are highlighted in a recent survey-cum-expository review study [8]. Some examples of publications on the extension of Sălăgean differential operators are included in [9,10], with examples of $q$-extensions in [11–18].

The theory of real and complex-order integrals and derivatives has been used in the study of geometric functions, and it has also shown potential for mathematical modeling and analysis of practical concerns in the applied sciences. Analyzing the dynamics of dengue transmission [19] and creating a novel model of the human liver [20] are both examples of studies that are included within the aforementioned field of research.

In particular, the family of integral operators related to the first-kind Lommel functions was introduced in [21] and is crucial for understanding both pure and applied mathematics. It is now possible to examine differential equations from the perspectives of functional analysis and operator theory due to differential operators. Differential operator properties are employed to solve differential equations using the operator technique. For the integral operators introduced in this work, several interesting geometric and mapping features are also deduced. In this line of study, we use the concepts of quantum operator theory and introduce the $q$-analogues of the differential operator, then consider this operator. We also introduce two new integral operators in this paper. From the viewpoints of operator theory and functional analysis, the study of differential equations utilizes operators, and with more investigation, it might be discovered that such operators play a role in solving partial differential equations.

In the open unit disc $U = \{z \in \mathbb{C} : |z| < 1\}$, let $\mathcal{A}$ stand for the collection of all analytic functions, and let every $f \in \mathcal{A}$ in this set have a series of the form:

$$f(z) = z + \sum_{j=2}^{\infty} a_j z^j, z \in U. \tag{1}$$

The class $T$ is a subclass of $\mathcal{A}$, and every $f \in T$ has a series of the form

$$f(z) = z - \sum_{j=2}^{\infty} a_j z^j, z \in U. \tag{2}$$

For $0 \leq \alpha < 1$, let $\mathcal{S}^*(\alpha)$ stand for the set of all star-shaped functions of order $\alpha$, which we define as follows:

$$\mathcal{S}^*(\alpha) = \left\{ f \in \mathcal{A} : Re\left(\frac{zf'(z)}{f(z)}\right) > \alpha \right\}.$$

For $\alpha = 0$,

$$\mathcal{S}^*(0) = \mathcal{S}^*.$$

The convolution of the functions $f, g \in \mathcal{A}$ is denoted by

$$(f * g)(z) = z + \sum_{j=2}^{\infty} a_j b_j z^j = (g * f)(z), \ z \in U,$$

where $f(z)$ is defined by Equation (1), and

$$g(z) = z + \sum_{j=2}^{\infty} b_j z^j.$$

**Definition 1** ([22]). *If $\mathcal{K}_1$ and $\mathcal{K}_2$ are two analytic functions in the open unit disk (U), if there is an analytic function $(u_0)$ in U, then $\mathcal{K}_1$ is subordinate to $\mathcal{K}_2$, $(\mathcal{K}_1 \prec \mathcal{K}_2)$ with*

$$u_0(0) = 0, \text{ and } |u_0(z)| < 1$$

*the set of all $z \in U$ then*

$$\mathcal{K}_1(z) = \mathcal{K}_2(u_0(z)).$$

*If $\mathcal{K}_2$ is univalent, then*

$$\mathcal{K}_1 \prec \mathcal{K}_2 \iff \mathcal{K}_1(0) = \mathcal{K}_2(0)$$

*and*

$$\mathcal{K}_1(U) \subseteq \mathcal{K}_2(U).$$

**Definition 2** ([22]). *Let $\psi : U \times \mathbb{C}^3 \longrightarrow \mathbb{C}$ and $h$ is univalent in $U$. If $s$ is analytic in $U$ and the following differential subordination conditions hold:*

$$\psi\left(s(z), zs'(z), z^2 s''(z); z\right) \prec h(z), \text{ for all } z \in U, \qquad (3)$$

*then $s$ is the solution of the differential subordination. Dominant refers to the univalent function (r) if $s \prec r$ for all $s$ satisfying (3). A dominant $\widetilde{r}$ satisfying $\widetilde{r} \prec r$ for all dominants $r$ of (3) is said to be the best dominant of (3). Up to a rotation of $U$, the best dominant is unique.*

Geometric function theory, q-difference equations, and q-integral equations are only a few examples of the recent generalization of quantum ($q$-) calculus across many areas of mathematics and science. Starting with the basics of $q$-calculus theory, Jackson [23] introduced the $q$-derivative and $q$-integral operators; then, Ismail et al. [24] defined $q$-starlike functions using the same ideas. After the $q$-difference operator was introduced, a rush of studies examined the $q$-analogues of other differential operators. In order to build a new class of analytic functions in the conic domain, Kanas and Raducanu [25] created the $q$-analogue of the Ruscheweyh differential operator. The multivalent generalizations were later provided by Arif et al. [26]. Using the basics of $q$-calculus, Zang et al. [27] constructed a generalized conic domain and studied a new category of $q$-starlike functions in this context. Geometric function theory (GFT) and $q$-calculus theory both have been the subject of a great deal of research by numerous mathematicians to date (for details, see [28–34]). It has been established that time-scale calculus, a more general branch of mathematics, involves quantum calculus. Time-scale calculus enables the investigation of dynamic equations according to a cogent framework in both discrete and continuous domains.

The main contribution of this study is the quantum calculus operator theory. We develop several new forms of $q$-analogues of the differential and integral operators using the fundamental principles of quantum calculus operator theory and the $q$-difference operator. Using these operators, we build many new classes of $q$-starlike and $q$-convex functions and investigate several interesting features of the analytic function ($f$) that belongs to these classes.

**Definition 3.** *Jackson [23] provided the following definition of the q-difference (or derivative) operator ($\partial_q$) for analytic functions ($f$), where $q \in (0,1)$.*

$$\begin{aligned}\partial_q f(z) &= \frac{f(qz) - f(z)}{(q-1)z}, \ z \neq 0, \\ &= 1 + \sum_{j=2}^{\infty} [j]_q a_j z^{j-1},\end{aligned} \qquad (4)$$

*where $[j]_q$ is the q-number and defined as:*

$$\begin{aligned}[j]_q &= \frac{1-q^j}{1-q} \\ &= 1 + q + q^2 + \ldots + q^{j-1}, \ j \in \mathbb{N}\end{aligned}$$

*and*

$$[0]_q = 0.$$

*The factorial of q, $[j]_q!$ is identified as follows:*

$$[j]_q! = [j]_q [j-1]_q [j-2]_q \ldots [2]_q [1]_q$$

*and*

$$[0]_q! = 1.$$

**Definition 4.** *Jackson [35] defined the q-integral for the function $f \in \mathcal{A}$ as follows:*

$$\int f(z)d_q(z) = (1-q)z \sum_{j=0}^{\infty} f\left(q^j z\right) q^j.$$

By using the same technique of the Al-Oboudi differential operator [36], now we define the q-analogues of the Al-Oboudi differential operator $(D_{\lambda,q}^m)$ for analytic functions as follows:

**Definition 5.** *For $\lambda \geq 0$, $q \in (0,1)$, $m, n \in \mathbb{N}$, and $f \in \mathcal{A}$, the operator $D_{\lambda,q}^m : \mathcal{A} \to \mathcal{A}$, is defined by*

$$\begin{aligned}
D_{\lambda,q}^0 f(z) &= f(z), \\
D_{\lambda,q}^1 f(z) &= (1-\lambda)f(z) + \lambda z \partial_q f(z) = D_{\lambda,q} f(z) \\
&\cdots \\
D_{\lambda,q}^m f(z) &= (1-\lambda)D_q^{m-1} f(z) + \lambda z \partial_q \left(D_q^{m-1} f(z)\right) = D_{\lambda,q}(D_{\lambda,q}^{m-1} f(z)).
\end{aligned}$$

After some simple calculation, we have

$$D_{\lambda,q}^m f(z) = z + \sum_{j=2}^{\infty} \left\{\lambda\left([j]_q - 1\right) + 1\right\}^m a_j z^j. \tag{5}$$

**Remark 1.** *For the function $(f)$ of the form (2), the series expansion of $D_{\lambda,q}^m$ is given by:*

$$D_{\lambda,q}^m f(z) = z - \sum_{j=2}^{\infty} \left\{\lambda\left([j]_q - 1\right) + 1\right\}^m a_j z^j.$$

**Remark 2.** *Specifically, when $\lambda = 1$, the operator $D_{\lambda,q}^m$ simplifies to the Sălăgean q-differential operator given by [37].*

**Remark 3.** *If $q \to 1-$, then we obtain the Al-Oboudi differential operator studied in [36].*

**Remark 4.** *If $\lambda = 1$, and $q \to 1-$, then we obtain the Sălăgean differential operator defined in [38].*

The Ruscheweyh $q$-differential operator $(R_q^n)$ was developed by Kanas and Raducanu utilizing fundamental concepts from operator theory in quantum mechanics. Very intriguing aspects of this operator in the conic domain were explored; they also created a new subclass of $q$-starlike functions connected to the conic domain.

**Definition 6** ([25]). *To define the operator $R_q^n : \mathcal{A} \to \mathcal{A}$ for $n \in \mathbb{N}$ and $f \in \mathcal{A}$, we write*

$$\begin{aligned}
R_q^0 f(z) &= f(z), \\
R_q^1 f(z) &= z \partial_q f(z) \\
&\cdots \\
R_q^n f(z) &= \frac{z \partial_q^n (z^{n-1} f(z))}{[n]!}, \quad z \in U
\end{aligned}$$

or

$$R_q^n f(z) = z + \sum_{j=2}^{\infty} \frac{\Gamma_q(j+n)}{[j-1]!\Gamma_q(1+n)} a_j z^j \qquad (6)$$

$$= z + \sum_{j=2}^{\infty} \frac{[n+1]_{j-1}}{[j-1]!} a_j z^j.$$

The standard quantum calculus has been extensively studied by numerous mathematicians, physicists, and engineers. Applications in areas including engineering, economics, mathematics, and other disciplines have helped $q$-calculus improve in a number of ways. If we consider the above facts about $q$-calculus in many areas, it is safe to assume that $q$-calculus has functioned as the interface between mathematics and physics throughout the last three decades. In addition, the $q$-calculus operator, the $q$-integral operator, and the $q$-derivative operator are used to build several classes of regular functions and play an intriguing role, since they are used and applied in many different branches of mathematics, including the theory of relativity, the calculus of variations, orthogonal polynomials, and basic hypergeometric functions. In [39], Akça et al. used the $q$-derivative and generated solutions to some differential equations. Therefore, we have also made use of $q$-calculus and provide certain important new types of $q$-analogues of differential and integral operators, as mentioned in this paper. Non-commutative $q$-calculus is a generalization of classical calculus as developed by Newton and Leibnitz. This $q$-derivative may be used with any function whose domain of definition does not include 0. When $q$ equals 1, the result simplifies to the standard derivative; that is, the results obtained by the $q$-differential and integral operators are quite effective and efficient.

Here, we define the $q$-analogues of differential operator $DR_{\lambda,q}^{m,n}$ by using the definition of convolution on the newly defined differential operator $D_{\lambda,q}^{m}$ and the Ruscheweyh $q$-differential operator $R_q^n$. This newly defined operator will help us to define two new integral operators introduced in this study.

**Definition 7.** *For $f \in \mathcal{A}$, $n,m \in \mathbb{N} = \{1,2,3\ldots\}$ and $\lambda \geq 0$, the q-analogues of differential operator $DR_{\lambda,q}^{m,n}$ is defined by*

$$DR_{\lambda,q}^{m,n} f(z) = D_{\lambda,q}^{m} f(z) * R_q^n f(z), \; z \in U. \qquad (7)$$

Using (5) and (6) in (7) and applying the definition of convolution, we obtain the following series expansion of $DR_{\lambda,q}^{m,n}$:

$$DR_{\lambda,q}^{m,n} f(z) = z + \sum_{j=2}^{\infty} \left\{ \lambda \left([j]_q - 1\right) + 1 \right\}^m \frac{\Gamma_q(j+n)}{[j-1]!\Gamma_q(1+n)} a_j^2 z^j, z \in U.$$

**Remark 5.** *The series expansion of $DR_{\lambda,q}^{m,n}$ for the function $(f)$ of type (2) is as follows:*

$$DR_{\lambda,q}^{m,n} f(z) = z - \sum_{j=2}^{\infty} \left\{ \lambda \left([j]_q - 1\right) + 1 \right\}^m \frac{\Gamma_q(j+n)}{[j-1]!\Gamma_q(1+n)} a_j^2 z^j, z \in U,$$

where $\lambda \geq 0$, $m,n \in \mathbb{N}$. The following identity holds for the function $f \in T$:

$$DR_{\lambda,q}^{m+1,n} f(z) = \left(1 - \frac{[\lambda]_q}{q^\lambda}\right) DR_{\lambda,q}^{m,n} f(z) + \left(\frac{[\lambda]_q}{q^\lambda}\right) z \partial_q \left(DR_{\lambda,q}^{m,n} f(z)\right). \qquad (8)$$

The following formulation introduces two new integral operators, $F_{\lambda,\gamma_1,\gamma_2,\ldots\gamma_l}^{m,n,q}$ and $G_{\lambda,\gamma_1,\gamma_2,\ldots\gamma_l}^{m,n,q}$, while considering the convolution operator $DR_{\lambda,q}^{m,n} f(z)$:

**Definition 8.** For functions $f_i \in T$, and $\gamma_i \in \mathbb{R}$, $i \in \{1,2,3\ldots,l\}$, the integral operators $F^{m,n,q}_{\lambda,\gamma_1,\gamma_2,\ldots\gamma_l}$ and $G^{m,n,q}_{\lambda,\gamma_1,\gamma_2,\ldots\gamma_l}$ are defined as follows:

$$F^{m,n,q}_{\lambda,\gamma_1,\gamma_2,\ldots\gamma_l} = \int_0^z \left(\frac{DR^{m,n}_{\lambda,q} f_1(t)}{t}\right)^{\gamma_1} \cdots \left(\frac{DR^{m,n}_{\lambda,q} f_l(t)}{t}\right)^{\gamma_l} d_q t \tag{9}$$

and

$$G^{m,n,q}_{\lambda,\gamma_1,\gamma_2,\ldots\gamma_l} = \int_0^z \left(\partial_q\left(\frac{DR^{m,n}_{\lambda,q} f_1(t)}{t}\right)\right)^{\gamma_1} \cdots \left(\partial_q\left(\frac{DR^{m,n}_{\lambda,q} f_l(t)}{t}\right)\right)^{\gamma_l} d_q t, \tag{10}$$

where

$$\lambda \geq 0, \ q \in (0,1), \ m, n \in \mathbb{N}, \ \text{and } z \in U.$$

**Remark 6.** For $\lambda = 0$, $m = 0$, and $q \to 1-$, we obtain the integral operators introduced by Breaz and Breaz in [40,41].

We establish several new types of $q$-starlike and $q$-convex functions by utilizing the $q$-difference operator and the $q$-analogues of the differential operator $DR^{m,n}_{\lambda,q}$ provided in Definition 7.

**Definition 9.** Let an analytic function $(f)$ of the form (2) be a member of class $R(\delta, q)$, if it satisfies the following inequality

$$\mathrm{Re}\left(\frac{z\partial_q\left(DR^{m,n}_{\lambda,q} f(z)\right)}{DR^{m,n}_{\lambda,q} f(z)}\right) < \delta, \ \text{for all } z \in U, \text{ and } \delta > 1.$$

**Definition 10.** Let an analytic function $(f)$ of the form (2) be a member of class $C(\delta, q)$ if it satisfies the following inequality

$$\mathrm{Re}\left(1 + \frac{z\partial_q^2\left(DR^{m,n}_{\lambda,q} f(z)\right)}{\partial_q\left(DR^{m,n}_{\lambda,q} f(z)\right)}\right) < \delta, \ \text{for all } z \in U, \text{ and } \delta > 1.$$

**Definition 11.** Let an analytic function $(f)$ of the form (2) be a member of class $RA(\beta, \mu, q)$, if

$$\left|\frac{z\partial_q\left(DR^{m,n}_{\lambda,q} f(z)\right)}{DR^{m,n}_{\lambda,q} f(z)} - 1\right| < \mu\left|\beta\left(\frac{z\partial_q\left(DR^{m,n}_{\lambda,q} f(z)\right)}{DR^{m,n}_{\lambda,q} f(z)}\right) - 1\right|, \ z \in U,$$

where

$$0 \leq \beta < 1, \ \text{and } 0 < \mu \leq 1.$$

**Definition 12.** Let an analytic function $(f)$ of the form (2) be a member of class $CA(\beta, \mu, q)$, if

$$\left|\frac{z\partial_q^2\left(DR^{m,n}_{\lambda,q} f(z)\right)}{\partial_q\left(DR^{m,n}_{\lambda,q} f(z)\right)}\right| < \mu\left|\beta\left(1 + \frac{z\partial_q^2\left(DR^{m,n}_{\lambda,q} f(z)\right)}{\partial_q\left(DR^{m,n}_{\lambda,q} f(z)\right)}\right) + 1\right|, \ z \in U,$$

where

$$0 \leq \beta < 1, \ \text{and } 0 < \mu \leq 1.$$

In the following definitions, we consider integral operators $F^{m,n,q}_{\lambda,\gamma_1,\gamma_2,\ldots\gamma_l}$ and $G^{m,n,q}_{\lambda,\gamma_1,\gamma_2,\ldots\gamma_l}$ given in Definition 8, and we define two new subclasses of $q$-convex functions:

**Definition 13.** *Let an analytic function ($f_i$, $i \in \{1,2,\ldots l\}$) of the form (2) be a member of class $LAF(\lambda, \beta, \mu, \gamma_1, \gamma_2, \ldots \gamma_l, q)$ if*

$$Re\left(1 + \frac{z\partial_q^2\left(F^{m,n,q}_{\lambda,\gamma_1,\gamma_2,\ldots\gamma_l}(z)\right)}{\partial_q\left(F^{m,n,q}_{\lambda,\gamma_1,\gamma_2,\ldots\gamma_l}(z)\right)}\right) \geq \beta\left|\frac{z\partial_q^2\left(F^{m,n,q}_{\lambda,\gamma_1,\gamma_2,\ldots\gamma_l}(z)\right)}{\partial_q\left(F^{m,n,q}_{\lambda,\gamma_1,\gamma_2,\ldots\gamma_l}(z)\right)}\right| + \mu, \; z \in U,$$

*where $\lambda \geq 0$, $\beta \geq 0$, $-1 \leq \mu \leq 1$, and $F^{m,n,q}_{\lambda,\gamma_1,\gamma_2,\ldots\gamma_l}(z)$ is defined by (9).*

**Definition 14.** *Let an analytic function ($f_i$, $i \in \{1,2,\ldots l\}$) of the form (2) be a member of class $LAG(\lambda, \beta, \mu, \gamma_1, \gamma_2, \ldots \gamma_l, q)$ if*

$$Re\left(1 + \frac{z\partial_q^2\left(G^{m,n,q}_{\lambda,\gamma_1,\gamma_2,\ldots\gamma_l}\right)}{\partial_q\left(G^{m,n,q}_{\lambda,\gamma_1,\gamma_2,\ldots\gamma_l}\right)}\right) \geq \beta\left|\frac{z\partial_q^2\left(F^{m,n,q}_{\lambda,\gamma_1,\gamma_2,\ldots\gamma_l}(z)\right)}{\partial_q\left(F^{m,n,q}_{\lambda,\gamma_1,\gamma_2,\ldots\gamma_l}(z)\right)}\right| + \mu, \; z \in U,$$

*where $\lambda \geq 0$, $\beta \geq 0$, $-1 \leq \mu \leq 1$, and $G^{m,n,q}_{\lambda,\gamma_1,\gamma_2,\ldots\gamma_l}(z)$ is defined in (10).*

This article is composed of four sections. We briefly reviewed some fundamental geometric function theory ideas, investigated some new $q$-analogues of differential and integral operators, and considered these operators to define a number of new subclasses of $q$-starlike and $q$-convex functions in Section 1 because they were important to our main finding. In Section 2, we provide some known lemmas and investigate some new lemmas that are used to prove our main results. In Section 3, we present our key findings, and in Section 4, we provide concluding remarks.

## 2. Set of Lemmas

Here, we provide some previously established lemmas and prove four new ones that are used in the proof of our key findings.

**Lemma 1** ([42])**.** *For convex univalent function $p$ and*

$$Re\left[\frac{1-\vartheta}{\vartheta} + 2p(z) + \left(1 + \frac{zp''(z)}{p(z)}\right)\right] > 0.$$

*If $f \in \mathcal{A}$ satisfies*

$$\frac{zf'(z)}{f(z)} + \vartheta z^2 \frac{f''(z)}{f'(z)} \prec (1-\vartheta)p(z) + \vartheta p^2(z) + \gamma z p'(z),$$

*then,*

$$\frac{zf'(z)}{f(z)} \prec p(z),$$

*where $0 < \vartheta \leq 1$, and $p(z)$ is the best dominant.*

**Lemma 2** ([42])**.** *Let an analytic function ($p$) be in the open unit disk ($U$) and*

$$p(0) = 1, \text{ and } h(z) = \frac{zp'(z)}{p(z)}$$

is starlike and univalent in $U$. If $f \in \mathcal{A}$ satisfies

$$\frac{(zf(z))''}{f'(z)} - 2\frac{zf'(z)}{f(z)} \prec h(z)$$

then,

$$\frac{z^2 f'(z)}{f^2(z)} \prec p(z),$$

where $p(z)$ is the best dominant.

**Lemma 3** ([22]). *Consider the case when $p$ is univalent and $\phi$ is analytic in the set of all $p(U)$. If*

$$\frac{zp'(z)}{\phi(p(z))}$$

is starlike and

$$\phi(\psi(z))z\psi'(z) \prec \phi(p(z))zp'(z), \ z \in U,$$

then,

$$\psi(z) \prec p(z),$$

where $p(z)$ is the best dominant.

**Lemma 4** ([43]). *For complex numbers, $\alpha, \beta$ and $\gamma$ and $\gamma \neq 0$. Let analytic functions $s$ and $p$ be in $U$, and $p$ be a convex univalent; suppose that*

$$Re\left[\frac{\alpha}{\gamma} + \frac{2\beta}{\gamma}p(z) + \left(1 + \frac{zp''(z)}{p(z)}\right)\right] > 0.$$

If $s(z) = 1 + c_1 z + \ldots$ is analytic in $U$ and

$$\alpha s(z) + \beta s^2(z) + \gamma z s'(z) \prec \alpha p(z) + \beta p^2(z) + \gamma z p'(z),$$

then, $s(z) \prec p(z)$, and the function $p(z)$ is the best dominant.

Now, we generalize the lemmas introduced in [22,43] by using the fundamentals of $q$-calculus operator theory.

**Lemma 5.** *Consider the case when $p$ is univalent and $\phi$ is analytic in the set of all $p(U)$. If*

$$\frac{z\partial_q p(z)}{\phi(p(z))} \qquad (11)$$

is starlike and

$$\phi(\psi(z))z\partial_q \psi(z) \prec \phi(p(z))z\partial_q p(z), \ z \in U, \qquad (12)$$

then, $\psi(z) \prec p(z)$, and $p(z)$ is the best dominant.

**Proof.** Suppose that $\phi$ is analytic in a domain containing $p(U)$ and $p$ is analytic in $U$. Letting $q \to 1-$ in (11) and (12) yields

$$\frac{zp'(z)}{\phi(p(z))},$$

which is starlike; then,

$$z\psi'(z)\phi(\psi(z)) \prec zp'(z)\phi(p(z)), \ z \in U.$$

Then, from the lemma in [22], we obtain $\psi(z) \prec p(z)$, and $p(z)$ is the best dominant. □

**Lemma 6.** *We assume that $p$ and $h$ are analytic in $U$ and that $h$ is convex and univalent in $U$, where $\alpha, \vartheta, \gamma \in \mathbb{C}$. Furthermore, we assume*

$$Re\left[\frac{\alpha}{\gamma} + \frac{2\vartheta}{\gamma}h(z) + \left(1 + \frac{z\partial_q^2 h(z)}{h(z)}\right)\right] > 0. \tag{13}$$

*If $p(z)$ is analytic in $U$ and*

$$\alpha p(z) + \vartheta p^2(z) + \gamma z \partial_q p(z) \prec \alpha h(z) + \vartheta h^2(z) + \gamma z \partial_q h(z), \tag{14}$$

*then, $p(z) \prec h(z)$, and $h(z)$ is the best dominant.*

**Proof.** Suppose that $p$ and $h$ are analytic in $U$. Letting $q \to 1-$ in (13) and (14), we have

$$Re\left[\frac{\alpha}{\gamma} + \frac{2\vartheta}{\gamma}p(z) + \left(1 + \frac{zp''(z)}{p(z)}\right)\right] > 0.$$

If $p(z)$ is analytic in $U$ and

$$\alpha p(z) + \vartheta p^2(z) + \gamma z p'(z) \prec \alpha h(z) + \vartheta h^2(z) + \gamma z h''(z), \; z \in U,$$

then, from the lemma in [43], we obtain $p(z) \prec h(z)$, and $h(z)$ is the best dominant. □

**Lemma 7.** *For $f_i(z) = z - \sum_{j=2}^{\infty} a_{i,j} z^j \in T$, $i \in \{1, 2, \ldots l\}$, we get*

$$\frac{z\partial_q^2\left(F_{\lambda,\gamma_1,\gamma_2,\ldots\gamma_l}^{m,n,q}(z)\right)}{\partial_q\left(F_{\lambda,\gamma_1,\gamma_2,\ldots\gamma_l}^{m,n,q}(z)\right)} = \sum_{i=1}^{l} \gamma_i \left( \frac{-\sum_{j=2}^{\infty}\left([j]_q - 1\right)\left\{\lambda\left([j]_q - 1\right) + 1\right\}^m \frac{\Gamma_q(j+n)}{[j-1]!\Gamma_q(1+n)} a_{i,j}^2 z^j}{1 - \sum_{j=2}^{\infty}\left\{\lambda\left([j]_q - 1\right) + 1\right\}^m \frac{\Gamma_q(j+n)}{[j-1]!\Gamma_q(1+n)} a_{i,j}^2 z^j} \right),$$

*where $F_{\lambda,\gamma_1,\gamma_2,\ldots\gamma_l}^{m,n,q}(z)$ is defined in (9).*

**Proof.** For $f_i(z) = z - \sum_{j=2}^{\infty} a_{i,j} z^j$, $i \in \{1, 2, \ldots l\}$, then

$$\partial_q\left(DR_{\lambda,q}^{m,n} f_i(z)\right) = 1 - \sum_{j=2}^{\infty} [j]_q \left\{\lambda\left([j]_q - 1\right) + 1\right\}^m \frac{\Gamma_q(j+n)}{[j-1]!\Gamma_q(1+n)} a_{i,j}^2 z^{j-1}.$$

We obtain

$$\partial_q\left(F_{\lambda,\gamma_1,\gamma_2,\ldots\gamma_l}^{m,n,q}(z)\right) = \left(\frac{DR_{\lambda,q}^{m,n} f_1(z)}{z}\right)^{\gamma_1} \ldots \left(\frac{DR_{\lambda,q}^{m,n} f_l(z)}{z}\right)^{\gamma_l},$$

so

$$\begin{aligned}\partial_q^2\left(F_{\lambda,\gamma_1,\gamma_2,\ldots\gamma_l}^{m,n,q}(z)\right) &= E_1\left(\partial_q\left(F_{\lambda,\gamma_1,\gamma_2,\ldots\gamma_l}^{m,n,q}(z)\right)\right)\frac{z}{DR_{\lambda,q}^{m,n} f_1(z)} \\ &\quad + \ldots + E_l\left(\partial_q\left(F_{\lambda,\gamma_1,\gamma_2,\ldots\gamma_l}^{m,n,q}(z)\right)\right)\frac{z}{DR_{\lambda,q}^{m,n} f_l(z)},\end{aligned}$$

where
$$E_i = \gamma_i \left( \frac{z\partial_q \left( DR_{\lambda,q}^{m,n} f_i(z) \right) - DR_{\lambda,q}^{m,n} f_i(z)}{z^2} \right).$$

We calculate the expression
$$\frac{z\partial_q^2 \left( F_{\lambda,\gamma_1,\gamma_2,\ldots\gamma_l}^{m,n,q}(z) \right)}{\partial_q \left( F_{\lambda,\gamma_1,\gamma_2,\ldots\gamma_l}^{m,n,q}(z) \right)} = \sum_{i=1}^{l} \gamma_i \left[ \frac{z\partial_q \left( DR_{\lambda,q}^{m,n} f_i(z) \right)}{DR_{\lambda,q}^{m,n} f_i(z)} - 1 \right].$$

We find
$$\frac{z\partial_q^2 \left( F_{\lambda,\gamma_1,\gamma_2,\ldots\gamma_l}^{m,n,q}(z) \right)}{\partial_q \left( F_{\lambda,\gamma_1,\gamma_2,\ldots\gamma_l}^{m,n,q}(z) \right)}$$

$$= \sum_{i=1}^{l} \gamma_i \left( \frac{z - \sum_{j=2}^{\infty} [j]_q \left\{ \lambda \left( [j]_q - 1 \right) + 1 \right\}^m \frac{\Gamma_q(j+n)}{[j-1]! \Gamma_q(1+n)} a_{i,j}^2 z^j}{z - \sum_{j=2}^{\infty} \left\{ \lambda \left( [j]_q - 1 \right) + 1 \right\}^m \frac{\Gamma_q(j+n)}{[j-1]! \Gamma_q(1+n)} a_{i,j}^2 z^j} - 1 \right)$$

$$= \sum_{i=1}^{l} \gamma_i \left( \frac{-\sum_{j=2}^{\infty} \left( [j]_q - 1 \right) \left\{ \lambda \left( [j]_q - 1 \right) + 1 \right\}^m \frac{\Gamma_q(j+n)}{[j-1]! \Gamma_q(1+n)} a_{i,j}^2 z^j}{z - \sum_{j=2}^{\infty} \left\{ \lambda \left( [j]_q - 1 \right) + 1 \right\}^m \frac{\Gamma_q(j+n)}{[j-1]! \Gamma_q(1+n)} a_{i,j}^2 z^j} \right)$$

$$= \sum_{i=1}^{l} \gamma_i \left( \frac{-\sum_{j=2}^{\infty} \left( [j]_q - 1 \right) \left\{ \lambda \left( [j]_q - 1 \right) + 1 \right\}^m \frac{\Gamma_q(j+n)}{[j-1]! \Gamma_q(1+n)} a_{i,j}^2 z^j}{1 - \sum_{j=2}^{\infty} \left\{ \lambda \left( [j]_q - 1 \right) + 1 \right\}^m \frac{\Gamma_q(j+n)}{[j-1]! \Gamma_q(1+n)} a_{i,j}^2 z^j} \right).$$

□

**Lemma 8.** *For $f_i(z) = z - \sum_{j=2}^{\infty} a_{i,j} z^j, i \in \{1,2,\ldots l\}$, we get*

$$\frac{z\partial_q^2 \left( G_{\lambda,\gamma_1,\gamma_2,\ldots\gamma_l}^{m,n,q}(z) \right)}{\partial_q \left( G_{\lambda,\gamma_1,\gamma_2,\ldots\gamma_l}^{m,n,q}(z) \right)} = -\sum_{i=1}^{l} \gamma_i \left( \frac{\sum_{j=2}^{\infty} [j]_q \left( [j-1]_q \right) \left\{ \lambda \left( [j]_q - 1 \right) + 1 \right\}^m \frac{\Gamma_q(j+n)}{[j-1]! \Gamma_q(1+n)} a_{i,j}^2 z^j}{1 - \sum_{j=2}^{\infty} [j]_q \left\{ \lambda \left( [j]_q - 1 \right) + 1 \right\}^m \frac{\Gamma_q(j+n)}{[j-1]! \Gamma_q(1+n)} a_{i,j}^2 z^j} \right),$$

*where $G_{\lambda,\gamma_1,\gamma_2,\ldots\gamma_l}^{m,n,q}(z)$ is defined in (10).*

**Proof.** For $f_i(z) = z - \sum_{j=2}^{\infty} a_{i,j} z^j, i \in \{1,2,\ldots l\}$, we obtain
$$\partial_q \left( G_{\lambda,\gamma_1,\gamma_2,\ldots\gamma_l}^{m,n,q}(z) \right) = \left( \partial_q \left( DR_{\lambda,q}^{m,n} f_1(z) \right) \right)^{\gamma_1} \ldots \left( \partial_q \left( DR_{\lambda,q}^{m,n} f_1(z) \right) \right)^{\gamma_l},$$
so
$$\partial_q^2 \left( G_{\lambda,\gamma_1,\gamma_2,\ldots\gamma_l}^{m,n,q}(z) \right) = \sum_{i=1}^{l} \gamma_i \left( \partial_q \left( G_{\lambda,\gamma_1,\gamma_2,\ldots\gamma_l}^{m,n,q}(z) \right) \right) \frac{\partial_q^2 \left( DR_{\lambda,q}^{m,n} f_i(z) \right)}{\partial_q \left( DR_{\lambda,q}^{m,n} f_i(z) \right)}.$$

We calculate the expression $\dfrac{z\partial_q^2\left(G^{m,n,q}_{\lambda,\gamma_1,\gamma_2,\ldots\gamma_l}(z)\right)}{\partial_q\left(G^{m,n,q}_{\lambda,\gamma_1,\gamma_2,\ldots\gamma_l}(z)\right)}$

$$\frac{z\partial_q^2\left(G^{m,n,q}_{\lambda,\gamma_1,\gamma_2,\ldots\gamma_l}(z)\right)}{\partial_q\left(G^{m,n,q}_{\lambda,\gamma_1,\gamma_2,\ldots\gamma_l}(z)\right)} = \sum_{i=1}^{l}\gamma_i\left[\frac{z\partial_q^2\left(DR^{m,n}_{\lambda,q}f_i(z)\right)}{\partial_q\left(DR^{m,n}_{\lambda,q}f_i(z)\right)}\right].$$

We find

$$\frac{z\partial_q^2\left(G^{m,n,q}_{\lambda,\gamma_1,\gamma_2,\ldots\gamma_l}(z)\right)}{\partial_q\left(G^{m,n,q}_{\lambda,\gamma_1,\gamma_2,\ldots\gamma_l}(z)\right)} = \sum_{i=1}^{l}\gamma_i\left(\frac{-\sum_{j=2}^{\infty}[j]_q([j-1]_q)\{\lambda([j]_q-1)+1\}^m\frac{\Gamma_q(j+n)}{[j-1]!\Gamma_q(1+n)}a_{i,j}^2 z^{j-1}}{1-\sum_{j=2}^{\infty}[j]_q\{\lambda([j]_q-1)+1\}^m\frac{\Gamma_q(j+n)}{[j-1]!\Gamma_q(1+n)}a_{i,j}^2 z^{j-1}}\right).$$

Hence,

$$\frac{z\partial_q^2\left(G^{m,n,q}_{\lambda,\gamma_1,\gamma_2,\ldots\gamma_l}(z)\right)}{\partial_q\left(G^{m,n,q}_{\lambda,\gamma_1,\gamma_2,\ldots\gamma_l}(z)\right)} = -\sum_{i=1}^{l}\gamma_i\left(\frac{\sum_{j=2}^{\infty}[j]_q([j-1]_q)\{\lambda([j]_q-1)+1\}^m\frac{\Gamma_q(j+n)}{[j-1]!\Gamma_q(1+n)}a_{i,j}^2 z^{j-1}}{1-\sum_{j=2}^{\infty}[j]_q\{\lambda([j]_q-1)+1\}^m\frac{\Gamma_q(j+n)}{[j-1]!\Gamma_q(1+n)}a_{i,j}^2 z^{j-1}}\right).$$

□

## 3. Main Results

We then provide necessary and sufficient criteria for the classes $LAF(\lambda,\beta,\mu,\gamma_1,\gamma_2,\ldots\gamma_l,q)$ and $LAG(\lambda,\beta,\mu,\gamma_1,\gamma_2,\ldots\gamma_l,q)$, where

$$\lambda \geq 0,\ \beta \geq 0,\ \text{and}\ -1 \leq \mu \leq 1.$$

**Theorem 1.** *For $i \in \{1,2,3\ldots l\}$, let $f_i \in T$. Then, $f_i \in LAF(\lambda,\beta,\mu,\gamma_1,\gamma_2,\ldots\gamma_l,q)$ if and only if*

$$\sum_{i=1}^{l}\gamma_i(\beta+1)\left(\frac{\sum_{j=2}^{\infty}([j]_q-1)\{\lambda([j]_q-1)+1\}^m\frac{\Gamma_q(j+n)}{[j-1]!\Gamma_q(1+n)}a_{i,j}^2 z^j}{1-\sum_{j=2}^{\infty}\{\lambda([j]_q-1)+1\}^m\frac{\Gamma_q(j+n)}{[j-1]!\Gamma_q(1+n)}a_{i,j}^2 z^j}\right) \leq 1-\mu, \qquad (15)$$

*where $\beta \geq 0,\ -1 \leq \mu \leq 1$.*

**Proof.** In order to demonstrate that (15) is true, we must prove that

$$\beta\left|\frac{z\partial_q^2\left(F^{m,n,q}_{\lambda,\gamma_1,\gamma_2,\ldots\gamma_l}(z)\right)}{\partial_q\left(F^{m,n,q}_{\lambda,\gamma_1,\gamma_2,\ldots\gamma_l}(z)\right)}\right| - \text{Re}\left(\frac{z\partial_q^2\left(F^{m,n,q}_{\lambda,\gamma_1,\gamma_2,\ldots\gamma_l}(z)\right)}{\partial_q\left(F^{m,n,q}_{\lambda,\gamma_1,\gamma_2,\ldots\gamma_l}(z)\right)}\right) \leq 1-\mu.$$

We have

$$\beta\left|\frac{z\partial_q^2\left(F_{\lambda,\gamma_1,\gamma_2,\ldots\gamma_l}^{m,n,q}(z)\right)}{\partial_q\left(F_{\lambda,\gamma_1,\gamma_2,\ldots\gamma_l}^{m,n,q}(z)\right)}\right| - Re\left(\frac{z\partial_q^2\left(F_{\lambda,\gamma_1,\gamma_2,\ldots\gamma_l}^{m,n,q}(z)\right)}{\partial_q\left(F_{\lambda,\gamma_1,\gamma_2,\ldots\gamma_l}^{m,n,q}(z)\right)}\right) \leq (\beta+1)\left|\frac{z\partial_q^2\left(F_{\lambda,\gamma_1,\gamma_2,\ldots\gamma_l}^{m,n,q}(z)\right)}{\partial_q\left(F_{\lambda,\gamma_1,\gamma_2,\ldots\gamma_l}^{m,n,q}(z)\right)}\right|.$$

Applying Lemma 7, we obtain

$$(\beta+1)\left|\frac{z\partial_q^2\left(F_{\lambda,\gamma_1,\gamma_2,\ldots\gamma_l}^{m,n,q}(z)\right)}{\partial_q\left(F_{\lambda,\gamma_1,\gamma_2,\ldots\gamma_l}^{m,n,q}(z)\right)}\right|$$

$$= (\beta+1)\sum_{i=1}^{l}\gamma_i\left|\frac{-\sum_{j=2}^{\infty}\left([j]_q-1\right)\left\{\lambda\left([j]_q-1\right)+1\right\}^m \frac{\Gamma_q(j+n)}{[j-1]!\Gamma_q(1+n)}a_{i,j}^2 z^{j-1}}{1-\sum_{j=2}^{\infty}\left\{\lambda\left([j]_q-1\right)+1\right\}^m \frac{\Gamma_q(j+n)}{[j-1]!\Gamma_q(1+n)}a_{i,j}^2 z^{j-1}}\right|$$

$$\leq (\beta+1)\sum_{i=1}^{l}\gamma_i\left\{\frac{\sum_{j=2}^{\infty}\left([j]_q-1\right)\left\{\lambda\left([j]_q-1\right)+1\right\}^m \frac{\Gamma_q(j+n)}{[j-1]!\Gamma_q(1+n)}a_{i,j}^2 |z^{j-1}|}{1-\sum_{j=2}^{\infty}\left\{\lambda\left([j]_q-1\right)+1\right\}^m \frac{\Gamma_q(j+n)}{[j-1]!\Gamma_q(1+n)}a_{i,j}^2 |z^{j-1}|}\right\}$$

$$\leq (\beta+1)\sum_{i=1}^{l}\gamma_i\left\{\frac{\sum_{j=2}^{\infty}\left([j]_q-1\right)\left\{\lambda\left([j]_q-1\right)+1\right\}^m \frac{\Gamma_q(j+n)}{[j-1]!\Gamma_q(1+n)}a_{i,j}^2}{1-\sum_{j=2}^{\infty}\left\{\lambda\left([j]_q-1\right)+1\right\}^m \frac{\Gamma_q(j+n)}{[j-1]!\Gamma_q(1+n)}a_{i,j}^2}\right\} \leq 1-\mu.$$

Therefore, we deduce

$$\beta\left|\frac{z\partial_q^2\left(F_{\lambda,\gamma_1,\gamma_2,\ldots\gamma_l}^{m,n,q}(z)\right)}{\partial_q\left(F_{\lambda,\gamma_1,\gamma_2,\ldots\gamma_l}^{m,n,q}(z)\right)}\right| - Re\left(\frac{z\partial_q^2\left(F_{\lambda,\gamma_1,\gamma_2,\ldots\gamma_l}^{m,n,q}(z)\right)}{\partial_q\left(F_{\lambda,\gamma_1,\gamma_2,\ldots\gamma_l}^{m,n,q}(z)\right)}\right) \leq 1-\mu,$$

or, equivalently,

$$Re\left(1+\frac{z\partial_q^2\left(F_{\lambda,\gamma_1,\gamma_2,\ldots\gamma_l}^{m,n,q}(z)\right)}{\partial_q\left(F_{\lambda,\gamma_1,\gamma_2,\ldots\gamma_l}^{m,n,q}(z)\right)}\right) \geq \beta\left|\frac{z\partial_q^2\left(F_{\lambda,\gamma_1,\gamma_2,\ldots\gamma_l}^{m,n,q}(z)\right)}{\partial_q\left(F_{\lambda,\gamma_1,\gamma_2,\ldots\gamma_l}^{m,n,q}(z)\right)}\right| + \mu.$$

Thus, $f_i \in LAF(\lambda,\beta,\mu,\gamma_1,\gamma_2,\ldots\gamma_l,q)$.

Contrarily, assume that $f_i \in LAF(\lambda,\beta,\mu,\gamma_1,\gamma_2,\ldots\gamma_l,q)$. Lemma 7 and (15) allow us to derive

$$1-\sum_{i=1}^{l}\gamma_i\left[\frac{\sum_{j=2}^{\infty}\left([j]_q-1\right)\left\{\lambda\left([j]_q-1\right)+1\right\}^m \frac{\Gamma_q(j+n)}{[j-1]!\Gamma_q(1+n)}a_{i,j}^2 |z^{j-1}|}{1-\sum_{j=2}^{\infty}\left\{\lambda\left([j]_q-1\right)+1\right\}^m \frac{\Gamma_q(j+n)}{[j-1]!\Gamma_q(1+n)}a_{i,j}^2 |z^{j-1}|}\right]$$

$$\geq \beta\left|\sum_{i=1}^{l}\gamma_i\frac{\sum_{j=2}^{\infty}\left([j]_q-1\right)\left\{\lambda\left([j]_q-1\right)+1\right\}^m \frac{\Gamma_q(j+n)}{[j-1]!\Gamma_q(1+n)}a_{i,j}^2 z^{j-1}}{1-\sum_{j=2}^{\infty}\left\{\lambda\left([j]_q-1\right)+1\right\}^m \frac{\Gamma_q(j+n)}{[j-1]!\Gamma_q(1+n)}a_{i,j}^2 z^{j-1}}\right| + \mu$$

$$\geq \beta\sum_{i=1}^{l}\gamma_i\left(\frac{\sum_{j=2}^{\infty}\left([j]_q-1\right)\left\{\lambda\left([j]_q-1\right)+1\right\}^m \frac{\Gamma_q(j+n)}{[j-1]!\Gamma_q(1+n)}a_{i,j}^2 z^{j-1}}{1-\sum_{j=2}^{\infty}\left\{\lambda\left([j]_q-1\right)+1\right\}^m \frac{\Gamma_q(j+n)}{[j-1]!\Gamma_q(1+n)}a_{i,j}^2 z^{j-1}}\right) + \mu,$$

which is equivalent to

$$\sum_{i=1}^{l} \beta \gamma_i \left[ \frac{\sum_{j=2}^{\infty} \left([j]_q - 1\right)\left\{\lambda\left([j]_q - 1\right) + 1\right\}^m \frac{\Gamma_q(j+n)}{[j-1]!\Gamma_q(1+n)} a_{i,j}^2 z^{j-1}}{1 - \sum_{j=2}^{\infty} \left\{\lambda\left([j]_q - 1\right) + 1\right\}^m \frac{\Gamma_q(j+n)}{[j-1]!\Gamma_q(1+n)} a_{i,j}^2 z^{j-1}} \right]$$

$$+ \sum_{i=1}^{l} \gamma_i \left[ \frac{\sum_{j=2}^{\infty} \left([j]_q - 1\right)\left\{\lambda\left([j]_q - 1\right) + 1\right\}^m \frac{\Gamma_q(j+n)}{[j-1]!\Gamma_q(1+n)} a_{i,j}^2 z^{j-1}}{1 - \sum_{j=2}^{\infty} \left\{\lambda\left([j]_q - 1\right) + 1\right\}^m \frac{\Gamma_q(j+n)}{[j-1]!\Gamma_q(1+n)} a_{i,j}^2 z^{j-1}} \right]$$

$$\leq 1 - \mu,$$

which reduces to

$$\sum_{i=1}^{l} (\beta + 1)\gamma_i \left[ \frac{\sum_{j=2}^{\infty} \left([j]_q - 1\right)\left\{\lambda\left([j]_q - 1\right) + 1\right\}^m \frac{\Gamma_q(j+n)}{[j-1]!\Gamma_q(1+n)} a_{i,j}^2 z^{j-1}}{1 - \sum_{j=2}^{\infty} \left\{\lambda\left([j]_q - 1\right) + 1\right\}^m \frac{\Gamma_q(j+n)}{[j-1]!\Gamma_q(1+n)} a_{i,j}^2 z^{j-1}} \right] \leq 1 - \mu,$$

Inequality (15) is found when $z \to 1-$ is on the real axis. □

For $q \to 1-$, we obtain known result that were proven in [44].

**Corollary 1** ([44]). *For $i \in \{1, 2, 3 \ldots l\}$, let $f_i \in T$. Then, $f_i \in LAF(\lambda, \beta, \mu, \gamma_1, \gamma_2, \ldots \gamma_l)$ if and only if*

$$\sum_{i=1}^{l} \gamma_i(\beta + 1) \left( \frac{\sum_{j=2}^{\infty} \{\lambda(j-1) + 1\}^m \frac{(n+j-1)!}{n!(j-2)!} a_{i,j}^2 z^j}{1 - \sum_{j=2}^{\infty} \{\lambda(j-1) + 1\}^m \frac{(n+j-1)!}{n!(j-1)!} a_{i,j}^2 z^j} \right) \leq 1 - \mu.$$

**Theorem 2.** *For $i \in \{1, 2, 3 \ldots l\}$, let $f_i \in T$. Then, $f_i \in LAG(\lambda, \beta, \mu, \gamma_1, \gamma_2, \ldots \gamma_l, q)$ if and only if*

$$\sum_{i=1}^{l} \gamma_i(\beta + 1) \left( \frac{\sum_{j=2}^{\infty} [j]_q [j-1]_q \{\lambda([j]_q - 1) + 1\}^m \frac{\Gamma_q(j+n)}{[j-1]!\Gamma_q(1+n)} a_{i,j}^2}{1 - \sum_{j=2}^{\infty} [j]_q \{\lambda([j]_q - 1) + 1\}^m \frac{\Gamma_q(j+n)}{[j-1]!\Gamma_q(1+n)} a_{i,j}^2} \right) \leq 1 - \mu,$$

*where $\beta \geq 0$, $-1 \leq \mu \leq 1$.*

**Proof.** Using Lemma 8 and the method used to prove Theorem 1, we arrive at Theorem 2. □

We now demonstrate some characteristics of the integral operators $F_{\lambda,\gamma_1,\gamma_2,\ldots\gamma_l}^{m,n,q}(z)$ and $G_{\lambda,\gamma_1,\gamma_2,\ldots\gamma_l}^{m,n,q}(z)$ for the families $R(\delta, q)$, $C(\delta, q)$, $RA(\beta, \mu, q)$, and $CA(\beta, \mu, q)$.

**Theorem 3.** *Let $f_i \in T$ and $\left|\frac{\partial_q \left(DR_{\lambda,q}^{m,n} f(z)\right)}{DR_{\lambda,q}^{m,n} f(z)}\right| < M_i$. If $f_i \in RA(\beta_i, \mu_i, q)$, then $F_{\lambda,\gamma_1,\gamma_2,\ldots\gamma_l}^{m,n,q}(z) \in \mathcal{D}(\delta')$, where*

$$\delta' = 1 + \sum_{i=1}^{l} \gamma_i \mu_i (\beta_i M_i + 1), \ z \in U,$$

*where*

$$\gamma_i \in R, \ \gamma_i > 0, \ i \in \{1, 2, 3 \ldots l\}.$$

**Proof.** As shown in (9), $F^{m,n,q}_{\lambda,\gamma_1,\gamma_2,\ldots\gamma_l} \in T$. Upon differentiating $F^{m,n,q}_{\lambda,\gamma_1,\gamma_2,\ldots\gamma_l}(z)$ as shown in (9), we obtain

$$\partial_q\left(F^{m,n,q}_{\lambda,\gamma_1,\gamma_2,\ldots\gamma_l}(z)\right) = \prod_{i=1}^{l}\left(\frac{DR^{m,n}_{\lambda,q}f(z)}{z}\right)^{\gamma_i}. \tag{16}$$

Taking the logarithmic differentiation of (16) and multiplying by $z$, we obtain

$$\frac{z\partial_q^2\left(F^{m,n,q}_{\lambda,\gamma_1,\gamma_2,\ldots\gamma_l}(z)\right)}{\partial_q\left(F^{m,n,q}_{\lambda,\gamma_1,\gamma_2,\ldots\gamma_l}(z)\right)} = \sum_{i=1}^{l}\gamma_i\left(\frac{z\partial_q\left(DR^{m,n}_{\lambda,q}f(z)\right)}{DR^{m,n}_{\lambda,q}f(z)}-1\right),$$

or, equivalently,

$$1+\frac{z\partial_q^2\left(F^{m,n,q}_{\lambda,\gamma_1,\gamma_2,\ldots\gamma_l}(z)\right)}{\partial_q\left(F^{m,n,q}_{\lambda,\gamma_1,\gamma_2,\ldots\gamma_l}(z)\right)} = 1+\sum_{i=1}^{l}\gamma_i\left(\frac{z\partial_q\left(DR^{m,n}_{\lambda,q}f(z)\right)}{DR^{m,n}_{\lambda,q}f(z)}-1\right). \tag{17}$$

By taking a real part from either side of (17), we obtain

$$Re\left(1+\frac{z\partial_q^2\left(F^{m,n,q}_{\lambda,\gamma_1,\gamma_2,\ldots\gamma_l}(z)\right)}{\partial_q\left(F^{m,n,q}_{\lambda,\gamma_1,\gamma_2,\ldots\gamma_l}(z)\right)}\right) = 1+\sum_{i=1}^{l}\gamma_i\left(Re\left(\frac{z\partial_q\left(DR^{m,n}_{\lambda,q}f(z)\right)}{DR^{m,n}_{\lambda,q}f(z)}\right)-1\right)$$

$$\leq 1+\sum_{i=1}^{l}\gamma_i\left|\frac{z\partial_q\left(DR^{m,n}_{\lambda,q}f(z)\right)}{DR^{m,n}_{\lambda,q}f(z)}-1\right|.$$

Since $f_i \in RA(\beta_i, \mu_i, q)$, we deduce that

$$Re\left(1+\frac{z\partial_q^2\left(F^{m,n,q}_{\lambda,\gamma_1,\gamma_2,\ldots\gamma_l}(z)\right)}{\partial_q\left(F^{m,n,q}_{\lambda,\gamma_1,\gamma_2,\ldots\gamma_l}(z)\right)}\right) < 1+\sum_{i=1}^{l}\gamma_i\mu_i\left|\beta_i\frac{z\partial_q\left(DR^{m,n}_{\lambda,q}f(z)\right)}{DR^{m,n}_{\lambda,q}f(z)}+1\right|$$

$$< 1+\sum_{i=1}^{l}\gamma_i\mu_i\beta_i\left|\frac{z\partial_q\left(DR^{m,n}_{\lambda,q}f(z)\right)}{DR^{m,n}_{\lambda,q}f(z)}\right|+\sum_{i=1}^{l}\gamma_i\mu_i\beta_i$$

$$< 1+\sum_{i=1}^{l}\gamma_i\mu_i(\beta_i M_i+1).$$

Furthermore,

$$\sum_{i=1}^{l}\gamma_i\mu_i(\beta_i M_i+1) > 0, \text{ and } F^{m,n,q}_{\lambda,\gamma_1,\gamma_2,\ldots\gamma_l}(z) \in \mathcal{D}(\delta'),$$

where

$$\delta' = 1+\sum_{i=1}^{l}\gamma_i\mu_i(\beta_i M_i+1), z \in U.$$

□

For $q \to 1-$, we obtain the result proven in [44].

**Corollary 2.** Let $\gamma_i \in R$, $\gamma_i > 0$, $i \in \{1,2,3\ldots l\}$, $f_i \in T$ and $\left|\frac{(DR_\lambda^{m,n} f(z))'}{DR_\lambda^{m,n} f(z)}\right| < M_i$. If $f_i \in RA(\beta_i, \mu_i)$, then $F_{\lambda,\gamma_1,\gamma_2,\ldots\gamma_l}^{m,n}(z) \in \mathcal{D}(\delta')$, where

$$\delta' = 1 + \sum_{i=1}^{l} \gamma_i \mu_i (\beta_i M_i + 1), \ z \in U.$$

The following is a corollary of Theorem 3 under the assumptions that $l = 1$, $\gamma_1 = \gamma$, $\delta_1 = \delta$, and $f_1 = f$.

**Corollary 3.** Let $f \in T$ and $\left|\frac{\partial_q f(z)}{f(z)}\right| < M$. If $f \in RA(\beta, \mu, q)$, then $\int_0^z \left(\frac{f(t)}{t}\right)^\gamma d_q(t) \in \mathcal{D}(\delta')$, where

$$\delta' = 1 + \gamma \mu (\beta M + 1),$$

and $\gamma \in R$, $\gamma > 0$, $z \in U$.

**Theorem 4.** Let $f_i \in T$. Then, $F_{\lambda,\gamma_1,\gamma_2,\ldots\gamma_l}^{m,n,q}(z) \in \mathcal{D}(\delta')$, where

$$\delta' = 1 + \sum_{i=1}^{l} \gamma_i (\delta_i - 1), \ z \in U$$

and

$$\gamma_i \in R, \ \delta_i > 1, \ \gamma_i > 0, \ i \in \{1,2,3\ldots l\}.$$

**Proof.** From (17), we have

$$Re\left(1 + \frac{z \partial_q^2 \left(F_{\lambda,\gamma_1,\gamma_2,\ldots\gamma_l}^{m,n,q}(z)\right)}{\partial_q \left(F_{\lambda,\gamma_1,\gamma_2,\ldots\gamma_l}^{m,n,q}(z)\right)}\right) = 1 + \sum_{i=1}^{l} \gamma_i Re\left(\frac{z \partial_q \left(DR_{\lambda,q}^{m,n} f_i(z)\right)}{DR_{\lambda,q}^{m,n} f_i(z)}\right) - \sum_{i=1}^{l} \gamma_i$$

$$< 1 + \sum_{i=1}^{l} \gamma_i \delta_i - \sum_{i=1}^{l} \gamma_i = 1 + \sum_{i=1}^{l} \gamma_i (\delta_i - 1).$$

Since $\delta_i > 1$, evidently, $\sum_{i=1}^{l} \gamma_i(\delta_i - 1) > 0$; hence, $F_{\lambda,\gamma_1,\gamma_2,\ldots\gamma_l}^{m,n,q}(z) \in \mathcal{D}(\delta')$, where

$$\delta' = 1 + \sum_{i=1}^{l} \gamma_i(\delta_i - 1), z \in U.$$

□

The following is a corollary of Theorem 4 under the assumptions that $l = 1$, $\gamma_1 = \gamma$, $\delta_1 = \delta$, and $f_1 = f$.

**Corollary 4.** Let $f \in R(\delta)$. Then, $\int_0^z \left(\frac{f(t)}{t}\right)^\gamma d_q(t) \in \mathcal{D}(\delta')$, where

$$\delta' = 1 + \gamma(\delta - 1)$$

and

$$\delta > 1, \ \gamma > 0, \ z \in U.$$

**Theorem 5.** Let $f_i \in \mathcal{D}(\delta_i)$. Then, $G^{m,n,q}_{\lambda,\gamma_1,\gamma_2,\ldots\gamma_l}(z) \in \mathcal{D}(\delta')$, where

$$\delta' = 1 + \sum_{i=1}^{l} \gamma_i(\delta_i - 1), \ z \in U$$

and

$$\gamma_i > 0, \ i \in \{1,2,3,\ldots,l\}, \ \delta_i > 1.$$

**Proof.** From the definition of $G^{m,n,q}_{\lambda,\gamma_1,\gamma_2,\ldots\gamma_l}(z)$ given by (10), we have

$$Re\left(1 + \frac{z\partial_q^2\left(G^{m,n,q}_{\lambda,\gamma_1,\gamma_2,\ldots\gamma_l}(z)\right)}{\partial_q\left(G^{m,n,q}_{\lambda,\gamma_1,\gamma_2,\ldots\gamma_l}(z)\right)}\right) = 1 + \sum_{i=1}^{l}\gamma_i Re\left(\frac{z\partial_q\left(DR^{m,n}_{\lambda,q}f_i(z)\right)}{DR^{m,n}_{\lambda,q}f_i(z)}\right) - \sum_{i=1}^{l}\gamma_i$$

$$< 1 + \sum_{i=1}^{l}\gamma_i\delta_i - \sum_{i=1}^{l}\gamma_i = 1 + \sum_{i=1}^{l}\gamma_i(\delta_i - 1).$$

Since $\delta_i > 1$, it seems to reason that $\sum_{i=1}^{l}\gamma_i(\delta_i - 1) > 0$ and that $G^{m,n,q}_{\lambda,\gamma_1,\gamma_2,\ldots\gamma_l}(z) \in \mathcal{D}(\delta')$, where

$$\delta' = 1 + \sum_{i=1}^{l}\gamma_i(\delta_i - 1), \ z \in U.$$

□

The following is a corollary of Theorem 5 under the assumptions $l = 1$, $\gamma_1 = \gamma$, $\delta_1 = \delta$, and $f_1 = f$.

**Corollary 5.** Let $f \in \mathcal{D}(\delta)$. Then, $\int_0^z \left(f'(t)\right)^\gamma d_q(t) \in \mathcal{D}(\delta')$, where

$$\delta' = 1 + \gamma(\delta - 1)$$

and

$$\gamma > 0, \ \delta > 1.$$

**Theorem 6.** Let $f_i \in DA(\beta_i, \mu_i, q)$ and $\left|\frac{\partial_q^2\left(DR^{m,n}_{\lambda,q}f(z)\right)}{\partial_q\left(DR^{m,n}_{\lambda,q}f(z)\right)}\right| < M_i$. Then, $G^{m,n,q}_{\lambda,\gamma_1,\gamma_2,\ldots\gamma_l}(z) \in \mathcal{D}(\delta')$, where

$$\delta' = 1 + \sum_{i=1}^{l}\gamma_i\mu_i(\beta_i M_i + 1)$$

and

$$\gamma_i \in R, \ \gamma_i > 0, \ z \in U, \ i \in \{1,2,3\ldots l\}.$$

**Proof.** The following is derived from the definition of $G^{m,n,q}_{\lambda,\gamma_1,\gamma_2,\ldots\gamma_l}$ in (10):

$$Re\left(1 + \frac{z\partial_q^2\left(G^{m,n,q}_{\lambda,\gamma_1,\gamma_2,\ldots\gamma_l}(z)\right)}{\partial_q\left(G^{m,n,q}_{\lambda,\gamma_1,\gamma_2,\ldots\gamma_l}(z)\right)}\right) \leq \sum_{i=1}^{l}\gamma_i\left|\frac{z\partial_q^2\left(DR^{m,n}_{\lambda,q}f(z)\right)}{\partial_q\left(DR^{m,n}_{\lambda,q}f(z)\right)}\right|$$

$$< \sum_{i=1}^{l}\gamma_i\mu_i\left|\beta_i\left(1 + \frac{z\partial_q^2\left(DR^{m,n}_{\lambda,q}f(z)\right)}{\partial_q\left(DR^{m,n}_{\lambda,q}f(z)\right)} + 1\right)\right| + 1$$

$$< 1 + \sum_{i=1}^{l} \gamma_i \mu_i \beta_i \left( 1 + \left| \frac{z \partial_q^2 \left( DR_{\lambda,q}^{m,n} f(z) \right)}{\partial_q \left( DR_{\lambda,q}^{m,n} f(z) \right)} \right| \right) + \sum_{i=1}^{l} \gamma_i \mu_i + 1$$

$$< \sum_{i=1}^{l} [\beta_i (1 + M_i) + 1] \gamma_i \mu_i + 1.$$

Because

$$\sum_{i=1}^{l} [\beta_i (1 + M_i) + 1] \gamma_i \mu_i > 0,$$

we draw the following conclusion

$$G_{\lambda,\gamma_1,\gamma_2,\ldots\gamma_l}^{m,n,q}(z) \in \mathcal{D}(\delta'),$$

where

$$\delta' = 1 + \sum_{i=1}^{l} [\beta_i (1 + M_i) + 1] \gamma_i \mu_i, \ z \in U.$$

□

For $q \to 1-$, we obtain the result proven in [44].

**Corollary 6** ([44]). *Let $\gamma_i \in R$, $\gamma_i > 0$, $i \in \{1,2,3\ldots l\}$, $f_i \in DA(\beta_i, \mu_i)$, and $\left| \frac{\left( DR_{\lambda,q}^{m,n} f(z) \right)''}{\left( DR_{\lambda,q}^{m,n} f(z) \right)'} \right| < M_i$. Then, $G_{\lambda,\gamma_1,\gamma_2,\ldots\gamma_l}^{m,n}(z) \in \mathcal{D}(\delta')$, where*

$$\delta' = 1 + \sum_{i=1}^{l} \gamma_i \mu_i (\beta_i M_i + 1), \ z \in U.$$

The following is a corollary of Theorem 6 under the assumptions $l = 1$, $\gamma_1 = \gamma$, $M_1 = 1$, and $f_1 = f$.

**Corollary 7.** *Let $f \in DA(\beta, \mu, q)$ and $\left| \frac{\partial_q f(z)}{f(z)} \right| < M$, where M is fixed. Then, $\int_0^z \left( f'(t) \right)^\gamma d_q(t) \in \mathcal{D}(\delta')$, where*

$$\delta' = 1 + \gamma \mu \beta [1 + M) + 1]$$

*and*

$$\gamma \in R, \ \gamma > 0, \ z \in U.$$

**Subordination Results:**
In this paper, we generalize Lemmas 1 and 2 to the operator $DR_{\lambda,q}^{m,n} f(z)$.

**Theorem 7.** *Assuming h is both convex and univalent, $\varsigma \neq 0$, and*

$$Re\left\{ \frac{(1-\varsigma)q^\lambda}{[\lambda]_q \varsigma} + \frac{2q^\lambda}{[\lambda]_q} h(z) + \left( 1 + \frac{z \partial_q^2 h(z)}{\partial_q h(z)} \right) \right\} > 0.$$

*If the differential subordination condition for $f \in T$ holds, then*

$$\left(\gamma \frac{DR_{\lambda,q}^{m+2,n} f(z)}{DR_{\lambda,q}^{m+1,n} f(z)} + 1 - \varsigma\right) \frac{DR_{\lambda,q}^{m+1,n} f(z)}{DR_{\lambda,q}^{m,n} f(z)}$$
$$\prec (1-\varsigma)h(z) + \varsigma h^2(z) + \frac{\varsigma [\lambda]_q}{q^\lambda} z \partial_q h(z) \qquad (18)$$

then,

$$\frac{DR_{\lambda,q}^{m+1,n} f(z)}{DR_{\lambda,q}^{m,n} f(z)} \prec h(z), \; z \in U.$$

**Proof.** Consider

$$p(z) = \frac{DR_{\lambda,q}^{m+1,n} f(z)}{DR_{\lambda,q}^{m,n} f(z)}, \; z \in U. \qquad (19)$$

We achieved

$$\frac{\partial_q p(z)}{p(z)} = \frac{DR_{\lambda,q}^{m,n} f(z)}{DR_{\lambda,q}^{m+1,n} f(z)} \left\{ \frac{\left(DR_{\lambda,q}^{m,n} f(z)\right) \partial_q \left(DR_{\lambda,q}^{m+1,n} f(z)\right) - DR_{\lambda,q}^{m+1,n} f(z) \partial_q \left(DR_{\lambda,q}^{m,n} f(z)\right)}{\left(DR_{\lambda,q}^{m,n} f(z)\right)^2} \right\}$$
$$= \frac{\partial_q \left(DR_{\lambda,q}^{m+2,n} f(z)\right)}{DR_{\lambda,q}^{m+1,n} f(z)} - \frac{\partial_q \left(DR_{\lambda,q}^{m+1,n} f(z)\right)}{DR_{\lambda,q}^{m,n} f(z)}.$$

Thus,

$$\frac{z \partial_q p(z)}{p(z)} = \frac{z \partial_q \left(DR_{\lambda,q}^{m+2,n} f(z)\right)}{DR_{\lambda,q}^{m+1,n} f(z)} - \frac{z \partial_q \left(DR_{\lambda,q}^{m+1,n} f(z)\right)}{DR_{\lambda,q}^{m,n} f(z)}. \qquad (20)$$

By using (8) in (20), we obtain

$$\frac{z \partial_q p(z)}{p(z)} = \frac{q^\lambda}{[\lambda]_q} \left(\frac{DR_{\lambda,q}^{m+2,n} f(z)}{DR_{\lambda,q}^{m+1,n} f(z)}\right) - \frac{q^\lambda}{[\lambda]_q}\left(1 - \frac{[\lambda]_q}{q^\lambda}\right) -$$
$$\frac{q^\lambda}{[\lambda]_q}\left(\frac{DR_{\lambda,q}^{m+1,n} f(z)}{DR_{\lambda,q}^{m,n} f(z)}\right) + \frac{q^\lambda}{[\lambda]_q}\left(1 - \frac{[\lambda]_q}{q^\lambda}\right).$$

$$\frac{[\lambda]_q}{q^\lambda}\left(\frac{z \partial_q p(z)}{p(z)}\right) = \left(\frac{DR_{\lambda,q}^{m+2,n} f(z)}{DR_{\lambda,q}^{m+1,n} f(z)}\right) - p(z)$$
$$\frac{DR_{\lambda,q}^{m+2,n} f(z)}{DR_{\lambda,q}^{m+1,n} f(z)} = \frac{[\lambda]_q}{q^\lambda}\left(\frac{z \partial_q p(z)}{p(z)} + \frac{q^\lambda}{[\lambda]_q} p(z)\right).$$

We deduce from (8) that

$$\frac{DR_{\lambda,q}^{m+1,n}f(z)}{DR_{\lambda,q}^{m,n}f(z)}\left\{\varsigma\frac{DR_{\lambda,q}^{m+2,n}f(z)}{DR_{\lambda,q}^{m+1,n}f(z)}+1-\varsigma\right\}$$

$$= p(z)\left\{\frac{\varsigma[\lambda]_q}{q^\lambda}\left(\frac{z\partial_q p(z)}{p(z)}+\frac{q^\lambda}{[\lambda]_q}p(z)\right)+1-\varsigma\right\}$$

$$= (1-\varsigma)p(z)+\varsigma p^2(z)+\frac{\varsigma[\lambda]_q}{q^\lambda}z\partial_q p(z).$$

Therefore, the differential subordination in (18) becomes

$$(1-\varsigma)p(z)+\varsigma p^2(z)+\frac{\varsigma[\lambda]_q}{q^\lambda}z\partial_q p(z)$$

$$\prec (1-\varsigma)h(z)+\varsigma h^2(z)+\frac{\varsigma[\lambda]_q}{q^\lambda}z\partial_q p(z).$$

Using Lemma 6, we obtain

$$\frac{DR_{\lambda,q}^{m+1,n}f(z)}{DR_{\lambda,q}^{m,n}f(z)} \prec h(z),$$

where $h$ is the best dominant. □

For $q \to 1-$, we obtain the result proven in [44].

**Corollary 8** ([44]). *Let $h$ be both convex and univalent, $\varsigma \neq 0$, and*

$$Re\left\{\frac{(1-\varsigma)}{\lambda\varsigma}+\frac{2}{\lambda}h(z)+\left(1+\frac{zh''(z)}{h'(z)}\right)\right\}>0.$$

*If $f \in T$ satisfies the differential subordination*

$$\frac{DR_\lambda^{m+1,n}f(z)}{DR_\lambda^{m,n}f(z)}\left(\varsigma\frac{DR_\lambda^{m+2,n}f(z)}{DR_\lambda^{m+1,n}f(z)}+1-\varsigma\right)$$

$$\prec (1-\varsigma)h(z)+\varsigma h^2(z)+\varsigma\lambda zh'(z),$$

*then*

$$\frac{DR_\lambda^{m+1,n}f(z)}{DR_\lambda^{m,n}f(z)} \prec h(z), \; z \in U.$$

**Theorem 8.** *For $h(0) \neq 0$, $\varsigma \neq 0$. Let $h$ be univalent in $U$ and $\frac{z\partial_q h(z)}{h(z)}$ be both univalent and starlike in $U$. If the differential subordination condition for $f \in T$ holds, then*

$$\frac{DR_{\lambda,q}^{m+2,n}f(z)}{DR_{\lambda,q}^{m+1,n}f(z)}-\varsigma\frac{DR_{\lambda,q}^{m+1,n}f(z)}{DR_{\lambda,q}^{m,n}f(z)}$$

$$\prec \frac{[\lambda]_q}{q^\lambda}\frac{z\partial_q h(z)}{h(z)}+1-\varsigma, \qquad (21)$$

then
$$\frac{z^{\varsigma-1} DR_{\lambda,q}^{m+1,n} f(z)}{\left(DR_{\lambda,q}^{m,n} f(z)\right)^{\varsigma}} \prec h(z), \; z \in U, \tag{22}$$

where the best dominant function is h.

**Proof.** Let
$$p(z) = \frac{z^{\varsigma-1} DR_{\lambda,q}^{m+1,n} f(z)}{\left(DR_{\lambda,q}^{m,n} f(z)\right)^{\varsigma}}, \tag{23}$$

which, when differentiated, yields

$$\partial_q p(z) = \left\{ \frac{z^{\varsigma-2}(\gamma-1)\left(DR_{\lambda,q}^{m+1,n} f(z)\right) + z^{\varsigma-1} \partial_q \left(DR_{\lambda,q}^{m+1,n} f(z)\right)}{\left(DR_{\lambda,q}^{m,n} f(z)\right)^{\varsigma}} \right\}$$
$$- \frac{\varsigma z^{\varsigma-1} \left(DR_{\lambda,q}^{m+1,n} f(z)\right) \partial_q \left(DR_{\lambda,q}^{m,n} f(z)\right)}{\left(DR_{\lambda,q}^{m,n} f(z)\right)\left(DR_{\lambda,q}^{m,n} f(z)\right)^{\varsigma}}.$$

Therefore,

$$\frac{z \partial_q p(z)}{p(z)} = \frac{\left(DR_{\lambda,q}^{m,n} f(z)\right)^{\varsigma}}{z^{\varsigma-1} DR_{\lambda,q}^{m+1,n} f(z)} \left\{ \begin{array}{c} \frac{z^{\varsigma-2}(\varsigma-1)\left(DR_{\lambda,q}^{m+1,n} f(z)\right) + z^{\varsigma-1} \partial_q \left(DR_{\lambda,q}^{m+1,n} f(z)\right)}{\left(DR_{\lambda,q}^{m,n} f(z)\right)^{\varsigma}} \\ - \frac{\varsigma z^{\varsigma-1} \left(DR_{\lambda,q}^{m+1,n} f(z)\right) \partial_q \left(DR_{\lambda,q}^{m,n} f(z)\right)}{\left(DR_{\lambda,q}^{m,n} f(z)\right)\left(DR_{\lambda,q}^{m,n} f(z)\right)^{\varsigma}} \end{array} \right\}$$
$$= (\varsigma - 1) + \frac{z \partial_q \left(DR_{\lambda,q}^{m+1,n} f(z)\right)}{DR_{\lambda,q}^{m+1,n} f(z)} - \varsigma \frac{z \partial_q \left(DR_{\lambda,q}^{m,n} f(z)\right)}{DR_{\lambda,q}^{m,n} f(z)}.$$

We deduce from (8) that

$$\frac{z \partial_q p(z)}{p(z)} = (\varsigma - 1) + \frac{q^{\lambda}}{[\lambda]_q} \left( \frac{DR_{\lambda,q}^{m+2,n} f(z)}{DR_{\lambda,q}^{m+1,n} f(z)} \right) - \frac{q^{\lambda}}{[\lambda]_q} \left( 1 - \frac{[\lambda]_q}{q^{\lambda}} \right)$$
$$- \varsigma \frac{q^{\lambda}}{[\lambda]_q} \left( \frac{DR_{\lambda,q}^{m+1,n} f(z)}{DR_{\lambda,q}^{m,n} f(z)} \right) + \varsigma \frac{q^{\lambda}}{[\lambda]_q} \left( 1 - \frac{[\lambda]_q}{q^{\lambda}} \right)$$
$$= \frac{q^{\lambda}}{[\lambda]_q} \left( \frac{DR_{\lambda,q}^{m+2,n} f(z)}{DR_{\lambda,q}^{m+1,n} f(z)} \right) - \varsigma \frac{q^{\lambda}}{[\lambda]_q} \left( \frac{DR_{\lambda,q}^{m+1,n} f(z)}{DR_{\lambda,q}^{m,n} f(z)} \right)$$
$$+ \frac{(\varsigma - 1)[\lambda]_q q^{\lambda} + q^{\lambda}(\varsigma - 1)\left(q^{\lambda} - [\lambda]_q\right)}{[\lambda]_q q^{\lambda}}$$
$$= \frac{q^{\lambda}}{[\lambda]_q} \left( \frac{DR_{\lambda,q}^{m+2,n} f(z)}{DR_{\lambda,q}^{m+1,n} f(z)} \right) - \varsigma \frac{q^{\lambda}}{[\lambda]_q} \left( \frac{DR_{\lambda,q}^{m+1,n} f(z)}{DR_{\lambda,q}^{m,n} f(z)} \right)$$
$$+ \frac{q^{\lambda}(\varsigma - 1)}{[\lambda]_q},$$

which corresponds to

$$\frac{DR^{m+2,n}_{\lambda,q}f(z)}{DR^{m+1,n}_{\lambda,q}f(z)} - \varsigma \frac{DR^{m+1,n}_{\lambda,q}f(z)}{DR^{m,n}_{\lambda,q}f(z)} = \frac{[\lambda]_q}{q^\lambda} \frac{z\partial_q p(z)}{p(z)} + (1-\varsigma).$$

According to hypothesis (21), we have

$$\frac{z\partial_q p(z)}{p(z)} \prec \frac{z\partial_q h(z)}{h(z)}.$$

By using Lemma 5, we obtain

$$\frac{z^{\varsigma-1} DR^{m+1,n}_{\lambda,q}f(z)}{\left(DR^{m,n}_{\lambda,q}f(z)\right)^\varsigma} \prec h(z),$$

where $h$ is the best dominant. □

For $q \to 1-$, we obtain the result proven in [44].

**Corollary 9** ([44]). *For $h(0) \neq 0$, $\varsigma \neq 0$. Let $h$ be univalent in $U$, and $\frac{zh'(z)}{h(z)}$ be univalent and starlike in $U$. The differential subordination condition is satisfied if and only if $f \in T$*

$$\frac{DR^{m+2,n}_{\lambda}f(z)}{DR^{m+1,n}_{\lambda}f(z)} - \varsigma \frac{DR^{m+1,n}_{\lambda}f(z)}{DR^{m,n}_{\lambda}f(z)}$$
$$\prec \lambda \frac{zh'(z)}{h(z)} + 1 - \varsigma,$$

*then*

$$\frac{z^{\varsigma-1} DR^{m+1,n}_{\lambda}f(z)}{\left(DR^{m,n}_{\lambda}f(z)\right)^\varsigma} \prec h(z), z \in U,$$

*where the best dominant function is $h$.*

## 4. Conclusions

This study presents a modification of previous work that used quantum calculus to better understand geometric function theory. In this study, first of all, in Section 1, we defined the convolution operator $DR^{m,n}_{\lambda,q}$ inspired by the $q$-Sălăgean operator and the Ruscheweyh $q$-differential operator. Then, using the operator $DR^{m,n}_{\lambda,q}$, two new integral operators, $F^{m,n,q}_{\lambda,\gamma_1,\gamma_2,...\gamma_l}(z)$ and $G^{m,n,q}_{\lambda,\gamma_1,\gamma_2,...\gamma_l}(z)$, were introduced. Some new subclasses of analytic functions were introduced by means of these operators. In Section 2, four innovative lemmas that are connected to the new integral operators and were used in the justifications of the first findings in Sections 3 were proven. In Section 3, we first determined the sufficient conditions in Theorems 1 and 2 for the functions from class $T$ to belong to classes $LAF$ and $LAG$. Next, in Theorems 3–6, we proved some new properties of the integral operators $F^{m,n,q}_{\lambda,\gamma_1,\gamma_2,...\gamma_l}(z)$ and $G^{m,n,q}_{\lambda,\gamma_1,\gamma_2,...\gamma_l}(z)$ for newly defined classes $R(\delta,q)$, $C(\delta,q)$, $RA(\beta,\mu,q)$, and $CA(\beta,\mu,q)$. We examined Theorems 7 and 8 by presenting the best dominants for certain differential subordinations. The results of this article are the generalizations discussed earlier in in [44].

Many new subclasses of analytic, meromorphic, and $p$-valent functions can be defined by utilizing the differential and integral operators introduced in this article, and a number of useful properties can be investigated for these classes.

Differential operators have allowed us to study differential equations from the perspective of operator theory and functional analysis. The use of differential operators allows for the solution of differential equations. In the future, research might be conducted to determine whether PDEs can be solved using these operators. These novel operators may be studied for potential applications in the applied sciences and other practical sciences, where similar results have been reported for numerous differential operators.

**Author Contributions:** Supervision, S.B.A.-S.; Methodology, A.A.A.; M.F.K.; Formal analysis, A.A.A.; K.M.; Writing, review and editing original draft, S.B.A.-S.; Funding acquisition, S.B.A.-S. All authors have read and agreed to the published version of the manuscript.

**Funding:** This manuscript was funded by Arab Open University (AOURG-2023-007).

**Data Availability Statement:** Not applicable.

**Acknowledgments:** The authors extend their appreciation to the Arab Open University for funding this work through research fund No. (AOURG-2023-007).

**Conflicts of Interest:** The authors declare no conflict of interest.

# References

1. Alexander, J.W. Functions which map the interior of the unit circle upon simple regions. *Ann. Math.* **1915**, *17*, 12–22. [CrossRef]
2. Alb Lupaş, A.; Oros, G.I. Differential Subordination and Superordination Results Using Fractional Integral of Confluent Hypergeometric Function. *Symmetry* **2021**, *13*, 327. [CrossRef]
3. Oros, G.I. Study on new integral operators defined using confluent hypergeometric function. *Adv. Differ. Equ.* **2021**, *2021*, 342. [CrossRef]
4. Alb Lupaş, A.; Oros, G.I. On Special Differential Subordinations Using Fractional Integral of Sălăgean and Ruscheweyh Operators. *Symmetry* **2021**, *13*, 1553. [CrossRef]
5. Cătaş, A.; Şendrţiu, R.; Iambor, L.F. Certain subclass of harmonic multivalent functions defined by derivative operator. *J. Comput. Anal. Appl.* **2021**, *29*, 775–785.
6. Oros, G.I. New differential subordinations obtained by using a differential-integral Ruscheweyh-Libera operator. *Miskolc Math. Notes* **2020**, *21*, 303–317. [CrossRef]
7. Páll-Szabó, A.O.; Wanas, A.K. Coefficient estimates for some new classes of bi-Bazilevič functions of Ma-Minda type involving the Sălăgean integro-differential operator. *Quaest. Math.* **2021**, *44*, 495–502.
8. Srivastava, H.M. Operators of basic (or $q$-) calculus and fractional $q$-calculus and their applications in geometric function theory of complex analysis. *Iran. J. Sci. Technol. Trans. A Sci.* **2020**, *44*, 327–344. [CrossRef]
9. Ibrahim, R.W.; Darus, M. New Symmetric Differential and Integral Operators Defined in the Complex Domain. *Symmetry* **2019**, *11*, 906. [CrossRef]
10. Ibrahim, R.W.; Elobaid, R.M.; Obaiys, S.J. Geometric Inequalities via a Symmetric Differential Operator Defined by Quantum Calculus in the Open Unit Disk. *J. Funct. Spaces* **2020**, *2020*, 6932739. [CrossRef]
11. Khan, B.; Srivastava, H.M.; Tahir, M.; Darus, M.; Ahmad, Q.Z.; Khan, N. Applications of a certain q-integral operator to the subclasses of analytic and bi-univalent functions. *AIMS Math.* **2021**, *6*, 1024–1039. [CrossRef]
12. Srivastava, H.M.; Khan, S.; Ahmad, Q.Z.; Khan, N.; Hussain, S. The Faber polynomial expansion method and its application to the general coefficient problem for some subclasses of bi-univalent functions associated with a certain q-integral operator. *Stud. Univ. Babeş-Bolyai Math.* **2018**, *63*, 419–436. [CrossRef]
13. Cotîrlă, L.I. New classes of analytic and bi-univalent functions. *AIMS Math.* **2021**, *6*, 10642–10651. [CrossRef]
14. Amini, E.; Omari, S.A.; Nonlaopon, K.; Baleanu, D. Estimates for coefficients of bi- univalent functions associated with a fractional q-difference operator. *Symmetry* **2022**, *14*, 879. [CrossRef]
15. Aldawish, I.; Swamy, S.R.; Frasin, B.A. A special family of m-fold symmetric bi-univalent functions satisfying subordination condition. *Fractal Fract.* **2022**, *6*, 271. [CrossRef]
16. Khan, S.; Hussain, S.; Naeem, M.; Darus, M.; Rasheed, A. A subclass of $q$-starlike functions defined by using a symmetric $q$-derivative operator and related with generalized symmetric conic domains. *Mathematics* **2021**, *9*, 917. [CrossRef]
17. Zhang, C.; Khan, S.; Hussain, A.; Khan, N.; Hussain, S.; Khan, N. Applications of $q$-difference operator in harmonic univalent functions. *AIMS Math.* **2021**, *7*, 667–680. [CrossRef]
18. Khan, M.F.; Goswami, A. Khan, S. Certain new subclass of multivalent q-starlike functions associated with $q$-symmetric calculus. *Fractal Fract.* **2022**, *6*, 367. [CrossRef]
19. Srivastava, H.M.; Jan, R.; Jan, A.; Deebai, W.; Shutaywi, M. Fractional-calculus analysis of the transmission dynamics of the dengue infection. *Chaos* **2021**, *31*, 053130. [CrossRef]
20. Baleanu, D.; Jajarmi, A.; Mohammadi, H.; Rezapour, S. A new study on the mathematical modelling of human liver with Caputo–Fabrizio fractional derivative. *Chaos Solitons Fract.* **2020**, *134*, 109705. [CrossRef]
21. Park, J.H.; Srivastava, H.M.; Cho, N.E. Univalence and convexity conditions for certain integral operators associated with the Lommel function of the first kind. *AIMS Math.* **2021**, *6*, 11380–11402. [CrossRef]

22. Miller, S.S.; Mocanu, P.T. *Differential Subordinations: Theory and Applications*; Series on Monographs and Textbooks in Pure and Applied Mathematics; Marcel Dekker: New York, NY, USA; Basel, Switzerland, 2000; Volume 225.
23. Jackson, F.H. On $q$-functions and a certain difference operator. *Trans. R. Soc. Edinb.* **1908**, *46*, 253–281. [CrossRef]
24. Ismail, M.E.H.; Merkes, E.; Styer, D. A generalization of starlike functions. *Complex Var. Theory Appl.* **1990**, *14*, 77–84. [CrossRef]
25. Kanas, S.; Raducanu, R. Some class of analytic functions related to conic domains. *Math. Slovaca* **2014**, *64*, 1183–1196. [CrossRef]
26. Arif, M.; Srivastava, H.M.; Umar, S. Some applications of a $q$-analogue of the Ruscheweyh type operator for multivalent functions. *RACSAM* **2019**, *113*, 1211–1221. [CrossRef]
27. Zhang, X.; Khan, S.; Hussain, S.; Tang, H.; Shareef, Z. New subclass of $q$-starlike functions associated with generalized conic domain. *AIMS Math.* **2020**, *5*, 4830–4848. [CrossRef]
28. Yousef, F.; Amourah, A.; Frasin, B.A.; Bulboacă, T. An Avant-Garde construction for subclasses of analytic bi-univalent functions. *Axioms* **2022**, *11*, 267. [CrossRef]
29. Srivastava, H.M.; Tahir, M.; Khan, B.; Ahmad, Q.A.; Khan, N. Some general classes of $q$-starlike functions associated with the Janowski functions. *Symmetry* **2019**, *11*, 292. [CrossRef]
30. Tang, H.; Khan, S.; Hussain, S.; Khan, N. Hankel and Toeplitz determinant for a subclass of multivalent $q$-starlike functions of order $\alpha$. *AIMS Math.* **2021**, *6*, 5421–5439. [CrossRef]
31. Noor, K.I.; Arif, M. Mapping properties of an integral operator. *Appl. Math. Lett.* **2012**, *25*, 1826–1829. [CrossRef]
32. Marin, M.; Ellahi, R.; Valse, S.; Bhatti, M.M. On the decay of exponential type for the solutions in a dipolar elastic body. *J. Taibah Univ. Sci.* **2020**, *14*, 534–540. [CrossRef]
33. Khan, S.; Hussain, S.; Darus, M. Inclusion relations of $q$-Bessel functions associated with generalized conic domain. *AIMS Math.* **2021**, *6*, 3624–3640. [CrossRef]
34. Jia, Z.; Khan, S.; Khan N.; Khan, B.; Muhammad, A. Faber polynomial coefficient bounds for -Fold symmetric analytic and bi-univalent functions involving q–calculus. *J. Funct. Spaces V* **2021**, *2021*, 5232467. [CrossRef]
35. Jackson, F.H. On $q$-definite integrals. *Pure Appl. Math. Q.* **1910**, *41*, 193–203.
36. Al-Oboudi, F.M. On univalent functions defined by a generalized Sălăgean operator. *Ind. J. Math. Math. Sci.* **2004**, *27*, 1429–1436. [CrossRef]
37. Govindaraj, M.; Sivasubramanian, S. On a class of analytic functions related to conic domains involving $q$-calculus. *Anal. Math.* **2017**, *43*, 475-487. [CrossRef]
38. Sălăgean, G.S. Subclasses of univalent functions. In *Complex Analysis—Fifth Romanian-Finnish Seminar*; Lecture Notes in Mathematics; Springer: Berlin/Heidelberg, Germany, 1983; Volume 1013, pp. 362–372.
39. Akça, H.; Benbourenane, J.; Eleuch, H. The $q$-derivative and differential equation. *J. Phys. Conf. Ser.* **2019**, *1411*, 012002. [CrossRef]
40. Breaz, D.; Breaz, N. *Two Integral Operators*; Studia Universitatis Babes-Bolyai Mathematica: Cluj-Napoca, Romania, 2002; Volume 13, p. 21.
41. Breaz, D.; Owa, S.; Breaz, N. A new integral univalent operator. *Acta Univ. Apul.* **2008**, *16*, 11–16.
42. Ravichandran, V. Certain applications of first order differential subordination. *Far East J. Math. Sci.* **2004**, *12*, 41–51.
43. Ravichandran, V.; Darus, M.; Khan, H.M.; Subramanian, K.G. Differential subordination associated with linear operators defined for multivalent functions. *Acta Math. Vietnam* **2005**, *30*, 113–121.
44. Lupas, A.A.; Loriana Andrei, L. Certain integral operators of analytic functions. *Mathematics* **2021**, *9*, 2586. [CrossRef]

**Disclaimer/Publisher's Note:** The statements, opinions and data contained in all publications are solely those of the individual author(s) and contributor(s) and not of MDPI and/or the editor(s). MDPI and/or the editor(s) disclaim responsibility for any injury to people or property resulting from any ideas, methods, instructions or products referred to in the content.

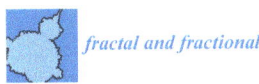

*fractal and fractional*

Article

# The Properties of Meromorphic Multivalent $q$-Starlike Functions in the Janowski Domain

Isra Al-Shbeil [1], Jianhua Gong [2,*], Samrat Ray [3], Shahid Khan [4], Nazar Khan [4] and Hala Alaqad [2]

1. Department of Mathematics, Faculty of Science, The University of Jordan, Amman 11942, Jordan
2. Department of Mathematical Sciences, United Arab Emirates University, Al Ain 15551, United Arab Emirates
3. Sai Balaji Education Society, Pune 411033, India
4. Department of Mathematics, Abbottabad University of Science and Technology, Abbottabad 22500, Pakistan
* Correspondence: j.gong@uaeu.ac.ae

**Abstract:** Many researchers have defined the $q$-analogous of differential and integral operators for analytic functions using the concept of quantum calculus in the geometric function theory. In this study, we conduct a comprehensive investigation to identify the uses of the Sălăgean $q$-differential operator for meromorphic multivalent functions. Many features of functions that belong to geometrically defined classes have been extensively studied using differential operators based on $q$-calculus operator theory. In this research, we extended the idea of the $q$-analogous of the Sălăgean differential operator for meromorphic multivalent functions using the fundamental ideas of $q$-calculus. With the help of this operator, we extend the family of Janowski functions by adding two new subclasses of meromorphic $q$-starlike and meromorphic multivalent $q$-starlike functions. We discover significant findings for these new classes, including the radius of starlikeness, partial sums, distortion theorems, and coefficient estimates.

**Keywords:** quantum (or $q$-) calculus; $q$-derivative operator; Sălăgean $q$-differential operator; meromorphic multivalent $q$-starlike functions; Janowski functions

**MSC:** Primary: 05A30; 30C45; Secondary: 11B65; 47B38

**Citation:** Al-Shbeil, I.; Gong, J.; Ray, S.; Khan, S.; Khan, N.; Alaqad, H. The Properties of Meromorphic Multivalent $q$-Starlike Functions in the Janowski Domain. *Fractal Fract.* **2023**, *7*, 438. https://doi.org/10.3390/fractalfract7060438

Academic Editors: Ivanka Stamova, Gheorghe Oros and Georgia Irina Oros

Received: 22 March 2023
Revised: 7 May 2023
Accepted: 20 May 2023
Published: 29 May 2023

**Copyright:** © 2023 by the authors. Licensee MDPI, Basel, Switzerland. This article is an open access article distributed under the terms and conditions of the Creative Commons Attribution (CC BY) license (https://creativecommons.org/licenses/by/4.0/).

## 1. Introduction and Definitions

Currently, researchers have given more attention to the study of $q$-calculus due to its applications in the fields of physics and mathematics. Before Ismail et al. [1] looked into the $q$-extension of the class of starlike functions, Jackson [2,3] was the first to consider some applications of $q$-calculus and define the $q$-analogue of the derivative and integral. After that, several scholars carried out great studies in geometric function theory (GFT). The $q$-Mittag–Leffler functions were specifically researched by Srivastava and others, and the authors of [4] also studied the class of $q$-starlike functions and looked into a third Hankel determinant. A recent survey-cum-expository review conducted by Srivastava [5] is also beneficial for researchers studying these subjects. In this review study, Srivastava [5] discussed applications of the fractional $q$-derivative operator in geometric function theory and provided some mathematical justifications. In their paper [6], Arif et al. defined and explored the $q$-derivative operator for multivalent functions, and [7] Zang et al. defined a generalized conic domain and then investigated a novel subclass of $q$-starlike functions using the definition of subordination and $q$-calculus operator theory. Recently, many well-known mathematicians have used $q$-calculus and studied some subclasses of analytic functions and their properties (see, for example, [8,9]). Recently, several authors published a series of studies [10–12] focusing on the classes of $q$-starlike functions connected to Janowski functions [13] from various angles.

The above works serve as the main inspiration for this article, which will first define a new $q$-analog of the Sălăgean differential operator for meromorphic multivalent functions.

By taking this operator into consideration, a new subclass of meromorphic multivalent functions related to Janowski functions is defined and studied, along with its geometric properties such as sufficient coefficient estimates, partial sums, distortion theorems, and the radius of starlikeness.

The set $\mathcal{M}(p)$ contains all meromorphic multivalent functions $h$ that are analytic in the punctured open unit disk

$$\mathbb{U}^* = \{\varsigma : \varsigma \in \mathbb{C} \text{ and } 0 < |\varsigma| < 1\},$$

and have the following series of representation:

$$h(\varsigma) = \frac{1}{\varsigma^p} + \sum_{i=0}^{\infty} a_{i+p} \varsigma^{i+p}, \quad (p \in \mathbb{N} = \{1, 2, ...\}). \tag{1}$$

In particular, if $p = 1$, then

$$h(\varsigma) = \frac{1}{\varsigma} + \sum_{i=1}^{\infty} a_i \varsigma^i, \tag{2}$$

In other words, we have

$$\mathcal{M}(1) = \mathcal{M},$$

which is the set of meromorphic univalent functions that are analytic in the punctured open unit disk.

A function $h \in \mathcal{MS}^*(p)$ is called a meromorphic multivalent starlike function if $h \in \mathcal{M}(p)$ satisfies the inequality

$$Re\left(-\frac{\varsigma h'(\varsigma)}{h(\varsigma)}\right) > 0.$$

A function $h \in \mathcal{MS}^*(p,\alpha)$ is called a meromorphic multivalent starlike functions of the order $\alpha$ $(0 \leq \alpha < 1)$ if $h \in \mathcal{M}(p)$ satisfies the inequality

$$Re\left(-\frac{\varsigma h'(\varsigma)}{h(\varsigma)}\right) > \alpha, \quad ((0 \leq \alpha < p)$$

In particular, we have

$$\mathcal{MS}^*(p,0) = \mathcal{MS}^*(p).$$

A function $h \in \mathcal{MC}(p)$ is called a meromorphic multivalent convex function if $h \in \mathcal{M}(p)$ satisfies the inequality

$$Re\left(-\left(1 + \frac{\varsigma h''(\varsigma)}{h'(\varsigma)}\right)\right) > 0. \quad (0 \leq \alpha < p)$$

A function $h \in \mathcal{MC}(p,\alpha)$ is called a meromorphic multivalent convex function of the order $\alpha$ $(0 \leq \alpha < p)$ if $h \in \mathcal{M}(p)$ satisfies the inequality

$$Re\left(-\left(1 + \frac{\varsigma h''(\varsigma)}{h'(\varsigma)}\right)\right) > \alpha.$$

In particular, we have

$$\mathcal{MC}(p,0) = \mathcal{MC}(p).$$

The basic ideas of these classes started in 1959 when Cluin [14] studied meromorphic schlicht functions. In 1963, Pommerenke [15] defined a class of meromorphic starlike functions and investigated coefficient estimates, and in [16], Royste studied meromorphic starlike multivalent functions for the first time and also found the same type of coefficient problems for the class of meromorphic starlike multivalent functions. In 1970, Miller [17] defined a class of meromorphic convex functions and investigated some generalized coefficient problems and other useful characteristics of meromorphic convex functions.

Cho and Owa [18] examined the partial sum for meromorphic $p$-valent functions, while Aouf et al. [19] determined a class of meromorphic $p$-valent functions and investigated the partial sums for meromorphic $p$-valent functions. In 2004, Srivastava [20] suggested some new classes of meromorphic multivalent functions and described some helpful features of meromorphic functions. Frasin and Maslina [21] investigated positive coefficients for a class of meromorphic functions.

A function $\varphi(z)$ is said to be in the class $P[F, \mathcal{K}]$ if it is analytic in $\mathbb{U}^*$ with $\varphi(z) = 1$ and
$$\varphi(z) \prec \frac{1 + Fz}{1 + \mathcal{K}z},$$

Equivalently, we can write
$$\left| \frac{\varphi(z) - 1}{F - \mathcal{K}\varphi(z)} \right| < 1.$$

Recalling certain definitions of the $q$-calculus operator theory would be helpful because they are essential for understanding this article. Unless otherwise stated, we assume the following throughout the article:
$$q \in (0,1), \quad -1 \leq \mathcal{K} < F \leq 1, \quad \text{and} \quad p \in \mathbb{N}.$$

**Definition 1** ([22]). *The $q$-number $[\zeta]_q$ is defined by*
$$[\zeta]_q = \begin{cases} \frac{1-q^\zeta}{1-q}, & (\zeta \in \mathbb{C}), \\ \sum_{k=0}^{i-1} q^k, & (\zeta = i \in \mathbb{N}), \end{cases}$$

*and for any non-negative integer $i$, we have*
$$[i]_q! = \begin{cases} [i]_q[i-1]_q[i-2]_q \ldots [2]_q[1]_q, & i \geq 1, \\ 1, & i = 0. \end{cases}$$

**Definition 2** ([2,3]). *Let $\mathcal{A}$ be the set of all analytic functions $h$ in the open unit disk*
$$\mathbb{U} = \{\varsigma : \varsigma \in \mathbb{C} \text{ and } |\varsigma| < 1\}$$

*and have the following series representation.*
$$h(\varsigma) = \varsigma + \sum_{i=2}^{\infty} a_i \varsigma^i.$$

*The $q$-derivative (or $q$-difference) $D_q$ is defined by*
$$(D_q h)(\varsigma) = \begin{cases} \frac{h(\varsigma) - h(q\varsigma)}{(1-q)\varsigma}, & (\varsigma \neq 0), \\ h'(0), & (\varsigma = 0). \end{cases} \tag{3}$$

*Equation (3) shows that if $h$ is differentiable at $\varsigma$, then*
$$\lim_{q \to 1^-} (D_q h)(\varsigma) = h'(\varsigma).$$

For $h \in \mathcal{A}$, and from Equation (3), we have

$$(D_q h)(\varsigma) = 1 + \sum_{i=2}^{\infty} [i]_q a_i \varsigma^{i-1}.$$

**Definition 3** ([23]). *The Sălăgean q-differential operator for $h \in \mathcal{A}$ is defined by*

$$\begin{aligned}
\mathcal{S}_q^0 h(\varsigma) &= h(\varsigma), \ \mathcal{S}_q^1 h(\varsigma) = \varsigma D_q h(\varsigma) = \frac{h(q\varsigma) - h(\varsigma)}{q-1}, \cdots, \\
\mathcal{S}_q^m h(\varsigma) &= \varsigma D_q\left(\mathcal{S}_q^{m-1} h(\varsigma)\right) = h(\varsigma) * \left(\varsigma + \sum_{i=2}^{\infty} [i]_q^m \varsigma^i\right), \\
&= \varsigma + \sum_{i=2}^{\infty} [i]_q^m a_i \varsigma^i.
\end{aligned}$$

Mahmood et al. extended the concept of the $q$-difference operator for $h \in \mathcal{M}$ and constructed a new subclass $\mathcal{MS}_q^*[F, \mathcal{K}]$ of meromorphic functions using the analogue of Definition 2:

**Definition 4** ([24]). *For $h \in \mathcal{M}$, the q-derivative (or q-difference) $D_q$ is defined by*

$$(D_q h)(\varsigma) = \frac{h(\varsigma) - h(q\varsigma)}{(1-q)\varsigma}. \tag{4}$$

For $h \in \mathcal{M}$, and from Equation (4), we have

$$(D_q h)(\varsigma) = \frac{-1}{q\varsigma^2} + \sum_{i=1}^{\infty} [i]_q a_i \varsigma^{i-1}, \ \forall \varsigma \in \mathcal{U}^*. \tag{5}$$

Using Equations (1) and (4), we extend the idea of the Sălăgean $q$-differential operator for meromorphic functions as follows:

**Definition 5.** *Let $h \in \mathcal{M}$. Then, the Sălăgean q-differential operator for a meromorphic function is given by*

$$\begin{aligned}
\mathcal{S}_q^0 h(\varsigma) &= h(\varsigma), \ \mathcal{S}_q^1 h(\varsigma) = D_q h(\varsigma) = \frac{h(q\varsigma) - h(\varsigma)}{(q-1)\varsigma}, \\
&\cdots \\
\mathcal{S}_q^m h(\varsigma) &= D_q\left(\mathcal{S}_q^{m-1} h(\varsigma)\right) \\
\mathcal{S}_q^m h(\varsigma) &= \frac{-1}{q\varsigma^2} + \sum_{i=1}^{\infty} [i]_q^m a_i \varsigma^{i-1}. 
\end{aligned} \tag{6}$$

**Definition 6.** *Let $h$ be a meromorphic multivalent function given by Equation (1). Then, the Sălăgean q-differential operator is given by*

$$\begin{aligned}
\mathcal{S}_{q,p}^0 h(\varsigma) &= h(\varsigma), \ \mathcal{S}_{q,p}^1 h(\varsigma) = D_q h(\varsigma) = \frac{h(\varsigma) - h(q\varsigma)}{(1-q)\varsigma}, \\
&\cdots \\
\mathcal{S}_{q,p}^m h(\varsigma) &= D_q\left(\mathcal{S}_{q,p}^{m-1} h(\varsigma)\right) \\
\mathcal{S}_{q,p}^m h(\varsigma) &= \frac{-1}{q^p \varsigma^{p+1}} + \sum_{i=0}^{\infty} [i+p]_q^m a_{i+p} \varsigma^{i+p-1}.
\end{aligned} \tag{7}$$

**Remark 1.** *By taking $p = 1$ in Equation (7), then we have the Sălăgean q-differential operator for $h \in \mathcal{M}$, which is given by Equation (6).*

In the case of the recently introduced Sălăgean q-differential operator $h \in \mathcal{M}$, we introduce a novel subclass of meromorphic q-starlike functions connected to Janowski functions.

**Definition 7.** *A function $h \in \mathcal{M}$ belongs to the class $\mathcal{MS}_q^*[m, F, \mathcal{K}]$ if*

$$\left| \frac{(\mathcal{K} - 1)\left(-\frac{\varsigma(\mathcal{S}_q^m h)(\varsigma)}{h(\varsigma)}\right) - (F - 1)}{(\mathcal{K} + 1)\left(-\frac{\varsigma(\mathcal{S}_q^m h)(\varsigma)}{h(\varsigma)}\right) - (F + 1)} - \frac{1}{1-q} \right| < \frac{1}{1-q}.$$

We provide a novel subclass of meromorphic q-starlike functions connected to Janowski functions in the context of the recently introduced Sălăgean q-differential operator $h \in \mathcal{M}(p)$.

**Definition 8.** *A function $h \in \mathcal{M}(p)$ belongs to the class $\mathcal{MS}_{q,p}^*[m, F, \mathcal{K}]$ if*

$$\left| \frac{(\mathcal{K} - 1)\left(-\frac{\varsigma(\mathcal{S}_{q,p}^m h)(\varsigma)}{h(\varsigma)}\right) - (F - 1)}{(\mathcal{K} + 1)\left(-\frac{\varsigma(\mathcal{S}_{q,p}^m h)(\varsigma)}{h(\varsigma)}\right) - (F + 1)} - \frac{1}{1-q} \right| < \frac{1}{1-q}.$$

**Remark 2.** *It can be easily observed that*

$$\mathcal{MS}_{q,1}^*(1, F, \mathcal{K}) = \mathcal{MS}_q^*(F, \mathcal{K}),$$

*which was introduced and studied by Mahmood et al. [24].*

**Remark 3.** *It is clear that*

$$\lim_{q \to 1-} \mathcal{MS}_{q,1}^*[m, F, \mathcal{K}] = \mathcal{MS}^*[F, \mathcal{K}],$$

*which was introduced and studied by Ali et al. [25].*

**Remark 4.** *For $q \to 1-$, $m = 1$, $F = 1$, and $\mathcal{K} = -1$, then*

$$\lim_{q \to 1-} \mathcal{MS}_{q,1}^*[1, -1] = \mathcal{MS}^*,$$

*where $\mathcal{MS}^*$ denotes the class of meromorphic starlike function.*

The sufficient condition for $h \in \mathcal{MS}_{q,p}^*[m, F, \mathcal{K}]$ is examined in Theorem 1, which can be used as a supporting result to research further findings. We will also look into the relationship between a function h of the type (Equation (1)) and the partial sums of its series

$$h_k(\varsigma) = \frac{1}{\varsigma^p} + \sum_{i=0}^{k} a_{i+p} \varsigma^{i+p}, \quad (k \in \mathbb{N}), \tag{8}$$

when the coefficients are sufficiently small.

## 2. Main Results

### 2.1. Sufficient Condition

**Theorem 1.** *If a function $h \in \mathcal{M}(p)$ of the form in Equation (1) satisfies the following condition, then $h \in \mathcal{MS}^*_{q,p}[m, F, \mathcal{K}]$:*

$$\sum_{i=0}^{\infty} 2\left([i+p]_q^m + 1\right) + \left|(\mathcal{K}+1)[i+p]_q^m - (F-1)\right| q^p |a_{i+p}|$$
$$\leq |(\mathcal{K}+1) - (F+1)q^p| + 2(1-q^p). \tag{9}$$

**Proof.** Supposing that Equation (9) is satisfied, then it is enough to prove that

$$\left| \frac{(\mathcal{K}-1)\left(-\frac{\varsigma(S_{q,p}^m h)(\varsigma)}{h(\varsigma)}\right) - (F-1)}{(\mathcal{K}+1)\left(-\frac{\varsigma(S_{q,p}^m h)(\varsigma)}{h(\varsigma)}\right) - (F+1)} - \frac{1}{1-q} \right| < \frac{1}{1-q}.$$

Now, we have

$$\left| \frac{(\mathcal{K}-1)\left(-\frac{\varsigma(S_{q,p}^m h)(\varsigma)}{h(\varsigma)}\right) - (F-1)}{(\mathcal{K}+1)\left(-\frac{\varsigma(S_{q,p}^m h)(\varsigma)}{h(\varsigma)}\right) - (F+1)} - \frac{1}{1-q} \right|$$

$$= \left| \frac{(\mathcal{K}-1)\left(-\frac{\varsigma(S_{q,p}^m h)(\varsigma)}{h(\varsigma)}\right) - (F-1)}{(\mathcal{K}+1)\left(-\frac{\varsigma(S_{q,p}^m h)(\varsigma)}{h(\varsigma)}\right) - (F+1)} - \frac{1+q-q}{1-q} \right|$$

$$= \left| \frac{-(\mathcal{K}-1)\varsigma\left(S_{q,p}^m h\right)(\varsigma) - (F-1)h(\varsigma)}{-(\mathcal{K}+1)\varsigma\left(S_{q,p}^m h\right)(\varsigma) - (F+1)h(\varsigma)} - 1 - \frac{q}{1-q} \right|$$

$$\leq \left| \frac{-(\mathcal{K}-1)\varsigma\left(S_{q,p}^m h\right)(\varsigma) - (F-1)h(\varsigma)}{-(\mathcal{K}+1)\varsigma\left(S_{q,p}^m h\right)(\varsigma) - (F+1)h(\varsigma)} - 1 \right| + \frac{q}{1-q}$$

$$= 2\left| \frac{\varsigma\left(S_{q,p}^m h\right)(\varsigma) + h(\varsigma)}{-(\mathcal{K}+1)\varsigma(S_{q,p}^m h)(\varsigma) - (F+1)h(\varsigma)} \right| + \frac{q}{1-q}$$

$$= 2\left| \frac{\left(1-\frac{1}{q^p}\right) + \sum_{i=0}^{\infty}\left(1 + [i+p]_q^m\right) a_{i+p} \varsigma^{i+p}}{(\mathcal{K}+1)\frac{1}{q^p} - (F+1) - \sum_{i=0}^{\infty}((\mathcal{K}+1)[i+p]_q^m - (F-1)) a_{i+p} \varsigma^{i+p}} \right| + \frac{q}{1-q}$$

$$= 2\left| \frac{\frac{(q^p-1)}{q^p} + \sum_{i=0}^{\infty}\left(1 + [i+p]_q^m\right) a_{i+p} \varsigma^{i+p}}{(\mathcal{K}+1)\frac{1}{q^p} - (F+1) - \sum_{i=0}^{\infty}((\mathcal{K}+1)[i+p]_q^m + (F+1)) a_{i+p} \varsigma^{i+p}} \right| + \frac{q}{1-q}$$

$$\leq 2\left( \frac{|q^p - 1| + \sum_{i=0}^{\infty}\left(1 + [i+p]_q^m\right) q^p |a_{i+p}|}{|(\mathcal{K}+1) - (F+1)q^p| - \sum_{i=0}^{\infty}|\{(\mathcal{K}+1)[i+p]_q^m - (F-1)\} q^p| |a_{i+p}|} \right) + \frac{q}{1-q}. \tag{10}$$

The inequality in Equation (10) is bounded by $\frac{1}{1-q}$ if

$$\sum_{i=0}^{\infty} 2\left([i+p]_q^m + 1\right) + \left|(\mathcal{K}+1)[i+p]_q^m - (F-1)\right| q^p |a_{i+p}|$$
$$< |(\mathcal{K}+1) - (F+1)q^p| + 2(1-q^p).$$

Thus, this completes the proof of Theorem 1. □

**Corollary 1.** *If a function $h \in \mathcal{M}(p)$ of the form in Equation (1) belongs to the class $\mathcal{MS}_{q,p}^*[m, F, \mathcal{K}]$, then*

$$a_{i+p} \leq \frac{|(\mathcal{K}+1) - (F+1)q^p| + 2(1-q^p)}{2\left([i+p]_q^m + 1\right) + \left|(\mathcal{K}+1)[i+p]_q^m - (F-1)\right| q^p}, \quad (i \in \mathbb{N}). \tag{11}$$

*This equality will satisfy the function*

$$h_i(\varsigma) = \frac{1}{\varsigma^p} + \frac{|(\mathcal{K}+1) - (F+1)q^p| + 2(1-q^p)}{2\left([i+p]_q^m + 1\right) + \left|(\mathcal{K}+1)[i+p]_q^m - (F-1)\right| q^p} \varsigma^{i+p-1}.$$

**Theorem 2.** *If a function $h \in \mathcal{M}$ of the form given in Equation (2) satisfies the following condition, then $h \in \mathcal{MS}_q^*[m, F, \mathcal{K}]$:*

$$\sum_{i=0}^{\infty} 2\left([i+1]_q^m + 1\right) + \left|(\mathcal{K}+1)[i+1]_q^m - (F-1)\right| q |a_{i+p}|$$
$$\leq |(\mathcal{K}+1) - (F+1)q| + 2(1-q). \tag{12}$$

By taking $p = 1$ and $m = 1$ in Theorem 1, then we have following known result, which was introduced in [24]:

**Corollary 2** ([24])**.** *If a function $h \in \mathcal{M}$ of the form in Equation (1) satisfies the following condition, then $h \in \mathcal{MS}_q^*[F, \mathcal{K}]$:*

$$\sum_{i=1}^{\infty} \Lambda(i, F, \mathcal{K}, q) |a_i| \leq Y(F, \mathcal{K}, q),$$

*where*

$$\Lambda(i, F, \mathcal{K}, q) = 2\left([i]_q + 1\right) + \left|(\mathcal{K}+1)[i]_q - (F-1)\right| q$$

*and*

$$Y(F, \mathcal{K}, q) = |(\mathcal{K}+1) - (F+1)q| + 2(1-q).$$

2.2. Distortion Inequalities

**Theorem 3.** *If $h \in \mathcal{MS}_{q,p}^*[m, F, \mathcal{K}]$, then*

$$\frac{1}{r^p} - \frac{|(\mathcal{K}+1) - (F+1)q^p| + 2(1-q^p)}{2\left([1+p]_q^m + 1\right) + \left|(\mathcal{K}+1)[1+p]_q^m - (F-1)\right| q^p} r^p$$
$$\leq |h(\varsigma)| \leq \frac{1}{r^p} + \frac{|(\mathcal{K}+1) - (F+1)q^p| + 2(1-q^p)}{2\left([1+p]_q^m + 1\right) + \left|(\mathcal{K}+1)[1+p]_q^m - (F-1)\right| q^p} r^p.$$

*This equality holds for the function*

$$h(\varsigma) = \frac{1}{\varsigma^p} + \frac{|(\mathcal{K}+1) - (F+1)q^p| + 2(1-q^p)}{2\left([1+p]_q^m + 1\right) + \left|(\mathcal{K}+1)[1+p]_q^m - (F-1)\right| q^p} \varsigma^p \quad at\ \varsigma = ir.$$

**Proof.** Let $h \in \mathcal{MS}^*_{q,p}[m, F, \mathcal{K}]$. Then, in light of Theorem 1, we have

$$2\Big([1+p]_q^m + 1\Big) + \Big|(\mathcal{K}+1)[1+p]_q^m - (F-1)\Big|q^p \sum_{i=1}^{\infty} |a_{i+p}|$$
$$\leq \sum_{i=1}^{\infty} 2\Big([i+p]_q^m + 1\Big) + \Big|(\mathcal{K}+1)[i+p]_q^m - (F-1)\Big|q^p |a_{i+p}|$$
$$< |(\mathcal{K}+1) - (F+1)q^p| + 2(1-q^p),$$

which yields

$$|h(\varsigma)| \leq \frac{1}{r^p} + \sum_{i=1}^{\infty} |a_{i+p}| r^{i-p} \leq \frac{1}{r^p} + r^p \sum_{i=1}^{\infty} |a_{i+p}|$$
$$\leq \frac{1}{r^p} + \frac{|(\mathcal{K}+1) - (F+1)q^p| + 2(1-q^p)}{2\Big([1+p]_q^m + 1\Big) + \Big|(\mathcal{K}+1)[1+p]_q^m - (F-1)\Big|q^p} r^p.$$

Similarly, we have

$$|h(\varsigma)| \geq \frac{1}{r^p} - \sum_{i=1}^{\infty} |a_{i+p}| r^{i-p}$$
$$\geq \frac{1}{r^p} - r^p \sum_{i=1}^{\infty} |a_{i+p}|$$
$$\geq \frac{1}{r^p} - \frac{|(\mathcal{K}+1) - (F+1)q^p| + 2(1-q^p)}{2\Big([1+p]_q^m + 1\Big) + \Big|(\mathcal{K}+1)[1+p]_q^m - (F-1)\Big|q^p} r^p.$$

Thus, this completes the proof of Theorem 3. □

**Theorem 4.** *If a function $h$ of the form in Equation (2) belongs to the class $\mathcal{MS}^*_q[m, F, \mathcal{K}]$, then*

$$\frac{1}{r} - \frac{|(\mathcal{K}+1) - (F+1)q| + 2(1-q)}{2\Big([2]_q^m + 1\Big) + \Big|(\mathcal{K}+1)[2]_q^m - (F-1)\Big|q} r$$
$$\leq |h(\varsigma)| \leq \frac{1}{r} + \frac{|(\mathcal{K}+1) - (F+1)q| + 2(1-q)}{2\Big([2]_q^m + 1\Big) + \Big|(\mathcal{K}+1)[2]_q^m - (F-1)\Big|q} r.$$

*This equality holds for the function*

$$h(\varsigma) = \frac{1}{\varsigma} + \frac{|(\mathcal{K}+1) - (F+1)q| + 2(1-q)}{2\Big([2]_q^m + 1\Big) + \Big|(\mathcal{K}+1)[2]_q^m - (F-1)\Big|q} \varsigma \quad \text{at } \varsigma = ir.$$

**Proof.** Here, we omit the proof of Theorem 4. It is similar to that of the proof of Theorem 3. □

For $p = 1$ and $m = 1$ in Theorem 3, then we have the known corollary given in [24]:

**Corollary 3 ([24]).** *If $h \in \mathcal{MS}^*_q[F, \mathcal{K}]$, then*

$$\frac{1}{r} - \frac{|(\mathcal{K}+1) - (F+1)q| + 2(1-q)}{2([2]_q + 1) + |(\mathcal{K}+1) - (F-1)|q} r$$
$$\leq |h(\varsigma)| \leq \frac{1}{r} + \frac{(\mathcal{K}+1) - (F+1)(1-q)}{2([2]_q + 1) + |(\mathcal{K}+1)[2]_q - (F-1)|q} r.$$

This equality holds for the function

$$h(\varsigma) = \frac{1}{\varsigma} + \frac{|(\mathcal{K}+1) - (F+1)q| + 2(1-q)}{2([2]_q + 1) + |(\mathcal{K}+1)[2]_q - (F-1)|q} \varsigma \quad \text{at } \varsigma = ir.$$

**Theorem 5.** *If* $h \in \mathcal{MS}^*_{q,p}[m, F, \mathcal{K}]$, *then*

$$\frac{1}{r^{p+1}} - \frac{(p+1)|(\mathcal{K}+1) - (F+1)q^p| + 2(1-q^p)}{2\left([1+p]^m_q + 1\right) + \left|(\mathcal{K}+1)[1+p]^m_q - (F-1)\right|q^p}$$
$$\leq |h(\varsigma)| \leq \frac{1}{r^{p+1}} + \frac{(p+1)|(\mathcal{K}+1) - (F+1)q^p| + 2(1-q^p)}{2\left([1+p]^m_q + 1\right) + \left|(\mathcal{K}+1)[1+p]^m_q - (F-1)\right|q^p}, \quad (|\varsigma| = r).$$

**Proof.** Here, we omit the proof of Theorem 5. Its proof is similar to that of the proof Theorem 3. □

For $p = 1$ and $m = 1$, then we have a known corollary introduced in [24]:

**Corollary 4** ([24]). *If* $h \in \mathcal{MS}^*_q[F, \mathcal{K}]$, *then*

$$\frac{1}{r^2} - \frac{2|(\mathcal{K}+1) - (F+1)q| + 2(1-q)}{2([2]_q + 1) + |(\mathcal{K}+1)[2]_q - (F-1)|q}$$
$$\leq |h'(\varsigma)| \leq \frac{1}{r^2} + \frac{2|(\mathcal{K}+1) - (F+1)q| + 2(1-q)}{2([2]_q + 1) + |(\mathcal{K}+1)[2]_q - (F-1)|q}, \quad (|\varsigma| = r).$$

### 2.3. Partial Sums for the Function Class $\mathcal{MS}^*_{q,p}[m, F, \mathcal{K}]$

In this section, we study the ratio of a function of the form in Equation (1) to its sequence of partial sums

$$h_k(\varsigma) = \frac{1}{\varsigma^p} + \sum_{i=0}^{k} a_{i+p} \varsigma^{i+p}$$

when the coefficients of $h$ are sufficiently small to satisfy the condition in Equation (9). We will investigate the sharp lower bounds for

$$Re\left(\frac{h(\varsigma)}{h_k(\varsigma)}\right), \quad \left(\frac{h_k(\varsigma)}{h(\varsigma)}\right), \quad Re\left(\frac{S^m_{q,p} h(\varsigma)}{S^m_{q,p} h_k(\varsigma)}\right) \text{ and } Re\left(\frac{S^m_{q,p} h_k(\varsigma)}{S^m_{q,p} h(\varsigma)}\right).$$

The sequence of partial sums of $h_k$ is denoted by

$$h_k(\varsigma) = \frac{1}{\varsigma^p} + \sum_{i=0}^{k} a_{i+p} \varsigma^{i+p}.$$

**Theorem 6.** *If a function* $h \in \mathcal{M}(p)$ *of the form in Equation (1) satisfies the condition in Equation (9), then*

$$Re\left(\frac{h(\varsigma)}{h_k(\varsigma)}\right) \geq 1 - \frac{1}{\chi_{k+p+1}} \quad (\forall \varsigma \in \mathbb{U}) \tag{13}$$

*and*

$$Re\left(\frac{h_k(\varsigma)}{h(\varsigma)}\right) \geq \frac{\chi_{k+p+1}}{1 + \chi_{k+p+1}}, \quad (\forall \varsigma \in \mathbb{U}), \tag{14}$$

*where*

$$\chi_{k+p} = \frac{2\left([k+p]^m_q + 1\right) + \left|(\mathcal{K}+1)[k+p]^m_q - (F-1)\right|q^p}{|(\mathcal{K}+1) - (F+1)q^p| + 2(1-q^p)}. \tag{15}$$

**Proof.** For the proof of the inequality in Equation (13), we set

$$\chi_{k+p+1}\left[\frac{h(\varsigma)}{h_j(\varsigma)} - \left(1 - \frac{1}{\chi_{k+p+1}}\right)\right]$$

$$= \frac{1 + \sum_{i=0}^{k} a_{i+p}\varsigma^{i+p-1} + \chi_{k+p+1}\sum_{i=k+1}^{\infty} a_{i+p}\varsigma^{i+p+1}}{1 + \sum_{i=0}^{k} a_{i+p}\varsigma^{i+p+1}}$$

$$= \frac{1 + q_1(\varsigma)}{1 + q_2(\varsigma)}.$$

If we fix

$$\frac{1 + q_1(\varsigma)}{1 + q_2(\varsigma)} = \frac{1 + w(\varsigma)}{1 - w(\varsigma)},$$

then after some simplification, we obtain

$$w(\varsigma) = \frac{q_1(\varsigma) - q_2(\varsigma)}{2 + q_1(\varsigma) + q_2(\varsigma)}.$$

We find that

$$w(\varsigma) = \frac{\chi_{k+p+1} \sum_{i=k+1}^{\infty} a_{i+p}\varsigma^{i+p-1}}{2 + 2\sum_{i=0}^{k} a_{i+p}\varsigma^{i+p+1} + \chi_{k+p+1}\sum_{i=k+1}^{\infty} a_{i+p}\varsigma^{i+p+1}}$$

and

$$|w(\varsigma)| \leq \frac{\chi_{k+p+1} \sum_{i=k+1}^{\infty} |a_{i+p}|}{2 - 2\sum_{i=0}^{k} |a_{i+p}| - \chi_{k+p+1}\sum_{i=k+1}^{\infty} |a_{i+p}|}.$$

Now, one can see that

$$|w(\varsigma)| \leq 1$$

if and only if

$$2\chi_{k+p+1}\sum_{i=k+1}^{\infty} |a_{i+p}| \leq 2 - 2\sum_{i=0}^{k} |a_{i+p}|,$$

which implies that

$$\sum_{i=0}^{k} |a_{i+p}| + \chi_{k+p+1}\sum_{i=k+1}^{\infty} |a_{i+p}| \leq 1. \tag{16}$$

Finally, to prove Equation (13), it is enough to show that the L.H.S. of Equation (16) is bounded above by $\sum_{i=0}^{\infty} \chi_{i+p}|a_{i+p}|$, which is equal to

$$\sum_{i=0}^{k} (1 - \chi_{i+p})|a_{i+p}| + \sum_{i=k+1}^{\infty} (\chi_{k+p+1} - \chi_{i+p})|a_{i+p}| \geq 0. \tag{17}$$

Hence, the proof of the inequality in Equation (13) is complete.

For the proof of the inequality in Equation (14), we fix

$$\left(1+\chi_{k+p}\right)\left(\frac{h_k(\varsigma)}{h(\varsigma)}-\frac{\chi_{k+p}}{1+\chi_{k+p}}\right)$$

$$=\frac{1+\sum\limits_{i=0}^{k}a_{i+p}\varsigma^{i+p-1}-\chi_{k+p+1}\sum\limits_{i=k+1}^{\infty}a_{i+p}\varsigma^{i+p-1}}{1+\sum\limits_{i=0}^{\infty}a_{i+p}\varsigma^{i+p-1}}$$

$$=\frac{1+w(\varsigma)}{1-w(\varsigma)},$$

where

$$|w(\varsigma)|\leq\frac{\left(1+\chi_{k+p+1}\right)\sum\limits_{i=k+1}^{\infty}|a_{i+p}|}{2-2\sum\limits_{i=0}^{k}|a_{i+p}|-\left(\chi_{k+p+1}-1\right)\sum\limits_{i=k+1}^{\infty}|a_{i+p}|}\leq 1. \qquad (18)$$

The inequality in Equation (18) is equivalent to

$$\sum_{i=0}^{k}|a_{i+p}|+\chi_{k+p+1}\sum_{i=k+1}^{\infty}|a_{i+p}|\leq 1. \qquad (19)$$

Finally, we can find that the L.H.S. in Equation (19) is bounded above by $\sum\limits_{i=0}^{\infty}\chi_{i+p}|a_{i+p}|$, and thus we have completed the inequality in Equation (14). Hence, the proof of Theorem 6 is complete. □

**Theorem 7.** *If $h \in \mathcal{M}(p)$ of the form in Equation (1) satisfies the condition in Equation (9), then*

$$Re\left(\frac{S_{q,p}^{m}h(\varsigma)}{S_{q,p}^{m}h_{p,k}(\varsigma)}\right)\geq 1-\frac{[k+p]_q^m}{\chi_{k+p+1}}, \quad (\forall \varsigma \in \mathbb{U})$$

*and*

$$Re\left(\frac{S_{q,p}^{m}h_{p,k}(\varsigma)}{S_{q,p}^{m}h(\varsigma)}\right)\geq \frac{\chi_{k+p+1}}{\chi_{k+p+1}+[k+p]_q^m}, \quad (\forall \varsigma \in \mathbb{U}),$$

*where $\chi_{k+p}$ is given by Equation (15).*

**Proof.** Here we omit the proof of Theorem 7. It is similar to that of Theorem 6. □

### 2.4. Partial Sums for the Function Class $MS_q^*[m, F, \mathcal{K}]$

We will study the ratio of a function of the form in Equation (1) to its sequence of partial sums

$$h_k(\varsigma)=\frac{1}{\varsigma}+\sum_{i=0}^{k}a_{i+1}\varsigma^{i+1}$$

when the coefficients of $h$ are sufficiently small to satisfy the condition in Equation (9). We will investigate the sharp lower bounds for

$$Re\left(\frac{h(\varsigma)}{h_k(\varsigma)}\right), \quad \left(\frac{h_k(\varsigma)}{h(\varsigma)}\right), \quad Re\left(\frac{S_q^m h(\varsigma)}{S_q^m h_k(\varsigma)}\right) \text{ and } Re\left(\frac{S_q^m h_k(\varsigma)}{S_q^m h(\varsigma)}\right).$$

The sequence of partial sums of $h_k$ is denoted by

$$h_k(\varsigma) = \frac{1}{\varsigma} + \sum_{i=0}^{k} a_{i+1}\varsigma^{i+1}.$$

**Theorem 8.** *If we let $h \in \mathcal{M}$ of the form in Equation (2) satisfy the condition in Equation (12), then*

$$Re\left(\frac{h(\varsigma)}{h_k(\varsigma)}\right) \geq 1 - \frac{1}{\chi_{k+2}} \quad (\forall \varsigma \in \mathbb{U})$$

*and*

$$Re\left(\frac{h_k(\varsigma)}{h(\varsigma)}\right) \geq \frac{\chi_{k+2}}{1 + \chi_{k+2}} \quad (\forall \varsigma \in \mathbb{U}),$$

*where*

$$\chi_{k+1} = \frac{2(1-\alpha)\left([k+1]_q^m + 1\right) + \left|(\mathcal{K}+1)[k+1]_q^m - (F-1)\right|q}{|(\mathcal{K}+1) - (F+1)q| + 2(1-q)}. \quad (20)$$

**Proof.** Here, we omit the proof for Theorem 8. It is similar to that of the proof for Theorem 7. □

**Theorem 9.** *If we let $h \in \mathcal{M}$ of the form in Equation (2) satisfy the condition in Equation (12), then*

$$Re\left(\frac{S_q^m h(\varsigma)}{S_q^m h_k(\varsigma)}\right) \geq 1 - \frac{[k+1]_q^m}{\chi_{k+2}}, \quad (\forall \varsigma \in \mathbb{U})$$

*and*

$$Re\left(\frac{S_q^m h_k(\varsigma)}{S_q^m h(\varsigma)}\right) \geq \frac{\chi_{k+2}}{\chi_{k+2} + [k+1]_q^m}, \quad (\forall \varsigma \in \mathbb{U}),$$

*where $\chi_{k+1}$ is given by Equation (20).*

**Proof.** Here, we omit the proof for Theorem 9. It is similar to that of the proof for Theorem 6. □

*2.5. Radius of Starlikeness*

In the next result, we obtain the radius of starlikeness for the class $\mathcal{MS}_{q,p}^*[m, F, \mathcal{K}]$:

**Theorem 10.** *Let the function $h$ with Equation (1) belong to the class $\mathcal{MS}_{q,p}^*[m, F, \mathcal{K}]$. If*

$$\inf_{i \geq 1} \left[\frac{(1-\alpha)2\left([i+p]_q^m + 1\right) + \left|(\mathcal{K}+1)[i+p]_q^m - (F-1)\right|q^p}{(i+p+1-\alpha)|(\mathcal{K}+1) - (F+1)q^p| + 2(1-q^p)}\right]^{\frac{1}{i+p}} = r$$

*is positive, then the function $h$ is $p$-valently meromorphically starlike to the order $\alpha$ in $|\varsigma| \leq r$.*

**Proof.** To prove the above result, we have to show that

$$\left|\frac{\varsigma h'(\varsigma)}{h(\varsigma)} + 1\right| \leq 1 - \alpha, \quad (0 \leq \alpha < 1) \quad \text{and} \quad |\varsigma| \leq r_1.$$

From the above inequality, we have

$$\left|\frac{\varsigma h'(\varsigma)}{h(\varsigma)} + 1\right| = \left|\frac{\sum_{i=0}^{\infty}(i+p+\alpha)a_{i+p}\varsigma^{i+p}}{\frac{1}{\varsigma^p} + \sum_{i=0}^{\infty} a_{i+p}\varsigma^{i+p}}\right|$$

$$\leq \frac{\sum_{i=0}^{\infty}(i+p+\alpha)|a_{i+p}||\varsigma|^{i+p}}{1 - \sum_{i=0}^{\infty}|a_{i+p}||\varsigma|^{i+p}}. \quad (21)$$

Hence, Equation (21) holds true if

$$\sum_{i=0}^{\infty}(i+p+\alpha)|a_{i+p}||\varsigma|^{i+p} \leq (1-\alpha)\left(1 - \sum_{i=0}^{\infty}|a_{i+p}||\varsigma|^{i+p}\right). \tag{22}$$

Now, we can set the inequality in Equation (22) as follows:

$$\sum_{i=0}^{\infty}\left(\frac{i+p+1-\alpha}{1-\alpha}\right)|a_{i+p}||\varsigma|^{i+p} \leq 1. \tag{23}$$

With the help of Equation (9), the inequality in Equation (23) is true if

$$\left(\frac{i+p+1-\alpha}{1-\alpha}\right)|\varsigma|^{i+p}$$
$$\leq \frac{(1-\alpha)2\left([i+p]_q^m+1\right) + \left|(\mathcal{K}+1)[i+p]_q^m - (F-1)\right|q^p}{|(\mathcal{K}+1) - (F+1)q^p| + 2(1-q^p)}. \tag{24}$$

By solving Equation (24) for $|\varsigma|$, we have

$$|\varsigma| \leq \left(\frac{(1-\alpha)2\left([i+p]_q^m+1\right) + \left|(\mathcal{K}+1)[i+p]_q^m - (F-1)\right|q^p}{(i+p+1-\alpha)|(\mathcal{K}+1) - (F+1)q^p| + 2(1-q^p)}\right)^{\frac{1}{i+p}}. \tag{25}$$

This completes the proof. □

## 3. Discussion

This section serves as an introduction to the conclusions section, we will specifically highlight the relevance of our primary findings and their applications. With a primary motive to consolidate the study of the famous convex function with starlike and convex functions, Govindaraj and Sivasubramanian in [23] involved the $q$-calculus operator and defined the Sălăgean $q$-differential operator for analytic functions. However, the meromorphic functions and meromorphic multivalent functions could not be defined with the other geometrically defined subclasses of $\mathcal{M}$ and $\mathcal{M}(p)$ using the same meromorphic $q$-analogue of the Sălăgean differential operator. For the functions in $\mathcal{M}$ and $\mathcal{M}(p)$, we smartly established a Sălăgean $q$-differential operator in this study so that normalization could be preserved.

When considering the Sălăgean $q$-differential operator for $h \in \mathcal{M}$, the family of functions $\mathcal{MS}_q^*[m, F, \mathcal{K}]$ (see Definition 7) is defined to include $q$-starlike functions, and the other family of functions $\mathcal{MS}_{q,p}^*[m, F, \mathcal{K}]$ (see Definition 8) is defined by using the Sălăgean $q$-differential operator for $h \in \mathcal{M}(p)$.

Another notable difference from earlier research is the fact that we found criteria for the classes of $\mathcal{MS}_q^*[m, F, \mathcal{K}]$ and $\mathcal{MS}_{q,p}^*[m, F, \mathcal{K}]$ that are more broadly applicable. Hence, if we let $p = 1$ and $m = 1$, then some of our results in Section 2 will reduce to results for the class of $q$-starlike functions introduced in [24]. The approach used by different authors in this paper in arriving at solutions to the challenges of the classes is the same. However, several novel and traditional results can be obtained as a special case of our main findings.

## 4. Conclusions

The extension and unification of various well-known classes of functions were the main objectives of this paper. In this article, we used the $q$-calculus operator theory, introduced the Sălăgean $q$-differential operator for meromorphic multivalent functions and defined two new subclasses of meromorphic multivalent functions in the Janowski domain. We investigated some interesting properties, such as coefficient estimates, partial sums, distortion theorems, and the radius of starlikeness. The technique and ideas of this paper may stimulate further research in the theory of multivalent meromorphic functions and further generalized classes of meromorphic functions can be defined and investigated for several other useful properties such as Hankal determinants, Feketo–Sezego problems, coefficient inequalities, growth problems, and many others.

**Author Contributions:** Conceptualization, I.A.-S., J.G., S.R.; Methodology, S.K., N.K. and H.A.; Validation, S.R. and S.K.; Formal Analysis, I.A.-S., J.G., S.R., S.K., N.K. and H.A.; Investigation, I.A.-S., J.G., S.R., S.K., N.K. and H.A.; Resources, N.K. and H.A.; Writing—Original Draft Preparation, I.A.-S., J.G., S.R., S.K., N.K. and H.A.; Writing —Review & Editing, I.A.-S., J.G., S.R., S.K., N.K. and H.A.; Project Administration, I.A.-S.; Funding Acquisition, J.G. All authors have read and agreed to the published version of the manuscript.

**Funding:** The authors acknowledge funding from UAE University (UPAR12S127).

**Data Availability Statement:** Not applicable.

**Conflicts of Interest:** The authors declare no conflict of interest.

# References

1. Ismail, M.E.-H.; Merkes, E.; Styer, D. A generalization of starlike functions. *Complex Var. Theory Appl.* **1990**, *14*, 77–84. [CrossRef]
2. Jackson, F.H. On $q$-definite integrals. *Q. J. Pure Appl. Math.* **1910**, *41*, 193–203.
3. Jackson, F.H. $q$-difference equations. *Amer. J. Math.* **1910**, *32*, 305–314. [CrossRef]
4. Srivastava, H.M.; Ahmad, Q.Z.; Khan, N.; Khan, N.; Khan, B. Hankel and Toeplitz determinants for a subclass of $q$-starlike functions associated with a general conic domain. *Mathematics* **2019**, *7*, 181. [CrossRef]
5. Srivastava, H.M. Operators of basic (or $q$-) calculus and fractional $q$-calculus and their applications in geometric function theory of complex analysis. *Iran. J. Sci. Technol. Trans. A Sci.* **2020**, *44*, 327–344. [CrossRef]
6. Arif, M.; Srivastava, H.M.; Uma, S. Some applications of a $q$-analogue of the Ruscheweyh type operator for multivalent functions. *Rev. De La Real Acad. De Cienc. Exactas Fis. Y Naturales. Ser. A. Mat.* **2019**, *113*, 1211–1221. [CrossRef]
7. Zhang, X.; Khan, S.; Hussain, S.; Tang, H.; Shareef, Z. New subclass of $q$-starlike functions associated with generalized conic domain. *AIMS Math.* **2020**, *5*, 4830–4848. [CrossRef]
8. Ur Rehman, M.S.; Ahmad, Q.Z.; Al-shbeil, I.; Ahmad, S.; Khan, A.; Khan, B.; Gong, J. Coefficient Inequalities for Multivalent Janowski Type q-Starlike Functions Involving Certain Conic Domains. *Axioms* **2022**, *11*, 494. [CrossRef]
9. Sharma, S.K.; Jain, R. On some properties of generalized $q$-Mittag Leffler function. *Math. Aeterna* **2014**, *4*, 613–619.
10. Al-shbeil, I.; Gong, J.; Shaba, T.G. Coefficients Inequalities for the Bi-Univalent Functions Related to q-Babalola Convolution Operator. *Fractal Fract.* **2023**, *7*, 155. [CrossRef]
11. Al-shbeil, I.; Gong, J.; Khan, S.; Khan, N.; Khan, A.; Khan, M.F.; Goswami, A. Hankel and Symmetric Toeplitz Determinants for a New Subclass of q-Starlike Functions. *Fractal Fract.* **2022**, *6*, 658. [CrossRef]
12. Saliu, A.; Al-Shbeil, I.; Gong, J.; Malik, S.N.; Aloraini, N. Properties of q-Symmetric Starlike Functions of Janowski Type. *Symmetry* **2022**, *14*, 1907. [CrossRef]
13. Janowski, W. Some extremal problems for certain families of analytic functions. *Ann. Polon. Math.* **1973**, *28*, 297–326. [CrossRef]
14. Clune, J. On meromorphic schlicht functions. *J. Lond. Math. Soc.* **1959**, *34*, 215–216. [CrossRef]
15. Pommerenke, C. On meromorphic starlike functions. *Pac. J. Math.* **1963**, *13*, 221–235. [CrossRef]
16. Royster, W.C. Meromorphic starlike multivalent functions. *Trans. Am. Math. Soc.* **1963**, *107*, 300–308. [CrossRef]
17. Miller, J.E. Convex meromorphic mappings and related functions. *Proc. Am. Math. Soc.* **1970**, *25*, 220–228. [CrossRef]
18. Cho, N.E.; Owa, S. Partial sums of certain meromorphic functions. *J. Inequal. Pure Appl. Math.* **2004**, *5*, 30.
19. Aouf, M.K.; Silverman, H. Partial sums of certain meromorphic $p$-valent functions. *J. Inequal. Pure Appl. Math.* **2006**, *7*, 116.
20. Srivastava, H.M.; Hossen, H.M.; Aouf, M.K. A unified presentation of some classes of meromorphically multivalent functions. *Comput. Math. Appl.* **1999**, *38*, 63–70.
21. Frasin, B.A.; Darus, M. On certain meromorphic functions with positive coefficients. *Southeast Asian Bull. Math.* **2004**, *28*, 615–623.
22. Gasper, G.; Rahman, M. *Basic Hypergeometric Series*; Cambridge University Press: Cambridge, UK, 1990.
23. Govindaraj, M.; Sivasubramanian, S. On a class of analytic functions related to conic domains involving $q$-calculus. *Anal. Math.* **2017**, *43*, 475–487. [CrossRef]
24. Mahmood, S.; Ahmad, Q.Z.; Srivastava, H.M.; Khan, N.; Khan, B.; Tahir, M. A certain subclass of meromorphically $q$-starlike functions associated with the Janowski functions. *J. Inequal. Appl.* **2019**, *2019*, 88. [CrossRef]
25. Ali, R.M.; Ravichandran, V. Classes of meromorphic alpha-convex functions. *Taiwan J. Math.* **2010**, *14*, 1479–1490. [CrossRef]

**Disclaimer/Publisher's Note:** The statements, opinions and data contained in all publications are solely those of the individual author(s) and contributor(s) and not of MDPI and/or the editor(s). MDPI and/or the editor(s) disclaim responsibility for any injury to people or property resulting from any ideas, methods, instructions or products referred to in the content.

Article

# Three General Double-Series Identities and Associated Reduction Formulas and Fractional Calculus

Mohd Idris Qureshi [1], Tafaz Ul Rahman Shah [1,2], Junesang Choi [3,*] and Aarif Hussain Bhat [1]

[1] Department of Applied Sciences and Humanities, Faculty of Engineering and Technology, Jamia Millia Islamia, A Central University, New Delhi 110025, India; miqureshi_delhi@yahoo.co.in (M.I.Q.); tafazuldiv@gmail.com (T.U.R.S.); aarifsaleem19@gmail.com (A.H.B.)

[2] University Institute of Engineering and Technology, Guru Nanak University, Hyderabad 501506, India

[3] Department of Mathematics, Dongguk University, Gyeongju 38066, Republic of Korea

* Correspondence: junesang@dongguk.ac.kr; Tel.: +82-010-6525-2262

**Abstract:** In this article, we introduce three general double-series identities using Whipple transformations for terminating generalized hypergeometric $_4F_3$ and $_5F_4$ functions. Then, by employing the left-sided Riemann–Liouville fractional integral on these identities, we show the ability to derive additional identities of the same nature successively. These identities are used to derive transformation formulas between the Srivastava–Daoust double hypergeometric function (S–D function) and Kampé de Fériet's double hypergeometric function (KDF function) with equal arguments. We also demonstrate reduction formulas from the S–D function or KDF function to the generalized hypergeometric function $_pF_q$. Additionally, we provide general summation formulas for the $_pF_q$ and S–D function (or KDF function) with specific arguments. We further highlight the connections between the results presented here and existing identities.

**Keywords:** Bailey quadratic transformation; generalized hypergeometric function; Kampé de Fériet's double hypergeometric function; series rearrangement technique; Srivastava–Daoust double hypergeometric function; Whipple transformations; left-sided Riemann–Liouville fractional integral

**MSC:** 26A33; 33C05; 33C20

## 1. Introduction and Preliminaries

The generalized hypergeometric series (or function) $_pF_q$ $(p, q \in \mathbb{Z}_{\geqslant 0})$, which is a natural generalization of the Gaussian hypergeometric series $_2F_1$, is defined by (see, e.g., [1–6])

$$_pF_q\left[\begin{array}{c}\mu_1, \mu_2, \ldots, \mu_p; \\ \nu_1, \nu_2, \ldots, \nu_q;\end{array} z\right] = {}_pF_q(\mu_1, \ldots, \mu_p; \nu_1, \ldots, \nu_q; z)$$
$$= {}_pF_q\left[\begin{array}{c}(\mu_p); \\ (\nu_q);\end{array} z\right] := \sum_{n=0}^{\infty} \frac{\prod_{j=1}^{p}(\mu_j)_n}{\prod_{j=1}^{q}(\nu_j)_n} \frac{z^n}{n!} \quad (1)$$

$$(\mu_k \in \mathbb{C} \ (k=1,\ldots,p), \ \nu_j \in \mathbb{C} \setminus \mathbb{Z}_{\leqslant 0} \ (j=1,\ldots,q)),$$

where $(\xi)_\eta$ $(\xi, \eta \in \mathbb{C})$ is the Pochhammer symbol defined in terms of gamma function $\Gamma$ (see, e.g., [5], pp. 2, 5), by

$$(\xi)_\eta = \frac{\Gamma(\xi+\eta)}{\Gamma(\xi)} = \begin{cases} 1 & (\eta=0, \xi \in \mathbb{C} \setminus \mathbb{Z}_{\leqslant 0}), \\ \xi(\xi+1)\cdots(\xi+n-1) & (\eta=n \in \mathbb{N}, \xi \in \mathbb{C}), \end{cases} \quad (2)$$

it being understood that $(0)_0 = 1$. Here and elsewhere, an empty product is interpreted as 1, and let $\mathbb{C}$, $\mathbb{R}$, and $\mathbb{Z}$ denote the sets of complex numbers, real numbers, and integers, respectively. Additionally, let $A_{\geq \ell}$, $A_{>\ell}$, $A_{\leq \ell}$, and $A_{<\ell}$ be the subsets of the set $A$ ($\mathbb{R}$ or $\mathbb{Z}$) whose elements are greater than or equal to, greater than, less than or equal to, and less than some $\ell \in \mathbb{R}$, respectively. In particular, let $\mathbb{N} := \mathbb{Z}_{\geq 1}$.

If $\mu_k \in \mathbb{Z}_{\leq 0}$ for some $k = 1, \ldots p$, then $_pF_q$ series terminates, that is, becomes a polynomial in $z$, and converges for all $z \in \mathbb{C}$. In case of $\mu_k \in \mathbb{C} \setminus \mathbb{Z}_{\leq 0}$ for some $k = 1, \ldots p$, the series $_pF_q$ in (1) becomes a polynomial of finite order. For the detailed convergence conditions for $_pF_q$ in (1), one can consult, for example, [7], p. 20.

The popularity and usefulness of the hypergeometric function $_2F_1$, as well as its generalized versions in one variable $_pF_q$, have motivated researchers to explore hypergeometric functions in multiple variables. Appell [8] initiated the study of hypergeometric functions in two variables by introducing the Appell functions $F_1$, $F_2$, $F_3$, and $F_4$ as generalizations of Gauss's hypergeometric function $_2F_1$. Subsequently, Humbert [9] investigated the confluent forms of these functions. A comprehensive list of these functions is available in standard literature, such as [10]. Kampé de Fériet [11] later expanded upon the work of Appell, generalizing the four Appell functions and their confluent forms to more general hypergeometric functions of two variables. Burchnall and Chaundy [12,13] introduced an abbreviation for the notation created by Kampé de Fériet for his double hypergeometric functions of superior order. In a slightly modified notation, Srivastava and Panda [14] (p. 423, Equation (26)) presented the definition of a more comprehensive double hypergeometric function than the one defined by Kampé de Fériet. This convenient generalization of the Kampé de Fériet function is defined as follows (see, for example, [7], p. 27):

$$F_{\ell:m;n}^{p:q;k}\left[\begin{array}{c}(a_p): \ (b_q); \ (c_k); \\ (\alpha_\ell): \ (\beta_m); \ (\gamma_n);\end{array} x, y\right]$$

$$= \sum_{r,s=0}^{\infty} \frac{\prod_{j=1}^{p}(a_j)_{r+s} \prod_{j=1}^{q}(b_j)_r \prod_{j=1}^{k}(c_j)_s}{\prod_{j=1}^{\ell}(\alpha_j)_{r+s} \prod_{j=1}^{m}(\beta_j)_r \prod_{j=1}^{n}(\gamma_j)_s} \frac{x^r}{r!} \frac{y^s}{s!}, \qquad (3)$$

where, for convergence,

(i) $p + q < \ell + m + 1$, $p + k < \ell + n + 1$, $|x| < \infty$, $|y| < \infty$,

or

(ii) $p + q = \ell + m + 1$, $p + k = \ell + n + 1$, and

$$\begin{cases} |x|^{1/(p-\ell)} + |y|^{1/(p-\ell)} < 1, & \text{if } p > \ell, \\ \max\{|x|, |y|\} < 1, & \text{if } p \leq \ell. \end{cases}$$

To gain further insight into the convergence properties of the double series in Equation (3), which encompasses conditional convergence as well, one can consult the research conducted by Hái et al. [15].

**Lemma 1.** *The following formula holds.*

$$F_{\ell:m;n}^{p:q;k}\left[\begin{array}{c}(a_p): \ (b_q); \ (c_k); \\ (\alpha_\ell): \ (\beta_m); \ (\gamma_n);\end{array} x, y\right] = F_{\ell:n;m}^{p:k;q}\left[\begin{array}{c}(a_p): \ (c_k); \ (b_q); \\ (\alpha_\ell): \ (\gamma_n); \ (\beta_m);\end{array} y, x\right]. \qquad (4)$$

*In particular,*

$$F_{\ell:m;n}^{p:q;k}\left[\begin{array}{c}(a_p): \ (b_q); \ (c_k); \\ (\alpha_\ell): \ (\beta_m); \ (\gamma_n);\end{array} x, x\right] = F_{\ell:n;m}^{p:k;q}\left[\begin{array}{c}(a_p): \ (c_k); \ (b_q); \\ (\alpha_\ell): \ (\gamma_n); \ (\beta_m);\end{array} x, x\right]. \qquad (5)$$

**Proof.** Observing the following fact is sufficient: Interchanging the summation indices $r$ and $s$ leaves the quantity on the right-hand side of Equation (3) unchanged. □

Srivastava and Daoust ([16], p. 199) introduced a generalization of the Kampé de Fériet function ([8], p. 150) by means of the double hypergeometric series (see also [17,18]):

$$F^{A:\, B;\, B'}_{C:\, D;\, D'}\left(\begin{array}{c}[(a_A):\vartheta,\varphi]:\ [(b_B):\psi];\ [(b'_{B'}):\psi'];\\ [(c_C):\delta,\varepsilon]:\ [(d_D):\eta];\ [(d'_{D'}):\eta'];\end{array} x, y\right)$$

$$= \sum_{m=0}^{\infty}\sum_{n=0}^{\infty} \frac{\prod_{j=1}^{A}(a_j)_{m\vartheta_j+n\varphi_j}\prod_{j=1}^{B}(b_j)_{m\psi_j}\prod_{j=1}^{B'}(b'_j)_{n\psi'_j}}{\prod_{j=1}^{C}(c_j)_{m\delta_j+n\varepsilon_j}\prod_{j=1}^{D}(d_j)_{m\eta_j}\prod_{j=1}^{D'}(d'_j)_{n\eta'_j}}\frac{x^m}{m!}\frac{y^n}{n!}, \qquad (6)$$

where the coefficients

$$\vartheta_1,\ldots,\vartheta_A;\ \varphi_1,\ldots,\varphi_A;\ \psi_1,\ldots,\psi_B;\ \psi'_1,\ldots,\psi'_{B'};\ \delta_1,\ldots,\delta_C;$$
$$\varepsilon_1,\ldots,\varepsilon_C;\ \eta_1,\ldots,\eta_D;\ \eta'_1,\ldots,\eta'_{D'} \qquad (7)$$

are real and positive. Let

$$\Delta_1 := 1 + \left(\sum_{j=1}^{C}\delta_j + \sum_{j=1}^{D}\eta_j\right) - \left(\sum_{j=1}^{A}\vartheta_j + \sum_{j=1}^{B}\psi_j\right)$$

and

$$\Delta_2 := 1 + \left(\sum_{j=1}^{C}\varepsilon_j + \sum_{j=1}^{D'}\eta'_j\right) - \left(\sum_{j=1}^{A}\varphi_j + \sum_{j=1}^{B'}\psi'_j\right).$$

Then

(i) The double power series in (6) converges for all complex values of $x$ and $y$ when $\Delta_1 > 0$ and $\Delta_2 > 0$.

(ii) The double power series in (6) is convergent for suitably constrained values of $|x|$ and $|y|$ when $\Delta_1 = 0$ and $\Delta_2 = 0$.

(iii) The double power series in (6) would diverge except when, trivially, $x = y = 0$ when $\Delta_1 < 0$ and $\Delta_2 < 0$.

The emergence of extensively generalized special functions, such as (3), has sparked intriguing research into their reducibility. The Kampé de Fériet function, in particular, has been studied extensively by many researchers for its reducibility and transformation formulas. Many reduction and transformation formulas for the Kampé de Fériet function can be found in the literature, as documented in various references, such as [19–42].

Buschman and Srivastava [19] provided insightful remarks on previous studies, specifically [43,44]. They employed a double-series manipulation technique, utilizing Whipple's transformation (see [45], Equation (7.1); see also [10], p. 190, Equation (1), [4], p. 90, Theorem 32):

$$_3F_2\left[\begin{array}{c}\alpha,\beta,\gamma;\\ 1+\alpha-\beta, 1+\alpha-\gamma;\end{array} z\right]$$
$$= (1-z)^{-\alpha}\,_3F_2\left[\begin{array}{c}\frac{\alpha}{2},\frac{\alpha+1}{2}, 1+\alpha-\beta-\gamma;\\ 1+\alpha-\beta, 1+\alpha-\gamma;\end{array} -\frac{4z}{(1-z)^2}\right] \qquad (8)$$

$$\left(\alpha-\beta,\alpha-\gamma \in \mathbb{C}\setminus\mathbb{Z}_{\leqslant -1};\ |z|<1,\ 4|z|/\{|1-z|^2\}<1,\ |\arg(1-z)|<\pi\right).$$

Through this approach, they introduced three double-series identities, which incorporated a bounded sequence of complex numbers. In addition, they [19] demonstrated that the application of double-series identities enables the provision of numerous reduction formulas for the Kampé de Fériet function, whether they are already known or newly discovered. Subsequently and concurrently, a number of papers have utilized series manipulation techniques along with, among several others, transformation formulas for $_2F_1$ (13) and (19) in Chan et al. [21]; the reduction formula for $_2F_1$ (15) in Karlsson [46]; a particular case of Euler's transformation formula for $_2F_1$ (12) in Karlsson [47]; terminating summation formulas for $_4F_3(1)$ (Equations (2.3), (2.4), (2.6), Tables 1 and 2, there) and the transformation formula for $_4F_3(1)$ (10) in Karlsson [30]; transformation formulas for $_2F_1$ (12) and (13) in Liu and Wang [48]; transformation formulas for $_2F_1$ ([22], Equations (2.8) and (2.9)) (cf. [10], p. 112, Equations (17) and (16), respectively), Whipple's transformation $_3F_2$ (8) and summation formula for a terminating $_3F_2(1)$ [22], Equation (3.2) (see also [49]), and Dougall's summation theorem for a terminating well-poised $_7F_6(1)$ [22], Equation (3.7) (see also [10], p. 189, Equation (4).4(8)), [50], p. 244, Equation (III. 14)) in Chen and Srivastava [22]; and terminating $_3F_2(\frac{4}{3})$ [51], Equation (1.3) (see also Gessel–Stanton summation theorem [52], Equation (5.21), and terminating $_3F_2(\frac{3}{4})$ [51], Equation (1.4) (see also [53], Equation (1.12)) in Qureshi et al. [51]. These papers have presented multiple or double-series identities, which have been employed to derive a range of reduction formulas for the Kampé de Fériet function and other intriguing identities for the $_pF_q$ functions.

Inspired by the aforementioned papers, especially [19], and utilizing Whipple's transformation formulas (refer to [45], p. 266, Equation (6.6))

$$_5F_4\left[\begin{matrix} -\frac{m}{2}, \frac{-m+1}{2}, E, 1-m-B-C, 1-m-D; \\ 1-m-B, 1-m-C, \frac{1+E-D-m}{2}, \frac{2+E-D-m}{2}; \end{matrix} 1\right]$$
$$= \frac{(D)_m}{(D-E)_m} {}_4F_3\left[\begin{matrix} -m, B, C, E; \\ 1-m-B, 1-m-C, D; \end{matrix} 1\right] \quad (9)$$

$$\left(m \in \mathbb{Z}_{\geq 0}; B, C \in \mathbb{C}\setminus\mathbb{Z}_{\geq 1-m}; D, \frac{1+E-D-m}{2}, \frac{2+E-D-m}{2} \in \mathbb{C}\setminus\mathbb{Z}_{\leq 0}\right)$$

and (see [54], p. 537, Equation (10.11); see also [30], Equation (2.5))

$$_4F_3\left[\begin{matrix} -m, X, Y, Z; \\ U, W, X+Y+Z+1-U-W-m; \end{matrix} 1\right]$$
$$= \frac{(U-X)_m(Y+Z+1-U-W-m)_m}{(U)_m(X+Y+Z+1-U-W-m)_m}$$
$$\times {}_4F_3\left[\begin{matrix} -m, W-Y, W-Z, X; \\ 1-m+X-U, U+W-Y-Z, W; \end{matrix} 1\right] \quad (10)$$

$$\left(m \in \mathbb{Z}_{\geq 0}; U, W, X+Y+Z+1-U-W-m, \atop 1-m+X-U, U+W-Y-Z, W \in \mathbb{C}\setminus\mathbb{Z}_{\leq 0}\right),$$

our objective is to introduce three double-series identities. These identities incorporating bounded sequences of complex numbers are derived using series rearrangement techniques and Pochhammer symbol identities. These issues are further discussed in Section 2. In Section 3, we employ these general double-series identities to establish three transformations of Srivastava–Daoust double hypergeometric functions. These transformations are expressed using Kampé de Fériet functions. By utilizing the left-sided Riemann–Liouville fractional integral on these identities in Sections 2 and 4, we demonstrate the capability to iteratively derive further identities of a similar nature. Section 5 further presents various new transformation formulae, such as Bailey's quadratic transformation formula, Clausen reduction formula, Gauss quadratic transformation formula, Karlsson reduction formula, Orr reduction formula, and Whipple quadratic transformation formula. We achieve this by using the following formulas.

**Required formulas**

Binomial theorem (see, e.g., [6], p. 44, Equation (8)):

$$(1-z)^{-\lambda} = \sum_{n=0}^{\infty} (\lambda)_n \frac{z^n}{n!} = {}_1F_0(\lambda;-;z) \tag{11}$$
$$(|z|<1,\ \lambda\in\mathbb{C},\ |\arg(1-z)|<\pi);$$

Euler's transformation formula (see, e.g., [3], p. 248, Equation (9.5.3), [1], p. 68, Equation (2.2.7)):

$$ {}_2F_1(\alpha,\beta;\gamma;z) = (1-z)^{\gamma-\alpha-\beta}\, {}_2F_1(\gamma-\alpha,\gamma-\beta;\gamma;z) \tag{12}$$
$$(|z|<1,\ \gamma\in\mathbb{C}\setminus\mathbb{Z}_{\leq 0},\ |\arg(1-z)|<\pi);$$

Pfaff–Kummer transformation formula (see, e.g., [3], p. 247, Equations (9.5.1) and (9.5.2), [1], p. 68, Equation (2.2.6)):

$$ {}_2F_1(\alpha,\beta;\gamma;z) = (1-z)^{-\alpha}\, {}_2F_1\left(\alpha,\gamma-\beta;\gamma;\frac{-z}{1-z}\right) \tag{13}$$
$$(|z|<1,\ |z|/|1-z|<1,\ \gamma\in\mathbb{C}\setminus\mathbb{Z}_{\leq 0},\ |\arg(1-z)|<\pi)$$

and

$$ {}_2F_1(\alpha,\beta;\gamma;z) = (1-z)^{-\beta}\, {}_2F_1\left(\beta,\gamma-\alpha;\gamma;\frac{-z}{1-z}\right) \tag{14}$$
$$(|z|<1,\ |z|/|1-z|<1,\ \gamma\in\mathbb{C}\setminus\mathbb{Z}_{\leq 0},\ |\arg(1-z)|<\pi);$$

A reduction formula (see, e.g., [4], p. 70, Equation (10)):

$$ {}_2F_1\left(\gamma,\gamma-\tfrac{1}{2};2\gamma;z\right) = \left(\frac{2}{1+\sqrt{1-z}}\right)^{2\gamma-1} \tag{15}$$
$$(|z|<1,\ 2\gamma\in\mathbb{C}\setminus\mathbb{Z}_{\leq 0});$$

Bailey transformation formula (see, e.g., [55], p. 251, Equation (4.22)):

$$ {}_2F_1(\alpha,\beta;2\beta;z) = (1-z)^{-\frac{\alpha}{2}}\, {}_2F_1\left(\tfrac{\alpha}{2},\beta-\tfrac{\alpha}{2};\beta+\tfrac{1}{2};\frac{-z^2}{4(1-z)}\right) \tag{16}$$
$$(|z|<1,\ |z|^2/\{4|1-z|\}<1,\ 2\beta\in\mathbb{C}\setminus\mathbb{Z}_{\leq 0},$$
$$\beta+\tfrac{1}{2}\in\mathbb{C}\setminus\mathbb{Z}_{\leq 0},\ |\arg(1-z)|<\pi);$$

Gauss transformation formula (see, e.g., [10], p. 111, Equation (2), and p. 112, Equation (18)):

$$ {}_2F_1\left(2\alpha,2\beta;\alpha+\beta+\tfrac{1}{2};z\right) = {}_2F_1\left(\alpha,\beta;\alpha+\beta+\tfrac{1}{2};4z(1-z)\right) \tag{17}$$
$$\left(|z|<1,\ 4|z(1-z)|<1,\ \alpha+\beta+\tfrac{1}{2}\in\mathbb{C}\setminus\mathbb{Z}_{\leq 0}\right);$$

Bailey product formula (see, e.g., [56], p. 383, Equation (7.4)):

$$ {}_2F_1(\alpha,\beta;\gamma;z)\, {}_2F_1(\gamma-\beta,1-\beta;\alpha-\beta+1;z) $$
$$ = (1-z)^{\beta-\alpha-\gamma}\, {}_4F_3\left[\begin{array}{c}\alpha,\gamma-\beta,\frac{\alpha+\gamma-\beta}{2},\frac{\alpha+\gamma-\beta+1}{2};\\ \gamma,\alpha+\gamma-\beta,\alpha-\beta+1;\end{array}\frac{-4z}{(1-z)^2}\right] \tag{18}$$

$$\left(|z|<1,\ 4|z|/|1-z|^2;\ \gamma,\alpha-\beta+1,\alpha+\gamma-\beta\in\mathbb{C}\setminus\mathbb{Z}_{\leq 0};\ |\arg(1-z)|<\pi\right).$$

Letting $\gamma \to \infty$ on both sides of (8) gives the following transformation formula ([10], Equation 2.11 (34)) (see also [21], p. 425, Equation (34)):

$$
{}_2F_1\left[\begin{array}{c}\alpha, \beta;\\ 1+\alpha-\beta;\end{array} z\right] = (1+z)^{-\alpha} {}_2F_1\left[\begin{array}{c}\frac{\alpha}{2}, \frac{\alpha+1}{2};\\ 1+\alpha-\beta;\end{array} \frac{4z}{(1+z)^2}\right] \tag{19}
$$

$$\left(\alpha - \beta \in \mathbb{C} \setminus \mathbb{Z}_{\leqslant -1};\ |z| < 1,\ 4|z|/\{|1+z|^2\} < 1,\ |\arg(1+z)| < \pi\right),$$

A number of reduction formulae for the Kampé de Fériet function, for example,

$$
\begin{aligned}
F_{0:q;s}^{0:p;r}&\left[\begin{array}{c}-:\ \alpha_1,\ldots,\alpha_p;\ \gamma_1,\ldots,\gamma_r;\\ -:\ \beta_1,\ldots,\beta_q;\ \delta_1,\ldots,\delta_s;\end{array} x, y\right]\\
&= {}_pF_q\left[\begin{array}{c}\alpha_1,\ldots,\alpha_p;\\ \beta_1,\ldots,\beta_q;\end{array} x\right] {}_rF_s\left[\begin{array}{c}\gamma_1,\ldots,\gamma_r;\\ \delta_1,\ldots,\delta_s;\end{array} y\right]
\end{aligned} \tag{20}
$$

(see, e.g., [7], p. 28, Equation (31));

$$
F_{q:0;0}^{p:1;1}\left[\begin{array}{c}\alpha_1,\ldots,\alpha_p:\ \nu;\ \sigma;\\ \beta_1,\ldots,\beta_q:\ -;\ -;\end{array} z, z\right] = {}_{p+1}F_q\left[\begin{array}{c}\alpha_1,\ldots,\alpha_p,\ \nu+\sigma;\\ \beta_1,\ldots,\beta_q;\end{array} z\right] \tag{21}
$$
$$(\beta_1,\ldots,\beta_q \in \mathbb{C} \setminus \mathbb{Z}_{\leqslant 0};\ |z| < 1\ (p = q))$$

(see, e.g., [8], pp. 23, 155, Equation (25), [57], p. 33, Equation (1.5.1.7));

$$
\begin{aligned}
F_{q:1;0}^{p:2;1}&\left[\begin{array}{c}\alpha_1,\ldots,\alpha_p:\ \lambda^*,\mu^*;\ \nu^*-\lambda^*-\mu^*;\\ \beta_1,\ldots,\beta_q:\ \nu^*;\ -;\end{array} z, z\right]\\
&= {}_{p+2}F_{q+1}\left[\begin{array}{c}\alpha_1,\ldots,\alpha_p,\ \nu^*-\lambda^*,\ \nu^*-\mu^*;\\ \beta_1,\ldots,\beta_q,\ \nu^*;\end{array} z\right]
\end{aligned} \tag{22}
$$
$$(\beta_1,\ldots,\beta_q,\nu^* \in \mathbb{C} \setminus \mathbb{Z}_{\leqslant 0};\ |z| < 1\ (p = q);\ |z| < \infty\ (p \leqslant q-1))$$

(see, e.g., [7], p. 28, Equation (34));

$$
\begin{aligned}
F_{q:1;1}^{p:2;2}&\left[\begin{array}{c}\alpha_1,\ldots,\alpha_p:\ g,h;\ g,h-1;\\ \beta_1,\ldots,\beta_q:\ g+h-\frac{1}{2};\ g+h-\frac{1}{2};\end{array} z, z\right]\\
&= {}_{p+3}F_{q+2}\left[\begin{array}{c}\alpha_1,\ldots,\alpha_p,\ 2g,\ 2h-1,\ g+h-1;\\ \beta_1,\ldots,\beta_q,\ g+h-\frac{1}{2},\ 2g+2h-2;\end{array} z\right]
\end{aligned} \tag{23}
$$
$$\left(\beta_1,\ldots,\beta_q,\ g+h-\tfrac{1}{2},\ 2g+2h-2 \in \mathbb{C} \setminus \mathbb{Z}_{\leqslant 0};\ |z| < 1\ (p = q)\right)$$

(see, e.g., [30], p. 34, Table 3(Ic), [7], p. 29, Equation (38));

A summation formula for ${}_3F_2$ (see, e.g., [58], p. 540, Entry (114)):

$$
{}_3F_2\left[\begin{array}{c}-\frac{m}{2},\ \frac{-m+1}{2},\ A;\\ B,\ \frac{3}{2}+A-B-m;\end{array} 1\right] = 4^{-m}\frac{(2B-2A-1)_m(2B+m-1)_m}{(B)_m(B-A-\frac{1}{2})_m} \tag{24}
$$

$$\left(m \in \mathbb{Z}_{\geqslant 0};\ B,\ \tfrac{3}{2}+A-B-m,\ B-A-\tfrac{1}{2} \in \mathbb{C} \setminus \mathbb{Z}_{\leqslant 0}\right);$$

The following generalized summation formulae for ${}_2F_1$:

Generalized Kummer first summation theorem (see [59], p. 828, Theorem 3):

$$
{}_2F_1\left[\begin{array}{c} C, D; \\ 1+C-D+m; \end{array} 1\right] = \frac{2^{m-2D}\Gamma(D-m)\Gamma(1+C-D+m)}{\Gamma(D)\Gamma(C-2D+m+1)}
$$
$$
\times \sum_{k=0}^{m}(-1)^k \binom{m}{k} \frac{\Gamma\left(\frac{C+k+m+1}{2}-D\right)}{\Gamma\left(\frac{C+k-m+1}{2}\right)}
$$
(25)

$\left(m \in \mathbb{Z}_{\geqslant 0},\ D-C \in \mathbb{C} \setminus \mathbb{Z}_{\geqslant m+1},\ \Re(D) < \frac{1+m}{2}\right);$

Generalized Kummer first summation theorem (see [59], p. 828, Theorem 4):

$$
{}_2F_1\left[\begin{array}{c} C, D; \\ 1+C-D-m; \end{array} -1\right] = \frac{2^{-m-2D}\Gamma(1+C-D-m)}{\Gamma(C-2D-m+1)}
$$
$$
\times \sum_{k=0}^{m} \binom{m}{k} \frac{\Gamma\left(\frac{C+k-m+1}{2}-D\right)}{\Gamma\left(\frac{C+k-m+1}{2}\right)}
$$
(26)

$\left(m \in \mathbb{Z}_{\geqslant 0},\ C-D \in \mathbb{C} \setminus \mathbb{Z}_{\leqslant m-1},\ \frac{1-m}{2} \leqslant \Re(D) < 1-\frac{m}{2}\right);$

Generalized Kummer second summation theorem (see [59], p. 827, Theorem 1):

$$
{}_2F_1\left[\begin{array}{c} C, D; \\ \frac{1}{2}(1+C+D+m); \end{array} \frac{1}{2}\right] = \frac{2^{D-1}\Gamma\left(\frac{C+D+m+1}{2}\right)\Gamma\left(\frac{C-D-m+1}{2}\right)}{\Gamma(D)\Gamma\left(\frac{C-D+m+1}{2}\right)}
$$
$$
\times \sum_{k=0}^{m}(-1)^k \binom{m}{k} \frac{\Gamma\left(\frac{D+k}{2}\right)}{\Gamma\left(\frac{C+k-m+1}{2}\right)}
$$
(27)

$\left(m \in \mathbb{Z}_{\geqslant 0},\ \frac{1}{2}(1+C+D+m) \in \mathbb{C} \setminus \mathbb{Z}_{\leqslant 0}\right);$

Generalized Kummer second summation theorem (see, e.g., [58], p. 491, Entry 7.3.7.2):

$$
{}_2F_1\left[\begin{array}{c} C, D; \\ \frac{1}{2}(1+C+D-m); \end{array} \frac{1}{2}\right] = \frac{2^{D-1}\Gamma\left(\frac{C+D-m+1}{2}\right)}{\Gamma(D)}
$$
$$
\times \sum_{k=0}^{m} \binom{m}{k} \frac{\Gamma\left(\frac{D+k}{2}\right)}{\Gamma\left(\frac{C+k-m+1}{2}\right)}
$$
(28)

$\left(m \in \mathbb{Z}_{\geqslant 0},\ \frac{1}{2}(1+C+D-m) \in \mathbb{C} \setminus \mathbb{Z}_{\leqslant 0}\right);$

Generalized Kummer third summation theorem (see [59], p. 828, Theorem 5):

$$
{}_2F_1\left[\begin{array}{c} C, 1-C+m; \\ D; \end{array} \frac{1}{2}\right] = \frac{2^{m-C}\Gamma(C-m)\Gamma(D)}{\Gamma(C)\Gamma(D-C)}
$$
$$
\times \sum_{k=0}^{m}(-1)^k \binom{m}{k} \frac{\Gamma\left(\frac{D-C+k}{2}\right)}{\Gamma\left(\frac{D+C+k}{2}-m\right)}
$$
(29)

$(m \in \mathbb{Z}_{\geqslant 0},\ D \in \mathbb{C} \setminus \mathbb{Z}_{\leqslant 0});$

Generalized Kummer third summation theorem (see [60], Equation (20)):

$$_2F_1\left[\begin{matrix} C, 1-C-m; \\ D; \end{matrix} \frac{1}{2}\right] = \frac{2^{-m-C}\Gamma(D)}{\Gamma(D-C)} \sum_{k=0}^{m} \binom{m}{k} \frac{\Gamma\left(\frac{D-C+k}{2}\right)}{\Gamma\left(\frac{D+C+k}{2}\right)} \quad (30)$$

$(m \in \mathbb{Z}_{\geq 0}, D \in \mathbb{C} \setminus \mathbb{Z}_{\leq 0})$,

which is the corrected version of [59], p. 828, Theorem 6.

Lastly, in Section 6, we derive a set of summation theorems with arguments of $1, -1, \frac{1}{2}, -\frac{1}{4}, -\frac{1}{8}$, and $-\frac{1}{16}$.

**Remark 1.** *It is intriguing to compare Entries 131 and 132 in ([61], p. 583) with the summation Formulas (29) and (30).*

*One can find the specific instances of Equations (29) and (30) in [62] (Equation (6) along with Table 3) for the values of m equal to 0, 1, 2, 3, 4, and 5.*

*The numerator parameters $-\frac{m}{2}$ and $\frac{-m+1}{2}$ of the $_5F_4$ on the left side of Equation (9) both yield negative integers if m is even and odd, respectively. The $_5F_4$ and $_4F_3$ on the left and right sides of Equation (9) exhibit properties of being Saalschützian and nearly poised, respectively.*

*Wolfram's MATHEMATICA has implemented the $_pF_q$ function as hypergeometric PFQ, which is appropriate for performing both symbolic and numerical computations.*

## 2. Three General Double-Series Identities

This section demonstrates three general double-series identities that involve bounded sequences by primarily utilizing Whipple transformations (9) and (10).

**Theorem 1.** *Let $\{\Psi(\mu)\}_{\mu=0}^{\infty}$ be a bounded sequence of complex (or real) numbers such that $\Psi(0) \neq 0$. Additionally, let $\alpha + \beta, \gamma, \delta \in \mathbb{C} \setminus \mathbb{Z}_{\leq 0}$. Then the following general double-series identity holds true:*

$$\sum_{m=0}^{\infty}\sum_{n=0}^{\infty} \Psi(2m+n) \frac{(\alpha)_{m+n}(\beta)_{m+n}\left(\frac{\gamma+\delta-1}{2}\right)_{m+n}\left(\frac{\gamma+\delta}{2}\right)_{m+n}}{(\gamma)_{m+n}(\alpha+\beta)_{m+n}(\delta)_{m+n}} \frac{(-4z^2)^m (4z)^n}{m!\, n!}$$
$$= \sum_{m=0}^{\infty}\sum_{n=0}^{\infty} \Psi(m+n) \frac{(\gamma+\delta-1)_{m+n}(\alpha)_m(\beta)_m(\alpha)_n(\beta)_n}{(\alpha+\beta)_{m+n}(\gamma)_m(\delta)_n} \frac{z^{m+n}}{m!\, n!}, \quad (31)$$

*provided that both sides of the double series are absolutely convergent.*

**Proof.** Let $\Xi_1(z)$ be the left member of (31). By using a double-series manipulation,

$$\sum_{m=0}^{\infty}\sum_{n=0}^{\infty} \Phi(m,n) = \sum_{n=0}^{\infty}\sum_{m=0}^{[\frac{n}{2}]} \Phi(m, n-2m), \quad (32)$$

where $\Phi : \mathbb{Z}_{\geq 0} \times \mathbb{Z}_{\geq 0} \to \mathbb{C}$ is a bounded function, and provided that both sides of the double series are absolutely convergent, we obtain

$$\Xi_1(z) = \sum_{n=0}^{\infty}\sum_{m=0}^{[\frac{n}{2}]} \Psi(n) \frac{(\alpha)_{n-m}(\beta)_{n-m}\left(\frac{\gamma+\delta-1}{2}\right)_{n-m}\left(\frac{\gamma+\delta}{2}\right)_{n-m}}{(\gamma)_{n-m}(\alpha+\beta)_{n-m}(\delta)_{n-m}} \frac{(-1)^m 4^{n-m} z^n}{m!\,(n-2m)!}. \quad (33)$$

Recall the following Pochhammer symbol identities:

$$(\lambda)_{n-k} = \frac{(-1)^k (\lambda)_n}{(1-\lambda-n)_k} \quad (k=0, 1, \ldots, n). \quad (34)$$

Setting $\lambda = 1$ in (34) gives

$$(n-k)! = \frac{(-1)^k n!}{(-n)_k} \quad (k = 0, 1, \ldots, n). \tag{35}$$

Additionally,

$$(\lambda)_{2n} = 2^{2n} \left(\frac{\lambda}{2}\right)_n \left(\frac{\lambda+1}{2}\right)_n \quad (n \in \mathbb{Z}_{\geq 0}). \tag{36}$$

Using (34)–(36) in (33), and expressing the inner sum in the resultant double series in terms of $_pF_q$ in (1), we have

$$\Xi_1(z) = \sum_{n=0}^{\infty} \Psi(n) \frac{(\alpha)_n (\beta)_n (\gamma+\delta-1)_{2n} z^n}{(\gamma)_n (\alpha+\beta)_n (\delta)_n \, n!}$$
$$\times {}_5F_4 \left[ \begin{array}{c} -\frac{n}{2}, \frac{-n+1}{2}, 1-\gamma-n, 1-\alpha-\beta-n, 1-\delta-n; \\ 1-\alpha-n, 1-\beta-n, \frac{3-\delta-\gamma-2n}{2}, \frac{2-\delta-\gamma-2n}{2}; \end{array} 1 \right]. \tag{37}$$

Applying Whipple transformation (9) to (37), with the aid of

$$(\lambda)_{m+n} = (\lambda)_m (\lambda+m)_n \quad (m, n \in \mathbb{Z}_{\geq 0}) \tag{38}$$

and (35), we obtain

$$\Xi_1(z) = \sum_{n=0}^{\infty} \Psi(n) \frac{(\alpha)_n (\beta)_n (\gamma+\delta-1)_n z^n}{(\alpha+\beta)_n (\delta)_n \, n!} {}_4F_3 \left[ \begin{array}{c} -n, \alpha, \beta, 1-\delta-n; \\ 1-\alpha-n, 1-\beta-n, \gamma; \end{array} 1 \right]$$
$$= \sum_{n=0}^{\infty} \Psi(n) \frac{(\alpha)_n (\beta)_n (\gamma+\delta-1)_n z^n}{(\alpha+\beta)_n (\delta)_n} \tag{39}$$
$$\times \sum_{m=0}^{n} \frac{(-1)^m (\alpha)_m (\beta)_m (1-\delta-n)_m}{(1-\alpha-n)_m (1-\beta-n)_m (\gamma)_m \, m! \, (n-m)!}.$$

Finally, using the following double-series manipulation,

$$\sum_{n=0}^{\infty} \sum_{m=0}^{n} \Phi(m,n) = \sum_{n=0}^{\infty} \sum_{m=0}^{\infty} \Phi(m, n+m), \tag{40}$$

where $\Phi : \mathbb{Z}_{\geq 0} \times \mathbb{Z}_{\geq 0} \to \mathbb{C}$ is a bounded function, and provided that both sides of the double series are absolutely convergent, and (34) on the right-hand side of (39), we prove (31). □

**Theorem 2.** *Let $\{\Psi(\mu)\}_{\mu=0}^{\infty}$ be a bounded sequence of complex (or real) numbers such that $\Psi(0) \neq 0$. Additionally, let $\beta + \delta$, $\gamma \in \mathbb{C} \setminus \mathbb{Z}_{\leq 0}$. Then the following general double-series identity holds true:*

$$\sum_{m=0}^{\infty} \sum_{n=0}^{\infty} \Psi(2m+n) \frac{(-1)^m (\alpha)_{m+n} (\beta)_m (\delta)_m (\gamma-\alpha)_m}{2^{2m} (\gamma)_m \left(\frac{\beta+\delta}{2}\right)_m \left(\frac{\beta+\delta+1}{2}\right)_m} \frac{z^{2m+n}}{m! \, n!}$$
$$= \sum_{m=0}^{\infty} \sum_{n=0}^{\infty} \Psi(m+n) \frac{(\gamma)_{m+n} (\alpha)_m (\beta)_m \, (\alpha)_n (\delta)_n}{(\beta+\delta)_{m+n} (\gamma)_m (\gamma)_n} \frac{z^{m+n}}{m! \, n!}, \tag{41}$$

*provided that both sides of the double series are absolutely convergent.*

**Proof.** Let $\Xi_2(z)$ be on the right-hand side of (41). A similar process of the proof of Theorem 1 with the aid of the identities (32) and (34)–(36) gives

$$\Xi_2(z) = \sum_{n=0}^{\infty} \Psi(n) \frac{(\alpha)_n z^n}{n!} {}_5F_4 \left[ \begin{array}{c} \frac{n}{2}, \frac{-n+1}{2}, \beta, \delta, \gamma-\alpha; \\ \gamma, 1-\alpha-n, \frac{\beta+\delta}{2}, \frac{\beta+\delta+1}{2}; \end{array} 1 \right]. \tag{42}$$

Applying Whipple transformation (9) to the right-hand side of (42) with the aid of (34) ($k = n$), we find

$$\Xi_2(z) = \sum_{n=0}^{\infty} \Psi(n) \frac{(\alpha)_n (\delta)_n z^n}{(\delta + \beta)_n n!} {}_4F_3 \left[ \begin{array}{c} -n, \alpha, \beta, 1-\gamma-n; \\ \gamma, 1-\alpha-n, 1-\delta-n; \end{array} 1 \right]$$
$$= \sum_{n=0}^{\infty} \Psi(n) \frac{(\alpha)_n (\delta)_n z^n}{(\delta + \beta)_n n!} \sum_{m=0}^{n} \frac{(-n)_m (\alpha)_m (\beta)_m (1-\gamma-n)_m}{(1-\alpha-n)_m (1-\delta-n)_m (\gamma)_m m!}. \quad (43)$$

Employing the double-series manipulation (40) to the last member of (43) and using (34) and (35) in the resultant expression, we obtain the desired identity (41). □

**Theorem 3.** *Let $\{\Psi(\mu)\}_{\mu=0}^{\infty}$ be a bounded sequence of complex (or real) numbers such that $\Psi(0) \neq 0$. Additionally, let $\alpha + \lambda, \alpha + \sigma, \beta + \lambda, \gamma \in \mathbb{C} \setminus \mathbb{Z}_{\leqslant 0}$. Then the following general double-series identity holds true:*

$$\sum_{m=0}^{\infty} \sum_{n=0}^{\infty} \Psi(m+n) \frac{(-1)^m (\alpha + \beta + \lambda + \sigma - 1)_{2m+n} (\alpha)_m (\gamma - \beta)_m}{(\alpha + \sigma)_m (\alpha + \lambda)_m (\gamma)_m} \frac{z^{m+n}}{m! \, n!}$$
$$= \sum_{m=0}^{\infty} \sum_{n=0}^{\infty} \Psi(m+n) \frac{(\alpha + \beta + \lambda + \sigma - 1)_{m+n} (\lambda + \beta)_{m+n} (\alpha + \beta - \gamma + \sigma)_m}{(\gamma)_{m+n} (\alpha + \lambda)_{m+n} (\alpha + \sigma)_m (\beta + \lambda)_n} \quad (44)$$
$$\times (\alpha)_m (\gamma - \alpha)_n (\lambda)_n \frac{z^{m+n}}{m! \, n!},$$

*provided that both sides of the double series are absolutely convergent.*

**Proof.** Let $\Xi_3(z)$ be the left-hand side of (44). Using the following double-series manipulation,

$$\sum_{m=0}^{\infty} \sum_{n=0}^{\infty} \Phi(m,n) = \sum_{n=0}^{\infty} \sum_{m=0}^{n} \Phi(m, n-m), \quad (45)$$

where $\Phi : \mathbb{Z}_{\geqslant 0} \times \mathbb{Z}_{\geqslant 0} \to \mathbb{C}$ is a bounded function, and provided that both sides of the double series are absolutely convergent, we obtain

$$\Xi_3(z) = \sum_{n=0}^{\infty} \sum_{m=0}^{n} \Psi(n) \frac{(-1)^m (\alpha + \beta + \lambda + \sigma - 1)_{m+n} (\alpha)_m (\gamma - \beta)_m z^n}{(\alpha + \sigma)_m (\alpha + \lambda)_m (\gamma)_m m! (n-m)!}. \quad (46)$$

Applying (35) and (36) to (46) and denoting the resultant expression in terms of ${}_pF_q$ in (1), we derive

$$\Xi_3(z) = \sum_{n=0}^{\infty} \Psi(n) \frac{(\alpha + \beta + \lambda + \sigma - 1)_n z^n}{n!}$$
$$\times {}_4F_3 \left[ \begin{array}{c} -n, \alpha + \beta + \lambda + \sigma - 1 + n, \alpha, \gamma - \beta; \\ \gamma, \alpha + \lambda, \alpha + \sigma; \end{array} 1 \right]. \quad (47)$$

Employing Whipple transformation (10) in (47), we find

$$\Xi_3(z) = \sum_{n=0}^{\infty} \Psi(n) \frac{(\alpha + \beta + \lambda + \sigma - 1)_n z^n}{n!} \frac{(\gamma - \alpha)_n (\lambda)_n}{(\alpha + \lambda)_n (\gamma)_n}$$
$$\times {}_4F_3 \left[ \begin{array}{c} -n, \alpha, 1 - \beta - \lambda - n, \alpha + \beta - \gamma + \sigma; \\ 1 + \alpha - \gamma - n, 1 - \lambda - n, \alpha + \sigma; \end{array} 1 \right] \quad (48)$$
$$= \sum_{n=0}^{\infty} \Psi(n) \frac{(\lambda)_n (\gamma - \alpha)_n (\alpha + \beta + \lambda + \sigma - 1)_n z^n}{(\alpha + \lambda)_n (\gamma)_n}$$
$$\times \sum_{m=0}^{n} \frac{(-n)_m (\alpha)_m (1 - \beta - \lambda - n)_m (\alpha + \beta - \gamma + \sigma)_m}{(1 + \alpha - \gamma - n)_m (1 - \lambda - n)_m (\alpha + \sigma)_m m!}.$$

Using (35) for $(-n)_m$ in the double series in (48) and employing the following double-series manipulation,

$$\sum_{n=0}^{\infty}\sum_{m=0}^{n} \Phi(m,n) = \sum_{m=0}^{\infty}\sum_{n=0}^{\infty} \Phi(m, n+m), \qquad (49)$$

where $\Phi : \mathbb{Z}_{\geq 0} \times \mathbb{Z}_{\geq 0} \to \mathbb{C}$ is a bounded function, and provided that both sides of the double series are absolutely convergent, we prove the desired identity (44). □

### 3. Transforming Srivastava–Daoust Functions to Kampé de Fériet Function

This section establishes three main transformations between the Srivastava–Daoust function in (6) and Kampé de Fériet function in (3) by utilizing the results in Section 2.

**Theorem 4.** *The following transformation formulas hold true:*

$$F_{E+3:0;0}^{D+4:0;0}\left(\begin{array}{l}[(d_D):2,1],[\alpha:1,1],[\beta:1,1],[\frac{\gamma+\delta-1}{2}:1,1],[\frac{\gamma+\delta}{2}:1,1]:-;-;\\ [(e_E):2,1],[\gamma:1,1],[\alpha+\beta:1,1],[\delta:1,1]:-;-;\end{array} -4z^2, 4z\right)$$

$$= F_{E+1:1;1}^{D+1:2;2}\left[\begin{array}{c}(d_D), \gamma+\delta-1: \alpha,\beta;\ \alpha,\beta;\\ (e_E), \alpha+\beta:\quad \gamma;\quad \delta;\end{array} z, z\right]; \qquad (50)$$

$$F_{E:3;0}^{D+1:3;0}\left(\begin{array}{l}[(d_D):2,1],[\alpha:1,1]:\quad [\beta:1],[\delta:1],[\gamma-\alpha:1];-;\\ [(e_E):2,1]:\quad [\gamma:1],[\frac{\beta+\delta}{2}:1],[\frac{\beta+\delta+1}{2}:1];-;\end{array} -\frac{z^2}{4}, z\right)$$

$$= F_{E+1:1;1}^{D+1:2;2}\left[\begin{array}{c}(d_D), \gamma: \alpha,\beta;\ \alpha,\delta;\\ (e_E), \delta+\beta:\ \gamma;\quad \gamma;\end{array} z, z\right]; \qquad (51)$$

$$F_{E:3;0}^{D+1:2;0}\left(\begin{array}{l}[(d_D):1,1],[\alpha+\beta+\lambda+\sigma-1:2,1]:\quad [\alpha:1],[\delta:1],[\gamma-\beta:1];-;\\ [(e_E):1,1]:\quad [\alpha+\lambda:1],[\alpha+\sigma:1],[\gamma:1];-;\end{array} -z, z\right)$$

$$= F_{E+2:1;1}^{D+2:2;2}\left[\begin{array}{c}(d_D), \alpha+\beta+\lambda+\sigma-1, \lambda+\beta:\ \alpha+\beta-\gamma+\sigma,\alpha;\ \lambda,\gamma-\alpha;\\ (e_E), \gamma, \alpha+\lambda:\quad \alpha+\sigma;\quad \lambda+\beta;\end{array} z, z\right], \qquad (52)$$

*where*

$$z \in \mathbb{R}_{>0},\ \Re(\xi)>0;\ e_1, e_2, \ldots, e_E, \delta, \gamma, \alpha+\beta, \alpha+\lambda, \alpha+\sigma, \beta+\delta, \beta+\lambda \in \mathbb{C}\setminus\mathbb{Z}_{\leq 0},$$

*provided that the other constraints for parameters and variable would follow from those in (3) and (6) so that the identities here are meaningful.*

**Proof.** Setting

$$\Psi(\mu) = \frac{(d_1)_\mu (d_2)_\mu \cdots (d_D)_\mu}{(e_1)_\mu (e_2)_\mu \cdots (e_E)_\mu} = \frac{\prod_{j=1}^{D}(d_j)_\mu}{\prod_{j=1}^{E}(e_j)_\mu} \quad (\mu \in \mathbb{Z}_{\geq 0})$$

on both sides of the general double-series identity (31), we obtain

$$\sum_{m=0}^{\infty}\sum_{n=0}^{\infty} \frac{\prod_{j=1}^{D}(d_j)_{2m+n}(\alpha)_{m+n}(\beta)_{m+n}\left(\frac{\gamma+\delta-1}{2}\right)_{m+n}\left(\frac{\gamma+\delta}{2}\right)_{m+n}(-4z^2)^m (4z)^n}{\prod_{j=1}^{E}(e_j)_{2m+n}(\gamma)_{m+n}(\alpha+\beta)_{m+n}(\delta)_{m+n}\, m!\, n!}$$

$$= \sum_{m=0}^{\infty}\sum_{n=0}^{\infty} \frac{\prod_{j=1}^{D}(d_j)_{m+n}(\gamma+\delta-1)_{m+n}(\alpha)_m(\beta)_m\,(\alpha)_n(\beta)_n\, z^{m+n}}{\prod_{j=1}^{E}(e_j)_{m+n}(\alpha+\beta)_{m+n}(\gamma)_m(\delta)_n\, m!\, n!},$$

which, upon expressing in terms of the Srivastava–Daoust function (6) for its left side and Kampé de Fériet function (3) for its right side, leads to (50).

Likewise, identities (51) and (52) can be demonstrated, but specific details have been omitted. □

## 4. Application of Fractional Calculus

This section demonstrates that the identities presented in Sections 2 and 3 can be converted into one another by employing the Riemann–Liouville fractional integrals. To do this, recall the left-sided Riemann–Liouville fractional integral and its related formula (see, e.g., [63], Equations (2.2.1) and (2.2.10), respectively):

$$\left(I_{0+}^{\xi} f\right)(z) := \frac{1}{\Gamma(\xi)} \int_0^z \frac{f(t)}{(z-t)^{1-\xi}}\, dt \quad (z \in \mathbb{R}_{>0};\, \Re(\xi) > 0), \tag{53}$$

and

$$\left(I_{0+}^{\xi} t^{\eta-1}\right)(z) = \frac{\Gamma(\eta)}{\Gamma(\eta+\xi)} z^{\eta+\xi-1} \quad (z \in \mathbb{R}_{>0};\, \Re(\xi) > 0,\, \Re(\eta) > 0). \tag{54}$$

Replacing $z$ by $t$ in the identities in Theorems 1–3, and applying the left-sided Riemann–Liouville fractional integral (53) to both sides of the resultant identities, with the aid of (54), we obtain the following identities, respectively. Here, we provide only a detailed proof of Theorem 5.

**Theorem 5.** *Let $\{\Psi(\mu)\}_{\mu=0}^{\infty}$ be a bounded sequence of complex (or real) numbers such that $\Psi(0) \neq 0$. Additionally, let $\alpha + \beta,\, \gamma,\, \delta \in \mathbb{C} \setminus \mathbb{Z}_{\leq 0};\, z \in \mathbb{R}_{>0},\, \Re(\xi) > 0$. Then the following general double-series identity holds true:*

$$\sum_{m=0}^{\infty}\sum_{n=0}^{\infty} \Psi(2m+n) \frac{(1)_{2m+n}(\alpha)_{m+n}(\beta)_{m+n}\left(\frac{\gamma+\delta-1}{2}\right)_{m+n}\left(\frac{\gamma+\delta}{2}\right)_{m+n}}{(\xi+1)_{2m+n}(\gamma)_{m+n}(\alpha+\beta)_{m+n}(\delta)_{m+n}} \frac{(-4z^2)^m (4z)^n}{m!\, n!}$$
$$= \sum_{m=0}^{\infty}\sum_{n=0}^{\infty} \Psi(m+n) \frac{(1)_{m+n}(\gamma+\delta-1)_{m+n}(\alpha)_m(\beta)_m\,(\alpha)_n(\beta)_n}{(\xi+1)_{m+n}(\alpha+\beta)_{m+n}(\gamma)_m(\delta)_n} \frac{z^{m+n}}{m!\, n!}, \tag{55}$$

*provided that both sides of the double series are absolutely convergent.*

**Proof.** Replacing $z$ by $t$ in (31), we obtain

$$\sum_{m=0}^{\infty}\sum_{n=0}^{\infty} \Psi(2m+n) \frac{(\alpha)_{m+n}(\beta)_{m+n}\left(\frac{\gamma+\delta-1}{2}\right)_{m+n}\left(\frac{\gamma+\delta}{2}\right)_{m+n}}{(\gamma)_{m+n}(\alpha+\beta)_{m+n}(\delta)_{m+n}} \frac{(-4)^m 4^n\, t^{2m+n}}{m!\, n!}$$
$$= \sum_{m=0}^{\infty}\sum_{n=0}^{\infty} \Psi(m+n) \frac{(\gamma+\delta-1)_{m+n}(\alpha)_m(\beta)_m\,(\alpha)_n(\beta)_n}{(\alpha+\beta)_{m+n}(\gamma)_m(\delta)_n} \frac{t^{m+n}}{m!\, n!}. \tag{56}$$

Applying the left-sided Riemann-Liouville fractional integral (53) to both sides of (56), we find

$$\sum_{m=0}^{\infty}\sum_{n=0}^{\infty}\Psi(2m+n)\frac{(\alpha)_{m+n}(\beta)_{m+n}\left(\frac{\gamma+\delta-1}{2}\right)_{m+n}\left(\frac{\gamma+\delta}{2}\right)_{m+n}}{(\gamma)_{m+n}(\alpha+\beta)_{m+n}(\delta)_{m+n}}\frac{(-4)^m 4^n \left(I_{0+}^{\xi}t^{2m+n}\right)(z)}{m!\,n!}$$
$$=\sum_{m=0}^{\infty}\sum_{n=0}^{\infty}\Psi(m+n)\frac{(\gamma+\delta-1)_{m+n}(\alpha)_m(\beta)_m(\alpha)_n(\beta)_n}{(\alpha+\beta)_{m+n}(\gamma)_m(\delta)_n}\frac{\left(I_{0+}^{\xi}t^{m+n}\right)(z)}{m!\,n!}. \tag{57}$$

Using (54) in (57), we derive

$$\sum_{m=0}^{\infty}\sum_{n=0}^{\infty}\Psi(2m+n)\frac{(\alpha)_{m+n}(\beta)_{m+n}\left(\frac{\gamma+\delta-1}{2}\right)_{m+n}\left(\frac{\gamma+\delta}{2}\right)_{m+n}}{(\gamma)_{m+n}(\alpha+\beta)_{m+n}(\delta)_{m+n}}\frac{(-4)^m 4^n z^{2m+n+\xi}\Gamma(2m+n+1)}{m!\,n!\,\Gamma(2m+n+1+\xi)}$$
$$=\sum_{m=0}^{\infty}\sum_{n=0}^{\infty}\Psi(m+n)\frac{(\gamma+\delta-1)_{m+n}(\alpha)_m(\beta)_m(\alpha)_n(\beta)_n}{(\alpha+\beta)_{m+n}(\gamma)_m(\delta)_n}\frac{\Gamma(m+n+1)\,z^{m+n+\xi}}{\Gamma(m+n+1+\xi)\,m!\,n!}. \tag{58}$$

Dividing both sides of (58) by $z^{\xi}$ and using (2) in the resultant identity, we obtain the desired identity (55). □

**Theorem 6.** *Let* $\{\Psi(\mu)\}_{\mu=0}^{\infty}$ *be a bounded sequence of complex (or real) numbers such that* $\Psi(0)\neq 0$. *Additionally, let* $\beta+\delta,\,\gamma\in\mathbb{C}\setminus\mathbb{Z}_{\leq 0}$; $z\in\mathbb{R}_{>0}$, $\Re(\xi)>0$. *Then the following general double-series identity holds true:*

$$\sum_{m=0}^{\infty}\sum_{n=0}^{\infty}\Psi(2m+n)\frac{(-1)^m\,(1)_{2m+n}\,(\alpha)_{m+n}(\beta)_m(\delta)_m(\gamma-\alpha)_m}{2^{2m}\,(\xi+1)_{2m+n}\,(\gamma)_m\left(\frac{\beta+\delta}{2}\right)_m\left(\frac{\beta+\delta+1}{2}\right)_m}\frac{z^{2m+n}}{m!\,n!}$$
$$=\sum_{m=0}^{\infty}\sum_{n=0}^{\infty}\Psi(m+n)\frac{(1)_{m+n}\,(\gamma)_{m+n}(\alpha)_m(\beta)_m(\alpha)_n(\delta)_n}{(\xi+1)_{m+n}\,(\beta+\delta)_{m+n}(\gamma)_m(\gamma)_n}\frac{z^{m+n}}{m!\,n!}, \tag{59}$$

*provided that both sides of the double series are absolutely convergent.*

**Theorem 7.** *Let* $\{\Psi(\mu)\}_{\mu=0}^{\infty}$ *be a bounded sequence of complex (or real) numbers such that* $\Psi(0)\neq 0$. *Additionally, let* $\alpha+\lambda,\,\alpha+\sigma,\,\beta+\lambda,\,\gamma\in\mathbb{C}\setminus\mathbb{Z}_{\leq 0}$; $z\in\mathbb{R}_{>0}$, $\Re(\xi)>0$. *Then the following general double-series identity holds true:*

$$\sum_{m=0}^{\infty}\sum_{n=0}^{\infty}\Psi(m+n)\frac{(-1)^m\,(1)_{m+n}\,(\alpha+\beta+\lambda+\sigma-1)_{2m+n}(\alpha)_m(\gamma-\beta)_m}{(\xi+1)_{m+n}\,(\alpha+\sigma)_m(\alpha+\lambda)_m(\gamma)_m}\frac{z^{m+n}}{m!\,n!}$$
$$=\sum_{m=0}^{\infty}\sum_{n=0}^{\infty}\Psi(m+n)\frac{(1)_{m+n}\,(\alpha+\beta+\lambda+\sigma-1)_{m+n}(\lambda+\beta)_{m+n}(\alpha+\beta-\gamma+\sigma)_m}{(\xi+1)_{m+n}\,(\gamma)_{m+n}(\alpha+\lambda)_{m+n}(\alpha+\sigma)_m(\beta+\lambda)_n} \tag{60}$$
$$\times (\alpha)_m\,(\gamma-\alpha)_n\,(\lambda)_n\frac{z^{m+n}}{m!\,n!},$$

*provided that both sides of the double series are absolutely convergent.*

By employing the identical procedure used to derive the identities in Theorem 4, we extend our analysis to the outcomes presented in Theorems 5–7, leading to the subsequent theorem.

**Theorem 8.** *The following transformation formulas hold true:*

$$F_{E+4:0;0}^{D+5:0;0}\left(\begin{array}{c}[(d_D):2,1],[1:2,1],[\alpha:1,1],[\beta:1,1],[\frac{\gamma+\delta-1}{2}:1,1],[\frac{\gamma+\delta}{2}:1,1]:-;-;\\ [\xi+1:2,1],[(e_E):2,1],[\gamma:1,1],[\alpha+\beta:1,1],[\delta:1,1]:-;-;\end{array}-4z^2,4z\right)$$

$$= F_{E+2:1;1}^{D+2:2;2} \begin{bmatrix} (d_D), 1, \gamma+\delta-1: & \alpha, \beta; & \alpha, \beta; \\ \xi+1, (e_E), \alpha+\beta: & \gamma; & \delta; \end{bmatrix} z, z \end{bmatrix}; \tag{61}$$

$$F_{E+1:3;0}^{D+2:3;0} \begin{pmatrix} [(d_D):2,1], [1:2,1], [\alpha:1,1]: & [\beta:1], [\delta:1], [\gamma-\alpha:1]; -; \\ [\xi+1:2,1], [(e_E):2,1]: [\gamma:1], [\frac{\beta+\delta}{2}:1], [\frac{\beta+\delta+1}{2}:1]; -; \end{pmatrix} -\frac{z^2}{4}, z \end{pmatrix}$$

$$= F_{E+2:1;1}^{D+2:2;2} \begin{bmatrix} (d_D), 1, \gamma: & \alpha, \beta; & \alpha, \delta; \\ \xi+1, (e_E), \delta+\beta: & \gamma; & \gamma; \end{bmatrix} z, z \end{bmatrix}; \tag{62}$$

$$F_{E+1:3;0}^{D+2:3;0} \begin{pmatrix} [(d_D):1,1], [1:1,1], [\alpha+\beta+\lambda+\sigma-1:2,1]: & [\alpha:1], [\delta:1], [\gamma-\beta:1]; -; \\ [\xi+1:1,1], [(e_E):1,1]: [\alpha+\lambda:1], [\alpha+\sigma:1], [\gamma:1]; -; \end{pmatrix} -z, z \end{pmatrix}$$

$$= F_{E+3:1;1}^{D+3:2;2} \begin{bmatrix} (d_D), 1, \alpha+\beta+\lambda+\sigma-1, \lambda+\beta: \alpha+\beta-\gamma+\sigma, \alpha; & \lambda, \gamma-\alpha; \\ \xi+1, (e_E), \gamma, \alpha+\lambda: & \alpha+\sigma; & \lambda+\beta; \end{bmatrix} z, z \end{bmatrix}, \tag{63}$$

where

$$z \in \mathbb{R}_{>0}, \Re(\xi) > 0; e_1, e_2, \ldots, e_E, \delta, \gamma, \alpha+\beta, \alpha+\lambda, \alpha+\sigma, \beta+\delta, \beta+\lambda \in \mathbb{C} \setminus \mathbb{Z}_{\leq 0},$$

provided that the other constraints for parameters and variable would follow from those in (3) and (6) so that the identities here are meaningful.

## 5. Certain Instances of Transformations (50)–(52)

This section demonstrates that certain special cases of transformations (50)–(52) result in the Bailey quadratic transformation, Clausen reduction formula, Gauss quadratic transformation, Karlsson reduction formula, Orr reduction formula, Whipple quadratic transformation, and several new transformations, which are given in the following examples.

**Example 1.** *Putting $D = E = 0$ and $\delta = \alpha + \beta - \gamma + 1$ in (50) and using the double-series manipulation (see, e.g., [64], p. 4, Equation (12))*

$$\sum_{m,n=0}^{\infty} \Phi(m+n) \frac{x^m y^n}{m!\, n!} = \sum_{p=0}^{\infty} \Phi(p) \frac{(x+y)^p}{p!}, \tag{64}$$

where $\Phi : \mathbb{Z}_{\geq 0} \to \mathbb{C}$ is a bounded function, and provided that both sides of the series are absolutely convergent, we obtain a product formula for $_pF_q$:

$$_4F_3 \begin{bmatrix} \alpha, \beta, \frac{\alpha+\beta}{2}, \frac{\alpha+\beta+1}{2}; \\ \gamma, \alpha+\beta, \alpha+\beta-\gamma+1; \end{bmatrix} 4z(1-z) \end{bmatrix}$$
$$= {}_2F_1 \begin{bmatrix} \alpha, \beta; \\ \gamma; \end{bmatrix} z \end{bmatrix} {}_2F_1 \begin{bmatrix} \alpha, \beta; \\ \alpha+\beta-\gamma+1; \end{bmatrix} z \end{bmatrix} \tag{65}$$

$(\alpha+\beta, \alpha+\beta-\gamma+1, \gamma \in \mathbb{C} \setminus \mathbb{Z}_{\leq 0}; |z| < 1, 4|z(1-z)| < 1).$

Identity (65) is due to Bailey ([56], p. 382, Equation (6.1)) (see also ([4], p. 275, Prob. 8)).

Setting $\gamma = \frac{\alpha+\beta+1}{2}$ in (65) and replacing $\alpha$ and $\beta$ by $2\alpha$ and $2\beta$ gives a formula for the square of $_2F_1$:

$$_3F_2 \begin{bmatrix} 2\alpha, 2\beta, \alpha+\beta; \\ 2\alpha+2\beta, \alpha+\beta+\frac{1}{2}; \end{bmatrix} 4z(1-z) \end{bmatrix} = \left\{ {}_2F_1 \begin{bmatrix} 2\alpha, 2\beta; \\ \alpha+\beta+\frac{1}{2}; \end{bmatrix} z \end{bmatrix} \right\}^2, \tag{66}$$

which, upon using Gauss transformation Formula (17), yields

$$_3F_2 \begin{bmatrix} 2\alpha, 2\beta, \alpha+\beta; \\ 2\alpha+2\beta, \alpha+\beta+\frac{1}{2}; \end{bmatrix} 4z(1-z) \end{bmatrix} = \left\{ {}_2F_1 \begin{bmatrix} \alpha, \beta; \\ \alpha+\beta+\frac{1}{2}; \end{bmatrix} 4z(1-z) \end{bmatrix} \right\}^2. \tag{67}$$

*Replacing $4z(1-z)$ by $z$ in (67) yields the well-known Clausen formula in [65] (see, e.g., [2], p. 86, Equation (4), [50], p. 75, Equation (2.5.7)).*

*Putting $\alpha = a$, $\beta = \delta = b$, and $\gamma = a + b + \frac{1}{2}$ in (88), and using the procedure illustrated in Example 13, we also acquire the Clausen formula.*

**Example 2.** *Putting $D = E = 0$ and $\gamma = \delta = \alpha$ in (50) and using (64), we obtain*

$$F_{1:0;0}^{1:1;1}\left[\begin{array}{c} 2\alpha - 1 : \beta; \beta; \\ \alpha + \beta : -;-; \end{array} z, z\right] = {}_2F_1\left[\begin{array}{c} \alpha - \frac{1}{2}, \beta; \\ \alpha + \beta; \end{array} 4z(1-z)\right] \tag{68}$$

$$(\alpha + \beta \in \mathbb{C} \setminus \mathbb{Z}_{\leqslant 0}; |z| < 1, 4|z(1-z)| < 1).$$

*Applying the reduction Formula (21) to the left-hand side of (68), we obtain*

$${}_2F_1\left[\begin{array}{c} 2\alpha - 1, 2\beta; \\ \alpha + \beta; \end{array} z\right] = {}_2F_1\left[\begin{array}{c} \alpha - \frac{1}{2}, \beta; \\ \alpha + \beta; \end{array} 4z(1-z)\right] \tag{69}$$

$$(\alpha + \beta \in \mathbb{C} \setminus \mathbb{Z}_{\leqslant 0}; |z| < 1, 4|z(1-z)| < 1),$$

*which, upon replacing $\alpha$ by $\alpha + \frac{1}{2}$, corresponds to Gauss transformation Formula (17).*

**Example 3.** *Putting $D = E = 0$ and $\gamma = \alpha$ $\delta = \beta$ in (50) and using (64) gives the first equality of the identity*

$$F_{1:0;0}^{1:1;1}\left[\begin{array}{c} \alpha + \beta - 1 : \beta; \alpha; \\ \alpha + \beta : -;-; \end{array} z, z\right] = {}_2F_1\left[\begin{array}{c} \frac{\alpha+\beta-1}{2}, \frac{\alpha+\beta}{2}; \\ \alpha + \beta; \end{array} 4z(1-z)\right]$$
$$= (1-z)^{1-\alpha-\beta} \tag{70}$$

$$(\alpha + \beta \in \mathbb{C} \setminus \mathbb{Z}_{\leqslant 0}; |z| < 1, 4|z(1-z)| < 1).$$

*Applying the reduction Formula (21) to the leftmost member of (70) yields the second equality of (70). Interestingly, the identity where $\beta = \alpha + 1$ in [48] (Equation (2.10)) is equivalent to the second equality of (70).*

**Example 4.** *Putting $D = E = 0$ and $\delta = 2\alpha + 2\beta - \gamma + 1$ in (50) and using (64), we acquire a reduction formula for the Kampé de Fériet function in (3):*

$$F_{1:1;1}^{1:2;2}\left[\begin{array}{cc} 2\alpha + 2\beta : & \alpha, \beta; \qquad \alpha, \beta; \\ \alpha + \beta : & \gamma; \quad 2\alpha + 2\beta - \gamma + 1; \end{array} z, z\right]$$
$$= {}_3F_2\left[\begin{array}{c} \alpha, \beta, \alpha + \beta + \frac{1}{2}; \\ \gamma, 2\alpha + 2\beta - \gamma + 1; \end{array} 4z(1-z)\right] \tag{71}$$

$$(\alpha + \beta, \gamma, 2\alpha + 2\beta - \gamma + 1 \in \mathbb{C} \setminus \mathbb{Z}_{\leqslant 0}; |z| < 1, 4|z(1-z)| < 1).$$

**Example 5.** *Putting $D = E = 0$ and $\gamma = \beta$ in (50) and using (64), we attain a reduction formula for the Kampé de Fériet function in (3):*

$$F_{1:0;1}^{1:1;2}\left[\begin{array}{c} \beta + \delta - 1 : \quad \alpha; \quad \alpha, \beta; \\ \alpha + \beta : \quad -; \quad \delta; \end{array} z, z\right] = {}_3F_2\left[\begin{array}{c} \alpha, \frac{\beta+\delta}{2}, \frac{\beta+\delta-1}{2}; \\ \alpha + \beta, \delta; \end{array} 4z(1-z)\right] \tag{72}$$

$$(\alpha + \beta, \delta \in \mathbb{C} \setminus \mathbb{Z}_{\leqslant 0}; |z| < 1, 4|z(1-z)| < 1).$$

*Setting $\delta = \alpha$ in (72) leads to identity (70).*

**Example 6.** *Putting $D = E = 0$ and $\delta = \gamma + 1$ in (50) and using (64), we gain a reduction formula for the Kampé de Fériet function in (3):*

$$F_{1:1;1}^{1:2;2}\left[\begin{array}{c}2\gamma: \alpha, \beta; \alpha, \beta; \\ \alpha+\beta: \gamma; \gamma+1;\end{array} z, z\right] = {}_3F_2\left[\begin{array}{c}\alpha, \beta, \gamma+\frac{1}{2}; \\ \alpha+\beta, \gamma+1;\end{array} 4z(1-z)\right] \tag{73}$$

$$(\alpha+\beta, \gamma \in \mathbb{C} \setminus \mathbb{Z}_{\leq 0}; |z| < 1, 4|z(1-z)| < 1).$$

Setting $\gamma = \alpha + \beta - \frac{1}{2}$ in (73) and using a particular case (Table 3, 1a) of the known general reduction formula $F_{q:1;1}^{p:2;2}[z,z] = {}_{p+3}F_{q+2}[z]$ in [30], Equation (3.2), we derive the following transformation formula:

$$_3F_2\left[\begin{array}{c}2\alpha, 2\beta, 2\alpha+\beta-1; \\ \alpha+\beta+\frac{1}{2}, 2\alpha+2\beta-1;\end{array} z\right] = {}_2F_1\left[\begin{array}{c}\alpha, \beta; \\ \alpha+\beta+\frac{1}{2};\end{array} 4z(1-z)\right] \tag{74}$$

$$\left(\alpha+\beta+\frac{1}{2}, 2\alpha+2\beta-1 \in \mathbb{C} \setminus \mathbb{Z}_{\leq 0}; |z| < 1, 4|z(1-z)| < 1\right).$$

**Example 7.** *Putting $D = E = 0$ and $\delta = \gamma - \beta$ and using the binomial theorem (11), we obtain a product formula of ${}_2F_1$'s:*

$$(1-z)^{-\alpha} {}_4F_3\left[\begin{array}{c}\alpha, \beta, \gamma-\alpha, \gamma-\beta; \\ \gamma, \frac{\gamma}{2}, \frac{\gamma+1}{2};\end{array} \frac{-z^2}{4(1-z)}\right]$$
$$= {}_2F_1\left[\begin{array}{c}\alpha, \beta; \\ \gamma;\end{array} z\right] {}_2F_1\left[\begin{array}{c}\alpha, \gamma-\beta; \\ \gamma;\end{array} z\right] \tag{75}$$

$$\left(\gamma \in \mathbb{C} \setminus \mathbb{Z}_{\leq 0}; |z| < 1, |z|^2/\{4|1-z|\} < 1\right),$$

which is a known formula due to Bailey [56], p. 382, Equation (6.3).

Applying Pfaff–Kummer transformation Formula (13) to the second ${}_2F_1$ on the right-hand side of (75), we obtain a product formula of ${}_2F_1$'s:

$$_4F_3\left[\begin{array}{c}\alpha, \beta, \gamma-\alpha, \gamma-\beta; \\ \gamma, \frac{\gamma}{2}, \frac{\gamma+1}{2};\end{array} \frac{-z^2}{4(1-z)}\right]$$
$$= {}_2F_1\left[\begin{array}{c}\alpha, \beta; \\ \gamma;\end{array} z\right] {}_2F_1\left[\begin{array}{c}\alpha, \beta; \\ \gamma;\end{array} \frac{-z}{1-z}\right] \tag{76}$$

$$\left(\gamma \in \mathbb{C} \setminus \mathbb{Z}_{\leq 0}; |z| < 1, |z|^2/\{4|1-z|\} < 1, |z|/|1-z| < 1\right),$$

which is another known formula due to Bailey [56], p. 383, Equation (7.2).

**Example 8.** *Putting $D = E = 0$ and $\gamma = \beta$ in (51) and using the binomial theorem (11), we deduce a reduction formula for the Kampé de Fériet function in (3):*

$$F_{1:0;1}^{1:1;2}\left[\begin{array}{c}\beta: \alpha; \alpha, \delta; \\ \beta+\delta: -; \beta;\end{array} z, z\right] = (1-z)^{-\alpha} {}_3F_2\left[\begin{array}{c}\alpha, \beta-\alpha, \delta; \\ \frac{\beta+\delta}{2}, \frac{\beta+\delta+1}{2};\end{array} \frac{-z^2}{4(1-z)}\right] \tag{77}$$

$$\left(\beta, \beta+\delta \in \mathbb{C} \setminus \mathbb{Z}_{\leq 0}; |z| < 1, |z|^2/\{4|1-z|\} < 1, |\arg(1-z)| < \pi\right).$$

Setting $\delta = \beta - 2\alpha$ in (77) and, via (5), using (22) in the resultant identity, we obtain a transformation formula for ${}_2F_1$:

$$_2F_1\left[\begin{array}{c}2\alpha, \beta-\alpha; \\ 2\beta-2\alpha;\end{array} z\right] = (1-z)^{-\alpha} {}_2F_1\left[\begin{array}{c}\alpha, \beta-2\alpha; \\ \beta-\alpha+\frac{1}{2};\end{array} \frac{-z^2}{4(1-z)}\right] \tag{78}$$

$$\left(2\beta-2\alpha, \beta-\alpha+\frac{1}{2} \in \mathbb{C} \setminus \mathbb{Z}_{\leq 0}; |z| < 1, |z|^2/\{4|1-z|\} < 1, |\arg(1-z)| < \pi\right),$$

which is a particular case of Bailey transformation Formula (16).

In view of (4), the reduction Formula (77) equals

$$F^{1:2;1}_{1:1;0}\left[\begin{matrix}\beta: & \alpha,\delta; & \alpha; \\ \beta+\delta: & \beta; & -;\end{matrix} z,z\right] = (1-z)^{-\alpha}\,_3F_2\left[\begin{matrix}\alpha,\beta-\alpha,\delta; \\ \frac{\beta+\delta}{2},\frac{\beta+\delta+1}{2};\end{matrix} \frac{-z^2}{4(1-z)}\right] \tag{79}$$

$$\left(\beta,\beta+\delta\in\mathbb{C}\setminus\mathbb{Z}_{\leqslant 0};\ |z|<1,\ |z|^2/\{4|1-z|\}<1,\ |\arg(1-z)|<\pi\right),$$

which is interesting to compare with the following known formula (see [27], Equation (2.2)):

$$F^{1:2;1}_{1:1;0}\left[\begin{matrix}\alpha: & \beta-\epsilon,\gamma; & \epsilon; \\ \beta: & \delta; & -;\end{matrix} z,z\right] = (1-z)^{-\alpha}\,_3F_2\left[\begin{matrix}\alpha,\beta-\epsilon,\delta-\epsilon; \\ \beta,\delta;\end{matrix} \frac{-z}{1-z}\right] \tag{80}$$

$$\left(\beta,\delta\in\mathbb{C}\setminus\mathbb{Z}_{\leqslant 0};\ |z|<1,\ |z|/|1-z|<1,\ |\arg(1-z)|<\pi\right).$$

**Example 9.** *Putting* $D = E = 0$ *and* $\delta = \beta$ *in (51) and using the binomial theorem (11), we obtain a reduction formula for the Kampé de Fériet function in (3):*

$$F^{1:2;2}_{1:1;1}\left[\begin{matrix}\gamma: & \alpha,\beta; & \alpha,\beta; \\ 2\beta: & \gamma; & \gamma;\end{matrix} z,z\right] = (1-z)^{-\alpha}\,_3F_2\left[\begin{matrix}\alpha,\gamma-\alpha,\beta; \\ \gamma,\beta+\frac{1}{2};\end{matrix} \frac{-z^2}{4(1-z)}\right] \tag{81}$$

$$\left(2\beta,\beta+\tfrac{1}{2},\gamma\in\mathbb{C}\setminus\mathbb{Z}_{\leqslant 0};\ |z|<1,\ |z|^2/\{4|1-z|\}<1,\ |\arg(1-z)|<\pi\right).$$

Setting $\gamma = \beta$ in (81) and the reduction formula of the Kampé de Fériet function (21) to the right-hand side of transformation (81) gives Bailey transformation Formula (16).

Additionally, as in obtaining (74), setting $\gamma = \alpha + \beta + \frac{1}{2}$ in (81), and using a particular case (Table 3, 1e) of the known general reduction formula ([30], Equation (3.2)), we obtain the following transformation formula:

$$_2F_1\left[\begin{matrix}2\alpha,\alpha+\beta; \\ 2\alpha+2\beta;\end{matrix} z\right] = (1-z)^{-\alpha}\,_2F_1\left[\begin{matrix}\alpha,\beta; \\ \alpha+\beta+\frac{1}{2};\end{matrix} \frac{-z^2}{4(1-z)}\right] \tag{82}$$

$$\left(\alpha+\beta+\tfrac{1}{2},2\alpha+2\beta\in\mathbb{C}\setminus\mathbb{Z}_{\leqslant 0};\ |z|<1,\ |z|^2/\{4|1-z|\}<1,\ |\arg(1-z)|<\pi\right).$$

**Example 10.** *Putting* $D = E = 0$ *and* $\delta = 2\gamma - 2\alpha - \beta$ *and using the binomial theorem (11), we attain a reduction formula for the Kampé de Fériet function in (3):*

$$F^{1:2;2}_{1:1;1}\left[\begin{matrix}\gamma: & \alpha,\beta; & \alpha,2\gamma-2\alpha-\beta; \\ 2\gamma-2\alpha: & \gamma; & \gamma;\end{matrix} z,z\right]$$
$$= (1-z)^{-\alpha}\,_3F_2\left[\begin{matrix}\alpha,\beta,2\gamma-2\alpha-\beta; \\ \gamma,\gamma-\alpha+\frac{1}{2};\end{matrix} \frac{-z^2}{4(1-z)}\right] \tag{83}$$

$$\left(2\gamma-2\alpha,\gamma-\alpha+\tfrac{1}{2},\gamma\in\mathbb{C}\setminus\mathbb{Z}_{\leqslant 0};\ |z|<1,\ |z|^2/\{4|1-z|\}<1,\ |\arg(1-z)|<\pi\right).$$

**Example 11.** *Putting* $D = E = 0$ *and* $\delta = \beta - 1$ *in (51) and using the binomial theorem (11), we acquire a reduction formula for the Kampé de Fériet function in (3):*

$$F^{1:2;2}_{1:1;1}\left[\begin{matrix}\gamma: & \alpha,\beta; & \alpha,\beta-1; \\ 2\beta-1: & \gamma; & \gamma;\end{matrix} z,z\right]$$
$$= (1-z)^{-\alpha}\,_3F_2\left[\begin{matrix}\alpha,\beta-1,\gamma-\alpha; \\ \gamma,\beta-\frac{1}{2};\end{matrix} \frac{-z^2}{4(1-z)}\right] \tag{84}$$

$$\left(\beta-\tfrac{1}{2},\gamma\in\mathbb{C}\setminus\mathbb{Z}_{\leqslant 0};\ |z|<1,\ |z|^2/\{4|1-z|\}<1,\ |\arg(1-z)|<\pi\right).$$

Setting $\gamma = 2\beta - 1$ in (84) and using the reduction Formula (20), we obtain a product formula for $_2F_1$'s:

$$(1-z)^{-\alpha} {}_3F_2\left[\begin{array}{c} \alpha, \beta - 1, 2\beta - \alpha - 1; \\ 2\beta - 1, \beta - \frac{1}{2}; \end{array} \frac{-z^2}{4(1-z)}\right]$$
$$= {}_2F_1\left[\begin{array}{c} \alpha, \beta; \\ 2\beta - 1; \end{array} z\right] {}_2F_1\left[\begin{array}{c} \alpha, \beta - 1; \\ 2\beta - 1; \end{array} z\right] \quad (85)$$

$\left(\beta - \frac{1}{2} \in \mathbb{C} \setminus \mathbb{Z}_{\leqslant 0}; |z| < 1, |z|^2/\{4|1-z|\} < 1, |\arg(1-z)| < \pi\right)$.

**Example 12.** *Putting $D = E = 0$ and $\delta = 2\gamma - 2\alpha - \beta - 1$ in (51) and using the binomial theorem (11), we gain a reduction formula for the Kampé de Fériet function in (3):*

$$F^{1:2;2}_{1:1;1}\left[\begin{array}{c} \gamma: \quad \alpha, \beta; \quad \alpha, 2\gamma - 2\alpha - \beta - 1; \\ 2\gamma - 2\alpha - 1: \quad \gamma; \quad \gamma; \end{array} z, z\right]$$
$$= (1-z)^{-\alpha} {}_3F_2\left[\begin{array}{c} \alpha, \beta, 2\gamma - 2\alpha - \beta - 1; \\ \gamma, \gamma - \alpha - \frac{1}{2}; \end{array} \frac{-z^2}{4(1-z)}\right] \quad (86)$$

$\left(\gamma, \gamma - \alpha - \frac{1}{2} \in \mathbb{C} \setminus \mathbb{Z}_{\leqslant 0}; |z| < 1, |z|^2/\{4|1-z|\} < 1, |\arg(1-z)| < \pi\right)$.

Setting $\gamma = 2\alpha + 1$ in (86) and using the reduction Formula (20), we deduce a product formula for $_2F_1$'s:

$$(1-z)^{-\alpha} {}_3F_2\left[\begin{array}{c} \alpha, \beta, 2\alpha - \beta + 1; \\ 2\alpha + 1, \alpha + \frac{1}{2}; \end{array} \frac{-z^2}{4(1-z)}\right]$$
$$= {}_2F_1\left[\begin{array}{c} \alpha, \beta; \\ 2\alpha + 1; \end{array} z\right] {}_2F_1\left[\begin{array}{c} \alpha, 2\alpha - \beta + 1; \\ 2\alpha + 1; \end{array} z\right] \quad (87)$$

$\left(\alpha + \frac{1}{2} \in \mathbb{C} \setminus \mathbb{Z}_{\leqslant 0}; |z| < 1, |z|^2/\{4|1-z|\} < 1, |\arg(1-z)| < \pi\right)$.

**Example 13.** *Putting $D = E = 1$, $d_1 = \delta + \beta$, and $e_1 = \gamma$ in (51) and using the reduction Formula (20), we obtain a reduction formula for the Srivastava–Daoust function in (6):*

$$F^{2:3;0}_{1:3;0}\left(\begin{array}{c} [\delta + \beta : 2, 1], [\alpha : 1, 1]: \quad [\beta : 1], [\delta : 1], [\gamma - \alpha : 1]; \quad -; \\ [\gamma : 2, 1]: \quad [\gamma : 1], [\frac{\beta + \delta}{2} : 1], [\frac{\beta + \delta + 1}{2} : 1]; \quad -; \end{array} -\frac{z^2}{4}, z\right)$$
$$= {}_2F_1\left[\begin{array}{c} \alpha, \beta; \\ \gamma; \end{array} z\right] {}_2F_1\left[\begin{array}{c} \alpha, \delta; \\ \gamma; \end{array} z\right]. \quad (88)$$

Setting $\alpha = a$, $\beta = b$, $\delta = b - 1$, and $\gamma = a + b - \frac{1}{2}$ in (88) gives

$$\sum_{n=0}^{\infty}\sum_{m=0}^{\infty} \frac{(2b-1)_{2m+n}(a)_{m+n}(b-1)_m(-1)^m(z)^{2m+n}}{\left(a+b-\frac{1}{2}\right)_{2m+n}\left(a+b-\frac{1}{2}\right)_m(4)^m m! n!}$$
$$= {}_2F_1\left[\begin{array}{c} a, b; \\ a+b-\frac{1}{2}; \end{array} z\right] {}_2F_1\left[\begin{array}{c} a, b-1; \\ a+b-\frac{1}{2}; \end{array} z\right],$$

which, upon utilizing the double-series manipulation (32) and then the Pochhammer symbol identity (34), yields

$$\sum_{n=0}^{\infty} \frac{(2b-1)_n(a)_n(z)^n}{\left(a+b-\frac{1}{2}\right)_n n!} {}_3F_2\left[\begin{array}{c} -\frac{n}{2}, \frac{-n+1}{2}, b-1; \\ a+b-\frac{1}{2}, 1-a-n; \end{array} 1\right]$$
$$= {}_2F_1\left[\begin{array}{c} a, b; \\ a+b-\frac{1}{2}; \end{array} z\right] {}_2F_1\left[\begin{array}{c} a, b-1; \\ a+b-\frac{1}{2}; \end{array} z\right]. \quad (89)$$

Applying the summation theorem for $_3F_2(1)$ (24) to the $_3F_2(1)$ in (89), we attain a product formula for $_2F_1$'s:

$$_3F_2\left[\begin{array}{c} 2a, 2b-1, a+b-1; \\ 2a+2b-2, a+b-\frac{1}{2}; \end{array} z\right] = {}_2F_1\left[\begin{array}{c} a, b; \\ a+b-\frac{1}{2}; \end{array} z\right] {}_2F_1\left[\begin{array}{c} a, b-1; \\ a+b-\frac{1}{2}; \end{array} z\right] \quad (90)$$

$$\left(2a+2b-2, a+b-\tfrac{1}{2} \in \mathbb{C} \setminus \mathbb{Z}_{\leqslant 0}; |z|<1\right),$$

which is due to Orr [66] (see also [50], p. 77, Equation (2.5.13)).

**Example 14.** *Putting* $\alpha = a+\frac{1}{2}$, $\beta = b-\frac{1}{2}$, $\delta = b+\frac{1}{2}$, *and* $\gamma = a+b+\frac{1}{2}$ *in* (88) *and performing the identical procedure as demonstrated in Example 13, we arrive at a known formula (see [30], p. 34, Table 3(Id))*:

$$_3F_2\left[\begin{array}{c} 2a, 2b+1, a+b; \\ 2a+2b, a+b+\frac{1}{2}; \end{array} z\right] = {}_2F_1\left[\begin{array}{c} a+\frac{1}{2}, b-\frac{1}{2}; \\ a+b+\frac{1}{2}; \end{array} z\right] {}_2F_1\left[\begin{array}{c} a+\frac{1}{2}, b+\frac{1}{2}; \\ a+b+\frac{1}{2}; \end{array} z\right] \quad (91)$$

$$\left(2a+2b, a+b+\tfrac{1}{2} \in \mathbb{C} \setminus \mathbb{Z}_{\leqslant 0}; |z|<1\right).$$

**Example 15.** *Putting* $\alpha = b$, $\beta = a+1$, $\delta = a$, *and* $\gamma = a+b+\frac{1}{2}$ *in* (88) *and following the same procedure shown in Example 13, we obtain a known formula (see [30], p. 34, Table 3(Ic))*:

$$_3F_2\left[\begin{array}{c} 2b, 2a+1, a+b; \\ 2a+2b, a+b+\frac{1}{2}; \end{array} z\right] = {}_2F_1\left[\begin{array}{c} a+1, b; \\ a+b+\frac{1}{2}; \end{array} z\right] {}_2F_1\left[\begin{array}{c} a, b; \\ a+b+\frac{1}{2}; \end{array} z\right] \quad (92)$$

$$\left(2a+2b, a+b+\tfrac{1}{2} \in \mathbb{C} \setminus \mathbb{Z}_{\leqslant 0}; |z|<1\right).$$

**Example 16.** *Putting* $D = E = 0$, $\beta = \alpha$, *and* $\gamma = 2\alpha + \lambda + \sigma - 1$ *in* (52) *and using the binomial theorem* (11), *we attain a product formula for* $_2F_1$'s:

$$(1-z)^{1-2\alpha-\lambda-\sigma}{}_4F_3\left[\begin{array}{c} \alpha, \alpha+\lambda+\sigma-1, \frac{2\alpha+\lambda+\sigma-1}{2}, \frac{2\alpha+\lambda+\sigma}{2}; \\ \alpha+\sigma, \alpha+\lambda, 2\alpha+\lambda+\sigma-1; \end{array} \frac{-4z}{(1-z)^2}\right]$$
$$= {}_2F_1\left[\begin{array}{c} 1-\lambda, \alpha; \\ \alpha+\sigma; \end{array} z\right] {}_2F_1\left[\begin{array}{c} \lambda, \alpha+\lambda+\sigma-1; \\ \alpha+\lambda; \end{array} z\right] \quad (93)$$

$$\left(\alpha+\sigma, \alpha+\lambda, 2\alpha+\lambda+\sigma-1 \in \mathbb{C} \setminus \mathbb{Z}_{\leqslant 0};\right.$$
$$\left.|z|<1, |z|^2/\{4|1-z|\} < 1, |\arg(1-z)| < \pi\right).$$

**Example 17.** *Putting* $D = E = 0$, $\gamma = \lambda + \beta$, *and* $\sigma = 1-\beta$ *and using the binomial theorem* (11), *we obtain a product formula for* $_2F_1$'s:

$$(1-z)^{-\alpha-\lambda}{}_4F_3\left[\begin{array}{c} \alpha, \lambda, \frac{\alpha+\lambda}{2}, \frac{\alpha+\lambda+1}{2}; \\ \alpha-\beta+1, \alpha+\lambda, \beta+\lambda; \end{array} \frac{-4z}{(1-z)^2}\right]$$
$$= {}_2F_1\left[\begin{array}{c} \alpha, \alpha-\lambda-\beta+1; \\ \alpha-\beta+1; \end{array} z\right] {}_2F_1\left[\begin{array}{c} \lambda, \beta-\alpha+\lambda; \\ \beta+\lambda; \end{array} z\right] \quad (94)$$

$$\left(\alpha-\beta+1, \alpha+\lambda, \beta+\lambda \in \mathbb{C} \setminus \mathbb{Z}_{\leqslant 0};\right.$$
$$\left.|z|<1, |z|^2/\{4|1-z|\} < 1, |\arg(1-z)| < \pi\right).$$

Setting $\lambda = \gamma - \beta$ in (94) and utilizing Euler transformation (12) in the $_2F_1$ on the resultant identity, we obtain a product formula for $_2F_1$'s due to Bailey [56], p. 383, Equation (7.4):

$$(1-z)^{\beta-\alpha-\gamma} {}_4F_3\left[\begin{array}{c} \alpha, \gamma - \beta, \frac{\alpha+\gamma-\beta}{2}, \frac{\alpha+\gamma-\beta+1}{2}; \\ \alpha - \beta + 1, \alpha + \gamma - \beta, \gamma; \end{array} \frac{-4z}{(1-z)^2}\right]$$
$$= {}_2F_1\left[\begin{array}{c} \alpha, \beta; \\ \gamma; \end{array} z\right] {}_2F_1\left[\begin{array}{c} 1-\beta, \gamma - \beta; \\ \alpha - \beta + 1; \end{array} z\right] \quad (95)$$

$$(\gamma, \alpha - \beta + 1, \alpha + \gamma - \beta \in \mathbb{C} \setminus \mathbb{Z}_{\leq 0};$$
$$|z| < 1, |z|^2/\{4|1-z|\} < 1, |\arg(1-z)| < \pi).$$

**Example 18.** *Putting $D = E = 0$ and $\beta = \alpha$ in (52) and using the binomial theorem (11), we acquire a reduction formula:*

$$F_{1:1;1}^{1:2;2}\left[\begin{array}{c} 2\alpha + \lambda + \sigma - 1 : \alpha, 2\alpha - \gamma + \sigma; \lambda, \gamma - \alpha; \\ \gamma : \alpha + \sigma; \alpha + \lambda; \end{array} z, z\right]$$
$$= (1-z)^{1-2\alpha-\lambda-\sigma} {}_4F_3\left[\begin{array}{c} \alpha, \gamma - \alpha, \frac{2\alpha+\lambda+\sigma-1}{2}, \frac{2\alpha+\lambda+\sigma}{2}; \\ \alpha + \lambda, \alpha + \sigma, \gamma; \end{array} \frac{-4z}{(1-z)^2}\right] \quad (96)$$

$$(\gamma, \alpha + \sigma, \alpha + \lambda \in \mathbb{C} \setminus \mathbb{Z}_{\leq 0}; |z| < 1, |z|^2/\{4|1-z|\} < 1, |\arg(1-z)| < \pi).$$

**Example 19.** *Putting $D = E = 0$ and $\gamma = \alpha + \beta + \lambda$ in (52) and using the binomial theorem (11), we gain a reduction formula:*

$$F_{2:1;0}^{2:2;1}\left[\begin{array}{c} \alpha + \beta + \lambda + \sigma - 1, \lambda + \beta : \alpha, \sigma - \lambda; \lambda; \\ \alpha + \beta + \lambda, \alpha + \lambda : \alpha + \sigma; -; \end{array} z, z\right]$$
$$= (1-z)^{1-\alpha-\beta-\lambda-\sigma} {}_3F_2\left[\begin{array}{c} \alpha, \frac{\alpha+\beta+\lambda+\sigma-1}{2}, \frac{\alpha+\beta+\lambda+\sigma}{2}; \\ \alpha + \beta + \lambda, \alpha + \sigma; \end{array} \frac{-4z}{(1-z)^2}\right] \quad (97)$$

$$(\alpha + \beta + \lambda, \alpha + \lambda, \alpha + \sigma \in \mathbb{C} \setminus \mathbb{Z}_{\leq 0};$$
$$|z| < 1, |z|^2/\{4|1-z|\} < 1, |\arg(1-z)| < \pi).$$

Applying the reduction Formula (22) to the left-hand side of (97), we obtain a transformation formula for $_3F_2$:

$$(1-z)^{1-\alpha-\beta-\lambda-\sigma} {}_3F_2\left[\begin{array}{c} \alpha, \frac{\alpha+\beta+\lambda+\sigma-1}{2}, \frac{\alpha+\beta+\lambda+\sigma}{2}; \\ \alpha + \beta + \lambda, \alpha + \sigma; \end{array} \frac{-4z}{(1-z)^2}\right]$$
$$= {}_3F_2\left[\begin{array}{c} \lambda + \beta, \alpha + \beta + \lambda + \sigma - 1, \sigma; \\ \alpha + \beta + \lambda, \alpha + \sigma; \end{array} z\right] \quad (98)$$

$$(\alpha + \beta + \lambda, \alpha + \sigma \in \mathbb{C} \setminus \mathbb{Z}_{\leq 0};$$
$$|z| < 1, |z|^2/\{4|1-z|\} < 1, |\arg(1-z)| < \pi),$$

which is a transformation formula of the type in (8) due to Whipple.

**Example 20.** *Putting $D = E = 0$ and $\sigma = \gamma - \alpha - \beta - \lambda + 1$ in (52) and using the binomial theorem (11), we deduce a reduction formula:*

$$F_{1:1;1}^{1:2;2}\left[\begin{array}{c} \beta + \lambda : \alpha, 1 - \lambda; \lambda, \gamma - \alpha; \\ \alpha + \lambda : \gamma - \beta - \lambda + 1; \beta + \lambda; \end{array} z, z\right]$$
$$= (1-z)^{-\gamma} {}_4F_3\left[\begin{array}{c} \alpha, \frac{\gamma}{2}, \frac{\gamma+1}{2}, \gamma - \beta; \\ \alpha + \lambda, \gamma - \beta - \lambda + 1, \gamma; \end{array} \frac{-4z}{(1-z)^2}\right] \quad (99)$$

$$(\alpha + \lambda, \gamma - \beta - \lambda + 1, \gamma, \beta + \lambda \in \mathbb{C} \setminus \mathbb{Z}_{\leq 0};$$
$$|z| < 1, |z|^2/\{4|1-z|\} < 1, |\arg(1-z)| < \pi).$$

**Example 21.** *Additionally, we can derive numerous reduction and transformation formulas by specializing the parameters in (52). For instance,*

(i) *Putting $(D = E = 0, \lambda = \gamma - \beta)$ or $(D = E = 0, \sigma = 1 - \beta)$ in (52) and using the binomial theorem (11), we can derive reduction formulas for $F_{1:1;1}^{1:2;2}$ of the similar type in (99).*

(ii) *Putting $(D = E = 0, \sigma = 0)$ or $(D = E = 0, \beta = 0)$ or $(D = E = 0, \lambda = 0)$ or $(D = E = 0, \gamma = \alpha)$ in (52) and using the binomial theorem (11) and the reduction Formula (22), we can attain certain transformation formulas of the type (8) due to Whipple.*

**Example 22.** (i) *It is interesting to recall a transformation formula for the Kampé de Fériet function (see [67], Equation (3.3)):*

$$F_{1:1;1}^{1:2;2}\left[\begin{matrix} b: & a,c; & a',c'; \\ c+c': & b; & b; \end{matrix} x,y\right]$$
$$= (1-x)^{-a}(1-y)^{-a'} F_{1:1;1}^{1:2;2}\left[\begin{matrix} b: & a,c; & a',c'; \\ c+c': & b; & b; \end{matrix} \frac{x}{1-x}, \frac{y}{1-y}\right], \tag{100}$$

*which can be used to provide some suitably altered formulas of (71), (73), (81), (83), (84), (86), (96), and (99). Additionally, Karlsson [46] (see also [30,47], [68], Equation (15)) presented a reduction formula from $F_{q:1;...;1}^{p:2;...;2}$ with equal variables and two more parameters per variable having certain relations to a single variable $_{p+2}F_{q+1}$.*

(ii) *Liu and Wang provided a number of reduction formulas for $F_{1:0;1}^{1:1;2}[z,z]$ in [48] (Equations (2.4), (2.11), (2.12), (2.13)), which are found to be distinct from (72) and (77).*

## 6. Summation Formulas for Kampé de Fériet and $_{p+1}F_p$

This section demonstrates specific general summation formulas for the Kampé de Fériet and $_{p+1}F_p$ with specified parameters and arguments $1, -1, \frac{1}{2}, -\frac{1}{4}, -\frac{1}{8}$, and $-\frac{1}{16}$, among many others.

**Instance 1.** *Putting $\alpha = a, \beta = b, \gamma = \frac{a+b+j+1}{2}$, and $z = \frac{1}{2}$ in (65) and using (27) and (28), we obtain the following general summation formula for $_4F_3(1)$:*

$$_4F_3\left[\begin{matrix} a,b,\frac{a+b}{2},\frac{a+b+1}{2}; \\ a+b,\frac{a+b+j+1}{2},\frac{a+b-j+1}{2}; \end{matrix} 1\right] = \left\{\frac{2^{b-1}\Gamma\left(\frac{a+b+j+1}{2}\right)\Gamma\left(\frac{a-b-j+1}{2}\right)}{\Gamma(b)\Gamma\left(\frac{a-b+j+1}{2}\right)}\right.$$
$$\times \sum_{r=0}^{j}(-1)^r\binom{j}{r}\frac{\Gamma\left(\frac{b+r}{2}\right)}{\Gamma\left(\frac{a+r-j+1}{2}\right)}\right\}\left\{\frac{2^{b-1}\Gamma\left(\frac{a+b-j+1}{2}\right)}{\Gamma(b)}\sum_{r=0}^{j}\binom{j}{r}\frac{\Gamma\left(\frac{b+r}{2}\right)}{\Gamma\left(\frac{a+r-j+1}{2}\right)}\right\}, \tag{101}$$

*where $j \in \mathbb{Z}_{\geq 0}$.*

**Instance 2.** *Putting $\alpha = a, \beta = 1 - a + j, \gamma = b$, and $z = \frac{1}{2}$ in (65) and using (29), we gain*

$$_4F_3\left[\begin{matrix} a, 1-a+j, \frac{1+j}{2}, \frac{2+j}{2}; \\ b, 1+j, 2+j-b; \end{matrix} 1\right]$$
$$= \left\{\frac{2^{j-a}\Gamma(a-j)\Gamma(b)}{\Gamma(a)\Gamma(b-a)}\sum_{r=0}^{j}(-1)^r\binom{j}{r}\frac{\Gamma\left(\frac{b-a+r}{2}\right)}{\Gamma\left(\frac{b+a+r}{2}-j\right)}\right\} \tag{102}$$
$$\times \left\{\frac{2^{j-a}\Gamma(a-j)\Gamma(2+j-b)}{\Gamma(a)\Gamma(2+j-b-a)}\sum_{r=0}^{j}(-1)^r\binom{j}{r}\frac{\Gamma\left(\frac{2+j-b-a+r}{2}\right)}{\Gamma\left(\frac{2+j-b+a+r}{2}-i\right)}\right\},$$

*where $j \in \mathbb{Z}_{\geq 0}$.*

**Instance 3.** Putting $\alpha = a$, $\beta = 1 - a + j$, $\gamma = 2a - j + k$, and $z = -1$ in (76) and using (25) and (29), we attain

$$_4F_3\left[\begin{array}{c} a, 1-a+j, a-j+k, 3a-2j+k-1; \\ 2a-j+k, \frac{2a-j+k}{2}, \frac{1+2a-j+k}{2}; \end{array} -\frac{1}{8}\right] = \left\{\frac{2^{k-2+2a-2j}}{\Gamma(1-a+j)}\right.$$

$$\times \frac{\Gamma(1-a+j-k)\Gamma(2a-j+k)}{\Gamma(3a-2j+k-1)} \sum_{r=0}^{k}(-1)^r\binom{k}{r}\frac{\Gamma\left(\frac{a+r+k+1}{2}-1+a-j\right)}{\Gamma\left(\frac{a+r-k+1}{2}\right)}\right\} \quad (103)$$

$$\times \left\{\frac{2^{j-a}\Gamma(a-j)\Gamma(2a-j+k)}{\Gamma(a)\Gamma(a-j+k)} \sum_{r=0}^{j}(-1)^r\binom{j}{r}\frac{\Gamma\left(\frac{a-j+r+k}{2}\right)}{\Gamma\left(\frac{3a-j+r+k}{2}-j\right)}\right\},$$

where $j, k \in \mathbb{Z}_{\geqslant 0}$.

**Instance 4.** Putting $\alpha = a$, $\beta = 1 - a - j$, $\gamma = 2a + j + i$, and $z = -1$ in (76) and using (25) and (30), we acquire

$$_4F_3\left[\begin{array}{c} a, 1-a-j, a+j+k, 3a+2j+k-1; \\ 2a+j+k, \frac{2a+j+k}{2}, \frac{1+2a+j+k}{2}; \end{array} -\frac{1}{8}\right] = \left\{\frac{2^{k-2+2a+2j}}{\Gamma(1-a-j)}\right.$$

$$\times \frac{\Gamma(1-a-j-k)\Gamma(2a+j+k)}{\Gamma(3a+2j+k-1)} \sum_{r=0}^{k}(-1)^r\binom{k}{r}\frac{\Gamma\left(\frac{a+r+k+1}{2}-1+a+j\right)}{\Gamma\left(\frac{a+r-k+1}{2}\right)}\right\} \quad (104)$$

$$\times \left\{\frac{2^{-j-a}\Gamma(2a+j+k)}{\Gamma(a+j+k)} \sum_{r=0}^{j}\binom{j}{r}\frac{\Gamma\left(\frac{a+j+r+k}{2}\right)}{\Gamma\left(\frac{3a+j+r+k}{2}\right)}\right\},$$

where $j, k \in \mathbb{Z}_{\geqslant 0}$.

**Instance 5.** Putting $\alpha = a$, $\beta = 1 - a + j$, $\gamma = 2a - j - k$, and $z = -1$ in (76) and using (26) and (29), we derive

$$_4F_3\left[\begin{array}{c} a, 1-a+j, a-j-k, 3a-2j-k-1; \\ 2a-j-k, \frac{2a-j-k}{2}, \frac{1+2a-j-k}{2}; \end{array} -\frac{1}{8}\right]$$

$$= \left\{\frac{2^{-k-2+2a-2j}\Gamma(2a-j-k)}{\Gamma(3a-2j-k-1)} \sum_{r=0}^{k}\binom{k}{r}\frac{\Gamma\left(\frac{a+r-k+1}{2}-1+a-j\right)}{\Gamma\left(\frac{a+r-k+1}{2}\right)}\right\} \quad (105)$$

$$\times \left\{\frac{2^{j-a}\Gamma(a-j)\Gamma(2a-j-k)}{\Gamma(a-j-k)\Gamma(a)} \sum_{r=0}^{j}(-1)^r\binom{j}{r}\frac{\Gamma\left(\frac{a-j+r-k}{2}\right)}{\Gamma\left(\frac{3a-j+r-k}{2}-j\right)}\right\},$$

where $j, k \in \mathbb{Z}_{\geqslant 0}$.

**Instance 6.** Putting $\alpha = a$, $\beta = 1 - a - j$, $\gamma = 2a + j - k$, and $z = -1$ in (76) and using (26) and (30), we obtain

$$_4F_3\left[\begin{array}{c} a, 1-a-j, a+j-k, 3a+2j-k-1; \\ 2a+j-k, \frac{2a+j-k}{2}, \frac{1+2a+j-k}{2}; \end{array} -\frac{1}{8}\right]$$

$$= \left\{\frac{2^{-k-2+2a+2j}\Gamma(2a+j-k)}{\Gamma(-1+3a+2j-k)} \sum_{r=0}^{k}\binom{k}{r}\frac{\Gamma\left(\frac{a+r-k+1}{2}-1+a+j\right)}{\Gamma\left(\frac{a+r-k+1}{2}\right)}\right\} \quad (106)$$

$$\times \left\{\frac{2^{-j-a}\Gamma(2a+j-k)}{\Gamma(a+j-k)} \sum_{r=0}^{j}\binom{j}{r}\frac{\Gamma\left(\frac{a+j+r-k}{2}\right)}{\Gamma\left(\frac{3a+j+r-k}{2}\right)}\right\},$$

where $j, k \in \mathbb{Z}_{\geq 0}$.

**Instance 7.** Putting $\alpha = a$, $\delta = \beta = b$, $\gamma = 1 + a - b + j$, and $z = -1$ in (88) and using (25), we obtain

$$F_{1:2;0}^{2:2;0}\left(\begin{array}{c}[2b:2,1],[a:1,1]: \quad [b:1],[1-b+j:1]; \quad -; \\ [1+a-b+j:2,1]: \quad [1+a-b+j:1],[\frac{2b+1}{2}:1]; \quad -;\end{array}-\frac{1}{4},-1\right)$$
$$= \left\{\frac{2^{j-2b}\Gamma(b-j)\Gamma(1+a-b+j)}{\Gamma(b)\Gamma(a-2b+j+1)}\sum_{r=0}^{j}(-1)^r\binom{j}{r}\frac{\Gamma\left(\frac{a+r+j+1}{2}-b\right)}{\Gamma\left(\frac{a+r-j+1}{2}\right)}\right\}^2, \tag{107}$$

where $j \in \mathbb{Z}_{\geq 0}$.

**Instance 8.** Putting $\alpha = a$, $\delta = \beta = b$, $\gamma = 1 + a - b - j$, and $z = -1$ in (88) and using (26), we obtain

$$F_{1:2;0}^{2:2;0}\left(\begin{array}{c}[2b:2,1],[a:1,1]: \quad [b:1],[1-b-j:1]; \quad -; \\ [1+a-b-j:2,1]: \quad [1+a-b-j:1],[\frac{2b+1}{2}:1]; \quad -;\end{array}-\frac{1}{4},-1\right)$$
$$= \left\{\frac{2^{-j-2b}\Gamma(1+a-b-j)}{\Gamma(a-2b-j+1)}\sum_{r=0}^{j}\binom{j}{r}\frac{\Gamma\left(\frac{a+r-j+1}{2}-b\right)}{\Gamma\left(\frac{a+r-j+1}{2}\right)}\right\}^2, \tag{108}$$

where $j \in \mathbb{Z}_{\geq 0}$.

**Instance 9.** Putting $\alpha = a$, $\delta = \beta = b$, $\gamma = \frac{1+a+b+j}{2}$, and $z = \frac{1}{2}$ in (88) and using (27), we gain

$$F_{1:2;0}^{2:2;0}\left(\begin{array}{c}[2b:2,1],[a:1,1]: \quad [b:1],[\frac{1-a+b+j}{2}:1]; \quad -; \\ [\frac{1+a+b+j}{2}:2,1]: \quad [\frac{1+a+b+j}{2}:1],[\frac{2b+1}{2}:1]; \quad -;\end{array}-\frac{1}{16},\frac{1}{2}\right)$$
$$= \left\{\frac{2^{b-1}\Gamma(\frac{1+a+b+j}{2})\Gamma(\frac{1+a-b-j}{2})}{\Gamma(b)\Gamma(\frac{1+a-b+j}{2})}\sum_{r=0}^{j}(-1)^r\binom{j}{r}\frac{\Gamma\left(\frac{b+r}{2}\right)}{\Gamma\left(\frac{a+r-j+1}{2}\right)}\right\}^2, \tag{109}$$

where $j \in \mathbb{Z}_{\geq 0}$.

**Instance 10.** Putting $\alpha = a$, $\delta = \beta = b$, $\gamma = \frac{1+a+b-j}{2}$, and $z = \frac{1}{2}$ in (88) and using (28), we attain

$$F_{1:2;0}^{2:2;0}\left(\begin{array}{c}[2b:2,1],[a:1,1]: \quad [b:1],[\frac{1-a+b-j}{2}:1]; \quad -; \\ [\frac{1+a+b-j}{2}:2,1]: \quad [\frac{1+a+b-j}{2}:1],[\frac{2b+1}{2}:1]; \quad -;\end{array}-\frac{1}{16},\frac{1}{2}\right)$$
$$= \left\{\frac{2^{b-1}\Gamma(\frac{1+a+b-j}{2})}{\Gamma(b)}\sum_{r=0}^{j}\binom{j}{r}\frac{\Gamma\left(\frac{b+r}{2}\right)}{\Gamma\left(\frac{a+r-j+1}{2}\right)}\right\}^2, \tag{110}$$

where $j \in \mathbb{Z}_{\geq 0}$.

**Instance 11.** Putting $\alpha = a$, $\delta = \beta = 1 - a + j$, $\gamma = b$, and $z = \frac{1}{2}$ in (88) and using (29), we acquire

$$F_{1:2;0}^{2:2;0}\left(\begin{array}{c}[2-2a+2j:2,1],[a:1,1]: \quad [1-a+j:1],[b-a:1]; \quad -; \\ [b:2,1]: \quad [b:1],[\frac{3-2a+2j}{2}:1]; \quad -;\end{array}-\frac{1}{16},\frac{1}{2}\right)$$
$$= \left\{\frac{2^{j-a}\Gamma(a-j)\Gamma(b)}{\Gamma(a)\Gamma(b-a)}\sum_{r=0}^{j}(-1)^r\binom{j}{r}\frac{\Gamma\left(\frac{b-a+r}{2}\right)}{\Gamma\left(\frac{b+a+r}{2}-j\right)}\right\}^2, \tag{111}$$

where $j \in \mathbb{Z}_{\geq 0}$.

**Instance 12.** Putting $\alpha = a$, $\delta = \beta = 1 - a - j$, $\gamma = b$, and $z = \frac{1}{2}$ in (88) and using (30), we derive

$$F_{1:2;0}^{2:2;0}\left(\begin{array}{c}[2-2a-2j:2,1],[a:1,1]:\\{}[b:2,1]:\end{array}\begin{array}{c}[1-a-j:1],[b-a:1];\\{}[b:1],[\frac{3-2a-2j}{2}:1];\end{array}\begin{array}{c}-;\\-;\end{array}-\frac{1}{16},\frac{1}{2}\right)$$

$$= \left\{\frac{2^{-j-a}\Gamma(b)}{\Gamma(b-a)}\sum_{r=0}^{j}\binom{j}{r}\frac{\Gamma\left(\frac{b-a+r}{2}\right)}{\Gamma\left(\frac{b+a+r}{2}\right)}\right\}^{2}, \tag{112}$$

where $j \in \mathbb{Z}_{\geqslant 0}$.

**Instance 13.** Putting $\alpha = \frac{a}{2}$, $\beta = \frac{b}{2}$, and $z = \frac{1}{2}$ in (66) and using the classical Kummer second summation theorem (the case $m = 0$ of (28)), with the aid of a duplication formula for the gamma function (see, e.g., [5], p. 6),

$$\Gamma\left(\frac{1}{2}\right)\Gamma(2z) = 2^{2z-1}\Gamma(z)\Gamma\left(z+\frac{1}{2}\right), \tag{113}$$

we obtain

$$_3F_2\left[\begin{array}{c}a,b,\frac{a+b}{2};\\a+b,\frac{a+b+1}{2};\end{array}1\right] = \left\{\frac{\Gamma\left(\frac{1}{2}\right)\Gamma\left(\frac{a+b+1}{2}\right)}{\Gamma\left(\frac{a+1}{2}\right)\Gamma\left(\frac{b+1}{2}\right)}\right\}^{2}. \tag{114}$$

## 7. Concluding Remarks

In this article, we introduced three general double-series identities using Whipple transformations for $_4F_3$ and $_5F_4$ functions. By employing the left-sided Riemann–Liouville fractional integral on those results in Section 2, in Section 4, we showcased the potential to systematically derive additional identities of a similar nature through iterative processes. These identities were then utilized to derive transformation formulas between the Srivastava–Daoust double hypergeometric function (S–D function) and Kampé de Fériet's double hypergeometric function (KDF function) with equal arguments. We also demonstrated reduction formulas from the S–D function or KDF function to the $_pF_q$ function. Furthermore, we provided various general summation formulas for the $_pF_q$ and S–D function (or KDF function) with specific arguments. By following the steps presented in this article, additional reduction and summation formulas of similar types can be derived. We anticipate that these transformation and summation formulas, as well as those deducible from the same steps, will have applications in diverse fields, such as mathematical physics, statistics, and engineering sciences.

**Author Contributions:** Writing—original draft, M.I.Q., T.U.R.S., J.C. and A.H.B.; writing—review and editing, M.I.Q., T.U.R.S., J.C. and A.H.B. All authors have read and agreed to the published version of the manuscript.

**Funding:** This research received no external funding.

**Acknowledgments:** The authors wish to extend their heartfelt appreciation to the anonymous reviewers for their invaluable feedback. Their constructive and encouraging comments have greatly contributed to enhancing the quality of this paper.

**Conflicts of Interest:** The authors have no conflict of interest.

## References

1. Andrews, G.E.; Askey, R.; Roy, R. *Special Functions, Encyclopedia of Mathematics and its Applications 71*; Cambridge University Press: Cambridge, UK, 1999.
2. Bailey, W.N. *Generalized Hypergeometric Series*; Cambridge Math. Tract No. 32; Cambridge University Press: Cambridge, UK, 1935; Reprinted by Stechert-Hafner: New York, NY, USA, 1964.
3. Lebedev, N.N. *Special Functions and their Applications*; Silverman, R.A., Translator; Prentice-Hall, Inc.: Englewood Cliffs, NJ, USA, 1965.

4. Rainville, E.D. *Special Functions*; The Macmillan Co., Inc.: New York, NY, USA, 1960; Reprinted by Chelsea Publishing Co.: Bronx, NY, USA, 1971.
5. Srivastava, H.M.; Choi, J. *Zeta and q-Zeta Functions and Associated Series Integrals*; Elsevier Science Publishers: Amsterdam, The Netherlands; London, UK; New York, NY, USA, 2012.
6. Srivastava, H.M.; Manocha, H.L. *A Treatise on Generating Functions*; Halsted Press (Ellis Horwood Limited): Chichester, UK; John Wiley and Sons: New York, NY, USA; Chichester, UK; Brisbane, Australia; Toronto, ON, Canada, 1984.
7. Srivastava, H.M.; Karlsson, P.W. *Multiple Gaussian Hypergeometric Series*; Halsted Press (Ellis Horwood Limited): Chichester, UK; John Wiley and Sons: New York, NY, USA; Chichester, UK; Brisbane, Australia; Toronto, ON, Canada, 1985.
8. Appell, P.; de Fériet, J.K. *Fonctions Hypergéométriques et Hypersphériques-Polynômes d' Hermite*; Gauthier-Villars: Paris, France, 1926.
9. Humbert, P. The confluent hypergeometric functions of two variables. *Proc. R. Soc. Edinb.* **1920**, *4*, 73–96. [CrossRef]
10. Erdélyi, A.; Magnus, W.; Oberhettinger, F.; Tricomi, F.G. *Higher Transcendental Functions*; McGraw-Hill Book Co., Inc.: New York, NY, USA; Toronto, ON, Canada; London, UK, 1953; Volume I.
11. de Fériet, J.K. Les Functions hypergéométriques d'ordre supérieur à deux variables. *C. R. Acad. Sci.* **1921**, *173*, 401–404.
12. Burchnall, J.L.; Chaundy, T.W. Expansions of Appell's double hypergeometric functions. *Q. J. Math.* **1940**, *11*, 249–270. [CrossRef]
13. Burchnall, J.L.; Chaundy, T.W. Expansions of Appell's double hypergeometric functions (II). *Q. J. Math.* **1941**, *12*, 112–128. [CrossRef]
14. Srivastava, H.M.; Panda, R. An integral representation for the product of two Jacobi polynomials. *J. Lond. Math. Soc.* **1976**, *12*, 419–425. [CrossRef]
15. Hái, N.T.; Marichev, O.I.; Srivastava, H.M. A note on the convergence of certain families of multiple hypergeometric series. *J. Math. Anal. Appl.* **1992**, *164*, 104–115. [CrossRef]
16. Srivastava, H.M.; Daoust, M.C. On Eulerian integrals associated with Kampé de Fériet function. *Publ. Inst. Math.* **1969**, *9*, 199–202.
17. Srivastava, H.M.; Daoust, M.C. Certain generalized Neumann expansions associated with the Kampé de Fériet's function. *Nederl. Akad. Wetensch. Proc. Ser. A = Indag. Math.* **1969**, *31*, 449–457.
18. Srivastava, H.M.; Daoust, M.C. A note on the convergence of Kampé de Fériet's double hypergeometric series. *Math. Nachr.* **1972**, *53*, 151–159. [CrossRef]
19. Buschman, R.G.; Srivastava, H.M. Series identities and reducibility of Kampé de Fériet functions. *Math. Proc. Camb. Philos. Soc.* **1982**, *91*, 435–440. [CrossRef]
20. Carlitz, L. Summation of a double hypergeometric series. *Mat. Catania* **1967**, *22*, 138–142.
21. Chan, W.-C.C.; Chen, K.-Y.; Chyan, C.-J.; Srivastava, H.M. Some multiple hypergeometric transformations and associated reduction formulas. *J. Math. Anal. Appl.* **2004**, *294*, 418–437. [CrossRef]
22. Chen, K.-Y.; Srivastava, H.M. Series identities and associated families of generating functions. *J. Math. Anal. Appl.* **2005**, *311*, 582–599. [CrossRef]
23. Choi, J.; Rathie, A.K. On the reducibility of Kampé de Fériet function. *Honam Math. J.* **2014**, *36*, 345–355. [CrossRef]
24. Choi, J.; Rathie, A.K. Reducibility of the Kampé de Fériet function. *Appl. Math. Sci.* **2015**, *9*, 4219–4232. [CrossRef]
25. Choi, J.; Rathie, A.K. General summation formulas for the Kampé de Fériet function. *Montes Taures J. Pure Appl. Math.* **2019**, *1*, 107–128.
26. Chu, W.-C.; Srivastava, H.M. Ordinary and basic bivariate hypergeometric transformations associated with the Appell and Kampé de Fériet functions. *J. Comput. Appl. Math.* **2003**, *156*, 355–370. [CrossRef]
27. Cvijović, D.; Miller, A.R. A reduction formula for the Kampé de Fériet function. *Appl. Math. Lett.* **2010**, *23*, 769–771. [CrossRef]
28. Exton, H. On the reducibility of the Kampé de Fériet function. *J. Comput. Appl. Math.* **1997**, *83*, 119–121. [CrossRef]
29. Jain, R.N. Sum of a double hypergeometric series. *Mat. Catania* **1966**, *21*, 300–301.
30. Karlsson, P.W. Some reduction formulae for double power series and Kampé de Fériet functions. *Nederl. Akad. Wetensch. Proc. Ser. A = Indag. Math.* **1984**, *46*, 31–36.
31. Kim, Y.S. On certain reducibility of Kampé de Fériet function. *Honam Math. J.* **2009**, *31*, 167–176. [CrossRef]
32. Krupnikov, E.D. *A Register of Computer Oriented Reduction of Identities for Kampé de Fériet Function*; Novosibirsk, Russia, 1996.
33. Rakha, M.A.; Awad, M.M.; Rathie, A.K. On a reducibility of the Kampé de Fériet function. *Math. Methods Appl. Sci.* **2015**, *38*, 2600–2605. [CrossRef]
34. Saran, S. Reducibility of generalized Kampé de Fériet function. *Ganita* **1980**, *31*, 89–97.
35. Shanker, O. An integral involving the G-function and Kampé de Fériet function. *Proc. Camb. Philos. Soc.* **1968**, *64*, 1041–1044. [CrossRef]
36. Shanker, O.; Saran, S. Reducibility of Kampé de Fériet function. *Ganita* **1970**, *21*, 9–16.
37. Sharma, B.L. Sum of a double series. *Proc. Am. Math. Soc.* **1975**, *52*, 136–138. [CrossRef]
38. Sharma, B.L.; Abiodun, F.A. Some new summation formulae for hypergeometric series of two variable. *Rend. Istit. Mat. Univ. Trieste* **1976**, *8*, 94–100. Available online: http://hdl.handle.net/10077/6500 (accessed on 13 September 2023).
39. Singal, R.P. Transformation formulae for the modified Kampé de Fériet function. *Math. Stud.* **1972**, *40*, 327–330.
40. der Jeugt, J.V. Transformation formula for a double Clausenian hypergeometric series, its $q$-analogue, and its invariance group. *J. Comput. Appl. Math.* **2002**, *139*, 65–73. [CrossRef]
41. der Jeugt, J.V.; Pitre, S.N.; Rao, K.S. Multiple hypergeometric functions and $g$-$j$ coefficients. *J. Phys. A Math. Gen.* **1994**, *27*, 5251–5264. [CrossRef]

42. der Jeugt, J.V.; Pitre, S.N.; Rao, K.S. Transformation and summation formulas for double hypergeometric series. *J. Comput. Appl. Math.* **1997**, *83*, 185–193. [CrossRef]
43. Srivastava, H.M. A note on certain summation theorems for multiple hypergeometric series. *Simon Stevin* **1978**, *52*, 97–109.
44. Srivastava, H.M. Some generalizations of Carlson's identity. *Boll. Union Mat. Ital.* **1981**, *18*, 138–143.
45. Whipple, F.J.W. Some transformations of generalized hypergeometric series. *Proc. Lond. Math. Soc.* **1927**, *26*, 257–272. [CrossRef]
46. Karlsson, P.W. Reduction of certain multiple hypergeometric functions. *Nederl. Akad. Wetensch. Proc. Ser. A = Indag. Math.* **1982**, *44*, 285–287. [CrossRef]
47. Karlsson, P.W. Some reducible generalized Kampé de Fériet functions. *J. Math. Anal. Appl.* **1983**, *96*, 546–550. [CrossRef]
48. Liu, H.; Wang, W. Transformation and summation formulae for Kampé de Fériet series. *J. Math. Anal. Appl.* **2014**, *409*, 100–110. [CrossRef]
49. Sheppard, W.F. Summation of the coefficients of some terminating hypergeometric series. *Proc. Lond. Math. Soc.* **1912**, *10*, 469–478. [CrossRef]
50. Slater, L.J. *Generalized Hypergeometric Functions*; Cambridge University Press: Cambridge, UK; London, UK; New York, NY, USA, 1966.
51. Qureshi, M.I.; Paris, R.B.; Malik, S.H.; Shah, T.R. Two reduction formulas for the Srivastava-Daoust double hypergeometric function. *Palest. J. Math.* **2023**, *12*, 181–186.
52. Gessel, I.; Stanton, D. Strange evaluations of hypergeometric series. *SIAM J. Math. Anal.* **1982**, *13*, 295–308. [CrossRef]
53. Andrews, G.E. Connection coefficient problems and partitions. In *AMS Proceedings Symposia in Pure Mathematics 34*; Ray-Chaudhuri, D., Ed.; American Mathematical Society: Providence, RI, USA, 1979; pp. 1–24.
54. Whipple, F.J.W. Well-poised series and other generalized hypergeometric series. *Proc. Lond. Math. Soc.* **1926**, *25*, 525–544. [CrossRef]
55. Bailey, W.N. Products of generalized hypergeometric series. *Proc. Lond. Math. Soc.* **1928**, *28*, 242–254. . [CrossRef]
56. Bailey, W.N. Some theorems concerning products of hypergeometric series. *Proc. Lond. Math. Soc.* **1935**, *38*, 377–384. [CrossRef]
57. Exton, H. *Multiple Hypergeometric Functions and Applications*; Halsted Press (Ellis Horwood Limited): Chichester, UK; John Wiley and Sons: New York, NY, USA; Chichester, UK; Sydney, Australia; Toronto, ON, Canada, 1976.
58. Prudnikov, A.P.; Brychkov, Y.A.; Marichev, O.I. *Integrals and Series*; Gould, G.G., Translator; More Special Functions: Nauka Moscow, Russia, 1986; Volume III. (In Russian); Gordon and Breach Science Publishers: New York, NY, USA; Philadelphia, PA, USA; London, UK; Paris, France; Montreux, Switzerland; Tokyo, Japan; Melbourne, Australia, 1990.
59. Rakha, M.A.; Rathie, A.K. Generalizations of classical summation theorems for the series $_2F_1$ and $_3F_2$ with applications. *Integral Transform. Spec. Funct.* **2011**, *22*, 823–840. [CrossRef]
60. Choi, J.; Qureshi, M.I.; Bhat, A.H.; Majid, J. Reduction formulas for generalized hypergeometric series associated with new sequences and applications. *Fractal Fract.* **2021**, *5*, 150. [CrossRef]
61. Brychkov, Y.A. *Handbook of Special Functions, Derivatives, Integrals, Series and Other Formulas*; CRC Press: Boca Raton, FL, USA; Taylor & Fancis Group: Abingdon, UK; London, UK; New York, NY, USA, 2008.
62. Lavoie, J.L.; Grondin, F.; Rathie, A.K. Generalizations of Whipple's theorem on the sum of a $_3F_2$. *J. Comput. Appl. Math.* **1996**, *72*, 293–300. [CrossRef]
63. Kilbas, A.A.; Srivastava, H.M.; Trujillo, J.J. *Theory and Applications of Fractional Differential Equations*; Elsevier: North-Holland, The Netherlands, 2006.
64. Srivastava, H.M. Certain double integrals involving yypergeometric functions. *Jñānābha Sect. A* **1971**, *1*, 1–10.
65. Clausen, T. Ueber die Fälle, wenn die Reihe von der Form $y =$ etc. ein Quadrat von der Form $z =$ etc. hat. *J. Reine Angew. Math.* **1828**, *3*, 89–91. [CrossRef]
66. Orr, W.M.F. Theorems relating to the product of two hypergeometric series. *Trans. Camb. Philos. Soc.* **1899**, *17*, 1–15.
67. Carlitz, L. A summation theorem for double hypergeometric series. *Rend. Semin. Mat. Univ. Padova* **1967**, *37*, 230–233. Available online: http://www.numdam.org/item?id=RSMUP_1967__37__230_0 (accessed on 13 September 2023).
68. Srivastava, H.M. The sum of a multiple hypergeometric series. *Indag. Math.* **1977**, *80*, 448–452. [CrossRef]

**Disclaimer/Publisher's Note:** The statements, opinions and data contained in all publications are solely those of the individual author(s) and contributor(s) and not of MDPI and/or the editor(s). MDPI and/or the editor(s) disclaim responsibility for any injury to people or property resulting from any ideas, methods, instructions or products referred to in the content.

 *fractal and fractional*

Article
# Analytic Functions Related to a Balloon-Shaped Domain

Adeel Ahmad [1,†], Jianhua Gong [2,*,†], Isra Al-Shbeil [3,†], Akhter Rasheed [4,†], Asad Ali [1,†] and Saqib Hussain [4,†]

1. Department of Mathematics and Statistics, Hazara University Mansehra, Mansehra 21120, Pakistan; adeelayaz33@gmail.com (A.A.); asad_maths@hu.edu.pk (A.A.)
2. Department of Mathematical Sciences, United Arab Emirates University, Al Ain 15551, United Arab Emirates
3. Department of Mathematics, Faculty of Science, The University of Jordan, Amman 11942, Jordan; i.shbeil@ju.edu.jo
4. Department of Mathematics, COMSATS University Islamabad, Abbottabad 22060, Pakistan; akhter@cuiatd.edu.pk (A.R.); saqibhussain@cuiatd.edu.pk (S.H.)
* Correspondence: j.gong@uaeu.ac.ae
† These authors contributed equally to this work.

**Abstract:** One of the fundamental parts of Geometric Function Theory is the study of analytic functions in different domains with critical geometrical interpretations. This article defines a new generalized domain obtained based on the quotient of two analytic functions. We derive various properties of the new class of normalized analytic functions $\mathcal{X}$ defined in the new domain, including the sharp estimates for the coefficients $a_2, a_3$, and $a_4$, and for three second-order and third-order Hankel determinants, $\mathcal{H}_{2,1}\mathcal{X}, \mathcal{H}_{2,2}\mathcal{X}$, and $\mathcal{H}_{3,1}\mathcal{X}$. The optimality of each obtained estimate is given as well.

**Keywords:** analytic function; subordination; sharp upper bound; Hankel determinant; generalized domain

## 1. Introduction

Let $\mathcal{A}$ be the class of all analytic functions $\mathcal{X}$ defined in the open unit disc $\mathbf{U} = \{z \in \mathbb{C} : |z| < 1\}$ with $\mathcal{X}(0) = 0$ and $\mathcal{X}'(0) = 1$. Thus, each analytic function in $\mathcal{A}$ has the following Taylor series representation

$$\mathcal{X}(z) = z + \sum_{t=2}^{\infty} a_t z^t. \qquad (1)$$

Let $\mathcal{S}$ be the subclass of all analytic functions in $\mathcal{A}$ that are univalent in $\mathbf{U}$.

An analytic function $\mathcal{X}$ is said to be subordinate to an analytic function $\mathbf{g}$ in $\mathbf{U}$, denoted as $\mathcal{X} \prec \mathbf{g}$, if there exists a Schwarz function $\xi$ that is analytic in $\mathbf{U}$ with $\xi(0) = 0$ and $|\xi(z)| < 1$, such that $\mathcal{X}(z) = \mathbf{g}(\xi(z))$. In particular (see [1]), if $\mathbf{g}$ is univalent in $\mathbf{U}$, then $\mathcal{X} \prec \mathbf{g}$ if and only if

$$\mathcal{X}(0) = \mathbf{g}(0) \quad \text{and} \quad \mathcal{X}(\mathbf{U}) \subset \mathbf{g}(\mathbf{U}).$$

Using the concept of subordination, many subclasses have been defined and studied, such as $\mathcal{S}^*, \mathcal{C}, \mathcal{K}$ and $\mathcal{R}$ of starlike, convex, close to convex, and functions with bounded turnings, respectively. See [2–6] for the new results about more subclasses.

For two analytic functions $\mathcal{X}$ and $\zeta$ in $\mathcal{A}$ with the series representation of $\mathcal{X}$ given in (1) and $\zeta(z) = z + \sum_{t=2}^{\infty} b_t z^t$, the convolution (Hadamard product) $\mathcal{X} * \zeta$ is defined by

$$(\mathcal{X} * \zeta)(z) = z + \sum_{t=2}^{\infty} a_t b_t z^t = (\zeta * \mathcal{X})(z). \qquad (2)$$

Shanmugam [7] generalized the idea of Padmanabhan et al. [8] and introduced the general form of function class $\mathcal{S}_h^*(\varphi)$ as follows

$$\mathcal{S}_h^*(\varphi) = \left\{ \mathcal{X} \in \mathcal{A} : \frac{z(\mathcal{X} * h)'(z)}{(\mathcal{X} * h)(z)} \prec \varphi(z), \quad z \in \mathbf{U} \right\},$$

where $h$ is a fixed function in $\mathcal{A}$ and $\varphi$ is a convex univalent function on $\mathbf{U}$ with $\varphi(0) = 1$ and $Re(\varphi(z)) > 0$.

Ma and Minda [9] defined a more general form of function class $\mathcal{S}^*(\varphi)$ by applying for some restrictions $h(z) = \frac{z}{1-z}$ (and hence $\mathcal{X} * h = \mathcal{X}$) with $\varphi(0) = 1$ and $\varphi'(0) > 0$. The generic form of Ma and Minda-type class of starlike functions is defined as

$$\mathcal{S}^*(\varphi) = \left\{ \mathcal{X} \in \mathcal{A} : \frac{z\mathcal{X}'(z)}{\mathcal{X}(z)} \prec \varphi(z), \quad z \in \mathbf{U} \right\}. \tag{3}$$

In recent years, many authors have established important subfamilies of analytic functions by varying $\varphi(z)$ in $\mathcal{S}^*(\varphi)$, and they proved significant geometric properties of those subfamilies. For details, see [10–14].

We discuss the following two classes that have some interesting geometric properties.

(i) For $\varphi_1(z) = \sqrt{1+z}$, the class $\mathcal{S}^*(\varphi)$ becomes $\mathcal{S}_L^*$, which was introduced by Sokol and Stankiewicz [15], and it contains those functions $\mathcal{X} \in \mathcal{A}$ such that $\frac{z\mathcal{X}'(z)}{\mathcal{X}(z)}$ lies in the region bounded by the right half of the lemniscate of Bernoulli defined by $|z^2 - 1| < 1$.

(ii) For $\varphi_2(z) = \frac{2}{1+e^{-z}}$, the class $\mathcal{S}^*(\varphi)$ becomes $\mathcal{S}_{sig}^*$, which was defined and investigated by Geol et al. [16]. Geometrically, a function $\mathcal{X} \in \mathcal{S}_{sig}^*$ if and only if $\frac{z\mathcal{X}'(z)}{\mathcal{X}(z)}$ lies in the region defined by $\{w \in \mathbb{C} : |\log(\frac{w}{2-w})| < 1\}$.

By taking inspiration from all of the previous works mentioned, we introduce the following new class of analytic functions by using the quotient of $\varphi_1(z) = \sqrt{1+z}$ and $\varphi_2(z) = \frac{2}{1+e^{-z}}$.

**Definition 1.** *Let $\mathcal{X} \in \mathcal{A}$, given in (1). We say $\mathcal{X} \in \mathcal{R}_{sl}$ if it satisfies the following condition*

$$\mathcal{X}'(z) \prec \frac{2\sqrt{1+z}}{1+e^{-z}}, \quad z \in \mathbf{U}. \tag{4}$$

Geometrically, each $\mathcal{X} \in \mathcal{R}_{sl}$ maps the open unit disc into a balloon-shaped domain, which is symmetric about the real axis, as shown in the following Figure 1.

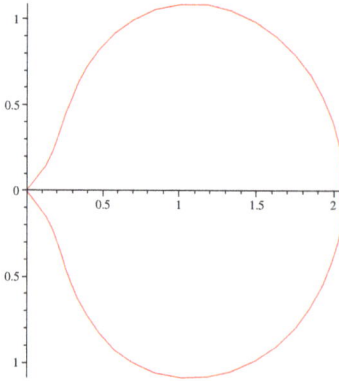

**Figure 1.** The geometry of the function $\phi(z) = \frac{2\sqrt{1+z}}{1+e^{-z}}$.

For $\mathcal{X} \in \mathcal{A}$ and $n, k \geq 0$, Pommerenke [17] defined the $k^{th}$ order Hankel determinant $\mathcal{H}_{k,n}$ by

$$\mathcal{H}_{k,n}(\mathcal{X}) = \begin{vmatrix} a_n & a_{n+1} & \cdots & a_{n+k-1} \\ a_{n+1} & a_{n+2} & \cdots & a_{n+k} \\ \cdot & \cdot & & \cdot \\ \cdot & \cdot & & \cdot \\ \cdot & \cdot & & \cdot \\ a_{n+k-1} & a_{n+k} & \cdots & a_{n+2(k-1)} \end{vmatrix}. \tag{5}$$

Recently, finding the sharp upper bounds of the Hankel determinants $\mathcal{H}_{k,n}(\mathcal{X})$ for certain $n$ and $k$ for various subfamilies of analytic functions has been identified as an interesting and important problem. Many researchers have observed sharp upper bounds of Hankel determinants for many subfamilies of analytic functions. In particular, the upper bounds of second and third-order Hankel determinants have been estimated in [18–23] for several subclasses of normalized analytic function.

Hayman [24] was the first to give the sharp inequality for $\mathcal{X} \in \mathcal{S}$, and subsequently proved that $|\mathcal{H}_{2,n}(\mathcal{X})| \leq \lambda\sqrt{n}$, where $\lambda > 0$. This inequality is further explained in [25] and showed that $|\mathcal{H}_{2,2}(\mathcal{X})| \leq \lambda$, where $1 \leq \lambda \leq \frac{11}{3}$.

Janteng et al. [26] determined the sharp bounds of $\mathcal{H}_{2,2}(\mathcal{X})$ for the subfamilies of $\mathcal{K}$, $\mathcal{S}^*$, and $\mathcal{R}$. Babalola [27] studied a third-order Hankel determinant for the subclasses of $\mathcal{S}^*$ and $\mathcal{C}$, while Zaprawa [28] amended Babalola's results and gave the following estimates, which it is believed may not be the best possible results.

$$|\mathcal{H}_{3,1}(\mathcal{X})| \leq \begin{cases} \frac{49}{540} & (\mathcal{X} \in \mathcal{K}), \\ 1 & (\mathcal{X} \in \mathcal{S}^*), \\ \frac{41}{60} & (\mathcal{X} \in \mathcal{R}). \end{cases}$$

Kwon et al. [29] improved this determinant for starlike functions as $|\mathcal{H}_{3,1}(\mathcal{X})| \leq \frac{8}{9}$. Zaprawa et al. [30] extended his work by estimating $|\mathcal{H}_{3,1}(\mathcal{X})| \leq \frac{5}{9}$ for $\mathcal{X} \in \mathcal{S}^*$.

Arif et al. [31] calculated the sharpness of the bounds of the coefficients and $\mathcal{H}_{3,1}(\mathcal{X})$ for a subfamily of starlike functions related to sigmoid functions; see [32] for the modified sigmoid functions. Orhan et al. [33] estimated the sharp Hankel determinants for a subfamily of analytic functions associated with the lemniscate of Bernoulli. Moreover, Shi et al. [34,35] estimated the sharpness of Hankel determinants for the functions with bounded turning associated with a petal-shaped domain and inverse functions, respectively.

Moreover, the estimation of various bounds can be considered for many classes of functions; for example, see [36–38].

It is natural to ask what the upper bounds for the analytic functions in the newly defined class $\mathcal{R}_{sl}$ related to the coefficients of the Taylor series representation (1) and Hankel determinants are.

The aim and novelty of this article are the sharp upper bounds of the modulus of the coefficients $a_2, a_3$, and $a_4$ and the second-order and third-order Hankel determinants, $\mathcal{H}_{2,1}\mathcal{X}, \mathcal{H}_{2,2}\mathcal{X}$, and $\mathcal{H}_{3,1}\mathcal{X}$, for the analytic functions in the new class $\mathcal{R}_{sl}$.

## 2. A Set of Lemmas

Let $\mathcal{P}$ represent the class of analytic functions $p$, such that $p(0) = 1$, $Re(p(z)) > 0$ for $z \in \mathbf{U}$, which has the following Taylor series form,

$$p(z) = 1 + \sum_{t=1}^{\infty} c_t z^t. \tag{6}$$

The subsequent Lemmas 1–4 will help to demonstrate our main findings, where $c_t, c_{t+k}$, and $c_{t+2k}$ for $t, k \in \mathbb{N}$ are coefficients of the Taylor series (6).

**Lemma 1** ([17]). *Let $p \in \mathcal{P}$. Then, the following inequalities hold true*

$$|c_t| \leq 2 \text{ for } t \geq 1, \tag{7}$$
$$|c_{t+k} - \rho c_t c_k| < 2 \text{ for } 0 \leq \rho \leq 1, \tag{8}$$
$$\left|c_{t+2k} - \rho c_t c_k^2\right| \leq 2(1+2\rho), \text{ for } 0 \leq \rho \leq 1, \tag{9}$$

*and*

$$\left|c_2 - \frac{c_1^2}{2}\right| \leq 2 - \frac{|c_1^2|}{2}. \tag{10}$$

**Lemma 2.** *Let $p \in \mathcal{P}$. Then there exists $q$, $\gamma$, and $\mu \in \mathbb{C}$ with $|q| \leq 1$, $|\gamma| \leq 1$, and $|\mu| \leq 1$ such that*

$$c_2 = \frac{1}{2}\left(c_1^2 + q\left(4 - c_1^2\right)\right), \tag{11}$$

$$c_3 = \frac{1}{4}\left(c_1^3 + 2c_1 q\left(4 - c_1^2\right) - \left(4 - c_1^2\right)c_1 q^2 + 2\left(4 - c_1^2\right)\left(1 - |q|^2\right)\gamma\right), \tag{12}$$

*and*

$$c_4 = \frac{1}{8}\left(\begin{array}{c} c_1^4 + q\left(4 - c_1^2\right)(4q + (q^2 - 3q + 3)c_1^2) - 4\left(4 - c_1^2\right)\left(1 - |q|^2\right)(c(q - 1)\gamma \\ -\mu\left(1 - |\gamma|^2\right) + \bar{q}\gamma^2) \end{array}\right). \tag{13}$$

The inequalities given in (11)–(13) are due to [17,39,40], respectively.

**Lemma 3** ([39]). *If $p \in \mathcal{P}$, $0 \leq R \leq 1$, and $R(2R - 1) \leq S \leq R$, then the following inequality holds true*

$$\left|c_3 - 2Rc_1c_2 + Sc_1^3\right| \leq 2. \tag{14}$$

**Lemma 4** ([41]). *Let $\alpha, \beta, \gamma,$ and $\lambda$ satisfying the conditions $0 < \alpha < 1$, $0 < \lambda < 1$, and*

$$8\lambda(1-\lambda)\left[(\alpha\beta - 2\gamma)^2 + (\alpha(\lambda+\alpha) - \beta)^2\right] + \alpha(1-\alpha)(\beta - 2\lambda\alpha)^2 \leq 4\alpha^2(1-\alpha)^2\lambda(1-\lambda).$$

*Let $p \in \mathcal{P}$ be given in (6), then the following inequality holds true*

$$\left|\gamma c_1^4 + \lambda c_2^2 + 2\alpha c_1 c_3 - \frac{3}{2}\beta c_1^2 c_2 - c_4\right| \leq 2. \tag{15}$$

### 3. Main Results

**Theorem 1.** *Let $\mathcal{X} \in \mathcal{R}_{sl}$. Then, the following inequalities for the coefficients in (1) are true.*

$$|a_2| \leq \frac{1}{2}, \quad |a_3| \leq \frac{1}{3}, \quad |a_4| \leq \frac{1}{4}, \quad \text{and} \quad |a_5| \leq \frac{1}{5}.$$

*The sharpness of these inequalities can be obtained using the function*

$$\mathcal{X}'_n(z) = \frac{2\sqrt{1+z^n}}{1+e^{-z^n}}, \ n \in \mathbb{N}.$$

In particular, if $n = 1, 2, 3$, and $4$, then we have

$$\mathcal{X}_1 = \int_0^z \left(\frac{2\sqrt{1+t}}{1+e^{-t}}\right) dt = z + \frac{1}{2}z^2 + \frac{1}{24}z^3 - \frac{1}{96}z^4 - \frac{11}{1920}z^5, \quad (16)$$

$$\mathcal{X}_2 = \int_0^z \left(\frac{2\sqrt{1+t^2}}{1+e^{-t^2}}\right) dt = z + \frac{1}{3}z^3 + \frac{1}{40}z^5 - \frac{1}{168}z^7, \quad (17)$$

$$\mathcal{X}_3 = \int_0^z \left(\frac{2\sqrt{1+t^3}}{1+e^{-t^3}}\right) dt = z + \frac{1}{4}z^4 + \frac{1}{56}z^7, \quad (18)$$

$$\mathcal{X}_4 = \int_0^z \left(\frac{2\sqrt{1+t^4}}{1+e^{-t^4}}\right) dt = z + \frac{1}{5}z^5. \quad (19)$$

**Proof.** As $\mathcal{X} \in \mathcal{R}_{ls}$, from (4), we obtain

$$\mathcal{X}'(z) = \frac{2\sqrt{1+\xi(z)}}{1+e^{-\xi(z)}}. \quad (20)$$

Then, (1) gives

$$\mathcal{X}'(z) = 1 + 2a_2 z + 3a_3 z^2 + 4a_4 z^3 + 5a_5 z^4 \ldots. \quad (21)$$

Let $p \in \mathcal{P}$ be written by

$$p(z) = \frac{1+\xi(z)}{1-\xi(z)} = 1 + c_1 z + c_2 z^2 + c_3 z^3 + c_4 z^4 + \ldots.$$

This implies that

$$\xi(z) = \frac{1}{2}c_1 z + \left(\frac{1}{2}c_2 - \frac{1}{4}c_1^2\right)z^2 + \left(\frac{1}{8}c_1^3 - \frac{1}{2}c_1 c_2 + \frac{1}{2}c_3\right)z^3$$
$$+ \left(\frac{1}{2}c_4 - \frac{1}{2}c_1 c_3 - \frac{1}{4}c_2^2 - \frac{1}{16}c_1^4 + \frac{3}{8}c_1^2 c_2\right)z^4 + \ldots.$$

Then,

$$\frac{2\sqrt{1+\xi(z)}}{1+e^{-\xi(z)}} = 1 + \left(\frac{1}{2}c_1\right)z + \left(\frac{1}{2}c_2 - \frac{7}{32}c_1^2\right)z^2 + \left(\frac{1}{2}c_3 - \frac{7}{16}c_1 c_2 + \frac{17}{192}c_1^3\right)z^3$$
$$+ \left(\frac{-203}{6144}c_1^4 + \frac{17}{64}c_1^2 c_2 - \frac{7}{16}c_1 c_3 - \frac{7}{32}c_2^2 + \frac{1}{2}c_4\right)z^4 + \ldots. \quad (22)$$

It follows from (21) and (22) that

$$a_2 = \frac{1}{4}c_1, \quad (23)$$

$$a_3 = \frac{1}{6}c_2 - \frac{7}{96}c_1^2, \quad (24)$$

$$a_4 = \frac{17}{768}c_1^3 - \frac{7}{64}c_1 c_2 + \frac{1}{8}c_3, \quad (25)$$

$$a_5 = \frac{-203}{30720}c_1^4 + \frac{17}{320}c_1^2 c_2 - \frac{7}{80}c_1 c_3 - \frac{7}{160}c_2^2 + \frac{1}{10}c_4. \quad (26)$$

Using Lemma 1, (23) and (24) imply

$$|a_2| \leq \frac{1}{2} \text{ and } |a_3| \leq \frac{1}{3}.$$

By (25),
$$|a_4| = \frac{1}{8}\left|c_3 - \frac{7}{8}c_1c_2 + \frac{17}{96}c_1^3\right|.$$

Using Lemma 3, we obtain
$$|a_4| \leq \frac{1}{4}.$$

From (26), we have
$$|a_5| = \frac{1}{10}\left|\frac{203}{3072}c_1^4 + \frac{7}{16}c_2^2 + 2\left(\frac{7}{16}\right)c_1c_3 - \frac{17}{32}c_1^2c_2 - c_4\right|.$$

By applying Lemma 4,
$$|a_5| \leq \frac{1}{5}.$$

□

**Theorem 2.** *Let* $\mathcal{X} \in \mathcal{R}_{ls}$. *Then, the sharp upper bound for the following second-order Hankel determinant is given by*
$$|\mathcal{H}_{2,1}(\mathcal{X})| \leq \frac{1}{3}. \tag{27}$$

*The function (17) gives the sharpness of the inequality (27).*

**Proof.** Applying to the identities (23) and (24),
$$\left|a_3 - a_2^2\right| = \frac{1}{6}\left|c_2 - \frac{13}{16}c_1^2\right|.$$

Using Lemma 1, we obtain
$$|\mathcal{H}_{2,1}(\mathcal{X})| \leq \frac{1}{3}.$$

It is easy to verify that the function (17) gives the sharpness of the inequality (27). □

**Theorem 3.** *Let* $\mathcal{X} \in \mathcal{R}_{ls}$. *Then, the sharp upper bound for the following second-order Hankel determinant is given by*
$$|\mathcal{H}_{2,2}\mathcal{X}| \leq \frac{1}{9}. \tag{28}$$

*The function (17) gives the sharpness of the inequality (28).*

**Proof.** By the identities (23)–(25),
$$\left|a_2a_4 - a_3^2\right| = \left|\frac{1}{4608}c_1^4 - \frac{7}{2304}c_1^2c_2 + \frac{1}{32}c_3c_1 - \frac{1}{36}c_2^2\right|.$$

Now, using Lemma 2, we have
$$\left|a_2a_4 - a_3^2\right| = \frac{1}{4608}\left|-32t^2q^2 - 36tq^2c_1^2 - 72\gamma tc_1\left(1-q^2\right) + tqc_1^2 - 2c_1^4\right|.$$

Using the triangular inequality by taking $|c_1| = c \in [0,2]$, $t = 4 - c^2$, $|\gamma| \leq 1$, and $|q| = b \in [0,1]$.

$$\left|a_2a_4 - a_3^2\right| \leq \frac{1}{4608}\left(32\left(4-c^2\right)^2b^2 + 36\left(4-c^2\right)b^2c^2 + 72c\left(4-c^2\right)\left(1-b^2\right) + \left(4-c^2\right)bc^2 + 2c^4\right).$$

Let

$$F(b,c) = \frac{1}{4608}\left(32\left(4-c^2\right)^2 b^2 + 36\left(4-c^2\right)b^2c^2 + 72c\left(4-c^2\right)\left(1-b^2\right) + \left(4-c^2\right)bc^2 + 2c^4\right).$$

Then

$$\frac{\partial F}{\partial b} = \frac{1}{4608}\left(4-c^2\right)\left(256b + 8bc^2 - 144bc + c^2\right) \geq 0,$$

which shows that $F(b,c)$ is an increasing function for all $b \in [0,1]$ and $c \in [0,2]$. Thus, the maximum value occurs at $b=1$. Consequently,

$$F(b,c) \leq F(1,c) = \frac{1}{4608}\left(32\left(4-c^2\right)^2 + 36\left(4-c^2\right)c^2 + \left(4-c^2\right)c^2 + 2c^4\right). \tag{29}$$

Let

$$G(c) = 32\left(4-c^2\right)^2 + 36\left(4-c^2\right)c^2 + \left(4-c^2\right)c^2 + 2c^4,$$

which implies

$$\frac{\partial G}{\partial c} = -12c\left(c^2 + 18\right) \leq 0,$$

this shows that $G(c)$ is a decreasing function for all $c \in [0,2]$, and the maximum value occurs at $c = 0$. By referring to (29), we can deduce the required inequality,

$$|\mathcal{H}_{2,2}\mathcal{X}| = \left|a_2 a_4 - a_3^2\right| \leq \frac{1}{9}.$$

It is also easy to verify that the function (17) provides the sharpness of the inequality (28). □

**Theorem 4.** *Let $\mathcal{X} \in \mathcal{R}_{ls}$. Then, we have the sharp upper bound for the following third-order Hankel determinant.*

$$|\mathcal{H}_{3,1}\mathcal{X}| \leq \frac{1}{16}. \tag{30}$$

*The sharpness of this inequality can occur according to the function given in (18).*

**Proof.** From (5), we have

$$\mathcal{H}_{3,1}(\mathcal{X}) = 2a_2 a_3 a_4 - a_3^2 a_5 - a_3^3 + a_3 a_5 - a_4^2. \tag{31}$$

Taking $c_1 = c$ in the identities (23)–(26), we have

$$\mathcal{H}_{3,1}(\mathcal{X}) = \frac{1}{1105920}\begin{pmatrix} -16c^6 - 309c^4 c_2 + 1944c^3 c_3 - 246c^2 c_2^2 - 14976c^2 c_4 \\ -13184c_2^3 + 18432c_2 c_4 - 17280c_3^2 + 25632cc_2 c_3 \end{pmatrix}. \tag{32}$$

Also, taking $4 - c^2 = t$ in Lemma 2, we can simplify the terms in (32).

$$
\begin{aligned}
-309c^4c_2 &= -\frac{309}{2}c^6 - \frac{309}{2}tqc^4, \\
1944c^3c_3 &= 486c^6 - 486tc^4q^2 + 972tc^4q + 972\left(1 - |q|^2\right)t\gamma c^3, \\
-246c^2c_2^2 &= -\frac{123}{2}c^6 - 123c^4tq - \frac{123}{2}c^2t^2q^2, \\
-14976c^2c_4 &= -1872c^6 - 1872tc^4q^3 + 5616tc^4q^2 - 5616tc^4q + 7488\left(1 - |q|^2\right)tc^3q\gamma \\
&\quad -7488\left(1 - |q|^2\right)tc^3\gamma - 7488tc^2q^2 + 7488\left(1 - |q|^2\right)tc^2q\gamma^2 \\
&\quad -7488\left(1 - |q|^2\right)t\left(1 - |\gamma|^2\right)\mu c^2, \\
-13184c_2^3 &= -1648c^6 - 4944c^4tq - 4944c^2t^2q^2 - 1648t^3q^3, \\
18432c_2c_4 &= 1152c^6 + 1152c^4tq^3 - 3456c^4tq^2 + 4608c^4tq - 4608\left(1 - |q|^2\right)c^3tq\gamma \\
&\quad + 4608\left(1 - |q|^2\right)c^3t\gamma + 1152c^2t^2q^4 - 3456c^2t^2q^3 + 3456c^2t^2q^2 + 4608c^2tq^2 \\
&\quad - 4608\left(1 - |q|^2\right)c^2tq\gamma^2 + 4608\left(1 - |q|^2\right)\left(1 - |\gamma|^2\right)\mu c^2 t - 4608\left(1 - |q|^2\right)ct^2q^2\gamma \\
&\quad + 4608\left(1 - |q|^2\right)ct^2q\gamma + 4608t^2q^3 - 4608\left(1 - |q|^2\right)t^2q^2\gamma^2 \\
&\quad + 4608\left(1 - |q|^2\right)\left(1 - |\gamma|^2\right)\mu t^2 q, \\
-17280c_3^2 &= -1080c^6 + 2160c^4tq^2 - 4320c^4tq - 4320c^3\left(1 - |q|^2\right)t\gamma - 1080c^2t^2q^4 \\
&\quad + 4320c^2t^2q^3 - 4320c^2t^2q^2 + 4320c\left(1 - |q|^2\right)t^2q^2\gamma - 8640c\left(1 - |q|^2\right)t^2q\gamma \\
&\quad - 4320\left(1 - |q|^2\right)^2 t^2\gamma^2, \\
25632cc_2c_3 &= 3204c^6 - 3204c^4tq^2 + 9612c^4tq + 6408\left(1 - |q|^2\right)\gamma c^3t - 3204c^2t^2q^3 \\
&\quad + 6408c^2t^2q^2 + 6408\left(1 - |q|^2\right)\gamma ct^2q.
\end{aligned}
$$

Substituting the simplified terms into (32),

$$
\mathcal{H}_{3,1}(\mathcal{X}) = \frac{1}{1105920}\begin{pmatrix} 26c^6 - 720c^4tq^3 + 630c^4tq^2 + \frac{69}{2}c^4tq + 2880c^3\left(1 - |q|^2\right)tq\gamma \\ +180c^3\left(1 - |q|^2\right)t\gamma + 2880c^2\left(1 - |q|^2\right)tq\gamma^2 - 288c\left(1 - |q|^2\right)t^2q^2\gamma \\ -2880c^2\left(1 - |\gamma|^2\right)\left(1 - |q|^2\right)\mu t - 2340c^2t^2q^3 + \frac{1077}{2}c^2t^2q^2 - 2880c^2tq^2 \\ +2376c\left(1 - |q|^2\right)t^2q\gamma - 4320\left(1 - |q|^2\right)^2 t^2\gamma^2 - 4608\left(1 - |q|^2\right)t^2q^2\gamma^2 \\ +72c^2t^2q^4 + 4608\left(1 - |\gamma|^2\right)\left(1 - |q|^2\right)t^2q - 1648t^3q^3 + 4608t^2q^3 \end{pmatrix}.
$$

Since $t = 4 - c^2$,

$$
\mathcal{H}_{3,1}(\mathcal{X}) = \frac{1}{1105920}\left[m_1(c, q) + m_2(c, q)\gamma + m_3(c, q)\gamma^2 + \varphi(c, q, \gamma)\mu\right],
$$

where

$$
\begin{aligned}
m_1(c, q) &= 26c^6 - \frac{1}{2}\left(4 - c^2\right)q\begin{pmatrix}(4 - c^2)q(1384c^2q - 144c^2q^2 - 1077c^2 + 3968q) + \\ 5760c^2q - 1260c^4q + 1440c^4q^2 - 69c^4\end{pmatrix}, \\
m_2(c, q) &= -36c\left(4 - c^2\right)\left(1 - |q|^2\right)\left(2\left(4 - c^2\right)q(4q - 33) - 80c^2q - 5c^2\right), \\
m_3(c, q) &= -288\left(4 - c^2\right)\left(1 - |q|^2\right)\left(\left(4 - c^2\right)\left(q^2 + 15\right) - 10c^2q\right), \\
\varphi(c, q, \gamma) &= 576\left(4 - c^2\right)\left(1 - |q|^2\right)\left(1 - |\gamma|^2\right)\left(8\left(4 - c^2\right)q - 5c^2\right).
\end{aligned}
$$

Let $|\gamma| = y$ and $|\mu| \leq 1$, then

$$|\mathcal{H}_{3,1}(\mathcal{X})| \leq \frac{1}{1105920}\left[|m_1(c,q)| + |m_2(c,q)|y + |m_3(c,q)|y^2 + |\varphi(c,q,\gamma)|\right]$$
$$\leq \frac{1}{1105920}[\mathcal{G}(c,q,y)], \tag{33}$$

where
$$\mathcal{G}(c,q,y) = n_1(c,q) + n_2(c,q)y + n_3(c,q)y^2 + n_4(c,q)\left(1 - y^2\right),$$

with

$$n_1(c,q) = 26c^6 + \frac{1}{2}\left(4 - c^2\right)q\left[\begin{array}{c}(4-c^2)q(1384c^2q + 144c^2q^2 + 1077c^2 + 3968q) \\ +5760c^2q + 1260c^4q + 1440c^4q^2 + 69c^4\end{array}\right],$$

$$n_2(c,q) = 36c\left(4 - c^2\right)\left(1 - |q|^2\right)\left[\left(4 - c^2\right)q(8q + 66) + 80c^2q + 5c^2\right],$$

$$n_3(c,q) = 288\left(4 - c^2\right)\left(1 - |q|^2\right)\left[\left(4 - c^2\right)\left(q^2 + 15\right) + 10c^2q\right],$$

$$n_4(c,q) = 576\left(4 - c^2\right)\left(1 - |q|^2\right)\left[8q\left(4 - c^2\right) + 5c^2\right].$$

To find the maximum values of the function $\mathcal{G}(c,q,y)$ within the closed cuboid $\triangle = [0,2] \times [0,1] \times [0,1]$, we need to examine the function $\mathcal{G}(c,q,y)$ inside the cuboid, on its faces and along its edges. Let us divide the analysis into the following three cases.

I. **Interior points of cuboid**

Now, we find the maximum value of $\mathcal{G}(c,q,y)$ within the cuboid's interior.

Let $(c,q,y) \in [0,2) \times [0,1) \times (0,1)$. By differentiating $\mathcal{G}(c,q,y)$ with respect to $y$, we obtain

$$\frac{\partial \mathcal{G}}{\partial y} = \left(\begin{array}{c}36c(4-c^2)\left(1 - |q|^2\right)[(4-c^2)q(8q+66) + 5c^2(16q+1)] \\ +576y(4-c^2)\left(1 - |q|^2\right)[(4-c^2)(q-15) + 10c^2](q-1)\end{array}\right).$$

Putting $\frac{\partial \mathcal{G}}{\partial y} = 0$, gives

$$y = \frac{c\left[2q(4-c^2)(4q+33) + 5c^2(16q+1)\right]}{16[(4-c^2)(15-q) - 10c^2](q-1)} = y_1.$$

If $y_1$ is a critical point inside $\triangle$, then $y_1 \in (0,1)$, which is possible only if

$$5c^3(16q+1) + 2cq\left(4 - c^2\right)(4q+33) + 16\left(4 - c^2\right)(15-q)(1-q) < 160(1-q)c^2, \tag{34}$$

and

$$c^2 > \frac{4(15-q)}{25-q}. \tag{35}$$

To identify the critical point, we need to find a solution that satisfies the inequalities (34) and (35). Let $g(q) = \frac{4(15-q)}{25-q}$ with $g'(q) = -\frac{40}{(25-q)^2} < 0$, which shows that $g(q)$ is a decreasing function, so

$$c^2 > \frac{7}{3}.$$

It follows from the simple calculations that (34) is not held for $q \in \left[\frac{15}{32}, 1\right)$. As a result, it can be concluded that the function $\mathcal{G}(c,q,y)$ does not possess any critical points within the interior of the cuboid $[0,2) \times \left[\frac{15}{32}, 1\right) \times (0,1)$.

Suppose $(c, q, y)$ is a critical point of $\mathcal{G}$ in the interior of the cuboid, satisfying the conditions $q \in \left[0, \frac{15}{32}\right)$ and $y \in (0, 1)$ which leads us to $c^2 > g\left(\frac{15}{32}\right) = \frac{372}{157}$. It can also be observed that

$$n_1(c, q) \leq n_1\left(c, \frac{15}{32}\right) = \vartheta_1(c).$$

Since $1 - q^2 \leq 1$ and $0 < q < \frac{15}{32}$, we have

$$\begin{aligned} n_2(c, q) &\leq 36(4 - c^2)\left[(4 - c^2)\left(8c\left(\frac{15}{32}\right)^2 + 66c\left(\frac{15}{32}\right)\right) + 5\left(16\left(\frac{15}{32}\right) + 1\right)c^3\right], \\ &= \frac{1024}{799}n_2\left(c, \frac{15}{32}\right) = \vartheta_2(c). \end{aligned}$$

Similarly, we obtain

$$n_j(c, q) \leq \frac{1024}{799}n_j\left(c, \frac{15}{32}\right) = \vartheta_j(c) \quad (j = 3, 4).$$

It follows that

$$\mathcal{G}(c, q, y) \leq \vartheta_1(c) + \vartheta_4(c) + \vartheta_2(c)y + (\vartheta_3(c) - \vartheta_4(c))y^2 = \Psi(c, y).$$

Differentiating with regard to "$y$", we have

$$\frac{\partial \Psi}{\partial y} = \vartheta_2(c) + 2(\vartheta_3(c) - \vartheta_4(c))y.$$

Consider

$$\vartheta_3(c) - \vartheta_4(c) = 288(4 - c^2)\left(\frac{7905}{256} - \frac{13\,345}{1024}c^2\right) \leq 0, \quad c \in \left(\sqrt{\frac{372}{157}}, 2\right).$$

Then, for all $c \in \left(\sqrt{\frac{372}{157}}, 2\right)$ and $y \in (0, 1)$, we have

$$\begin{aligned} \frac{\partial \Psi}{\partial y} &= \vartheta_2(c) + 2(\vartheta_3(c) - \vartheta_4(c))y \\ &\geq \vartheta_2(c) + 2(\vartheta_3(c) - \vartheta_4(c)) \\ &= 36(4 - c^2)\left(\frac{1255}{128}c^3 - \frac{13345}{64}c^2 + \frac{4185}{32}c + \frac{7905}{16}\right) \\ &\geq 0. \end{aligned}$$

Thus, we obtain

$$\Psi(c, y) \leq \Psi(c, 1) = \vartheta_1(c) + \vartheta_2(c) + \vartheta_3(c) = \zeta(c),$$

where

$$\zeta(c) = -\frac{1269383}{131\,072}c^6 - \frac{11295}{32}c^5 + \frac{32362695}{16\,384}c^4 - \frac{13185}{4}c^3 - \frac{210375495}{8192}c^2 + \frac{37665}{2}c + \frac{2348865}{32}.$$

It can be seen that $\zeta'(c) \neq 0$, for any $c \in \left(\sqrt{\frac{372}{157}}, 2\right)$. Also, $\zeta(c)$ is a decreasing function and its maximum value occurs at $c \approx 1.53928554$, which is 37,437.

**II. On the six faces of the cuboid**

Next, we proceed to examine the maximum value of the function $\mathcal{G}(c, q, y)$ on all six faces of the cuboid $\triangle$.

(i) On the face $c = 0$: $\mathcal{G}(0, q, y)$ becomes

$$h_1(q, y) = 31744q^3 + \left(4608(q-1)(q-15)y^2 + 73728q\right)\left(1 - q^2\right),$$

then

$$\frac{\partial h_1}{\partial y} = -9216y\left(q^2 - 1\right)(q-1)(q-15) \neq 0 \text{ for } y \in (0, 1),$$

which implies that $h_1$ does not have any optimal points within the interval $(0, 1) \times (0, 1)$.

(ii) On the face $c = 2$, we have

$$\mathcal{G}(2, q, y) = 1664 \tag{36}$$

(iii) On the face $q = 0$, $\mathcal{G}(c, 0, y)$ becomes

$$h_2(c, y) = 26c^6 + 180c^3y\left(4 - c^2\right) + 7200c^4y^2 - 2880c^4 - 46080c^2y^2 + 11520c^2 + 69120y^2,$$

then $\frac{\partial h_2}{\partial y} = 0$ gives

$$y = \frac{c^3}{16(5c^2 - 12)} = y_0. \tag{37}$$

For the provided range of $y$, $y_0 \in (0, 1)$, if $c > c_0 \approx 1.5491933$.

Also, $\frac{\partial h_2}{\partial c} = 0$ gives

$$12c\left(13c^4 - 75c^3y + 2400c^2y^2 - 960c^2 + 180cy - 7680y^2 + 1920\right) = 0. \tag{38}$$

Putting (37) in (38), we obtain

$$14925c^9 - 1222920c^7 + 7916976c^5 - 17694720c^3 + 13271040c = 0.$$

Solving for $c$ within the range $(0, 2)$, we find that $c \approx 1.4228$. This indicates that there is no optimal solution for $\mathcal{G}(c, 0, y)$.

(iv) On the face $q = 1$: $\mathcal{G}(c, 1, y)$ becomes

$$h_3(c, y) = -820c^6 + 334c^4 + 4264c^2 + 31744,$$

then $\frac{\partial h_3}{\partial c} = 0$ gives a critical point $c \approx 1.208$, where $h_3$ attains its maximum value; that is,

$$h_3(c, y) \leq 36129. \tag{39}$$

(v) On the face $y = 0$: $\mathcal{G}(c, q, 0)$ becomes

$$\begin{aligned}h_4(c, q) &= 72c^6q^4 - 28c^6q^3 - \frac{183}{2}c^6q^2 - \frac{69}{2}c^6q + 26c^6 - 576c^4q^4 - 5280c^4q^3 \\ &\quad -1788c^4q^2 + 4746c^4q - 2880c^4 + 1152c^2q^4 + 32064c^2q^3 + 8616c^2q^2 \\ &\quad -36864c^2q + 11520c^2 - 41984q^3 + 73728q.\end{aligned}$$

Thus,

$$\begin{aligned}\frac{\partial h_4}{\partial c} &= 432c^5q^4 - 168c^5q^3 - 549c^5q^2 - 207c^5q + 156c^5 - 2304c^3q^4 - 21120c^3q^3 - 7152c^3q^2 \\ &\quad +18984c^3q - 11520c^3 + 2304cq^4 + 64128cq^3 + 17232cq^2 - 73728cq + 23040c,\end{aligned}$$

$$\begin{aligned}\frac{\partial h_4}{\partial q} &= 288c^6q^3 - 84c^6q^2 - 183c^6q - \frac{69}{2}c^6 - 2304c^4q^3 - 15840c^4q^2 - 3576c^4q + 4746c^4 \\ &\quad +4608c^2q^3 + 96192c^2q^2 + 17232c^2q - 36864c^2 - 125952q^2 + 73728.\end{aligned}$$

Computation shows that the system of equations $\frac{\partial h_4}{\partial c} = 0$ and $\frac{\partial h_4}{\partial q} = 0$ has no solutions in $(0,2) \times (0,1)$.

(vi) On the face $y = 1$: $\mathcal{G}(c,q,1)$, becomes

$$
\begin{aligned}
h_5(c,q) &= 72c^6q^4 - 28c^6q^3 - \frac{183}{2}c^6q^2 - \frac{69}{2}c^6q + 26c^6 - 288c^5q^4 + 504c^5q^3 + 468c^5q^2 \\
&\quad - 504c^5q - 180c^5 - 864c^4q^4 + 2208c^4q^3 - 8700c^4q^2 - 2742c^4q + 4320c^4 \\
&\quad + 2304c^3q^4 + 7488c^3q^3 - 3024c^3q^2 - 7488c^3q + 720c^3 + 3456c^2q^4 - 16320c^2q^3 \\
&\quad + 52392c^2q^2 + 11520c^2q - 34560c^2 - 4608cq^4 - 38016cq^3 + 4608cq^2 + 38016cq \\
&\quad - 4608q^4 + 31744q^3 - 64512q^2 + 69120.
\end{aligned}
$$

It follows that

$$
\begin{aligned}
\frac{\partial h_5}{\partial c} &= 432c^5q^4 - 168c^5q^3 - 549c^5q^2 - 207c^5q + 156c^5 - 1440c^4q^4 + 2520c^4q^3 + 2340c^4q^2 \\
&\quad - 2520c^4q - 900c^4 - 3456c^3q^4 + 8832c^3q^3 - 34\,800c^3q^2 - 10\,968c^3q + 17\,280c^3 \\
&\quad + 6912c^2q^4 + 22\,464c^2q^3 - 9072c^2q^2 - 22\,464c^2q + 2160c^2 + 6912cq^4 - 32\,640cq^3 \\
&\quad + 104\,784cq^2 + 23\,040cq - 69\,120c - 4608q^4 - 38\,016q^3 + 4608q^2 + 38\,016q,
\end{aligned}
$$

$$
\begin{aligned}
\frac{\partial h_5}{\partial q} &= 288c^6q^3 - 84c^6q^2 - 183c^6q - \frac{69}{2}c^6 - 1152c^5q^3 + 1512c^5q^2 + 936c^5q - 504c^5 \\
&\quad - 3456c^4q^3 + 6624c^4q^2 - 17\,400c^4q - 2742c^4 + 9216c^3q^3 + 22\,464c^3q^2 - 6048c^3q \\
&\quad - 7488c^3 + 13\,824c^2q^3 - 48\,960c^2q^2 + 104\,784c^2q + 11\,520c^2 - 18\,432cq^3 - 114\,048cq^2 \\
&\quad + 9216cq + 38\,016c - 18\,432q^3 + 95\,232q^2 - 129\,024q.
\end{aligned}
$$

Also, the computation indicates that the system of equations $\frac{\partial h_5}{\partial c} = 0$ and $\frac{\partial h_5}{\partial q} = 0$ has no solutions in $(0,2) \times (0,1)$.

**III. On the twelve edges of the cuboid**

Finally, we need to find the maximum values of $\mathcal{G}(c,q,y)$ along the twelve edges.

(i) On $q = 0$ and $y = 0$: $\mathcal{G}(c,0,0)$ becomes

$$h_6(c) = 26c^6 - 2880c^4 + 11520c^2,$$

then $\frac{\partial h_6}{\partial c} = 0$ gives the critical point $c \approx 1.4343$, where the maximum value is obtained as follows.

$$h_6(c) \leq 11737. \tag{40}$$

(ii) On $q = 0$ and $y = 1$: $\mathcal{G}(c,0,1)$ becomes

$$h_7(c) = 26c^6 - 180c^5 + 4320c^4 + 720c^3 - 34560c^2 + 69120.$$

It is clear that $\frac{\partial h_7}{\partial c} \leq 0$, for all $c \in [0,2]$. This indicates that $h_7(c)$ is a decreasing function and attains its maximum value at $c = 0$.

$$h_7(c) \leq 69120. \tag{41}$$

(iii) On $q = 0$ and $c = 0$: $\mathcal{G}(0,0,y)$ becomes

$$h_8(y) = 66816y^2 + 2304.$$

Therefore, $\frac{\partial h_8}{\partial c} > 0$ for the interval $[0,1]$, which shows that $h_8(y)$ is an increasing function. As a result, it attains its maximum value at $y = 1$; that is,

$$h_8(y) \leq 69120. \tag{42}$$

As the terms $\mathcal{G}(c,1,1)$ and $\mathcal{G}(c,1,0)$ are free from $q$, that is

$$h_9(c) = \mathcal{G}(c,1,0) = \mathcal{G}(c,1,1) = -56c^6 - 5778c^4 + 16488c^2 + 31744.$$

Putting $\frac{\partial h_9}{\partial c} = 0$, we find a critical point $c \approx 1.1825$. At this critical point, $h_9(c)$ achieves its maximum value, which is

$$h_9(c) \leq 43349. \tag{43}$$

(iv) On $q = 1$ and $c = 0$: $\mathcal{G}(0,1,y)$ becomes

$$h_{10}(y) = \mathcal{G}(0,1,y) = 31744.$$

(v) On $c = 2$:

$$\mathcal{G}(2,0,y) = \mathcal{G}(2,1,y) = \mathcal{G}(2,q,1) = \mathcal{G}(2,q,0) = 1664.$$

(vi) On $c = 0$ and $y = 0$: $\mathcal{G}(0,q,0)$ becomes

$$h_{11}(q) = -1024q\left(41q^2 - 72\right),$$

and calculation shows that $\frac{\partial h_{11}}{\partial q} \leq 0$ for all $q \in [0,1]$, which means $h_{11}(q)$ is a decreasing function and maximum value occurs at $q = 0$; that is,

$$h_{11}(q) \leq 0. \tag{44}$$

(vii) On $c = 0$ and $y = 1$: $\mathcal{G}(0,q,1)$ becomes

$$h_{12}(q) = -4608q^4 + 31744q^3 - 64512q^2 + 69120.$$

Let $\frac{\partial h_{12}}{\partial q} = 0$, we then find a critical point $q = 0$, where the function $h_{12}(q)$ achieves its maximum value,

$$h_{12}(q) \leq 69120. \tag{45}$$

Therefore, we can conclude that

$$\mathcal{G}(c,q,y) \leq 69120.$$

And hence, we reach the following inequality as described by (33),

$$|\mathcal{H}_{3,1}(\mathcal{X})| \leq \frac{1}{16}.$$

□

## 4. Conclusions

In the present article, we defined a class of analytic functions by considering the ratio of two well-known functions. We investigated the sharp upper bounds of the modulus of coefficients $a_2, a_3$, and $a_4$; and the sharp upper bounds for the modulus of three second-order and third-order Hankel determinants, $\mathcal{H}_{2,1}\mathcal{X}$, $\mathcal{H}_{2,2}\mathcal{X}$, and $\mathcal{H}_{3,1}\mathcal{X}$, for the normalized analytic functions $\mathcal{X}$ belonging to the newly defined class. These findings contribute to the existing body of knowledge and provide valuable insights for further research in the field. This work provides a direction to define more interesting generalized domains and to extend to new subclasses of starlike and convex functions by using quantum calculus.

**Author Contributions:** Conceptualization, A.A. (Adeel Ahmad), J.G., I.A.-S., A.R., A.A. (Asad Ali) and S.H.; Methodology, A.A. (Adeel Ahmad), J.G., I.A.-S., A.R., A.A. (Asad Ali) and S.H.; Formal analysis, A.A. (Adeel Ahmad), J.G., I.A.-S., A.R., A.A. (Asad Ali) and S.H.; Investigation, A.A. (Adeel Ahmad), J.G., I.A.-S., A.R., A.A. (Asad Ali) and S.H.; Writing—original draft, A.A. (Adeel Ahmad),

J.G., I.A.-S., A.R., A.A. (Asad Ali) and S.H.; Writing—review & editing, A.A. (Adeel Ahmad), J.G., I.A.-S., A.R., A.A. (Asad Ali) and S.H.; All authors have read and agreed to the published version of the manuscript.

**Funding:** This research was funded by United Arab Emirates University with UAEU Program for Advanced Research (UPAR12S127).

**Data Availability Statement:** No new data were created or analyzed in this study. Data sharing is not applicable to this article.

**Conflicts of Interest:** The authors declare no conflict of interest.

## References

1. Al-Shbeil, I.; Gong, J.; Shaba, T.G. Coefficients Inequalities for the Bi-Univalent Functions Related to q-Babalola Convolution Operator. *Fractal Fract.* **2023**, *7*, 155. [CrossRef]
2. Khan, M.F.; Al-Shbeil, I.; Khan, S.; Khan, N.; Haq, W.U.; Gong, J. Applications of a q-Differential Operator to a Class of Harmonic Mappings Defined by q-Mittag–Leffler Functions. *Symmetry* **2022**, *14*, 1905. [CrossRef]
3. Saliu, A.; Al-Shbeil, I.; Gong, J.; Malik, S.N.; Aloraini, N. Properties of q-Symmetric Starlike Functions of Janowski Type. *Symmetry* **2022**, *14*, 1907. [CrossRef]
4. Ur Rehman, M.S.; Ahmad, Q.Z.; Al-Shbeil, I.; Ahmad, S.; Khan, A.; Khan, B.; Gong, J. Coefficient Inequalities for Multivalent Janowski Type q-Starlike Functions Involving Certain Conic Domains. *Axioms* **2022**, *11*, 494. [CrossRef]
5. Murugusundaramoorthy, G. Fekete–Szegő Inequalities for Certain Subclasses of Analytic Functions Related with Nephroid Domain. *J. Contemp. Math. Anal.* **2022**, *57*, 90–101. [CrossRef]
6. Khan, M.G.; Khan, B.; Gong, J.; Tchier, F.; Tawfiq, F.M.O. Applications of First-Order Differential Subordination for Subfamilies of Analytic Functions Related to Symmetric Image Domains. *Symmetry* **2023**, *15*, 2004. [CrossRef]
7. Shanmugam, T.N. Convolution and Differential subordination. *Int. J. Math. Math. Sci.* **1989**, *12*, 333–340. [CrossRef]
8. Padmanabhan K.S.; Parvatham, R. Some applications of differential subordination. *Bull. Aust. Math. Soc.* **1985**, *32*, 321–330. [CrossRef]
9. Ma, W.C.; Minda, D. A unified treatment of some special classes of univalent functions. In *Proceedings of the Conference on Complex Analysis*; Li, Z., Ren, F., Yang, L., Zhang, S., Eds.; International Press: New York, NY, USA, 1992; pp. 157–169.
10. Cho, N.E.; Kumar, V.; Kumar, S.S.; Ravichandran, V. Radius problems for starlike functions associated with the sine function. *Bull. Iran. Math. Soc.* **2019**, *45*, 213–232. [CrossRef]
11. Kumar, S.S.; Arora, K. Starlike functions associated with a petal-shaped domain. *arXiv* **2020**, arXiv:2010.10072.
12. Mendiratta, S.; Nagpal, V.; Ravichandran, V. On a subclass of strongly starlike functions associated with exponential function. *Bull. Malays. Math. Sci. Soc.* **2015**, *38*, 365–386. [CrossRef]
13. Mundula, M.; Kumar, S.S. On subfamily of starlike functions related to hyperbolic cosine function. *J. Anal.* **2023**, *31*, 2043–2062. [CrossRef]
14. Sharma, K.; Jain, N.K.; Ravichandran, V. Starlike functions associated with cardioid. *Afr. Mat.* **2016**, *27*, 923–939. [CrossRef]
15. Sokol, J.; Stankiewicz, J. Radius of convexity of some subclasses of strongly starlike functions. *Zeszyty Naukowe Oficyna Wydawnicza Al. Powstáncow Warszawy* **1996**, *19*, 101–105.
16. Geol, P.; Kumar, S.S. Certain class of starlike functions associated with modified sigmoid function. *Bull. Malays. Math. Sci. Soc.* **2020**, *43*, 957–991. [CrossRef]
17. Pommerenke, C.; Jensen, G. *Univalent Functions*; Vandenhoeck and Ruprecht: Gottingen, Germany, 1975.
18. Riaz, A.; Raza, M.; Binyamin, M.A.; Saliu, A. The second and third Hankel determinants for starlike and convex functions associated with Three-Leaf function. *Heliyon* **2023**, *9*, 12748. [CrossRef] [PubMed]
19. Bansal, D.; Maharana, S.; Prajapat, J.K. Third order Hankel determinant for certain univalent functions. *J. Korean Math. Soc.* **2015**, *52*, 1139–1148. [CrossRef]
20. Krishna, D.V.; Venkateswarlu, B.; RamReddy, T.Third Hankel determinant for bounded turning functions of order alpha. *J. Niger. Math. Soc.* **2015**, *34*, 121–127. [CrossRef]
21. Singh, G. On the second Hankel determinant for a new subclass of analytic functions. *J. Math. Sci. Appl.* **2014**, *2*, 1–3.
22. Al-Shbeil, I.; Gong, J.; Khan, S.; Khan, N.; Khan, A.; Khan, M.F.; Goswami, A. Hankel and Symmetric Toeplitz Determinants for a New Subclass of q-Starlike Functions. *Fractals Fract.* **2022**, *6*, 658. [CrossRef]
23. Orhan, H.; Deniz, E.; Raducanu D. The Fekete–Szegö problem for subclasses of analytic functions defined by a differential operator related to conic domains. *Comput. Math. Appl.* **2010**, *59*, 283–295.
24. Hayman, W.K. On second Hankel determinant of mean univalent functions. *Proc. Lond. Math. Soc.* **1968**, *3*, 77–94. [CrossRef]
25. Obradović, M.; Tuneski, N. Hankel determinants of second and third order for the class $S$ of univalent functions. *Math. Slovaka* **2021**, *71*, 649–654. [CrossRef]
26. Janteng, A.; Halim, S.A.; Darus, M. Coefficient inequality for a function whose derivative has a positive real part. *J. Inequal. Pure Appl. Math.* **2006**, *7*, 50.
27. Babalola, K.O. On $\mathcal{H}_3(1)$ Hankel determinant for some classes of univalent functions. *Inequal. Theory Appl.* **2010**, *6*, 1–7.

28. Zaprawa, P. Third Hankel determinants for subclasses of univalent functions. *Mediterr. J. Math.* **2017**, *14*, 10. [CrossRef]
29. Kwon, O.S.; Lecko, A.; Sim, Y.J. The bound of the Hankel determinant of the third kind for starlike functions. *Bull. Malays. Math. Sci. Soc.* **2019**, *42*, 767–780. [CrossRef]
30. Zaprawa, P.; Obradović, M.; Tuneski, N. Third Hankel determinant for univalent starlike functions. *Rev. R. Acad. Cienc. Exactas Fís. Nat. Ser. A Mat.* **2021**, *49*, 115. [CrossRef]
31. Arif, M.; Marwa, S.; Xin, Q.; Tchier, F.; Ayaz, M.; Malik, S.N. Sharp coefficient problems of functions with bounded turning subordinated by sigmoid function. *Mathematics* **2022**, *10*, 3862. [CrossRef]
32. Khan, M.G.; Ahmad, B.; Murugusundaramoorthy, G.; Chinram, R.; Wali Khan Mashwani, W.K. Applications of Modified Sigmoid Functions to a Class of Starlike Functions. *J. Funct. Spaces* **2020**, *2020*, 8844814. [CrossRef]
33. Orhan, H.; Çağlar, M.; Cotîrlă, L.-I. Third Hankel determinant for a subfamily of holomorphic functions related with lemniscate of Bernoulli. *Mathematics* **2023**, *11*, 1147. [CrossRef]
34. Shi, L.; Arif, M.; Rafiq, A.; Abbas, M.; Iqbal, J. Sharp bounds of Hankel determinant on logarithmic coefficients for functions of bounded turning associated with petal-shaped domain. *Mathematics* **2022**, *10*, 1939. [CrossRef]
35. Shi, L.; Arif, M.; Abbas, M.; Ihsan, M. Sharp bounds of Hankel determinant for the inverse functions on a subclass of bounded turning functions. *Mediterr. J. Math.* **2023**, *20*, 156. [CrossRef]
36. Kanas, S.; Răducanu, D. Some class of analytic functions related to conic domains. *Math. Slovaca* **2014**, *64*, 1183–1196. [CrossRef]
37. Abd El-Hamid, H.A.H.; Rezk, M.; Ahmed, A.M.; AlNemer, G.; Zakarya, M.; El Saify, H.A. Dynamic Inequalities in Quotients with General Kernels and Measures, *J. Funct. Spaces* **2020**, *2020*, 5417084. [CrossRef]
38. Ahmed, A.M.; Saker, S.H.; Kenawy, M.R.; Rezk, H.M. Lower Bounds on a Generalization of Cesaro Operator on Time Scales, *Dyn. Contin. Discret. Impuls. Syst. Ser. A Math. Anal.* **2021**, *28*, 345–355.
39. Libera, R.J.; Zlotkiewicz, E.J. Coefficient bounds for the inverse of a function with derivative in *P*. *Proc. Am. Math. Soc.* **1983**, *87*, 251–257. [CrossRef]
40. Kwon, O.S.; Lecko, A.; Sim, Y.J. On the fourth coefficient of functions in the Carathéodory class. *Comput. Methods Funct. Theory* **2018**, *18*, 307–314. [CrossRef]
41. Ravichandran, V.; Verma, S. Bound for the fifth coefficient of certain starlike functions. *Comptes Rendus Math.* **2015**, *353*, 505–510. [CrossRef]

**Disclaimer/Publisher's Note:** The statements, opinions and data contained in all publications are solely those of the individual author(s) and contributor(s) and not of MDPI and/or the editor(s). MDPI and/or the editor(s) disclaim responsibility for any injury to people or property resulting from any ideas, methods, instructions or products referred to in the content.

MDPI
St. Alban-Anlage 66
4052 Basel
Switzerland
www.mdpi.com

*Fractal and Fractional* Editorial Office
E-mail: fractalfract@mdpi.com
www.mdpi.com/journal/fractalfract

Disclaimer/Publisher's Note: The statements, opinions and data contained in all publications are solely those of the individual author(s) and contributor(s) and not of MDPI and/or the editor(s). MDPI and/or the editor(s) disclaim responsibility for any injury to people or property resulting from any ideas, methods, instructions or products referred to in the content.

www.ingramcontent.com/pod-product-compliance
Lightning Source LLC
LaVergne TN
LVHW070426100526
838202LV00014B/1540